Sardinia

THE ROUGH GUIDE

There are more than one hundred and fifty Rough Guide titles
covering destinations from Amsterdam to Zimbabwe

Forthcoming titles include
Croatia • Cuba • Las Vegas • Rome • Switzerland

Rough Guide Reference Series
Classical Music • Drum 'n' Bass • European Football • House
The Internet • Jazz • Music USA • Opera • Reggae
Rock Music • World Music

Rough Guide Phrasebooks
Czech • Dutch • Egyptian Arabic • European • French • German
Greek • Hindi & Urdu • Hungarian • Indonesian • Italian • Japanese
Mandarin Chinese • Mexican Spanish • Polish • Portuguese • Russian
Spanish • Swahili • Thai • Turkish • Vietnamese

Rough Guides on the Internet
www.roughguides.com

Rough Guide Credits

Text Editor:	Chris Schüler
Series Editor:	Mark Ellingham
Editorial:	Martin Dunford, Jonathan Buckley, Jo Mead, Kate Berens, Amanda Tomlin, Ann-Marie Shaw, Paul Gray, Helena Smith, Judith Bamber, Olivia Eccleshall, Orla Duane, Ruth Blackmore, Sophie Martin, Geoff Howard, Claire Saunders, Gavin Thomas, Alexander Mark Rogers, Polly Thomas, Joe Staines, Lisa Nellis, Andrew Tomicíc (UK), Mary Beth Maioli (US)
Online Editors:	Kelly Cross (US)
Production:	Susanne Hillen, Andy Hilliard, Link Hall, Helen Ostick, Julia Bovis, Michelle Draycott, Katie Pringle, Robert Evers
Picture Research:	Louise Boulton
Cartography:	Melissa Baker, Maxine Repath, Nichola Goodliffe, Ed Wright
Finance:	John Fisher, Gary Singh, Ed Downey, Mark Hall
Marketing & Publicity:	Richard Trillo, Niki Smith, David Wearn (UK); Jean-Marie Kelly, Myra Campolo, Simon Carloss (US)
Administration:	Tania Hummel, Charlotte Marriott, Demelza Dallow

Acknowledgements

Thanks are due to the many enthusiastic and well-informed guides who shared their knowledge of and passion for Sardinia with me. In Britain, Kate Hughes's input was greatly appreciated – thanks. At Rough Guides, Chris Schüler was a great editor, and unfailingly polite in the face of mangled deadlines, while Judy Pang, Laurence Larroche and The Map Studio, Romsey, Hants made a fine job of the typesetting, proofreading and cartography respectively. Thanks also to Michelle Draycott for the picture research.

This first edition published January 2000 by Rough Guides Ltd, 62–70 Shorts Gardens, London WC2H 9AB.

Distributed by the Penguin Group:

Penguin Books Ltd, 27 Wrights Lane, London W8 5TZ.

Penguin Books USA Inc, 375 Hudson Street, New York 10014, USA.

Penguin Books Australia Ltd, 487 Maroondah Highway, PO Box 257, Ringwood, Victoria 3134, Australia.

Penguin Books Canada Ltd, 10 Alcorn Avenue, Toronto, Ontario, Canada M4V 1E4.

Penguin Books (NZ) Ltd, 182–190 Wairau Road, Auckland 10, New Zealand.

Printed in England by Clays Ltd, St Ives PLC

Typography and original design by Jonathan Dear and The Crowd Roars.

Illustrations throughout by Edward Briant.

Sardinia

THE ROUGH GUIDE

Written and researched by
Robert Andrews

THE ROUGH GUIDES

Help us update

We've gone to a lot of trouble to ensure that this first edition of the *Rough Guide to Sardinia* is completely up to date and accurate. However, things do change: hotels and restaurants come and go, opening hours are notoriously fickle, and prices are extremely volatile. We'd appreciate any suggestions, amendments or contributions for future editions of the guide. We'll credit all letters and send a copy of the next edition (or any other *Rough Guide*) for the best.

Please mark all letters "Rough Guide to Sardinia Update" and send to:
Rough Guides, 62–70 Shorts Gardens, London WC2H 9AB or
Rough Guides, 375 Hudson St, 3rd floor, New York, NY 10014.

Email should be sent to:
mail@roughguides.co.uk

Online updates about *Rough Guide* titles can be found on our Web site at *www.roughguides.com*

The Author

Robert Andrews lived in Italy for six years, and returns there two or three times a year. Interested mainly in the south and in the islands in particular, he has written various articles and co-authored the Rough Guide to Sicily. Now based in Bristol, he also compiles dictionaries of quotations.

> This book is dedicated to my favourite holiday companions:
> Jo, Quincy and Evelina.

Rough Guides

Travel Guides • Phrasebooks • Music and Reference Guides

We set out to do something different when the first Rough Guide was published in 1982. Mark Ellingham, just out of University, was travelling in Greece. He brought along the popular guides of the day, but found they were all lacking in some way. They were either strong on ruins and museums but went on for pages without mentioning a beach or taverna. Or they were so conscious of the need to save money that they lost sight of Greece's cultural and historical significance. Also, none of the books told him anything about Greece's contemporary life – its politics, its culture, its people, and how they lived.

So with no job in prospect, Mark decided to write his own guidebook, one which aimed to provide practical information that was second to none, detailing the best beaches and the hottest clubs and restaurants, while also giving hard-hitting accounts of every sight, both famous and obscure, and providing up-to-the-minute information on contemporary culture. It was a guide that encouraged independent travellers to find the best of Greece, and was a great success, getting shortlisted for the Thomas Cook travel guide award, and encouraging Mark, along with three friends, to expand the series.

The Rough Guide list grew rapidly and the letters flooded in, indicating a much broader readership than had been anticipated, but one which uniformly appreciated the Rough Guides' mix of practical detail and humour, irreverence and enthusiasm. Things haven't changed. The same four friends who began the series are still the caretakers of the Rough Guide mission today: to provide the most reliable, up-to-date and entertaining information to independent-minded travellers of all ages, on all budgets.

We now publish 100 titles and have offices in London and New York. The travel guides are written and researched by a dedicated team of more than 100 authors, based in Britain, Europe, the USA and Australia. We have also created a unique series of phrasebooks to accompany the travel series, along with the acclaimed series of music guides, and a best-selling pocket guide to the Internet and World Wide Web. We also publish comprehensive travel information on our Web site: *www.roughguides.com*

Contents

List of maps

MAP SYMBOLS

- - - -	Chapter division boundary	ᴠ	Spa
▬ ▪ ▪	Provincial boundary	▲	Peak
▬▬	Highway	⌒⌒	Mountains
══	Main road	♦	Point of interest
──	Minor road	Ⅹ̲	Campsite
───	Unpaved road	◉	Hotel
⊞⊞⊞	Steps	◼	Restaurant
▬▬	Railway	✕	Airport
▪▪▪▪	Wall	★	Bus stop
— —	Ferry route	ⓘ	Tourist office
∿∿	Waterway	⊠	Post office
♠	Church (regional maps)	ℭ	Telephone
⑃	Archeological site	▮	Building
∴	Ruins	⊞	Church (town maps)
♆	Castle	▨	Park
◖	Cave	▨	National park
♦	Museum	⊡	Cemetery

Sardinia's mysterious nuraghic culture to the Roman theatre and Pisan citadel. The best Roman and Carthaginian ruins, however, stand a short journey outside town at **Nora**, evidence of the importance with which the island was regarded. Many of the Mediterranean powers that occupied the island were drawn to its mines, still visible throughout the regions of **Sulcis** and **Iglesiente**, which make up Sardinia's southwestern corner. Off the Sulcis coast, the islands of **Sant'Antíoco** and **San Pietro** provide more archeological remains as well as some prime beaches, while the southern littoral and the Iglesiente's **Costa Verde** are among Sardinia's most scenic coasts.

The island's only extensive plain, the **Campidano**, separates Iglesiente from **La Marmilla**, a hilly country holding some spectacular nuraghic sites, including Sardinia's biggest, **Su Nuraxi**. East of Cágliari, the rugged **Sarrabus** area is fringed by more acres of clean sandy beaches, with resort facilities concentrated in the towns of **Villasimius** and **Muravera**. On the western coast, the province of **Oristano** holds an abundance of nuraghic, Carthaginian and Roman remains, the most important of which – the ruins of **Tharros** – lie on the **Sinis peninsula**, whose lagoons and beaches form a protected habitat for aquatic birds. North of here, **Bosa** is a low-key but attractive fishing port on a river, and **Alghero** attracts much of the island's tourist trade while retaining its distinctive Catalan character, the result of intense settlement 500 years ago. **Stintino**, on the island's northwestern tip, lies near some beaches of jaw-dropping beauty.

Inland, **Sássari** is Sardinia's second city, making a good base to tour some of the Pisan churches which are scattered throughout the Logudoro area south and east of here. On the north coast, picturesque **Castelsardo** is the chief town of **Anglona**, a territory indelibly associated with the Doria family of Genoa. Bordering it, **Gallura** is a dramatically craggy zone whose interior is swathed in cork forests and whose indented coast includes the **Costa Smeralda**. A host of less celebrated but equally enticing stretches of rocky or sandy shore lie nearby, clustered around such centres as **Santa Teresa di Gallura** – the chief port for connections with Corsica – on Sardinia's northern tip, and **Palau**, embarcation point for trips to the **Maddalena archipelago**, whose crystalline waters are also a magnet for boatloads of visitors in summer. Further down the coast, **Olbia** is the main entry point for most of the seasonal swarms from the mainland, though it lacks much charm.

Apart from this top section, Sardinia's eastern coast is largely inaccessible, the sheer cliff walls punctuated by a few developed spots such as **Cala Gonone** and by the small-scale ferry port of **Arbatax**. The huge central province of **Nuoro** occupies most of the mountainous interior, and is the best place to encounter the last remnants of the island's rural culture, particularly its costumes and village festivals. If your image of Sardinia is all shaggy sheep and off-beat folklore – the kind of place depicted in films like *Padre*

Padrone – then these bleak slopes and isolated villages probably fit the bill. This is especially true in the central area known as **Barbagia**, where the sparse population is concentrated in small, insulated villages, few of which warrant spending much time in, though they provide an excellent opportunity to view the quiet life of the interior at first hand, and make useful bases for mountain rambles. Although Sardinia's peaks are not particularly high by European standards (no mountain exceeds 2000m), the terrain can be both awesome and forbidding, particularly in the central ring of the **Gennargentu** mountains, which are often blanketed in snow between November and March.

When to go

The only strong advice which can be given with respect to when to visit Sardinia is to avoid the month of August at all costs. Travelling at this time is by no means unbearable, but the negative factors make a convincing argument for opting for any other time of the year if at all possible – not least the heat, crowds, increased prices, frayed tempers and the difficulty in finding the best accommodation. June, July and September can also be oppressively hot, but there is nothing like the kind of holiday frenzy of the peak weeks. You can count on swimming fairly comfortably at any time between May and late September, nor will you be considered excessively eccentric if you take dips during the winter months. Unless you're camping, there is much to be said for travelling in Sardinia in winter, when the weather can be warm and clear and tourism is refreshingly scarce. Some of the best festivals take place in December, January and February, though the diminished daylight hours in this period can limit your freedom of movement, and you may find many facilities closed for the winter. If walking appeals, spring and autumn provide the most colourful landscape, the most limpid air and the best chances to observe wildlife.

Sardinia climate table

Sardinia's climate varies considerably between the coast and the inland areas. The following table therefore gives average temperatures (°C) and rainfall (in centimetres) for Cágliari, on the south coast, and the high inland region of the Barbagia.

	Jan	Feb	Mar	Apr	May	Jun	Jul	Aug	Sep	Oct	Nov	Dec
Cágliari												
Temperature	10	11	12.5	14.5	18	24	25	25.5	23	18.5	14	12
Rainfall	4.4	4	3.9	3.5	3.5	0.8	0.5	0.8	3	5	6	7
Barbagia												
Temperature	4	5	7	10	14	19	23	22	19	15	9	6
Rainfall	15.5	15	14	11.5	10	3.5	1.5	1.5	6	10.5	15	18

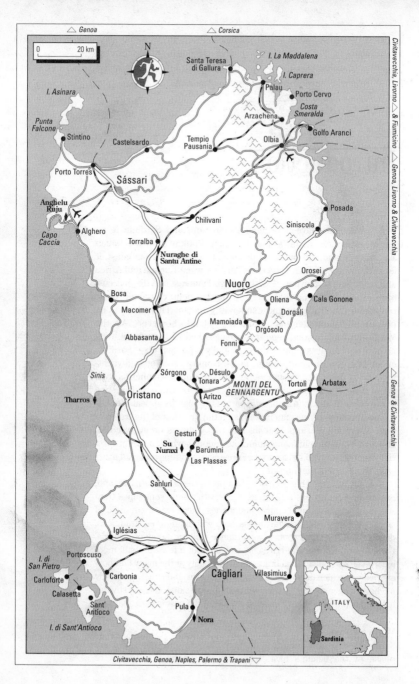

0   20 km

N

I. La Maddalena

Santa Teresa
di Gallura

I. Caprera

Palau

Porto Cervo

I. Asinara

Arzachena

*Costa
Smeralda*

Punta
Falcone

Stintino

Castelsardo

Tempio
Pausania

Olbia

Golfo Aranci

Porto Torres

Sássari

Anghelu
Ruju

Chilivani

Posada

Alghero

Siniscola

Capo
Caccia

Torralba

**Nuraghe di
Santu Antine**

Orosei

Nuoro

Oliena

Cala Gonone

Bosa

Macomer

Dorgáli

Mamoiada

Orgósolo

Abbasanta

Fonni

Sinis

Sórgono

Désulo

Tonara

*MONTI DEL
GENNARGENTU*

Tortolì

Arbatax

Tharros ⚓

Oristano

Aritzo

Gesturi

**Su
Nuraxi** ⬇

Barúmini

Las Plassas

Sanluri

Muravera

Iglésias

Portoscuso

I. di
San Pietro

Carloforte

Carbonia

Cágliari

Villasimius

Calasetta

Sant'
Antioco

Pula

I. di Sant'Antioco

Nora

ITALY

Sardinia

Introduction

A ll islands have a peculiar fascination, and Sardinia is no exception. Lying a little less than 200km from the Italian mainland and the same distance from the Tunisian coast, it is, in the words of D.H. Lawrence, "lost between Europe and Africa and belonging to nowhere." With its own language and distinct customs, the island boasts a fiercely independent character while remaining unmistakably and exuberantly Italian. There is nothing particularly homogenous about the island, however. As the Mediterranean's second biggest island after Sicily – though, with 1.6 million people, less than a third of Sicily's population – Sardinia encompasses a range of diverse faces, from the stereotyped yachting elite of the fabled Costa Smeralda to the simple shepherd's society of the mountainous interior. The fact that you can pass from one to the other in less than an hour is part of the island's appeal. Neither image of course represents more than a tiny fraction of the true picture. There are glorious beaches and rocky shores on every coast, and also dramatic cliffs and numerous lagoons which account for a rich diversity of wildlife, as do the forested mountains and wild *macchia* that carpets the interior.

Not only the island but each of its four provinces of Cágliari, Oristano, Sássari and Nuoro has this range, while within – or sometimes transcending – these administrative boundaries, there exists a mosaic of smaller entities, historical territories each with its different traditions, dialects and historical roots – for instance Gallura, Logudoro, Sulcis, Campidano, Arborea and Barbagia, to name but a few. At a still more local level, each village celebrates its individuality at the many flamboyant festivals which take place throughout the year. Ranging from rowdy medieval pageants to dignified religious processions, these festivities help to keep tradition alive in an island where the past is inescapable.

Where to go
Sardinia's capital, **Cágliari**, is the best place to find traces of every phase of the island's past, from the idiosyncratic statuettes of

The Basics

Getting there from Britain

Much the easiest way to get to Sardinia from Britain is to fly, and prices for charter flights compare well with the long rail/ferry option. Still, arriving by sea has much to commend it, helping to give a sense of Sardinia as an island, though the ferries can get uncomfortably congested in high season.

By plane

Direct flights – either to Olbia or Fertilia (near Alghero) in the north of the island, or Cágliari in the south – take around two and a half hours from London.

The cheapest way to fly is by direct **charter**, though you'd be advised to book some weeks in advance in high season (Easter, July & Aug). Flight-only deals to Cágliari, Fertilia or Olbia cost from around £200–250 return in high season; outside the summer months, when flights are far less frequent, you probably won't find anything much under £200. There are daily summer departures from the various London airports (1–2 weekly in summer from Manchester), down to once or twice a week in the winter.

These flights are available from the numerous specialist **agencies** (see p.4) that deal with charter flights. If you're prepared to book at the last minute, you might find some very good deals indeed, though seat availability is limited – so if you're committed to certain dates, book ahead. Apart from the agencies, other places to check for budget flights are the classified sections in the weekend newspapers, especially the *Guardian*, the *Sunday Times* and the *Observer*; and, if you live in London, *Time Out* magazine or the *Evening Standard*. Teletext, Ceefax and the Internet are also good sources of information. If you're under 26 or a student, contact the **youth/student travel specialists** STA Travel and Usit CAMPUS (see p.4) for cheap deals.

Some agents can sell you an **open-jaw** return, flying to one airport and returning from another – a good idea if you want to make your way across the island (or to Sardinia from somewhere else in Italy), and generally no more expensive than a

---

Flights from the Italian mainland to Sardinia

Most flights to Sardinia start from the Italian mainland, connecting all three of Sardinia's major airports – Fertilia (for Alghero), Olbia and Cágliari – with Rome, Bologna and Milan. Most arrive at Cágliari: the most frequent flights are between Rome and Cágliari (about 8–12 daily), and Cágliari also has flights from Genoa (2 daily); Naples (2 daily); Turin (1 daily); Venice (1 daily) and Verona (1 daily). There is also at least 1 flight daily to **Cágliari** from Catania and Palermo in Sicily. **Olbia** has at least 3 arrivals daily from Rome, 2 from Milan, 1 from Bologna and Pisa, and 3 from Rome; **Fertilia** has at least 4 from Rome and 3 from Milan.

The chief carriers are Alitalia and Meridiana; other lines are Alpi Eagles (from Venice and Verona) and Air Dolomiti (from Genoa). Flight time is about an hour Rome–Cágliari, about 70min Milan–Fertilia. Fares vary according to season and according to how much advance booking you are able to give: the cheapest fares are between Rome and Olbia, amounting to about L100,000 for a single. Purchasing the tickets in Italy – either from a travel agent or direct from the airline – is usually cheaper than buying from abroad.

---

standard charter return. Consider a **package deal** (see p.9), too, which takes care of flights and accommodation for an all-in price.

It may also be worth looking at cheap flights to **other Italian destinations**: Fiumicino, Rome's main airport, is only about four hours by fast ferry from Olbia, for example.

Scheduled flights with Alitalia, British Airways or Meridiana are more expensive, though only

one (Meridiana) goes direct. Others are routed via Italian mainland airports (usually Milan or Rome), which could mean a total journey time of anything up to five hours if you have to wait for a connecting internal flight (flight time from the mainland to Sardinia is about an hour). However, scheduled services to the mainland are very frequent (several times daily), though almost all are from one of the London airports.

AIRLINES AND AGENCIES IN BRITAIN

AIRLINES

Alitalia, 4 Portman Square, London W1H 9PS ☎0171/602 7111.

British Airways, 156 Regent St, London W1R 5TA; Victoria Place, Victoria Station, SW1W 9SJ; 146 New St, Birmingham B2 4HN; 41–43 Deansgate, Manchester M3 2AY; 66 Gordon St,

Glasgow G1 3RS; 32 Frederick St, Edinburgh EH2 2JR. For all enquiries ☎0345/222 111 (24hr line).

Meridiana, 15 Charles II St, London SW1Y 4QU ☎0171/839 2222.

TRAVEL AGENCIES

Alpha Flights, 37 King's Exchange, Tileyard Rd, London N7 9AH ☎0171/609 8188.

APA Travel, 138 Eversholt St, London NW1 ☎0171/387 5337.

Council Travel, 28a Poland St, London W1V 3DB ☎0171/437 7767.

CTS Travel, 44 Goodge St, London W1P 2AD ☎0171/636 0031.

Italflights, 125 High Holborn, London WC1V 6QA ☎0171/405 6771.

Italia nel Mondo, 6 Palace St, London SW1E 5HY ☎0171/828 9171.

Italy Sky Shuttle, 227 Shepherds Bush Rd, London W6 7AS ☎0181/748 1333.

LAI, 185 King's Cross Rd, London W6 7AS ☎0171/837 8492.

STA Travel, 86 Old Brompton Rd, London SW7 3LQ ☎0171/581 4132; 117 Euston Rd, London NW1 2SX ☎0171/465 0485; 38 Store St, London WC1E 7BZ ☎0171/580 7733; 11 Goodge St, London W1P 1FE ☎0171/436 7779; 30 Upper Kirkgate, Aberdeen AB10 1BA ☎01224/658 222; 38–39 North St, Brighton BN1 1RH ☎01273/728 282; 25 Queen's Rd, Bristol BS8 1QE ☎0117/929 4399; 38 Sidney St, Cambridge CB2 3HX ☎01223/366 966; 11 Duke St, Cardiff CF1 2AY ☎01222/382 350; 27 Forrest Rd, Edinburgh EH1 2QH ☎0131 226

7747; 184 Byres Rd, Glasgow G12 8SN ☎0141/338 6000; 88 Vicar Lane, Leeds LS1 7JH ☎0113/244 9212; 75 Deansgate, Manchester M3 2BW ☎0161/834 0668; 9 St Mary's Place, Newcastle NE1 7PG ☎0191/233 2111; 36 George St, Oxford OX1 2OJ ☎01865/792 800; plus branches on university campuses throughout Britain. Flights only. Web site *www.sta-travel.com/*

Travel Bug, 597 Cheetham Hill Rd, Manchester M8 5EJ ☎0161/721 4000.

Usit CAMPUS, 52 Grosvenor Gardens, London SW1W 0AG ☎0171/730 3402; 110 High St, Old Aberdeen AB24 3HE ☎01224/273 559; 541 Bristol Rd, Selly Oak, Birmingham B29 6AU ☎0121/414 1848; 61 Ditchling Rd, Brighton BN1 4SD ☎01273/570 226; 39 Queen's Rd, Clifton, Bristol BS8 1QE ☎0117/929 2494; 5 Emmanuel St, Cambridge CB1 1NE ☎01223/324 283; 20 Fairfax St, Coventry CV1 5RY ☎01203/225 777; 53 Forrest Rd, Edinburgh EH1 2QP ☎0131/668 3303; 122 George St, Glasgow G1 1RF ☎0141/553 1818; 166 Deansgate, Manchester M3 3FE ☎0161/833 2046; 105–106 St Aldates, Oxford OX1 1DD ☎01865/242 067; 340 Glossop Rd, Sheffield S10 2HW ☎0114/275 2552; plus branches in YHA shops and on university campuses all over Britain. Flights only.

Meridiana flies 1–3 times a week between April and October (on Saturdays from April 3, also Tuesdays from April 27, also Fridays from July 2) from London Gatwick to Olbia: the cheapest current return fare is around £246 in the high season, about £226 in the low (April to mid-July and mid-Sept to Oct); ask about discounts for students and under-25s. British Airways, flying daily from Heathrow, Gatwick and Manchester, charge about £385 return in high season, £311 in low season, though fares vary considerably according to times and dates. Alitalia fly daily from Heathrow, Gatwick and Stansted via Rome or Milan to Cágliari, and charge from about £230 return, with special student discounts in some periods. The full fare on any of these scheduled flights would in fact be nearer £700 return – discounts mean that restrictions apply, for example the requirement to book at least one or two weeks ahead and to stay at least one Saturday night; a ticket validity of one month allowing for no date changes, and either no refund or only a partial one on cancellation. It's always worth checking for seasonal special deals, and booking tickets through a travel agent rather than the airline direct will often reduce the price considerably.

On arrival, you will find shops and cafés at all the airports, and regular public transport departures into town. Each of the three main airports has a tourist information office open daily, and a bank open only during normal banking hours, but equipped with a cash machine for local currency. Taxis and most of the car rental agencies can also be found at the airports.

By train

Travelling by **train to Sardinia** from Britain is marginally cheaper than flying and allows you the possibility of breaking your journey. However, it won't save a huge amount of money when you take into account eating and drinking costs en route, and it can also be something of an endurance test: the journey from London across the Channel by ferry, through France to the nearest ports of Marseille, Toulon, Genoa and Livorno takes a minimum of nine hours, including at least one change of trains, depending on which of the three possible routes you take. It's well worth **reserving a seat** (currently £2–10 for each train you travel on), if not a **couchette bed** (around £15) for at least part of the journey – and you should do both well in advance.

Fares vary according to the route taken, but the ordinary second-class **return fare** on the fastest route (using Eurostar via Paris) to Genoa will cost you £223, to Marseilles or Toulon £129; all tickets are valid for two months and should be booked at least a week ahead. Under-26s can buy **discounted Billet International de Jeunesse (BIJ) tickets** through Wasteels (address below), which allow as many stopovers as you like over a two-month period; these currently cost around £130 return to Marseille and Toulon £130 to Genoa, and £138 to Livorno. All of these prices apply to the slower ferry crossing from Dover or Folkestone. Under-26s travelling from **outside London** can also arrange discounted connecting fares to get them to London; alternatively, they qualify for reduced-price tickets if they join the train at the Channel ports. Any of these tickets are available at offices in Victoria Station, London, from youth/student agents, or direct from Rail Europe or Wasteels. Obviously, if you choose to travel the London–Paris section of the route by Eurostar from London Waterloo, the total fare will be considerably more.

Given these prices, you might consider investing in an **InterRail** pass, which for those under 26 costs from £209 for one month's unlimited rail travel throughout Europe. The pass is zoned (Italy is grouped with Turkey, Greece and Slovenia), and gives discounts on cross-Channel services and free passage on the Bríndisi–Corfu–Patras route to Greece – though it's not actually a lot of help once you've arrived in Sardinia, since the rail network isn't that extensive (see "Getting Around", p.26). There's a version for over-26s too, costing £279. The InterRail pass is available from

---

Rail Ticket Agencies

Citalia ☎ 0891/715 151.

Eurostar European Passenger Services (reservations) ☎ 0990/186 186.

Italian State Railways (enquiries) ☎ 0171/724 0011; timetables and general information on the Web at *www.fs-on-line.com/*

Rail Europe 179 Piccadilly, London W1V 0BA ☎ 0990/848 848.

Ultima Travel 424 Chester Rd, Little Sutton, Ellesmere Port CH10 3RB ☎ 0151/339 6171.

Wasteels ☎ 0171/834 7066.

CROSS-CHANNEL TICKETS

Eurotunnel ☎ 0990/353 535. To Calais.

Hoverspeed, Dover ☎ 0990/240 241. To Boulogne and Calais.

P&O Stena Line ☎ 0990/980 980. To Calais and Dieppe.

Sea France ☎ 0990/980 980. To Calais.

AGENTS FOR FERRIES TO ITALY

Corsica Ferries, c/o Viamare, Graphic House, 2 Sumatra Rd, London NW6 1PU ☎ 0171/431 4560.

Grandi Navi Veloci, c/o Viamare, see above.

Moby Lines, c/o Viamare, see above.

SNCM, c/o Southern Ferries, 179 Piccadilly, London W1 ☎ 0171/491 4968.

Tirrenia Line, c/o Serena Holidays, 40–42 Kenway Rd., London SW5 0RA ☎ 0171/373 6548.

CROSSING FROM THE ITALIAN MAINLAND

Tirrenia run most of the services to Sardinia from the Italian mainland and Palermo and Trápani in Sicily. The prices given are the cheapest one-way high-season fares (for reclining chair or deck class). Berths in shared cabins cost about L20,000 more. Car fares given here are for vehicles less than 4m length, calculate another L30,000 for cars longer than 3.5 or 4m.

FERRIES (*Traghetti*) FROM ITALY

Route	Company	Frequency	Length of crossing	Single fare passenger	Car
Civitavecchia–Arbatax	Tirrenia	2 weekly	10hr 30min	L69,000	L125,000
Civitavecchia–Cágliari	Tirrenia	1 daily	14hr 30min–17hr	L70,500	L140,500
Civitavecchia–Golfo Aranci	FS	2 daily	8hr	L80,000 (June–Sept)	L160,000
Civitavecchia–Golfo Aranci	Sardinia Ferries	3–7 weekly	7hr	L45–84,000 (April–Jan)	L94–147,000
Civitavecchia–Olbia	Tirrenia	6–7 weekly	8hr	L33,900	L138,000
Genoa–Arbatax	Tirrenia	1–2 weekly	16hr 30min–19hr	L78,500	L140,500
Genoa–Cágliari	Tirrenia	2 weekly	20hr	L95,500 (mid-June to mid-Sept)	L130,500
Genoa–Olbia	Grandi Navi Veloci	1 daily	10hr	L130,000 (late June to mid-Sept)	L200,000
Genoa–Olbia	Tirrenia	3–7 weekly	13hr 15min	L76,500	L140,500
Genoa–Porto Torres	Grandi Navi Veloci	1 daily	10hr	L136,000 (late June to mid-Sept)	L205,000
Genoa–Porto Torres	Tirrenia	5–7 weekly	13hr	L76,500	L140,500
Livorno–Golfo Aranci	Sardinia Ferries	1–2 daily	9–10hr	L90,000 (April–Sept)	L205,000
Livorno–Olbia	Moby	6 weekly–2 daily	10hr	L96,000	L205,000

Route	Company	Frequency	Length of crossing	Single fare passenger	Car
Napoli–Cágliari	Tirrenia	1–2 weekly	15hr 30min–16hr 15min	L71,500	L140,500
Napoli–Palau	Linee Lauro	1–2 weekly	14hr	L140,000	L230,000 (mid-June to Sept)
Palermo–Cágliari	Tirrenia	1 weekly	13hr 30min	L66,500	L140,500
Trápani–Cágliari	Tirrenia	1 weekly	11hr 30min	L66,500	L140,500

"FAST" OR "EXPRESS" FERRIES (*mezzi veloci*) FROM ITALY

Daytime crossings take the shortest time. Fares vary according to season and speed of mezzo veloce.

Route	Company	Frequency	Length of crossing	Single fare passenger	Car
Civitavecchia–Golfo Aranci	Sardinia Ferries	2 daily	3hr 30min	L63–98,000	L152–207,000 (June–Sept)
Civitavecchia–Olbia	Tirrenia	6 weekly–3 daily	4–6hr	L55–80,000	L140–160,000
Fiumicino–Arbatax	Tirrenia	2 weekly	4hr 45min	L85,000	L130,000 (mid-June to Aug)
Fiumicino–Golfo Aranci	Tirrenia	2–3 daily	4hr–5hr 30min	L55–80,000	L140–160,000 (mid-June to Aug)
Genoa–Olbia	Tirrenia	1–2 daily	6hr	L131,000	L166,000 (mid-June to Sept)
Genoa–Porto Torres	Tirrenia	2 daily	6hr	L131,000	L166,000 (mid-June to Aug)
La Spezia–Golfi Aranci	Tirrenia	1 daily	5hr 30min	L112,500	L165,000 (mid-June to Aug)

CROSSING FROM FRANCE, CORSICA AND TUNISIA

In summer, you could cross to Bastia, Corsica, with Corsica Ferries (from La Spezia or Pisa) or Moby (from Genoa, Livorno or Piombino), then make your way down to Bonifacio (178km) from which it's a short crossing to Sardinia. There are also seasonal crossings from Porto Vecchio in Corsica, and year-round from Tunis.

Route	Company	Frequency	Length of crossing	Single fare passenger	Car
Bonifacio (Corsica)–Santa Teresa di Gallura	Moby	4–10 dailly	50min	L18,000	L60,000 (April–Sept)
Bonifacio (Corsica)–Santa Teresa di Gallura	Saremar	2–4 daily	50min	L16,000	L55,000
Marseille–Porto Torres	SNCM	2–3 monthly	12hr 45min–15hr 30min	£44	£77 (April–Sept)
Porto Vecchio (Corsica)–Palau	TRIS	1–2 weekly	2hr 30min	L24,000	L60,000 (April–Sept)
Toulon–Porto Torres	SNCM	1 weekly	10hr 15min–15hr 30min	£44	£77 (April–Sept)
Tunis–Cágliari (via Trápani)	Tirrenia	1 weekly	35hr 30min	L107,000	L171,000

British Rail stations and youth/student travel agencies, and you need to have been resident in Europe for at least six months to qualify.

Finally, senior citizens holding a Senior Citizen Railcard (£18) can purchase a **Rail Europe Senior Card** for £5, which allows 30 percent discounts on rail fares covering more than one country, plus 30 percent off most ferry crossings. Specific details and tickets from British Rail stations.

For details of passes for use solely within Italy, see p.27.

By bus

You can travel to Sardinia by **bus** as far as the ferry crossing at Marseille and Toulon using **National Express Eurolines** (☎0990/808 080) from London. A daily service departs from Victoria Coach Station at 6pm, arriving at Marseille the next day at 2.15pm local time, and at Toulon an hour later (respectively £101 and £109 for the return trip; children pay half price). Buses use the ferry crossing, which is included in the price.

By car: the ferries and Eurotunnel

The standard cross-Channel **ferry/hovercraft** links are between Dover and Calais or Boulogne (with Hoverspeed, P&O Stena or Sea France), Folkestone and Boulogne (Hoverspeed), or Newhaven and Dieppe (P&O Stena or Hoverspeed). Crossing using Eurotunnel from Folkestone to Calais (24hr service, departures every 15min at peak periods) will speed up the initial part of the journey.

The shortest **ferry crossing** to Sardinia is by "Fast Ferry" or "Express Ferry" from Genoa, Civitavecchia and Fiumicino, though only the Tirrenia Civitavecchia–Olbia route is served by these outside the summer months. Considerably cheaper regular ferries run year-round from these and other mainland Italian and Sicilian ports, and there are also direct SNCM ferries from Marseille and Toulon in France. Marseille, Toulon and Nice also have regular connections with Corsica, from whose southern tip there are frequent ferry links to Sardinia, providing you with an interesting exercise in comparing and contrasting the two islands.

Specialist Tour Operators in Britain

Alternative Travel Group, 69–71 Banbury Rd, Oxford OX2 6PE ☎01865/315 678. Inclusive seven-day walking holidays (April/May & Oct) in the mountains around Oliena, near Nuoro; costly (around £995, excluding flights) but well organized.

Citalia, Marco Polo House, 3–5 Lansdowne Rd, Croydon, Surrey CR9 1LL ☎0181/686 0677. Packages in the poshest places, including the Costa Smeralda, Santa Margherita di Pula and Villasimius, between May and September, with prices starting from about £800 per person per week, double that in August. Car rental is also laid on.

Holiday Options, Independent Air Travel Ltd., Martlett Heights, 49 The Martletts, Burgess Hill, West Sussex RH15 9NJ ☎01444/244 411. Hotels and self-catering apartments in the best of Sardinia's resorts, mainly in the north of the island.

Interhome, 383 Richmond Rd, London TW1 2EF ☎0181/891 1294. Holiday homes throughout Sardinia, including apartments in Stintino and Santa Teresa di Gallura for 4 people at around £650 in peak season.

Magic of Italy, 227 Shepherds Bush Rd, London W6 7AS ☎0181/748 7575. Tailor-made packages throughout the island, including apartments and farm accommodation, two-centre holidays, or just fly-drive deals.

Ramblers Holidays, Box 43, Welwyn Garden City, Herts AL8 6PQ ☎01707/331 133. Half-board walking holidays based in Fonni and Dorgali, near Nuoro in the eastern interior (one week, £470, two weeks £620–648). Departures in May–June and Sept.

Sardatur, 125 High Holborn, London WC1V 6QA ☎0171/242 2455. Hotels and self-catering villas and apartments in the Santa Margherita di Pula area, the Costa Smeralda and Alghero, plus a fly-drive option where you can choose different lodgings all over the island.

Voyages Ilena, 1 The Old Garden, The Lanterns, Bridge Lane, London SW11 3AD ☎0171/924 4440. Villas, apartments and hotels in the prime holiday areas of northeast Sardinia, Alghero and around, and the south-west and southeast.

Any travel agent can provide up-to-date cross-Channel schedules and make advance bookings (essential in high season if you're driving). For the Italian crossings, contact the companies or their agents; more details on all these routes are given in the box on pp.6–7. In the low season, watch out for **special offers** on the Italian ferries if you're buying a return ticket on your outward journey; check with the agent.

Something to bear in mind when calculating driving costs is that **motorway tolls** can add another £40 or so per car driving from Calais to the French coast, and about £10 more between the French border and Genoa. Driving in Italy is more expensive than just about anywhere else in Europe, with inflated fuel prices (see p.28) and high rental charges (p.29).

Package holidays

If you don't want to move around so much, it's always worth looking at **travel-plus-accommodation** package holidays. Many companies offer travel at rates as competitive as any you could find on your own, and any travel agent can fill you in on

all the latest offers. Most packages are to Alghero and Stintino in the northwest of the island, Santa Teresa di Gallura and the Costa Smeralda region in the northeast, Santa Margherita di Pula in the southwest, and the area around Villasimius in the southeast. You'll also see holidays in the interior, often used by **specialist holiday operators**, mostly dealing with walking tours, but also skiing and riding (see box opposite). These don't come cheaply: accommodation, food, local transport and the services of a guide are nearly always included, and a week's half-board holiday can cost from £750 per person, full-board as much as £1300. It's obviously cheapest to go out of season, something to be recommended anyway as the resorts and sights are much less crowded, and the sea is often warm enough to bathe in as early as May and as late as October.

If you want to rent a car in Sardinia, it's well worth checking with tour operators before you leave as some **fly-drive deals** work out very cheaply. See the box opposite for operator's addresses; and see p.29 for more car-rental details.

Getting there from Ireland

There are no direct flights from Ireland to Sardinia; you must either travel via London, or via a major Italian city such as Milan or Rome.

The cheapest current high-season return fares **from Dublin** to either Cágliari or Fertilia (booked at least seven days in advance) are around IR£390 return; otherwise your best bet is to get to London and then catch a Sardinia-bound plane from there. There are numerous daily flights to London with Ryanair, Aer Lingus, British Airways and British Midland. The cheapest are Ryanair's, which cost from around IR£70 for a return to Gatwick, Luton or Stansted, though the bus and underground journeys across London may make the total cost greater than flying direct to Heathrow. **From Belfast**, there are British Airways and British Midland flights to Heathrow, but the cheapest service is the Jersey European run to Gatwick or Stansted, at £70–90 return. (For information on flights to Sardinia from the Italian mainland, see p.3.)

For the best **youth/student deals** from either Dublin or Belfast, and for information about rail passes, contact Usit (see box below).

AIRLINES AND AGENTS IN IRELAND

AIRLINES

Aer Lingus, 40 Upper O'Connell St, Dublin ☎01/844 4747; 2 Academy St, Cork ☎021/327 155; 136 O'Connell St, Limerick ☎061/474 239.

Alitalia, 4–5 Dawson St, Dublin ☎01/677 5171.

British Airways, Belfast reservations ☎0345/222 111; Dublin reservations ☎1800/626 747.

British Midland, Belfast reservations ☎0870/607 0555; Dublin reservations ☎01/283 8833.

Jersey European Airways, Belfast reservations ☎01232/457 2004.

Ryanair, Dublin reservations ☎01/609 7800.

AGENTS

Thomas Cook, 11 Donegal Place, Belfast BT1 5AJ ☎01232/554 455; 118 Grafton St, Dublin 2 ☎01/677 1721. Mainstream package holiday and flight agent, with occasional discount offers.

Usit, 19–21 Aston Quay, O'Connell Bridge, Dublin 1 ☎01/677 8117; 66 Oliver Plunkett St, Cork ☎021/270 900; Fountain Centre, College St, Belfast BT1 6ET ☎01232/324 073. Student and youth specialist.

Getting there from the USA and Canada

Although there are no direct flights from North America to Sardinia, you can fly to the Italian mainland from a number of cities. The main points of entry are Rome and Milan, from either of which there are plenty of connecting flights to Sardinia. Many airlines and agents also offer open-jaw tickets, enabling you to fly into one Italian city and out from another.

It might be a good idea to take advantage of the wide choice of well-priced flights available from all over North America to various **European cities** (particularly in Britain or Germany), as there's a greater range of options for reaching Sardinia from there. **Flying** is the most straightforward way to get from Britain to Sardinia, and prices are competitive; see p.3 for full details. If you're interested in seeing more of Europe on the way, the long **rail** journey may be more appealing – see p.14 for details of the **Eurail** pass, which you'll need to purchase before you leave home.

Shopping for tickets

Barring special offers, the cheapest fare is usually an **Apex** ticket, although this will carry certain restrictions: you have to book – and pay – at least 21 days before departure, spend at least seven days abroad (maximum stay three months), and you tend to get penalized if you change your schedule. There are also winter **Super Apex** tickets, sometimes known as "Eurosavers" – slightly cheaper than an ordinary Apex, but limiting your stay to between seven and 21 days. Some airlines also issue **Special Apex** tickets to people younger than 24, often extending the maximum stay to a year. Many airlines offer youth or student fares to **under-25s**; a passport or driving licence are sufficient proof of age, though these tickets are subject to availability and can have eccentric booking conditions. It's worth remembering that most cheap return fares involve spending at least one Saturday night away, and that many will only give a percentage refund if you need to cancel or alter your journey – check the restrictions carefully before buying a ticket.

You can normally cut costs further by going through a **specialist flight agent** – either a **consolidator**, which buys up blocks of tickets from the airlines and sells them at a discount, or a **discount agent**, which deals in blocks of tickets offloaded by the airlines, and often offers special student and youth fares and a range of other travel-related services such as insurance, rail passes, car rentals and tours. Bear in mind, though, that penalties for changing your plans can be stiff.

Some agents specialize in **charter flights**, which may be cheaper than anything available on a scheduled flight, but again departure dates are fixed and withdrawal penalties are high (check the refund policy). If you travel a lot, **discount travel clubs** are another option – the annual membership fee may be worth it for benefits such as cut-price air tickets and car rental. Finally, **students** should be able to take advantage of discounted air fares from various travel agencies; while a couple of agencies (see box overleaf) also offer very cheap **courier** flights – though these carry severe restrictions on trip duration and the amount of luggage allowed.

Don't automatically assume that tickets purchased through a travel specialist will be cheapest – once you get a quote, check with the airlines and you may turn up an even better deal. Be advised also that the pool of travel companies is swimming with sharks – exercise caution and never deal with a company that demands cash up-front or refuses to accept payment by credit card.

Regardless of where you buy your ticket, the **fare** will depend on the season, and are highest between June and August; they drop during the "shoulder" seasons, September–October and April–May, and you'll get the best prices during the low season, November to March (excluding Christmas and New Year when prices are hiked up and seats are at a premium). Note also that flying on **weekends** ordinarily adds US$60

(CAN$80) to the round-trip fare, while **taxes** added to each fare usually run to another US$35 (CAN$55–65); price ranges quoted below assume midweek travel.

From the USA

Alitalia, the Italian national airline, offers the widest choice of routes between the USA and Italy, flying direct every day from New York, Boston, Miami, Chicago and Los Angeles to Milan and Rome. As for **American-based airlines**, Delta Airlines flies daily from New York non-stop, and also from Chicago and Los Angeles to Rome and Milan with stopovers in either New York or a European city; TWA flies daily from LA and Chicago via New York to Milan and Rome; American Airlines flies daily direct to Milan from Chicago and Miami; and Continental flies daily from Newark to Rome and Milan.

AIRLINES AND OPERATORS IN NORTH AMERICA

AIRLINES

Air Canada ☎1-800/776-3000; in Canada ☎1-888/247 2262; *www.aircanada.ca/*

Air France ☎1-800/237-2747; in Canada ☎1-800/667 2747; *www.airfrance.fr/*

Alitalia ☎1-800/223-5730; in Canada ☎1-800/361 8336; *www.alitalia.com/*

American Airlines ☎1-800/433-7300; *www.americanair.com/*

British Airways ☎1-800/247-9297; in Canada ☎1-800/243 6822; *www.british-airways.com/*

Canadian Airlines ☎1-800/426-7000; in Canada ☎1-800/665 1177; *www.cdnair.ca/*

Continental Airlines ☎1-800/231-0856; *www.flycontinental.com/*

Delta Airlines ☎1-800/241-4141; in Canada ☎1-800/221 1212; *www.delta-air.com/*

Iberia in US & Canada ☎1-800/772-4642; *www.iberia.com/*

Icelandair ☎1-800/223-5500; *www.icelandair.is/*

Northwest/KLM ☎1-800/374-7747; in Canada ☎1-800/581 6400; *www.klm.com/*

Lufthansa ☎1-800/645-3880 or 1-800/399-LUFT; in Canada ☎1-800/563 5954; *www.lufthansa.com/*

Sabena ☎1-800/955-2000; *www.sabena-usa.com/*

SAS ☎1-800/221-2350; *www.flysas.com/*

Swissair ☎1-800/221-4750; in Canada ☎1-800/267 9477; *www.swissair.com/*

TWA ☎1-800/892-4141; *www.twa.com/*

DISCOUNT TRAVEL OPERATORS

Air Brokers International, 323 Geary St, Suite 411, San Francisco, CA 94102 ☎1-800/883-3273, *www.airbrokers.com/* Consolidator.

Air Courier Association, 15000 W 6th Ave, Suite 203, Golden, CO 80401 ☎303/278-8810, *www.aircourier.org/* Courier flight broker, often with flights from New York to Milan or Rome.

Airhitch, 2472 Broadway, Suite 200, New York, NY 10025 ☎212/864-2000; *www.airhitch.org/* Standby-seat broker: for a set price, they guarantee to get you on a flight as close to your preferred destination as possible, within a week.

Cheap Tickets, 115 E 57th St, Suite 1510, New York, NY 10022 ☎1-800/377-1000. Discounted tickets for international destinations.

If you want to **stop over in Europe**, it's worth considering one of the European airlines with services to Italy, including: Air France (via Paris); British Airways (via London); Iberia (via Madrid); Icelandair (via Luxembourg); Lufthansa (via Frankfurt or München); Northwest/KLM (via Amsterdam); Sabena (via Brussels); Swissair (via Zürich); and SAS (via Copenhagen) – all of which have services to at least Rome and Milan.

Direct flights to Italy take around 9 hours from New York or Boston, 12 hours from Chicago, and 15 hours from Los Angeles; for the **connection to Sardinia** add on another 1–3 hours, depending on the service, plus any time spent waiting for the connection itself.

The basic round-trip **fares to Rome or Milan** vary little between airlines, though it's always worth asking about special promotions. Generally, the cheapest round-trip fare, travelling midweek in low season, starts at around US$650 from New York or Boston to Rome, rising to around US$750 during the shoulder season, and to about US$950 during the summer. Flights from LA work out about US$200 on top of these round-trip fares; from Miami and Chicago, add on about US$100.

Sardinian cities with airports include Cágliari, Olbia and Alghero. Fares with Alitalia from Rome or Milan to any one of these are in the range of US$180–300, with no student discounts available. (For information on flights to Sardinia from the Italian mainland, see p.3.)

From Canada

The only airlines to fly direct to Italy **from Canada** are Alitalia, which flies daily from Toronto and Montréal to Rome or Milan for a low-season fare of CAN$1060 midweek, increasing to around

Council Travel, Head Office: 205 E 42nd St, New York, NY 10017 ☎1-800/2COUNCIL; in New York ☎212/822-2700; *www.counciltravel.com/* Student and youth travel organization offering discounted airfares, rail passes and travel gear. For over-26s, it acts like a regular travel agency.

Educational Travel Center, 438 N Frances St, Madison, WI 53703 ☎1-800/747-5551; *www.edtrav.com/* Student/youth discount agent with good prices on flights to Rome and Milan.

Encore Travel Club, 4501 Forbes Blvd, Lanham, MD 20706 ☎1-800/444-9800; *www.emitravel.com/* Discount travel club.

Last Minute Travel Club, 100 Sylvan Rd, Woburn, MA 01801 ☎1-800/LAST-MIN.Travel club specializing in standby deals.

New Frontiers/Nouvelles Frontières Head offices: 12 E 33rd St, New York, NY 10016 ☎1-800/366-6387; 1001 Sherbrook East, Suite 720, Montréal, H2L 1L3 ☎514/526-8444. French discount travel firm with summer charters to Rome. Other branches in LA, San Francisco and Québec City.

STA Travel Head office: 5900 Wiltshire Blvd, Suite 2110, Los Angeles, CA 90036 ☎1-800/777-0112; *www.sta-travel.com/* Worldwide specialist in independent travel for students and under-26s only, with branches in the New York, San Francisco and Boston areas.

TFI Tours International Head office: 34 W 32nd St, 12th Floor, New York, NY 10001 ☎1-800/745-8000. Consolidator; other offices in Las Vegas, San Francisco, Los Angeles.

Travac, Head office: 989 6th Ave, 16th Floor, New York, NY 10018 ☎1-800/872-8800 or ☎212/563-3303; *www.travac.com/* Consolidator and charter broker. Will fax current fares from their fax line (☎1-888/872-8327).

Travel Avenue, 10 S Riverside Plaza, Suite 1404, Chicago, IL 60606 ☎1-800/333-3335; *www.tipc.com/* Discount travel agent.

Travel Cuts 187 College St, Toronto, ON M5T 1P7 ☎1-800/667-2887, in the US ☎1-877/247-888; *www.travelcuts.com/* Branches all over Canada, plus an office in San Francisco (☎414/247-1800). Specialists in student fares, IDs and travel services.

Travelers Advantage, 3033 S Parker Rd, Suite 900, Aurora, CO 80014 ☎1-800/548-1116. Discount travel club.

UniTravel, 11737 Administration Drive, Suite 120, St Louis, MO 63146 ☎1-800/325-2222. Consolidator.

Worldtek Travel, 111 Water St, New Haven, CT 06511 ☎1-800/243-1723; *www.worldtek.com/* Discount travel agency.

CAN$1320 in high season (expect to pay upwards of CAN$100–200 extra for weekend travel at any time of the year); and Canadian Airlines, which flies to Rome from Toronto (daily except Mon & Sat) and Montréal (Mon & Sat only) for around CAN$756 in low season and CAN$1070 in high season. Remember to add on another CAN$150 return or so for any connecting flights to Sardinia. Flights to Italy take around 9 hours from the eastern Canadian cities, 15 hours from the west. Other airlines to consider are British Airways (daily flights from Toronto, Montréal and Vancouver – via London – to Rome); Lufthansa (daily, a direct Calgary, Montréal, Toronto, Vancouver – via Frankfurt – to Milan, Rome or Venice service); and Northwest/KLM (daily from Montréal and Toronto to Milan and Rome via Amsterdam).

Packages and organized tours

There are dozens of companies operating **group travel** and **tours** in Italy, ranging from full-blown luxury escorted tours to small groups sticking to specialized itineraries. However, specifically Sardinian options are less common, though the agencies listed below usually offer tours at least partly based on the island. If you're happy to stay in one (or two) places, you can also, of course, simply book a hotel-plus-flight deal, or, if you're keener to self-cater, rent a villa or a farmhouse for a week or two. Prices vary wildly, so check what you are getting for your money (many don't include the cost of the air fare). Reckon on paying at least US$1500 for a ten-day touring vacation without flight, and up to as much as US$4000 for a fourteen-day escorted specialist package with flight.

Travelling by rail

If you're interested in seeing more of Europe en route to Sardinia, travelling by **train** may be appealing, though you'll have to plan ahead as rail passes usually have to be purchased before you leave home. A **Eurail Pass** (allowing unlimited free train travel in Italy and sixteen other countries) is not likely to pay for itself if you're planning to stick to Sardinia alone, since the train network there is rather limited, though for anyone planning to see more of Italy on the way there or back it's ideal. It costs US$554 for fifteen days, US$718 for 21 days, US$1260 for two months, and US$1558 for three months.

If you're under 26, you can save money with a **Eurail Youthpass**, which is valid for second-class travel and is available in fifteen-day ($388), 21-day ($499), one-month ($623), two-month ($882) and three-month ($1089) increments. If you're travelling with one to four other companions, the joint **Eurail Saverpass** is available in fifteen-day ($470), 21-day ($610), one-month ($756), two-month ($1072), and three-month ($1324) increments. You stand a better chance of getting your money's worth out of a **Eurail Flexipass**, which is good for a certain number of travel days in a two-month period. This, too, comes in first-class and under-26/second-class versions: ten days cost US$654/458; and fifteen days, US$862/599. Again, parties of two to five can save fifteen percent with the **Eurail Saver Flexipass** with travel within a two-month period for ten days ($556) and fifteen days ($732).

North Americans are also eligible to purchase more specific passes valid for travel in Italy only, for details of which see "Getting Around", p.26.

Specialist Operators in North America

Adventure Center, 1311 63rd St, Suite 200, Emeryville, CA 94608 ☎1-800/227-8747.

American Express Vacations, PO Box 619008, MD 5268; DFW Airport, Texas 75261-9008 ☎1-800/241-1700. Individual and escorted programmes to Italy; they can also plan city stays, offering competitive hotel rates.

Archaeological Tours, 271 Madison Ave, New York, NY 10016 ☎212/986-3054. Fully escorted archeological tours to Sardinia, Corsica and Malta for 19 days; around US$4000.

CIT Tours, 342 Madison Ave, New York, NY 10173 ☎1-800/CIT-TOUR; in Canada ☎514/845-9101 or ☎1-800/387-0711 in Toronto, and 1-800/361-7799 in Montréal. Specialize exclusively in tours to Italy.

Italiatour, ☎1-800/237-0517 or ☎1-800/845-3365. In conjunction with Alitalia, offers fly-drive tours, and escorted and individual programs.

Globus-Cosmos, 5301 South Federal Circle, Littleton, CO 80123 ☎1-800/221-0090; *www.cosmostours.com/* Escorted and individual tours; prices start at US$1300.

Rail Contacts in North America

DER Travel Services, 9501 W Devon Ave, Suite 301, Rosemont, IL 60018 ☎ 1-800/421-2929. Eurail and Italian passes.

Forsyth Travel Library, 1750 East 131st St, P.O. Box 480800, Kansas City, MO, 64148 ☎ 1/800-367-7984; *www.forsyth.com/* Eurail passes.

Italian State Railways, c/o CIT Tours, 342 Madison Ave, Suite 207, New York, NY 10173 ☎ 1-800/223-7987; in LA ☎ 310/338-8616. Eurail and Italian passes.

Rail Europe, 226 Westchester Ave, White Plains, NY 10604 ☎ 1-800/438-7245, *www.raileurope.com/* Official Eurail agent in North America; also sells a wide range of European regional and individual country passes.

ScanTours, 3439 Wade St, Los Angeles, CA 90066 ☎ 1-800/223-7226. Eurail and Italian passes.

Getting there from Australia and New Zealand

The easiest way to get to Sardinia from Australia is to fly direct to the island's capital Cágliari, though you will have more choice and may find a cheaper flight if you travel to a big Italian city and pick up an internal flight from there. Coming from New Zealand, you'll have no choice but to travel via mainland Italy, as there are no direct flights to Sardinia.

Shopping for tickets

The cheapest fares from Australia to Italy are with Gulf Air, which flies from **Sydney to Rome** (A$1350 low season), or Thai Airways, which flies via Bangkok to Rome (A$1460 low season). Alitalia has fares departing from Adelaide, Brisbane, Canberra, Melbourne and Sydney, flying via Singapore to Milan or Rome (A$1540 low season, A$2150 high season). Fares are also available on Alitalia through to Cágliari, with a stopover in either Milan or Rome (A$1600–2400). Flights with Qantas and British Airways from Sydney to Rome start at A$1760 return. Low season is generally January–March and October–November; high season covers April and August to mid-September; peak season is mid-May to end July and mid to end December.

The best deals from **Auckland to Rome** are with Thai Airways via Bangkok ($NZ1950–2400). There are also flights with Qantas-Alitalia (NZ$2350–2700).

A Rome–Sardinia flight will cost around A$260–340 return. (For more information on flights to Sardinia from the Italian mainland, see p.3.)

As far as **Round-the-World** fares go, you should be able to get four to six stopovers worldwide (including Rome) for A$2350–2800 /

NZ$2700–3300. The best deals are with the One World consortium (British Airways, Qantas, American Airlines, Canadian Airlines and Cathay Pacific); routings are offered on a zoned (A$2000–3100/NZ$2700–3700) or mileage basis (A$2500–3000/NZ$3090–3550). Round-the-World tickets from Sydney on Qantas and Alitalia via Asia to Rome, including a side-trip to Cágliari and returning via the USA start at A$2670. The Star Alliance (between Ansett, Air New Zealand,

---

AIRLINES AND AGENTS IN AUSTRALIA AND NEW ZEALAND

AIRLINES

Alitalia, 32 Bridge St, Sydney ☎ 1300 653 747; 6/229 Queen St, Auckland ☎ 09/379 4457

Gulf Air, 64 York St, Sydney ☎ 02/9321 9199

Qantas, 70 Hunter St, Sydney ☎ 13 13 13; 154 Queen St, Auckland ☎ 09/357 8900 or 0800/808 767

Thai Airways, 75 Pitt St, Sydney ☎ 1300/651 960; 22 Fanshaw St, Auckland ☎ 09/377 3886

SPECIALIST AGENTS

European Travel Office, 133 Castlereagh St, Sydney ☎ 02/9267 7727; 122 Rosslyn St, West Melbourne ☎ 03/9329 8844; 407 Great South Rd, Auckland ☎ 09/525 3074. Air tickets plus accommodation packages from camping to villas.

Italia Mia, 101 Bridport Rd, Melbourne ☎ 03/9682 8098. Small-group package holidays, with a gastronomic and cultural slant.

Italian Travel Bureau (CIT), 123 Clarence St, Sydney ☎ 02/9267 1255, plus other offices in Melbourne, Brisbane, Adelaide and Perth. Specialists in flights and package deals. Web site at *www.cittravel.com.au/*

DISCOUNT TRAVEL AGENTS

Anywhere Travel, 345 Anzac Parade, Kingsford, Sydney ☎ 02/9663 0411 *anywhere@ozemail.com.au/*

Budget Travel, 6 Fort St, Auckland; other branches around the city ☎ 09/366 0061; 0800/808040.

Destinations Unlimited, 3 Milford Rd, Milford, Auckland ☎ 09/373 4033.

Flight Centres, Australia: ☎ 13 16 00 or 13 31 33 (24 hours), Level 11, 33 Berry St, North Sydney ☎ 02/9241 2422; Bourke St, Melbourne ☎ 03/9650 2899; Brisbane ☎ 07/3229 9211 plus other branches nationwide. Web site at *www.flightcentre.com/* New Zealand: National Bank Towers, 205–225 Queen St, Auckland ☎ 09/209 6171; Shop 1M, National Mutual Arcade, 152 Hereford St, Christchurch ☎ 03/379 7145; 50-52 Willis St, Wellington ☎ 04/472 8101; other branches countrywide.

STA Travel Australia: fastfare telesales ☎ 1300/360 960; nearest branch ☎ 13 17 76; 855 George St, Sydney ☎ 02/9212 1255; 256 Flinders St, Melbourne ☎ 03/9654 7266; *trav-eller@statravelaus.com.au/*; other offices in state capitals and major universities. Web site *www: statravelaus.com.au/*

New Zealand: Travellers' Centre, 10 High St, Auckland ☎ 09/309 0458; 233 Cuba St, Wellington ☎ 04/385 0561; 90 Cashel St, Christchurch ☎ 03/379 9098; other offices in Dunedin, Palmerston North, Hamilton and major universities.

Student Uni Travel, 92 Pitt St, Sydney ☎ 02/9232 8444; branches in state capitals.

Thomas Cook, Australia: telesales ☎ 1800/063 913; nearest branch ☎ 13 17 71; 175 Pitt St, Sydney ☎ 02/9248 6100; 257 Collins St, Melbourne ☎ 03/9650 2442; branches in other state capitals.

New Zealand: Shop 250a St Luke's Square, Auckland ☎ 09/849 2071.

Trailfinders, 8 Spring St, Sydney ☎ 02/9247 7666

Travel.com.au, 76–80 Clarence St, Sydney ☎ 02/9249 5444; *consultant@travel.com.au* Web site at *www.travel.com.au/*

Air Canada, Lufthansa, SAS, Thai Airways, United Airlines and Varig Brazilian Airlines) has mileage based fares (A$2699–3209/NZ$3000–3500).

Travelling by rail

There are a couple of European **rail passes** that can only be purchased before leaving home. Before you go, consider carefully how much travelling you are going to be doing; the rail network in Sardinia itself is limited and the passes only really begin to pay for themselves if you intend to see more of Italy and the rest of the Europe on the way.

The **Eurail Youthpass**, for under-26s only, costs A$597/NZ$698 for fifteen days unlimited travel, A$777/NZ$910 for 21 days, A$961/NZ$1124 for one month, A$1361/NZ$1592 for two months, and A$1681/NZ$1967 for three months. If you're over 26 you'll have to buy the first-class version,

which also comes in fifteen-day (A$854/NZ$999), 21-day (A$1108/NZ$1296), one-month (A$1372/NZ$1605), two-month (A$1943/NZ$2273) and three-month (A$2400/NZ$2808) increments. **Eurail Flexipass** is good for a certain number of days' travel in a two-month period and also comes in youth/first-class versions; ten days cost A$705/1007 (NZ$825/1178), and fifteen days A$929/1327 (NZ$1086/1553).

A scaled-down version of the Flexipass, the **Europass** (again available in either youth or first-class versions) allows travel in France, Germany, Italy, Spain and Switzerland and costs from A$343/518 (NZ$401/606) for five days in two months to A$804/1185 (NZ$940/1386) for fifteen days in two months. The passes are available in Australia from Rail Plus ☎03/96428644, or 1300/555 003, *info@railplus.com.au/* In New Zealand from Thomas Cook ☎09/263 7260.

Red tape and visas

British, Irish and other EU citizens can enter Sardinia and stay as long as they like on production of a valid passport. Citizens of the United States, Canada, Australia and New Zealand need only a valid passport, too, but are limited to stays of three months. All other nationals should consult the relevant embassies about visa requirements.

Legally, you're required to register with the police within three days of entering Italy, though if you're staying at a hotel this will be done for you. Although the police in some towns have become more punctilious about this, most would still be amazed at any attempt to register yourself down at the local police station while on holiday. However, if you're going to be living here for a while, you may as well do it; see p.57 for more details.

Italian Embassies and Consulates Abroad

Australia: Level 45, 1 Macquarie Place, Sydney 2000, NSW ☎02/9392 7900; 509 St Kilda Rd, Melbourne ☎03/9867 5744; 12 Grey St, Yarralumla, ACT ☎02/6273 3333.

Britain: 38 Eaton Place, London SW1 8AN ☎0171/235 9371; 32 Melville St, Edinburgh EH3 7HA ☎0131/226 3631; 111 Piccadilly, Manchester M1 2HY ☎0161/236 9024.

Canada: 275 Slater St, Ottawa, Ontario K1P 5H9 ☎613/232-2401; 3489 Drummond St, Montréal, Québec H3G 1X6 ☎514/849-

8351; 136 Beverley St, Toronto ☎416/977-1566.

Ireland: 63–65 Northumberland Rd, Dublin ☎01/660 1744; 7 Richmond Park, Belfast ☎01232/668 854.

New Zealand: 34 Grant Rd, Thorndon, Wellington ☎04/473 5339.

USA: 690 Park Ave, New York ☎212/737-9100 or 439-8600; 12400 Wilshire Blvd, Suite 300, Los Angeles ☎310/820-0622; 1601 Fuller St NW, Washington DC ☎202/328-5500.

Insurance

■

As an EU country, Italy has free reciprocal health agreements with other member states, but even if you're covered by this you're strongly advised to take out travel insurance to cover you against loss or theft during your travels. Some kind of travel insurance is essential for all non-EU citizens.

Before you purchase any insurance, check what you have already. Some credit cards offer insurance benefits if you use them to pay for your holiday tickets. North Americans, in particular, may find themselves covered for medical expenses and loss, and possibly loss of or damage to valuables, while abroad, as part of a family or student policy.

For medical treatment and drugs, keep all the receipts and claim the money back later. If you have anything stolen (including money), **register** the loss immediately with the local police – without their report you won't be able to claim. Note also that very few insurers will arrange on-the-spot payments in the event of a major expense or loss; you will usually be reimbursed only after going home.

British and Irish cover

Most travel agents and tour operators will offer you insurance when you book your flight or holiday. These policies are usually reasonable value, though as ever, you should check the small print. If you feel the cover is inadequate, or you want

to compare prices, any travel agent, insurance broker or bank should be able to help. If you have a good "all risks" home insurance policy it may well cover your possessions against loss or theft even when overseas, and many private medical schemes also cover you when abroad – make sure you know the procedure and the helpline number.

In Britain and Ireland, **travel insurance schemes** are sold by almost every travel agent or bank, and by specialist insurance companies, all of which offer two weeks' basic cover in Italy for around £20, one month for around £30. Good-value policies are issued by Usit CAMPUS (Usit in Ireland) or STA Travel (see p.4 and 10); Endsleigh Insurance (97–107 Southampton Row, London WC1B 4AG ☎0171/436 4451); Liverpool Victoria (County Gates, Bournemouth, Dorset BH1 2NF ☎01202/292 333); or Columbus Travel Insurance (17 Devonshire Square, London EC2M 4SQ ☎0171/375 0011). Columbus also do an annual multi-trip policy, which offers twelve months' cover for around £50, as do Thomas Cook (45 Berkeley St, London W1X 5AE 0845/600 5454); American Express (0800/700 737) are slightly more expensive at £65.

North American cover

Holders of official **student/teacher/youth cards** are entitled (outside the US) to accident coverage and hospital in-patient benefits. **Students** will often find that their student health coverage extends during the vacations and for one term beyond the date of their last enrolment. Bank and credit cards (particularly American Express) often have certain levels of medical or other insurance included, and travel insurance may also be included if you use a major credit or charge card to pay for your trip. **Homeowners' or renters'** insurance often covers theft or loss of documents, money and valuables while overseas, though conditions and maximum amounts vary from company to company. **Canadians** are usually covered for medical mishaps overseas by their provincial health plans.

After exhausting the possibilities above, you might want to contact a **specialist travel insur-**

Travel Insurance Companies in North America

Access America ☎ 1-800/284-8300.

Carefree Travel Insurance US only ☎ 1-800/323 3149.

Council Travel ☎ 1-800/2COUNCIL, *www.counciltravel.com/*

Desjardins Travel Insurance Canada only ☎ 1-800/463 7830.

International Student Insurance Service (ISIS), sold by STA Travel ☎ 1-800/777-0112.

Travel Guard ☎ 1-800/826-1300.

Travel Insurance Services ☎ 1-800/937-1387.

Worldwide Assistance ☎ 1-800/821-2828.

ance company; your travel agent can usually recommend one, or see the box above. Policies are comprehensive (accidents, illnesses, delayed or lost luggage, cancelled flights, etc), but maximum pay-outs tend to be meagre. The best deals are usually to be had through student/youth travel agencies – ISIS policies, for example, cost US$60 for fifteen days (depending on coverage), US$110 for a month, US$165 for two months, or up to US$665 for a year.

Australasian cover

Travel insurance is available from most travel agents (see p.16) or direct from insurance companies (see below), for periods ranging from a few days to a year or even longer. Most policies are similar in premium and coverage – but if you plan to indulge in high-risk activities such as mountaineering, bungee jumping or scuba diving without a certificate, check the policy carefully to make sure you'll be covered. A typical policy will cost around A$190/NZ$230 for one month to A$300/NZ$340 for two months.

In Australasia policies are issued by: AFTA, 144 Pacific Highway, North Sydney ☎ 02/9956 4800; Cover-More Insurance Services, Level 9, 32 Walker St, North Sydney ☎ 02/9202 8000 or 1800/251 881, and 57 Simon St, Auckland ☎ 09/377 5958; Ready Plan, 141–147 Walker St, Dandenong, Victoria ☎ 1300/555 017, and 10/63 Albert St, Auckland ☎ 09/300 5333; and by UTAG, 122 Walker St, North Sydney ☎ 02/9744 7833 or 1800/809 462 or through STA Travel (see box on p.16)

Costs, money and banks

Sardinia isn't cheap compared with other Mediterranean holiday spots, though it is still noticeably less expensive than mainland Italy – you'll find that food and accommodation especially are good value.

Average costs

If you're watching your budget – camping, buying some of your own food in the shops and markets – you could get by on as little as £20–30/US$35–50 a day; a more realistic **average daily budget** is around £35–50/US$55–80 a day, including hotel accommodation and some travel costs; while on £50–60/US$80–100 a day you could be living pretty comfortably. Most basic things are fairly inexpensive: a pizza and a beer cost around £3.50-5/$6-8.25 just about everywhere, a full meal with wine from around £12/$20; buses and trains are relatively cheap and distances between towns small; and hotel rooms in the cities start at around £17/$28 a double. It's the snacks and drinks that add up: eating ice creams and drinking soft drinks or coffee all costs around the same price (if not more) as at home. And if you sit down to do any of this, it'll cost around 30 percent more.

Of course, these prices are subject to where and when you go, and whether you're alone. You'll pay more in summer for rooms, while accommodation and food in the Costa Smeralda are downright expensive, and the offshore Maddalena islands can also be quite costly. On the whole, the interior is cheap, though don't expect much choice of places to stay and eat. **Out of season** you'll find lower accommodation prices in nearly all the small hotels and *pensioni*. However, **single accommodation** can be hard to come by: what there is tends to fill quickly and you'll often have to pay most of the price of a double room. There are no **reductions** or discounts for students or young people in Sardinia: it's the one place where an ISIC card is no use at all; under-18s and over-65s, on the other hand, get into museums and archeological sites free everywhere.

Money and banks

The most painless way of dealing with your money is by using **credit**, **charge** or **cash cards**, which, in conjunction with your personal identification number (PIN), give you access to cash dispensers (*bancomat*). Found even in small towns, these accept all major cards, with a minimum withdrawal of L50,000 and a maximum of L300,000–500,000 per day. Cards can also be used for cash advances over the counter in banks and for payment in most hotels, restaurants, petrol stations and some shops; for all these transactions you will pay a fee of 1.5 percent, but the rate of exchange will be in your favour. Remember that all cash advances on a credit card are treated as loans, with interest accruing daily from the date of withdrawal. To block any lost or **stolen card** in Italy, call ☎ 167.822.056.

An alternative option is to carry your money in the form of **travellers' cheques**, available from any British high street bank, whether or not you have an account, as well as post offices and some building societies. Most American and Canadian banks sell American Express cheques, and they're widely accepted; your local bank will probably also sell one or more of the other brands. To find the nearest bank that sells a particular brand, or to buy cheques by phone, call the following numbers: American Express (☎ 1-800/673-3782), Citicorp (☎ 1-800/645-6556), MasterCard International/Thomas Cook (☎ 1-800/223-7373), Visa (☎ 1-800/227-6811). The usual fee for travellers' cheque sales is 1 or 2 percent, and it pays to get them in either sterling or dollars. Make sure to keep the purchase agreement and a record of cheque serial numbers safe and separate from the cheques themselves. In the event that cheques are lost or stolen, the issuing company will expect you to report the loss forthwith to their nearest office; most companies claim to replace lost or stolen cheques within 24 hours.

You'll usually – though not always – pay a small commission when you **exchange money** using travellers' cheques – again around 1 percent of the amount changed, although some

---

Currency

Italy is one of eleven countries who have opted to join the European Monetary Union and, from January 1, 1999, began to phase in the single European currency, the **euro**. Initially, however, it will only be possible to make paper transactions in the new currency (if you have, for example, a euro bank or credit-card account), and the normal unit of currency will remain the lira (plural lire), always abbreviated as L. Euro notes and coins are scheduled to be issued at the beginning of 2002, and to replace the lira entirely by the end of that year.

You get notes for L1000, L2000, L5000, L10,000, L50,000 and L100,000; and coins for L50, L100, L200 and L500. L50 and L100 coins in particular come in a variety of forms. It's an idea to have at least some Italian money for when you first arrive, and you can buy lire in advance from most banks.

Exchange rates: 1 euro is equal to L1936. At the time of writing you'll get around L2800 to the pound sterling and L1600 to the US$.

Wire Services

Australia American Express MoneyGram
☎ 1800/230 100; Western Union ☎ 1800/649 565.

Britain Western Union ☎ 0800/833 833.

New Zealand American Express MoneyGram: Auckland ☎ 09/379 8243; Wellington ☎ 04/499 7899 or 473 7766; Western Union: Auckland ☎ 09/270 0050.

USA and Canada American Express MoneyGram ☎ 1-800/543-4080; Western Union ☎ 1-800/325-6000.

banks will make a standard charge per cheque regardless of its denomination – usually around L6000. It's worth knowing that Thomas Cook offices don't charge for cashing their own cheques, and American Express offices don't charge for cashing anyone's cheques. Note too that main post offices in Italy will accept and cash American Express cheques.

It's an idea to have at least some Italian **cash** for when you first arrive. You can buy lire over the counter in British banks; most American banks will need a couple of days' notice. Try and get some smaller-denomination currency for bus or taxi rides from your point of disembarkation: if you don't have the right money, it's up to you to find it – a general rule throughout Italy.

The main **banks** you'll see in Sardinia are the Banco di Sardegna, Banco di Sássari, and the Banca Commerciale Italiana. **Banking hours** vary slightly from town to town, but generally banks are open Monday to Friday, 8.30am–1.20pm and 3–4pm. Outside these times you can change travellers' cheques and cash at large hotels and the main airports. Some banks open on Saturday mornings as well; check the text and city Listings sections.

If you run out of money abroad, or there is some kind of emergency, the quickest way to get **money sent out** is to use a wire service (see box). This can take minutes; find the local Western Union office on the toll-free number ☎ 167/464 464. Charges are on a sliding scale, £14 for £50–100, £42 for £500–700. Getting money sent from your bank at home takes much longer and costs around £15 for a five- to seven-day transfer, or £20 for a two- to three-day transfer.

Health matters

EU citizens can take advantage of Italy's health services under the same terms as the residents of the country. You'll need form E111, available from any main post office. The Australian Medicare system also has a reciprocal health care arrangement with Italy. However, you should also take out ordinary travel insurance – certainly if you're a non-EU citizen (see "Insurance", p.18, for more details).

Vaccinations are not required. However, cholera and typhoid jabs are a wise precaution if you intend to continue to North Africa – in which case make sure you also have an up-to-date polio booster. Otherwise, Sardinia doesn't present too many health worries: the worst that's likely to happen to you is suffering from the extreme heat in summer or from an upset stomach (shellfish is the usual culprit). Tap water is perfectly safe to drink (unless there's a sign saying "*acqua non potabile*"), though bottled water is available everywhere.

Pharmacies

An Italian **pharmacist** (*farmacia*) is well-qualified to give you advice on minor ailments, and to dispense prescriptions. There's generally one open all night in the bigger towns; they work on a rota system, and you should find the address of the one currently open on any *farmacia* door or listed in the local paper. Condoms (*profilático*) are available over the counter from all pharmacists and some supermarkets; the Pill (*la píllola*) is available on prescription only.

Doctors and hospitals

If you need treatment, go to a **doctor** (*médico*); every town and village has one. Ask at a pharmacy, or consult the local *Págine Gialle* (*Yellow Pages*) under *Azienda Unità Sanitaria Locale* or *Unità Sanitaria Locale*, or *Pronto Soccorso*. The *Págine Gialle* also list some specialist practitioners in such fields as acupuncture and homeopathy, the latter much more common in Italy than in many countries. If you're eligible, take your E111 with you to the doctor's: this should enable you to get free treatment and prescriptions for medicines at the local rate – about 10 percent of the price of the medicine. For repeat medication, take any empty bottles or capsules with you to the doctor's – the brand names often differ.

If you get taken **seriously ill**, or involved in an accident, hunt out the nearest **hospital** and go to the Pronto Soccorso (casualty) section, or phone ☎113 and ask for "*ospedale*" or "*ambulanza*". Hospital standards don't differ significantly from clinics at home. Throughout the guide, you'll find listings for pharmacists, hospitals and emergency services in all the major cities.

Incidentally, try to avoid going to the **dentist** (*dentista*) while you're in Sardinia. These aren't covered by the *mutua* or health service, and for the smallest problem they'll make you pay through the teeth. Take local advice, or consult the local *Yellow Pages*.

If you don't have a spare pair of glasses, take a copy of your prescription with you; an **optician** (*óttico*) will be able to make you up a new pair should you lose or damage them.

Information and maps

Before you leave, it's worth calling the Italian State Tourist Office (ENIT) for a selection of maps and brochures, though don't go mad – much of it can easily be picked up later in Sardinia. Worth grabbing are any accommodation listings and town plans they may have for the area you're interested in, as well as a camping brochure.

Tourist offices

The main Sardinian tourist organization is ESIT (Ente Sardo Industrie Turistiche), with an information office in Cágliari. Most Sardinian towns, and the three principal airports' have a **tourist office**: either an APT or EPT (Azienda Promozione Turistica/Ente Provinciale per il Turismo), a provincial branch of the state organization, or an AAST (Azienda Autónoma di Soggiorno e Turismo), a smaller local outfit. When there isn't either an APT/EPT or AAST there

---

Sardinia on the Net

Italian **Web sites** have proliferated in recent years and provide a wealth of information; these are some of the more useful ones for Sardinia. Other relevant Internet addresses are given on p.24 (ENIT) and p.33 (IYHA).

Alitalia
www.alitalia.it/
Alitalia routes and schedules in English.

Hello Sardinia
www.hellosardinia.it/
Online edition of the free monthly magazine (see p.24) with events, articles, itineraries and general information on the island, in Italian.

In Italy
www.initaly.com/
Well produced, with detailed information on the whole country; the Sardinia section covers history, culture, festivals, travel and services.

Italian Ministry for Arts and the Environment
www.beniculturali.it/
Museums, temporary exhibitions, performances and so on, in Italian.

Italian State Railways (FS)
www.fs-on-line.com/
Timetable information in Italian and English.

Italian Yellow Pages
www.paginegialle.it/

La Nuova Sardegna
www.lanuovasardegna.it/
Online local newspaper, with local news, weather, transport timetables, features on food, etc.

Sardegna in Italy
www.sardegnainitaly.com/
Articles on towns, artists and local issues, plus photos and recipes.

Sardinia Net
www.sardinia.net/
Links to all the most useful web sites, including the EU-sponsored Tirso site, with ferries and flight timetables, hotels and campsites, and info on routes and itineraries.

Sardinia Travel Net
www.vol.it/stn
General information on accommodation and features in a site still needing improvement.

Italian State Tourist Offices (ENIT)

Australia: apply to the consulate, Level 45, 1 Macquarie Place, Sydney 2000, NSW ☎02/9392 7900.

Canada: 1 Placeville Marie, Suite 1914, Montréal, Québec H3B 2C3 ☎514/866-7667.

Ireland: 47 Merrion Square, Dublin 2 ☎01/766 397.

New Zealand: apply to the embassy, 34 Grant Rd, Thorndon, Wellington ☎04/473 5339.

UK: 1 Princes St, London W1R 8AY ☎0171/408 1254.

USA: 630 Fifth Ave, Suite 1565, New York, NY 10111 ☎212/245-5618, brochure requests 212/245-4822; 500 North Michigan Ave, Suite 2240, Chicago, Illinois 60611 ☎312/644-0996, brochure requests 312/644-0990; 12400 Wilshire Blvd, Suite 550, Los Angeles, CA 90025 ☎310/820-1898, brochure requests 310/820-0098.

Note: ENIT is on the Web at *www.enit.it/*

will sometimes be a Pro Loco office, which will have much the same kind of information, though these generally keep much shorter hours. All of these vary in degrees of usefulness, and away from the main cities and tourist areas the staff aren't likely to speak English. But you should always be able at least to get a free town plan, accommodation lists and a local listings booklet in Italian, and some will reserve you a room and sell tickets for performances in archeological sites and seats at festas. You will also see **unofficial tourist offices** in some places, offering a host of other services such as car hire, apartment rental, excursions, etc., as well as dispensing lots of free information.

Likely summer **opening hours** are Monday to Friday 9am to 1pm and 4 to 7pm, Saturday 9am to 1pm, but check the text for more details. If the tourist office isn't open and all else fails, the local telephone office and most bars with phones carry a copy of the local *Tuttocittà*, a listings and information magazine which details addresses and numbers of most of the organizations you're likely to want to know about, as well as having indexed street maps for local towns and adverts for restaurants and shops. Note, too, that there is an island-wide toll-free telephone service giving tourist information during office hours: ☎167/013 153.

Another useful source of information is the free monthly **magazine** *Hello Sardinia*, aimed at both tourists and locals wanting to explore the island, with a calendar of events, articles on places of interest and itineraries, written in Italian but much of it easy to understand. Pick up the magazine at airports, tourist offices and some hotels; they also have a Web site (see p.23).

Maps

The best large-scale **road map** of Sardinia is published by the Touring Club Italiano (*Sardegna*, 1:200,000), usually available from the outlets listed in the box opposite. Otherwise, the Automobile Club d'Italia (see "Cars", p.28) issues a good, free 1:275,000 road map, available from the State Tourist Offices, while local tourist offices in Sardinia often have road maps of varying quality to give away.

For **hiking**, you'll need at least a scale 1:100,000 map (better 1:50,000), though there's not much around – again, check with one of the specialist map shops listed opposite or with the Club Alpino Italiano, Via Fonseca Pimental 7, 20121 Milan ☎02.2614.1378. For specific towns, the maps we've printed should be fine for most purposes, though local tourist offices also often hand out reasonable town plans and regional maps.

MAP OUTLETS

AUSTRALIA

Mapland, 372 Little Bourke St, Melbourne, VIC 3000 ☎03/9670 4383.

The Map Shop, 16a Peel St, Adelaide, SA 5000 ☎08/8231 2033.

Perth Map Centre, 891 Hay St, Perth, WA 6000 ☎08/9322 5733.

Travel Bookshop, Shop 3, 175 Liverpool St, Sydney, NSW 2000 ☎02/9261 8200.

Worldwide Maps and Guides, 187 George St, Brisbane, QLD 4000 ☎07/3221 4330.

BRITAIN

Blackwell's Map and Travel Shop, 53 Broad St, Oxford OX1 3BQ ☎01865/792 792.

Daunt Books, 83 Marylebone High St, London W1M 3DE ☎0171/224 2295; 193 Haverstock Hill, London NW3 4QL ☎0171/794 4006.

Heffers Map Shop, 3rd Floor, in Heffers Stationery Department, 19 Sidney St, Cambridge, CB2 3HL ☎01223/568 467.

Italian Bookshop, 7 Cecil Court, London WC2N 4EZ ☎0171/240 1634.

James Thin Melven's Bookshop, 29 Union St, Inverness, IV1 1QA ☎01463/233 500.

John Smith and Sons, 57–61 St Vincent St, Glasgow G2 5TB ☎0141/221 7472.

Newcastle Map Centre, 55 Grey St, Newcastle upon Tyne, NE1 6EF ☎0191/261 5622.

Stanfords*, 12–14 Long Acre, London WC2E 9LP ☎0171/836 1321; at Usit CAMPUS, 52 Grosvenor Gardens, London SW1W 0AG; 156 Regent St, London W1R 5TA ☎0171/434 4744; 29 Corn St, Bristol BS1 1HT ☎0117/929 9966.

The Map Shop, 30a Belvoir St, Leicester, LE1 6QH ☎0116/247 1400.

The Travel Bookshop, 13–15 Blenheim Crescent, London W11 2EE ☎0171/229 5260.

Waterstone's, 91 Deansgate, Manchester, M3 2BW ☎0161/832 1992.

Maps by mail or phone order are available from Stanfords ☎0171/836 1321.

CANADA

Curious Traveller Travel Bookstore, 101 Yorkville Ave, Toronto, ON M5R 1C1 ☎1-800/268 4395.

Open Air Books and Maps, 25 Toronto St, Toronto, ON M5C 2R1 ☎416/363 0719.

International Travel Maps, 555 Seymour St, Vancouver, BC V6B 3J5 ☎604/687 3320.

IRELAND

Hodges Figgis Bookshop, 56–58 Dawson St, Dublin 2 ☎01/677 4754.

Waterstone's, Queens Bldg, 8 Royal Ave, Belfast BT1 1DA ☎01232/247 355; 7 Dawson St, Dublin 2 ☎01/679 1415.

NEW ZEALAND

Specialty Maps, 58 Albert St, Auckland ☎09/307 2217.

USA

Book Passage, 51 Tamal Vista Blvd, Corte Madera, CA 94925 ☎415/927-0960.

The Complete Traveler Bookstore, 199 Madison Ave, New York, NY 10016 ☎212/685-9007; 3207 Fillmore St, San Francisco, CA 94123 ☎415/923-1511.

California Map & Travel Center, 3312 Pico Blvd, Santa Monica, CA 90405 ☎310/396-6277.

The Globe Corner Bookstore, 28 Church St, Cambridge, MA 02138 ☎617/497-6277 and 500 Boylston St, Boston, MA 02116 ☎617/859-8008. Orders also accepted at *www.globecorner.com/._*

Phileas Fogg's Books, Maps and More, 87 Stanford Shopping Center, Palo Alto, CA 94304 ☎1-800/233-FOGG in California; ☎1-800/533-FOGG elsewhere in USA.

Rand McNally*, 444 N Michigan Ave, Chicago, IL 60611 ☎312/321-1751; 150 E 52nd St, New York, NY 10022 ☎212/758-7488; 595 Market St, San Francisco, CA 94105 ☎415/777-3131; 7988 Tysons Corner Center, Maclean, VA, 22102 ☎202/223-6751.

Sierra Club Bookstore, 6014 College Ave, Oakland, CA 94618 ☎510/658-7470.

Travel Books & Language Center, 4437 Wisconsin Ave NW, Washington, DC 20016 ☎1-800/220-2665.

Note: Rand McNally now has 24 stores across the US; call ☎1-800/234-0679 for the location of your nearest store.

Getting around

Although distances aren't especially large in Sardinia, getting around by public transport is not always easy. The rail system is slow, few buses run on Sunday and route information can be frustratingly difficult to extract, even from the bus and train stations themselves. On the positive side, public transport prices are among the cheapest in Europe.

Although general points are covered below, each chapter's "Travel Details" section has the full picture on transport schedules and frequencies. Note that these refer to regular working day schedules, ie Monday to Saturday; services may be much reduced, or even non-existent, on Sundays. Note also that comments such as "every 30min" are approximations – on the railways in particular, there are occasional gaps in the schedule.

One thing to bear in mind is that travelling by train is not the best way to see all of the island. Some stations are miles away from their towns while much of the east and centre of Sardinia is only accessible by bus or car. Driving, biking and walking are the best modes for exploring anywhere off the beaten path, though it makes sense to use public transport for direct jouneys between towns. It's useful to know that in case of strikes, there are always a small number of essential transport services guaranteed to run, though these can become very jammed.

Trains

Sardinia's **train network** connects all the major towns, though few of the intermediate stops are very useful. The main lines are operated by Italian State Railways, Ferrovie dello Stato (FS), and by two independent companies, Ferrovie Meridionali della Sardinia (FMS) and Ferrovie della Sardinia (FdS, also known as Ferrovie Sarde or Ferrovie Complementari Sarde). FMS runs a service between Cágliari, Iglésias and Carbónia, while FdS operates various lines: the Sássari–Alghero branch line, the Nuoro–Macomer–Bosa route, Tempio Pausánia–Palau, and an internal route linking Cágliari, Sórgono, Mandas and Arbatax. On this last line, steam trains take over in summer, when it is known as the *trenino verde*, otherwise these smaller lines are diesel-driven, and therefore noisy and not the smoothest of rides. You might get two carriages if you're lucky, and these fill quickly at certain times, for example for the school runs in the morning and at lunchtime; FS trains too get busy at these times. On the whole the trains leave punctually, and arrive within ten minutes or so of the scheduled time.

All trains in Sardinia are either Diretto or Regionale: Diretto trains are less longer-distance, calling only at larger stations, while the Regionale services (also called Locale) cover shorter distances, stopping at every station. Smoking is not permitted in any part of Regionale trains, and there are moves afoot to ban it on all trains. Note that train tickets must be validated – ie punched in machines scattered around the station and platforms, soon to be introduced on the trains themselves – within 6 hours for distances of less than 200km, or 24 hours for distances over 200km. Failure to do this may land you with an on-the-spot fine of around L50,000. If you don't have time to buy a ticket you can simply board your train and pay the conductor, though it'll cost around 30 percent more this way.

As well as the boards displayed at stations ("Departures" are *Partenze*, "Arrivals" *Arrivi*,

---

Information on all FdS trains can be found on the Web at *www.ferroviesardegna.it/*

"Delayed" *In Ritardo*), a timetable is useful, even if you use it only to discover exactly how late your train is. The Sardinian routes are covered by FS's booklet, *In Treno Sardegna*, issued twice-yearly and free from most train stations, and there are also sheets given out for individual routes. Pay attention to the timetable notes, which may specify the dates between which some services run (*Si effetua dal . . . al . . .*), or whether a service is seasonal (*periódico*), denoted by a vertical squiggle; *feriale* is the word for the Monday to Saturday service, symbolized by two crossed hammers, *festivo* means that a train runs only on Sundays and holidays, with a cross as its symbol.

Prices are very reasonable. Tickets are charged by the kilometre; the longest trip you can make on the island, the 300km loop from Olbia to Cágliari costs less than L25,000 for a second-class ticket, though most of the journeys you'll make will be much shorter and cheaper. **Bikes** can be carried on trains marked with a bicycle symbol on the timetables for a L5000 supplement.

Rail passes and discounts

The Europe-wide **InterRail** and **Eurail** passes (see p.5, p.14 and p.17) give unlimited travel on the FS network only, not the private lines. These are the passes that are most likely to prove useful, but if you're undertaking an intensive bout of rail travel elsewhere in Italy, you might want to invest in one of the many passes exclusive to the FS system.

Travellers from the UK have a choice of three **Freedom/Euro-Domino** passes for the Italian network – three days' unlimited rail travel for £104 (£84 for under-26s), five days' for £134 (£106 for under-26s), or ten days' for £187 (£145 for under-26s). They include a 30–50 percent discount for cross-Channel ferries and for journeys to other European Channel ports.

North Americans and Australians can buy the similar **Italy Flexi-Railcard**, valid for four days' travel within a nine-day period (US$ 216/CAN$313/A$170); eight days within 21 (US$302/CAN$439/A$238); or twelve days within 30 (US$389/CAN$562/A$306).

Note that all the above passes should be bought before you leave home, and that you should allow at least a week for processing before you can use them; see p.5 for the relevant agents.

In addition, there are two specific **Italian passes**, also available before you leave from the rail agencies listed in the relevant "Getting There" sections above, or from major train stations in Italy. The **Biglietto Turistico Libera Circolazione** is valid for unlimited travel on all FS trains, excluding "Pendolino" (a first-class inter-city service); for eight days it costs from £120/US$266/A$227; for fifteen days £146/US$332/A$284; for 21 days £168/US$386/A$329; and for 30 days £200/US$465/A$397. You must have the station ticket office validate the first journey you make before boarding the train. The **Chilométrico** ticket, valid for up to five people, gives 3000km worth of travel on a maximum of twenty separate journeys; it costs around L246,000, but you have to pay supplements on faster trains – and you're very unlikely to cover that sort of distance on a Sardinian holiday anyway.

Other **discounts** on normal fares are for large **groups** (6–24 people get a discount of 20 percent, more than 25 people get 30 percent), **children** (50 percent discount for 4–12 year-olds), and **under-4s** travel free provided they do not occupy a seat. If you're going to be spending a long time in Sardinia or Italy, the **Cartaverde** for under-26s, and the **Carta d'argento** for over-60s, come into their own. Valid for one year, these cards cost L40,000, give a 20 percent discount on any fare, and are available from main train stations in Italy.

Buses

Sardinia is served by an extensive network of **buses** (*autobus* or *pullman*) covering almost every town and village and a good number of beaches too, though schedules can be sketchy and much reduced on Sundays. Prices and some journey times compare favourably with the trains, with a Sássari to Oristano trip costing around L12,500, taking about 2hr 15min.

The main, state-run **bus company**, ARST, operates a comprehensive service covering local routes from the main cities of Cágliari, Oristano, Sássari, Nuoro and Olbia, while the biggest private company, PANI, runs fast services between these main cities with a limited number of stops in between. Other private companies stick mainly to specific areas, such as Ferrovie Meridionali della Sardegna (FMS) in the southwest and Ferrovie della Sardegna (FdS) around Sássari and Alghero, while Olbia airport is connected by

Nuragica buses to Sássari, by Deplanu to Nuoro, and by Turmo to Alghero – details in the text. Note that some services covering beach areas and archeological zones only operate during the summer, and that lots of services are linked to school/market requirements – sometimes meaning a frighteningly early start, last departures in the afternoon, and occasionally no buses at all during school holidays.

City **bus terminals** are all very central and most buses make stops at the local train station – if you want the bus station, ask for the *autostazione*. **Timetables** are rarely available to be given out: schedules are posted up at the bus stops and stations. Wherever possible, you buy **tickets** before boarding, from ARST offices and local bars, though if everywhere's closed you can buy tickets on board. For longer hauls (and if you want to be sure of a place), it's worth buying them in advance. Bus stops are often quite difficult to track down; if you want directions, ask *dov'è la fermata dei pullman?* If you want to get off a bus, ask *posso scéndere?*; "the next stop" is *la próssima fermata*.

City buses are always cheap, usually charging a flat fare of around L1100, and worth mastering for quick rides across town. Invariably you need a ticket *before* getting on. Buy them in bars, *tabacchi*, or from the kiosks and vendors at bus terminals and stops, and then validate them in the machine on board. Checks are occasionally made by inspectors who can charge a spot fine in the region of L50,000. Smoking is strictly prohibited.

A few bus services are operated by one of the railway companies, usually on the periphery of the rail network. These are detailed in the train timetables and in the text.

Cars

Car travel across the island can be very quick as long as you follow the main roads. Minor roads can be narrow, very bendy and often confusing, though they are often the most interesting or spectacular. The island has no motorways or autostradas, and therefore no tolls; instead, good dual carriageways, or superstradas, run for most of the routes linking Cágliari, Oristano, Olbia, Sássari and Nuoro. The straightest and fastest is the SS131, aka the Carlo Felice highway, after the Savoyan king who commissioned it. Extending along the length of the island, from Cágliari via Oristano and Sássari as far as Porto Torres, this is rarely congested, though occasionally poorly lit and surfaced; beware of tricky junctions.

Other superstradas branch off east to Nuoro and Olbia, others link Cágliari with Iglésias, Carbónia and Sant'Antíoco, and Nuoro with the northeast coast. Most other roads are of the twisty variety, and going can be slow, particularly along the coasts in summer (the SP125 running behind the Costa Smeralda between Olbia and Santa Teresa di Gallura is especially gruesome). It is Sardinia's secondary roads that are the most rewarding to explore, however, and you should avoid at all costs travelling along these after dark: not only because you would miss the often extraordinary scenery that is the principal reason for using them, but you'll need to exercise maximum caution in following the twists and turns, and considerably increase your journey time.

At all times while driving in rural areas, be prepared for a flock of sheep or a panniered horse round the next bend. In remoter parts, there are *strade bianche*, or "white roads" – little more than rough tracks which can continue for hours, seemingly going nowhere; these can become very rocky, and should not be negotiated with a low axle. Signposting on these lanes is nonexistent, and it's easy to lose one's direction. Nonetheless, they are perfect for spontaneous wandering, and can lead to excellent places to get out and walk, not to mention the splendid beaches often lying at the end of them.

Italy is one of the most expensive countries in Europe in which to buy **fuel**: it's around L1800/litre for unleaded (*senza piombo*) and L1900/litre leaded (*super*). Fuel stations are spaced at fairly regular intervals along the superstradas, and there are pumps in most towns and villages. Although many of the remoter ones are closed 1–4pm and after 7.30pm, and often on Sunday or one other day of the week, an increasing number – particularly in towns – have self-serve dispensers which take L10,000 notes. Make sure your notes aren't dog-eared or the machines won't accept them. If your tank is filled before all your prepaid fuel is dispensed, you can punch for a receipt and ask for a refund when the station is open. Almost all stations accept major credit cards.

For **documentation** you need a valid driving licence, an international green card of insurance, and, if you are a non-EU licence holder, an international driving permit. It's *compulsory* to carry your car documents and passport while you're driving, and you'll be required to present them if you're stopped by the police – not an uncommon occurrence. You are also required to carry a portable triangular danger sign, available in Britain from most AA, RAC or Automobile Club d'Italia (ACI) offices, in Australia from NRMA, RACQ and RACV offices, in the US from the AAA, and in Canada from the CAA.

Rules of the road are straightforward: drive on the right; at junctions, where there's any ambiguity, give precedence to vehicles coming from the right, and observe the speed limits (50kph in built-up areas, 110kph on country roads). Note that some road customs are markedly different from what you may be used to: flashing headlights, for example, are *not* a signal to allow you priority, but on the contrary mean *look out, I'm coming!*

If you **break down**, dial ☎116 at the nearest phone and tell the operator where you are, the type of car and your registration number. The nearest office of the ACI will send someone out to fix your car, though it's not a free service. If you need towing anywhere it will cost a fairly substantial sum, though temporary membership of ACI gives free or discounted tows and repairs: write to ACI (Via Marsala 8, 00185 Roma; ☎06.499.8234); alternatively, arrange cover with a motoring organization in your country before you leave. Any ACI office in Sardinia can tell you where to get **spare parts** for your particular car.

Car rental in Sardinia is expensive, around £250/$400 per week for a Fiat Panda plus fuel, with unlimited mileage, from one of the major international firms (addresses are detailed in the city listings), but usually less from local companies. Best of all, though, is to arrange it in conjunction with your flight/holiday – most travel agents or tour operators can provide details; as can the **rental companies** (see below for numbers), which all have offices at each of the main airports.

Although **car crime** is on a lower level than in most of mainland Italy, it's prudent not to leave anything visible in the car when you leave it, including the radio. If you're taking your own vehicle, consider installing a detachable car-radio, and always depress your aerial and tuck in your wing mirrors. The main cities and ports have **garages** where you can leave your car, a safe enough option. At least the car itself is unlikely to be stolen if it's got a right-hand drive and a foreign numberplate: they're too conspicuous to be of much use to thieves.

As **parking** spaces are rare and small, good parking skills are an asset. The task is easier in the early afternoon, when towns are quiet, or at

CAR RENTAL AGENCIES

AUSTRALIA		UK	
Avis	☎1800/225 533	Avis	☎0990/900 500
Budget	☎1300/362 848	Budget	☎0800/181 181
Hertz	☎1800/550 067	Hertz	☎0990/996 699
Renault Eurodrive	☎02/9299 3344	Holiday Autos	☎0990/300 400
IRELAND		USA AND CANADA	
Avis	☎01/605 7500	Auto Europe	☎1-800/223-5555
Budget	☎0800/973 159	Avis	☎1-800/331-1084
Europcar	☎01/614 2800	Budget	☎1-800/527-0700
Hertz	☎0990/996 699	Dollar	☎1-800/421-6868
Holiday Autos	☎01/872 9366	Europe by Car ☎1-800/223-1516; in New York 212/581-3040; in Canada ☎1-800/252-9401. Rentals available only on mainland Italy.	
NEW ZEALAND		Hertz ☎1-800/654-3001; in Canada, except Toronto ☎1-800/263 0600; in Toronto ☎416/620 9620.	
Avis	☎09/526 2847		
Budget	☎09/375 2222		
Hertz	☎09/367 6350		

night; if you're renting, it makes sense to choose a small car. Most towns have strictly enforced restrictions regarding where you can park – usually between blue lines. Seek out the parking attendant and buy a ticket for as long as you think you'll be parked; it's not expensive, usually L1000 for the first hour, L2000 for subsequent hours. If you park in a *zona di rimozione*, your car will most likely be towed away; and if you've chosen a street that turns into a market by day, you'll be stuck until it closes down.

Hitch-hiking (*autostop*) is not widely practised in Sardinia and is not recommended as a means of getting around the island. It's very definitely not something that women should do on their own, particularly in the more out-of-the-way places; also be warned that cars will sometimes stop to offer you a lift if you're standing alone at a bus stop. If you are hitching, travel in pairs, and always ask where the car is headed before you commit yourself (*Dov'è diretto?*). If you want to get out, say *Mi fa scéndere?*

However you get around on the roads, **watch the traffic**. Driving in Sardinia is not the competitive sport that it can be in Rome, Naples or Sicily, but neither is dilatory or indecisive driving much tolerated. Nonetheless, anyone used to negotiating mainland Italy's roads will find Sardinia a doddle, and **pedestrians** accustomed to being treated as human skittles will be pleasantly surprised to find that drivers actually stop at pedestrian crossings and respect red lights. Local pedestrians also respect signals, and especially in Cágliari and Sássari, where traffic is heavy and constant, you will find that it's a lot less stressful to wait with everyone else for the signal to cross.

Bikes

Surprisingly few people use **bicycles** in Sardinia, and the possibilities for hiring them are scarce. Seaside resorts like Alghero and Santa Teresa di Gallura and some of the offshore islands are the best bet, and some hotels have rental facilities – check the text for details – though you may find

other outlets sprouting up in summer; the charge is usually around L10,000 per day. If you use a bike, take extra care and make yourself conspicuous, since the very rarity of cyclists means people won't be looking out for you. Prepare too for some arduous uphill peddling.

The roads are perfect for petrol-assisted cruising however, and have become a favourite touring ground for squads of bikers from Germany and Switzerland. Again, renting **motorbikes** is difficult, though most places that rent out bicycles also rent out **mopeds** and **scooters**. If you opt for one of these, remember that the smaller models are not suitable for any kind of long-distance travel, though they're ideal for buzzing around towns and beaches; expect to pay from L30,000 a day. Crash helmets are compulsory, though you'll see many Sards just riding with one slung over one arm.

Ferries

You'll use **ferries** to get to the offshore islands, from Palau for La Maddalena and Calasetta or Portovesme for San Pietro. The main companies are Traghetti Isole Sarde (TRIS), ☎0789.708.631 in Palau, ☎0781.855.849 in San Pietro, and Saremar, ☎0781.854.005 in San Pietro, ☎0781.88.430 in Calasetta, ☎0781.509.065 in Portovesme, ☎0789.754.788 in Santa Teresa di Gallura. Departures are at least hourly, there are more in high season, and summer also sees a night-time service for anyone dining out on the opposite shore, for example. All take vehicles, and if you are transporting yours it makes sense to get to the port early to be sure of a place (things can get quite congested in August, especially); some offices are only open 20min before departure. Frequencies are listed in the text and in "Travel Details", p.136 and p.309. Saremar (☎0789.754.156) and Moby ·Lines (☎0789.751.449) also operate daily services between Santa Teresa di Gallura and Bonifacio in Corsica, and all seaside holiday centres offer boat tours of the coast and islands.

Accommodation

On the whole, accommodation in Sardinia is considerably cheaper than in the rest of Italy. There's a whole range of places in all price categories, and on average you'll pay from around £18–30/$30–50 a night for two. If you're watching your budget, a (very) few youth hostels, some private rooms and many campsites are all possibilities – for more on which see below.

All types of accommodation are officially graded, their tariffs fixed by law. In tourist areas, on the offshore islands and in big cities there's often a low-season and high-season price. All prices of hotels and campsites should be listed in the local accommodation booklets provided by the tourist office and posted on the door of the room. If the prices don't correspond, demand to know why, and don't hesitate to report infractions to the tourist office. Loopholes do exist, however: in summer especially, when demand for accommodation exceeds supply, hotels are prone to add a breakfast charge to the price of the room,

whether you take breakfast or not. There's nothing you can do about it; just make sure you know exactly how much you're going to be paying before you accept the room.

Hotels

Hotel accommodation, while normally abundant in the main towns and tourist areas, tends to thin out in remoter areas, and especially inland. It's worthwhile phoning ahead to book if you're heading for a one-hotel town, and reserve a room in any hotel as early as possible if you're travelling in high season.

The cheapest hotel-type accommodation is a **locanda** – basic, but on the whole clean and safe, and nearly always corresponding to our category ①, ie under L60,000 for a double room without bath/shower; in many cases you'll find prices to be lower than this, occasionally as little as L35,000 for a double. More common are regular hotels, either a **pensione** or **albergo** (plural *alberghi*), the distinction between which has become obsolete since *pensioni* – the smaller, family-run establishments – have grown more professional, while still keeping the name. All come graded with from one to five stars, and a double room in a one-star hotel usually falls into our price category ① – you'll be paying L40,000–50,000 without bath/shower and around L60,000 with a bath/shower. Most two-stars fall into the ② and ③ categories, and once you're up to three-star level and beyond, you will pay prices corresponding to categories ④ and ⑤.

Accommodation Price Codes

The hotels listed in this guide have been coded according to price. The codes represent the cheapest available double room in high season (Easter & June–Aug). In cheaper hotels the rooms usually come without en-suite bathroom or shower; some of these places will also have a few en-suite rooms, for which you'll pay more – usually the next category up in price. Higher category hotels nearly always have only en-suite rooms. Out of season, you'll often be able to negotiate a lower price than those suggested here. The categories are:

① under L60,000	③ L90,000–120,000	⑤ L150,000–200,000	⑦ L250,000–300,000
② L60,000–90,000	④ L120,000–150,000	⑥ L200,000–250,000	⑧ over L300,000

In resorts and especially on the Costa Smeralda, four-star hotels can charge pretty much what they like, which means prices in categories ⑥, ⑦ and ⑧ are the norm. The three five-stars on the island are all here, where prices start at L900,000. That said, there are some bargains among the luxury hotels which remain open outside the summer season, many dropping their room rates by as much as 40 percent to attract custom. Quirks in the official grading system mean that you can sometimes pay around the same in a one- or two-star hotel as in a basic *locanda*, or that the same price elsewhere gets you a bathroom included: always ask to see the room before you take it (*posso vedere?*), and in the cheaper places check if there's hot water available (*c'è acqua calda?*).

There are few **single rooms** available, and these are often occupied during the week by workers and commercial travellers. In high season especially, lone travellers will often pay most (if not all) the price of a double. **Three or more people** sharing a room should expect to pay around 35 percent on top of the price of a double room.

In the cheaper places you may be able to negotiate a lower rate if you're staying for any length of time (ask *c'è uno sconto per due/tre/quattro notti?*).

Private rooms, apartments and farm stays

Certain tourist resorts, especially Alghero and Stintino, also have **private rooms** in people's houses for rent, which often come equipped with kitchen. Ask in local bars, shops and tourist offices, check the text for details and watch for signs saying "*cámere*" (rooms). Depending on the season and location, you'll pay anything from L30,000–50,000 per person a night.

For longer-term stays, you can also rent holiday **apartments** in Alghero and Stintino, and remoter places such as the island of La Maddalena or the Barbágia region. Although it's horrendously expensive in the summer – over L1 million a month even for a one-bedroom place – there are real bargains to be had in May or late September, and during the winter; ask in the tourist offices or a local estate agency (*agenzia immobiliare*), and keep an eye out for local advertisements.

The **agriturismo** scheme, in which cottages and farmhouses in villages or the countryside offer informal bed and breakfast, has grown considerably in recent years, and you'll often find various activities also available, such as horse riding, hunting and mountain-biking, plus escorted walks and excursions. The main disadvantage of these places is their remoteness from anything going on that isn't to do with the mountains or the sea, while the tendency of some agriturismi to expand and standardize, offering impersonal service, detracts from one of the main reasons to stay in them in the first place. However, agriturismi are useful when you're stuck for a room, and are ideal for remoter beaches and villages, and for getting close to the Sardinian countryside. Some genuinely provide a face-to-face encounter with Sards and offer more authentic country cooking than most places on the tourist track. A room for two will cost from around L60,000 a night, and a three-course dinner another L30,000 or so each. A few agriturismi are detailed in the guide, and local tourist offices can tell you of all the suitable places in the district. Bookshops also have comprehensive lists, or else buy *Agriturismo Sardegna* from a newsstand (L8000), a magazine with full descriptions and photos of a selection of these properties. Published annually – and difficult to find outside Cágliari in wintertime – it's written in Italian, German and English and contains a wealth of other practical information for travellers. Alternatively, contact one of the agriturismo associations directly: *Agriturist* ☎070.303.486; *Terranostra* ☎070.668.367, and *Turismo Verde* ☎070.373.73.

Campsites and youth hostels

Camping is popular in Sardinia, with about ninety officially graded sites dotted around the island's coasts and on the islands of La Maddalena and San Pietro. There are no official sites in Sardinia's interior, though the coastal sites are sometimes a fair walk from the sea. Facilities range from the most rudimentary to the full gamut of shops, disco, pool and watersports, and many offer bungalows, caravans or cabins with cooking facilities at reasonable rates. Campers can expect to pay around L10,000–15,000 per person plus L3,000–10,000 for a pitch, and a bungalow or caravan would cost L40,000–100,000 a night. Addresses, telephone numbers and rates are listed in accommodation booklets, as are the sites' months of opening (only a handful stay open between October and April), though bear in mind that

Youth Hostel Associations

Note: the Italian Youth Hostel Association (AIG) is on the Web at *www.hostels-aig.org/* and *www.travel.it/hostels*

AUSTRALIA
Australian Youth Hostels Association, 422 Kent St, Sydney ☎ 02/9261 1111.

BRITAIN
Youth Hostel Association (YHA), Trevelyan House, 8 St Stephen's Hill, St Alban's, Herts AL1 2DY ☎ 01727/855 215; Scottish Youth Hostel Association, 7 Glebe Crescent, Stirling FK8 2JA ☎ 01786/51 181.

CANADA
Hostelling International/Canadian Hostelling Association, 205 Catherine St, Suite 400, Ottawa, ON K2P 1C3 ☎ 613/237 7884, or 1-800/663 5777 everywhere except Newfoundland.

IRELAND
An Oige, 61 Mountjoy St, Dublin 7 ☎ 01/830 4555; Youth Hostel Association of Northern Ireland, 22 Donegal Rd, Belfast BT12 5JN ☎ 01232/324 733.

ITALY
Associazione Italiana Alberghi per la Gioventù, Via Cavour 44, 00184 Roma ☎ 06.487.1152, fax 06.488.0492.

NEW ZEALAND
Youth Hostels Association of New Zealand, 173 Gloucester St, Christchurch ☎ 03/379 9970.

USA
Hostelling International-American Youth Hostels (HI-AYH), 733 15th St NW, Suite 840, PO Box 37613, Washington, DC 20005 ☎ 202/783-6161.

---

these months – also detailed in the text – are flexible, and campsites generally open or close whenever they want, depending on business. And don't assume there will always be available space: the better sites fill up quickly in the summer months. If you want to be sure, phone first. Full details of all the campsites are contained in the book *Campeggi e Villagi Turistici in Italia*, published by the Touring Club Italiano (Corso Italiano 10, 20122 Milan ☎ 02/852.6245) and available from bookshops.

By and large, **camping rough** is a non-starter: it's frowned on in the tourist areas and on the off-shore islands, and regarded with outright suspicion in the interior (Sards are especially wary of the danger of forest fires). Occasional possibilities are detailed in the text; anywhere else you're likely to attract the unwelcome attention of the local police.

Official Hostelling International (HI) **youth hostels** are sparse, having dwindled to just three, all in the northwest of the island, in Porto Torres, Fertilia (near Alghero) and Bosa. Another is under construction outside Nuoro, to open possibly in 2000 or 2001. It's hardly worth joining just to use these (which, out of season, probably won't want to see membership cards anyway), though there are perks – discounts on rail travel, student cards, car hire and books, chiefly – and temporary membership is usually available for around L5,000. If you want full membership, contact your home hostelling organization (see box above). Always phone ahead: availability is limited at all times, though in the summer months they are almost permanently full to capacity. Charges are L14,000 for a dormitory bed, the same for an evening meal.

Food and drink

Eating and drinking are refreshingly good-value in Sardinia, and the quality usually high. Often, even the most out-of-the-way village will boast somewhere you can get a good, solid lunch, while towns like Cágliari and Alghero can keep a serious eater happy for days. If you stay away from the few ruinously expensive places, a full meal with good local wine generally costs around L30,000 a head, though there are often much cheaper set-price menus available: see below for more detailed prices.

The lists below will help you find your way around supermarkets and menus, but don't be afraid to ask to look if you're not sure what you're ordering. Also, check our lists of specialities, some of which crop up in nearly every restaurant.

The basics of Sardinian cuisine

Historically, the twin pivots of traditional **Sardinian cuisine** were land- and sea-based local produce, and this continues to be the principal distinction today. Mutton, beef, game, boar, horsemeat and ass are the staples of the cooking in the interior, while the coasts rely on whatever can be fished out of the sea – tuna, seabass and sardines all figure heavily. Add to these the basic ingredients of Italian cooking – pasta, tomato sauce, olives and fresh vegetables – and a choice of seasonal fruit and sheep's cheese. Some of the most famous Italian wines hail from

Sardinia – wine was already being made on the island at the time of the Phoenicians – and a meal is often rounded off with *dolci*, traditional biscuits of almonds and honey.

The mild winters and long summers mean that fruit and vegetables are less seasonal than in northern Europe, and are much bigger and more impressive: strawberries appear in April, oranges are available right through the winter, and even bananas are grown on a small scale. Unusual and unexpected foods and fruit are a bonus too: prickly pears (introduced from Mexico by the Spanish), artichokes, asparagus, wild mushrooms and wafer bread are common, while foreign elements have been introduced to specific areas – couscous on the island of San Pietro, and Catalan dishes in Alghero.

Breakfasts, snacks and ice cream

Most Sardinians start the day in a bar, their **breakfast** consisting of a milky coffee (cappuccino), and the ubiquitous *cornetto* – a jam-, custard- or chocolate-filled croissant, which you usually help yourself to from the counter. Bigger bars or a patisserie (*pasticceria*) will have more choice, but breakfast in a hotel (*prima colazione*) will be a limp (and expensive) affair, usually worth avoiding.

At other times of the day, **rolls** (*panini*) can be pretty substantial, packed with any number of fillings. Most bars sell these, though you'll get fresher stuff by going into an *alimentari* (grocer's shop) and asking them to make you one from whatever they've got on hand: you'll pay around L3000–5000 each. Bars may also offer **sandwiches** (*tramezzini*), ready-made sliced white bread sandwiches with mixed fillings – lighter and less appetizing than your average *panino*. Toasted sandwiches (*toste*) are common too: in a sandwich bar you can get whatever you like put inside them; in bars which have a sandwich toaster you're more likely to be offered a variation on cheese with ham or tomato.

Apart from sandwiches, other prepared takeaway food is pretty thin on the ground. You'll get most of the things already mentioned, plus small pizzas, portions of prepared pasta, chips, even full hot meals, in a **távola calda**, a sort of stand-up snack bar that's at its best in the morning when everything is fresh. The bigger towns have them, often combined with normal bars, and there's sometimes one in main train stations.

You'll get more adventurous ingredients in **markets** – good bread, fruit, pizza slices and picnic food, such as cheese, salami, olives, tomatoes and salads. Some markets sell traditional takeaway food from stalls, usually things like boiled artichokes, cooked octopus, sea urchins and mussels, and *focacce* – oven-baked pastry snacks either topped with cheese and tomato, or filled with spinach, fried offal or meat. For picnics, some tinned and bottled things are worth looking out for too: sweet peppers (*peperoni*), baby squid (*calamari*), seafood salad (*insalata di mare*) and preserved vegetables. You'll find **supermarkets** in most towns; look out for the "two-for-the-price-of-one" offers on items such as tinned fish, meat, biscuits and soft drinks. Island-wide store chains with food halls are Standa and Upim.

You'll probably end up with an **ice cream** (*gelato*) at some point: in summer, a cone (*un cono*) is an indispensable accessory to the evening *passeggiata*, and many people eat a dollop of ice cream in a brioche for breakfast. Most bars have a fairly good selection, but for real choice go to a **gelateria** where the range is a tribute to the Italian imagination and flair for display. If they make their own on the premises, there'll be a sign saying *produzione propria*. You'll have to go by appearance rather than attempt to decipher their exotic names, many of which don't mean much even to Italians; you'll find it's often the basics – chocolate, lemon, strawberry and coffee – that are best. There's no trouble in identifying the finest *gelateria* in town: it's the one that draws the crowds.

Pizzas

As elsewhere in Italy, **pizza** in Sardinia comes flat and not deep-pan, and the choice of toppings is fairly limited – none of the pineapple-and-sweet-corn variations beloved of foreign pizzerias. It's also easier to find pizzas cooked in the traditional way, in wood-fired ovens (*forno a legna*), rather than squeaky-clean electric ones, so that the pizzas arrive blasted and bubbling on the surface, with a distinctive charcoal taste. However, because of the time it takes to set up

and light the wood-fired ovens, these pizzas are usually only served at night, except on Sundays and in some resorts in summer.

Pizzerias, which range from a stand-up counter to a fully-fledged sit-down restaurant, on the whole sell just pizzas and drinks, usually chips, sometimes salads; a basic cheese and tomato pizza costs around L6000, something a bit fancier between L7000 and L10,000. To follow local custom, it's quite acceptable to cut it into slices and eat it with your hands, washing it down with a beer or Coke rather than wine. You'll also get pizzas in larger towns and tourist areas in a hybrid pizzeria-ristorante, which serves meals too and is slightly more expensive. Check our list of pizzas on p.38 for what you get on top of your dough.

Meals: lunch and dinner

Full **meals** are much more elaborate affairs. These are generally served in a **trattoria** or a **ristorante**, though these days there's often a fine line between the two: traditionally, a trattoria is cheaper and more basic, offering good home-cooking (*cucina casalinga*), while a ristorante is more upmarket (tablecloths and waiters). The main differences you'll notice, though, are more to do with opening hours and the food on offer. In small towns and villages a trattoria is usually best at lunch time and often only open then – there probably won't be a menu and the waiter will simply reel off a list of what's on that day. In large towns both will be open in the evening, though there'll be more choice in a ristorante, which will always have a menu. In either, a pasta course, meat or fish, fruit and a drink, should cost around L25,000–40,000 (fish pushes up the price), though watch out for signs saying *menu turístico, pranzo turístico* or *pranzo completo*. This is a limited set menu including wine which can cost as little as L12,000, but is usually more in the region of L18,000–25,000. Classier ristoranti will charge around L50,000–80,000 per head, including quality wine, and these are often worth going out of your way for.

Other types of eating place include those usually found in tourist resorts, that flaunt themselves as a trattoria-ristorante-pizzeria; *távole calde*, for warmed-up snacks (see above), *spaghetterie*, which specialize in pasta dishes, and *birrerie* – pubs with snacks and music, often the haunts of the local youth. Lastly, when you tire, if that is possible, of the Sardinian diet, you might try out one of the many **Chinese restaurants** which have sprouted in most large towns in the last few years. They're at least as good as the ones in Britain, and are significantly cheaper than most Italian restaurants. Many eating places close for three or four weeks in November or February.

Traditionally, a **meal** (lunch is *pranzo*, dinner is *cena*) starts with an **antipasto** (literally "before the meal"): you'll only find this in restaurants, at its best when you circle around a table and pick from a selection of cold dishes, main items including stuffed artichoke hearts, olives, salami, anchovies, seafood salad, aubergine in various guises, sardines and mixed rice. A plateful will cost around L8000–10,000, but if you're moving on to pasta and the main course, you'll need quite an appetite to tackle it.

As far as the **menu** goes, it starts with soup or pasta, **il primo**, usually costing from L6,000–12,000, and moves on to **il secondo**, the meat or fish dish, which ranges roughly from L12,000–18,000. This course is generally served alone except for perhaps a wedge of lemon or tomato. Vegetables and salads (**contorni**) are ordered and served separately and often there won't be much choice: potatoes will usually come as chips (*patatine fritte*), but you can also find them boiled (*lesse*) or roast (*arroste*), while salads are simply green (*verde*) or mixed (*mista*), usually with tomato. Bread (**pane**), which in Sardinia comes in a variety of forms – though rarely brown (*integrale*) – will be served with your meal. Used in ceremonies as well as for everyday needs, Sardinian bread can be thin and crispy or soft, floury and delicately shaped, and differs markedly from place to place.

If there's no menu, the verbal list of what's available can be a bit bewildering, but if you don't hear anything you recognize just ask for what you want: everywhere should have pasta with tomato sauce (*pomodoro*) or meat sauce (*al ragù*).

Afterwards, you'll usually get a choice of fruit (*frutta*), while in a ristorante, you'll probably be offered other desserts (*dolci*) as well. Sardinia is renowned for its almond-based sweets, though they are not always available; most restaurants will only have fresh fruit salad (*macedonia*) and fresh or packaged ice cream and desserts – in common with the rest of Italy, Sardinia has embraced the mass-produced, packaged sweets produced by such brands as Ranieri – *tiramisù*, *tartufo* and *zuppa inglese* are the most common; some of them aren't bad, but they're a poor substitute for the real thing.

It's useful to know that you don't have to order a full meal in trattorias and most restaurants. Asking for just pasta and a salad, or the main course on its own, won't outrage the waiter. Equally, asking for a dish listed as a first course as a second course, or having pasta followed by pizza (or vice versa), won't be frowned upon.

Something to watch for is **ordering fish**, which will usually be served by weight (usually per 100g, *all'etto*) – if you don't want the biggest one they've got, ask to see what you're going to eat and check the price first.

The bill... and tipping

At the **end of the meal**, ask for the bill (*il conto*). In many trattorias this doesn't amount to much more than an illegible scrap of paper, and if you want to be sure you're not being ripped off, ask

---

Meal Prices

For a general idea of what various meals cost in Sardinia, see "Lunch and dinner" and "Pizzas" above. All prices are approximate, based on prices in 1999. In the accounts of any large town or city in the guide, recommended restaurants are **graded** according to the following scale:

Inexpensive: under L25,000   Expensive: L40,000–70,000

Moderate: L25,000–40,000   Very expensive: over L70,000

These prices reflect the per person cost of a **full meal including wine and cover charge** – usually consisting of pasta, main course, salad or vegetable, dessert or fruit, and coffee. Obviously, in every restaurant, you'll be able to eat for less than the upper price limit if you only have a couple of courses; and in pizzerias you'd rarely be able to spend more than L20,000 a head even if you wanted to. The price categories are simply intended as a guide to what you could spend if you pushed the boat out in each restaurant.

In the guide, **telephone numbers** are only given for restaurants where it's necessary to reserve a table in advance. Outside Cágliari, Olbia and Alghero – and not always there – the staff are unlikely to speak English, so you may have to get someone to ring for you.

to have a receipt (*una ricevuta*), something they're legally obliged to give you anyway (see Directory, p.61). Nearly everywhere, you'll pay cover (*pane e coperto*), which amounts to L1500–3000 per person; service (*servizio*) will be added as well in most restaurants, another 10 percent – though up to 15 percent or even 20 percent in some places. If service is included, you won't be expected to tip; otherwise leave 10 percent, though bear in mind that the smaller places – pizzerias and trattorias – won't expect this.

Vegetarians – a few pointers

Some **vegetarians** might find their food principles stretched to the limit in Sardinia. If you're a borderline case, the abundance of excellent fish and shellfish and the knowledge that nearly all eggs and meat are free-range might just push you over the edge. On the whole, though, it's not that difficult if you're committed. Most pasta sauces are based on tomatoes or dairy products and it's easy to pick a pizza that is meat- (and fish-) free. Most places can be persuaded to cook you eggs in some shape or form, or provide you with a big mixed salad.

The only real problem is one of comprehension: many people don't know what a vegetarian is. Saying you're vegetarian (*sono vegetariano/a*) and asking if the dish has meat in it (*c'è carne dentro?*) is only half the battle: poultry and especially *prosciutto* are regarded by many waiters as barely meat at all. Better is to ask what the dish is made with (*com'è fatto?*) before you order, so that you can spot the offending "non-meaty" meat. Remember even "vegetarian" minestrone and risotto are cooked with meat stock.

If you're a **vegan**, you'll be in for a hard time, though pizzas without cheese are a good standby, and the fruit is excellent. Soups are usually made with a fish or meat broth. However, you'll have absolutely no success explaining to anyone why you're a vegan – an incomprehensible concept to a Sardinian.

Drink

Although Sard children are brought up on wine, there's not the same emphasis on dedicated **drinking** here as there is in Britain or America. You'll rarely see drunks in public, young people don't make a night out of getting wasted, and women especially are frowned upon if they're seen to be indulging. Nonetheless, there's a wide choice of alcoholic drinks available in Sardinia, at low prices; soft drinks come in multifarious hues, thanks to the abundance of fresh fruit, and there's also mineral water and crushed ice drinks: you'll certainly never be stuck if you want to slake your thirst.

Coffee, tea and soft drinks

One of the most distinctive smells in a Sardinian street is the aroma of fresh **coffee**, usually wafting out of a bar (many trattorias and pizzerias don't serve hot drinks). It's always excellent: the basic choice is either small, black and very strong (an *espresso*, or just *caffè*), or weaker, white and frothy (a *cappuccino*), but there are other varieties, too. A *caffelatte* is an *espresso* in a big cup filled up to the top with hot milk. If you want your *espresso* watered down, ask for a *caffè lungo*; with a shot of alcohol – and you can ask for just about *anything* in your coffee – is *caffè corretto*; with a drop of milk is *caffè macchiato* ("stained"). If you want to be sure of a coffee without sugar, ask for *caffé senza zúcchero*. Most places also sell decaffeinated coffee (ask for Hag, even when it isn't); while in summer you'll probably want to have your coffee cold (*caffè freddo*). In holiday centres, you might find *granita di caffè* in summer – cold coffee with crushed ice and topped with cream (*senza panna* if you prefer it without).

As for **tea**, it's best in summer when you can drink it iced (*tè freddo*) usually mixed with lemon; it's excellent for taking the heat off. Hot tea (*tè caldo*) comes with lemon (*con limone*) unless you ask for milk (*con latte*). **Milk** itself is drunk hot as often as cold, or you can get it with a dash of coffee (*latte macchiato*), and in a variety of flavoured drinks (*frappé*) too.

Alternatively, there are various **soft drinks** (*analcóliche*) to choose from. A **spremuta** is a fresh fruit juice, squeezed at the bar, usually orange, lemon or grapefruit. You might need to add sugar to a lemon juice (*spremuta di limone*), but orange juice (*spremuta di arancia*) is usually sweet enough on its own, especially the crimson-red

ITALIAN FOOD TERMS

Basics and snacks

aceto	vinegar	*maionese*	mayonnaise	*patatine fritte*	chips
aglio	garlic	*marmellata*	jam	*pepe*	pepper
biscotti	biscuits	*olio*	oil	*pizzetta*	slice of pizza
burro	butter	*olive*	olives		to take
caramelle	sweets	*pane*	bread		away
cioccolato	chocolate	*pane*	wholemeal	*riso*	rice
focaccia	oven-baked snack	*integrale*	bread	*sale*	salt
formaggio	cheese	*panino*	bread roll/	*uova*	eggs
frittata	omelette		sandwich	*yogurt*	yoghurt
gelato	ice cream	*patatine*	crisps/potato	*zúcchero*	sugar
grissini	bread sticks		chips	*zuppa*	soup

Antipasti and starters

antipasto misto	mixed cold meats, seafood and cheese (plus a mix of other things in this list)	*mortadella*	salami-type cured meat with white nuggets of fat; in Sardinia, often with pistachios
caponata	mixed aubergine, olives, tomatoes	*pancetta*	bacon
caprese	tomato and mozzarella cheese salad	*peperonata*	grilled green, red or yellow peppers stewed in olive oil
insalata di mare	seafood salad (usually squid, octopus and prawn)	*pomodori ripieni*	stuffed tomatoes
insalata russa	"Russian salad"; diced vegetables in mayonnaise	*prosciutto*	ham
		salame	salami
insalata di riso	rice salad	*salmone/tonno/ pesce spada affumicato*	smoked salmon/tuna/ swordfish
melanzane alla parmigiana	fried aubergine in tomato sauce with parmesan cheese		

Pizzas

biancaneve	"black and white"; mozzarella and oregano	*frutti di mare*	seafood; usually mussels, prawns, squid and clams
calzone	folded pizza with cheese, ham and tomato	*margherita*	cheese and tomato
		marinara	tomato and garlic
capricciosa	literally "capricious"; topped with whatever they've got in the kitchen, usually including baby artichoke, ham and egg	*Napoli/ Napoletana*	tomato, anchovy and olive oil (often mozzarella, too)
		quattro formaggi	"four cheeses", usually mozzarella, fontina, gorgonzola and gruyère
cardinale	ham and olives	*quattro stagioni*	"four seasons"; the toppings split into four separate sections, usually including ham, peppers, onion, mushrooms, artichokes, olives, egg, etc
diávolo	spicy, with hot salami or Italian sausage		
funghi	mushroom; tinned, sliced button mushrooms unless it specifies fresh mushrooms, either *funghi freschi* or *porcini*	*romana*	anchovy and olives

The first course (*il primo*): soups

brodo	clear broth	*pasta e fagioli*	pasta soup with beans
minestrina	any light soup	*pastina in brodo*	pasta pieces in clear broth
minestrone	thick vegetable soup	*stracciatella*	broth with egg

Pasta...

cannelloni	large tubes of pasta, stuffed	*ravioli*	ravioli
farfalle	literally "bow"-shaped pasta; the word also means "butterflies"	*rigatoni*	large, grooved tubular pasta
		risotto	cooked rice dish, with sauce
fettuccine	narrow pasta ribbons	*spaghetti*	spaghetti
gnocchi	small potato and dough dumplings	*spaghettini*	thin spaghetti
lasagne	lasagne	*tagliatelle*	pasta ribbons, another word for *fettucine*
maccheroni	macaroni (tubular pasta)		
pappardelle	pasta ribbons	*tortellini*	small rings of pasta, stuffed with meat or cheese
pasta al forno	pasta baked with minced meat, eggs, tomato and cheese	*vermicelli*	very thin spaghetti (literally "little worms")
penne	smaller version of *rigatoni*		

...and the sauce (*salsa*)

aglio e olio	tossed in garlic and olive oil	*panna*	cream
(e peperoncino)	(and hot chillies)	*parmigiano*	parmesan cheese
amatriciana	cubed pork and tomato sauce (originally from Rome)	*pesto*	ground basil, pine nut, garlic and pecorino sauce
arrabiata	spicy tomato sauce, with chillies	*pomodoro*	tomato sauce
		puttanesca	"whorish"; tomato, anchovy, olive oil and oregano
bolognese	meat sauce		
burro e salvia	butter and sage	*ragù*	meat sauce
carbonara	cream, ham and beaten egg	*vóngole (veraci)*	clam and tomato sauce (fresh clams in shells, usually served with oil and herbs)
frutta di mare	seafood		
funghi	mushroom		

The second course (*il secondo*): meat (*carne*)

agnello	lamb	*maiale*	pork
ásino	ass, donkey	*manzo*	beef
bistecca	steak	*montone*	mutton
capretto	young goat	*monzette*	snails
cavallo	horse	*ossobuco*	shin of veal
cervello	brain	*pollo*	chicken
cinghiale	wild boar	*polpette*	meatballs
coniglio	rabbit	*rognoni*	kidneys
costolette/cotolette	cutlets/chops	*salsiccia*	sausage
fegatini	chicken livers	*saltimbocca*	veal with ham
fégato	liver	*scaloppina*	escalope (of veal)
involtini	steak slices, rolled and stuffed	*spezzatino*	stew
		tacchino	turkey
lepre	hare	*trippa*	tripe
lingua	tongue	*vitello*	veal
lumache	snails		

continued overleaf

ITALIAN FOOD TERMS (continued)

Fish (*pesce*) and shellfish (*crostacei*)

Note that *surgelati* or *congelati* written on the menu next to a dish means "frozen" – it often applies to squid and prawns.

acciughe	anchovies	*déntice*	dentex (like	*rospo*	monkfish
anguilla	eel		sea bass)	*sampiero*	John Dory
aragosta	lobster	*gamberetti*	shrimps	*sàrago*	bream
arselle	clams	*gámberi*	prawns	*sarde*	sardines
bottarga	salted and dried	*granchio*	crab	*seppie*	cuttlefish
	eggs of mullet	*merluzzo*	cod	*sgombro*	mackerel
	and tuna	*múggine*	mullet	*sógliola*	sole
baccalà	dried salted cod	*orata*	gilthead	*sp'gola*	sea-bass
calamari	squid	*óstriche*	oysters	*tonno*	tuna
céfalo	grey mullet	*pesce spada*	swordfish	*triglie*	red mullet
cozze	mussels	*polpo/pólipo*	octopus	*trota*	trout
dattile	razor clams	*ricci di mare*	sea urchins	*vóngole*	clams

Vegetables (*contorni*) and salad (*insalata*)

aspáragi	asparagus	*cetriolo*	cucumber	*orígano*	oregano
basílico	basil	*cipolla*	onion	*patate*	potatoes
bróccoli	broccoli	*fagioli*	beans	*peperoni*	peppers
cápperi	capers	*fagiolini*	green beans	*piselli*	peas
carciofi	artichokes	*finocchio*	fennel	*pomodori*	tomatoes
carciofini	artichoke hearts	*funghi*	mushrooms	*radicchio*	red chicory
carotte	carrots	*insalata*	green salad/	*spinaci*	spinach
cavolfiori	cauliflower	*verde/mista*	mixed salad	*zucca*	pumpkin
cávolo	cabbage	*melanzane*	aubergine/	*zucchini*	courgettes
ceci	chickpeas		eggplant		

Desserts (*dolci*)

amaretti	macaroons	*zabaglione*	dessert made	*zuppa inglese*	trifle
gelato	ice cream		with eggs,		
macedonia	fruit salad		sugar and		
torta	cake, tart		Marsala wine		

Cheese

caciocavallo	a type of dried, mature mozzarella cheese	*mozzarella*	soft white cheese, traditionally made from buffalo's milk
dolce sardo	dry, hard shepherd's cheese, often going into sandwiches	*parmigiano*	parmesan cheese
		pecorino	strong-tasting hard sheep's
fontina	mild northern Italian cheese used in cooking and in rolls		cheese, either *romano* or *sardo*, both from Sardinia
fiore sardo	sheep's cheese frequently used in cooking	*provolone*	cheese with grooved rind, either mild or tasty
gorgonzola	soft, strong, blue-veined cheese	*ricotta*	soft white cheese made from ewe's milk, used in sweet or savoury dishes
grana	hard cheese often used instead of *parmigiano* on pastas and soups		

Fruit and nuts

albicocche	apricots	*ciliegie*	cherries	*melone*	melon
ananas	pineapple	*fichi*	figs	*néspole*	medlars
anguria/		*fichi d'India*	prickly pears	*pere*	pears
coccómero	water melon	*frágole*	strawberries	*pesche*	peaches
arance	oranges	*limone*	lemon	*pignoli*	pine nuts
banane	bananas	*mándorle*	almonds	*pistacchio*	pistachio nut
cacchi	persimmons	*mele*	apples	*uva*	grapes

Cooking terms and useful words

affumicato	smoked	*grattugiato*	grated
alla brace	barbecued	*alla griglia*	grilled
arrosto	roast	*al marsala*	cooked with *marsala* wine
ben cotto	well done	*milanese*	fried in egg and breadcrumbs
bollito/lesso	boiled	*pizzaiola*	cooked with tomato sauce
brasato	cooked in wine	*ripieno*	stuffed
cotto	cooked (not raw)	*sangue*	rare
crudo	raw	*allo spiedo*	on the spit
al dente	firm, not overcooked	*stracotto*	braised, stewed
ferri	grilled without oil	*surgelato*	frozen
al forno	baked	*in úmido*	stewed
fritto	fried	*al vapore*	steamed

Sardinian specialities: starters, breads and cheeses

sa burrida	bits of dogfish boiled and marinated in garlic, parsley, walnuts and vinegar	*sa fregula*	couscous-type pasta either in a meat stock or dry with mussels or clams
culurgiones	ravioli stuffed with potato, cheese, garlic and mint	*pane carasau*	crisp wafer bread, often served with olive oil and salt to add flavour
malloreddus	gnocchetti, or pasta shaped in little shells, with various toppings, for example *alla campidanese*, a spicy sausage sauce.	*pane frattau*	carasau bread soaked in tomato sauce with pecorino and an egg, typically from Mamoiada
fainè	chickpea pizza to a Genoan recipe, served plain, or with onion, sausage or anchovy (not usually available in summer)	*spianadas*	soft round bread from the Logudoro district, often served with sausages
		zuppa/suppa cuata	bread, cheese and tomato soup

Sardinian specialities: main courses

aragosta catalana	lobster in sauce as served in Alghero	*cuscus*	a version of north African couscous, a speciality of the island of San Pietro, usually served with a fish and vegetable sauce
cashcà	couscous-type wheat semolina steamed with meat, vegetables or fish, as prepared in Carloforte on San Pietro	*fritto misto*	a standard seafood dish; deep-fried prawns and calamari rings in batter
sa còrdula	roasted sheep's entrails		

continued overleaf

ITALIAN FOOD TERMS (continued)

fritto di pesce	as above but also with other fried fish, like sardines and whitebait	*panadas*	pastry rolls filled with meat, fish and vegetables, or all three, originating in Assémini, near Cágliari
giogghe	snails boiled and then fried with garlic, parsley and paprika	*pécora in capotta*	mutton boiled with vegetables, garlic and rosemary, typical of the Nuoro area
gran premio	horsemeat steak		
grigliata di pesce	a mixed fish grill, usually quite substantial and expensive	*porceddu/ porcheddu*	young pig roasted whole on a spit with myrtle leaves
sa merca	salted mullet from the Cabras lagoon, cooked in herbs	*stufato di capretto*	chunks of kid casseroled with wine, artichokes and saffron
monzette	small snails roasted with salt, a speciality of Sássari	*zuppa di pesce*	a big dish of mixed fish in rich wine-based soup

Sweets and desserts

aranciatte/ aranzada	very sweet confection available from Nuoro, made with almonds, oranges and honey	*seadas/sebadas*	fried ricotta-filled pastry bubbles soaked in honey
pardulas/ casadinas	cheese-based pastries flavoured with saffron, vanilla and the peel of citrus fruit	*torrone*	crystallized almonds and honey, the best from the Barbágia villages of Tonara and Aritzo

variety, made from blood oranges. You can also have orange and lemon mixed (*mischiato*). A **frullato** is a fresh fruit shake, often made with more than one fruit. A **granita** (a crushed-ice drink) comes in several flavours other than coffee. Otherwise, there's the usual range of fizzy drinks and concentrated juices; Coke is prevalent, but the home-grown Italian alternative, Chinotto, is less sweet – good with a slice of lemon. **Tap water** (*acqua normale*) is drinkable everywhere and you won't pay for it in a bar. But **mineral water** (*acqua minerale*) is the usual choice, either still (*senza gas* or *naturale*) or fizzy (*con gas, gassata* or *frizzante*).

Beer, wines and spirits

Beer (*birra*) is usually a lager-type brew which comes in a third of a litre (*píccolo*) or two thirds of a litre (*grande*) bottles: commonest (and cheapest) are the Italian brand, Peroni, and the Sardinian Ichnussa, both of which are fine, if a bit weak. A small (33cl) bottle of Ichnussa beer costs

about L2500 in a bar or restaurant, a larger (66cl) bottle L3500–4500; if this is what you want, ask for *birra nazionale*, otherwise you'll be given the more expensive imported beers, like Carlsberg and Becks. In some bars and bigger restaurants and in all *birrerias* you also have a choice of draught lager (*birra alla spina*), sold in units of 25cl (*píccola*) and 50cl (*media*), measure for measure more expensive than the bottled variety. In some places you might find so-called "dark beers" (*birra nera, birra rossa* or *birra scura*), which have a slightly maltier taste, and in appearance resemble stout or bitter. These are the dearest of the draught beers, though not necessarily the strongest.

With just about every meal you'll be offered **wine** (*vino*), either red (*rosso*) or white (*bianco*), labelled or local. If you're unsure and want the local stuff, ask for *vino locale*: on the whole it's fine, often served straight from the barrel in jugs or old bottles and costing as little as L4000–8000 a litre.

Bottled wine is much more expensive, though still good value; expect to pay from around L12,000 a bottle in a restaurant, more like L15,000–20,000 in places like Alghero. One peculiarity is that bars don't tend to serve wine **by the glass** – when they do, you'll pay around L2000. A standard dry red available everywhere but mainly produced around Dorgali and the eastern regions, is Cannonau; others to watch for are Vermentino, a tangy white from Gallura; Campidano di Terralba (red and white), from Oristano province; Mandrolisai, a bitter red but smoother rosé from the Sulcis region; the fruity dry white Nuragus from the provinces of Cágliari and Oristano; Torbato, an aromatic white served chilled with fish, from around Alghero; Semidano, a dry white from the Campidano, and Monica, a strong dry red, best drunk young.

Sardinia produces good **dessert wines**, the most famous being Vernaccia, sweet or dry, honey-coloured, with a bitter-almond taste, from the Tirso river area around Oristano. If you're heading to Bosa, watch out for mellow Malvasia, also served as a table wine, and also produced around Cágliari. Sweet white Moscato comes from Cágliari, Sorso-Sénnori and Tempio Pausánia, while the Alghero territory produces Anghelu Ruju, one of the strongest and best dessert wines, a sweet red with cherry and cinnamon aromas.

Fortified wine is fairly popular too: Martini (red or white) and Cinzano are nearly always available; Cynar (an artichoke-based sherry) and Punt'e Mes are other common aperitifs. If you ask for a Campari-Soda you'll get a ready-mixed version in a little bottle; a slice of lemon is a *spicchio di limone*; ice is *ghiaccio*.

All the usual **spirits** are on sale and known mostly by their generic names, except brandy which you should call *cognac* or ask for by name. The best Italian brandies are Stock and Vecchia Romagna; for all other spirits, if you want the cheaper Italian stuff, again, ask for *nazionale*. A generous shot costs around L4000–5000. Among the **liqueurs**, favourite in Sardinia is *mirto*, made from the leaves and berries of wild myrtle, which you should drink chilled; the red is rated more highly than the white. There's also the standard selection of **amari** (literally "bitters"), an after-dinner drink served with (or instead of) coffee. It's supposed to aid digestion, and is often not bitter at all, but can taste remarkably medicinal. The favourite brand is Averna, but there are

dozens of different kinds. **Other strong drinks** available are *grappa di mirto*, almost pure alcohol, from distilled myrtle husks; *Fil'e Ferru*, a fiery grappa-like concoction brewed in the interior, and, though not especially Sardinian, *sambuca* – a sticky-sweet, aniseed liqueur, traditionally served with one or more coffee beans in it and set on fire, though only tourists are likely to experience this these days.

Where to drink

Bars in Sardinia are either functional stops or social centres. You'll come to the first category for drinking on the hoof, a coffee in the morning, a quick beer or cup of tea. Social bars have tables and a greater range of snacks, and are amenable to whiling away part of a morning or afternoon, reading or people-watching. Most bars don't stay open much after 9pm, though practice varies from place to place, and hours are prolonged in summer. As in bars throughout the Mediterranean, there are no set licensing hours and children have free access. Most have a public phone and won't object to you using that or their toilet facilities, even if you're not drinking there.

If you're just having a drink at a stand-up bar, pay first at the cash desk (*la cassa*), present your receipt (*scontrino*) to the bar person and give your order. If there's no cashier, pay either before or after being served. If you're sitting down, wait for someone to take your order, and there'll usually be a 25–35-percent service charge (shown on the price list as *távola*); you're often expected to pay the bill on being served. If you don't know how much a drink will cost, there should be a list of prices (the *listino prezzi*) behind the bar or *cassa*. When you present your receipt, it's customary to leave an extra L100 on the counter – though no one will object if you don't.

For more **serious drinking**, most people go out and eat as well, at a pizzeria or restaurant, and spin the meal out accordingly if they want a few more beers. Otherwise, they repair to a **birreria** (literally "beer shop"), where people go just to drink, though often they sell food too. These are where you'll find young people at night, listening to music or glued to rock videos; they're often called "pubs", although they bear little relation to their British namesakes. In tourist areas, bars and cafés (*caffè*) are more like the real European thing and they're open later, but they're more expensive than the common-or-garden bar. Other places to get a drink are an **enoteca**, a rudimentary wine bar selling cheap local wine by the glass and a **bar-pasticceria**, which sells wonderful cakes and pastries too, and a **távola calda** in a railway station always has a bar.

Drinks

acqua minerale	mineral water	*succo di frutta*	concentrated fruit juice,
aranciata	orangeade		sometimes sugared
bicchiere	glass	*tè*	tea
birra	beer	*tónico*	tonic water
bottiglia	bottle	*vino*	wine
caffè	coffee	*rosso*	red
cioccolata calda	hot chocolate	*bianco*	white
ghiaccio	ice	*rosato*	rosé
granita	iced coffee/fruit drink	*secco*	dry
latte	milk	*dolce*	sweet
limonata	lemonade	*litro*	litre
selz	soda water	*mezzo*	half litre
spremuta	fresh fruit juice	*quarto*	quarter litre
spumante	sparkling wine	*salute!*	cheers!

Post, phones and the media

Post office opening hours are usually Monday–Saturday 8.30am–6pm; smaller towns won't have a service on a Saturday and everywhere post offices close at noon on the last day of the month. If you want stamps, you can buy them in *tabacchi* too, as well as in some gift shops in the tourist resorts. The Italian postal service is one of the tardiest in Europe – if your letter is urgent, consider spending extra for the express service.

Letters can be sent **poste restante** to any main post office in Sardinia, by addressing them "Fermo Posta" followed by the name of the town. When collecting something, take your passport, and if your name doesn't turn up make sure they check under middle names and initials.

Telephones

Public **telephones**, mostly run by Telecom Italia, come in various forms, usually with clear instructions printed on them (in English, too). For the most common type, you'll need L100, L200 or L500 coins. You need at least L200 to start a call, even to toll-free numbers (the money is refunded at the end of the call). **Telephone cards** (*schede telefóniche*) are available for L5000, L10,000 and L15,000 from *tabacchi* or news stands. They're accepted in most Sardinian phone booths – in fact some will only take cards. Note that the perforated corner of these cards must be torn off before they can be used. Bars will often have a phone you can use, though these often take coins only: look for the yellow phone symbol. Alternatively you could find a Telecom Italia or other office (listed in the text in the larger towns) or a bar with a *cabina a scatti*, a soundproofed and metered kiosk: ask to make the call and pay at the end. You can do the same at hotels, but they normally charge 25 percent more. Phone **tariffs** are among the most expensive in Europe; they're at their dearest on Monday to Friday between 8.30am and 1pm, but cheapest between 10pm and 8am Monday to Saturday and all day Sunday.

You can make **international calls** from any booth that accepts cards, and from any other booth labelled "*interurbano*"; the minimum charge for an international call is L2000. The cheapest way to make them is to get a Global Calling Card issued by AT&T (☎1-800/225-5288), an MCI WorldCom card (☎1-800/955-0925), a BT Charge Card (☎0800/345 144), or a Cable & Wireless Calling Card (☎0500/100 505). All are free, and they work in the same way – just ring the company's international operator (see the box below), who will connect you free of charge and add the cost of the connected call to your domestic bill. Alternatively, use a special **international phone card** (*carta telefónica internazionale*) available from post offices for L12,500, L25,000, L50,000 and L100,000; all cardphones accept them, but before each call you need to dial ☎1740 and the PIN number on the back of the

---

COUNTRY DIRECT SERVICES

Australia: Telstra ☎1800/626 008; Optus ☎1300/300 300

Ireland: ☎172 0353

New Zealand: Telecom ☎04/382 5818.

UK: BT ☎172 0044; Cable and Wireless ☎172 0544

USA and Canada: AT&T ☎172 1011; MCI ☎172 1022; Sprint ☎172 1877

INTERNATIONAL TELEPHONE CODES

For direct **international calls from Italy**, dial the country code (given below), the area code (minus its first 0, where applicable), and finally the subscriber number.

Australia: 61	**New Zealand:** 64	**USA and Canada:** 1
Ireland: 353	**UK:** 44	

CALLING SARDINIA FROM ABROAD

Dial the access code ☎0011 from Australia, Canada and the US, ☎00 from Britain, Ireland and New Zealand; then 39 (for Italy); then the area code *including the first zero* (the major towns are listed below); and then the subscriber number. If calling **within Sardinia** the area code must always be used, even when dialling locally; all telephone numbers listed in the Guide include the relevant code.

Alghero ☎079	**Costa Smeralda** ☎0789	**Sássari** ☎079
Arbatax ☎0782	**Nuoro** ☎0784	**Villasimius** ☎070
Bosa ☎0785	**Olbia** ☎0789	
Cágliari ☎070	**Oristano** ☎0783	

ITALIAN PHONE NUMBERS

Telephone numbers change with amazing frequency in Italy. The latest innovation has been to merge the local code with the individual number, so that it is necessary to dial the entire number wherever you are. If in doubt, consult the local directory – there's a copy in most bars, hotels and, of course, telephone offices. Numbers beginning ☎147 and ☎167 are reduced tariff or free, and ☎170 will get you through to an English-speaking operator.

card. To make a **collect/reversed charge** call (*cári-co al destinatario*) dial ☎172 followed by the country code (see box on p.45), which will connect you to an operator in your home country.

Mobile phones work on the GSM European standard. You will hardly see an Italian without one, but if you are going to join them make sure you have made the necessary arrangements before you leave – which may involve paying a hefty (refundable) deposit. Your phone should lock onto one of the two Italian frequencies – Omnitel or Tim – according to which is strongest.

Fax and email

Nearly every Italian town has a **fax office**, but the cost is fairly high: for faxes within Italy, expect to pay L3000 for the first page and L2000 for each subsequent page, plus the cost of the call; for international faxes it's about L6000 for the first and L4000 for subsequent pages, plus the cost of the call.

There are no central "internet cafés" in Sardinia, but there is normally somewhere in each of the major cities where you can send or receive email, for a minimal cost. Ask at the local tourist office for the current places. Travelling with a laptop and a modem can enable you to log in to your own service provider, but it's advisable to check before you leave whether this is possible.

The media

Sards number among Italy's most avid readers of **newspapers**. You'll find the main national papers on any newsstand: *La Repubblica* is middle-to-left with a lot of cultural coverage; *Il Corriere della Sera* is authoritative and rather right wing; *L'Unità* is the former Communist Party organ, also strong on culture; *Il Manifesto*, a more radical and readable left-wing daily, and the pink *Gazzetta dello Sport*, essential reading for the serious sports fan.

Most people, however, prefer Sardinian **local papers**, which offer outsiders good insights into local concerns as well as being useful for transport timetables, entertainments listings, festival announcements, etc. There are two main ones: *L'Unione Sarda*, most read in Cágliari and the south of the island, and *La Nuova Sardegna*, also called "La Nuova", favoured in Sássari and the north. There is little to tell between them in terms of content, and each has local editions for each of the main towns. Note that Monday editions are almost exclusively devoted to sport, with no coverage of other events. **English-language newspapers** can be found in Cágliari, Sássari, Oristano, Nuoro, Olbia, Porto Cervo and Alghero, at the train station and the main piazza or corso, usually a day or two late.

If the opportunity arises, take a look at Italian **TV** to sample the pros and cons of deregulation in television. The three state-run channels, RAI 1, 2 and 3, have got their backs against the wall in the face of the massive independent onslaught, led by the Euromogul Berlusconi. The output is generally pretty bland, with a heavy helping of Brazilian soaps, American sitcoms and films, and ghastly Italian cabaret shows, though the RAI channels have less advertising and mix some good reporting in among the dross. RAI 3 has the most intelligent coverage, and broadcasts Sardinian news programmes. Of the local channels, *Videolina* is most popular in Cágliari, *Sardegna Uno* in the north, *TeleSardegna* around Nuoro, and *Tele Regione* transmits everywhere. Advertising is constant on all stations.

The situation in **radio** is even more anarchic, with the FM waves crowded to the extent that you can pick up a new station just by walking down the corridor. Again, the RAI stations are generally more professional, though daytime listening is virtually undiluted non-stop dance music. RAI 3, on 97.3 Mhz FM, has classical and jazz music, and afternoons devoted to themes such as Brazilian or Celtic music.

Opening hours and public holidays

Basic hours for most shops and businesses in Sardinia are Monday to Saturday from 8 or 9am to around 1pm, and from around 4pm to 7 or 8pm, though some offices work to a more standard European 9am–5pm day. Everything, except bars and restaurants, closes on Sunday, though you might find pasticcerias, and fish shops in some coastal towns, open until Sunday lunchtime.

Other disrupting factors are **national holidays** and local **saints' days** (see Festivals, p.48). Local religious holidays don't generally close down shops and businesses, but they do mean that accommodation space will be tight. However, everything, except bars and restaurants, will be closed on the national holidays shown in the box.

PUBLIC HOLIDAYS

January 1 New Year's Day

January 6 Epiphany

Good Friday

Easter Monday

April 25 Liberation Day

May 1 Labour Day

August 15 Ferragosto; Assumption of the Blessed Virgin Mary

November 1 Ognissanti (All Saints)

December 8 Immaculate Conception of the Blessed Virgin Mary

December 25 Christmas Day

December 26

Churches, museums, nuraghi and other archeological sites

The rules for visiting **churches** are much as they are all over the Mediterranean. Dress modestly, which usually means no shorts, and covered shoulders for women, and avoid wandering around during a service. Most churches open around 7 or 8am for Mass and close around noon, opening up again at 4–5pm, and closing at 7pm; more obscure ones will only open for early morning and evening services; some only open on Sunday and on religious holidays. Other churches, which have become fully-fledged tourist stops, are open all day every day, for example the Pisan churches of Santa Trinità di Saccárgia, near Sássari, and San Gavino, in Porto Torres. Occasionally you'll come across churches, monasteries or convents **closed for restoration** (*chiuso per restauro*). Some of these are long-term closures, though you might be able to persuade a workman or priest/curator to show you around, even if there's scaffolding everywhere.

Museums are generally open daily from 9am to 1pm, and again for a couple of hours in the afternoon on certain days; likely closing day is Monday, while they close slightly earlier on Sunday, usually 12.30pm. **Archeological sites** are usually open from 9am until an hour before sunset, in practice until around 4pm in winter, 7pm in summer. Again, they are sometimes closed on Monday. The more important **nuraghi** are fenced off and have set times (usually 9am–sunset) and an admission charge. The vast majority are open to anyone at all hours, though if you need to cross private land to reach them, it's best to ask first.

Festivals and entertainment

Sardinia's festivals – *feste* or *sagre* – are high points of the island's cultural life, and excellent opportunities to view traditional costumes and hear local music. While many are religious in origin – mostly feast days for saints having a special role for a particular locality – others are purely secular, often celebrating the harvest or simply perpetuating ancient games and competitions. These are still basically unchanged in the smaller towns and villages, though some have evolved into much larger affairs spread over three or four days, and others have been developed with an eye to tourism.

In all, masks and costumes play a prominent role, the first representing a variety of functions and traditions and injecting an eerie theatricality into the event, the second an emblem of local identity. Horses, too, are usually present, and often the main protagonists of the proceedings. Many events attract groups of singers and dancers from surrounding villages, usually competing to win a prize for their performance, and special food and sweets are consumed at stalls. Local people spend months preparing for the occasion, and they're well worth scheduling into your visit.

Sardinia has a number of *chiese novene*, remote churches open only for nine days a year when **pilgrimages** take place. The best-known of these are Sant'Antine, outside Sédilo, and San Salvatore, on the Sinis peninsula, where pilgrims gather at the beginning of July and the beginning of September respectively – both places are in Oristano province.

Aside from the festivals, there's a fair selection of cultural events happening throughout the year in Sardinia. **Concerts** and **dramatic performances** are sometimes held at outdoor venues in summer, and **films**, too, can be enjoyed under the stars. The ESIT office in Cágliari (see p.72) or any of the provincial tourist offices can tell you about forthcoming events.

Festivals

January
16–17 Sant'Antonio's (St Anthony's) day is celebrated in dozens of Sardinian villages, usually with bonfires, since the saint is supposed, Prometheus-like, to have given the gift of fire to men after he had stolen it from hell. The liveliest celebrations are at the villages of Abbasanta, near Oristano, and Mamoiada, Bitti, Lodè, Orosei and Lula, around Nuoro.

19–20 Among the villages commemorating **San Sebastiano**'s day are Turri and Ussana, both in Cágliari province, and Bulzi, inland from Castesardo. Again, bonfires, processions and holy singing are the order of the day, usually ending up with wine and food being shared.

February
3 San Biagio's day in Gergei, near Barúmini (north of Cágliari), sees the festival of **Su Sessineddu**, named after the *sessini* – reed frames on which sweets, fruits and flowers are hung and attached to the horns of oxen. This is primarily a children's festival, which involves seeing who can scoff the most goodies before staggering home.

Carnival
Traditionally the **Carnival** period starts with Sant'Antonio's day on 17 January, but in practice most of the action takes place over three days climaxing on Shrove Tuesday, most often in February. Although the occasion is intended as a prelude to the abstinence of Lent (*carne vale* =

farewell to meat), most Carnival celebrations smack of the pagan. Children raid their family trunks or, in richer households, get stuff hired or bought for them to wear as fancy dress. Masks are worn – Sardinia has a particularly impressive range – producing a somewhat sinister effect.

In Mamoiada, south of Nuoro, the three-day festival features music, dancing and the distribution of wine and sweets, climaxing in the ritual procession of the *issohadores* and *mamuthones* representing respectively hunters and hunted. The latter are clad in shaggy sheepskin jerkins, their faces covered in chilling black wooden masks, their backs hidden beneath dozens of sheep-bells with which they create a jangling, discordant clamour. Meanwhile the "hunters" lasso bystanders who are supposed to appease them with gifts of wine (but rarely do).

Oristano's **Sa Sartiglia** is wildly different, a medieval pageant involving much horseback racing and a jousting competition in which masked and mounted "knights" attempt to ram their swords through a hanging ring, called *sartija* – a Spanish word which gives its name to the festival. The whole three-day event is directed by the *componidori*, also white-masked and dressed in an elaborate frilly costume.

Various other strange goings-on take place during this period: a six-day festival at Bonorva, between Oristano and Sássari, includes masked processions, dances and ritual burnings of puppets; Bosa, south of Alghero, holds another six-day event, with theatrical funeral processions and costumed searches for the *Giolzi*, spirit of Carnival and sexuality; the normally taciturn mountain village of Tempio Pausánia, in Gallura, bursts into life with masks and floats as another symbolic puppet is incinerated; while frenetic horse races are held at Santu Lussurgiu, in the mountains north of Oristano.

March

March is traditionally bereft of merry-making on account of Lent, though Muravera (on the coast east of Cágliari) holds its **Sagra dell'Agrume** to mark the citrus fruit (*agrumi*) harvest. Traditional Sardinian dances are performed as peasant carts trundle through town. It's always held on a Sunday, though the date varies.

April

23 Several villages on the island celebrate **San Giorgio**'s day: Bonnanaro, south-east of Sássari,

is the scene of religious processions and prayers conducted entirely in Sard; Bitti, a mountain village north of Nuoro, has a horseback procession in traditional costume and renditions of mournful shepherds' songs; and Onifai, near Orosei, holds horseback processions, dances and poetry competitions.

Easter

Usually occuring in April, **Easter** is a time of holy processions throughout the island. One of the most dramatic celebrations files through Iglesias almost daily for a week, beginning on the Tuesday of Easter week, culminating in a re-enactment of the Passion, with all the local guilds represented. Other places with distinctive rites include Alghero; Castelsardo; Sássari; Oliena, near Nuoro, and Santu Lussurgiu, north of Oristano, where fifteenth-century Gregorian chants are sung on Good Friday.

On the first Sunday after Easter religious processions and musical events take place in Alghero and Valledoria (near Castelsardo), and the Sunday following sees three days of events to commemorate the feast day of **Sant'Antíoco.** These are naturally most exuberant in the town named after him, but impressive celebrations are also held in Dolianova, outside Cágliari; Gavoi, a village in the Barbagia region southwest of Nuoro; Mogoro, south of Oristano; Ulassai, south of Lanusei on the island's eastern seaboard; and Villasor, northwest of Cágliari.

May

1–4 May's biggest event, if not the whole year's, is Cágliari's feast day in honour of the martyr **Sant'Efisio.** In one sense this festival belongs to all Sardinia since costumed delegations with extravagantly decorated ox-drawn carts are sent from dozens of villages throughout the island to accompany the image of the saint through the streets of the capital in memory of its delivery from plague in 1656. The procession takes two days to reach Sant'Efisio's church, 40km down the coast near the ruins of Roman Nora, site of the saint's martyrdom, then returns. It's one of the best opportunities to see a good selection of the island's costumes out at the same time.

15 Olbia's yearly extravaganza commemorates another martyr, **San Simplicio**, its patron saint, and consists of fireworks, the distribution of sweets and wine, and various games and water competitions.

Ascension Day The penultimate Sunday of May sees more costumed revelry, this time in Sássari, though without any of the religious overtones of Cágliari's festa. Many of the same costumes that appeared there can be seen at this pageant, **La Cavalcata**, which, as its name suggests, has a distinctly horsy flavour to it, culminating in grand equestrian stunts in the afternoon. The occasion originated with the successful repulse of a Muslim raid around the year 1000.

29 In the countryside outside Onaní, northeast of Nuoro, traditional Sardinian dances take place for three consecutive days and nights.

Pentecost Sunday – a movable feast 50 days after Easter – sees four days of celebration at Porto Torres, including an impressive procession carrying plaster images of the town's martyred saints from the clifftop church of Balai to the Pisan basilica of San Gavino. On the following day the saints are transported to the sea and there's a huge fish fry-up. One of the features of this festival is a boat-race involving teams from five of the main seaside towns on Sardinia's northern coast, and there is also a costumed parade.

Suelli, north of Cágliari, likewise has a prolonged celebration of Pentecost, beginning the Friday before, when the entire population exits from the town and spends the night in the fields gathering wood, singing songs and dancing. The wood collected gets brought into the town, and a bonfire is lit on Pentecost Sunday, amid costumed processions and games.

June

2 The island's most important **horse fair** takes place outside Santu Lussurgiu, north of Oristano, around the Romanesque church of San Leonardo.

Second Sunday Fonni, south of Nuoro, hosts a festival devoted to the "Blessed Virgin of the Martyrs" – **Beata Vérgine dei Mártiri**. Costumes and processions on horseback are the main features.

15 San Vito, outside Muravera (on the coast east of Cágliari), honours its saint with three days of spirited feasting.

24 A pre-Christian feast day marking the summer solstice coincides with **St John the Baptist's day** and is celebrated in more than fifty villages all over Sardinia with the usual processions, dances, songs and poetry competitions. Among the villages are Bonorva, between Oristano and Sássari; Buddusò, in the Galluran mountains between Olbia and Nuoro; Escalaplano, a mountain village between Cágliari and Lanusei; Fonni (see above), and nearby Gavoi.

29 Ss Peter and Paul are commemorated in a score of Sardinian villages, notably Ollolai and Orgósolo, both south of Nuoro; Terralba, south of Oristano, and Villa San Pietro, on the coast south of Cágliari.

July

6–8 Locals at Sédilo, between Oristano and Nuoro, indulge their passion for horses with characteristic gusto in the three-day **S'Ardia di Costantino**, in honour of the Roman emperor (and saint) Constantine. The reckless horse-racing guarantees plenty of thrills and spills and attracts thousands of fans.

25 Orosei, on the coast east of Nuoro, stages one of the most important of the island's many **poetry competitions**, in which contestants recite or sing verses.

31 There are three days of frolics at Musei, just off the Iglesias–Cágliari road, in honour of the founder of the Jesuit order, St Ignatius of Loyola (**Sant'Ignazio**); it has all the usual festival paraphernalia, usually kicking off on the nearest Sunday to the 31st.

August

This is the month when tourists flood into the island, emigrés return for the summer, and all the resorts devote every last lira to entertainment. The high point comes in the middle of the month with Ferragosto, a bank holiday that is celebrated more exuberantly than Christmas.

First Sunday On the first Sunday of the month Bosa hosts various events in honour of **Santa Maria del Mare**, with an emphasis on the water, including a river procession and various watersports.

15 Mid-August, or **Ferragosto**, is the day when villages all over Italy erupt with dazzling fireworks displays to mark the festival of the Madonna: the Assumption, or Assunta. Some of Sardinia's Ferragosto celebrations are coupled with another festival, as in Sássari's spectacular **I Candelieri**. The event – which had its origin in the fifteenth century when plague was averted by divine intervention – starts on the 14th, and takes its name from the huge candles carried through thronged streets amid delirious dancing. Each candle represents one of the city's guilds, whose traditional colours are emblazoned on the candlesticks along with the tools and symbols of the trade.

A similar festa is held in the nearby village of Nulvi, also starting on the 14th, but with just three candles (here representing shepherds, farmers and craftsmen) which are preceded by twelve monks – representing the apostles – singing medieval hymns. The Madonna herself is wheeled around town on the 15th, and there follows some sort of religious ceremony every day until the 22nd.

In Golfo Aranci, north of Olbia, the regular Ferragosto festivities are combined with a **Sagra del Pesce**, a fishing festa involving the consumption of much seafood.

Other Ferragosto events worthy of mention are held at Dorgali and Orgósolo, both in the Nuoro region, and Guasila, north of Cágliari.

Penultimate Sunday of August Nuoro's **Sagra del Redentore** includes parades and the most important of the island's costume competitions. This is the biggest of the festivals in Sardinia's mountainous Barbagia district.

29 The second, religious part of Nuoro's annual festival features a procession up to the statue of Christ the Redeemer on top of nearby Monte Ortobene. On the same day, St John the Baptist has a second holy day celebrated in several villages, notably Orotelli, west of Nuoro, and San Giovanni di Sinis, west of Oristano.

September

Formerly the first month of the year according to the old Sardinian calendar, September marks the return to work and is the traditional time for contracts to be sealed and marriages made.

First Sunday The lagoon town of Cabras, near Oristano, re-enacts the rescue of its statue of **San Salvatore** from raiders in the sixteenth century: an army of barefoot young men dressed in white sprint the 8km from the saint's sanctuary into town with the saint borne aloft.

7–17 Santa Maria de Sauccu Two separate processions take off from Bortigali, near Macomer, to a sanctuary 10km away in the mountains, the venue for dances, picnics and poetic competitions over the next nine days.

8 The **Madonna** is venerated in Ales, a village southeast of Oristano, when her statue is brought

out amid much fanfare no less than six times in three days.

Second Sunday: Nostra Signora di Regnos Altos Not for the first time in the year, the banners and bunting are strung across the narrow lanes of Bosa's old centre; once the religious formalities are out of the way, tables are laid and much food is guzzled and drink quaffed.

Last Sunday of September More than 100,000 devotees every year come to pay their tributes to **Santa Greca**. in five days of festivities at Decimomannu, outside Cágliari.

October

4 The village of Alà dei Sardi, nestled in the mountains between Nuoro and Olbia, takes to the fields and spends two days attending open-air masses, eating and feasting in honour of **St Francis**.

Last Sunday of October The **Sagra delle Castagne**, or chestnut fair, is held at Aritzo in the heart of the Barbagia mountains. The smell of the cooking nuts permeates the air around here for days.

November–December

The end of the year is a lean time for outdoor festivals, though a few saints are remembered, notably St Andrew on the last day of November.

1–2 November Tuttisanti, or All Saints Day, is a public holiday, and is followed by the **Day of the Dead**, a time of mourning observed all over the Catholic world. Families troop en masse to the local cemetery where loved ones are buried; in parts of Sardinia, the table is laid and the favourite dishes of the deceased are served up and left overnight. Apparently, just the odours are enough to satisfy them.

Christmas

Christmas Eve and **Christmas Day**, comparatively recent introductions, are not the big commercial affair they are in some countries. This is primarily a family event; fish is normally eaten on Christmas Eve, and lamb is the traditional fare on Christmas Day, followed by *panettone*, a dry, sweet cake.

Music and dance

The island's archeological remains provide spectacular settings for **concerts**, usually classical, and there are regular events by local and visiting international orchestras in the theatres at Cágliari and Sássari. The **opera** season runs from January to June, the best venues being the Teatro Cívico in Cágliari and Sássari. Smaller theatres in all the main towns and cities also have music programmes, with a season of classical music in Alghero every August and a festival of sacred **choral music** in the Pisan church of San Gavino in Porto Torres during the first week of September.

Unaccompanied harmony singing, in fact, forms a central part of Sardinia's musical tradition, and you'll come across it at many of the local festivals. Most village singing groups either belong to the *coros* (choral) or *tenores* (four-part) traditions, and the latter groups, in particular, have made quite an impact internationally in recent years. Festivals are also a good place to see **traditional instruments** being played; if you miss them there are plenty of examples to be seen in museums. Apart from drums and accordion, the most distinctive instrument is the *launeddas*, a simple, polyphonic triple pipe made from reed.

Together with an accordion, drum and guitar, the *launeddas* is the usual accompaniment to **Sardinian dancing**, a curiously twitchy spectacle, in which the feet perform a constant fast rhythm while the rest of the body remains still. The group (usually composed of men and women) might have to sustain the synchronized movement for a long time, exercising flawless control during the elaborate sequence – definitely worth catching if you get the chance.

There's no specific Sardinian **rock music** scene. Radio and TV are dominated by mainstream Italian chart music which is mostly ballads, bland dance music and Europop, or British and American hits. The island has made more impact in the field of **jazz**, contributing some big names to the Italian and European scenes – for example the trumpeter Paolo Fresu, who has accentuated the Sard connection in his work. Some big, international jazz and rock names do come to Sardinia, and, in summer especially, some of the more enterprising local councils sponsor open-air concerts in public squares or parks. Alghero stages a **world music** festival during August, using mainly outdoor venues.

Theatre and cinema

Regular **theatre** is popular in Sardinia. Most performances, unsurprisingly, take place in the main cities of Cágliari and Sássari, the Teatro Cívico in each place being the premier venue for mainstream works. Smaller theatres in both cities and some other towns stage more experimental material, while summer sees open-air performances in Cágliari's Anfiteatro Romano, amid the ruins of Nora and Tharros, and at Villasimius.

There are **cinemas** in most towns, though all English-language films are dubbed into Italian. An alternative in summer to the indoor movie houses are the open-air film shows that take place in some towns and tourist resorts, detailed in the text. The island of Tavolara, east of Olbia, hosts a unique **film festival** every year in mid-July, with open-air screenings of new, mainly low-budget Italian films. You can reach the island by boat from Porto San Paolo; for programmes, see the festival Web site: *web.tin.it/cinematavolara/*

Activities

It is possible to have a quiet, passive holiday in Sardinia, but the island also offers numerous possibilities to participate in a range of activities, chief among these hiking, riding and watersports. There is just one ski run, in the Gennargentu mountains near Fonni (see pp.330–331), the season extending from December to March. Further south, around Íttiri, the rockscape has become a magnet for free climbers. Biking is described on p.30. You'll find public tennis courts in most towns and attached to hotels, with racquets sometimes available for rent.

Hiking

Walking – ie serious **hiking** – was until recently a fairly rare phenomenon in Sardinia, and there are no long-distance paths and few marked routes. Nonetheless, the island has some of the most magnificent walking country in Europe, including the Gorropu canyon (see p.344), Sopramonte, south of Nuoro (p.324), and, still further south, the Gennargentu mountains (pp.329–334). But almost every part of Sardinia offers scope for serious or casual hikes, and there are scores of hiking cooperatives who will supply **guides** for walks of all levels of difficulty. Phone numbers for some of these are given in the text; others may be contacted through local tourist offices, such as that at Nuoro (see p.316), which can also supply itineraries and rough maps, or else the Sardinian branch of the *Associazione Italiana Guide Ambientali Escursionistiche* (AIGE ☎0783.57.155).

We've described some simple hikes in the guide (see p.324 and p.344). Remember to bring suitable footwear, headwear and a good supply of water, and that long-distance hikes are inadvisable without an experienced guide. For maps, see pp.24–25.

Riding

Horses and Sardinia have been an item for centuries, and Sards have long been acknowledged as among Italy's finest riders. There's ample evidence of this on display in the festivals which feature equestrian skills, notably in Oristano province, and in the **riding** courses and excursions available throughout the island. The largest of the riding operations is also in Oristano province, at Ala Birdi (see p.178); it organizes courses and a range of treks through pinewoods and on the nearby beaches, and can provide information on riding activities over the whole island. The Barbágia, too, provides myriad possibilities for mountain riding, for example from Su Gologone, near Oliena and Nuoro (see p.325). You'll find other stables throughout the island. Rates depend on the length of the excursion and whether or not you are part of a group.

Watersports

You'll find a full range of **watersports** available on most coasts as soon as the beaches start filling up in summer. **Scuba diving** is offered by small firms in most holiday centres, as is **water-skiing**, though this has been supplanted in many places by **windsurfing**, for which the favourite spot is Porto Puddu, near Palau. All of these activities are often available from the bigger hotels, even for non-residents, and from some campsites. Prices can be high – up to L60,000 per hour for tuition, less for simple rental of equipment. **Surfers** tend to congregate at Capo Mannu on the Sinis peninsula, near Oristano.

Sailing is another favourite summer pastime, particularly on the Costa del Sud and Costa Smeralda, and around the Maddalena archipelago. This is a high-spending pursuit in Sardinia, however, and most enthusiasts will have to make do with joining a group with a full crew to do the actual sailing. Ask at tourist offices in Olbia, Pula, Palau and Porto Cervo about companies offering these expeditions.

Police and trouble

Mention crime in Sardinia to most people and they think of bandits in the hills. The kidnapping of rich industrialists or members of their families has been the most high-profile felony practised on the island since it was found to be more lucrative than sheep-rustling, though it is still a comparatively rare event, and should not affect tourists at all. In the interior, road signs peppered with gunshot are more an indication of bored youth than anything more menacing, and the feuds which occasionally erupt between families are always "in-house" affairs.

In fact, Sardinia is one of Italy's safest regions, with a remarkably low level of violence, drunkenness and crime. Most **petty juvenile crime** is connected with drug addiction in the cities of Cágliari and Sássari. You can minimize the risk of falling victim to **muggings** or **pickpockets** by being discreet: don't flash anything of value, keep a firm hand on your camera, and carry shoulder-bags, as you'll see many Sardinian women do, slung across your body. It's a good idea, too, to entrust money and credit cards to hotel managers. On the whole it's common sense to avoid badly lit or deserted areas at night. Confronted with a robber, your best bet is to submit meekly: it's an excitable situation where panic can lead to violence – though very few tourists see anything of this.

The police

If the worst happens, you'll be forced to have some dealings with the **police**. In Sardinia, as in the rest of Italy, they come in many forms. The most innocuous are the **Polizia Urbana** or town police, mainly concerned with directing the traffic and punishing parking offences. The **Guardia di Finanza**, often heavily armed and screaming ostentatiously through the cities, are responsible for investigating smuggling, tax evasion and other similar crimes. Most conspicuous are the **Carabinieri** and **Polizia Statale**; no one knows what distinguishes their roles, apart from the fact that the Carabinieri – the ones with the blue uniforms – are organized along military lines and are a branch of the armed forces. They are also the butt of most of the jokes about the police, usually on the "How many Carabinieri does it take to…?" level. Each of the two forces is meant to act as a check and counter-balance to the other: a fine theory, though it results in much time-wasting and rivalry in practice.

Hopefully, you won't need to get entangled with either, but **in the event of theft**, you'll need to report it at the headquarters of the Polizia Statale, the **Questura**; you'll find their address in the local *Tuttocittà* magazine, and we've included details in the various city listings. The Questura is also where you're supposed to go to obtain a *permesso di soggiorno* **if you're staying** for any length of time, or a **visa extension** if you require one.

In any brush with the authorities, your experience will very much depend on the individuals you're dealing with. Apart from **topless bathing** (permitted, but don't try anything more daring) and **camping rough**, don't expect a soft touch if you've been picked up for any offence, especially if it's drug related: it's not unheard of to be stopped and searched if you're young and carrying a backpack, and Italy always has plenty of plain-clothes police and informers on the lookout for any suspicious activity.

Drugs are generally frowned upon by everyone above a certain age, and universal hysteria about *la droga*, fuelled by the epidemic of heroin addiction that has become a serious problem for Sardinia, means that any distinction between the "hard" and "soft" variety has become blurred. Theoretically, everything is illegal above the possession of a few grammes of cannabis or mari-

Emergencies

In an emergency, note the following national emergency telephone numbers:

☎ 112 for the police (Carabinieri).

☎ 113 for any emergency service (Soccorso Púbblico di Emergenze).

☎ 115 for the fire brigade (Vígili del Fuoco).

☎ 116 for road assistance (Soccorso Stradale).

juana "for personal use", though there's no agreed definition of what this means and you can expect at least a fine for this, possibly a stint in jail, for as long as it takes for them to analyze the stuff, draw up reports and wait for the bureaucratic wheels to grind. For the addresses of the nearest **foreign consulates** (UK; US, Irish, Australian, New Zealand, Canadian in Rome), see "Directory", p.50, though bear in mind that they're unlikely to be very sympathetic or do anything more than put you in touch with a lawyer.

Travellers with disabilities

Although most Sardinians are helpful enough if presented with a specific problem, the island is hardly geared towards accommodating travellers with disabilities, and there can be significant accessibility problems for anyone in a wheelchair wishing to visit archeological sites.

In the medieval city centres and old villages, few budget hotels have elevators, let alone ones capable of taking a wheelchair, and rooms have not been adapted for use by disabled visitors. The narrow cobbled streets, steep inclines, chaotic driving and parking are hardly conducive to a stress-free holiday either, while crossing the street in Cágliari is a trial at the best of times. That said, Sardinia presents a much less frenetic level of bustle and rush than other areas in Italy's south, while Alghero, the most popular resort, has a highly user-friendly grid of traffic-free streets.

However, there are things you can do to make your visit to Sardinia easier. Contacting one of the **organizations** listed below puts you in touch with a wide range of facilities and information that may prove useful. RADAR, for instance, issues a badge enabling disabled drivers to park more freely in Italy. Indeed, if the thought of negotiating your own way around the island proves too daunting, an **organized tour** may be the way to go: it will be more expensive than planning your own trip, but accommodation is usually in higher-category

hotels which should have at least some experience of and facilities for disabled travellers; while you'll also have someone on hand who speaks Italian to help smooth the way. You should also consult the list of specialist Sardinian tour operators on p.8 (Britain) or p.14 (North America): these will at least consider your enquiries and requests, though in the end they (and you) may conclude that certain resorts and destinations are not suitable for your needs.

At all times, it is vital to be honest – with travel agencies, insurance companies and travel companions. Know your limitations and make sure others know them. If you do not use a wheelchair all the time but your walking capabilities are limited, remember that you are likely to need to cover greater distances while travelling (often over rougher terrain and in hotter temperatures) than you are used to. If you use a wheelchair, have it serviced before you go and carry a repair kit.

Read your travel **insurance** small print carefully to make sure that people with a pre-existing medical condition are not excluded. Use your travel agent to make your journey simpler: airline or bus companies can cope better if they are expecting you, with a wheelchair provided at airports and staff primed to help. A **medical certificate** of your fitness to travel, provided by your doctor, is also extremely useful; some airlines or insurance companies may insist on it. Make sure that you have extra supplies of drugs – carried with you if you fly – and a prescription including the generic name in case of emergency. If there's an association representing people with your disability, contact them early in the planning process.

CONTACTS FOR PEOPLE WITH DISABILITIES

AUSTRALIA AND NEW ZEALAND

Access Able, *www.access-able.com/*

ACROD, PO Box 60, Curtin, ACT 2605 ☎02/6282 4333

Barrier Free Travel, 36 Wheatley St, North Bellingen, NSW 2454 ☎02/6655 1733

Disabled Persons Assembly, 173–175 Victoria St, Wellington ☎04/811 9100

Global Access, *www.geocities.com/Paris/1502/index/*

BRITAIN AND IRELAND

Disability Action Group, 2 Annadale Ave, Belfast BT7 3JH ☎01232/491 011. Information on access for disabled travellers abroad.

Holiday Care Service, 2nd Floor, Imperial Buildings, Victoria Rd, Horley, Surrey RH6 7PZ ☎01293/774 535. Holiday Care provides information on places catering to disabled people.

Irish Wheelchair Association, Blackheath Drive, Clontarf, Dublin 3 ☎01/833 8241. A national voluntary organization working with disabled people and offering related services for holidaymakers.

RADAR, 12 City Forum, 250 City Rd, London EC1V 8AS ☎0171/250 3222; Minicom ☎0171/250 4119. A good source of advice on holidays and travel abroad.

Tripscope, The Courtyard, Evelyn Rd, London W4 5JL ☎ & Minicom 0181/994 9294 or 08457/585 641. National telephone information service offering transport and travel advice, free of charge.

USA AND CANADA

Access First, 239 Commercial St, Malden, MA 02148 ☎1-800/557-2047; TTY ☎781/322-4842. Makes a specialty of trips to Italy.

Jewish Rehabilitation Hospital, 3205 Place Alton Goldbloom, Montréal, PQ H7V 1R2 ☎514/688 9550, ext 226. Guidebooks and travel information.

Mobility International USA, PO Box 10767, Eugene, OR 97440 ☎541/343-1284. Information and referral services, access guides, tours and exchange programmes. Annual membership US$35 (includes quarterly newsletter).

Society for the Advancement of Travelers with Handicaps (SATH), 347 5th Ave, Suite 610, New York, NY 10016 ☎212/447-7284 or 447-0027. Non-profit travel-industry referral service that passes queries on to its members as appropriate; allow plenty of time for a response.

Travel Information Service, Moss Rehabilitation Hospital, 1200 West Tabor Rd, Philadelphia, PA 19141 ☎215/456-9603, *www.mossresourcenet.org/* Telephone information and referral service.

Twin Peaks Press, Box 129, Vancouver, WA 98666 ☎206/694-2462 or 1-800/637-2256. Publisher of the *Directory of Travel Agencies for the Disabled* ($19.95), listing more than 370 agencies worldwide; *Travel for the Disabled* ($14.95); the *Directory of Accessible Van Rentals;* and *Wheelchair Vagabond* ($9.95), loaded with personal tips.

Wheels Up! ☎1-888/389-4335. Provides discounted airfare, tour and cruise prices for disabled travelers, and also publishes a free monthly newsletter.

Sexual harassment and women in Sardinia

Italy's reputation for sexual harassment of women is well known and well founded. Generally, though, things have improved radically in recent years, and Sardinia is one of the most relaxed parts of the Italian south in this respect.

If you're travelling on your own, or with another woman, you can expect to attract occasional unwelcome attention in bars, restaurants and on the beach. This pestering does not usually have any violent intent, but it's annoying and frustrating nevertheless. There are a few things you can do to ward it off, though you'll never be able to stop the car horns and wolf-whistles. Indifference is often the best policy, or try hurling a few simple retorts like *Lasciátemi in pace* ("Leave me alone"), though stronger language is not advised. As a last resort, don't hesitate to approach a policeman. Obviously, travelling with a man cuts out much of the more intense hassle, and perhaps the best strategy of all for a woman alone in Sardinia, where the sanctity of the family is still paramount, is to flaunt a wedding ring.

Finding work

With one of the highest unemployment rates of all the Italian regions, Sardinia offers few opportunities for finding work, although all EU citizens are eligible to do so.

The two main **bureaucratic requirements** for both working and living in Sardinia are a *libretto di lavoro* and *permesso di soggiorno*, respectively a work and residence permit, both available from the Questura (see p.54). For the first you must have a letter from your prospective employers saying they are prepared to take you on, for the second (which is also necessary if you want to buy a car or have a bank account in Italy) you'll need a passport, passport-sized photos and a lot of patience.

Teaching

The obvious choice is to **teach English**, for which the demand has expanded enormously in recent years. You can do this in two ways: freelance private lessons, or through a language school. **Private lessons** generally pay best, and you can charge up to L20,000–40,000 an hour, though there's scope for bargaining. Advertise in bars, shop windows and local newspapers, and, most importantly, get the news around by word-of-mouth that you're looking for work, emphasizing your excellent background, qualifications and experience. An advantage of private teaching is that you can start at any time of the year (summer especially is a good time because there are

schoolchildren and students who have to retake exams in September); the main disadvantage is that it can take weeks to get off the ground, and you need enough money to support you until then. You'll find the best opportunities for this kind of work in the tourist resorts and the bigger towns and cities.

Teaching in schools, you start earning immediately (though some schools can pay months in arrears). Teaching classes usually involves more hours per week, often in the evening, and for less per hour, though the amount you get depends on the school. For the less reputable places, you can get away without any qualifications and a bit of bluff, but you'll need to show a degree and a

---

WORK, STUDY AND VOLUNTEER PROGRAMMES

BRITAIN

Central Bureau for Educational Visits and Exchanges, 10 Spring Gardens, London SW1A 2BN ☎0171/389 4004. The Central Bureau administers a number of exchanges, including LINGUA (language training opportunities).

Commission of the European Communities, ☎0800/581 591. The information office produces a series of factsheets and booklets on

issues relating to work and study in Europe. See also their web site: *citizens.eu.int/*

European Programme, The Prince's Trust, 18 Park Square East, London NW1 4LH ☎0171/543 1365. Offers a number of "Go" grants to young people between 18 and 25 to work and study in Europe. Awards are usually made to disadvantaged or undereducated applicants.

ITALY

Ministero Lavoro e Previdenza Sociale, Divisone 11, Via Flavia 6, 1-00187 Roma. Job placement information. There is also *The*

Informer, an expatriate magazine containing current vacancy listings; available from Buro Service, Via de Imtigli 2, 20020 Arese, Milan.

USA

Institute of International Education, 809 UN Plaza, New York, NY 10017 ☎212/984-5413 (recorded information only), *www.iie.com/* Contact IIE's Publications Service to order its annual study abroad directory.

InterExchange Program, 161 Sixth Ave, New York, NY 10013 ☎212/924-0446, *www.interexchange.com/* Information on work programmes and au pair opportunities for non-US citizens.

Italian Cultural Institute, 686 Park Ave, New York, NY 10021 ☎212/879-4242; Suite 104, 1717 Massachusetts Ave NW, Washington DC 20036 ☎202/387-5161. Publishes a directory of study courses for English-speaking students and helps with job openings.

Office of Overseas Schools, US Department of State, Room 245, SA-29, Washington DC 20522-2902 ☎703/875-7800. Produces a list of schools for potential EFL teachers to contact.

Volunteers for Peace, 1034 Tiffany Rd, Belmont, VT 05730 ☎802/259-2759, *www.vfp.com/* Non-profit organization with links to a huge international network of "workcamps", two- to four-week programmes that bring volunteers together from many countries to carry out community projects. Most workcamps are in summer, with registration in April–May. Annual directory costs US$15.

TEFL certificate for the more professional language schools. For these, it's best to apply in writing from Britain (look for the ads in the *Guardian* and *The Times Educational Supplement*, and contact the *Italian Cultural Institute* at 39 Belgrave Square, London SW1X 8NX ☎0171/235 1461), preferably before the summer, though you can also find openings in September. If you're looking on the spot, sift through the *Yellow Pages* (*Págine Gialle*) and do the rounds on foot, asking to speak to the *direttore* or his/her secretary; don't bother to try in August when everything is closed. Strictly speaking, you could get by without any knowledge of Italian, but some definitely helps.

The best teaching jobs of all are with a university as a *lettore*, a job requiring fewer hours

than the language schools and generally offering a fuller pay packet. Universities need English-language teachers in most faculties and you should write to the individual faculties at the universities of Cágliari or Sássari (addressed to Ufficio di Personale). That said, success in obtaining a university teaching job usually depends on you knowing someone already in place – as with so many things in Sardinia.

Other options

If teaching's not up your street, there's the possibility of **bar/restaurant work** too – not the most lucrative of jobs, though you should make enough to keep you in Sardinia over the summer. You'll have to ask around for this type of work, and a knowledge of Italian is essential.

Directory

ADDRESSES Usually written as the street name followed by the number – eg Via Roma 69. Interno refers to the flat number – eg interno 5 (often abbreviated as int.). Always use postal codes.

AIRPORT TAX Around £20 for British and Italian airports combined, usually included in the price of your ticket.

BARGAINING Not really on in shops and restaurants, though you'll find you can get a "special price" for some rooms in cheap hotels if you're staying a few days; and that things like boat or bike rental and guided tours (especially out of season) are negotiable. In markets, you can haggle for everything except food, and you'll be taken for an imbecile if you don't bargain on craft items bought from individuals – ask for *uno sconto* ("a discount"). The craftwork for sale in the official chain of shops, ISOLA (addresses in Guide), is normally fixed-price.

BEACHES There are excellent beaches on every coast of Sardinia, most of them easy to find, the better-known ones indicated by brown signposts. You'll have to pay for access to the supervised beaches referred to as lidos, which offer deck chairs and parasols for a few thousand lire, with unlimited use of showers and toilets. In other places, you have to leave your vehicle in a private or council-run car park, for L5–10,000 a day. Most beaches are free but not always clean, especially during winter when some look like dumps; it's not worth anyone's while to clean them until the season starts at Easter. On the other hand, any beach that's remotely inaccessible should remain in a fairly pristine state. Some coasts are prone to invasions of jellyfish (*meduse*) in very warm weather. These are not dangerous, but can cause quite a sting, so take local advice.

CAMPING GAZ Easy enough to buy for the small portable camping stoves, either from hardware stores (*ferramenta*) or camping/sports shops. You can't carry canisters on aeroplanes.

CHILDREN Children are revered in Sardinia and will be welcomed and catered for in bars and restaurants (though be warned that there's no such thing as a smoke-free environment, with chain-smoking the norm). Hotels normally charge around 30 percent extra to put a bed or cot in your room, though kids pay less on trains (see p.27). Many coastal hotels are well-equipped for family holidays, and lay on a range of entertainments and activities for kids and parents. The main hazards when travelling with children in Sardinia are the heat and sun in summer. Sunblock can be bought at any chemist's, and bonnets or straw hats in most markets. Take advantage of the less intense periods – mornings and evenings – for travelling, and use the quiet of siesta time to recover flagging energy. The rhythms of the southern climate soon modify established patterns, and you'll find it more natural carrying on later into the night, past normal bedtimes. In summer, it's not unusual to see Sardinian children out at midnight, and not looking much the worse for it.

CIGARETTES The state monopoly brand – MS, jokingly referred to as Morte Sicura (Certain Death) – are the most widely smoked cigarettes, strong and aromatic and selling for around L4200 for a pack of twenty. Younger people tend to smoke imported brands, all of which are slightly more expensive at around L5200 per pack. You buy cigarettes from *tabacchi* (see below).

CONSULATES The following consular agencies can all be found at the respective embassies in Rome: Australia, Corso Trieste 25c (☎06.852 721); Canada, Via Zara 30 (☎06.445 981); Great Britain, Via XX Settembre 80a (☎06.482 5441); Ireland, Piazza Campitelli 3 (☎06.697 9121); New Zealand, Via Zara 28 (☎06.441 7171); USA, Via Veneto 121 (☎06.46 741).

DEPARTMENT STORES There are two main nationwide chains, Upim and Standa. Neither is particularly posh, and they're good places to stock up on toiletries and other basic supplies; branches of both stores sometimes have a food

hall attached. The Upim chain also runs the huge Rinascente store in Cágliari, selling higher-quality products. The long post-Christmas sales period is a good time to seek out bargains.

ELECTRICITY The supply is 220V, though anything requiring 240V will work. Most plugs have two round pins: a travel plug is useful.

ENTRANCE FEES The entrance fee for museums and sites is usually L4000–8000, although under-18s and over-60s get in free on production of documentary proof of age. Some sites insist on escorting you around, their running commentary – sometimes available in English – included in the price, and it's not expected that you hand over a tip.

GAY LIFE There's no openly gay scene in Sardinia outside a few scattered clubs, bars and beaches. There is a slightly more sympathetic atmosphere in parts of Cágliari and Sássari, and on the Costa Smeralda, where there is higher proportion of gay beaches. In this respect, Sardinia has much in common with the rest of the south of Italy, where attitudes towards homosexuality (male and female) are generally much less tolerant than in Rome or the industrial north. That said, there's no legally sanctioned discrimination against gays and what gay groups there are in Italy work at getting the public to accept and understand homosexuality. Also, it's worth noting that physical contact between men is fairly common in Sardinia, on the level of linking arms and kissing cheeks at greetings and farewells – though an overt display of anything remotely ambiguous is likely to be met by hostility. For general information, contact ARCI-Gay/ARCI-Lesbica, Piazza di Porta Saragozza 2, PO Box 692, 40100 Bologna ☎051.644.7054.

LAUNDRY There are currently no coin-operated launderettes in Sardinia, so you'll have to use a *lavanderia*, or service-wash laundry, where items are individually charged – say L5000 for a shirt, L8000 for a skirt or trousers – and are returned a day or two later immaculately ironed. Addresses are given in the Listings sections for cities. Although you can usually get away with it, washing clothes in your hotel room is disapproved of simply because the plumbing often can't cope, and the water supply itself may be limited in summer.

PUBLIC TOILETS Usually found in bars and restaurants, and you'll generally be allowed to use them whether you're eating and drinking or not. You'll find most places to be very clean,

Things to Take

A universal electric plug adaptor and a universal sink plug.

A flashlight.

Earplugs (for street noise in hotel rooms).

High-factor sun block.

Mosquito repellent and antiseptic cream.

A pocket alarm clock (for those early morning departures).

An inflatable neck rest, for long journeys.

A multi-purpose penknife.

A needle and some thread.

A towel (for cheaper hotels).

A water bottle for visiting hot, exposed archeological sites.

A hat.

A driving licence, if you have one.

though it's advisable not to be without your own toilet roll.

RECEIPTS Shops, bars and restaurants are all legally obliged to provide you with a receipt (*una ricevuta* or *uno scontrino*). Don't be surprised when it's thrust upon you, as they – and indeed you – can be fined if you don't take it.

TABACCHI These ubiquitous tobacco shops – recognizable by a sign displaying a white "T" on a black or blue background – also sell sweets, postcards and other writing equipment, stamps and sometimes bus tickets and toiletries.

TIME Sardinia (and Italy) is always one hour ahead of Britain except for one week at the end of September when the time is the same. Italy is seven hours ahead of Eastern Standard Time and ten hours ahead of Pacific Time.

WATER Safe to drink everywhere, and especially prized from mountain springs. You'll find bottled mineral water is on sale everywhere.

Part 2

The Guide

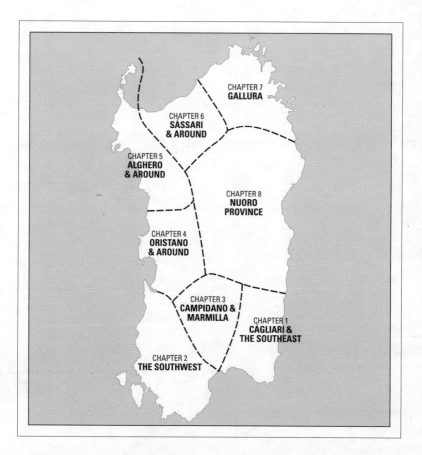

Chapter 1

Cágliari and the southeast

S
ituated at the centre of the broad curve of the Golfo di Cágliari, backed by lagoons and surmounted by an imposing ring of medieval walls, **Cágliari** is visually the most impressive of Sardinia's cities. As the island's capital since Roman times at least, it's also littered with the remains of two thousand years of history. Today, it remains Sardinia's busiest port, with the greatest concentration of industry. Intimidating as this may sound, Cágliari is much more than a mere administrative centre or urban sprawl, offering both chic sophistication and medieval charm in the raggle-taggle of narrow lanes crammed into its high citadel and port area. The city's old core is small and compact enough to amble about on foot, in between taking in its splendid and diverse collection of museums, absorbing archeological remains and historic churches. And, should you find yourself succumbing to sightseeing fatigue, you can unwind on the enormous expanse of sandy beach at nearby **Poetto**.

With Sardinia's best choice of hotels, Cágliari makes an ideal base for excursions further afield. One monument of immediate interest, the Romanesque church of **Dolianova**, stands in the fertile flatlands due north of Cágliari on the SS387. East of here lies the mountainous **Sarrabus** region, where the Monte dei Sette Fratelli reaches 1023m. Most of this zone is too desolate even for shepherds, though it attracts a rich birdlife and makes good walking country. What towns there are have been developed as holiday resorts on or close to the coast, notably **Villasimius**, 50km east of Cágliari and within easy reach of some of Sardinia's finest beaches. Sadly, the heavy presence of holiday homes has disfigured a large part of the coast, not least around the **Costa Rei**, Sardinia's most extensive beach development outside the Costa Smeralda. Come out of season though, and there's no distraction from the sea and sand.

Further north, near the mouth of the Flumendosa river, **Muravera** is another holiday centre lacking much intrinsic interest but within a short drive of more superb beaches. You could reach the town directly from

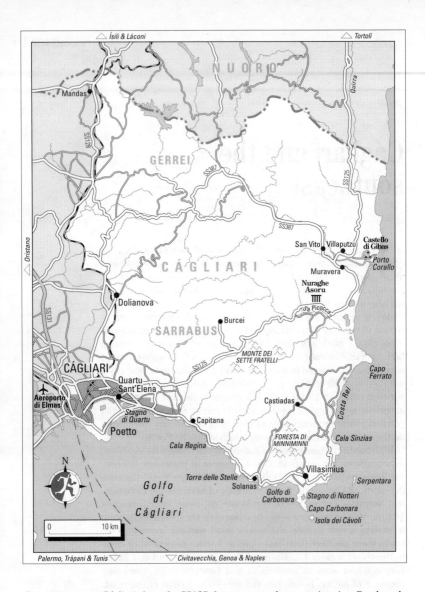

For more
information on
bus and train
connections,
see Travel
Details, p.101.

Cágliari along the SS125 that traverses the empty interior. Good roads exist for most areas you might want to visit, though a four-wheel drive would be useful for the remoter mountain tracks (non-asphalted roads are marked white on maps). **Public transport** links are adequate for Villasimius, Muravera and the coast, all of which are served by ARST buses, while local FdS trains depart frequently from Cágliari's sec-

THE GUIDE: CHAPTER 1

Accommodation Price Codes

The hotels listed in this guide have been coded according to price. The codes represent the cheapest available double room in high season (Easter & June–Aug). In cheaper hotels the rooms usually come without en-suite bathroom or shower; some of these places will also have a few en-suite rooms, for which you'll pay more – usually the next category up in price. Higher category hotels nearly always have only en-suite rooms. Out of season, you'll often be able to negotiate a lower price than those suggested here. The categories are:

① under L60,000   ④ L120,000–150,000   ⑦ L250,000–300,000

② L60,000–90,000   ⑤ L150,000–200,000   ⑧ over L300,000

③ L90,000–120,000   ⑥ L200,000–250,000

ondary station in Piazza Repúbblica to Dolianova; at Mandas, the line splits for Sórgono, in the centre of the Barbagia, or Arbatax, the port on Sardinia's east coast.

Cágliari

Viewing **CÁGLIARI** from the sea at the start of his Sardinian sojourn in 1921, D.H. Lawrence compared it to Jerusalem: "strange and rather wonderful, not a bit like Italy". Today, still crowned by an old centre squeezed within a protective ring of Pisan fortifications, Cágliari retains a very different identity from mainland towns of an equivalent size, distinguished by its less frenetic pace and unusual setting: the calm lagoons (*stagni*) that almost surround the city and form the habitat for cranes, flamingos and cormorants.

Almost all the wandering you will want to do in Cágliari is encompassed within the four oldest quarters of the city: Castello, Marina, Stampace and Villanova. You will probably spend most time in the old citadel, **Castello**, not for its hotels (there are none), but for the city's flamboyant cathedral and best museums. Beneath the citadel walls, Via Manno – scene of the smartest evening promenades you'll see in Sardinia – drops down through the noisier Piazza Yenne and Largo Carlo Felice to the seafront **Marina** quarter, where most of the shops, restaurants, banks and hotels are located, as well as a couple of absorbing historical remains. At the bottom of the town, the arcades of Via Roma are still the city's favourite venue for sitting with an ice cream or a cup of coffee in view of the port.

West of Largo Carlo Felice, the **Stampace** district contains some of the city's oldest churches; just a short distance away are the city's best Roman remains, a theatre and a residential complex from the imperial era. And if **Villanova**, the area extending east of Castello and Marina, is somewhat less picturesque, it does hold two of

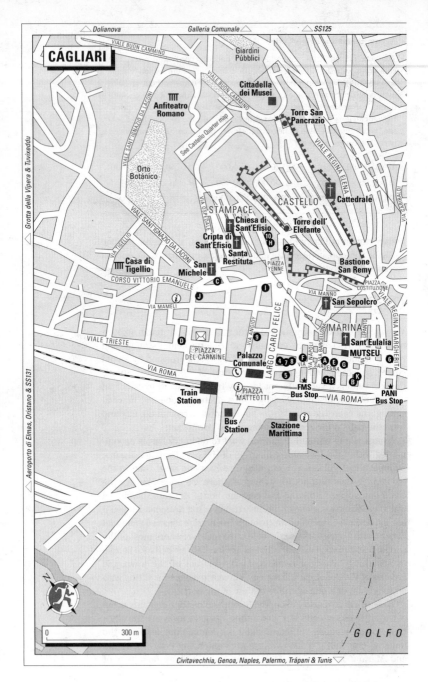

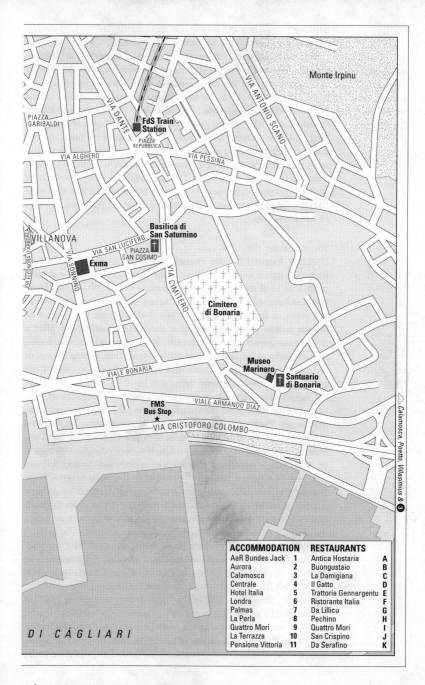

ACCOMMODATION
AeR Bundes Jack	1
Aurora	2
Calamosca	3
Centrale	4
Hotel Italia	5
Londra	6
Palmas	7
La Perla	8
Quattro Mori	9
La Terrazza	10
Pensione Vittoria	11

RESTAURANTS
Antica Hostaria	A
Buongustaio	B
La Damigiana	C
Il Gatto	D
Trattoria Gennargentu	E
Ristorante Italia	F
Da Lillicu	G
Pechino	H
Quattro Mori	I
San Crispino	J
Da Serafino	K

Cágliari

Handy bus maps are available free from the tourist offices.

Sardinia's most important religious monuments, the ancient church of San Saturnino and the Santuario di Bonaria.

You can easily walk between the main points of interest in Cágliari, though there are some useful **bus routes** which can might help on the longer traipses: the most useful is #10, running between Viale Trento to the west of the city and Piazza Garibaldi to the east, taking in Corso Vittorio Emanuele, Piazza Yenne, Via Manno and Piazza Costituzione. Other useful routes from Piazza Matteotti are #6, running up to the Castello and beyond to the Giardini Públici, and #8 going to the Roman amphitheatre. Tickets are available from the kiosk in Piazza Matteotti and from some *tabacchi*, either for single journeys (*biglietto semplice*, L1100 or L1300, depending on route) or for unlimited rides over two hours (*biglietto válido due ore*, L1500), timed from when you punch the ticket for your first journey, on board the bus.

Some history

Probably founded by the Phoenicians, who gave it the name of Karalis, Cágliari became a colony of the Carthaginians, and was their main base until its capture by the Romans in 238 BC. As an important and flourishing *municipium*, the city was one of the major trading ports in the Mediterranean, but declined with the demise of Roman power, eventually falling to the Vandals and Goths. After a brief Byzantine revival, it was repeatedly plundered by the Saracens. The threat from marauders remained so great that, during the era of the *giudicati*, the site of Santa Igia, on a lagoon to the west of the city, was preferred as a more defensible base.

Cágliari's fortunes only revived in the middle of the thirteenth century after the local *giudichessa* granted the hill behind her capital to the Pisans. They walled and populated it, creating the citadel now known as Castello. It quickly became their principal base in Sardinia, and the fortifications – modern Cágliari's most conspicuous legacy of Pisan rule – were later extended to encompass the city's lower quarters. The formal cession of Sardinia to the Aragonese by Pope Boniface VIII in 1297 and a two-year siege of Cágliari by Alfonso d'Aragona led to the Pisan withdrawal from the city in 1326. Cágliari, however, retained its position under the Aragonese as Sardinia's capital, and the island's first university was opened here by Philip III in the early seventeenth century. Even so, absorption into the ramshackle Spanish empire proved a mixed blessing for Cágliari – in 1700 the city's population stood at a mere 15,000, fewer than when the Spanish first arrived more than three centuries earlier.

In 1708, during the War of the Spanish Succession, the city was bombarded by an English fleet and occupied in the name of Austria; twelve years later, along with the rest of the island, it came under the rule of the Piedmontese House of Savoy. During the eighteenth century, the city first began to creep out from behind its protective walls, which were dismantled in the quarters of Stampace, Marina and Villanova, to be replaced by the broad boulevards along which the traffic rumbles today. Although Cágliari repulsed an attack by French forces in 1793, the ideas of the French Revolution were infiltrating the island in other ways. The following year the so-called "Sardinian Revolution" broke out in Cágliari against the centralizing tendencies of the Savoyard government, and was brutally suppressed. But the city benefitted in time from the social and institutional reforms which filtered through the island under the Savoy dynasty, and, in common with the rest of the island, welcomed being integrated into the new kingdom of Italy in 1861.

More recently, in February and May 1943, heavy aerial bombardment destroyed nearly half the city. Many of the bomb sites have only recently been filled in, often with bold modernistic constructions which do not on the whole disrupt the harmony of the city centre. The real changes in the last twenty or thirty years have occurred on the northern outskirts of town, where new apartment blocks and businesses have mushroomed, since expansion in any other direction is restricted by the lagoons and the sea. Today, a brisk, confident city with a population of nearly a quarter of a million, Cágliari has the island's worst traffic – though without the clamorous chaos that would prevail in any mainland city of comparable size – the most engaging museums and monuments, and the broadest and most forward-looking cultural scene.

Cágliari is not a town to drive round: there is too much to absorb here without the added headache of negotiating its narrow streets, one-ways and pedestrian areas.

Arrival and information

Cágliari's **port** lies in the heart of the town, opposite Via Roma, the main thoroughfare; the Stazione Maríttima here has an information desk which opens to coincide with the arrival of boats. The **airport** sits beside the city's largest *stagno* (lagoon) 6km northwest of the centre: facilities include a **bank** (Mon–Fri 8.25am–1.25pm & 2.40–4.10pm) with a cash machine, and an **information desk** (daily: mid-June to mid-Sept 8am–8pm, mid-Sept to mid-June 9am–1pm & 4–6pm ☎070.240.200). A city bus service to Piazza Matteotti in the town centre runs at least every ninety minutes from 6.20am until midnight, taking fifteen minutes (tickets L1100 from the shop behind the information office); otherwise a taxi ride costs around L20,000–25,000 (more after 10pm).

If you're **driving into Cágliari** and wish to avoid parking fines, you'll need to pay the attendant (usually lurking in the vicinity) L1000 for the first hour, L2000 for every subsequent hour, almost everywhere in the centre (Mon–Sat 8.30am–1pm and 4–8pm). **PANI buses** from Oristano and Sássari stop on Via Roma, but all ARST buses use the **bus station** on Piazza Matteotti. This also serves as the terminus for most **local buses**, tickets for which are sold at the booth. The main FS **train station** is also located on Piazza Matteotti (FdS trains stop in the station at Piazza Repúbblica), and there's a handy tourist **information kiosk** (July & Aug daily 8am–8pm, Sept–June Mon–Sat 8am–2pm ☎070.669.255) in the square. The **main tourist office**, which dispenses information covering the whole of Sardinia, is at Via Mameli 97 (mid-May to Sept daily 8am–8pm; Oct–Nov & mid-Feb to March Mon–Sat 9am–7pm, Sun 9am–2pm; Dec to mid-Feb Mon–Fri 9.30am–5.30pm, Sat 9.30am–1.30pm; April to mid-May daily 9am–7pm ☎070.60.231). Any of Cágliari's information points should be able to provide an accommodation book covering the entire island, and may also stock *Appuntamenti*, a free booklet published quarterly giving the latest details on the city's sights as well as a calendar of events.

Accommodation

Most of Cágliari's **hotels** are in or around the Marina district, nearest to the sea. Availability may be restricted in high season, and single rooms are at a premium at all times (though easiest to find at weekends). The cheapest choices lie on or around the narrow Via Sardegna, running parallel to Via Roma. If you want to stay near a beach, head for Calamosca, near Poetto. The nearest campsite is at Capitana, a 40-minute bus ride east along the coast (see pp.95–96).

AeR Bundes Jack, Via Roma 75 (☎ & fax 070.667.970). One of Cágliari's best mid-range choices, centrally located above the arcades on the third floor (there's a lift). Front-facing rooms have great views over the port, but suffer from traffic rumble; all are solidly furnished, with or without private bath. The family that runs it are friendly, and helpful with local information (they also run the marginally cheaper *Pensione Vittoria*, for which see opposite). ③.

Aurora, Salita Santa Chiara 19 (☎070.658.625). Cágliari's cheapest deal lies in a faded palazzo just up from Piazza Yenne. There are only six rooms, all clean but none with bath, and they're often full. No CCs. ①.

Calamosca, Viale Calamosca (☎070.371.628, fax 070.370.346). Right on the sea, this is an excellent choice for avoiding Cágliari's noisy centre, 2km away. It's also the nearest hotel to Poetto, Cágliari's summer suburb, so space here can be limited. The terrace overlooks a secluded cove near the lighthouse on Capo Sant'Elia, where there's a small beach; you can also swim off rocks from the hotel garden. Much the best rooms are those facing the sea, the same price as back-facing ones; all are spacious. The hotel's about 15min from the centre: take bus "PF" or "PQ" from Piazza Matteotti, changing to the frequent #11 at Stadio Amsicora – the bus stops right outside. ④.

Centrale, Via Sardegna 4 (☎070.654.783). Very basic but adequate hotel, without en suite facilities. No CCs. ②.

Hotel Italia, Via Sardegna 31 (☎070.660.510, fax 070.650.240). Smart, modern and characterless three-star with standard facilities including TVs in the rooms and a restaurant. Breakfast included in price. ④.

La Perla, Via Sardegna 18 (☎070.669.446). Almost identical to the other two budget choices at this end of Via Sardegna. Rooms have no view or private bathrooms, but they're quiet and clean. No CCs. ②.

Londra, Viale Regina Margherita 16 (☎070.669.083). At the eastern end of Via Sardegna, this basic third-storey pensione is run by a Londoner who's lived twenty-two years on the island – the rooms are a mite cramped but clean, and the atmosphere is friendly. No CCs. ①.

Palmas, Via Sardegna 14 (☎070.651.679). In price and level of comfort, this is a notch above the others in this cluster of budget lodgings off Largo Carlo Felice, though it's still a fairly ordinary, no-frills place, with shared facilities. No CCs. ②.

Quattro Mori, Via Angioy 27 (☎070.668.535). Ask to see a room before you book into this two-star just up from Piazza Matteotti – some are run-down and tatty, others more cheerful. ③.

La Terrazza, Via Santa Margherita 21 (☎070.668.652, fax 070.660.863). Above a Chinese restaurant near Piazza Yenne, this place has small over-priced rooms, with or without bath, but it's an acceptable last resort if everywhere else in the centre is full. ②.

Pensione Vittoria, Via Roma 75 (☎070.657.970, fax 070.667.970). Managed by the same people who run *AeR Bundes Jack* one floor below (see above), this has very similar, clean rooms with or without bath, though without air-conditioning (or heating in winter), TV or telephone; accordingly, prices are about L5000 cheaper. ②.

Castello

Secure on its hill, Cágliari's **Castello** district was traditionally the seat of Sardinia's administration, aristocracy and highest ecclesiastical offices. The intricate knot of alleys visible today, accessed from various points in its thick girth of walls, has altered little since the Middle Ages, though most of the dwellings date from much later. Dripping with washing strung across the balconies, many of the high blocks are run-down and don't admit much light, though the lack of fuss or traffic makes for an agreeable stroll through the long alleys of this homogenous quarter, either before or after visiting its major sights. While things get pretty ghostly at night, during the daytime there's a continuous hum of low-level activity in the antique shops, restorers' studios and watch-repairers'. Contrive an invitation into a private home, if you can; many of Castello's houses prove to be fascinating repositories of past building styles.

The most evocative entry to the district is from the monumental **Bastione San Remy** on Piazza Costituzione, the southern spur of the defensive walls, remodelled between 1899 and 1902. Its triumphal tone is diluted somewhat by the graffiti and weeds sprouting out of its walls, and by the groups of youths who collect here to make music and consume substances, but it's worth the haul up the grandiose flight of steps for the broad terrace above, offering fabulous vistas over the port and the lagoons and mountains beyond. You can catch some of the best views at sunset, though it makes a good place for a pause at any time, with shady benches conducive to picnics or siestas. A flea market sets up here most Sundays.

The Torre dell'Elefante

From the bastion, you can wander off in any direction to enter the tangled maze of Castello's steps and alleys. Leading off to the west,

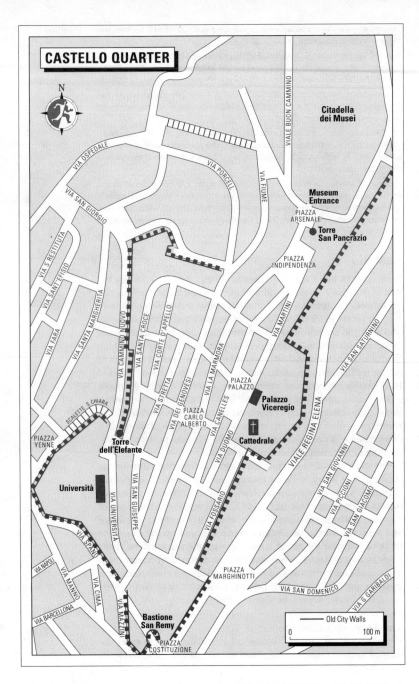

CASTELLO QUARTER

N

Citadella
dei Musei

VIALE BUON CAMMINO

VIA OSPEDALE

VIA PORCELL

VIA SAN GIORGIO

VIA FIUME

Museum
Entrance

PIAZZA
ARSENALE

Torre
San Pancrazio

VIA S RESTITUTA

VIA SANTEFISIO

VIA FARA

VIA SANTA MARGHERITA

VIA CAMMINO NUOVO

VIA SANTA CROCE

VIA CORTE D'APPELLO

VIA STRETTA

VIA DEI GENOVESI

VIA LA MARMORA

PIAZZA
INDIPENDENZA

VIA MARTINI

PIAZZA
PALAZZO

VIA SAN SATURNINO

PIAZZA
CARLO
ALBERTO

VIA CANELLES

Palazzo
Viceregio

SCALETTE S CHIARA

PIAZZA
YENNE

Torre
dell'Elefante

VIA DUOMO

Cattedrale

VIALE REGINA ELENA

Università

VIA SAN GIUSEPPE

VIA UNIVERSITA

VIA FOSSARIO

VIA SAN GIOVANNI

VIA PICCIONI

VIA SAN GIACOMO

VIA SPANO

VIA NAPOLI

VIA MANNO

VIA CIMA

VIA MAZZINI

PIAZZA
MARGHINOTTI

VIA BARCELLONA

Bastione
San Remy

PIAZZA
COSTITUZIONE

VIA SAN DOMENICO

VIA S GARIBALDI

Old City Walls

0   100 m

a copy of a lost painting by Rogier van der Weyden. The triptych was part of a collection of precious items stolen from the private apartments of Pope Clement VII during the sack of Rome in 1527, and brought to Cágliari by Catalan sailors, who confessed their guilt when their vessel was caught up in a fierce storm during the crossing from the mainland. The treasure was handed in to the archbishop of Cágliari, who returned it to the pope. Grateful to have recovered his other lost property, Clement subsequently presented the painting to the cathedral. Apart from the hunched, wan figure of the dead Christ in the central panel, the work depicts the Madonna and Saints Anne and Margaret, the latter holding a dragon. Next to this masterpiece, you may also see the powerful *Retablo della Crocefissione*, a six-panelled polyptych attributed to Michele Cavaro (1517–84) or, more probably, to his workshop.

Of the numerous tombs crammed into the cathedral, the most important is the incredibly elaborate fifteenth-century sepulchre of Martin II of Aragon in the left transept, and those of the Savoy royal family in the densely adorned subterranean **crypt** beneath the altar, which includes the tombs of Marie-Josephine of Savoy, wife of Louis XVIII of France, and the infant son of Vittorio Emanuele I of Savoy and Maria-Teresa of Austria, Carlo Emanuele, who died in 1799. This low, vaulted chamber is hewn directly out of the rock the cathedral stands on, though little of its surface has been left undecorated; the carvings include work by Sicilian artists of the Sardinian saints whose ashes were said to have been found under the church of San Saturnino (see p.84) in 1617.

The Palazzo Viceregio

The cathedral is flanked in one corner of the square by the graceful archbishop's palace, the work of the architect Davisto in 1769. He was also responsible for the **Palazzo Viceregio** (Tues–Sun 9am–1pm & 3–7pm; L4000), the second building to the left of the Cattedrale, once the official palace of the Piedmontese kings of Sardinia, though rarely inhabited by them, and now used for meetings of the provincial assembly. The three-storey building is also known as Palazzo Regio, though the large inscription at the top of the porticoed neoclassical facade names it the Palazzo del Governo, above a dedication to Carolus Emanuel III (Carlo Emanuele III, the Savoy king of Sardinia who reorganized many of the island's institutions and founded Carloforte, on San Pietro). Of the rooms open to the public, the grandiose entrance – hung with the unsmiling portraits of the Piedmontese viceroys who governed the island from this very spot – is the most sumptuous; the reception rooms upstairs have low chandeliers, gilt mirrors and painted ceilings, but the price of your ticket will be mainly going towards whatever exhibition is currently showing: recent subjects include "The Phoenicians in Sardinia" and the work of eighteenth-century Sard painter Marghinotti.

Via Università curves round the lower perimeter of the walls beneath the bombed-out shell of an old palazzo, past the main **university** building and the old **Seminario Tridentino**, both eighteenth-century. The road fetches up at the **Torre dell'Elefante**, which you can climb for the view (Tues–Sun 9am–4.30pm; free). Famed local architect Giovanni Capula designed the tower in 1307, a little later than the Torre San Pancrazio further up the hill (see p.77). Both are considered masterpieces of military engineering; together they formed the main bulwarks of Cágliari's defences, hastily erected by Pisa against the Aragonese threat, and tested in the siege of the city just twelve years later. The sheer, unbattlemented walls are constructed of great blocks of off-white granite. Like the other Pisan towers, the Torre dell'Elefante has a half-finished look, with the side facing the old town completely open. As you walk through, notice the surviving gate mechanism and the spiky gate itself, menacingly poised over the entrance. A small carving of an elephant on a plinth on one side gives the tower its name.

The Cattedrale

Following the line of walls north from the Bastione San Remy, you'll soon reach the nucleus of the Castello district – **Piazza Palazzo**, an elongated area not enhanced by its use as the quarter's main car park. The buildings which line the square are mostly eighteenth-century, though the **Cattedrale Santa Maria del Castello** (daily 8am–12.30pm & 4–8pm) at one end of it has a more venerable history. Dating originally from the thirteenth century, it later, as D.H. Lawrence put it, went through "the mincing machine of the ages, and oozed out Baroque and sausagey". Nothing of this, however, is visible in the present frontage – Lawrence's sausages went back into the mincer in 1933, to be replaced by the present tidy pastiche of a typical Pisan Romanesque arcaded facade.

The **interior** shows a mixture of Gothic and Baroque elements, the ornate painted ceiling rising to a trim cupola. The nave is lined with shallow side chapels, the third on the right holding a vivid sculpture of devils being cast to hell by San Michele. The pair of massive stone **pulpits** which flank the main doors are adorned with carved reliefs showing scenes from the life of Jesus, including the *Adoration of the Magi*, the *Baptism*, the *Sermon on the Mount* and the *Last Supper*. They were originally crafted around 1160 by Guglielmo da Pisa as a single piece, which graced Pisa's cathedral for a century and a half before being presented to Cágliari, where it was divided in the seventeenth century. The same sculptor's set of lions – four fierce-looking creatures devouring their prey – adorns the steps leading up to the altar.

The church's finest painting, the fifteenth-century *Tríttico di Clemente VII*, stands to the right of the altar (though it is sometimes moved). Its authorship is unknown, though it is thought to be the work of different Flemish artists at different times, and may be

Cágliari

Antonio Pacinotti, professor at the university's Physics Institute 1873–81, is credited with inventing the world's first dynamo.

The Torre San Pancrazio

At the opposite end of Piazza Palazzo, along Via Martini, the smaller Piazza Indipendenza is overlooked by the best restored of Cágliari's fortified towers, the **Torre San Pancrazio** (Tues–Sun summer 9am–1pm & 3–7pm, winter 9am–4.30pm, last admissions 15min before closing; free; under-12s not admitted). Very similar in design to the Torre dell'Elefante (see p.75), and like that one open at one side, the tower repays the climb up four levels with magnificent views over the old town and port, extending south as far as the refinery at Sarroch and the sliver of land holding the remains of Nora (see pp.110–111). The tower, which rises to 36m, dates from 1305, as attested by a marble plaque near the entrance, and was the work of the renowned Pisan-Cagliaritan military architect Giovanni Capula. It subsequently became a prison and later still an observatory, when Alberto di Lamármora, Sardinia's greatest nineteenth-century all-round scientist, placed star-gazing and cartographic instruments on its top in 1835.

The tower stands above the Porta di San Pancrazio gateway, usually busy with cars passing through Piazza dell'Arsenale, where a plaque records the brief visit made to Cágliari by the Spanish author of Don Quixote, Miguel de Cervantes, in 1573, shortly before his capture and imprisonment by Moorish pirates.

The Cittadella dei Musei

From Piazza dell'Arsenale, a fortified arched gateway gives access to the **Cittadella dei Musei**, a museum and study complex erected on the site of the former royal arsenal. The modern concrete cunningly incorporates parts of the older structure and has been softened by greenery. Foremost of the city's principal museums housed here is the **Museo Archeologico** (daily: April–Sept 9am–2pm & 3–8pm, Oct–March 9am–7pm; L4000), a must for anyone interested in Sardinia's past. The island's most important Phoenician, Carthaginian and Roman finds are gathered together, including jewellery and coins, busts and statues of gods and muses, and funerary items from the sites of Nora (see pp.110–111), Tharros (pp.173--175) and Sant'Antíoco (pp.119–220). A Phoenician bronze statue of Hercules highlights the strong trading links that stretched across the Mediterranean to Italy in the fourth century BC, and to Etruria and Greece before then.

Everything else pales, however, beside the museum's greatest pieces, the creations of Sardinia's **nuraghic culture**. Of these, the most eye-catching is a series of bronze statuettes, or *bronzetti*, ranging from about thirty to ninety centimetres in height, spindly and highly stylized but packed with invention and quirky humour. Representing warriors and hunters, athletes, shepherds, nursing mothers, bulls, stags and other wild animals, these figures were votive offerings, made to decorate the inside of temples, and later

For more
information
on Sardinia's
nuraghic
culture, see
box on
pp.148–149.

buried to protect them from the hands of foreign predators. You can recognize the chieftain by his cloak and raised right arm, and the warriors by their extravagantly horned helmets. Looking surprisingly modern, the figurines constitute the main source of information about this obscure phase of the island's history. Other nuraghic items have a more primitive look: fragments of pots, axe-heads, jewellery and various domestic implements.

The other collections housed in the museum complex contrast wildly with each other, and each is worth exploring. The smallest is also the most surprising: the **Mostra di Cere Anatomiche** (Tues & Thurs 4–7pm and during exhibitions; free) displays 23 gruesome wax models of anatomical sections, modern reproductions of early nineteenth-century works by the Florentine Clemente Susini (the originals are in the university). One of the most striking items in this macabre grouping is a cutaway pregnant woman showing the foetus within the womb.

Further up, another building holds the **Museo d'Arte Siamese** (Tues–Sun 9am–1pm & 4–7pm; L4000), a wonderful assemblage of items from Southeast Asia collected by a local engineer who spent twenty years in what is now Thailand. Chinese bowls and boxes sit alongside Japanese statuettes and a fearsome array of weaponry, but most of the work is from Siam, including vases, silk paintings and ink drawings featuring vivid portrayals of Hindu and Buddhist legends.

Lastly, the Cittadella dei Musei contains a **Pinacoteca** (daily 8.30am–7.30pm; L4000) with an excellent collection of primarily Catalan and Italian religious art from the fifteenth and sixteenth centuries. Pick up a free catalogue with English translation on the way in. The paintings, well displayed on three levels, have mostly been brought here from local churches; they include wooden altar-pieces by the foremost Sard painters of the time, Pietro Cavaro and Antonio Mainas, as well as Flemish work and even a Sienese *Madonna* that ended up in Cágliari on account of a mistaken attribution. Works to look out for include a *Giudizio Universale* (Last Judgment), showing distinct African elements, by the Sard Mastro di Olzai, and, next to each other on the top level, a trio of large, multi-panelled altar-works: the *Retablo di San Bernardino* by Joan Figuera and Rafael Thomas, an *Annunciazione* by Joan Mates and a *Visitazione* by Joan Barcelo. The lowest floor displays a collection of traditional Sardinian jewellery – amulets, necklaces, earrings and rosaries – worked in silver and gold, mostly dating from the nineteenth century.

The Galleria Comunale d'Arte

From Piazza Arsenale, walk though the Porta di San Pancrazio and down Viale Regina Elena to reach the Giardini Púbblici, a brief area of flat greenery below the walls of the Castello. At one end of it, Cágliari's **Galleria Comunale d'Arte** (Tues–Sun summer 9am–1pm and 4–7pm, winter 9am–5pm; L5000) offers a more contemporary slant on Sardinia and its people. Rolling exhibitions of Sard artists take place alongside a permanent collection of some of the island's best modern artworks. Among the most notable of these are a collection of paintings by Tarquinio Sini (1891–1943), a clever caricaturist of the 1920s who specialized in *contrasti* – unlikely encounters between traditionally-garbed Sards and bright young flappers of the day – and, from a decade later, Giuseppe Biasi (1885–1945), who drew upon his experiences in Africa to produce work influenced by Gauguin and Matisse. Among the pieces by other artists, the portraits of Sards and the island landscapes illustrate different versions of the Sard experience and the tensions between the island and the outside world. Bronzes from the 1960s recall nuraghic *bronzetti*, while works from the 1970s and 80s show women artists such as Mirella Mitelli and Rosanna Rossi – represented by some strongly coloured abstracts – beginning to make their mark in Sardinia.

Marina

Like Castello, the lanes of the **Marina** quarter are narrow and dark, but unlike those in the upper town, these streets are always animated, busy with the coming and going from the city's biggest grouping of restaurants and hotels. Marina's proximity to the docks meant that it was heavily bombed during World War II, the damage still starkly visible in places; elsewhere, the bombed-out buildings have been replaced by brazen modern constructions, startling apparitions in the predominantly medieval layout. One of the victims of the bombardment was the very un-Sardinian **Palazzo Comunale** or Municipio (town hall) that presides over Piazza Matteotti. White and pinnacled, with bronze eagles and heraldic devices, this nineteenth-century neo-Gothic concoction with hints of Art Nouveau was rebuilt to match its pre-war appearance. The upstairs rooms, which can be seen at most weekends (Sat 4–8pm; Sun 9am–1pm; free), contain some notable tapestries and works by the sixteenth-century painters Antonio Mainas and Pietro Cavaro, among others.

Elsewhere, within the area bounded by Largo Carlo Felice, Viale Regina Margherita, Via Roma and the Castello, Marina preserves a number of sequestered treasures within its many churches. **Sant'Eulalia**, in the piazza of the same name, is currently closed for renovation, but its principal interest, the museum and archeological area beneath the church, remains open. The most remarkable part of the **Museo del Tesoro e Area Archeologica di Sant'Eulalia**, abbreviated to MUTSEU (Tues–Sun 10am–1pm & 5–8pm; L4000), is the subterranean complex directly under the altar of the church, in which a fragment of the Roman city dating from the first century AD has been unearthed. A raised walkway provides a good overview of the broad limestone slabs of a wide road. The absence of wheel-ruts suggests that it was probably not a major thoroughfare; it's more likely to have been a pedestrian avenue giving access to a major temple.

In the heart of Marina, Via Baylle holds Sardinia's two oldest salumerie (delicatessens): Vaghi, here since 1902, and the slightly younger Pisu.

Hopefully the ongoing excavations will reveal the answer. Another road leads down towards the port, and there are also a couple of wells and even a public urinal. Most of the walls now visible belong to the medieval city that arose on the ruins of the Roman one, which had been abandoned at some time between the sixth and eighth centuries.

Upstairs, the **Treasury** displays priestly mantles and fine silverware, as well as a couple of interesting paintings: one, a fourteenth-century *Madonna and Child*, is Tuscan in style, with additions by a Sard artist of the sixteenth century; the other, a Flemish *Ecce Homo* of the seventeenth century, has been painted on both sides, the rear of the canvas giving a close-up of Christ's gorily flayed back.

Climbing further up Marina's backstreets, drop into the church of **San Sepolcro** in the eponymous piazza off Via Dettori. The building was re-opened at the end of 1998 after a 28-year closure, during which the surprisingly spacious interior was painstakingly restored and its treasures cleaned up. The most eye-popping of these is the huge gilded altarpiece covering one entire wall, created in the seventeenth century to hold a Madonna revered by the wife of one of the Spanish viceroys after a supposed miracle. The viceroy had to alter the church drastically to fit the gigantic wooden structure inside, which he did by knocking through two chapels built into the rock, accounting for the church's unorthodox shape. Grates in the floor allow you to peer into what was once a paleochristian burial ground.

Stampace and the Roman remains

Lying to the west of Largo Carlo Felice, the quarter of **Stampace** has given its name to Cágliari's – and Sardinia's – most influential school of art. Founded by Pietro Cavaro (died 1537), the *scuola di Stampace* affected painting throughout Sardinia in the sixteenth century, where the impact of the Renaissance was slow to arrive. It included artists such as Antioco Mainas and Pietro's son Michele Cavaro, and drew much of its inspiration from Spain, blending the influence of Raphael with late Gothic elements. Major works by members of the school can be seen in Cágliari's Pinacoteca (see p.78) and Oristano's Antiquarium Arborense (see p.164); few examples remain in Stampace itself, though the district's churches are still redolent of the tight-knit community that gave birth to the *scuola*.

At the top of Largo Carlo Felice, **Piazza Yenne** was the site of the old Porta Stampace before the destruction of the quarter's walls. The cobbled square now forms a pedestrianized enclave to one side of the thick traffic of the Carlo Felice highway, Sardinia's main north-south artery (now the SS131). A pair of monuments recall the building of the highway, though the bronze statue of its instigator, King Carlo Felice, dressed in Roman garb, for some reason gestures away from the road. Across the street, a pointed ball on top of a simple stone column indicates the true start of the highway, up **Corso Vittorio Emanuele**. Cágliari's best Roman remains are reached along this busy thoroughfare, which begins broad but soon narrows as it runs through Stampace, lined with a lively diversity of shops and restaurants.

Stampace's churches

Running off the top of Piazza Yenne parallel to Corso Vittorio Emanuele, Via Azuni gives access to four of Stampace's historic churches. On the right, the monumental white neoclassical facade of the **Church of Sant'Anna** (Tues–Sat 8am–1pm, 3–7pm, Sun 7.30–10.30am & 5–8pm), with its two tiers of Corinthian columns, stands atop a grand flight of steps. The present building was begun during the Savoy era in 1785, on the site of an earlier Pisan church, though not completely finished until the 1930s. Faithfully reconstructed after serious damage during the bombing raids of 1943, the late Baroque design is marked by strong Piedmontese features. The airy interior holds a fourteenth-century wooden crucifix from the Stampace church of San Francesco (destroyed by fire in the nineteenth century), a statue of Amedeo di Savoia by Andrea Galassi, the *sassarese* sculptor responsible for the statue of Carlo Felice in Piazza Yenne, and a painting by the nineteenth-century Sard master Giovanni Marghinotti, depicting *Christ the Saviour*.

To the left of Sant'Anna, the narrow Via Sant'Efisio leads north past the piazzetta and church of **Santa Restituta**, whose simple facade fronts a mainly sixteenth-century structure. Further up the street, the **Cripta di Sant'Efisio** constitutes a far older relic of the city (Tues–Sun summer 9am–1pm & 5–8pm, winter 8.30am–5.30pm; free). From a doorway on the left, steps lead down to the crypt, which was originally one of the many hypogea or cisterns of the Punic-Roman city of Karalis. According to tradition, Efisius, a Roman soldier from Asia Minor, was imprisoned here before being taken to Nora to be decapitated. You can see the column where he was supposedly bound, an object of worship for local believers. There is evidence of a church in existence here as far back as the fifth century; more recently, the crypt served as an air-raid shelter and rubbish dump. If the entrance is closed, go round the corner to the church, where there may be someone to show you around.

The present **Chiesa di Sant'Efisio** (same hours as crypt) is a small affair, built in the eighteenth century and intimately connected with the martyr and the Festa di Sant'Efisio, which starts here (see box on p.82). The second chapel on the right holds the effigy of the saint that provides the focal point of the procession, and the holy cross carried at Easter is in the third chapel on the right. A wooden altar on the left side of the church has a more dashing image of the saint in the guise of a bearded, armoured figure with a plumed helmet. The cannonballs embedded in the walls at the back of the church were fired by the French fleet during their attack on Cágliari in 1793 – the fleet's flight was another miracle attributed to Sant'Efisio.

Festa di Sant'Efisio

Popularly represented as a flamboyant knight with a plumed helmet, Sant'Efisio was born in Elia, Asia Minor, and served as a soldier in the Roman army during the reign of the emperor Diocletian (283–310). According to tradition, he was sent to Sardinia to combat the tribes of the Barbagia in the interior. Having refused to renounce his Christian faith, he was imprisoned in the hypogeum that is now the crypt of the Stampace church that bears his name, then taken to Nora where he was beheaded in 303. A cult soon grew up around the saint, increasing over the centuries with the attribution of various miracles to him – notably the rescue of the city from a plague in 1652 and the repulsion of the French attack on Cágliari in 1793.

Since saving the city from plague, the saint has been commemorated annually at the beginning of May in Sardinia's biggest religious festival, the **Festa di Sant'Efisio**. Setting forth from Sant'Efisio church on the morning of May 1, a solemn procession embarks on the long walk to Nora, 40km south along the coast, bearing the holy statue of the saint which is kept in the church. As it makes its way through Cágliari, it is preceded by a long column of costumed participants from every part of the island, sometimes mounted, often accompanied by traditional singing and the playing of drums and instruments such as the *launeddas* (shepherd's pipes). The costumed part of the procession melts away once it reaches Via Pula, south of the train station, but the holy statue continues with a small retinue, joined for part of its way by villagers and bands in the places it passes through, before arriving at Nora on the evening of the following day. After religious services have taken place, the statue departs from the church at Nora on the evening of May 3, entering Cágliari the next evening to a much more muted reception.

The festa is a spectacular affair, and a great chance to view a panoply of traditional costumes from the villages, as well as to hear authentic Sard music at first hand. If you can't be present for the whole four-day event, the May 1 festivities are the highlight, for which you might consider a ticket for a bandstand seat, giving a high, unimpeded view of the proceedings: the stadium-type seats erected around Piazza Matteotti cost between L10,000 and L25,000: the AAST tourist office at Via Mameli 97 (☎070.664.195) sometimes deals directly with ticket sales, alternatively they can give you the number of the organization currently handling sales. This is also the main information point for any other queries regarding the festivities. It's worth booking accommodation in advance if you're planning to be in Cágliari during the first four days of May.

Return back to Via Azuni to reach the triple-arched facade of the church of **San Michele** at the end of this street (Mon–Sat 7.30–11am & 5–8pm, Sun 7.30–11am & 7–8pm). Consecrated by the Jesuits in 1738, the highly ornamented building is one of Sardinia's most opulent examples of the Baroque. The striking porticoed facade gives a foretaste of the majestic interior, a densely stuccoed and painted octagonal space, sumptuously marbled and topped by a frescoed cupola. On the steps outside, a richly decorated pulpit – said to have been used by Charles V before setting off on his expedition against Tunis in 1535 – stands on four Corinthian columns.

The Anfiteatro Romano and Orto Botánico

Cágliari

Theatre and opera performances are held in Cágliari's Anfiteatro Romano from July to September. See p.92 for more information.

With its entrance on Viale Sant'Ignazio da Láconi, the **Anfiteatro Romano** (summer Mon–Sat 9am–1pm & 4–8pm, Sun 9am–1pm & 2.30–5pm; winter daily 9am–5pm; free) is reachable from Castello on Viale Buon Cammino, or from Stampace by walking up from Corso Vittorio Emanuele. Cut out of solid rock in the second century AD, the amphitheatre could hold the entire city's population of about 10,000. Despite its state of decay (much of the site was cannibalized to build churches in the Middle Ages), you can still see the trenches for the animals, the underground passages and several rows of seats.

Turning left out of the amphitheatre, walk down Viale Sant'Ignazio da Láconi to the **Orto Botánico** (daily: April–Sept 8am–1.30pm & 3–6.30pm, Oct–March 8am–1.30pm; L1000), one of Italy's most famous botanical gardens, with over 500 species of Mediterranean and tropical plants, including examples of carob trees, lentisks, holm oaks, as well as yuccas, palms, papyrus, cacti and some carnivorous species. The collection was initiated in the seventeenth century, and transferred to this site in the second half of the nineteenth century. Incidentally, the writer Italo Calvino's mother later became director of the gardens. Informative guided visits take place (sometimes in English) on the second and fourth Sunday of each month at 11am, but you don't need to be a plant enthusiast to enjoy this quiet and shady retreat, especially on a sizzling afternoon.

The Casa di Tigellio

On the other side of Viale Sant'Ignazio da Láconi, a railed enclosure on Via Tigellio shields another remnant of Cágliari's Roman era. The **Casa di Tigellio** (Mon–Sat 9am–1pm; free) was traditionally held to be the villa of Tigellius, a Sardinian poet whose singing and versifying were appreciated by the Roman Emperor Augustus, but loathed by perhaps better judges such as Horace and Cicero. However, the excavations have brought to light a later villa of the second and third centuries, quite a substantial complex arranged on either side of a narrow lane, though it's difficult to make much sense of the site, a litter of calcareous blocks, in its present state. On one side, a set of thermal baths is identifiable by the raised floor of the hypocaust; opposite stand three buildings with tetrastyle porticos from the imperial era. The first, the atrium, where guests were received, has two Ionic columns and a *tablinum* (room giving onto atrium) with mosaic decorations, and is paved with black and white mosaics. The "stuccoed house" has remnants of patterned decoration on the walls, while of the third, few traces remain. The overall effect is rather spoiled by the crowd of twentieth-century apartment blocks all around, and there is no attempt to explain the site very fully, though there are plans to display finds in an exhibition room on the site. Meanwhile excavations continue, sometimes throwing up oddments like the lapidary monuments from nearby tombs currently displayed here. If the site is closed, you can get much of the gist of it from the railings.

Villanova

Although much of the quarter of **Villanova** is modern and traffic-thronged, the streets to the east of Viale Regina Margherita hold two important religious sites of great historical interest. On the slopes of **Monte Irpinu**, east of Piazza Garibaldi and accessible from Viale Europa or Via Pietro Leo, Cágliari's biggest public garden affords the city's best views.

The Basilica di San Saturnino

At one end of the broad Piazza San Cosimo, just off the busy Via Dante, the fifth-century **Basilica di San Saturnino** (Tues–Sun 9am–1pm & 3.30–7.30pm; free) is one of Sardinia's two oldest churches (see p.173 for details of the other, San Giovanni di Sinis near Oristano) and one of the most important surviving examples of early Christian architecture in the Mediterranean. The basilica was erected on the spot where the Christian martyr Saturninus met his fate during the reign of Diocletian (283–310). The building sustained severe bombardment in World War II, and today the weathered stone of the tall, domed structure is offset by the modernistic darkened glass which makes up most of three sides. Despite this, the church retains an unmistakable Middle Eastern flavour, with its palm trees and cupola.

The monument is entered through an open atrium within which a palm is surrounded by various pieces of flotsam from the past: numerous pillars, seven cannonballs, fragments of Roman sarcophagi and slabs of stone carved with Latin inscriptions. The church's

---

The Trenino Verde

Small-gauge trains of the Ferrovie delle Sardegna company (FdS) – also known as Ferrovie Sarde, or Ferrovie Complementari Sarde – provide a slow but scenic trawl through the island's interior. From the station in Cágliari's Piazza Repubblica, eight trains daily run to Mandas in about 90 minutes (with four continuing to Ísili); but the really interesting part is the separate service between Mandas and Arbatax, the port on Sardinia's eastern coast (April Sun only, currently at 10.30am; May–Sept at least once daily). The Mandas–Arbatax stretch takes four and a half hours, a meandering, often tortuous and stomach-churning journey through the beautiful highlands of the Sarcidano and Barbagia Seulo. Reckon on about seven hours for the whole journey, for a fare of less than L35,000. It's a good way to see some of Sardinia's remotest tracts and to reach the island's eastern port, though the laborious slog can be daunting and excruciatingly slow. For timetables, ask at the FdS station, or call ☎070.580.246 or the toll-free 167.865.042.

---

stark interior, of ponderous dimensions, is empty of any decoration or distraction, though the glass walls allow you to see the necropolis which is still being excavated, the tombs clearly visible on either side of the nave.

Turn left up Via Cimitero, behind Piazza San Cósimo, to reach Piazza Repubblica, site of the FdS station. Nearby on Via San Lucífero, **Exma** (daily: summer 9am–1pm & 5pm–midnight, winter 9am–8pm; L5000) is Cágliari's former *mattatoio*, or slaughter-house, now converted into an exhibition centre, arranged around an open space in which jazz and classical concerts are performed all year in summer (small-scale concerts are held indoors all year). As well as the one permanent exhibition tracing the restoration and transformation of the old building, there are usually two other shows, mainly featuring the work of Sard artists. There's also a good café and bookshop on either side of the entrance.

For informa-tion about exhibitions and concerts at Exma, enquire at the bookshop or at the tourist office (see p.72).

The Santuario di Bonaria

Turning right down Via Cimitero from Piazza San Cósimo leads past the **cimitero di Bonaria**, where there are several monumental tombs and mausoleums, to Viale Bonaria and Piazza Bonaria. Here, the fourteenth-century **Santuario di Bonaria** (Mon–Sat 7am–noon & 4.30–7.30pm, Sun 9–noon & 6–8pm, 7–9pm in summer) occupies a commanding spot looking out to sea above Viale Armando Diaz. Valued for its clean air ("*Buon'aria*") and for its distance from Cágliari's pestilential conditions, this was an important military base for the Aragonese during their efforts to prise the Pisans out of Cágliari. The fortifications quickly evolved into a significant city and port with a population of 6000, and Bonaria was even for a while the seat of the archbishop and of the administrative organization of the kingdom of Sardinia and Corsica. It was only when the Catalans were persuaded to transfer to Cágliari's castle in 1336, ten years after the Pisans were finally expelled from there, that Bonaria's fortifications were abandoned, and a few decades later they were in ruins.

Prosperity returned, however, following the recovery of a leg-endary image of Our Lady of Bonaria from a shipwreck. When a Spanish trading vessel was caught in a storm on the way to Italy in 1370, its crew jettisoned everything on board in their efforts to save themselves, including one chest which refused to sink, and which had a miraculously becalming effect on the waters. When the chest washed up ashore, at the spot below the sanctuary marked by a col-umn, it was found to contain an image of the Madonna holding a child in one hand, a lit candle in the other. The ship's grateful sur-vivors built the sanctuary in her honour, which soon became a place of pilgrimage, of special significance to all sailors who have tradi-tionally invoked the Madonna di Bonaria as protectress, and for whom the church sheltering her image continues to be a reassuring beacon on the approach to Cágliari's harbour.

The sanctuary has always been tended by monks of the Mercedari order, who arrived in Sardinia around 1300 from Barcelona, under the protection of the Aragonese royal house. The order specialized in negotiating the liberation of Christian slaves from pirate kidnappers, usually by means of ransoms. One of their last missions was the rescue of the hundreds of inhabitants of the island of San Pietro captured by North African pirates at the end of the eighteenth century, and held as slaves in Tunis for fifteen years. A handful of Mercedari monks still run the sanctuary, inhabiting the convent to the left.

Viceroys, bishops and popes – including John Paul II – have traditionally paid their respects to the Madonna di Bonaria, and in recent centuries the approach to the church has been aggrandized by a geometric swathe of steps. It is the adjacent **basilica** which in fact dominates the scene, its neoclassical front completely overwhelming the plain lines of the sanctuary to its left. The basilica, begun in 1704, had all of its frescos, stuccos and precious decoration devastated by a bomb in World War II, though its marbled interior has been restored, and today it soaks up the overflow from the ceremonies next door.

In the **santuario** itself, it is the holy image that commands attention, conserved on the high altar in the Gothic apse. The statue of the Madonna and Child, both crowned, is fashioned from a single piece of locust-tree wood, finely carved and painted. The first chapel on the right has an even more ancient and much venerated statue, the Madonna del Mirácolo, which has stood here since the church was built in 1325.

In the middle of the apse hangs a small ivory model ship; dating from 1400, just thirty years after the arrival of the Madonna di Bonaria, it is the oldest of the gifts donated to the sanctuary by shipwrecked sailors as a token of thanksgiving for their survival. The model is significant in that it depicts one of the first examples of an Italian ship with a single stern rudder, as opposed to the lateral rudders mainly used at that time. More mysteriously, it is also said to signal the direction of winds in the gulf.

The little ship provides a foretaste of the collection in the church museum, housed on the first floor above the adjoining monastery's cloister. The **Museo Marinaro** (daily 9.30am–noon & 4.30–6pm; L2000) consists largely of a diverting hoard of ex-voto model ships, most of them dating from the eighteenth century and later. They form an important chronicle of both evolving nautical styles and maritime art. Amid shelf-fulls of silver galleons, clippers, steamers, warships, Arab dhows and assorted fishing boats – some in bottles – there are several French, US and British ships reproduced, including an *Ark Royal*, which burned in 1587 (and here made of matches), a *Bounty* and a couple of *Cutty Sarks*. There are also eighteenth- and nineteenth-century paintings of dramatic shipwreck scenes, many painted with the initials VFGA, standing for *votum feci gratiam* *abui* ("I made a pledge and received grace"), or PGR, *per grazia ricevuta*.

Cágliari

If you want to reach the Santuario di Bonaria from Piazza Matteotti by bus, take any one bound for Poetto, or the frequent #5 from Via Roma, which stops right in Piazza Bonaria.

Other gifts are from liberated slaves, and some from nobles and sovereigns, such as the golden crown offered in 1816 by King Vittorio Emanuele I and Queen Maria Teresa, and a silver anchor given by Queen Margherita di Savoia on the safe return of an expedition to the North Pole in 1899. Apart from the nautical exhibits, the museum also holds a miscellany of other objects of local interest, including finds from the excavation immediately to the west of the sanctuary: nuraghic odds and ends (obsidian blades and ceramics), a few Punic coins from the sixth to the third centuries BC, clay figurines, fragments of sarcophagi, amphorae and cinerary urns from the third century BC to the first century AD. You'll also see a cistern from the Aragonese castle built here in 1325, used by the monks of the convent until the beginning of the twentieth century, as well as swords and arms donated by soldiers. One unexpectedly gruesome display case contains the mummified bodies of four members of the noble Alagon family, who died of plague in 1604, the three adults and child still fully clothed.

The sanctuary's original Aragonese belltower is visible from the park at the back of the church. There's a good bar in the piazza below it for coffees and cakes (see p.91)

West along Via Sant'Avendrace

West of Piazza Matteotti, Via Roma turns into Viale Trieste, joining Viale Trento to become Via Sant'Avendrace. This has always been Cágliari's main route inland, and the traffic flows thick and fast past smog-begrimed palazzi. Unpromising though these untidy suburbs may appear, the district does harbour two **ancient monuments**, which are well worth the short bus ride (#1 from Largo Carlo Felice, Corso Vittorio Emanuele or Via Mameli every five or ten minutes, or the #9 from Piazza Matteotti approximately every fifteen minutes).

Grotta della Vípera

Shortly after the junction with Viale Trieste (the bus stop is opposite the CRAI supermarket), a grand quarried rock marks the **Grotta della Vípera** (summer Tues–Sun 9am–1pm & 2–6pm, winter Tues–Sun 9am–5pm; free), more properly known as the Sepolcro di Attilia Pomptilla. The popular name derives from the two snakes decorating the classical pediment surmounting the entrance to this shrine, which commemorates the much-loved wife of a Roman official, Cassius Philippus, during the reign of Nero (AD 54–68). She was apparently a woman of exemplary goodness, according to the Greek and Latin inscriptions found at the spot, though you'll need to get someone to point out what's left of the faint carvings. The work of time has erased much of the elaborate tomb that once stood here, its atrium and columns long disappeared, and the site now is little more than a shallow grotto, with collapsed passages leading off into the rock – now filled with water – and a sea of pigeon droppings (keep a wary eye up). Even if the grotto is closed, you can still see quite a lot through the gates.

Tuvixeddu

A far more impressive site lies at the top of this calcareous mass, accessible from a flight of cracked concrete steps 200m further up Via Sant'Avendrace on the right (turn right at the top). The high, boulder-strewn wasteland is honeycombed with tombs chiselled out of the rock. This extensive burial place is the Punic necropolis of **Tuvixeddu** (always open; free), used between the sixth century BC and the first century AD, first by Carthaginians and then by their Roman successors; much of the wealth of archeological evidence it has yielded up can be seen in Cágliari's Museo Archeologico (see p.77).

The neat square or oblong chambers are either hewn out of the vertical rockface on multiple levels or cut sheer into the ground – watch your step among the grass and cactus. A few of the chambers, mostly consisting of single or twin tombs, display much-eroded carvings, in particular of a warrior who might be the Punic divinity Sid, curer of all ills. Dark corridors are tantalizingly visible at the bottom of the deep ground-dug tombs, though you'd need ladders and torches to explore this hidden network.

The whole area – one of the most complete and intricate Punic remains on the island – is shockingly neglected, all work to maintain, protect and open up the site having been stalled for years while a property dispute is unresolved. In the meantime, despite the litter of plastic bags and broken glass and the complete absence of explanatory signs, the site is still a fascinating place to wander about, and the high ground offers good views over the gulf. You'll need more than flip-flops to explore the higher tombs.

Poetto and Calamosca

When you need a break and a bathe, head for the suburb of **Poetto**, a fifteen-minute bus ride (bus "PF" or "PQ") from Piazza Matteotti past Cágliari's Sant'Elia football stadium. Poetto has 6km of fine sandy beach (the Spiaggia di Quartu), with small bars and showers conveniently located nearby. Behind the beaches are the choppy waters of the **Stagno di Quartu** lagoons, north of which stands the town of Quartu Sant'Elena itself, now little more than an industrial suburb of Cágliari.

The liveliest of Poetto's beaches is at the southernmost end, where there's the tidy **Marina Píccola** – an anchorage for boats and an area for concerts and outdoor cinema in July and August. Other spots along this beach strip can get equally raucous throughout the summer. "PF" or "PQ" buses run along the whole length of it, allowing you to take your pick of the various stretches of sand, though there's little to distinguish between them, and all have similar facilities. Some, clearly marked, are reserved for the police or air force.

If you don't have your own shade with you, it would make sense to bathe from one of the lidos lining the beach, where you pay a standard daily rate (about L5000) for entry and use of showers and toilets. Parasols cost around L8000 for the day, deck-chairs L5000, and from the same places it's usually possible to rent pedalos, canoes and surf-bikes (respectively about L15,000, L8000 and L12,000 per hour). Other facilities available at numerous points further along the beach include windsurfing and sailing.

Though bars and other refreshment stops are ten a penny in Poetto, there's less choice when it comes to eating in the area; the main lido, *D'Aquila*, however, has a mediocre restaurant, *Da Pietrino* (closed Thurs in winter) which overlooks the sea, and there's also the Chinese *Draco d'Oro* close by. The next-door *Stabilimento Il Lido* also has a pizzeria and disco, open summer only.

The Sella del Diávolo

The **Sella del Diávolo** ("Devil's Saddle") rears above the marina at Poetto's southern end, most of the rocky promontory a military zone and therefore off-limits. Its name is connected with a legend relating how the Archangel Gabriel won a battle here against the devil himself (the name of Cágliari's gulf, Golfo degli Ángeli, is also a reference to this celestial tussle). On the western side of this outcrop – for which you need to backtrack along Via Poetto, then turn left into Viale Calamosca – a lighthouse overlooks the **Calamosca** locality, little more than a small sandy cove with one good hotel (see p.72). It can get crowded on this small beach, but if you wanted a quick dip from Cágliari, this is the nearest patch of sand to the centre. To get here by public transport, take any of the "P" buses from Cágliari, changing at the Amsicora stadium for bus #11, which leaves every half-hour.

Shopping

Via Manno, descending from the Bastione di San Remy to Piazza Yenne, is the place to find **boutiques** and fashion shops. In Castello, Via La Mármora, below the cathedral, has a concentration of galleries and **antiques shops**. In the lower town, Via Sardegna has a couple of army surplus shops with a range of equipment for campers and travellers, cheap T-shirts and other practical items. On Via Roma, Rinascente is a quality department store with a good stock of most things (Mon 2–8.30pm, Tues–Sat 9am–8.30pm), while the arcades harbour mainly Senegalese traders hawking everything from leather handbags and African masks to lighters and nail-clippers. Via Roma's newspaper kiosks sell foreign **newspapers and magazines**, including same-day English titles.

The island's biggest antiques and crafts fairs take place annually at the Fiera Campionaria at Viale Diaz 221 (take any bus to Poetto to get here). Antiques are traded for nine days between October and November; contact the tourist office for other dates.

Sardinian **craftwork** is sold in numerous shops in the Castello and Marina districts; the best selection can be found in the government-sponsored ISOLA shop on Via Berchidda, though prices here are quite steep. If it's **antique and curio markets** you're after, Piazza del Carmine becomes a scene of low-level haggling on the first Sunday of the month, as does Piazza Carlo Alberto (in front of the cathedral) on the second and fourth Sundays, while there's a **flea-market** on the Bastione di San Remy every Sunday except during August; all are finished by lunchtime. On Via Francesco Cocco Ortu, a brief walk north of Castello, the vivacious San Benedetto **covered market** is open every morning from Monday to Friday and all day Saturday for foodstuffs and household goods of every description on two floors. A bigger **outdoor food market** sprawls around the Stadio Sant'Elia, west of the centre, on Sundays. For bookshops and supermarkets, see "Listings", on p.93.

Eating, drinking and nightlife

Cágliari has the best range of **restaurants** on the island, most clustered around Via Sardegna in the Marina quarter. Many don't start serving until 8.30–9pm and are full within thirty minutes, so pass by earlier to make a booking if you want to be sure of a particular place. You'll find a similar choice of food everywhere, almost invariably traditional Sard recipes with a strong fishy emphasis, though the local places have been joined in recent years by a host of authentic Chinese restaurants, providing the island's only real alternatives to the local fare, if you wanted a change – and they're always cheap. One of the best is detailed below, others are on Via Sardegna, Via Cavour, Corso Vittorio Emanuele and Via Leonardo Alagon (west of Via Sonnino). For a fast-food **snack**, make for Piazza Yenne, where the grotto-like pizzeria and *távola calda* called *Downtown* makes a useful lunch-stop.

Restaurants
Antica Hostaria, Via Cavour 60 (☎070.665.870). Upmarket though not over-formal ristorante, with antique trimmings. Meat and fish are given equal billing, and are usually good. You'll spend around L50,000 a head, if you include the wine available in bottles only (from L14,000). Closed Sun. Expensive.

Buongustaio, Via Concezione 7. Off the main restaurant strip close to the port, this is a notch up from the other cheapies in the neighbourhood, reflected in the smarter clientele. It still has comparatively low prices, and there's a L22,000 tourist menu, though you'll find much better dishes *à la carte*. Closed Mon evening & Tues. Moderate.

La Damigiana, Corso Vittorio Emanuele 115. Unpretentious wood-panelled neighbourhood trattoria for good fixed-price meals in this area. Closed Mon evening. Inexpensive.

Il Gatto, Viale Trieste 15 (☎070.663.596). Try this spacious, vaulted pizzeria and restaurant outside the main dining zone, off Piazza del Cármine. It's a little more innovative than most, but has the usual selection of seafood or meat dishes all immaculately prepared, plus a huge range of desserts and imported bottled beer. Closed Sat lunch & Sun all day. Moderate.

Trattoria Gennargentu, Via Sardegna 60c. The plain narrow rooms have a slightly rustic flavour. Good Sardinian staples with low prices, though portions can be small. Closed Sun. Moderate.

Ristorante Italia, Via Sardegna 30 (☎070.657.987). Rated first-floor restaurant strong on fish, with very reasonable prices but dull, old-fashioned feel. Closed Sun. Moderate.

Da Lillicu, Via Sardegna 78 (☎070.652.970). A fashionably bare dining area in the heart of Marina is the place for this straight-talking Sard trattoria, with plain marble tables. The food is basic but reliably good, with a limited menu of local meat and fish specialities, and a bigger choice of antipasti. Gets packed out, so needs booking. Closed Sun. Moderate.

Pechino, Via Santa Margherita 19. One of Cágliari's best Chinese restaurants, offering a L15,000 fixed-price dinner and such dishes as *ánatra pechinese*, Peking Duck. Inexpensive.

Quattro Mori, Via Angioi 93. Just off Corso Vittorio Emanuele, this place is snobbish and over-priced, but offers good Sard dishes. Closed Sun evening & Mon. Expensive.

San Crispino, Corso Vittorio Emanuele 190. Despite plaudits it has won, this modern place can be mediocre with lacklustre service. Horse and donkey feature strongly among the meat dishes. Closed Mon. Moderate.

Da Serafino, entrances at both Via Sardegna 109 and Via Lepanto 6. Unfancy trattoria with low prices, popular with younger locals. Closed Thurs. Inexpensive.

Bars and birrerias

Cágliari is well endowed with drink stops, starting with the cafés under the arcades of Via Roma, most of which add a 10–30 percent service charge. For a morning coffee or afternoon tea, Piazza Yenne is a pleasant, relatively traffic-free place to sit out, getting quite lively at *passeggiata* time. The Castello quarter is worth exploring after dark for new bars and *birrerie* opening up. In summer, **Poetto** offers a gaudier atmosphere, a blitz of bars, pizzerias, fairgrounds and ice-cream kiosks by the sea to provide an evening's entertainment. In Cágliari, good **ice cream** can be had from *Tutto Gelato*, Corso Vittorio Emanuele 244 (closed Tues).

Antico Caffè, Piazza Costituzione. Old coffee shop with character next to the Bastione San Remy. There are outdoor tables, though the traffic can be oppressive. Good lunches available.

Caffè Libarium Nostrum, Via Santa Croce 33. Low-roofed and beamed place with lots of atmosphere in Castello. Snacks served. Closed Mon.

Caffè Mediterraneo, Viale Armando Diaz, opposite the Santuario di Bonaria. Great coffee-and-pastries spot attached to the *Mediterraneo* hotel, where locals congregate before, during and after work. Sit outside in summer. Ice creams available.

Le More, Via Napoli 13, entrance also at Via Barcellona 4. Brick, beamed *birreria* off Via Roma, with snacks all day and live music some evenings, usually Fri. Closed Sun.

Il Merlo Parlante, Via Portascalas. Tucked up an alley off Corso Vittorio Emanuele, this boisterous *birreria* offers draught beers, music and *panini* until 2am. Open evenings only.

Nuovo Caffè Torino, Via Roma 121. Under the arcades, good pastries and table service at 30 percent.

Old Coffee, Via La Mármora 91. Traditional-looking bar near the cathedral, with small marble tables and snacks served.

Bar Olympia, Via Roma 77. A cinema foyer that doubles as a daytime bar, serving good cappuccinos and without any surcharge for waiter service.

Sotto La Torre, Piazza San Giuseppe. This series of elegantly beamed and furnished rooms lies right opposite the Torre dell'Elefante, agreeable surroundings for a long cappuccino by day and cocktails or beers till late at night. Buns and snacks also make this a good breakfast or lunch spot. Closed Wed.

Festivals and entertainments

Apart from Sant'Efisio (see box, p.82), Cágliari has a few other **festivals** which are worth catching if you can plan it. In February or March, **Carnevale** is always a rowdy affair, kicking off with a carousal through the streets of Castello on the first official day of the season – a long procession with dancing and extravagantly costumed shenanigans, all accompanied by *sa ratantina*, a deafening drum tattoo. **Easter** is also taken seriously in Cágliari, with a procession from the church of Sant'Efisio up to the cathedral taking place on the morning of Easter Monday, and cowled columns trailing through town on Easter Friday and Easter Sunday.

The new brutalist Teatro Comunale (also called Teatro Cívico) in Via Sant'Alenixedda, north of Castello, is the main venue for **theatre** performances (ticket office open Mon–Sat 10am–2pm & 5–8pm; ☎070.452.0033). The smaller-scale Teatro Alfieri also stages a full winter programme of performances ranging from Shakespeare to the Alice stories at Via della Pineta 29 (☎070.301.1378), as does Teatro delle Saline on Via La Palma (☎070.341.322), both on the eastern side of town; for more experimental theatre performances, consult the programme at the Teatro dell'Arco in Via Portoscalas 47 (☎070.663.288). Most performances begin at 7.30pm, tickets around L10,000–15,000 for the smaller places, L20,000 rising to L400,000 for the Teatro Comunale.

In summer, the Anfiteatro Romano is the venue for performances of **music and ballet**: tickets cost L20,000 to sit on the hard stone, or L40,000 for stalls. Call ☎070.408.2230 or 070.408.2249, or ask at the tourist office for details. The Exma complex on Via San Lucífero hosts chamber music and soloists (☎070.666.399), but the main venue for classical **concerts** (Oct–Dec) and **opera** (Jan–June) is, again, the Teatro Comunale (see above). Open-air **rock concerts** are held regularly in summer at the Fiera Campionaria, Viale Diaz 221. Mainstream **films** are screened at cinemas in Via Roma and Via San Lucífero, while Cineclub Namaste is an arts cinema showing foreign-language films at Via Ospedale 4, and **open-air cinema** takes place

at Poetto's Marina Píccola nightly in August at 9.30pm (tickets
L6000). Pick up the *Appuntamenti* booklet published every three
months for information on upcoming concerts and other events,
available from Cágliari's tourist offices.

Listings

Airlines Alitalia, Via Caprera 12 (☎070.60.101); Meridiana, Via Rossi 27
(☎070.669.161); Ati, Aeroporto di Elmas (☎070.240.169).

Airport Aeroporto di Elmas (☎070.240.047).

Banks Cágliari's centre has a choice of banks, all with cash machines. Most are
on or around Largo Carlo Felice, including Banco Nazionale di Lavoro, Banco
di Nápoli and Crédito Italiano, open about 9am–1.20pm & 2.30–3.30pm. Hay
Elettronica Service at Via Napoli 8, off Via Roma, can change money and is the
local agent for Western Union transfers, open Mon–Sat 9am–1pm &
4.30–8pm.

Bookshops Dessi, at Corso Vittorio Emanuele 32, has a good range of books
including English-language publications and stuff on Sardinia, open Mon
4–7.30pm, Tues–Sat 9am–1pm & 4–7.30pm.

Bus companies ARST, Piazza Matteotti (☎167.865.042); PANI, Piazza
Dársena 4 (6.30–7am, 8–8.30am, 9am–2.15pm & 5.30–7pm, Sun
1.30–2.15pm & 5.30–7pm; ☎070.652.326); FMS buses for Iglésias and
Carbonia depart from outside the bar at Viale Cristóforo Colombo 24
(☎070.666.121), which sells tickets; they also stop near the Spano pharmacy
on Via Roma (tickets from the nearby newspaper kiosk).

Car rental Europcar, Aeroporto di Elmas (☎070.240.126); Eurorent,
Aeroporto di Elmas (☎070.240.129); Hertz, Piazza Matteotti 8
(☎070.651.078); Maggiore-Budget, Aeroporto di Elmas (☎147.867.067);
Matta, Aeroporto di Elmas (☎070.240.050); Pinna, Aeroporto di Elmas
(☎070.240.276); Ruvioli, Via dei Mille (☎070.658.955).

Ferries Saremar, Via Mameli 40 (☎070.67.901); Tirrenia, Via Campidano 1
(☎070.666.065).

Hospital Via Peretti 21 (☎070.543.266).

Laundry Coin-operated *lavanderia* at Via Ospedale 109 (daily until 9.30pm).
Service wash at Sun Showers, Vico Malta 2, off Piazza del Cármine (Mon–Sat
8.30am–1.15pm & 4–8pm).

Post office Piazza del Cármine (Mon–Sat 8am–7pm).

Supermarket Upim, Via Mannu (Mon 4–8pm, Tues–Sat 9am–1pm & 4–8pm).

Taxi Ranks at the airport and Piazza Matteotti; Coop Radio Taxi 4 Mori
(☎070.400.101). For the long haul to Villasimius, expect to pay around
L120,000 from Cágliari.

Telephones Unstaffed office at Via Angioy 6 (daily 8am–10pm).

Train information FS in Piazza Matteotti (☎147.888.088 daily 7am–9pm);
FdS in Piazza Garibaldi (☎070.580.246 or 167.865.042 during office hours).

Travel agents CTS, Via Balbo 4 (☎070.488.260); Sardamondial, at Via Roma
9 (☎070.668.094) can arrange bus and train tickets as well as flights and ferries, while Viaggi Orrù, at Via Roma 95 (☎070.659.858) can arrange train
tickets but not buses.

Sarrabus

Although Poetto may do for a morning dip or an evening out, it probably won't meet your requirements for the perfect beach – and you don't need to go very far from Cágliari to find something nearer the mark. Nor will you have to venture far before meeting some of the island's wildest interior landscape: the mountainous regions north and east of the island's capital provide the perfect opportunity to get lost on remote and highly scenic roads.

Heading north from Cágliari, you might make a brief stop at the agricultural centre of **Dolianova**, whose attractive Romanesque ex-cathedral is the most important artistic monument in this part of Sardinia. In contrast to the ordered plains hereabouts, most of the **Sarrabus** region, occupying Sardinia's southeastern corner, is refreshingly wild and sparsely populated, with few roads passing through. Best reached from the minor road threading northeast from Dolianova, or direct from Cágliari along the SS125, the heart of this zone is empty of human habitation, with all development squeezed along the coast. Here, ranks of identical-looking holiday homes have scarred long stretches of the rocky shore, with the biggest concentration around the resort of **Villasimius**, a fully-fledged holiday town on the eastern tip of the Golfo di Cágliari.

Despite the desecration, there are still unforgettable views to be enjoyed along the coasts hereabouts, over isolated coves and rocky promontories, enhanced by a generous scattering of Spanish watchtowers. There are also some superb beaches to swim off – the most idyllic golden sands can be found along the **Costa Rei**, north of Villasimius. Again, the natural beauty is compromised by thick colonies of unsightly tourist homes, and you must persevere towards **Capo Ferrato**, 30km north of Villasimius, to find emptier stretches. Beyond the cape, another seemingly endless beach extends for 12km as far as **Porto Corallo**, a port and small holiday resort in the process of development. The only centre in these parts is **Muravera**, a dull inland town with a traffic problem, though it makes a good place to find accommodation. Elsewhere in Sarrabus, Villasimius holds the area's best choice of hotels and restaurants. Campers will have an easier time of it, with a handful of good sites scattered along the coast.

Dolianova and around

Fifteen kilometres north of Cágliari, the market town of **DOLIANOVA** lies in a plain off the SS387. Though it's mostly a workaday local centre with a few handsome nineteenth-century palazzi, it does have one interesting relic: the local church, formerly a cathedral, reached through an archway signposted off its main thoroughfare. Occupying one side of the large courtyard or small piazza, the **Chiesa di San Pantaleo** (daily 10am–noon & 3.30–7pm) is topped by a short belltower and sports blind arcading running right round the walls, sculpted with eroded stone carvings – mainly of animals, plants, moons and some human forms. Begun between 1150 and 1160 by a team who had previously worked on the church of Santa Giusta, outside Oristano (see p.175), the grey stone exterior was completed by Arab architects a century later, accounting for its *mudéjar* style, which mixes Romanesque, Gothic and Arab elements. Next to the entrance, a Roman sarcophagus protrudes incongruously from the main body of the church, suspended on slender columns.

The **interior** is decorated with an impressive array of murals, one of them depicting Christ crucified on what looks like the tree of life; it is in fact an *álbero genealógico*, a favourite theme in medieval art showing Abraham and the prophets, though a quarter of it is missing. Next to this, an oriental-looking *ancona*, or six-panelled altarpiece, shows the martyrdom of San Pantaleo, probably the work of an unknown Spanish painter in the sixteenth century. There's a horribly immolated Christ on one wall of the church, and at the back, a stone *baldacchino* (canopy) which, like the wonky columns of the nave, is crudely carved with figures of animals, angels and a man and woman embracing.

You can rejoin the SS387 north of Dolianova, where at Sant'Andrea Frius you can choose between branching left onto the SS547 to Mandas and the heart of the Barbagia, or staying with the SS387 as it twists into the highlands of **Gerrei**, a little-visited mountain area north of Sarrabus. An even smaller road links Dolianova directly with the main village in these parts, **San Nicolò Gerrei**, a 33km drive without a building to be seen. Either of the latter options is tempting for the often exhilarating mountain scenery, though they're both fairly arduous routes, with few villages along the way and no hotels. You can continue north beyond Ballao, or follow the road east along the path of the Flumendosa river, eventually reaching the coast near Muravera (see p.99).

The Dolianova region is renowned for its olives and olive oil, and for its wines, which include Nuragus, Moscato and Malvasia.

The Golfo di Cágliari

Thankfully, the main roads east out of Cágliari quickly bypass the snarled-up centre of **Quartu Sant'Elena**, separated from the northern curve of the Poetto beaches by the brown waters of the Stagno di Quartu. The road soon narrows as it traces the littoral eastward along the **Golfo di Cágliari**, and can get congested with traffic, especially in summer. Much of the coming and going is accounted for by the swelling carpet of holiday villas covering a substantial section of the rocky slopes. Despite these hostile factors, it's still a pretty drive, with good views across the gulf back to Cágliari and the western shore. The coast grows progressively emptier and, despite the closeness of Cágliari, it's still possible to find inlets for a relatively secluded dip. The nearest **campsite** to Cágliari lies in one of its nicer sections in the **Capitana** district, about 6km from Quartu Sant'Elena's beach and not too far from beaches to either side. The *Pini e Mare* (mid-June to mid-Sept; ☎070.803.103, fax 070.812.125) also has four-person cabins available for L70,000–100,000 a night – though campers will find better sites around Villasimius (see below).

East of here, there are good beaches tucked away at **Cala Regina**, **Torre delle Stelle** and **Solanas** – the prettiest village on this stretch, next to one of the sentinel towers that dot the entire coast. East of Capo Boi, the **Golfo di Carbonara** also holds scraps of beach, sometimes visible from the mainly high coastal, though it's difficult to ignore the intrusions of the holiday industry, for the most part four-star hotels and drab rows of peach-coloured villas. The only accommodation to hand charges handsomely for the superb locations, and you would do better to push on to Villasimius, which has many far cheaper choices.

The Golfo di Carbonara was named after the charcoal produced in the forests in the vicinity; a byproduct was the black powder added to gunpowder for its damp-proof qualities, favoured by Nelson among others.

Villasimius

Not so long ago a nondescript village, **VILLASIMIUS** gets incredibly lively in summer, when it's a hotbed of bars, boutiques, pizzerias and revving scooters – the rest of the time it slumbers, and visitors between October and May may find most facilities closed-up. The main road through town is Viale Umberto, leading to Piazza Gramsci and the smaller Piazza Generale Incani. From here, Via del Mare leads down to the sea, the nearest stretch of beach just 1.5km away at **Simius**, facing the offshore isles of **Serpentara**, a long strip of bare rock, and the more southerly **Isola dei Cávoli**. Boat tours round these islands leave from the beach in summer. Simius is the most developed of the area's bathing spots, dominated by luxury hotels; you can find wilder sections walking south towards **Capo Carbonara**, where the eastern shore of this thin peninsula is backed by the calm **Stagno di Notteri**, a stopover for flamingoes in winter, and the **Fortezza Vecchia**, a square Spanish watchtower from 1590. You can drive here by turning right out of Villasimius and following the road for two or three kilometres. This is also the road for the **Marina di Villasimius**, a new yachting port on the Golfo di Carbonara, and for **Spiaggia di Riso**, another magnificent stretch of sand surrounded by turquoise and aquamarine waters, close to a campsite (see opposite).

Practicalities

The best **place to stay** in Villasimius is the *Stella d'Oro* (☎070.791.255; ③), off Piazza Gramsci at Via Vittorio Emanuele 25. Rooms are regular and clean, and a good fish restaurant occupies an internal courtyard. Other choices are the much smarter *Blu Marlin*, Via Giotto 7 (☎ & fax 070.790.310; ⑤), a small place offering reasonable low-season deals, and cheapest of all, *Sa Tankitta* at Via Umberto 240 (☎070.791.338; ②), with only six rooms with shared bathrooms, and a restaurant. If you want to stay nearer the sea, hotel prices soar into the luxury bracket, though there is a good campsite, *Spiaggia di Riso* (April–Oct; ☎070.791.052), located right on the beach of the same name on Capo Carbonara, with four- or five-person bungalows to rent at L180,000–270,000 per night. Other campsites are north of town at Cala Sinzias (see below).

If you want to eat in Villasimius, there are **restaurants** practically on every corner: among the best are the moderately-priced *Stella d'Oro* (see opposite) and *La Página*, on Piazza Generale Incani, while the *Carbonara* is a sober fish restaurant with slightly steeper prices at Via Umberto 54 (closed Wed in winter). A food **market** operates on Saturday mornings in Via Donatello, next to the Carabinieri barracks.

A small office at Via Marconi 12 dispenses **local information** and has some literature on the area (summer Mon–Sat 9am–1pm & 4–7.30pm, winter Mon–Fri 9am–12.30pm & 3–7.30pm, Sat 9am–12.30pm; ☎070.791.546). The Carboni agency at Via Umberto 44 (☎070.790.376) rents out **cars, scooters and moun-tain bikes**: a Fiat Punto costs around L150,000 a day, scooters are L60,000, bikes L15,000–20,000. The Banco di Sardegna on Piazza Gramsci (Mon–Fri 8.20am–1.20pm & 2.35–3.35pm) has a cash machine to **change money**, and the **post office** is at Via del Mare 72 (open Mon–Fri 8.10am–1.20pm, Sat 8.10am–12.30pm, last day of month closes noon). The main **bus stop** is on Piazza Gramsci for ARST buses, and Vacca Viaggi also run a beach service from here to Capo Boi and Porticciolo (and vice versa) five times daily in summer.

The Costa Rei

West of Villasimius, the road dips and swings as it follows the con-tours of the coast, affording glorious views towards the islands of Serpentara and Isola dei Cávoli. The first good beach lies eighteen circuitous kilometres along this road, at **Cala Sinzias**, a broad swathe of sand cupped within the arms of a small bay, virtually empty of visible constructions. There are two campsites here, however, *Limone Beach* (☎070.995006), usually open March–November, and, right in front, *Garden Cala Sinzias* (April–Sept; ☎070.995.037), both with bungalows and caravans available, and the *Limone Beach* also has cheaper tents to rent.

A short distance north of here begins the long ribbon of beaches that make up the **Costa Rei**. If your taste is for shimmering expans-es of fine white sand but not for the area's full-on holiday mania, just make sure you're here outside the months of June–September, when things have simmered down and prices have fallen. Almost all of the available accommodation is in villas rented out by the week booked through agencies in Villasimius – when they're not block-booked by package companies – though there are some **hotels** which might appeal to families, for example the *Albaruja Hotel* on Via Cristóforo Colombo (☎070.991.557, fax 070.991.459; ⑥), which has villa accommodation near a pool and tennis courts. In common with all other hotels here, it requires at least half-board in high season, and it's closed October–May. At the other end of the scale, the *Capo Ferrato* campsite (April–Sept; ☎070.991.012) has bungalows available; it's right by a broad sweep of sand, though perhaps too close to the dreary ranks of orange and pink holiday villas for comfort. There are windsurfing and canoeing facilities nearby, and you'll find a few **supermarkets** along here if you want to pick up some food.

At the top end of this bay, there are remoter scraps of sandy beach towards **Capo Ferrato**; these may be reached via dirt tracks running off the road parallel to the coast. The only place around here for **food and refreshments** is the *Capo Ferrato* bar/pizzeria, which serves roast chicken alongside the panini and pizzas (closed Tues Oct–May). Not too far distant is the *Porto Pirastu* campsite (April–Sept; ☎070.991.437), with bungalows to rent by the sea; ARST buses from Cágliari stop right outside the bar. A short way north of here, the asphalt degenerates into a dusty track that winds behind the pine-clad Capo Ferrato to the next bay, and more premium beaches.

Castidias

In Castidias, contact the Cooperativa Monte dei Sette Fratelli (Via Centrale, ☎070.994. 7200 or 0338.280.4305) for guided excursions in the Foresta di Minniminni and on Monte dei Sette Fratelli. A 100km ride in an off-roader, taking about 5hr, is charged at L80,000 per person (negotiable).

Inland of the Costa Rei, the land is flat and verdant. Signposted 7km west of the main road, **CASTIDIAS** is a straggle of buildings around the flaking pink walls of an abandoned penal colony set up in the nineteenth century. There's not much more than a bar here, but it makes a good target for trips inland, and a starting point if you want to explore the **Foresta di Minniminni**, a couple of kilometres to the south. This protected area of holm oak and thick *macchia* is only passable on foot, donkey or, to an extent, in four-wheel-drive vehicles. As well as the ubiquitous arbutus, juniper and cyclamen of the *macchia*, the area holds two plantations of pine trees left by the inmates of the penal colony, one from 1875, when they arrived, the second from when the colony was closed down in 1956. Though the summit of Monte Minniminni is not high at 723m, it affords wonderful views over the surrounding coast.

Monte dei Sette Fratelli

An alternative road to Muravera from Cágliari – and the quickest route if you're heading up Sardinia's eastern coast – is via the SS125, a tortuous mountain road that cuts through the heart of **Sarrabus**, the interior of Sardinia's southeast corner. It's a highly scenic drive but can be slow-going if you're stuck behind a truck or caravans. The road passes through one of the emptiest regions on the island, rising through the often dramatic **Monte dei Sette Fratelli** ("Seven Brothers") range, whose steep slopes are either *macchia*-covered or forested with cork oak. If you want to strike out on foot, there are plenty of opportunities to stop along the way, though it's difficult to climb very high without expert guidance. Look out for the rare *cervo sardo*, the short Sardinian stag for which this is a protected zone.

The region is utterly uninhabited but for a couple of isolated settlements. About 20km northeast of Quartu Sant'Elena, a good road left wanders 7km up to **Burcei**, a small village at a height of 648m, famed for its cherries. To the right of the SS125, a track meanders south for about a kilometre to the **Convento de Sette Fradi**, a small, walled monastery deep in the forest. A tarmacked road leads 6km to the Caserma Vecchia, a Forestry Corps station from which it's possible to reach the 1023-metre peak in a couple of hours; beware of rapidly falling nights if you decide to do any roaming around here.

Nuraghe Asoru

Soon after this junction, the SS125 descends through the desolate gorge of the Picocca river, littered with monolithic boulders. After another 16km the road levels out and passes the **Nuraghe Asoru** (also called *Nuraghe S'Oro*), unmissable on the left-hand side of road. Built between the tenth and eighth centuries BC in a dominating position over the surrounding plain and the inland approaches, it's the only nuraghe worthy of note in southeastern Sardinia, which evidently proved too barren even for this hardy folk. There's a small internal courtyard, and a hole in the coarse masonry of the wall reveals a bench running all around its interior. In perfect condition since its 1976 restoration, the nuraghe's lovely tawny colour is in perfect harmony with its surroundings.

For more on Sardinia's nuraghic culture, see pp.148–149.

Muravera and around

The Riu Sa Picocca flows into a flat, fertile area, with thick groves of citrus and lesser growths of almonds and other fruit and nut trees. The SS125 swings close to the coast and the beach of San Giovanni before heading inland again to enter **MURAVERA**, the only town in these parts. It's an unprepossessing place, centred on the main Via Roma – a constant stream of traffic alongside which pedestrians are squeezed onto minuscule pavements.

Although heavily dependent on the local tourist industry, for which it serves as a centre, Muravera also thrives as an agricultural town, and is known as the island's citrus capital. It has close links with two nearby villages, and all three have gained a certain renown for the authenticity of the rural produce, such as honey, wine and *dolci*. They are also famed for the preservation of their local traditions, as shown in their much respected local festivals, whose ebullience goes some way to compensating for the essentially drab appearance of the villages themselves.

In Muravera itself, the biggest **festival** is the Sagra degli Agrumi (Citrus Fair) on the first or second Sunday before Easter – usually in March or April – to celebrate the end of winter, marked by parades of peasant wagons laden with fruit; the other main dates are around August 28, when the music and costumed frolics last four days, and December 6, for two days of poetry competitions, singing and dancing. **San Vito**, 4.5km north of Muravera, makes a rewarding place to visit on its saint's day, June 15, on the first Sunday in August, and during the marathon five days of poetry and singing competitions and concerts that take place around the third Sunday in October; while you should drop in on **Villaputzu**, 3.5km north of Muravera, around the second Sunday in October for four days of costumed processions and traditional dances.

From San Vito, the SS387 curls inland along the course of the Flumendosa river and into the hilly Gerrei region, a panoramic route into the interior (see p.95). East of the undistinguished village of Villaputzu, the river joins the sea near **Porto Corallo** where, on the approximate site of a long-disappeared Phoenician port, work is currently under way to recreate a small harbour, this time for pleasure craft. On the left of the road stand the scanty remains of the hilltop **Castello di Gibas**, less a castle than a fortification, erected by the Spanish together with the cylindrical tower that overlooks Porto Corallo. The latter was the scene of one of the last battles against North African pirates, when the locals succeeded in driving back their attackers in 1812. To the south of the river mouth, a broad strand of sand stretches southwards, backed by eucalyptus woods; it's a popular spot in fine weather, with picnic tables and a bar/pizzeria and gelateria close at hand.

North of Muravera, the road follows the course of the Quirra river, parallel to the coast and separated from it by a wall of mountains. It's a fertile area, much of it cultivated, with scattered nut trees adding a blaze of blossom in early spring. Twenty-two kilometres north of Muravera, the road crosses the Cágliari–Nuoro provincial boundary on its way north to the village of Tertenia and the Ogliastra region around Tortolì (see p.344).

Practicalities

Despite being the main centre for this holiday region, Muravera has a surprising lack of accommodation and good places to eat. There are only two **hotels** in town, both along the main Via Roma. The most central at no. 31, the *Corallo* (☎070.993.0502, fax 070.993.0298; ④), is also the smartest, with fifty-odd clean and functional rooms. A few doors towards the south, opposite the petrol station at Piazza Libertà 3, *Sa Férula* is dowdier but adequate (☎070.993.0237; ③). If you want to stay near the sea, you'll have to camp. A couple of kilometres south of town, the *Quattro Mori* **campsite** (Easter–Sept; ☎070.999.110) has small self-catering villas available for rent for up to L170,000 per night in high season, less than half that outside July and August. A kilometre or two further down, another campsite, *Torre Salinas* (April to mid-Oct; ☎070.999.032) has cheaper tents and caravans for rent at L30,000–75,000 a night. Both have sports facilities and pizzerias, and both offer riding excursions.

Restaurants are easy to find in the summer season, less so in winter. At Via Roma 257 (the northern end of the drag), *Su Nuraxi* is one place that stays open all year and provides a reliable if unexceptional menu of the usual items, with fast, friendly service, and a wood-fired oven for good pizzas (closed Wed Oct–May; no CCs; moderate). Further up in this direction, opposite the *Polizia Stradale* station at the northern end of town *Sa Foredda* is a more upmarket restaurant with Sard specialities (closed Tues). For snacks, the *Paderi* bar at Via Roma 63 has crepes and ice cream (closed Mon in winter), and there is also good ice cream at *L'Oasi* north of the centre. *Rockburgers* at Via Roma 128 (closed Mon) has pizzas and beers as well as burgers. For a bop, *Discobar Corallo* has funk and Latin American dance music on Fridays, or try *Tiffany* pub, opposite the post office on Via Europa. At Porto Corallo, refreshment is provided by the *Top Sound* bar/pizzeria/ristorante, open all year, which also has a lively disco in summer. This is also the main place in the neighbourhood for tobacco, telephones, bus tickets and newspapers.

Turn down Via Europa off Via Roma to find Muravera's tourist office on Piazza Sardegna, which can provide you with a list of alternative accommodation if everywhere else is full, in the form of agriturismi and apartments (Mon–Sat 9am–1pm & 4–8pm, open later and on Sun in July & Aug; ☎070.993.0760). There's a post office nearby on Via Europa which also has exchange facilities (Mon–Fri 7.50am–1pm, Sat 8.10am–12.30pm), or use the Banco di Sardegna, back on the main street, which has a cash machine (8.20am–1.20pm & 2.35–3.35pm). Car hire is available from G.M. Angioi at Via Roma 112 (☎070.993.0570), and Francesco Musiu at Via Matteotti 23 (☎070.993.0741). Take away with you some of Muravera's fresh produce, sold at the fruit market off Via Roma on Monday mornings.

Travel Details

TRAINS

Cágliari to: Carbonia (Mon–Sat 3 daily; 1hr); Ísili (FdS; 4 daily; 1 hr 50min); Dolianova (FdS 10 daily; 35min); Iglesias (Mon–Sat 12 daily, Sun 5; 1hr); Mandas (FdS; 8 daily; 90min); Oristano (hourly; 1hr–1hr 40min); Sanluri (every 1 or 2hr; 50min); Sássari (3 daily; 3hr 40min–4hr).

BUSES

Cágliari to: Barúmini (Mon–Sat 3 daily, Sun 2; 1hr 35min–2hr); Buggerru (1 daily; 2hr 20min); Burcei (Mon–Sat 6 daily; 1hr 10min); Calasetta (Mon–Sat 5 daily, Sun 4; 2hr 20min–2hr 50min); Capitana (Mon–Sat 9 daily, Sun 6; 40min); Capo Ferrato (6–7 daily; 2hr 15min); Carbonia (Mon–Sat 7 daily, Sun 4; 1hr 30min–2hr); Costa Rei (Mon–Sat 8 daily, Sun 6; 2hr 5min); Iglesias (8–9 daily; 55min–1hr 15min); Muravera (Mon–Sat 11 daily, Sun 3; 1hr 35min–2hr 50min); Nuoro (4 daily; 3hr 35min); Oristano (5 daily; 1hr 35min); Porto

Torres (2 daily; 4hr 20min); Portovesme (3 daily; 1hr 20min–2hr); Sanluri (hourly; 45min–1hr 5min); Sant'Antíoco (Mon–Sat 5 daily, Sun 4; 2hr 10min–2hr 30min); Sássari (7 daily; 3hr 15min–3hr 50min); Villasimius (Mon–Sat 9 daily, Sun 6; 1hr 25min).

Costa Rei to: Cágliari (Mon–Sat 8 daily, Sun 6; 2hr 5min); Muravera (Mon–Sat 3–4 daily; 45min); Villasimius (2–7 daily; 30min–1hr 10min).

Muravera to: Cágliari (Mon–Sat 11 daily, Sun 3; 1hr 35min–2hr 50min); Costa Rei (Mon–Sat 3–4 daily; 45min).

Villasimius to: Cágliari (Mon–Sat 9 daily, Sun 6; 1hr 25min); Castiadas (Mon–Fri 3 daily; 1hr 10min); Costa Rei (2–7 daily; 30min–1hr 10min); Muravera (3 daily; 1hr 20min–1hr 50min).

FERRIES

Cágliari to: Civitavecchia (1 daily; 14–15hr); Genoa (mid-June to mid-Sept 2 weekly; 21hr); Naples (1–2 weekly; 16hr 15min); Palermo (1 weekly; 13hr 30min); Trápani (1 weekly; 11hr 30min); Tunis (1 weekly; 35hr 30min).

Chapter 2

The southwest

S ardinia's **southwest** forms a rugged wedge of land that juts south of the main body of the island into the Mediterranean, its craggy coastline ameliorated by some fine beaches. Forests cling to the slopes of its predominantly mountainous landscape, which is densely strewn with towns, temples and fortifications founded by Phoenicians, settled by Carthaginians and occupied by Rome. The best preserved ruins are at **Nora**, a Roman harbour town dramatically situated on a promontory overlooking the Golfo di Cágliari. The Carthaginian remains at **Sant'Antíoco** occupy an equally evocative location on an island tethered to Sardinia's coast by a road causeway; the isle, and its neighbour **San Pietro**, are among the area's most appealing destinations, with long sandy beaches and a distinctive offshore atmosphere.

Sant'Antíoco was the principal city of the old territory of **Sulcis**, the name still used to denote the westernmost slab of southwest Sardinia. Historically, the region's importance was due mainly to the mining of ores and minerals, which continues to play a prominent role in Sardinia's economy today. The industry was given a boost by Mussolini, who, in his drive for Italian self-sufficiency, founded the inland town of **Carbónia**, just below another ancient Carthaginian settlement on **Monte Sirai**, whose hilltop site enjoys stunning views over sea and mountain.

The **Iglesiente** territory to the north shows more evidence of mineworks, often in a poignant state of abandon, especially around its main town of **Iglésias**, which makes an attractive base for exploring the area. The Roman **Témpio di Antas**, a short distance north of here, owes its fine state of preservation to its remote valley location, while some of Sardinia's choicest **beaches** lie to the west, where the **Pan di Zúcchero** outcrop sprouts dramatically out of the sea. There is more superlative swimming to be had off the area's **southern coast**, where, from Santa Margherita di Pula to Capo Spartivento, there is an almost unbroken succession of beaches. West of **here,** Sardinia's southernmost littoral, the **Costa del Sud**, offers fewer bathing opportunities, though its highly scenic sequence of inlets

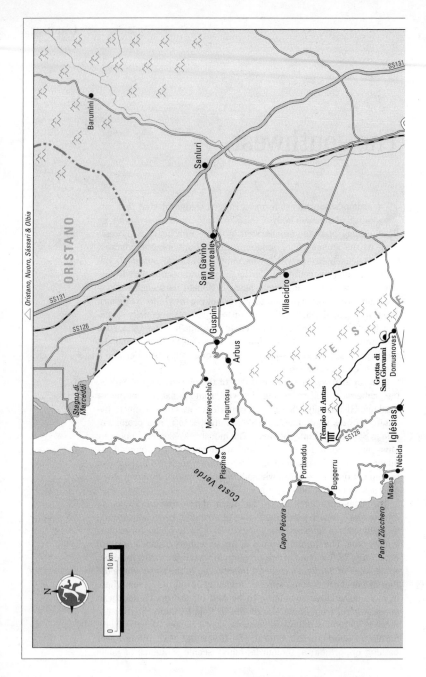

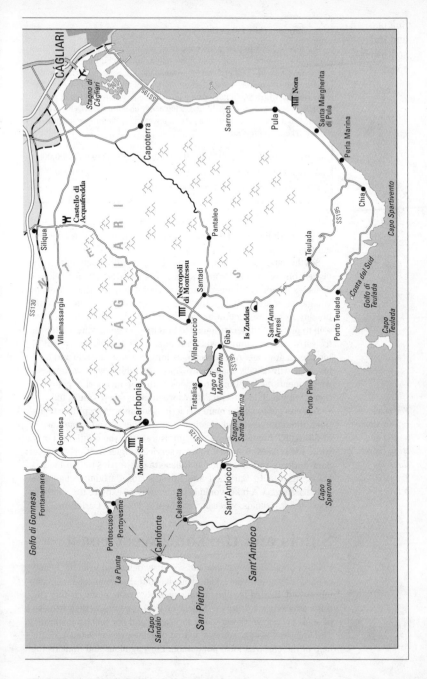

CÁGLIARI

Stagno di
Cágliari

SS195

Capoterra

Sarroch

Pula

IIII Nora

Santa Margherita
di Pula

Perla Marina

Capo Spartivento

Chia

SS195

Castello di
Acquafredda

Siliqua

SS130

Villamassargia

Pantaleo

Necropoli
di Montessu

Santadi

Is Zuddas

Sant'Anna
Arresi

Teulada

Costa del Sud

Golfo di
Teulada

Porto Teulada

Capo
Teulada

Villaperuccio

Giba

SS195

S U L C I S

Carbonia

Gonnesa

Tratalias

Lago di
Monte Pranu

Stagno di
Santa Caterina

Porto Pino

IIII
Monte Sirai

SS126

Golfo di Gonnesa

Fontanamare

Portoscuso

Portovesme

Calasetta

Sant'Antioco

Capo
Sperone

La Punta

Carloforte

Sant'Antioco

Capo
Sándalo

San Pietro

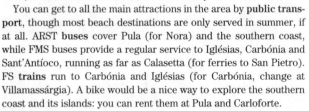

Accommodation Price Codes

The hotels listed in this guide have been coded according to price. The codes represent the cheapest available double room in high season (Easter & June–Aug). In cheaper hotels the rooms usually come without en-suite bathroom or shower; some of these places will also have a few en-suite rooms, for which you'll pay more – usually the next category up in price. Higher category hotels nearly always have only en-suite rooms. Out of season, you'll often be able to negotiate a lower price than those suggested here. The categories are:

① under L60,000   ④ L120,000–150,000   ⑦ L250,000–300,000

② L60,000–90,000   ⑤ L150,000–200,000   ⑧ over L300,000

③ L90,000–120,000   ⑥ L200,000–250,000

studded with Pisan and Spanish watchtowers is more than adequate compensation.

Southwestern Sardinia is a compact region, and much of it can be visited on excursions from Cágliari. But with so much to see, it deserves a more prolonged tour, with hotel stops in the towns and villages en route. Although the area includes several well-developed holiday resorts, **accommodation** can be on the thin side. You'd do well to plan your itinerary ahead to be sure of staying where you want to, especially in summer when some seaside places are booked up months in advance. All the same, as long as you're mobile and flexible, you will usually manage to find somewhere with vacancies – we've mentioned options in places with not much else going for them, but which are useful last resorts if everywhere else is full.

For more information on bus and train connections, see Travel Details, p.136.

You can get to all the main attractions in the area by **public transport**, though most beach destinations are only served in summer, if at all. ARST **buses** cover Pula (for Nora) and the southern coast, while FMS buses provide a regular service to Iglésias, Carbónia and Sant'Antíoco, running as far as Calasetta (for ferries to San Pietro). FS **trains** run to Carbónia and Iglésias (for Carbónia, change at Villamassárgia). A bike would be a nice way to explore the southern coast and its islands: you can rent them at Pula and Carloforte.

Sulcis and the southwest coast

Pockets of development have not seriously detracted from the beauty of Sardinia's **southwest coast**, while its hinterland remains practically untouched. Settled by Phoenicians as early as the ninth century BC, this was once the territory of **Sulcis**, an important link in their network of trade routes which extended to France and the Iberian peninsula. The area was also a valuable source of minerals, extracted with the help of the enslaved local population. Carthaginians and Romans followed in the wake of the Phoenicians, all keen to exploit the lucrative mines.

Following the **southern coast** down from Cágliari, you should make the archeological site at **Nora**, 35km to the south on the SS195, your first stop. The nearest town, **Pula**, is the main centre for the surrounding area, including **Santa Margherita di Pula**, where thick swathes of eucalyptus and pine provide a lush setting for one of Sardinia's most luxurious holiday enclaves. If it's swimming you're after, you'd do better to continue to **Chia** and beyond, where broad, dune-backed beaches stretch south as far as **Capo Spartivento**.

The craggy, undeveloped **Costa del Sud** runs west from here, a string of tranquil coves interspersed with a few patches of sand. There is more tourist activity at **Porto Pino**, but little in the way of hotels and restaurants even here. For these, the inland towns of **Teulada** and **Giba** are the best bet, though they are not particularly inspiring places. Giba, at least, has attractions in the vicinity: the SS195 takes you west from here to **Tratalias**, site of a well-preserved Romanesque church, while **Santadi**, 10km east of Giba, has a small museum of folklore and the impressive **Is Zuddas** caves nearby.

The capital of Sulcis was **Sant'Antíoco**, which stands on an island of the same name. You could spend the best part of a day exploring the various relics of its long past, though you'd need more time to poke around the local coastline, with its scattering of good beaches. Alternatively, you could continue straight through to the island's northern port of **Calmest**, embarcation point for the smaller island of **San Pietro**, 5km across the strait. The main town, **Carloforte**, has an attractive seafront, and there are beaches and beauty spots within easy reach.

Both islands have developed into well-frequented holiday destinations, though they are very relaxed out of season. Endowed with some first-class beaches, they make an attractive place to hide out for a couple of days without fear of brushing up against holiday villages or mega tourist complexes. If you're thinking of staying, it's worth penetrating outside the islands' main towns for the small selection of **hotels** and **campsites** next to the sea. Given the local preference for rented holiday houses, however, hotel accommodation is on the scarce side, and you'd do well to book ahead. If you're really stuck, there's usually more availability at **Portoscuso**, an off-putting industrialized town on the Sardinian mainland, though once you're past the chimneys, its fishing harbour and centre aren't at all bad. The large town of **Carbónia**, 10km inland, is equally unprepossessing, but again, there's curiosity value in the time-frozen Fascist architecture, and there are a couple of good museums here too, one of them showing finds from the nearby Carthaginian site on **Monte Sirai**. A visit to the remains of this impregnable fortress is highly recommended, affording stupendous views out to the islands and inland.

ARST **buses** from Cágliari run every hour or so along the coast to Pula, some continuing on to Chia, then turning inland towards Teulada. There's a less frequent service along the Costa del Sud in summer only, and a summer bus connection between Teulada and **Porto di Teulada**, its tiny coastal offshoot, where there's a beach and a useful campsite and agriturismo. Carbónia is on the **train** line from Cágliari, though the station is a local bus ride from the centre. Carbónia and Sant'Antíoco are served by regular FMS **buses** from Cágliari, which leave from the terminal at Via Cristóforo Colombo 24, behind Piazza Deffenu. The bus to Sant'Antíoco continues to Calasetta, from which frequent **ferries** cross the short distance to San Pietro. Carloforte is also linked by equally frequent ferries with Portoscuso (or rather its port, Portovesme) on the Sardinian mainland, the most convenient crossing for travellers to or from Carbónia and Iglésias.

The road to Pula

The road south of Cágliari runs past and over the extensive complex of lagoons known as the **Stagno di Cágliari**. Picked over by angular flamingos and swooping cormorants, the brown, occasionally choppy waters also attract legions of fishermen, often perched in rows over the bridges, spinning their curious hand-made reels. The peaceful scene disappears as the smoking towers of the refinery at **Macchiareddu** hove into view on the banks of the lagoon. Undeterred by its ominous presence, a small beach resort has grown up at **Lido di Capoterra**. The only reason to stop here, however, would be to dine at its renowned fish **restaurant**, *Su Cardiga e Su Schironi*. Close enough to Cágliari to draw in the crowds, it's reckoned to be one of the island's best, though prices remain refreshingly low: a smallish but exquisite *risotto alla pescatora*, for example, costs just L10,000, and other fish dishes are L6000 per hundred grams. Treat the menu as a guide only: fish are available according to what's in season, and can be prepared in any way (☎070.71.652; closed Mon except evenings in summer).

Capoterra itself, 5km inland, is the starting point for the one very minor road running through the range of mountains, some of them rising to over 1000m, that occupies the interior here. It's a laborious drive, mostly on a stony surface, running some 40km to Santadi (see p.115), but it allows you to glimpse the wildest and remotest part of the Iglesiente mountains, forested with oak and thick with coloured and scented maquis – especially evocative in winter or spring.

A few kilometres down a dirt road from Capoterra, a protected wildlife zone has been established around the woody slopes of **Monte Arcosu**, destined to become the core of a national park. Its chief purpose is to provide a sheltered habitat for the *cervo sardo* (deer), now an unusual sight in Sardinia though common before the twentieth century. Other rare wildlife includes martens, wildcats and boars, not to mention kestrels, buzzards, hawks and even golden eagles. Where the granite slopes are not forested with holm oaks, there is a thick mantle of Mediterranean *macchia* which is crossed by waymarked paths. There's a Visitor Centre (usually closed Aug–Sept) with information on walks; if you want a guide, contact *Cooperativa Il Caprifoglio* (summer only; ☎070.968.714), or the local WWF branch (☎070.670.308).

Ten kilometres south from Lido di Capoterra, the vast oil and chemical refinery at **Sarroch** is the biggest industrial complex on the whole island, its malevolent tangle of pipes, container drums and flaming chimneys covering an enormous area that nudges into the village itself, filling the air with acrid odours. The villagers – most of them dependent on the works for their livelihood – don't complain, but it's a zone for anyone else to rush through with windows wound up. All the same, if you're really stuck for somewhere to stay near Pula (a not uncommon occurrence in summer), there's a comfortable and economical little hotel here, the *Lanterna Verde*, on the main road leading towards the sea (☎070.900.396; ②).

Pula

Keep going past the smoking chimneys and foul air for another 7km to reach **PULA**, a large inland village that's become something of a tourist centre thanks to its proximity to the seaside archeological site at Nora (see p.110). Apart from its hotels and restaurants, the village makes an essential stop, either before or after a visit to Nora, on account of its **Museo Archeologico** (daily: April–Oct 9am–8pm; Nov–March 9am–6pm; L4000, or L7000 including site at Nora), signposted at Corso Vittorio Emanuele 67. Although the display is small and poorly labelled – the most significant finds are in the archeological museum at Cágliari – the plans and explanations (in Italian) help put the site into context. Most of the items were fished out of the sea, notably the crusty amphorae and pottery fragments – Phoenician, Iberian, Greek, Gallic and Punic – in which oil and other produce was transported from the European mainland and North Africa. Other exhibits include Roman capitals and some stelae from Nora's Punic tophet, dating from the fifth to third centuries BC.

Practicalities

Hourly ARST **buses** connect Cágliari with Pula, of which two a day continue to Nora in summer. If you're not on one of these and want to go straight to the site, get off the bus at Pula's Via Corinaldi, from which there are six departures daily (fewer in winter) on local services #1 or #2 – alternatively walk or hitch the 4km. Coming by bus from the south, get off at Pula's Municipio just up from the museum, for the same local bus service.

Pula has a couple of budget **hotels**, cheapest the *Quattro Mori*, a one-star locanda at Via Cágliari 10 (☎070.920.9124; ③; May–Sept;

no CCs), whose nine simple rooms include singles with and without private bath, and doubles all with shared facilities. Nearer the centre, a few doors down at Via Cágliari 2, the larger *Sandalyon* has more comfort and slightly higher prices (☎ & fax 070.920.9151; ③). The ten boxy rooms (one's a triple) all have private bathroom, and come with TV and telephone; there's an outdoor pizzeria/ristorante, and breakfast is included in the price June–September. Other choices in the neighbourhood lie 3km away at Nora (see below).

There are several **restaurants** in town, including the smartish *Eleonora* at Via Nora 35, which has outdoor seating in a narrow courtyard; a less formal pizzeria, *L'Incontro*, lies a short distance away on the central Piazza del Pópolo. Across the square from here, you can enjoy wonderful **ice creams**, *frappés* and yoghurt concoctions at *Crazy Art* (closed Mon in winter).

An old villa on Piazza del Pópolo, Casa Frau, houses Pula's **Pro Loco** (☎070.920.8224; June–Sept daily 9am–1pm & 8pm–midnight, Oct–May Mon–Fri 9am–1pm), but the all-purpose private tourist office, Le Torri, is more help, near one of the Cágliari bus stops on the corner of Via Nora and Via Corinaldi (☎ & fax 070.920.8373; Mon–Sat 9am–12.30pm & 4.30–7.30pm, Sun in summer 9am–12.30pm). Apart from issuing general information on the locality, they rent out **cars, bicycles and motorbikes**, and also **apartments** in or around town, if you were thinking of staying a week or more in the area. Car rental rates are comparatively low (starting at L500,000 per week), though you can rent bikes more cheaply (for about L10,000 a day) at Serra (signed Biciclette Legnani) at Corso Vittorio Emanuele 68. **Change money** at Le Torri, or at the banks on Via Lamármora.

July and August see plenty of action in Pula's Piazza del Pópolo, with **concerts** and dances almost nightly and free art **exhibitions** in Casa Frau, while there's a programme of nightly **open-air films** at the Cine Arena, on Via Santa Croce (behind the Municipio off Corso Vittorio Emanuele), starting at 9.45pm. Entertainments are also organized at Nora's Roman theatre (see below).

Nora

Founded by the Phoenicians and settled later by Carthaginians and Romans, **Nora** was abandoned after the third century AD. Now partly submerged under the sea, the site requires some imagination to grasp its former scale, but, overlooked by a defensive tower built by the Spanish in the sixteenth century, its position on the tip of a peninsula gives it plenty of atmosphere.

The Phoenicians who first settled the site in the ninth and eighth centuries BC were clearly drawn by its strategic location on the Capo di Pula promontory, dominating the Golfo di Cágliari from its southwestern approaches. Controlled by Carthage from the sixth century BC, the city expanded to become the biggest urban centre on the island, a position it retained after it was taken by the Romans in 238 BC, under whom it became provincial capital for the whole island. However, the gradual incursion of the sea meant that the site became increasingly precarious, and the arrival on the scene of the Vandals in the fifth century AD led to its abandonment.

The archeological site

Today, a good part of the **site** (daily: April–Oct 9am–8pm; Nov–March 9am–6pm; L4000, or L7000 including Pula museum) is immersed beneath the waves. As for the rest, crashed arches and walls give some idea of the original size of the buildings, but little has survived above ground level apart from some solitary Roman columns. Evidence of the long Carthaginian dominion is particularly scanty, despite the intense commercial activity suggested by the foundations of warehouses and the contents of tombs dug up here, though on a slight elevation you can see the ruins of a temple dedicated to Tanit, goddess of fertility. Other Punic remnants, among them an inscription featuring the first recorded use of the name Sardinia, can be viewed in Cágliari's museum. Most of the remainder belongs to the Roman period, including, near the Spanish watchtower, a temple, with a single column still standing, and a small theatre – much reconstructed, but splendidly sited, and still used for concerts. Further on, four upright columns mark a patrician's villa, surrounded by numerous one- and two-room dwellings. The villa's well-preserved black, white and ochre-coloured mosaic floors are Nora's most arresting sights; the opulence of their simple but splendid designs – taken together with the town's four sets of baths and good network of roads with their drainage system still intact – suggests something of the importance of this Roman outpost.

Free **tours** of the excavations, in Italian, take place whenever there are enough people to make a group and the guides are available; otherwise you can get a pretty good picture by wandering about under your own steam, aided by diagrams and bilingual explanations.

Concerts – mainly classical – take place in Nora's Roman theatre in July and August. Tickets cost around L15,000 and can be bought at the gate or in advance: contact the tourist offices in Cágliari or Pula, or call ☎070.408.2230.

Around Nora

Immediately north of the archeological site, the exquisite sandy bay of **Spiaggia di Nora** is lapped by crystal-clear water, though this can rapidly transform into day-tripper hell in season. Following the bay north for 500 metres or so, you'll come to another beach at **Su Guventeddu**. Behind the bay stands the rather ordinary-looking **church of Sant'Efísio**, built by Vittorini monks in the eleventh century on the site of the saint's martyrdom. Efisius, a Roman soldier of the third century who converted to Christianity, was credited with staunching an outbreak of plague in 1656, since when the church has been the ultimate destination of Cágliari's Mayday procession (see p.82). A new facade robs the church's front of much of its flavour, but the inside is more pleasing: a narrow nave lined with thick pillars and round arches.

South of the archeological site (to the right of the entrance), a placid circle of water, the **Laguna di Nora**, shelters a small nature reserve and, on a rocky causeway, a learning centre with an **aquarium** and exhibition rooms (June–Sept daily 10am–1.30pm & 5–6.30pm, 4–5.30pm in Sept; L8000). Aimed at school parties and other groups, the 90-minute guided tour around the centre uses audio-visual displays to explain the local ecology, and there is a somewhat irrelevant section on dolphins, whales and turtles. Supervised snorkelling and canoe trips on the lagoon are also offered; in winter the place only opens for bookings (☎070.920.9544).

Practicalities

If you want a **meal** in the area, *L'Approdo* is a pizzeria/ristorante with an outdoor terrace opposite the church of Sant'Efísio – a touristy place, but useful for a snack. For a quality – but moderately priced – repast, head for *Su Guventeddu*, a small pensione a kilometre up the road back to Pula. At just a hundred metres from the beach of the same name, this makes a good place **to stay**: rooms are clean and modern, all with TV, telephone and private bath (☎070.920.9092; ③). Buses #1 and #2 stop directly outside, connecting Nora with Pula. The nearest **campsites** are in Santa Margherita di Pula (see below), on the #2 bus route.

Santa Margherita di Pula

The **SANTA MARGHERITA DI PULA** locality constitutes a southern Sardinian version of the Costa Smeralda, though marginally more downmarket and decidedly less picturesque. Like its northern counterpart, this élite retreat has no history prior to the 1960s, owing its existence primarily to the presence, just outside Pula, of the luxury *Is Molas* golf course and a cluster of three- and four-star **hotels**, discreetly concealed among the trees and accessible from the main SS195 coast road. Though way out of the league of most people, these can be useful places for changing money if you're caught short; even so, if you do fancy a splurge, most offer quite good-value low-season discounts. The biggest and flashiest of them is the *Forte Village*, with pools, sports facilities, shops and restaurants spread over a huge area and catering largely to package groups (mid-April to mid-Nov; ☎070.92.171, fax 070.921.246; ⑨). If you're in the luxury stakes, however, you might prefer the more select *Flamingo* (late April to mid-Oct; ☎070.920.8361, fax 070.920.8359; L140–180,000 low season, L180–240,000 high), where you can stay in rooms in the main building or in detached villas; the half-board requirement bumps up the price. At the other end of the scale are the area's two **campsites**, next to each other on the minor seafront road beyond the pinewoods: the one nearer to Nora is *Flumendosa* (☎ & fax 070.920.8364), while *Cala d'Ostia*

(April–Sept; ☎070.921.470), which is closer to the wide sandy beach of the same name. Bus #2 from Pula and Nora stops right outside the sites. You don't need to be a lira millionaire to eat around here: try the *Urru* bar-restaurant, on the road between the SS195 and the seafront, or the *Ranch Is Morus*, further along the same road, which offers meals and horse-riding (☎0330.739.428).

Chia and around

Like Santa Margherita di Pula, **CHIA** is a dispersed locality without any centre as such. The interesting bit lies at the end of the minor road branching left off the main SS195, 10km beyond Santa Margherita; it's signposted "Torre di Chia". You'll soon see the **Pisan watchtower** after which the place is named; it stands above one of the best **beaches** on the southern coast, a perfect sandy arc with a small lagoon behind. Around the tower have been found the remains of the fourth-century-BC Phoenician and Carthaginian town of **Bythia**, mentioned in Ptolemy's *Geography* but never attaining the same importance as Nora or Tharros. Traces of the settlement were uncovered during a storm in 1933, including some tombs and parts of a temple probably dedicated to the Egyptian deity Bes, but systematic excavation has revealed little of importance. A climb up the tower affords marvellous views south down the coast, taking in a range of inviting beaches. Just behind the Chia beach, there's a handy three-star **campsite**, *Torre Chia* (June–Sept; ☎070.923.0054, fax 070.923.0055), equipped with a tennis court and also small villas for up to four people, available for rent for L105,000 a night in June and September, rising to L175,000 in peak season. Immediately south of Chia, the immense beach of **Sa Colonia** makes an irresistible spot for a dip, and there's the *Gabbiano* **pizzeria/ristorante** behind.

A series of lagoons and sandy bays unfurls as you head south from Chia, right up to the point at **Capo Spartivento**. There are a couple of **hotels** here – the last for a while – including the relatively cheap *Su Giudeu* (☎070.923.0260, fax 070.923.0002; ②); comfortable and modern, it requires half- or full board in summer (and non-residents can eat in the **restaurant** here). The road to the cape ends at the last good beaches on this stretch of coast, backed by unshaded car parks which charge between June and September (L5000 for the day, or L3000 for the afternoon). There's also a **horse-riding** facility here, *Maneggio da Eros* (☎070.923.6037).

The Costa del Sud

West of Capo Spartivento, the road runs briefly inland, then climbs and swoops for some 20km along the largely deserted **Costa del Sud**, one of Sardinia's most scenic drives. To the north, groves of olive and eucalyptus give way to a backdrop of bare mountains, while the jagged coast of the **Golfo di Teulada** presents a procession of indented bays punctuated by lonely Spanish watchtowers. It can be a rewarding hike, though walkers will need to follow much of the route by road, making it something of a grind. Much of the time, too, the sea is difficult or impossible to reach, though swimming is possible from rocks or the few strips of sand along the way. **Tuerredda**, a stop on the ARST bus route, is one of the more populated bathing spots, with parking facilities and a bar/pizzeria. Next, the road skirts round **Malfatano**, a deep bay providing shelter for boats and some scraps of beach. A right turn here leads to the jetty and beaches of **Porto Teulada**, an anchorage for fishing boats and pleasure craft, where you can have *panini* and beers at a kiosk in summer, go diving or rent dinghies, canoes or pedalos. The port is also the embarkation point for a tour by yacht of the coast as far as Capo Teulada, Sardinia's southernmost point at the far end of the Golfo di Teulada; call ☎0368.377.3523 for details.

Beyond Porto Teulada, there are more alluring beaches at and around **Tramatzu**, and a well-appointed and therefore popular campsite, *Porto Tramatzu* (June–Sept; ☎070.927.1022). There's a much smaller inland site at *Agrifenu*, a peaceful agriturismo signposted off the Porto Teulada turn-off about a kilometre up a track; they have eight self-catering **rooms for rent** (☎070.928.3013; ②).

Teulada and around

Back on the main SS195, a right turn leads to the small inland town of **TEULADA**, its drowsy air enlivened by odd pieces of sculpture dotted around its streets and squares. Sculptors come from all over the world to compete in the town's annual exhibition; they're given a block of local marble, granite or trachyte in June, when the theme – usually locally-inspired – is announced. The pieces are finished by September, and then placed around the village. Other than sculpture, Teulada is distinguished for its **handicrafts**, available for sale in various shops in the centre, in particular embroidery, tapestries, carpets, cork objects and terracotta pipes. The only **place to stay** is the *Sebera*, on Via San Francesco, which has ten simple rooms and a restaurant (☎070.927.0876, fax 070.927.0020; ④), though you might prefer **to eat** at the *Antica Trattoria del Vico* in Vico Primo Mártiri, which specializes in goat and other Sard dishes – there's a set menu for L26,000 (closed Tues Sept–June; no CCs). You can **change money** at the *Banco di Sardegna*, which has a cash machine.

West of Teulada, the SS195 loops inland of the cliffy coast and Sardinia's southernmost tip, **Capo Teulada**, which is occasionally used for military exercises and effectively inaccessible. A right turn at the village of **Sant'Anna Arresi** (the last stop on the bus route from Cágliari) brings you to the pinewoods, lagoons and beaches of **Porto Pino**. It's a favourite spot for day-trippers from the towns and villages nearby, and the shady picnic spots and dazzling sand beaches can get a bit claustrophobic, but the place is less busy on weekdays outside August. Right behind the main beach, there's a **campsite**, *Sardegna*, with bungalows available (mid-May to Sept; ☎0781.967.013).

Giba and around

Some 8km north of Sant'Anna Arresi, the village of **GIBA** stands at a crossroads just below the **Lago di Monte Pranu**. Like almost all Sardinia's lakes, this was artificially created, formed by a barrage on the Palmas river. You can see something of it from the track leading north from the main crossroads at Giba, but it's hardly worth the detour, since the route is slow and unsignposted, presenting plenty of opportunity to get lost. Neither is there much reason to hang around in Giba itself, barring a useful if unexceptional hotel, the *Rosella*, with a good restaurant attached (☎070.964.029; ②); if you lodge here, make sure you get an inward-facing room to avoid the traffic noise.

A right turn at the Giba junction leads 10km east to **Santadi**, an agricultural centre on the banks of the Rio Mannu. The otherwise nondescript village is famous for its *matrimonio maureddino*, a re-enactment of a Mauretanian wedding on the first Sunday of August, said to derive from an African colony settled here during the Roman era; contact the **Pro Loco** on Via Veneto for details (Mon–Fri 9am–1pm & 4–7pm; ☎0781.955.441). If you do stop here, you might as well drop in on the **Museo Etnográfico Sa Domu Antiga** on Via Mazzini (Mon–Fri 9am–12.30pm, sporadic afternoon opening; free), a grand name for a small house typical of the rustic dwellings of the Sulcis region. The courtyard shows a ragbag of traditional items of rural life, including a loom, bread-making equipment and agricultural tools, but it's all sadly neglected, and not a patch on the ethnographic exhibits at Sant'Antíoco (see p.120).

Santadi's Coop Fillirea (Via Mazzini 37, ☎ & fax 0781.955.983) can arrange excursions into the surrounding area, with a special emphasis on local history, wildlife, rural culture and gastronomy.

Is Zuddas and Pantaleo

A more engaging attraction can be found 8km south of Santadi, off the SP70: the **Is Zuddas** grottoes (April–Sept daily 9am–noon & 2.30–6pm; Oct–March Mon–Sat tours at noon & 4pm, Sun 9am–noon & 2.30–6pm; L10,000). Hour-long guided tours through the five main chambers of this cave system reveal how the slow work of millennia has created stalagmites to resemble frozen cascades, organ pipes and Walt Disney characters; the delicate white spiky aragonite, which grows here in apparent contradiction of the laws of gravity, is especially lovely. The relative coolness of the caves (16°C) makes them a welcome respite from a boiling sun; an English-speaking tour guide is usually on hand.

Travelling east out of Santadi, following signs for *Bosco di Pantaleo*, you'll soon come (after 7km) to **Pantaleo**, a cluster of buildings amid a small wood. The main attraction here is the *Su Commeo* **restaurant**, housed in an old coal-processing plant, and specializing in local mountain dishes including roast or grilled pork. Ring first in winter to make sure they're open (☎0781.955.822; no CCs). You could always drop by on the way through the mountains to or from Capoterra (p.108): the dirt road begins shortly after Pantaleo.

Montessu

West of Santadi and 3km north of the village of Villaperuccio, off the SP293 Giba–Siliqua road, is one of Sardinia's most important prenuraghic burial sites: the necropolis of **Montessu** (daily 9am–6.30pm; L5000). Hewn out of a natural amphitheatre of trachyte rock by people of the Ozieri culture of the fourth and third millennia BC, the forty-odd tombs – popularly called *domus de janas*, or "fairy-houses" – show diverse forms. The square openings either in the top or sides were originally sealed with stone doors (one is still in place); four have wide canopies, behind which circular areas are marked out by stones, probably used for funerary rites. Several of the clean-cut chambers contain niches and small annexes, but their most interesting feature is the sacred symbols cut into the walls: graffiti, reliefs and incisions linked to earth cults, mostly representing the mother goddess and bull god. The best are visible in the **Tomba delle Spirali**, showing a cluster of alien-looking spirals, possibly the "eyes" of the goddess, and the **Tomba delle Corna**, with multiple horn shapes.

Linked to the same complex is a group of **menhirs** up to five metres tall situated in the open country about a kilometre south of Villaperuccio, in the **Terrazzu** district. Associated with obscure fertility rites, the stark monoliths are conspicuous landmarks amid the flat cultivated fields.

Tratalias

Heading west, a short diversion from the SS195 Giba-to-Sant'Antíoco road brings you to **Tratalias**, once an important centre in the area, as attested by its Romanesque church of **Santa Maria** (Mon–Tues 9am–2pm, Wed–Sun 9am–2pm & 4–8pm, reduced times in winter), which was consecrated in 1213 as cathedral for the entire Sulcis region. The well-preserved building – located in the Vecchio Borgo, the shabby, medieval quarter outside the newer town – fuses Pisan and French styles, with a small rose window and, curiously, a section of an external staircase at the top of its simple square facade. There's more of the staircase visible inside, where the thick columns and plain bricks are topped by a wooden roof, though all the finery has long since disappeared. Elsewhere in the Vecchio Borgo, a few palazzi near the church preserve their medieval lines, but most of the historic buildings have been pulled down to make way for the new town.

Sant'Antíoco

The island of **Sant'Antíoco** is joined to the Sardinian mainland by a three-kilometre isthmus that meets the coast 8km west of Tratalias. This causeway has existed since Carthaginian times, though the last section now runs over a modern bridge, which dwarfs the adjacent remains of its Roman predecessor. The waters of the **Stagno di Santa Caterina** on the right are the occasional habitat of flamingoes, and you may also spot cormorants and herons. The lagoon is associated with the local legend of two lovers, a monk and a nun, who, attempting to elope to the island, were turned to stone in mid-flight in a visitation of divine disapproval. The petrified figures – rocks or *faraglioni* – are in fact prenuraghic menhirs, thought to have been associated with fertility rites. Popularly named **Su Para** and **Sa Mongia** ("the monk" and "the nun"), the pair are stranded in the middle of an open field: take a side track on the left just after crossing the bridge to view them.

The port area of **Sant'Antíoco town** lies at the end of the new bridge, a low-key harbour for yachts, fishing vessels and freighters. All but sailors, however, bypass the port in favour of the historical centre in the upper town; to reach it, continue on the road from the bridge, the long Via Nazionale (becoming Via Roma and Corso Vittorio Emanuele). Most of the places of interest lie at the top of the town, at the end of Via Regina Margherita. The SS126 continues north of here towards Calasetta; to reach the island's southern zone, turn left soon after the bridge (signposted *spiagge*). The road south follows the coast past bays and beaches before swinging over to the island's rocky western shore. Only primitive tracks cross the hilly interior.

Some history

Founded around the eighth century BC, the core of Sant'Antíoco's upper town has been continuously inhabited since Phoenician times. As a defensible anchorage commanding the whole of Sardinia's southwest coast, it was an important base both for the Carthaginians and the Romans, who shipped the mining products of the inland region – chiefly lead and zinc – from here. The town's Carthaginian name, Sulki, was later extended to cover the whole mainland area, while for the Romans, it was Plumbea, after the nearby lead mines. The present name refers to Saint Antiochus, a North African martyr who was said to have endured the most gruesome tortures and death by drowning only to rise from the dead and undertake the conversion of the islanders to Christianity. During the Second Punic War, the port hosted the Carthaginian fleet, for which it was punished by the Roman victors, losing many of its privileges. The importance of the mines on the mainland, however, ensured that it continued to flourish until the Middle Ages, when, in common with much of Sardinia, the town fell victim to pirates and Saracen raids. The port's strategic importance was recognized during the French Revolutionary Wars, and Nelson's flagship, the *Vanguard*, berthed here after suffering severe damage in a storm, shortly before the Battle of the Nile in 1798. The vessel was re-rigged in four days, though Nelson deplored the fact that, on account of Sardinia's recently declared neutrality, the ship's company was not allowed ashore. "We are refused the rights of humanity," he wrote to Lady Nelson. More recently, Mussolini's expansion of Sardinia's mining industry injected new life into the town's shipping activities, and a new harbour was constructed which continues in use today.

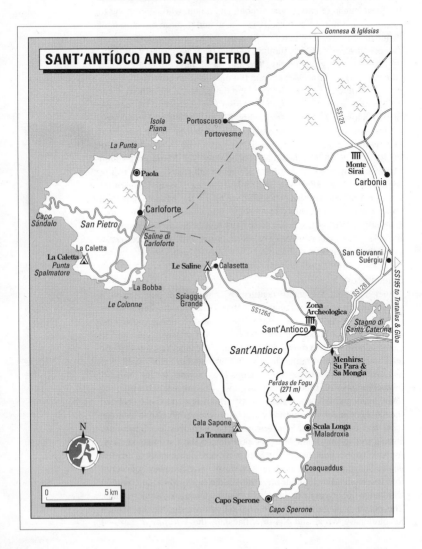

Arrival, information and accommodation

FMS **buses** from the Sardinian mainland stop on Sant'Antíoco's Piazza Repubblica before continuing on to Calasetta. For information and tickets, ask in the *Sanitari* chemist on the corner. The piazza also has a stop for the orange **minibuses** which provide a summer service to the south-coast beaches, leaving every fifteen minutes or so from the piazza and other stops in town. For beaches in the north of the island, some FMS buses continue on beyond Calasetta as far as Spiaggia Grande.

The **tourist office** is on Piazza Repubblica (June–Sept 9am–noon & 5–9pm; Oct–May 10am–noon & 4.30–6.30pm; ☎0781.82.031). A few steps away, at Via Nazionale 82, lies one of the town's only two **hotels**, the small *Moderno* (☎0781.83.105, fax 0781.840.252; ③). In the upper town, there's the posher *Eden* (☎ & fax 0781.840.768; ④), right next to the main church on Piazza Parrocchia. **Change money** at one of the two banks on Sant'Antíoco's Piazza Umberto, both with cash machines, or there's one just off Piazza Italia on Via Roma.

The town

At the top of Via Regina Margherita, the **church of Sant'Antíoco** makes a good place to begin a tour of the old town. Hidden behind the dilapidated facade of a bishop's palace, the Romanesque construction dates from the twelfth century, and is built over Christian catacombs. Near the entrance to the church, look out for a statue of the saint himself, who was interred in the catacombs – a second burial, after his miraculous resurrection. The entrance to the **catacombs** (Mon–Sat 9am–noon & 3–6pm, also 7–8pm in summer, Sun 10–11am & 4–8pm; L4000) lies in the right transept. Early Christians enlarged these in the sixth century from an existing Carthaginian *hypogeum* (underground vault). Guides are on hand to tour the dark and dingy corridors, pitted with numerous low-ceilinged mini-chambers and graves in which authentic skeletons are displayed, along with reproductions of the ceramic objects unearthed during excavation. Fragments of primitive frescoes survive on some walls.

One hundred metres down Via Regina Margherita, the small **Museo Archeologico** (archeological zone and museum daily 9am–1pm & 3.30–7pm in summer, 3.30–6pm in winter; L8000 including ethnographic museum, tophet and archeological zone) shows a sample of the finds from the hilltop excavations, a tiny fraction of what is claimed to be one of the largest collections of Carthaginian ware outside Carthage itself, most of it currently stashed away out of view until a new on-site museum has been completed. Nonetheless, it's worth making a stop here for the few exhibits – mainly inscribed stelae, ceramics and items of jewellery found within the Punic necropolis, along with maps and diagrams of the archeological site. The reproduction of a section of the tophet at one end of the room seems unnecessary, however, when the real thing lies just a few minutes away. To see this, cross the road and follow signs up Via Castello, a side road outside the church. On the way, you'll pass the **Forte Su Pisu** (also called the *Fortino Sabaudo*, or just *Castello*), part of a Piedmontese fortification built in 1812; three years later its garrison was massacred by corsairs. Beyond the tower is the main part of the *zona archeologica*, commanding a lofty view of the sea and Sardinian mainland. At the top of the site stand the meagre remains of the **Punic acropolis**, little more than a few truncated columns and the surviving blocks of what once must have been massive walls. There is more interest in the enclosed area below, where a **Punic necropolis** has been excavated, consisting of numerous narrow subterranean chambers of one or two rooms, each accessible via a flight of steps. Well-informed guides explain (in Italian) the structure and use of the tombs, and steer visitors into the more accessible ones. There is little evidence here of the Phoenicians, for whom cremation was the preferred method of disposing of their dead.

About 500m further north, another hilltop holds Sant'Antíoco's extensive **Punic tophet** (same hours as museum), or burial site, dedicated to the Carthaginian goddess Tanit. The rocky site is centred on the ruined walls of a sanctuary surrounded by a scattering of funerary urns, many of them modern reproductions. The original urns were long held to contain the ashes of sacrificed first-born children, but this is now thought to have been Roman propaganda: the ashes, it seems, were the cremated remains of children still-born or dead from natural causes. At the summit of the site stand the massive square blocks of a Punic temple.

There's a quite different tone in the last museum included in the price of your ticket, located about 350m back towards the town on Via Necrópoli (signposted). The small but engrossing **Museo Etnográfico** (daily: 9am–1pm & 3.30–7pm, 3.30–6pm in winter) is little more than one capacious room crammed to the rafters with examples of rural culture – tools, agricultural implements, craftwork, bread- and pasta-making equipment, most of them only recently superseded by modern machinery – all enthusiastically explained (in Italian) by a guide.

Eating, drinking and nightlife

There is a wide choice of **restaurants** in town that makes up for their sparsity elsewhere on the island. One of the best is on the seafront near the bridge, *La Laguna* at Lungomare Vespucci 37, which offers quality – mainly seafood – meals at moderate-to-expensive prices (☎0781.83.286; closed Tues). Nearer the centre, on Viale Trento, *Il Cantuccio* has similar prices but a more upscale ambience, with modern art on the walls (☎0781.82.166). Of the numerous **pizzerias** lining Via Nazionale and Via Roma, the bamboo-roofed garden restaurant attached to the *Moderno* hotel at Via Nazionale 82 is one of the most popular. For something quieter, go round the corner to Via Toscana, where the *birreria*/pizzeria *Askos* serves the regular range of pizzas for about L8000, plus the seafood-rich *Askos* for L13,000. For a twist on the pizza theme, seek out *Caligola*, on Via Garibaldi (off Piazza Umberto), where the decor is cod Roman and the pizzas have names such as *Colosseo* and *Centuri*. Despite the gimmickry, the pizzas aren't at all bad, and you can eat at pavement tables in summer (closed Wed). Quick **snacks** are available from the bars on Piazza Italia, though for ices, chocolate croissants and good coffee, the *Bar Nuovo Sport* on Corso Vittorio Emanuele can't be beat. Tuesday is **market day** in Sant'Antíoco, the stalls spreading below Piazza Italia as far as the seafront.

Summer sees a full programme of evening entertainments, including **concerts** in July and August on Piazza Umberto and Piazza Italia, and **open-air films** at the *Cinema in Laguna*, just below Piazza Repubblica on Lungomare Vespucci, starting at 9.45pm. Most people, however, content themselves with the slow promenade through the centre of town, sucking ice creams and pausing at the many pavement bars along the way.

The rest of the island

Outside town, the **island of Sant'Antíoco** mainly consists of *macchia*-covered slopes, with a few white houses dotted among the vineyards and scrub. Most of the **beaches** lie on the southern and eastern shores, accessible from the road running south out of town: take a left turn after 5km for some of the best, signposted **Maladroxia**. You'll soon come to an attractive cove fringed by a strip of sand, though there is more space further on at Maladroxia's enclosed bay. It's overlooked by one of the island's best budget **hotel** choices, the *Scala Longa*, with seven simple rooms (each with shower), a panoramic terrace, and a rather uninspired restaurant; you may be asked to take half- or full board in summer (☎0781.817.202; ②).

The road ends at the bay. By continuing on the main coastal road, you'll meander round the island's highest point, **Perdas de Fogu** (271m), from which hikers can enjoy the distant views stretching out over the Sardinian mainland. Another turn-off to the left leads to one of Sant'Antíoco's best beaches at **Coaquaddus**, equipped with deck chairs and parasols to hire, and a couple of bars. Much of the coastline around here is high and rocky, especially at the southern tip of the island at **Capo Sperone**, occupied by a solitary watchtower and a luxury **hotel** – the family-orientated *Capo Sperone*, with its own pool and a range of sports facilities, but fairly steep prices (☎0781.809.000, fax 0781.809.015; ⑨). Non-guests can swim at the nearby beach, walking down from the tower.

Bathing spots on the remoter **western side of the island** are harder to find: the best is probably **Cala Sapone**, a well-sheltered bay

The biggest date on the island's calendar is the Festa di Sant'Antíoco, taking place around the second Sunday after Easter; a prolonged four-day affair, it features traditional songs, poetry recitations and dancing, ending in a procession to the sea and fireworks.

with one of Sant'Antíoco's two **campsites** alongside, *Tonnara* (☎0781.809.058), open all year and with two- and four-room bungalows available. Beyond here the going gets slow as the road loses its asphalt, and access is easiest from the north.

Calasetta

At the island's northern extremity, Sant'Antíoco's second town and port, **CALASETTA**, lies 10km from the main town. The right-angled grid of lanes here holds little of interest, but a brief distance southwest, **La Salina** offers a dune-backed sand beach, or follow the crowds to **Spiaggia Grande**, a couple of kilometres further down, where umbrellas, deck-chairs and boats are available to rent, and there is a bar serving refreshments. The road becomes a dirt track soon after.

If you want to stay in Calasetta, the *FJBY* is the nearest **hotel** to the port at Via Solferino 83 (☎0781.88.444, fax 0781.887.089; ③); further out, the three-star *Cala di Seta* offers very reasonable rates at Via Regina Margherita 61 (☎0781.88.304, fax 0781.31.538; ④), while the smaller *Bellavista* stands above a lovely arc of beach a short walk north of town (☎ & fax 0781.88.211; ③). All three hotels have **restaurants**; if you don't want to eat at one of these, *L'Approdo*, right on the port, specializes in seafood, or you can just have a drink at the outdoor tables. The smaller of the island's two **campsites**, *Le Saline*, lies next to La Salina beach (☎0781.88.615, in winter ☎0781.88.489).

For your onward journey from Calasetta, TRIS or Saremar **ferries** make the 5km hop to San Pietro roughly every hour (40min; L4000 per person); if you're in a car in August, make sure you're here in good time, as you'll need to queue. From mid-July to mid-September, Delcomar ferries also make night-time crossings between Calasetta and Carloforte every 90 minutes (L4000 per person; tickets on board).

San Pietro

The dialect in **San Pietro** is pure Piedmontese, two and a half centuries after the Savoyan king Carlo Emanuele III invited a colony of Ligurians to settle here. They had been evicted from the island of Tabarca, near Tunisia, and were hardly relocated here before suffering the further misfortune of being abducted in one of the last great pirate raids. The hapless settlers eventually returned to the island on payment of a hefty ransom by the king, who formally established them at Carloforte in 1750. Ligurian elements remain in the local cuisine and dialect, and some of the buildings hark back to Genoan styles of architecture.

San Pietro sits exactly on the thirty-ninth parallel, for which there is an observatory situated on the outskirts of town.

San Pietro today preserves a laid-back pace in the face of boatloads of holidaymakers who flood the island every summer. Avoid the peak months to see the island at its best, and to be sure of finding accommodation. Although the island's eastern seaboard is not exactly enhanced by the prospect of Portoscuso's smoky industrial works on the Sardinian mainland opposite, the few beaches off the southern coast are pleasantly secluded, while the high western shore vaunts some exquisite panoramas as well as one or two great places for swimming and snorkelling. The cliffy terrain here provides sanctuary for a protected species of falcon, recalling the island's former names – Enosim, as it was known by the Carthaginians, and Accipitrum by the Romans, both of which refer to the numbers of sparrow hawks that once dwelt here. The present name derives from a legend according to which Saint Peter washed up here after being shipwrecked (a claim made by dozens of other Mediterranean islands), subsequently teaching the locals new fishing techniques. The most notorious kind of fishing performed on San Pietro now, however, is the annual slaughter of tuna fish, *La Mattanza*, which takes place in May and June (see box).

The island's only town, **Carloforte** (named after Carlo Emanuele), is attractive and lively in summer, its open port giving it a carefree feel. Water-polo matches take place in cordoned-off sections of the port, and dockside booths offer boat tours round the island. Facing the port, most of the town's activity is concentrated on Piazza Carlo Emanuele, a broad area holding numerous bars, the tourist office and a bank. From here, Corso Battellieri runs south along the seafront to a wide and placid lagoon that marks the town's southern limit.

Dotted with white houses, most of the island is covered with *macchia* that gives way to bare craggy or round peaks, the slopes rising to a height of about 200m. The best route for exploring the sparsely populated interior is along the twisty road leading across the island from Carloforte to the western shore at **Capo Sándalo**. This rugged

---

La Mattanza: San Pietro's tuna bloodbath

Though the annual tuna massacre is also enacted on Sant'Antíoco (at Punta Maggiore, southwest of Calasetta), San Pietro's age-old rite of *La Mattanza* is a much bigger, grosser affair. Nets are laid down as early as March, but the killing mainly takes place in May and June, when the tuna are passing through the northern straits on their way to their mating grounds in the eastern Mediterranean. Channeled through a series of nets culminating in the *camera della morte*, or death-chamber, the fish are bludgeoned to death as the net is slowly raised.

The *Mattanza* – the word is from Spanish roots ("the killing") – has a mixture of different origins. The methods are identical to those used at other places where the Ligurians settled, such as the Égadi Islands off Sicily's western tip, but there's also a strong Arab influence evident in the use of titles like *Raís* (Arab for chief), referring to the coordinator of the operation. Although deplored by many for its brutality, the practice attracts crowds of spectators every season, and has even been appropriated as a selling-point by the tourist office. All the same, the gory details of the grim ritual are played down in the numerous restaurants that serve up the tuna at dinner: it's an island speciality, naturally.

---

beauty spot on the western tip affords memorable views along the coast, most of which is inaccessible without a boat, though the road running **south out of Carloforte** winds round to a popular beach at **La Caletta** (also called Spalmatore), where there's a cluster of houses and a campsite (see below). More rough strips of beach lie sheltered in a series of inlets on the island's southeastern edge, for example **La Bobba**, where the twin rock formations known as *Le Colonne* spring abruptly out of the sea. **North of Carloforte**, a six-kilometre road (bear left at the Agip garage) ends up at **La Punta**, a bracing spot on San Pietro's exposed northern corner, looking towards the offshore **Isola Piana**. This is the venue for the annual tuna slaughter, but you can see the old *tonnare*, or tuna fisheries, at any time.

Practicalities

Most of the island's facilities are located in Carloforte. Opposite the port, the main Piazza Carlo Emanuele III holds the ferry offices, a bank where you can change money, and San Pietro's **tourist office** (summer Mon–Sat 9am–1pm & 3.30–7.30pm, winter Mon–Sat 10am–12.30pm; ☎0781.854.009). They can help you with accommodation and provide a list of **rooms for rent**, a useful option if you are stuck without a booking in summer. Carloforte's most stylish **hotel** is undoubtedly the ornate, Art Nouveau *Hieracon* at Corso Cavour 63 (☎0781.854.028; ④), a few minutes' walk up from Piazza Carlo Emanuele; some rooms have harbour views, and there's a restaurant. In the other direction, overlooking the port on Corso Battellieri, there's another three-star, the *Riviera* (☎0781.854.004, fax 0781.856.552; ⑤); the town's only cheapish choice lies further south, near the lagoon, the plain and friendly *California*, at Via Cavallera 5, about ten minutes' walk from the port (☎0781.854.470; ③; no CCs).

Elsewhere on the island, there are just three hotels, all inland. One of them, the three-star *Paola*, signposted off the road to La Punta 3km north of town, offers surprisingly cheap rates, probably due to its relative distance from the sea (about a ten-minute walk), though it enjoys a great view (☎0781.850.098, fax 0781.852.104; ④). You can **camp** near the sea at *La Caletta* (June–Sept; ☎0781.852.112), 8km southwest of Carloforte and reachable on a regular bus service (summer only).

Carloforte has no shortage of fish **restaurants**, most on the expensive side. In all, tuna features on the menu in summer, while *zuppa di pesce* is a speciality priced at L25–35,000. Couscous – a variation on the Tunisian version – is another island speciality worth sampling. One of the best fish restaurants is just up from Piazza Carlo Emanuele, *Da Nicolò*, at Corso Cavour 32 (☎0781.854.048), with outdoor seating and quite high prices: the *Cus Cus Carlofortino*, for example, weighs in at L18,000. More moderate places include the award-winning *Al Tonno di Corsa*, at Via Marconi 47, and *Da*

Vittorio, on Corso Battellieri (both closed Mon in winter). Otherwise, there is plenty of choice when it comes to pizzas and fast food on and around the main piazza. For **drinks**, the modish *Barone Rosso* at Via Venti Settembre 26 has loads of character and stays open till the small hours in summer (closed Mon in winter); *L'Oblo* at Via Garibaldi 23 is another pub which also offers a good-value tourist menu (closed Wed).

During the first week of September, Carloforte hosts an **international festival** of film, music, theatre and dance, with nightly performances by big-name companies or stars (tickets L5000 or L20,000 for the whole week). Contact the tourist office for details. The **Festa di San Pietro** is another highlight of the year: a picturesque procession of boats taking place at the end of June.

A summer **bus service** links Carloforte with La Punta, Capo Sándalo and La Caletta, with a stop on Piazza Carlo Emanuele. An ideal way to see the island would be **by bicycle or scooter**, for which you'll find a hire shop at Corso Cavour 28, *Viracaruggi*, offering scooters for L50,000 a day and mountain bikes for L20,000; in winter, when the shop closes, call ☎0368.305.5554. If you're moving on to the Sardinian mainland from Carloforte, **ferries** leave once or twice an hour on the 30-minute crossing to Portvesme, the port next to the industrial plant at Portoscuso.

Sulcis and the southwest coast

One of the best ways to explore San Pietro's coast is by boat. Tours depart from Carloforte at 10.30am and 3pm daily in summer, visiting all the most important grottoes and some secluded beaches. Tickets (L20,000 per person) can be bought from the port-side kiosk (☎0781.854.2 44).

Portoscuso

The smoking stacks of **PORTOSCUSO** are the biggest blot on the otherwise undeveloped coast of Sulcis. Built as an aluminium extraction plant after coal exports dried up following World War II, Portoscuso looks worse from afar than it does close up, and does not suffer from the chemical-tainted air that permeates Sarroch. There's an attractive fishing port where you can see the old tuna fisheries, and even if there's nothing else of particular interest, Portoscuso does have a range of useful facilities: Avis and Hertz **car hire** agencies on the main road into town, a Banco di Sardegna with a cash machine, and a couple of good **hotels**. Cheapest of these is the simple *Mistral* on Via de Gásperi above its own restaurant (☎0781.509.230; ②; no CCs), though there's not much difference pricewise between this and the much plusher and quieter *Panorama* (☎ & fax 0781.508.077; ③), a three-star hotel on the main Via Giúlio Césare with rooms overlooking the pretty fishing port, but without a restaurant.

Carbónia

Mussolini's push for self-sufficiency in the 1930s led to a series of initiatives to boost Sardinia's economy, the most ambitious of which was the founding of **CARBÓNIA** in 1938 as a coal-mining centre. With the dwindling of mining operations since the 1950s, mainly due to the costs of extraction and the poor quality of "Sulcis coal", the town has lost much of its raison d'être, but it's still worth a visit on account of its historical interest – you can sense the Duce's presence in the orderly streets of regimented workers' houses that give the place such an un-Sardinian air – and its excellent museums of archeology and paleontology.

Far from being the fulcrum of local industry that Mussolini had intended, Carbónia now has a high level of unemployment, which gives the place a somewhat somnolent air. At the centre of town, the broad, shapeless **Piazza Roma** is dominated by the red tower of San Ponziano (a copy of the campanile of the cathedral of Aquileia) and the stout, foursquare Municipio. Leading down off the piazza, modern shops and restaurants line Viale Gramsci, but any vitality that this and the neighbouring streets might possess is soon dissipated as they give way to anonymous, right-angled residential quarters.

A drink in a pavement café on Piazza Roma should be enough to absorb the atmosphere before striking out down Via Nápoli to the Giardino Púbblico, site of Carbónia's **Museo Archeologico** (Tues–Sun 9am–1pm & 4–8pm; L4000, or L7000 with Museo Paleontologico). Housed in the former residence of the director of the local mining operations, this well-displayed collection consists mainly of finds from Monte Sirai (see opposite). The most noteworthy exhibits are from the tombs found in the necropolis there: bone, silver and gold ornaments from the sixth century BC; an iron dagger, and a necklace made of bone and shells. In one corner of the museum, a computer gives a good overview of the excavations, allowing you to view the site as it must have once appeared and home in on details, with full explanations (in Italian). There are also objects from further afield, including a smattering of pre-nuraghic items from the so-called Bonnanaro culture – necklaces and domestic implements – and Phoenician and Carthaginian amphorae from Sant'Antíoco.

Across the park, in Via Campania, take time to view the **Museo Paleontologico-Speleologico** (Tues–Sun 9am–1pm & 4–8pm; L4000, or L7000 with Museo Archeologico), a couple of rooms filled with rock specimens, fossils and cave-delving bric-a-brac. Even a total ignorance of paleontology, mineralogy and speleology shouldn't prevent the items here eliciting some interest: the Sulcis area holds the oldest fossils anywhere in Italy, and the display is augmented by non-Italian material donated from around the world, such as echinoids, or sea-urchins, from Mexico. The paleontological section progresses in a chronological order, the oldest exhibits being trilobites from 590–225 million years ago. Ammonites from the mesozoic era (225–65 million years ago) are followed by corals, fish, fossilized wood and even four ants in amber. From the quaternary period (about a million years ago), a fossilized tree trunk, a skeletal reconstruction of the *Prolagus sardus* rodent unique to Sardinia (a sort of tailless rabbit extinct for the last thousand years), and the jaws and tusk of a dwarf elephant from the Palermo area take us up to the present. The speleological collection is smaller, mainly photos and diagrams of local cave complexes, and a few glass cases containing bits and pieces of equipment.

Practicalities

Carbónia's Piazza Roma is the terminus for **buses** from Cágliari, Iglésias and Sant'Antíoco, and for the regular local buses that connect the train station a couple of kilometres below town. There are no hotels here (the nearest are at Gonnesa, p.134, Portoscuso, p.125, and Iglésias, p.128), but if you want **to eat**, *La Paninoteca* provides sit-down ice creams and snacks on Viale Gramsci; for a full meal, go round the corner to the *Ristorante Bovo* on Via Costituente, where they have an extensive and very reasonably-priced menu (closed Sun).

Monte Sirai

Four kilometres northwest of Carbónia, off the SS126 Iglésias road, a poorly-marked turning leads up to the high, flat top of **Monte Sirai** (there is no bus service). Ejecting a pre-existent nuraghic settlement, Phoenicians occupied the site around the eighth century BC. They were displaced in turn by Carthaginians at the end of the sixth century BC, who made this their principal military base in the whole of Sardinia. The Romans then occupied the site, but abandoned it at the end of the second century AD for reasons which have never been identified.

The strategic advantages of the location are immediately obvious: from a height of nearly 200m, it dominates the surrounding tracts of sea and land for an immense distance. Today the view encompasses the stacks and industrial paraphernalia of Portoscuso as well as the islands of Sant'Antíoco and San Pietro, but it is still a thrilling vantage point. The **site** (9am–1hr before sunset; L5000) was first excavated in 1966 by a Tunisian team, which unearthed three streets of terraced houses, of which only the foundations remain; everything else, made of mud and straw, had long since disappeared. Later, the tombs of a substantial necropolis came to light, marked with the symbols of Tanit, the Phoenician goddess: a circle, horizontal line and triangle, resembling if anything a character from *Charlie Brown*. Some of the tombs can be entered, and you can see Tanit's symbol – for some reason upside down – in tomb number five. Apart from the red rubble of the crumbled walls, there is little left to see here of the Phoenician/Carthaginian settlement; anyway, the main interest lies in the glorious location, with dwarf palms and olive trees bent almost double under the force of the *maestrale* wind; the panorama is best at sunset.

The Iglesiente

The Iglesiente is the name for the mainly mountainous and sparsely populated region north of Sulcis, centred on the town of **Iglésias**, 25km north of Carbónia and 57km due west of Cágliari. Though it lacks much tourist infrastructure, this inland town is the biggest and liveliest in the area, with a handful of medieval churches worth looking into and the impressive ruins of a huge mine on the outskirts. The Iglesiente coast benefits from the lack of development, though the tourist industry is beginning to wake up to the charms of the highly scenic **Golfo di Gonnesa**, swamping the old mining town of **Buggerru** with holiday villas. Elsewhere, the coast maintains an almost pristine feel, nowhere more than on the **Costa Verde** – acres of untrammelled sand washed by uncontaminated sea.

Public transport facilities are rudimentary throughout the region, though Iglésias is connected to Cágliari by **train** and FMS **bus**, and there are infrequent ARST and FMS bus services from Iglésias to the coast. For all practical purposes, however, you need your own transport to do any exploring.

Iglésias

Surrounded by mine-shafts and quarries gouged out of the red rock, the principal city of the Iglesiente region, **IGLÉSIAS**, is an appealing place to stop, with a decidedly Spanish-tinged atmosphere, especially during its flamboyant Easter festivities. The town is also a viable base for exploring the clutch of beach resorts a short drive away, which have little in the way of accommodation. In fact, there's not a great choice in Iglésias either, but since the place is way off the tourist trail, there's a good chance of finding room in one of its three hotels.

Best known for its numerous churches, of which a good number survive, Iglésias was formerly known as Villa di Chiesa. Its livelihood has depended more on its **mining** operations, however; indeed, the town owes its foundation to the notorious Pisan Count Ugolino della Gherardesca (see box on p.130), who re-opened the old Roman mines in the thirteenth century. Gold, silver, iron, zinc and lead have all been extracted here at different times, making Iglésias the chief mining centre of Sardinia, despite bearing small resemblance to the stereotyped image of a grimy mining town.

Arrival, information and accommodation

The main **FS train station** is on Via Salvatore, while all out-of-town buses stop at the **Giardini Púbblici**, on Via Oristano (tickets and timetables from the bar opposite the stop). Both of these entry points are a five-minute walk from **Piazza Quintino Sella**, the centre of the new town. The **Pro Loco** is housed in the public library just off Piazza Sella on Via Gramsci (Mon–Fri 9.30am–1pm & 4–7pm, Sat

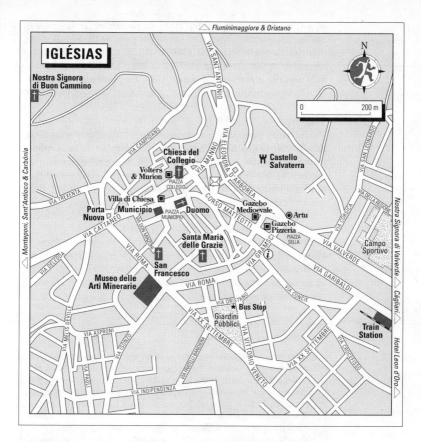

9am–12.30pm; ☎0781.41.795) – worth calling in on for a town map, but good for little else. Two **banks** on Piazza Sella – at the bottom, and at the junction with Corso Matteotti – have exchange facilities and cash machines.

Of the **hotels** in Iglésias – all three-star – the most central is the *Artu* (☎0781.22.492, fax 0781.22.546; ④) at Piazza Sella 15, which can't be bettered either for its premium location or for its small garage (parking is generally problematic in Iglésias). Rooms are spacious and clean, and there's a bar and restaurant. Next out is the similarly-priced *Leon d'Oro* (☎0781.33.531, fax 0781.33.530; ④), a flashy, business-traveller's hotel boasting a pool, but it's a bit of a hike to reach at Corso Colombo 72, on the eastern side of town (follow Via Crocefisso, running along the south side of the rail tracks). A third hotel, *Il Sillabario* (☎0781.33.830, fax 0781.33.790; ④), also geared towards expense-account travellers, is even further out, 6km east of town on the main SS130, so only useful to drivers. If you're coming this far out you might

The best Web site for general information on Iglésias, including museums, exhibitions, transport and a street map, is iglesias. tiscalinet.it

as well cut your bills by staying at the far pleasanter *Lo Sperone*, an *agriturismo* clearly signposted just below town on the SS126 south, opposite the Masua turn-off (☎0781.36.247; ②; no CCs). It's a relaxed spot, convenient for the Fontanamare beach (see p.134) and they also run a **stables**. Otherwise, there's a *pensione* at Gonnesa, 7km further south (p.134).

The town

The focus of the action in the modern town is the central **Piazza Sella**, named after the local benefactor and vintner Quintino Sella, whose Sella & Mosca wine is one of Sardinia's best. Surrounded by roads, the piazza is a lively forum by day, and the noisy meeting place of a throng of people every night. At the top end of the square, what's left of the ruined Aragonese (originally Pisan) **Castello Salvaterra** crowns a knoll, its impact softened by landscaped flowerbeds. The castle is currently closed except for occasional exhibitions.

The old town's labyrinth of lanes and traffic-free squares runs off Piazza Sella's western side. Pedestrianized Corso Matteotti is the main artery, threading through the heart of the *città vecchia* almost as far as the sequestered **Piazza Município**, the only true square in the old town and one of the few really typical Italian piazzas on the

---

Ugolino della Gherardesca

Iglésias enjoyed its greatest prosperity under the rule of the Gherardesca family, one of the foremost Tuscan dynasties, whose lands included the counties of Gherardesca, Donoratico, and Montescudaio, near Pisa. At the beginning of the thirteenth century, they led the pro-imperial Ghibelline party of the Pisan republic against the pro-papal Guelf party led by the Visconti family of Milan, but **Ugolino della Gherardesca** (died 1289) became the most reviled member of the family by switching allegiance from the Ghibellines to the Guelfs. Having assumed control as the tyrannical master of Pisa, he soon alienated his allies, and was eventually accused of treason in 1288 by the archbishop Ruggieri degli Ubaldini, who wanted to revive the republican order. Imprisoned in the tower of Gualandi along with two of his sons and two of his grandsons, Ugolino was said to have eaten his own children before himself dying of starvation, an event depicted in numerous works of art, most famously in Dante's *Divina Commedia*, in which the poet encounters the tyrant frozen in the ice of the ninth circle of hell (*Inferno*, canto 33); Archbishop Ruggieri's also there.

Ugolino is remembered with more affection in Iglésias, where, in the course of exploiting the area's mineral resources, he succeeded in introducing Tuscan methods of planning and political organization. The resulting statutory code of local rights was enshrined in a *Breve*, or law book, a meticulously drafted volume which is viewable on application in the town's Archivio Stórico, in Via delle Cárceri, near the church of Santa Maria delle Grázie (Mon–Fri 9am–1pm & 4–7pm, Sat 9am–1pm & 5–8pm; ☎0781.24.850). Ugolino's son, Guelfo, was imprisoned in the Castello di Acquafredda (see p.133).

---

whole island. It's an elegant composition, with the town hall taking up one entire side opposite the cathedral and bishop's palace, which are joined by a harmonious enclosed bridge. The **Duomo** itself (daily 8am–1pm & 5–7pm, but usually closed Thurs) shows a mixture of Pisan and Aragonese styles, reflecting the two dominant (and warring) powers in Iglésias during the Middle Ages, though the building wasn't completed until the seventeenth century. The bell in the squat tower was cast by the great Tuscan sculptor Andrea Pisano in 1337. In the low-vaulted, sparsely-decorated interior, the main interest is in the corroded angels carved on the capitals, and, more spectacularly, the huge gilded altar piece in the left transept. This was carved in the seventeenth century to hold the relics of Saint Antiochus, removed here for safekeeping from the church at Sant'Antíoco during a spate of pirate raids. However, the bones – which were kept behind the curtain in the middle panel – were forcibly reclaimed in the nineteenth century after the clerics of Iglésias refused to return them. An image of the saint adorns the front of the sculpture, his hands blackened, according to legend, from the barrel of pitch in which he had been forced to hide to escape persecution; and Saint Antiochus appears again in the painting behind the altar in the bottom left corner, opposite Saint Clare.

Across the piazza from the Duomo, take Via Pullo to reach the church of **San Francesco** (daily 9–11am & 5–7pm), a predominantly Catalan-Gothic structure built between the fourteenth and sixteenth centuries. Behind a minimalist facade of pinkish trachyte stone, pierced through with three circular windows, the nave has a wooden ceiling and seven chapels on each side, each framed by an ogival arch. Off Via Zecca, the tiny Piazza Manzo holds a much humbler church, **Santa Maria delle Grazie** (daily 9–11am & 5–7pm), its medieval base incongruously topped by a Baroque upper portion, squeezed between houses on either side.

The other historic churches of Iglésias can be a labour to reach, but you might make an effort to track down **Nostra Signora di Valverde**, behind the station near the cemetery. Dating from the end of the thirteenth century, the facade is similar to that of the Duomo, though here the austerity is relieved by lively carvings of animals. Lastly, on the hill behind this city of churches stands the simple white **Nostra Signora di Buoncammino**, reconstructed in 1968 according to its original eighteenth-century design. It's well worth the drive or hike (up a track off Via Campidano, off the Fluminimaggiore road) for the excellent views of the town and its surrounding mountains if nothing else.

The more down-to-earth side of Iglésias is represented by its Art Nouveau-style mining institute on Via Roma, which houses the **Museo delle Arti Minerárie** (Fri–Sun 7–9.30pm; free). The museum displays mining machinery and recreations of the pit face, though the real attraction here is the 8000-odd specimens of the minerals dug up out of the rock in the area. It's worth checking times of opening before heading out to this exhibition, since it keeps erratic hours: contact the tourist office or call ☎0781.22.304 for the latest update. If you're really keen on the industrial archeology of the area, you should make a point of seeing the evocative site at **Monteponi**, a vast desolate area of mineworkings west of town, visible as you enter Iglésias on the SS126. The place was abandoned surprisingly recently – given the extent of its decay – in 1992, when most of the operation was transferred across to Campo Pisano, visible across the valley. For tours of the ruins, contact Cooperativa La Gherardesca opposite the church of San Francesco at Via Don Minzoni 62 (Mon–Fri 9am–1pm & 4–7pm; ☎0781.33.850). Costs are worked out according to the length of tour, number of people, and so on; a two- to three-hour tour, for example, might cost L7–15,000 per person.

The enthusiastic guides of Cooperativa La Gherardesca can reveal esoteric niches of Iglésias you wouldn't easily find on your own. Costs start from around L5000 per head.

Eating, drinking and entertainment

It is not only hotels that Iglésias lacks: the town isn't so hot on **restaurant** facilities, either. The best location – though not necessarily the best food or prices – can be found at the *Villa di Chiesa* on Piazza Municipio, where you can eat in the square in summer (closed Mon Oct–June). For indoor atmosphere, choose *Gazebo Medioevale*, a medievally styled brick-vaulted hall at Via Musio 27, off Corso Matteotti; there's a regular restaurant menu with moderate prices and again, somewhat mediocre food (closed Sun; no CCs). The same family runs a plainer pizzeria one alley down the Corso, on Vico Matteotti (evenings only; no CCs). Both are closed for two weeks in August/September. The *Volters & Murion* pub, with outdoor seating on Piazza Collegio, offers an all-in fish meal for L18,000, or you might just come here for a late-night **drink** (closed Tues Oct–May; no CCs). Finally, to stock up on do-it-yourself meals, there's an indoor **market** open Monday–Saturday mornings up from the Pro Loco on Via Gramsci.

In summer, outdoor concerts take place at various points of the old town, and there's open-air cinema in Piazza Collegio. The Pro Loco has a full list of events.

Iglésias Festivals

Iglésias comes into its own during its famous **Easter festivities**, when processions weave solemnly between the churches of the old town in a tradition that dates back to the seventeenth century. Marching to the rhythm of traditional instruments, the white robed, sometimes cowled, cortège (the dress is known as *baballotti*) performs this ritual during the whole of Easter week, though the highlight is the second procession, Christ's funeral, on Good Friday evening. Another traditional ceremony, I Candelieri, takes place on or around August 15. As in the better-known *festa* at Sássari that occurs on the same day (see box on p.227), seven (sometimes eight) huge candles, one for each section of the city, are borne through the streets in the evening, from the Chiesa del Collegio to the cathedral, to be returned eight days later. If you're thinking of visiting Iglésias at any of these times, fix up your accommodation first.

Old town Cágliari

The waterfront at Bosa

Musicians playing *launeddas*

Santa Trinità di Saccargia, near Sássari

The festival of Sa Sartiglia, Oristano

A reservoir in a wooded valley near Iglésias

Piazza d'Italia, Sássari

Old town and cathedral, Cágliari

Fishing boats at Castelsardo

Capo Caccia, near Alghero   The ancient city at Nora

Around Iglésias: the Grotta di San Giovanni and the Témpio di Antas

The SS130 dual carriageway runs due east of Iglésias over mainly flat terrain, connecting drivers with Cágliari in less than an hour. If you're not in a hurry, make a detour at Domusnovas, 10km east of Iglésias. Signposted at the back of the village, a small road straggles 4km to the **Grotta di San Giovanni**, a 750m-long natural rock tunnel large enough for you to drive through. It's the only example of such a phenomenon in Italy, and a disconcerting, rather eerie experience. Beyond the tunnel there's a bar and restaurant, and thick woods which provide some nice picnicking spots, though you can't penetrate far into the tangled vegetation. The road soon deteriorates to a dirt track that climbs high into the mountains. In theory it's feasible to follow this road as far as the Témpio di Antas, but in practice there are no markers and it's easy to get lost: the preferable route is north from Iglésias (see below).

Further east along the Cágliari road, look out for the ruins of the **Castello di Acquafredda**, on a jagged elevation 4km south of Siliqua. Built in the thirteenth century, the castle was the prison for Guelfo, son of Ugolino della Gherardesca (see box on p.130). If you want to stretch your legs, it's a steep but intensely panoramic climb to the top.

Fifteen kilometres north of Iglésias, a right turn off the twisty mountain road to Fluminimaggiore (the SS126) wanders down a valley to the remote **Témpio di Antas**, a Roman temple built on the site of a nuraghic and later Carthaginian sanctuary. Its Punic origins are thought to date back to around 500 BC, but it probably assumed its final form in the third century AD. As an inscription records, the Romans dedicated the temple to Sardus Pater Babay, a local deity worshipped as the father of the Sards in the kind of synthesis of imperial and local cults that was practised throughout the Roman Empire. The Ionic-style columns are still standing, topped by a simple pediment, and you can see inside the remains of the sacred chambers, while rooms and houses used by the priests and other members of the ethnically mixed population are faintly visible behind. It's an idyllic spot, the air full of the aromas of the *macchia* and the jangle of distant goat bells, spoiled only by the pylons and cables strung across the valley.

A little way north of the Témpio di Antas, the **Grotta Su Mannau** (daily: April to June & mid-Sept to Oct 9.30am–7.30pm; July to mid-Sept 9.30am–6.30pm; L7000) is one of the most accessible of the many grottoes scattered throughout this area. A tourist trail penetrates for 350m, enough to see some spectacular rock formations, while cavers can go for about a kilometre inside the mountain. Tours last 50 minutes, leaving every half hour. In winter, call Fluminimaggiore's Società Su Mannau Grotte, Via Vittorio Emanuele 81 (☎0781.580.189 or 0347.687.748) for bookings. The organization will also provide information about guided walks and expeditions to the grotto.

The Iglesiente coast

West of Iglésias, the remote villages and beaches on the coast have few transport links with the outside world, but are easily accessible under your own steam. The villages and resorts here are hardly the attraction anyway: the real appeal is the refreshing emptiness of the coast, either cliff-hung tracts or wildernesses of bare dunes. Getting to the best places may involve a lengthy haul along dirt roads, so make sure your vehicle is in good working order. Accommodation, too, is scarce: all options have been listed here, though you should be prepared to travel to a hotel or campsite.

The Golfo di Gonnesa

The coast of the **Golfo di Gonnesa** is mainly high and cliffy, with the exception of one good beach which attracts crowds from Iglésias and from inland **Gonnesa**, 9km southwest of Iglésias. This fairly unremarkable village has a useful **hotel**, the basic but clean and friendly *Frau*, next to the *Bar La Piazzetta* on Via della Pace (☎0781.45.104; ①; no CCs); there's a restaurant here too, and a bank nearby.

From the SS126, a road branches west to the long sandy beach at **Fontanamare**, just 4km from Gonnesa. It's a popular bathing spot, with bars and a pizzeria open in summer, but quiet the rest of the time. There are no other facilities until you reach the nearby village of **Nébida**, high above the coast, at the far end of which the *Pan di Zúcchero* hotel offers simple **accommodation**, including some rooms with good views and a restaurant (☎0781.47.114; ②). A small lane next to the hotel dives steeply down to a tiny sandy cove, **Porto Banda**, where two large *faraglioni*, needle-shaped stacks of rock, poke up from the sea. Elsewhere in the village, next to a public garden and sports ground, a path rounding a cliff face gives access to a **belvedere** offering the area's best views of the sheer coast on either side, as far as the Pan di Zúcchero *scoglio* to the north (see below). Below this path, at the bottom of a 400-step descent, the **Laveria La Mármora** is an impressive structure from 1897, used for filtering and washing mine products. Now abandoned, the building can only be entered with a guide (contact Cooperativa La Gherardesca in Iglésias, p.132). A **bar** built into a grotto on the cliff path, *Café del Operáio*, serves drinks and snacks until late.

North of Nébida, the mountain road winds three or four kilometres on to **Masua**. Another huge mining site dominates the knot of houses here, dedicated to extracting zinc and lead, the two main products of this region. Below, a lovely but restricted beach backed by shade-giving rocks and ruined walls faces the colossal outcrop known as the **Pan di Zúcchero**, whose prodigious white hulk is depicted on countless postcards. Owing its name, "Sugarloaf", to its unique shape, it's said to be the oldest such *scoglio*, or rock formation, in Italy. From Masua, where there are bars and a pizzeria, a tortuous road climbs inland; it's mostly untarmacked, though work is currently being carried out to upgrade it.

Ten kilometres along, **Buggerru** is a fishing port and tourist resort superimposed on another old mining centre. Once accessible only by sea, Buggerru was largely self-sufficient during its mining days; it was the first place in Sardinia to have a regular electrical system, and the miners enjoyed health and recreational facilities long before such practices were introduced by other companies. Today, the ram-shackle remains of the mine buildings overlooking a regimented marina packed with small pleasure boats are the most attractive thing about this overdeveloped resort, though there are some superb **beaches** in the vicinity. The most solitary of these is at **Cala Domestica**, little more than a deep, sheltered sandy inlet (bring your own shade) four or five kilometres south of Buggerru; alternatively, you can head north to the much wider **Portixeddu**, a sweeping swathe of sand with little or no construction nearby. Eight hundred metres inland of here, *Ortus de Mari* offers **camping** with minimal facilities (June–Sept; ☎0781.54.964), the only site on this stretch of coast. The road ends a little further north at **Capo Pécora**, a good deserted spot with a small stony beach.

The Costa Verde

There is little that's "green" about the **Costa Verde**, stretching north from Capo Pécora, most of it consisting of arid rock, scrub and sand. Access is from the SS126, either from the village of Gúspini, from where a road twists for 25km to the desolate coast, or, 13km further south, via the dirt road threading westwards from the deserted mining town of **Ingurtosu**. If your car can stand it, this is the preferable route; it's shorter, and allows a stop at the ghostly ruins of this once vibrant community. Nine kilometres below, the road emerges on the coast at **Piscinas**, a barren spot, about as remote as it gets in Sardinia, with superb swimming. Apart from a few traces of nine-teenth-century mineworks, there is nothing here but immense sand dunes – and the thankfully subdued *Hotel Le Dune* (☎070.977.130, fax 070.977.230; ⑦). If you can afford the bill (with prices ranging from L115–160,000 per person for half-board) at this chic luxury retreat, it would be a fabulous place to hole up for a few days. If not, you may be grateful for the bar, which serves *panini*, and (expen-sive) restaurant facilities, which are available to anyone – there's absolutely nowhere else to eat around here. If you don't want to pay to stay, free camping would be feasible in this out-of-the-way area.

From Piscinas, another dirt road follows the coast north, passing more dune-backed sands and perfect seas, until it meets civilization among the holiday homes of Marina di Arbus. There are shops and restaurants here, and more stupendous beaches to the north. One of these, **Funtanazza**, below and out of sight of an eyesore of a ruined 1950s holiday complex, lies along a private road that is barred at night, but otherwise open to anyone. Another 10km north, **Torre dei Corsari** has another broad sand beach with high dunes. The towering

One of Sardinia's most productive mining areas was centred on Montevecchio, 10km west of Gúspini on the road to the coast. The grand, mostly well-preserved buildings stand at Villaggio Gennas, Villaggio Telle and Laveria Sanna, in the hills around Montevecchio. For guided tours, call ☎0368.538. 997.

cliffs beyond, ending at **Capo Frasca**, are inaccessible by land, though there is a causeway across the Stagno di Marceddi to the east, from which you pass into Oristano province.

Travel Details

TRAINS

Carbónia to: Cágliari (Mon–Sat 3 daily; 1hr); Villamassárgia (Mon–Sat 13 daily, Sun 4; 25min).

Iglésias to: Cágliari (Mon–Sat 12 daily, Sun 5; 1hr); Villamassárgia (Mon–Sat 14 daily, Sun 7; 10min).

Villamassárgia to: Cágliari (Mon–Sat 15 daily, Sun 7; 45min); Carbónia (Mon–Sat 11 daily, Sun 4; 20min); Iglésias (Mon–Sat 13 daily, Sun 7; 10min).

BUSES

Calasetta to: Cágliari (Mon–Sat 4 daily, Sun 2; 2hr 10min–2hr 30min); Carbónia (Mon–Sat 8–14 daily, Sun 3; 50min–1hr); Iglésias (Mon–Sat 2–4 daily; 1hr 25min–1hr 45min); Sant'Antíoco (Mon–Sat 9–13 daily, Sun 4; 20–25min).

Carbónia to: Cágliari (Mon–Sat 5 daily, Sun 2; 1hr 20min–1hr 40min); Calasetta (Mon–Sat 4–5 daily, Sun 6; 50min); Iglésias (Mon–Sat 8–9 daily, Sun 7; 45min); Portoscuso (Mon–Sat 9–14 daily, Sun 4; 45min); Sant'Antíoco (Mon–Sat 4–5 daily, Sun 6; 30min).

Giba to: Portopino (Mon–Sat 1–4 daily; 20min).

Iglésias to: Buggerru (Mon–Sat 6–7 daily, Sun 4; 1hr 15min); Cágliari (Mon–Sat 8–10 daily, Sun 6; 1hr); Calasetta (4–5 daily; 1hr 45min); Carbónia (Mon–Sat 8–9 daily, Sun 7; 45min); Fontanamare (Mon–Sat 10 daily, Sun 3; 17min); Gonnesa (Mon–Sat 3–4 daily, Sun 1; 20min); Masua (Mon–Sat 10 daily, Sun 3; 20min); Nébida (Mon–Sat 10 daily, Sun 3; 25min); Portixeddu (Mon–Sat 6–7 daily, Sun 4; 1hr 5min); Portoscuso/Portovesme (Mon–Sat 5–9 daily, Sun 1; 1hr 20min); Sant'Antíoco (Mon–Sat 3–4 daily, Sun 6; 1hr 10min).

Portoscuso/Portovesme to: Cágliari (Mon–Sat 3 daily, Sun 2; 1hr 50min–2hr 10min); Carbónia (Mon–Sat 9–14 daily, Sun 4; 45min); Iglésias (Mon–Sat 8 daily, Sun 1; 1hr 30min).

Pula to: Cágliari (Mon–Sat 1–2 hourly, Sun 5–7 daily; 50min); Santa Margherita di Pula (Mon–Sat hourly, Sun 6–7 daily; 10min); Chia (Mon–Sat hourly, Sun 6–7 daily; 25min); Teulada (Mon–Sat 6–9 daily, Sun 5–6 daily; 1hr).

Sant'Antíoco to: Cágliari (Mon–Sat 4 daily, Sun 2; 1hr 50min–2hr 10min); Calasetta (Mon–Sat 9–13 daily, Sun 4; 20–25min); Carbónia (Mon–Sat 8–14 daily, Sun 3; 30min); Iglésias (Mon–Sat 3–4 daily, Sun 6; 1hr 20min).

Teulada to: Porto di Teulada (summer only, Mon–Sat 3 daily, Sun 1; 15min).

FERRIES

Calasetta to: Carloforte (hourly; 40min).

Carloforte to: Calasetta (hourly; 40min); Portovesme (1–2 hourly; 30min).

Portovesme to: Carloforte (1–2 hourly; 30min).

Chapter 3

Campidano and
La Marmilla

The plain of **Campidano**, which lies to the northwest of Cágliari, is Sardinia's richest agricultural region, the beneficiary of numerous rivers as well as an extensive drainage and reclamation scheme and anti-malaria programme. Its flatness was exploited by King Carlo Felice in the 1820s when he routed the long highway which still bears his name, through the region. This road, now the fast SS131 dual carriageway, is essential if you're hurrying northward, though you might miss some spots of historic and scenic interest lying on or just off Sardinia's main artery.

Many of these could be visited on brief excursions out of Cágliari, the nearest of them being the lovely early Romanesque church at **Uta** and the "open-air museum" of **San Sperate**, both villages to the west of the main route. Campidano's biggest town, **Sanluri**, 45km up from Cágliari, holds the island's best-preserved medieval castle, a linchpin of the Sard-Aragonese conflict that embroiled Sardinia during the fourteenth and fifteenth centuries. The much more derelict **Castello di Monreale** caps a hill a little way northwest of here, close to one of Sardinia's oldest thermal baths outside **Sárdara**.

East of the SS131, in the northern reaches of the province of Cágliari, the uniformity of Campidano gives way to the hill country of **La Marmilla**. Named after the mammary-shaped elevations that characterize the landscape, the zone has some of the island's most important nuraghic remains, such as **Genna Maria**, near Villanovaforru, and the biggest and most famous of all, **Su Nuraxi**. If you have no time to see any of the island's other nuraghic monuments, make a point of visiting this one, a good taste of the primitive grandeur of the island's only indigenous civilization. The site lies a kilometre outside the village of **Barúmini**, 50km north of Cágliari and served by infrequent bus services from the capital.

To the north, La Marmilla ends at the high tableland of **Giara di Gésturi**, an uninhabited region that is one of the last refuges of Sardinia's miniature wild ponies. You'll need a little luck and a lot of

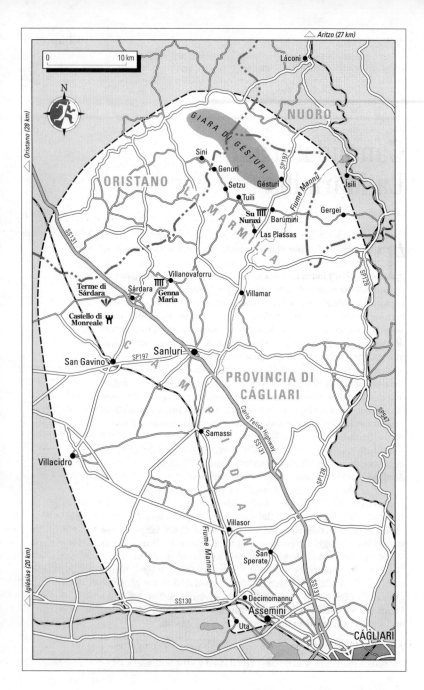

cunning to spot these shy creatures, but in any case it's an excellent spot for walking, and in the spring the area is a regular stopover for migrating birds.

Situated well off Sardinia's main tourist track, these areas have a serious shortage of accommodation and restaurants. The few useful **hotels** are detailed here, though a much larger choice can be found in Cágliari, Oristano and the Bárbagia, which are probably your ultimate destinations on your way through the area. All the stops mentioned in this chapter could be visited from these places, either as day trips or en route to other places further north in the provinces of Nuoro or Oristano. The snag for non-drivers is access. Although **buses** do reach most of the smaller villages, services are often extremely sketchy. **Trains** between Cágliari and Oristano follow the same trajectory as the SS131, though they don't stop anywhere very useful, except for Decimomannu, which is close to Uta and San Sperate, and San Gavino, handy for Sanluri and Sárdara.

For more information on bus and train connections, see Travel Details, p.152.

Campidano

If the plain of **Campidano**, which extends featurelessly for a hundred kilometres between Cágliari and Oristano, lacks the scenic drama of Sardinia's more mountainous zones, it still packs quite a weight of history. If you have a loose schedule, you might make a brief detour from the Carlo Felice highway to visit the Romanesque church of Santa Maria outside the village of **Uta**, about 20km out of Cágliari off the SS130 Iglésias road. You could combine it with a tour of the gallery of murals and sculptures on display at **San Sperate**, 12km northeast. Otherwise, speed up the SS131 to **Sanluri**, holding Sardinia's only continuously inhabited medieval castle, one of the last strongholds of resistance against the Aragonese aggressors. Today it is the home of the counts of Villa Santa, who have created within an absorbing museum that recalls another struggle against foreign oppression, the

Risorgimento – Italy's lurch to nationhood in the nineteenth century. Note that opening times to the castle are severely restricted, so you'll need to time your visit here if you want to see inside. Further up the SS131, **Sárdara** is known for its weaving industry and its curative waters, appreciated since nuraghic times.

The Campidano has few **hotel** options; if you want to make an overnight stop, try the small selection in Sárdara and Sanluri. All places mentioned here are accessible on frequent ARST **buses** from Cágliari; PANI buses from Cágliari and Oristano are the quickest way to reach Sanluri and Sárdara. By **train**, both towns are close to the station at San Gavino, 9km west of Sanluri and 7km south of Sárdara; Sanluri's own station has less frequent connections and is 5km southwest of town anyway; buses and taxis can transport you from the stations into town.

Uta and San Sperate

West of Cágliari, the small towns of Decimomannu and Assémini are renowned for their decorated ceramic output as well as for their eel-filled *panadas* (pasta cakes), though neither place has much else to merit more than a quick passage through. Six kilometres west of those towns, however, on the other side of the Mannu river flowing into the Stagno di Cágliari, the agricultural centre of UTA has perhaps southern Sardinia's loveliest Romanesque church, built by the Vittorini monks from Marseille around 1140. **Santa Maria** (May–Sept daily 9am–12.30pm & 3–8.30pm) stands by itself at the eastern end of the village, its light stonework embellished with arcading running round under the roof, at the base of which human heads, rams, dogs, stags, calves and various abstract devices are chiselled. This florid Provençal style is fused with Pisan elements, apparent in the portals and the bare interior, where two columns of perfect round arches have well-restored capitals. The Benedictine Vittorini house was as instrumental in diffusing Romanesque building styles in the south of Sardinia as the Tuscans and Lombards were in the island's north – its great influence proceeding from the good relations with the papacy and the Sardinian *giudici* that the order enjoyed after 1089, when it was assigned the churches of San Saturno in Cágliari, Sant'Efisio in Nora and Sant'Antíoco in the town of the same name. Eventually, the Vittorini even took over control of Cágliari's salt pans.

Make a circuit round the church's outside to appreciate the intricate carving of the figures and differently-coloured stones used in Santa Maria's construction. During the last week of August, the **Festa di Santa Lucia** is celebrated with a procession to the church of peasant carts, or *traccas*.

Six kilometres northeast of Decimomannu, **SAN SPERATE** is famous for its murals and sculptures. The startling images daubed over the walls of houses are not as vibrant as those in Orgósolo, near Nuoro (see p.325), but there are still some fine works to be seen, in

Fuelled by the nearby military base at Decimomannu, one of Sardinia's biggest concentration of discos is clustered in and around Assémini. The hottest places are currently Eurogarden (Via Trieste 15); Kilton (Piazza Don Bosco 5); K2 (Via Sardegna 2), and Woodstock (Via Sicilia).

a variety of styles, including *trompe l'oeil* domestic scenes, portraying an older, simpler if far more parochial society. The village also has several open-air sculptures by Sardinia's best-known contemporary sculptor, **Pinuccio Sciola**, born in San Sperate in 1942. Sciola works almost exclusively in Sardinian trachyte, whose mutating, seasoned appearance makes it particularly appropriate for his outdoor pieces, which in form resemble nothing so much as menhirs and even nuraghic *tombe dei giganti* burial stones.

Sanluri

Occupying a commanding position in the hinterland between the *giudicati* of Arborea and Cágliari, 45km to the southeast, **SANLURI** grew around the castle built here in the thirteenth century. Now named the **Castello di Eleonora d'Arborea** after Sardinia's warrior queen, who lived a century later (see pp.162–163), the castle was the venue for a treaty signed by her father Mariano IV and the Aragonese king, Pedro IV. Though this allowed the *giudice* of Arborea a measure of peace, it turned out to be merely a breathing space. Eleonora herself spent a lifetime in arms against the Aragonese with some success, but in 1409, after her death, Pedro's son, Martino, won a definitive victory at Sanluri against forces commanded by the new *giudice*, Gugliemo, husband of Eleonora's younger sister. This defeat marked the end of Arborea's resistance, and was followed by the swift occupation of almost the whole island by Aragonese forces.

The castle, a square keep surrounded by railings and fir trees, lies on the main road through the centre of Sanluri. Modern artillery pieces have been arranged on the tidy verge, but little else is revealed from outside, the high walls and four crenellated turrets (the two facing north are purely decorative) enclosing a small internal courtyard. Inside, the **Museo Risorgimentale** (March to mid-June & Oct–Dec Sun 9.30am–1pm & 3pm–sunset; mid-June to Sept Mon–Thurs 4.30–9pm) has a much wider ambit than Italy's struggle for independence in the nineteenth century, though much of it has a strong military flavour. First established by the local count, Generale Nino Villa Santa, the motley collection of curios, portraits and trophies reflects the enthusiasm of an amateur collector, though in fact it represents the fruits of various donors in the 1920s. The two floors are joined by a fine staircase, and the beamed rooms are richly furnished with rugs, tables, dressers and paintings, mainly from the eighteenth century. The soldierly theme is strongest in the two largest rooms, one above the other: the ground-floor Salone delle Milizie has photos, flags, maps and armaments from Garibaldi's campaigns against the Austrians and the Carso and Piave fronts during World War I; above, the impressively spacious Salone della Giustizia, with a Gothic-Aragonese window, focuses on the little-known Italian-Turkish war of 1911–12, Mussolini's Ethiopian campaign of 1936, Fascist mementos, and oddments from World War II, including English postcards. Other rooms hold an engaging miscellany, notably a collection of some 400 wax figurines, some dating as far back as the sixteenth century, and some by the master in the field Clemente Susini, whose works are also on display in Cágliari (see p.78). Other items to look out for include Napoleonic memorabilia, for example sabres used by Napoleon Bonaparte and his brother-in-law Joachim Murat, and an iron bed belonging to the Genoan Doria dynasty.

Further down Via Carlo Felice, prominently sited on an elevation near the centre of town, the sixteenth-century church of San Rocco stands close to another idiosyncratic collection, the **Museo Etnográfico Cappuccino** (Mon, Wed & Fri 9am–noon & 4–6pm; free), attached to a Franciscan convent and dedicated to the work of the Capuchin friars in Sardinia since 1591. On two floors, vestments, psalters and items of religious art mingle with a more practical selection of workaday items, evoking the highly active part this community played on the island in a variety of occupations. Basketwork, woodworking tools and even a collection of some sixty watches reflect the diversity of crafts with which the Franciscans occupied themselves, in accordance with the precepts eschewing idleness laid down by their order. There are also a few archeological finds from the Campidano area, mainly jewellery and coins, and a statue thought to represent the Roman Emperor Tiberius.

Practicalities

There are usually a couple of taxis lurking outside Sanluri's **train station**, 5km southwest of the centre, also a stop on some bus routes heading into town. For lunches or evening meals, head for *La Rosy*, a **ristorante/pizzeria** marked out by its lime green exterior at Via Carlo Felice 510 (☎070.930.7957; closed Fri). It's modern and capacious and does a good range of reasonably-priced meals. If you want to stay in Sanluri, the functional *Mirage* **hotel** (☎070.930.7100; ②) lies 100m further on, just by the exit onto the Carlo Felice highway (SS131) at the northern end of the village. Open all year, the hotel also houses the *Moulin Rouge* nightclub. Outside Sanluri, on the Carlo Felice road, the even less character-ful *Motel Ichnusa* has rooms with or without bath and a restaurant (☎070.930.7073; ①). Other possibilities lie outside town, in the village of Serrenti, 10km south down the SS131, where the *Campidano* hotel offers absurdly cheap but very basic facilities at Via Gramsci 38 (☎ & fax 070.915.9021; no CCs; ①), and at Samassi, about the same distance due south of Sanluri (also a stop on the rail line), where another *Campidano* (☎070.938.8121; no CCs; ②) lies near the station at Viale Stazione 29, with a restaurant. There are a couple of **banks** with exchange facilities in Sanluri's centre.

Before leaving Sanluri, pick up a loaf of the local bread. Huge and flavoursome, it's renowned throughout the Campidano.

Sárdara and the Castello di Monreale

Nine kilometres northwest of Sanluri on the SS131, **SÁRDARA** clusters around a handful of relics from the nuraghic, Roman and medieval periods. At the top of a flight of steps in the centre of the village stands the attractive fourteenth-century church of **San Gregorio**; the tall, narrow facade with its graceful rose window mixes Romanesque and Gothic styles. Late Gothic workmanship dominates in the fifteenth-century church of **Sant'Anastasia**, at the village's highest point and close to a much more ancient centre of worship, the **témpio nurághico**. Constructed in basalt and calcareous bricks, this sacred well dates from the eleventh or tenth centuries BC and is known locally as Funtana de is Dolus, or "Fountain of Pains", on account of the various ailments its waters were supposed to cure. The site, which is fenced off and cannot be entered, has yielded some notable finds, including heavily ornate water jugs, some of them to be seen in the **Museo Cívico** in Sárdara's ex-town hall on Piazza Libertà (Mon–Sat 9am–1pm; free).

The waters around Sárdara were not only valued by Sardinia's prehistoric people. The village lies close to the spa complex known to the Romans as Acquae Neapolitanae, now called the Complesso Termale di Santa Maria Is Acquas, or more simply the **Terme di Sárdara**. Lying amid pine and eucalyptus groves a couple of kilometres west of the village, the five hot springs are rich with sodium bicarbonate water that is still used to treat liver and digestive complaints. Next to the modern hotel complex (see below), the late Gothic church of **Santa Maria Is Acquas** is the venue for a festival deriving from a pagan water cult, taking place on the penultimate Monday of September.

Two kilometres to the south, the **Castello di Monreale** was one of Arborea's key strongholds, equidistant from Cágliari and Oristano and controlling the routes between those cities. The squat ruins crown a hillock overlooking the surrounding plain – an evocative backdrop, even if the sparse remains don't really merit closer exploration. Back in the village, there is an economical **hotel**, the *Sárdara* at Via Cedrino 5 (☎070.938.7811; no CCs; ②), which also has a restaurant. The spa hotel at Terme di Sárdara, eponymously named, is much pricier but you get use of all the facilities, sometimes at an extra cost (☎070.938.7200, fax 070.938.7025; ⑤).

Five kilometres south of the Castello di Monreale, and seven or eight kilometres south of Sárdara, **San Gavino Monreale** is one of the larger villages of the Campidano, site of a foundry for the lead and zinc ores extracted from the nearby mines. The village itself holds little interest, though the otherwise unremarkable fourteenth-century church of **San Gavino** hit the headlines in 1983 when portraits of the four most prominent figures of the *giudicato* of Arborea – Mariano IV, his daughter Eleonora d'Arborea (see p.141), her husband Brancaleone Doria and her brother Ugone III – were discovered in the

San Gavino is Sardinia's main centre of saffron (zafferano) production. Harvested the same day or soon after the violet-coloured Crocus Sativus has flowered, the plant is used as a dye and in cooking.

apse, the only contemporary likenesses known to exist (but unfortunately presently unviewable). The village might also prove a useful overnight stop: it's got a central station on the Cágliari–Oristano train line, and there's a decent one-star **hotel** on Piazza Césare Battista 25 (☎070.933.9053; ①), with rooms with or without private bath, and a restaurant.

La Marmilla

On the confines of Oristano and Nuoro provinces, the mildly hilly region known as **La Marmilla** is a feast of scenic variety after the monotonous plains of Campidano. Its very name, thought to derive from *mammella*, or breast, conjures up the shape of the land, the flat expanses interrupted by small, solitary protuberances, often round and regular in appearance. Traditionally a cereal-growing area, it's a zone rich in nuraghi, including two of Sardinia's most important sites – one, the recently unearthed **Genna Maria**, dating from the middle of the second millennium BC, outside the village of **Villanovaforru**, where a museum exhibits the huge quantity of graceful ceramics and other finds from the site covering a period of eight centuries. Far more striking, however, is the great nuraghic complex of **Su Nuraxi**, outside the village of **Barúmini**. It is best reached via the local SS197 leading northeast from Sanluri, a route which takes in the distinctive conical hill at **Las Plassas**, just south of Barúmini. Clearly visible on the round summit, the fragments of a twelfth-century castle are a landmark for miles around.

Beyond Barúmini, you could spend an invigorating afternoon tramping through the woods and scrubland covering the high plain of the **Giara di Gésturi**. It shelters a variety of birdlife and other fauna and flora, most famously a breed of miniature wild pony. Carless hikers can explore a good part of the plateau on foot from one of the bordering villages of Tuili, Setzu, Sini, Genuri or Gésturi, all accessible on local bus routes, as are both Barúmini and Villanovaforru.

Villanovaforru and Genna Maria

Roads trail north and east from Sanluri and Sárdara into the hills of Marmilla. At its southern fringes, the village of **VILLANOVAFORRU** was a Spanish foundation of the seventeenth century. The village has a spruce appearance, testimony to its importance as a grain market for the surrounding area. In Villanovaforru's centre, a tastefully restored villa on Piazza Costituzione holds the **Museo Archeológico** (Tues–Sun 9.30am–1pm & 3.30–6pm, 3.30–7pm in summer; L6000 including Genna Maria). It's well worth a visit by anyone also going to the nearby archeological site or anyway interested in the prehistory of the whole Marmilla zone, exhibiting some of the earliest evidence of local settlements in the Iron and Bronze Ages. The well-lit displays mostly consist of the contents of prenuraghic and nuraghic tombs: a procession of ritual vases, oil lamps (some boat-shaped), myriad brooches and necklaces, and assorted ceramics, sometimes painted with complex geometric patterns. Many of the items are distinctively polished, an effect attained using specially crafted bones. Finds from Su Nuraxi (see p.146) are well represented, and one room is entirely devoted to Carthaginian and Roman objects, including coins, the clay contents of a Punic tomb found at Villamar and part of a Roman millstone. Many of the artifacts were for domestic use, others testify to the intense religious and commercial activity that characterized this region until the Middle Ages. The importance of water to the local communities is reflected in the abundance of containers yielded up, often with elegantly curving designs.

Though stripped of its original furnishings, the villa's interior retains its beamed ceilings, arched walls and a central well on the ground floor. Behind it, the small **Museo Cívico** (same times as Museo Archeológico; free) hosts occasional exhibitions to do with the town and the region. The slow-moving village has little else to detain you, though a couple of bars and *alimentari* on or within a few steps of the piazza can provide refreshments.

Occupying the summit of the Marmilla's highest hill (408m), the **Nuraghe di Genna Maria** (summer 9.30am–12.30pm & 3.30–7pm, winter 9.30–1pm & 3.30–6pm; L6000 including archeological museum) commands far-reaching views over the surrounding area. A kilometre west of Villanovaforru, a left turn off the Collinas road leads to a car park from which it's a short but fairly steep climb up, the path lined on both sides with pungent rosemary and other herbs. The site itself covers an extensive area dominated by a central ruined tower and the surrounding circular structures of a village. The remains are in worse condition than some of Sardinia's other nuraghic monuments, partly a result of the use of local sandstone as building material, but this still ranks among the island's most important sites, not least for the quantity of finds it has yielded. First excavated between 1951 and 1954 by Sardinia's greatest archeologist, Giovanni Lilliu, but only fully revealed in 1977, the site is still the subject of digs. A raised walkway above the walls, in parts 3m high, allows you to look down on the chambers and passages of the main building, and the lower walls encircling the crowd of small rooms pressed up against it.

The difficulties of building on this elevated site are shown in the many successive stages of construction. The central keep (*mastio*) was erected during the first phase, possibly as early as the fifteenth century BC, while the quadrilobate bastion and part of the curtain wall (*antemurale*) certainly go back to the thirteenth century BC. A new phase extended over the thirteenth and twelfth centuries BC, while the village dwellings were built between the twelfth and ninth centuries BC, the beginning of Sardinia's Iron Age. Finally, the curtain wall was completed during the ninth and eighth centuries BC. The village, some

For more on Sardinia's nuraghic culture, see pp.148–149.

La Marmilla

of whose buildings have a central courtyard, was also inhabited in Carthaginian and Roman periods until the third century AD.

To one side of the site, a new stone-built construction shelters diagrams illustrating how the complex might once have looked, while one map shows how densely the Marmilla is filled with other nuraghic settlements. From this high windy spot, you can sight many of the hills and areas defined on the map, the most significant landmark being the flat and high Giara di Gésturi, northward (see p.150).

The area is desperately short of **accommodation**, although a short lane right opposite the turn-off to the site leads to *Le Colline* (☎070.930.0123, fax 070.930.0134; ②), a smart, friendly hotel, flat and modern, with great views on all sides.

Sardinian x's are pronounced either with a "sh" sound, or like the French "j". "Su Nuraxi" is thus pronounced "Su Nurashi" or "Su Nuraji".

Barúmini and Su Nuraxi

East of Villanovaforru stretches a varied landscape of cultivated fields interspersed with some pasturage, all overlooked by a horizon of knobbly brown peaks. The most prominent feature for miles around is the extraordinary conical hill of **Las Plassas** (274m), with fragments of the twelfth-century **castello di Marmilla** sticking up like broken teeth on its round pinnacle. The hill is a perfect example of the bosomy bumps characteristic of the Marmilla region. To get closer, take a left turn off the straight SS197, just before the Agip petrol station at the southern entrance to the hamlet of **Las Plassas**; alternatively a brown signpost in the village points you in the same direction. Five hundred metres along, opposite the majolica-tiled dome of the seventeenth-century church of **Santa Maria Maddalena**, a path weaves up the hillside to the scanty ruins: there is little to see of the castle itself, but the view makes it worth the brief spurt of exercise necessary to reach it. Traces of a previous nuraghic settlement have been unearthed below the castle.

Barúmini, 3km to the north of Las Plassas, is a larger though still nondescript village rather overshadowed by the fame of the nuraghic site lying just outside it. On the crossroads at the centre, the slightly offbeat seventeenth-century church of **Santa Tecla** has a swirling rose window and battlements on a square facade. Turn left here for the site of **Su Nuraxi** (daily 9am–dusk; L8000), just 500m east, the dark-grey stone of its imposing central structure surrounded by a tight mesh of walled dwellings separated by a web of lanes. Its dialect name means simply "the nuraghs", and not only is it the largest nuraghic site on the island, it's also one of the oldest, dating from around 1500 BC. Its size and complexity have attracted more funding than any other nuraghic site, and, having been continuously excavated since 1949, there is plenty to take in. Su Nuraxi was a palace complex at the very least – possibly even a capital city, though its origins remain largely obscure. The whole area is thought to have been covered with earth by Sards and Carthaginians at the time of the Roman conquest, accounting for its excellent state of preservation.

All visitors to the site are escorted by a guide who can supply a knowledgeable commentary (usually available in English), and will warn you to keep off the walls, which demand to be clambered over. The first traces of human settlement date from the middle Bronze Age (sixteenth–thirteenth centuries BC), the place was destroyed in the seventh century BC, then rebuilt and resettled until the Roman period. In between, the complex was constantly being expanded, with towers added to the central bastion, which were joined by a stone wall. The bulky **central tower** originally reached 21m (now shrunk to about 14.5m), and contained three rooms, one above the other, of which two remain. At the end of a corridor, the "tholos-type" lower chamber has alcoves once lined with cork, and an opening halfway up the walls suggesting the existence of a wooden flight of stairs to reach the next storey. To reach this room now you have to backtrack along the elaborate network of passageways and rugged steps connecting the various inner chambers. The top storey is vanished, allowing access to a good viewpoint over the whole site. Next to the central tower on ground level, a deep crescent-shaped **courtyard** holds a well still containing water, and gives onto three of the four external towers which form the corners of the quadrilobate outer defences, part of a second phase of construction, probably in the thirteenth or twelfth centuries. The height of the walls enclosing this courtyard was raised at a later period, an alteration clearly visible in the contrast between the more regular masonry of the later work and the rougher-hewn stones of the lower parts.

The outer walls were strengthened between the twelfth and tenth centuries BC, and encompassed within a further line of defence: a polygonal **curtain wall** studded with (now roofless) round towers. The same period saw the expansion of the settlement, though most of the **nuraghic village** dates from later, between the tenth and sixth centuries, when the nucleus of the settlement was already in a state of decay. Scattered around the curtain walls, it's a dense, untidy outgrowth of over 200 circular and horseshoe-shaped buildings, all now roofless, but many reconstructed to a height of about two metres. In appearance these huts must have resembled the small stone-roofed shepherd's *pinneddas* still used today in some parts of Sardinia (see p.180).

In the village, the Renaissance-influenced **Palazzo Zapata** (also called Casa degli Zapata), former residence of a Spanish family granted the fiefdom of La Marmilla in 1541, is destined to hold finds from the site when restoration work is complete. Until that time, there are a few exhibits and diagrams at the **Convento dei Cappuccini** (daily: summer 9am–1pm & 3.30–7pm, winter 10am–1pm & 3–6pm; free), a signposted left turn on the southbound Villamar road, marked out by its square campanile and stout clock tower. There is currently much more material to be seen at the archeological museum at Villanovaforru (see p.144), though you can see some elegant water containers and other pottery items, and a computer programme

Sardinia's Nuraghic Culture

Of all the vestiges of Sardinia's multi-faceted history, only those of the **nuraghic civilization** are unique to the island. They are also the most ubiquitous – raw, imposing landmarks scattered thickly in every corner of the island, inescapable reminders of the enigmatic society that once flourished here. Originating in a time before foreign invasion changed the course of the island's history, they have become an enduring image of the true, unconquered Sardinia.

The nuraghic culture held sway for well over a millennium, from around 1800 BC until the Carthaginian conquest in 535 BC, though in certain areas of the interior it continued until the Roman invasion of 238 BC. Traditionally, the nuraghic period is divided into five phases, from the Early Bronze Age (1800–1500 BC) to the Late Iron Age (500–238 BC). During the earliest two phases there was a gradual transition from the preceding Bonnánaro culture until, around 1200 BC, isolated single-towered structures had been built throughout the island. Over the next three centuries, these grew more elaborate; villages mushroomed around the original fortified structures, craftwork grew more refined and trading contacts expanded. This third phase is widely regarded as the golden age of nuraghic culture. However, the fourth phase, or "aristocratic period", saw the gradual waning of nuraghic influence. The Phoenicians had already established trading contacts with Sardinia by 850 BC, founding colonies on the coasts, and the arrival of the Carthaginians led inexorably to the absorption of the islanders' culture by the new dominant power. In coastal regions in particular, the nuraghic culture was completely replaced by the more urban, militaristic regimes of Carthage and subsequently Rome.

Leaving no written record, the nuraghic people are known to us primarily through their artifacts – most conspicuously, the nuraghi themselves. These round towers taper inwards to resemble a truncated cone (their very roundness was cited by nineteenth-century historians as the distinguishing mark of the "barbarian" peoples as against the linearity of "classical" cultures). The majority were built between 1500 and 500 BC, both for defensive purposes and as habitations, of large blocks of stone; though no cement was used, many are still standing some 3000 years later.

The earliest nuraghs consisted of little more than a single room in one circular tower; later they developed to include several chambers on two or three levels, to which were added other towers linked by walls to form bastions like those in medieval castles, trilobate (triangular) or quadrilobate (square) in groundplan. In the main inner chamber, often of a "tholos" (beehive-shape) design, niches or alcoves were hollowed out for effigies, storage or sentry-posts. Designs grew more elaborate: **Su Nuraxi**, outside Barúmini, encompasses thirteen towers, while **Nuraghe Arrubiu** south of Orroli, currently being excavated, has at least sixteen. Though no nuragh has yet been dug up intact, the central tower in many still exceeds 10m in height; in the case of some, like the **Nuraghe Santu Antine** at Torralba, an original height of over 20m has been calculated.

Alongside these monuments, mention must be made of **Nuraghe Losa**, near Abbasanta, and **Genna Maria**, in La Marmilla. You don't need to venture far to encounter these relics, however; nuraghi can be seen everywhere on the island – on roadsides, perched on hills, stranded amidst a sea of *macchia*, often sited in the least expected of places. Sardinia has about 7000 of these constructions, although archeologists have estimated that their number may once have exceeded 10,000. They have been variously defined as dwellings, fortresses, temples, mausoleums, memorials, palaces, grain stores and even observatories. Most archeologists now accept, however, that the majority were fortified houses serving mainly (though not exclusively) to defend Sards from other Sards. Similar structures are found in the Balearic Islands, in Corsica – perhaps influenced by the Sards – and on Pantelleria, an island between Sicily and North Africa.

The nuraghi themselves are only one part of the whole picture. **Sacred wells** also played an important part in the social customs of these early Sards – good examples can be seen at Sárdara, in the Campidano, and Santa Cristina, northeast of Oristano. Nuraghic burials have also provided a wealth of material and insights. At first, the nuraghic people continued to use the burial places favoured by their predecessors: the rock-cut tombs known as *domus de janas* (literally "fairy-dwellings"), of which the **Anghelu Ruju** complex outside Alghero, dating from about 1750 BC, is one of the most notable examples. Later, they preferred to bury their dead collectively in "gallery tombs" or the so-called *tombe dei giganti* ("Giants' Tombs"), megalithic constructions with extended horn-shaped arms. These are common in the Macomer area, though one of the best examples, **Coddu Vecchiu**, lies near Arzachena, north of Olbia.

As for **nuraghic society**, almost everything we know is still highly speculative. It was primarily a shepherds' and farmers' culture, though changes in building patterns suggest that an aristocracy of sorts developed between 1400 and 1000 BC. The ruling elite must have exercised a tight social control over the local tribes, and slaves and servants were probably used. Later, communities intermingled: Phoenician and Punic pottery and Roman remains have been found together with nuraghic artifacts at many sites, evidence in some cases of continuous habitation until the fifth century AD. Nuraghic society was initially thought to be quite self-contained, but the discovery of many items from far afield has convinced archeologists that it was part of a Mediterranean-wide trading network from earliest times, connected with such centres as Etruria, Cyprus and Crete.

The finds chiefly consist of bronze jewellery and sculptures, the most engaging items being the diminutive **statuettes** or *bronzetti*. These mostly represent warriors and noble figures, though some show considerable fantasy: humans with four arms and eyes, for example, or bulls with human heads. Interestingly, only one example of a horse has been found; the ox is the favourite animal. Two styles have been identified, one rigid and geometric, showing a possible influence from Armenia or Iran, the other loose and *popolaresco*, showing influences from Cyprus, Syria and the eastern Mediterranean. All display deep religious sensibility: hung on walls or laid next to the deceased in tombs, they were probably intended as offerings to the divinity. Nuraghic *bronzetti* can be seen in London's British Museum, Cágliari's **Museo Archeológico** (p.77), Sássari's **Museo Sanna** (p.231) and the nuraghic museum at **Torralba** (p.256).

Our knowledge of the nuraghic people owes much to **Alberto di Lamármora** (1789–1863), explorer, birdwatcher, geologist and archeologist, who filled many of the gaps in its complex social and architectural history, showing that the nuraghi were gradually enlarged rather than built in one go. In the twentieth century, **Antonio Taramelli** systematically excavated the larger nuraghi as well as setting up the archeological sections of the museums at Cágliari and Sássari, while **Giovanni Lilliu** has been the leading light on the subject in more recent times. Conferences and exhibitions in 1926 and 1949 first began to stimulate the outside interest in this arcane culture, and the mass of finds recovered from Lilliu's excavation of Su Nuraxi in 1951–55 brought its treasures to a wider world. Much remains to be discovered, and continuing excavations promise a fuller picture of this unique civilization.

La Marmilla shows a reconstructed image of the monument from different perspectives, homing in on details of its design accompanied by a spoken multilingual commentary.

There's a **bar** across the road from Su Nuraxi (closed Thurs in winter) where you can pick up drinks and, in summer, *panini*; the adjoining **restaurant**, *Il Funghetto* (closed Mon) does fuller meals. There's nowhere to stay in Barúmini: the nearest hotels are at Villanovaforru, Sanluri (see p.141) and Ísili (pp.336–337). The village is connected by two–three **buses** daily, calling here en route to Désulo, Láconi and Samugheo.

La Giara di Gésturi

North of Barúmini, the high tableland of the **Giara di Gésturi**, or *Sa Jara*, is an ever-present feature of the landscape. Roughly 12km long, covering some 42 square kilometres at a maximum height of 560m, it is the largest of a series of basalt plateaux thrown up in ancient eruptions – the most noteworthy others are the Giara di Siddi and that of Serri – and the subject of plans to protect it as a natural reserve. The area is controlled now by rangers, but is uncrossed by any roads. There are, though, tarmacked tracks winding up from the villages at its base, leading to places where you can leave your vehicle. The Giara ("plateau") is fairly bare on its lower flanks, but as you climb you'll come across thicker brushwood and groves of twisted cork trees. On the flat summit, the impervious basalt rock has created *paulis*, or depressions, which fill up with rainwater to create ponds; these, together with the thick vegetation, help to provide a perfect terrain for a variety of **wildfowl**, from buzzards to bee-eaters. Spring is the best season to visit, when the area is at its greenest and a magnet for migrating birds.

The plateau has also become home to goats and wild boars, though the most rarely seen beasts are those which appear most frequently on the tourist literature – packs of **wild ponies**, or *cavallini* (in dialect, *is quaddedus*). At the last count there were around 500 of the diminutive creatures, which measure less than 130cm at shoulder height; a smaller number live in the Arca di Noe protected zone at Porto Conte, near Alghero (see p.209). Their origins are not known but they are thought to have links with oriental breeds, possibly introduced by the Phoenicians 3000 years ago. Though free to roam at will, the ponies are generally claimed by local farmers – the branding ceremony is one of the highlights of the year. You're allowed to wander where you please over the rough terrain (you'll need stout shoes), though you might also consider hooking up with an experienced **guide**, whose services are charged at about L35,000 per hour or L20,000 per person per hour on horseback. Rates are infinitely negotiable, depending on time, numbers and season. Ask in the bars of the low-lying villages, or one of the forest rangers, normally stationed in shacks near the car parks.

Access to the area is easiest from the villages of Génuri, Setzu, Tuili and Gésturi. One to two ARST **buses** from Cágliari and Barúmini link Tuili and Gésturi daily, while Génuri and Setzu have two daily weekday connections to Sanluri and one to Oristano. None has much in the way of restaurants or even information facilities.

Tuili

The most interesting of the villages circling the Giara di Gésturi is TUILI, 3km west of Su Nuraxi's site, whose church of **San Pietro** contains a real treasure. Lying opposite a ramshackle old villa, the church is easily locatable by its neat, round-topped belltower. Within the unprepossessing exterior, the **retablo di San Pietro** occupies the whole of a chapel at the back of the right-hand aisle. Painted by the mysterious Maestro di Castelsardo, this vividly coloured polyptych is considered to be his best work, and his only one to bear a date – 1500, according to a legal document specifying his fee. Its style is predominantly Gothic, with few signs of the impact of the Renaissance. Against richly detailed landscapes, the central panels show Christ crucified and the Madonna with saints; on the left, St Michael slaying the devil and St Peter are depicted, on the right are St James and St Paul, respectively above and below. Considered by some to be Sardinia's finest work of medieval art, it's a solemn and absorbing painting, the facial expressions and garments superbly rendered. To appreciate it in the church's dim interior, ask someone to turn on the lights (the switch is behind the painting on the left). The rest of the building is also richly painted – there's another *retablo* on the corresponding chapel on the other side of the nave, dated 1534, painted by another anonymous artist, more evidence of rich local patronage.

Come to Tuili at the end of August if you want to see the miniature ponies of the Giara di Gésturi rounded up and branded.

The village has a couple of other lavishly endowed churches, as well as bars and a Banco di Sardegna. There's not much else: the whole place lies in the lee of the Giara di Gesturi, rising bare to the north, towards which there are unmissable signs indicating "Altopiano della Giara". A **Centro Visite** at the back of the village has been long closed, but may reopen for information on the Giara.

Gésturi

North of Barúmini, the campanile of **Santa Teresa d'Ávila** dominates the village of **GÉSTURI**. The church is reckoned to be Sardinia's very latest example of the Catalan Gothic style, dating from 1674. The main road through the village has a useful **bar and pizzeria**, *Fra Nicola* (closed Mon), where you also arrange **excursions on the Giara di Gésturi** on foot, bike or horseback (☎070.936.9425). There are the same brown signs to the *Altopiano della Giara* as Tuili, but again, nowhere to find general information. Gésturi is a stop on the ARST bus routes from Cágliari to Désulo, Láconi and Samugheo, the same services which run through Barúmini.

Travel Details

TRAINS

Sanluri to: Cágliari (every 1 or 2 hours; 50min); Oristano (Mon–Sat 8 daily, Sun 5; 45min).

San Gavino to: Cágliari (hourly; 35min–1hr); Oristano (hourly; 40min).

BUSES

Barúmini to: Cágliari (Mon–Sat 3 daily, Sun 2; 1hr 35min–2hr); Gésturi (Mon–Sat 3 daily, Sun 1; 10min); Láconi (Mon–Sat 1 daily; 35min); Tuili (1 daily; 5min).

Gésturi to: Barúmini (Mon–Sat 3 daily, Sun 1; 10min); Cágliari (Mon–Sat 3 daily, Sun 2; 1hr 30min–2hr 10min); Sanluri (Mon–Sat 2 daily, Sun 1; 45min); Tuili (1 daily; 12min).

Sanluri to: Aritzo (1 daily; 2hr); Barúmini (Mon–Sat 2 daily, Sun 1; 30–45min); Cágliari (Mon–Sat 1–2 hourly; 45min–1hr 15min); Gésturi (Mon–Sat 2 daily, Sun 1; 40–55min); Láconi (Mon–Sat 2 daily, Sun 1; 1hr 5min–1hr 20min); Oristano (Mon–Sat 2 daily; 1hr 10min); Sárdara (Mon–Sat 10–11 daily; Sun 5; 10–30min); Tuili (Mon–Sat 3 daily; 35–50min).

San Sperate to: Cágliari (Mon–Sat 5–10 daily, Sun 1; 30min).

Sárdara to: Cágliari (hourly, Sun 4; 1hr 5min); San Gavino (Mon–Sat 2–4 daily; 15min); Sanluri (Mon–Sat 10–11 daily; Sun 5; 10–30min).

Tuili to: Barúmini (1 daily; 5min); Cágliari (Mon–Sat 2 daily, Sun 1; 1hr 40min–2hr); Gésturi (1 daily; 12min); Sanluri (Mon–Sat 3 daily; 35–50min); Sárdara (Mon–Sat 1 daily; 40min).

Uta to: Cágliari (Mon–Sat 8–11 daily, Sun 1; 40min).

Villanovaforru to: Cágliari (Mon–Sat 3 daily; 1hr 25min–1hr 50min); San Gavino (Mon–Sat 2–3 daily; 30min); Sanluri (Mon–Sat 2 daily; 25min); Sárdara (Mon–Sat 4–6 daily; 15min); Tuili (Mon–Sat 1 daily; 25min).

Chapter 4

Oristano province

Sardinia's smallest province, **Oristano**, was created as recently as 1974 out of bits hacked off the provinces of Cágliari and Nuoro, but it roughly corresponds to the much older entity of Arborea, the medieval *giudicato* which championed the Sardinian cause in the struggle against the Spaniards. Then as now, the city of **Oristano** was the region's main town, and today it retains more than a hint of medieval atmosphere, mixed with equal measures of a burgeoning youth culture and an antiquated and blinkered parochialism. In most respects, however, Oristano's tone is small-town and pedestrian-friendly, making it an undemanding stop with some engaging monuments and an enjoyable museum in which to spend a couple of hours.

Many of the museum's best exhibits are from the venerable Punic-Roman town of **Tharros**. It's one of the best-preserved classical sites on the island, and especially worth a visit if you are giving Nora a miss. As at Nora, the ruins are scattered across a prong of land surrounded by water. The **Sinis Peninsula** on which Tharros stands makes an easy excursion from Oristano and holds much else worth exploring. The **lagoons** which have attracted some of Sardinia's most abundant birdlife are also the place to see the coracle-like flat-bottomed *fassonis* – truncated, rush-constructed boats still used by the lagoon's fishermen and hunters, or just for local races. The peninsula's western coast provides some of the province's most alluring **beaches**, while there are also a pair of ancient churches which merit a look. One of these, **San Giovanni di Sinis**, just north of Tharros, is paleochristian, middle-eastern in appearance, and one of the island's two oldest churches, while the nearby **San Salvatore** interweaves an extraordinary mix of pagan and Christian strands, and is also the destination of an annual barefoot race fom the nearby lagoonside town of **Cabras**.

Inland lie a couple of engrossing nuraghic remnants – **Santa Cristina**, site of both a perfectly preserved sacred well and an impressive if ramshackle nuraghe amid ancient olive groves, and the monumental site at **Losa**, outside the village of **Abbasanta**. There are

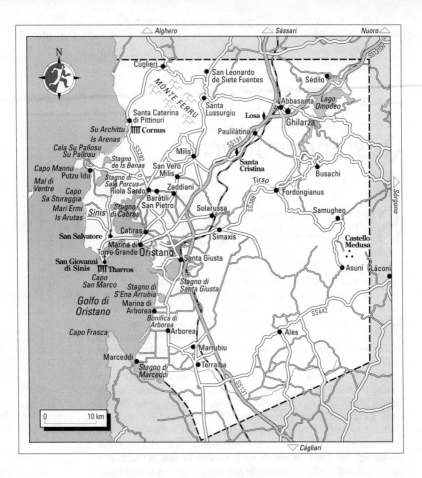

more Roman traces at nearby **Fordongianus**, a system of baths on the banks of the Tirso river. North of Oristano, the agreeably remote but still easily accessible archeological site at **Cornus** was the scene of a historic Roman victory. The nearby resort of **Santa Caterina di Pittinuri** is flanked by some good beaches. South of the city, don't miss the basilica of **Santa Giusta**, one of the earliest of Sardinia's Pisan-Romanesque churches.

For more information on bus and train connections, see Travel Details, p.188.

Neither of the nuraghic sites is much more than a twenty-minute drive northeast from Oristano on the SS131; Santa Caterina is about the same distance up the SS292, running inland of Sinis, while the Roman baths are slightly longer on the smaller SS338 eastwards. **Public transport** won't get you very far for any of the remoter archeological sites, though you can at least rely on buses from Oristano (which is on the main north–south rail line) to Tharros in summer,

THE GUIDE: CHAPTER 4

and there are regular links to Fordongianus, Santa Caterina di Pittinuri and Santa Giusta. For other destinations, non-drivers should be able to negotiate a reasonable taxi fare, especially if there are three or four of you.

The province is richly endowed with **annual festivals**, mostly with a horsey theme: Oristano's medieval **Sa Sartiglia** at Carnival time is the most famous of these, and well worth going out of your way for, but there are smaller, less trumpeted affairs at **Sédilo**, northeast of Abbasanta, and **Santu Lussúrgiu**, in the wooded folds of Monte Ferru.

Some history

In prehistoric times, the area that subsequently became Oristano province was the cradle of an active **nuraghic culture**. The complexes of Nuraghe Losa and Santa Cristina are only the most visible remnants of this civilization; in fact the area around Paulilátino has the highest concentration of nuraghi anywhere on the island, and the Sinis peninsula, too, was the scene of much construction. The arrival of the **Phoenicians** in the second half of the eighth century halted the growth of the nuraghic culture; the archeological evidence suggests that while Phoenician ways largely supplanted the local culture, the two peoples lived chiefly in harmony. The Phoenicians' main base was at Tharros, which was to remain the centre of commercial and political activity for the best part of the next two millennia.

Phoenicians and Sards joined forces against **Carthaginian incursions** during the sixth century BC, and both peoples suffered as a result of the Punic triumph. As the island passed under the direct control of Carthage following the treaty with Rome of 509 BC, North African colonies were established at Neapolis, on the southern coast of the Golfo di Oristano, and at Cornus, near present-day Cúglieri. As elsewhere on the island, the partial integration of the indigenous people into the Phoenician/Carthaginian cultural framework took its course, and it was a combined force of Sards and Carthaginians that suffered a decisive defeat by the **Romans** at Cornus in 216 BC, an event which helped to bring about the total occupation of Sardinia by Rome. The Oristano region was thoroughly penetrated by the new rulers, as evidenced by the thermal baths of Forum Traiani, now Fordongianus. Tharros was revitalized by the new conquerors, and remained the local capital until its decline and eventual evacuation in the face of Arab assaults during the second half of the first millennium.

Most of the inhabitants of Tharros resettled inland at Oristano, which became the principal power base during the **Middle Ages**, and the capital of one of Sardinia's four *giudicati* (sovereign states) in the tenth century. In common with the others, the **Giudicato of Arborea** was created as a result of a complex of conventions between the noble families and the local judicial structures; its authority, however, depended on the endless power shifts and temporary alliances that characterized the centuries of rivalry beween Pisa, Genoa and Aragon throughout the island. Arborea reached its zenith during the thirteenth and fourteenth centuries, first under **Mariano II** (d.1298), and later at the forefront of the island's resistance to the Aragonese. **Eleonora d'Arborea** emerged as the champion of independence in the few areas of the island that remained free of Aragonese domination. Her fortitude and success ensured that she would become one of the greatest figures in Sardinia's history, though her near-legendary fame is also due to the **Carta de Logu**, a body of laws promulgated by her in 1390, which formed the basis of Sardinia's legislative structure until 1817.

For more on Eleonora, see box on pp.162–163.

After Eleonora's death in 1404, anti-Aragonese resistance fell apart, and her realms joined the rest of the island under Aragonese – and subsequently Spanish – colonial rule. Arborea itself disappeared, while Oristano sank into provincial oblivion, languishing in neglect until Sardinia was taken on by the **Piedmontese** in the eighteenth century. The linking of Oristano to the Carlo Felice Highway (now the SS131) in the 1820s gave the town a much-needed boost, and some programmes of social reform were attempted, but other problems – principally the malarial marshland which increasingly encroached on large tracts of this otherwise fertile land – were not addressed until **Mussolini**'s initiatives got under way after 1924. His land reclamation scheme south of Oristano was sustained by colonies of settlers from northern Italy, centred on the new town he originally called "Mussolinia" – later renamed Arborea, as if to reclaim the town itself for the local population. Despite the slow but steady development, however, the area did not achieve **provincial status** until 1974, and Oristano's population still hasn't risen in line with the expansion of Cágliari and Sássari.

Oristano: the city

The city of **ORISTANO**, 100km northwest of Cágliari, is a flat, unprepossessing place whose old walls have been mostly replaced by busy traffic arteries. The centre has a relaxed yet purposeful ambience, and although it lies 4km from the sea, the town shares with Cágliari an air of being surrounded by water, on account of the lagoons and irrigation systems which helped to make it the centre of a richly productive agricultural zone, fuelling its growth and prosperity.

In the centre, Oristano's **Duomo** is as old as anything in town, dating from the early thirteenth century, though a seventeenth-century refashioning has given it an opulent Baroque flavour. The medieval stamp is more evident in the central Piazza Roma, where the **Torre di Mariano II** has been a sturdy survivor of the city's chequered fortunes since its erection in the thirteenth century; another remnant of the old defences, the **Portixedda**, lies a short walk away. But the old town's most essential attraction is the marvellous repository of prehistoric and classical finds and medieval works of art at the local museum, the **Antiquarium Arborense**, one of Sardinia's top three or four collections.

For more on Sa Sartiglia, see box on pp.166–167.

The best time to be in Oristano is for the colourful medieval **Sa Sartiglia**, a vivid, highly ritualized horseback competition at Carnival. Advance bookings are essential if you hope to get **accommodation** during that time; indeed, they're a good idea at any period, since hotel space is scarce. Oristano is better provided with **restaurants** and **bars**, and the local cuisine makes good use of the area's agricultural produce and seafood.

Arrival, information and accommodation

Oristano's **train station** is situated at the eastern end of town, a twenty-minute walk from the centre, to which it is linked by local buses that run every twenty minutes or so. Buy tickets (L1100 per ride) at the bar outside the station in Piazza Ungheria: the bus stop is across the road from here. Buses of the Linea Rossa and Linea Verde ("Red" and "Green" lines) end their run at Piazza Mariano, from where it's a five-minute walk up Via Mazzini to Piazza Roma. However, it's always worth telling the driver your intended destination, as the route may run via a nearer, more useful stop. Alternatively, there are **taxis** stationed in Piazza Ungheria; the fare, on the meter, should be less than L10,000 to any destination in town.

Oristano's **bus station** is more central, on Via Cágliari with access onto Via Episcopio, off Via Vittorio Emanuele. All ARST buses pull in here, also making a stop at the train station, though PANI buses from Cágliari, Nuoro and Sássari stop at Via Lombardia 30, where their office is at the *Blu Bar* (closed Sun). When the bar is closed, you can buy tickets on board. Piazza Roma is a five-minute walk from here on Via Tirso.

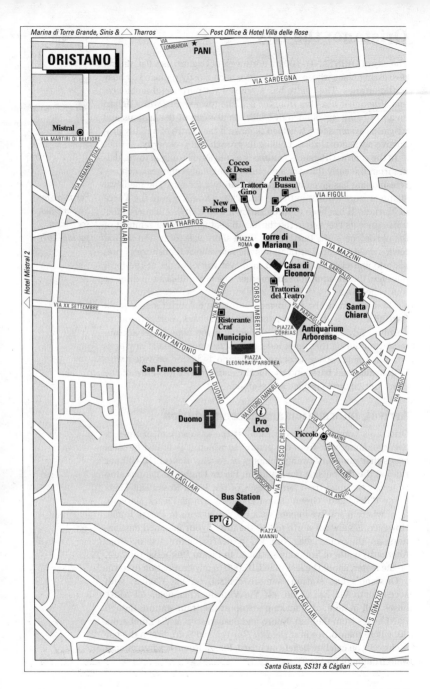

ORISTANO

★ PANI

VIA LOMBARDIA

VIA SARDEGNA

● Mistral

VIA MÁRTIRI DI BELFIORE

VIA ARMANDO DIAZ

VIA TIRSO

VIA CAGLIARI

■ Cocco
& Dessi

■ Fratelli
Bussu

■ Trattoria
Gino

VIA FIGOLI

■ New
Friends

■ La Torre

VIA THARROS

PIAZZA
ROMA

● Torre di
Mariano II

VIA MAZZINI

◆ Casa di
Eleonora

VIA GARIBALDI

△ Hotel Mistral 2

VIA DE CASTRO

CORSO UMBERTO

■ Trattoria
del Teatro

VIA XX SETTEMBRE

VIA SANT'ANTONIO

■ Ristorante
Craf

■ Municipio

VIA PARPAGLIA

✝ Santa
Chiara

◆ Antiquarium
Arborense

PIAZZA
CORRIAS

PIAZZA
ELEONORA D'ARBOREA

VIA AZUNI

San Francesco ✝

VIA DUOMO

VIA ANGIOY

Duomo ✝

VIA VITTORIO EMANUELE

(i) Pro
Loco

VIA FRANCESCO CRISPI

● Piccolo

VIA DEL CARMINE

VIA MARTIGNANO

VIA ANGIOI

VIA CAGLIARI

VIA PESCURO

Bus Station ■

EPT (i)

PIAZZA
MANNU

VIA CAGLIARI

VIA S. IGNAZIO

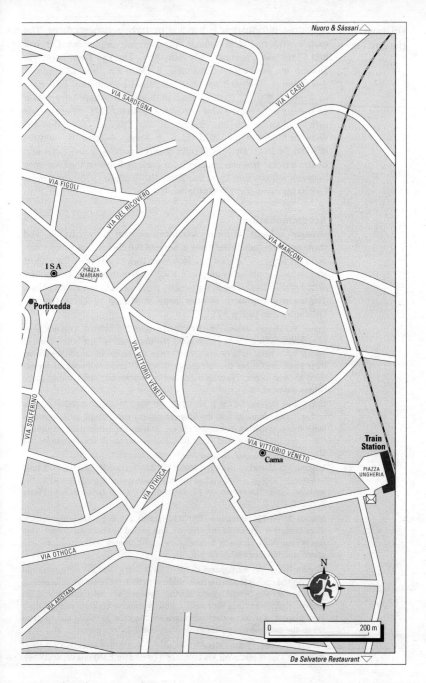

Nuoro & Sássari △

VIA SARDEGNA

VIA V. CASU

VIA FIGOLI

VIA DEL RICOVERO

VIA MARCONI

ISA ◉

PIAZZA
MABIANO

● Portixedda

VIA VITTORIO VENETO

VIA SOLFERINO

VIA OTHOCA

VIA VITTORIO VENETO

Cama ◉

Train
Station

PIAZZA
UNGHERIA

VIA OTHOCA

N

VIA ARISTANA

0   200 m

Da Salvatore Restaurant ▽

Oristano: the city

Tourist information is handled by three separate offices. The mobile office on Piazza Roma is only open July–September, Carnival and Christmas, generally daily 8am–8pm. The **Pro Loco** is off Via Duomo at Via Vittorio Emanuele 8 (Mon–Fri 9am–12.30pm & 4–7.30pm, 4.30–8pm in summer, Sat 9am–12.30pm, also 4.30–8pm in summer; ☎0783.70.621). Both of these offices have information on the city only; for the whole province, go to the **EPT**, a fourth-floor office opposite the bus station at Via Cágliari 278 (Mon–Fri 8am–2pm, Tues & Wed also 5–8pm, 4–7pm in winter; ☎0783.74.191). **Drivers** should observe parking restrictions and obtain a ticket from an attendant for parking between the blue lines between 8.30am and 1pm, and from 4 to 7.30pm (L700 for 30min, L1200 for one hour, L3000 for two hours).

Accommodation

Oristano is badly off for accommodation, with just six **hotels**, and these are often full. What's more, none of the choices has much character, or any view to speak of. However, they're adequate for a short stay, which is probably all you'll want to give this town. During the *Sa Sartiglia* festivities in particular, you'll need to book way ahead. The nearest **campsite** is 6km away at Marina di Torre Grande, Oristano's lido (see p.171).

Cama, Via Vittorio Véneto (☎0783.74.374, fax 0783.74.375). This dull business-travellers' hotel is convenient for the train station (just 500m towards town), but a hefty walk (about 15min) from the centre of things. Rooms on three levels are OK but strictly functional, with TV and telephone and decent-sized shower-rooms. There is a bar but no restaurant, and parking space behind the hotel. ③.

ISA, Piazza Mariano 50 (☎ & fax 0783.360.101). Though the place is not as bad as it looks from outside, the fifties architecture and bland, soulless rooms make this a somewhat depressing choice. At least it's comfortable, capacious (there are 56 rooms), and close to the town centre at the bottom of Via Mazzini. ③.

Mistral, Via Mártiri di Belfiore (☎0783.212.505, fax 0783.210.058). A grey five-storey block in a dull part of town, this three-star appeals mostly to the business class. The rooms are bright, and it's not too far to walk to Piazza Roma. ④.

Mistral 2, Via XX Settembre (☎0783.210.389, fax 0783.211.000). Pricier, more upmarket version of the *Mistral*, and owned by the same people. This one is even more pointedly business-orientated, though the large pool might entice you. Mountain bikes for hire. ⑤.

Píccolo Hotel, Via Martignano 19 (☎0783.71.500). Oristano's cheapest and most central choice is also the most difficult to find, tucked away in an area of unmarked streets behind Piazza Martini, between Via del Cármine and Via Angioy (signposted from Via Angioy). Run by a chatty Venetian woman, it's a quiet place with small rooms (bathrooms are tiny); the plumbing and electrics are on the dodgy side, and the whole place could do with a facelift. ③.

Villa delle Rose, Piazza Italia (☎0783.310.101, fax 0783.310.117). A good choice on a quiet piazza off Via Lombardia (useful for PANI bus connections).

Piazza Roma is a 10-minute walk away, and there's a city bus stop right outside on the *Linea Verde* for connections with Piazza Mariano and the train station. Rooms are solidly furnished, each with a spacious bathroom. Part of the hotel is occasionally used as an old folks' home. ③.

The town: the central sights

Oristano is initially disorientating, with few straight roads connecting the major landmarks. The principal squares of the town centre are **Piazza Mariano**, terminus of most local bus routes and marked out by a white war memorial; **Piazza Roma**, unmistakeable with its fortified medieval tower, and the pedestrianized **Piazza Eleonora d'Arborea**, site of the municipio in the heart of the old town. All the main sights are encompassed by this triangle, and lie just a few minutes' walk from one another.

Piazza Eleonora and around

Presiding over the **Piazza Eleonora d'Arborea** in front of Oristano's Neoclassical town hall, the marble statue of Eleonora strikes a symbolic pose that recalls the town's greatest hour. Sculpted in 1881, the statue shows the *giudichessa* with the scroll bearing the famous *Carta de Logu* with which she is associated, while inset panels depict her various victories (see box, pp.162–163).

At the western end of the elongated piazza, four stout Ionic columns front the nineteenth-century church of **San Francesco**. Designed by the eminent Cagliaritan architect Gaetano Cima, the building incorporates the remains of a much older construction, traces of which – Gothic arches and Corinthian columns – are visible on the right-hand side, where the adjoining convent is now occupied by a military office. The most compelling item within the church's capacious domed interior is the so-called *Crocifisso di Nicodemo*, housed in a Neoclassical marble altar on the left side. Carved in the fourteenth century by an unknown Catalan, the crucifix is considered one of the most precious and influential wooden sculptures on the whole island; the powerful carving of an emaciated, sunken-eyed Christ, his skin scored by cuts and raw abrasions, is drenched with emotion.

Otherwise the church has little to detain you, unless there is someone around to allow you into the sacristy to see the central panel of Pietro Cavaro's polyptych of Saint Francis receiving the stigmata, the rest of which is now in the Antiquarium Arborense (see p.164). The space in front of San Francesco forms the main arena for Oristano's annual *Sa Sartiglia* festivities (see box on pp.166–167).

The narrow pedestrianized Corso Umberto links Piazza Eleonora with Piazza Roma, where pavement bars cluster around the base of the crenellated **Torre di Mariano II**. Also known as the Torre di San Cristóforo, the tower was erected by one of Oristano's greatest rulers, the *giudice* Mariano II in 1290; the inscription recording this

event is on display in the Antiquarium Arborense. The bastion originally formed the fulcrum of Oristano's medieval fortifications. The
walls to which it was joined were demolished at the end of the nineteenth century; the gateway through it, the **Porta Mariano** or **Porta
Manna**, was the city's northern gate. When the tower is open, you
can climb the three levels (daily Aug–Sept and festivals 10am–noon
& 3–5pm; free) to view the huge bell at the top – last rung when
Oristano became a province in the 1970s – and, on a clear day, for
vistas of the sea.

The only other survivor of the city's defences is the squat
Portixedda ("little gate"), off Via Garibaldi at the bottom of Via
Mazzini (daily 9am–1pm & 4–7pm, 4–9pm in summer; free). This
was one of two towers protecting the western approaches into town.
Though much smaller than the Torre di Mariano II, and generally
lacking that tower's impact, the Portixedda has recently been reno-

---

Eleonora d'Arborea

As the only one of Sardinia's medieval *giudici* to enjoy any significant success against the island's aggressors, Eleonora of Arborea (c.1340–1404)
is the best-known and best-loved of Sardinia's rulers. Occupying a sort of
"Joan of Arc" role in the popular imagination, she also made significant
contributions to the evolution of civil rights on the island with her pro-
mulgation of a book of law in Oristano, which eventually became the
benchmark of local freedoms throughout Sardinia.

Eleanora's father, the *giudice* Mariano IV (reigned 1346–76) – himself a
Catalan – was required by the Aragonese king Pedro IV to send his two
daughters to be married to local aristocrats. One, Beatrice, was matched
with Amerigo VI of Narbonne, but Mariano allowed Eleonora to be wedded
instead, in 1366 or 1367, to the Genoan Brancaleone Doria, scion of Spain's
main rivals in Sardinia at that time, who were also nominally Aragon's vas-
sals. Eleonora spent most of the following fifteen years in Castelsardo (then
called Castelgenovese) and Genoa itself, where she ingratiated herself with
the Doge and laid the foundations of a future anti-Aragonese alliance, only
returning to her native city in 1383 to assume the regency of the *giudicato*
following the assassination of her brother, Ugone. As the wife of a vassal of
Aragon, she was able to negotiate a delicate balance of power and a degree
of independence, allowing her space to concentrate on the concerns of her
subjects. In a short time she had acquainted herself with the entire *giudicato*, her tours round the Oristanese territory greeted with enthusiastic
acclaim. Her popular appeal was no doubt enhanced by the ten years of tax
exemptions she granted to the downtrodden population, exhausted by the
economic hardship induced by the long period of war. Of more lasting benefit was her formulation in 1395 of a legal code (*Carta de Logu*) covering
every aspect of civil legislation, which was only made possible by her years
of struggle to protect the *giudicato's* independence. In fact, Eleonora's
political instincts proved to be as great as her legislative gifts. Despite the
imprisonment of her husband by the Aragonese (an event interpreted by
some as his desertion to the enemy), she refused to bow to his captors'

---

vated and holds a small exhibition on Oristano's defensive system. Climb to the top from the entrance in Via Garibaldi for the rather limited views around town.

Just off Piazza Roma, at Via Parpaglia 6–12, take a glance at the building still referred to on some maps as the **Casa di Eleonora**. In fact, this fine house, now derelict, could not have been Eleonora's home as it was built over a century after her death, but it remains a good if sorely neglected example of sixteenth-century architecture. Eleonora is said to be interred in the fourteenth-century church of **Santa Chiara**, in the parallel Via Garibaldi.

The Duomo

Oristano's **Duomo** (daily: April–Oct 8am–1pm & 4–7pm; Nov–March 7am–1pm & 3–6.30pm) stands in its own square off Via Duomo, behind Piazza Eleonora. With its detached octagonal, onion-roofed

---

demands, preferring to leave Brancaleone to his own devices. Her intransigence paid off, bringing about a treaty in 1388 that returned to Aragon the cities occupied by Arborea, but also guaranteed independence for the territory she governed, and even returned Brancaleone to the fold. From her new position of strength, Eleonora forged a tactical alliance with the Genoans and launched a new offensive against the Spanish, as a result of which, Brancaleone, with Genoan help, even managed to occupy Sássari on her behalf.

Eleanora's military achievements collapsed soon after her death from plague in 1404, and the Aragonese were able to occupy the last of Sardinia's *giudicati* to remain independent. Her reign marked the final glorious period of Sardinian independence, even if, in reality, that freedom was severely circumscribed. Eleonora herself was hampered on all sides, and for all the contribution that the *Carta de Logu* made to the status of women in her society and in future times, her powers were constantly restricted by her gender and her role as regent for infant male heirs. In the context of these limitations, Eleonora's victories resound ever greater.

The statue of Eleonora of Arborea in Oristano's Piazza Eleonora depicts her bearing the *Carta de Logu* represented as a brief scroll, but in fact this work for which the *giudichessa* is remembered comprises 198 chapters, covering every aspect of contemporary life. First mooted by her father Mariano IV, the *Carta* focused on both practical and wider issues, in the process defining the legal status and rights of people at every level of society, including children, slaves and – in particular detail – women. The book was far ahead of its time in its range and application, combining the roles of rural, civil and penal codes, and it remains the most enduring legacy of Eleonora's reign. Adopted by the Aragonese in 1421, it was later extended throughout the island, and remained in force until the enactment of the Carlo Felice code by the Piedmontese in 1817. As the eighteenth-century English lawyer and traveller John Tyndale put it: "The framing of a body of laws so far in advance of those of other countries, where greater civilization existed, must ever be the brightest ornament in the diadem of the Giudichessa."

belltower, dating from the fourteenth century, and the seminary (built in 1712) next door, it forms an atmospheric ensemble. The present building is mostly the result of a Baroque-era renovation; the only parts to have survived from the original thirteenth-century cathedral are sections of the apses.

The Duomo's spacious if fussy **interior** has three ornate chapels on either side of the nave. The first on the right has a painted wooden statue of the *Annunziata*, or Annunciation of the Madonna, thought to be by Nino Pisano (c.1315–68). Full of expression, the statue is surrounded by a majolica and gilt altar busy with *putti*. The two marble panels in front of it were carved by an anonymous Catalan in the fourteenth or fifteenth century: on the left, figures of prophets, an *Annunciation* and *Christ in Judgment*; on the right, Paul and the Apostles, and saints Antonio Abate and Chiara. Far more interesting, however, are the other sides of the slabs, carved 300 years earlier: here you can see eleventh-to-twelfth-century sculptures in the Byzantine tradition, illustrating biblical scenes, including, on the right, a portrayal of Daniel in the lions' den.

The transepts are dominated by large Neoclassical altars at either end, and, on the right, the fourteenth-century Cappella del Rimedio survives from the Duomo's earlier incarnation. Two fierce marble lions salvaged from an ancient pulpit flank the steps leading up to the main altar, behind which the raised presbyterium has large nineteenth-century canvases above wooden Renaissance choirstalls.

Antiquarium Arborense

A handsome sixteenth-century merchant's house on Piazzetta Corrias, just off Via Parpaglia, holds one of Sardinia's most absorbing museums – Oristano's **Antiquarium Arborense** (July–Sept daily 10am–8pm, Tues & Thurs closes at 11.30pm, Oct–June daily 9am–8pm; L4000). As well as featuring rotating exhibitions of its extensive collection of nuraghic, Phoenician, Roman and Greek artefacts, the museum gives permanent space to Tharros and its occupants, and has a good gallery of medieval art (though this may in the future be relocated in the Galleria Comunale on Via Sant'Antonio).

The **ground floor** contains the museum's earliest exhibits, from the prenuraghic and nuraghic eras, including a quantity of neolithic blades, axeheads and spearheads – many of obsidian or flint – from the Sinis peninsula, and a small collection of jewellery, bone hairpins and other personal items recovered from tombs. More gripping is the wealth of material from Carthaginian Tharros, much of it from burial sites, including masks to ward off the evil eye, elegantly shaped *askoi* (curved vessels), and terracotta figurines, mostly from the fifth century BC and often Ionic Greek in inspiration. There are equally numerous exhibits from the Roman period in Tharros: pins, plates, ceramic objects, bottles and myriad other glass containers including first-century-AD cinerary urns from northern Italy and Gaul. One display case is devoted to items of foreign manufacture found in Tharros tombs, including Cretan, Etruscan and mainland Greek ceramics.

The Antiquarium's **first floor** holds an imaginative reconstruction of Roman Tharros as it might have appeared at its maximum extent, in the fourth century AD, to a scale of 1:200. Around it, texts (in Italian) explain the various buildings and monuments: the port, baths, amphitheatre, the tetrastyle Doric temple, the houses, roads, aqueduct and excavated tombs. Display cases on the balcony surrounding the model show funerary items from a Phoenician necropolis excavated at San Giovanni di Sinis (see p.173) from the seventh and sixth centuries BC, plus amphorae, brooches, oil burners and other objects from Tharros and Cabras, including relics of the Byzantine era (sixth–seventh century AD), including oil lamps, possibly made in Egypt, and little jugs with circular fluting.

Next door to this room, the air-conditioned **pinacoteca** houses a small but interesting collection of medieval and Renaissance art. The chief exhibits come from the studio of the *cagliaritano* Pietro Cavaro, one of Sardinia's best painters from this era. His most outstanding work, the nine-panelled *Retablo del Santo Cristo* (1533), previously in Oristano's church of San Francesco, depicts the most important Franciscan saints, portrayed with great subtlety and sensitivity. The central panel of this polyptych, showing Saint Francis receiving the stigmata, has been left in the sacristy of San Francesco (see p.161).

There are two other famous *retabli* (paintings on wood) here, the *Madonna dei Consiglieri* by Antioco Mainas (also from Cágliari) in 1564–5, depicting five white-bearded town councillors around the Madonna and baby Jesus, with Saint Andrew and John the Baptist, and the much earlier *Retablo di San Martino*, two parts of a triptych (the third long disappeared) by an anonymous Catalan in the first half of the fifteenth century. The right panel shows Saint Martin in the act of cutting off part of his cloak to give to a beggar, and the top one shows the saint's consecration as bishop. The gallery also contains various lapidary inscriptions commemorating episodes in the construction of the city, including one recording Mariano II's strengthening of its defences at the end of the thirteenth century.

Restaurants

Oristano has plenty of decent **restaurants**, most within a short walk of the centre. Prices are generally reasonable, and the best places concentrate on fresh produce from the nearby sea, the surrounding lagoons, and the fertile hinterland. You might finish your meal with a glass of the area's celebrated *Vernaccia* dessert wine.

Cocco & Dessi, Via Tirso 31 (☎0783.300.720). Oristano's fanciest restaurant has five eating spaces, including a gazebo, a balcony and a non-smoking room. The whole place resembles a cinema foyer, but the food is excellent, best experienced on one of their sampling menus costing between L40,000 and L50,000 (excluding drinks). Closed Mon. Expensive.

Ristorante Craf, Via de Castro (☎0783.70.669). Oristano's only restaurant with any atmosphere specializes in local dishes, especially meat, including horse and ass. Vegetarian dishes include the delicious *risotto alla bonar-cadese*, with mushrooms. The atmosphere is chic without being too formal. Closed Mon and all Aug. Moderate–expensive.

Fratelli Bussu, Piazza Roma 54. This place combines a fast-food *panini* bar and, at the back, a straightforward trattoria offering unexceptional restaurant fare and pizzas at reasonable prices. A large video screen televises football matches and soaps. Service can be sluggish at weekends. Closed Tues in winter. No CCs. Moderate.

Trattoria Gino, Via Tirso 13. This central and reliable eaterie off Piazza Roma has a good-value menu with traditional Sardinian items like *ravioli sardi* (made with butter and sage) and *sebadas* (cheese-filled pastry-cases topped with honey). Closed Sun. Moderate.

New Friends, Via Tirso 16. Stand-up fast-food joint for hot dogs, pizzas, chips and sandwiches, open until midnight. Closed Mon. Inexpensive.

Da Salvatore, Via Carbonia 1 (☎0783.357.134). The remote location of this place off the main restaurant area means that it is often empty, which is a

---

Sa Sartiglia

Oristano's flamboyant **Sa Sartiglia** festival is the biggest date in the town's calendar, prepared months in advance and the subject of intense speculation – some complain it's the only thing that moves this insular, narrow-visioned town. The event takes place between the last Sunday of the Carnival period and the following Tuesday (Shrove Tuesday), usually in February.

The abstruse rituals of the festival perhaps originated with knights on the Second Crusade, who may have brought the trappings of Saracen tournaments to Sardinia in the twelfth century. On the other hand, it could be a Spanish import – a similar annual festival, *La Sortilla*, is held on the island of Menorca in June. Whatever the case, similarly lavish feasts were held for Oristano's ruling knights at regular intervals throughout the year during the Spanish domination, and in time these celebrations took on a more theatrical aspect, finally merging with the annual Carnival revelries. With all participants in the various stages of the ceremonies masked and costumed, the whole three-day affair exudes a theatrical spirit unrivalled by Sardinia's other festivals.

The main events take place on the first and third days, staged by the guilds of San Giovanni (representing the farmers) and San Giuseppe (the carpenters) respectively. Each event is presided over by a white-masked arbiter known as **Su Componidori**, selected from among the "knight" contestants according to his riding prowess. The *Componidori* represents the continuation of the *giudice*'s role and is decked out in a bizarre pastiche of medieval garb – the process of dressing him is itself a highly formal ceremony, according to precise rules. The beribboned *Componidori* initiates the proceedings riding up and down the sanded track on Via Duomo, blessing the track, contenders and audience alike with a bouquet of violets, after which the joust commences, involving a succession of mounted charges with the aim of lancing with a rapier a star-shaped ring – *stella* or *sartiglia* – suspended three metres above the ground. Each charge is her-

shame, considering the good fish and low prices. The restaurant lies on the southern outskirts of town, signposted to the right on the main road into town from Santa Giusta; the Linea Rossa bus route passes nearby. Moderate.

Trattoria del Teatro, Via Parpaglia. Touristy and slapdash, this place is a useful last resort; it serves pizzas with novelty toppings such as pineapple and fish in the evenings and Wednesday lunchtimes, though traditional pizzas are also available. Closed Sun. Moderate.

La Torre, Piazza Roma. For a cheap and basic pizza, head for this popular place where the speciality is *pizza ai funghi porcini*. Gets very lively on weekends. Closed Mon. Inexpensive.

Bars and nightlife

Oristano has plenty of decent **bars** to while away an afternoon or evening, of which one, *Lolamundo*, has late-night sounds. For anything more frenetic, head for *Gaudi* at Via Tirso 171, open winter weekends only until 4am, playing a varied and variable menu. At

---

alded by a fanfare of drums and trumpets, and followed by groans of disappointment or wild cheering according to whether the ring is speared or missed; traditionally, more hits represent a better chance of a good harvest and thus good luck for the townspeople. The ring has a diameter of 33mm, but after a record 20 rings were lanced in 1999, there were calls to reduce the diameter. There has also been criticism of the attention given to the number of hits, at the expense of the style and grace of the run-up.

After the *corse alla stella*, the afternoon is given over to **Le Pariglie** – hair-raising horseback stunts, usually taking place on a sanded track along Via Mazzini, with prizes given to the greatest equestrian feats. The whole rigmarole is repeated two days later for the *gremio* of San Giuseppe, while on the second day a relatively new event takes place – the **Sartigliedda**, dedicated to younger riders mounted on the miniature horses of the Giara di Gésturi (see p.150). Other highlights of the festa include the proclamation at the beginning of each day to announce the opening of the proceedings, read out by a mounted herald accompanied by a squadron of drummers and trumpeters (normally around 10am in Piazza Roma and Piazza Eleonora), and singing and traditional dancing in Piazza Eleonora on the eve of the festivities and at the end of them.

Although the festival draws big crowds, both locals and tourists, it is usually possible to get a view of the events, though the best vantage point is from the grandstand seats on Via Duomo and Via Mazzini (tickets cost around L35,000, or L5000 for the Sartigliedda, available from the Pro Loco). If you can't or don't want to attend the whole three-day event, Tuesday is the best day to be here, when the crowds are smaller. It's worth asking to be present at the *vestizione* or formal dressing of the *componidori* which generally takes place in Via Aristana for the San Giovanni *sartiglia*, and in the church of San Efisio for San Giuseppe's – though, with limited space, this may not be an option. A similarly elaborate ceremony, the *svestizione*, or disrobing, takes place at the end of each day.

---

other times, you'll have to venture out of the centre, where there are two **discotheques** to the south of town. The nearest is *Killtime* in Via Garibaldi, Santa Giusta (see p.175), which draws a regular crowd, though the accent is on easy listening. A few kilometres further down, on the SS126 near Terralba (p.178), the air-conditioned *Why Not Disco* has six dance and video areas catering to diverse tastes, including "Hard Core Progressive" and "Crazy Karaoke".

Bar Azzurro, Piazza Roma. Central bar with snacks and a sit-down area. Closed Wed.

Bar Eleonora, Piazza Eleonora. A great breakfast bar or coffee stop at any time, with *cornetti*, pastries and *pizzette*, and comfortable seating.

Latte e Miele, Via de Castro 14. Nice sit-down café (service adds 25 percent to the bill), with *cornetti* and pastries. Closed Sun.

Lolamundo Café, Piazzetta Corrias. Stylish bar which makes a useful pre- or post-*Antiquarium* stop. It's also good for daytime snacks and late-night drinking, with tables in the piazza and DJs Thursday–Saturday evenings until midnight or 1am. Closed Sun.

Tira Tardi, Via Sardegna 15. Just off Via Tirso, this lively *birreria* has DJs, and serves some 40 bottled beers, plus *panini*. Open until late, closed Tues.

Listings

Ambulance *Croce Rossa* (☎0783.74.318).

Banks Central banks with cash machines include the Banca Nazionale di Lavoro (Mon–Fri 8.20am–1.20pm & 3–4.30pm) and Banco di Nápoli (Mon–Fri 8.20am–1.35pm & 3.05–3.50pm, Sat 8.20–11.50am) on Piazza Roma, and Banca Commerciale Italiana (Mon–Fri 8.20am–1.35pm & 3–4.30pm, Sat 8.20–11.50am).

Bike rental Mountain bikes available at the *Mistral 2* hotel (see p.160).

Buses PANI for Cágliari, Mácomer, Porto Torres, Sássari: Via Lombardia 30 (☎0783.212.268); ARST for everywhere else: Via Cágliari 102 (☎0783.78.001).

Books Good range of guides and some English-language books from *La Pergamena*, Via Vittorio Emanuele 24, open Mon–Fri 9am–1pm & 4.30–8pm, Sat 9am–1pm. In Corso Umberto, *Gulliver* is open Mon–Fri 9.30am–1pm & 4–8pm, Sat 9.30am–1pm.

Buses Information on local transport ☎0783.357.183.

Laundry Lavasecco Ecológico, Via Vittorio Veneto 55a charges about L5000 for shirts, L8000 for trousers or dresses.

Left luggage Facilities at the train station will probably have opened by the time you read this. Opening hours should be Mon–Sat 8am–8pm; L5000 per piece per 12 hours is the standard rate.

Markets Clothes, household goods and fruit'n'veg Mon–Sat mornings on Via Aristana, near the train station. There's an antiques and curiosity market in Piazza Eleonora (sometimes held in Via Garibaldi).

Pharmacy See rota posted on pharmacy doors for current late-night opening.

Post office The main office is outside the train station on Piazza Ungheria (Mon–Fri 8.15am–5.30pm, Sat 8.15am–1pm, closes at noon last day of month), where you can also change cash and American Express travellers' cheques. More central branches are in the gallery off Via Tirso for telegrams and faxes only

(Mon–Sat 8.15am–7.40pm), and on Via Liguria (Mon–Sat 8.15am–7.40pm), north of the centre off Via Lombardia, but there are no change facilities at these.

Supermarkets *Upim* on Via Mazzini (Mon–Sat 9am–1pm & 4–8pm). There is no food hall, but there is a food supermarket, *Vinci*, across the road (Mon–Fri 8.15am–8pm, Sat 8.15am–2pm).

Tours Sardinian Way, at Via Carmine 14 (☎0783.75.172), organizes excursions in the area and riding and sailing activities.

Train information All trains ☎147.888.088.

Travel agency Tharros Viaggi, Via Cágliari (☎0783.73.389), arranges tickets for air, sea and rail journeys.

The Sinis peninsula

For many people, Oristano is just a stop en route to the Punic and Roman city of **Tharros**, one of the island's most important archeological sites from this era. The ruined city is superbly situated by the sea, 20km west of town. Don't be deterred from exploring the rest of the **Sinis peninsula**, however, for this low-lying wedge of land at the northern end of the Golfo di Oristano rewards spending a little more time. Fringed with beaches and punctuated by lagoons where reserves have been established to protect the birds which nest here for part of the year, Sinis is physically unlike anywhere else in Sardinia, though its natural beauty can be spoiled by the streams of other visitors in the summer.

The marshes and lagoons teem with fish, a continuous source of income for the locals, who have perfected the art of negotiating the watery terrain on reed-built craft, or *fassonis*. There is evidence of these in use since prehistoric times, and though they are now mainly taken out for ceremonial occasions, you may still see the flimsy-looking vessels on remote backwaters. Resembling truncated canoes, but guided from an upright position punt-style, it is said that they can be assembled in minutes by experts.

A museum in the peninsula's main town of **Cabras** gives a good overview of the history and geography of the area, though there is little other reason to hang about here apart from the useful facilities, which include a couple of hotels. Accommodation is otherwise extremely sparse in Sinis, though the campsite at **Marina di Torre Grande**, the nearest beach area to Oristano, can be fun in summer. Tharros is served by three ARST **buses** daily in summer, and there are good year-round connections to Cabras and Marina di Torre Grande, otherwise public transport is sparse.

Cabras

Spread along the eastern shore of the Stagno di Cabras lagoon, **CABRAS** has a tranquil feel, a low-key, low-built town, unruffled by much commotion. Lacking any central piazza or other focal point, the town has a discursive, rather aimless ambience. The castle belonging to the *giudici* of Arborea which once stood here has almost completely disappeared – scanty traces lie behind the seventeenth-century parish church of **Santa Maria**, whose bulky domed profile is the townscape's only distinctive feature. If the occasion arises, take a peek through one of the doorways giving onto the courtyards around which the low, flat local dwellings, typical of the region, were constructed.

The site has been settled since Sardinia's earliest prehistory, as shown by the abundance of archeological finds thrown up in the area. Most recently, work around the southern mouth of the lagoon – at Kukkuru S'Arriu, or Cúccuru is Arrius, three or four kilometres south of Cabras – has revealed a huge shrine and necropolis with finds going back to the Bonu Ighinu culture of the fourth millennium BC. Only since the late 1990s have these been documented and displayed in the **Museo Cívico** at Via Tharros 190 (Tues–Sun 9am–1pm & 3–7pm; L5000), on the banks of the lagoon near the southwest entrance to town. The collection is worth an unhurried investigation, the exhibits well displayed on the ground floor of the modern purpose-built block. As well as the nuraghic and prenuraghic items from throughout the Sinis peninsula, there are shelves full of objects from Tharros – including a Roman milestone, stelae, needles, amphoras and vases – and a good part of the museum space is also given over to temporary exhibitions relating to the area, such as local archives, etchings and the lagoon culture. The museum explains plenty about the ecology and flora of the peninsula too, and gives a close-up look at the wonderful *fassonis*. When you've had your fill, take a breather along the eucalyptus-fringed lagoonside outside the museum.

At Cabras you can find one of the oldest-known dishes on the whole island: sa merca, salted mullet cooked in herbs. The dialect name suggests a Phoenician ancestry.

The *stagni* are abundant sources of fish, especially eels and mullet, which you can sample at any of the town's **restaurants** – for example *La Lanterna*, an amenable ristorante/pizzeria near the museum at Via Tharros 119 (closed Tues). A **birreria** next door offers cool drinks and stays open late. If you're looking for a **hotel**, *Hotel Summertime* (☎0783.392.089; ②), up by the museum, offers rooms with or without bath; the other hotel in Cabras is *El Sombrero* on the other side of town at Corso Italia 26 (☎0783.290.659, fax 0783.290.234; ③); both places are plain and clean. If these are full, there are also several houses in town offering **agriturismo**, for example Eligia Simbula at Via Oristano 15 (☎0783.391.048), who asks about L60,000 per person for dinner, bed and breakfast, and *Perdagruxi*, Via Trieste 6 (☎0783.391.617), charging about L35,000 per person for bed and breakfast, or L55,000 including dinner; rates drop out of season.

Cabras has a couple of **banks** with cash machines on the main drag, Crédito Italiano and Banco di Napoli. A **regatta** of the *fassonis* takes place on the Cabras lagoon in August, and the town participates in the barefoot race to San Salvatore during the first weekend of September (see below) – good, but hot, times to be here.

Marina di Torre Grande

The main lido for both Oristano and Cabras, **MARINA DI TORRE GRANDE** is located 8km west of the provincial capital along the SP1. It's a lively place to visit of an evening if you're spending any time in Oristano, mainly for its animated bars and pizzerias and the late-night scene along the seafront. Evening life kicks off with a buzzing *passeggiata* along Lungomare Eleonora d'Arborea, which runs for about a kilometre behind the beach, lined with ranks of holiday homes on the landward side – all of them shut up in winter – and dwarf palms and the view across the gulf to Tharros on the other. The resort is centred on the solid cylindrical Aragonese watchtower for which it is named, a focus for the bikes and blaring radios of Oristano's youth.

Among the many **restaurants**, which fill up fast in summer, the *Maestrale* does good seafood and has a terrace on the seafront (closed Mon in winter). If this is heaving, there are plenty of other trattorias and pizzerias around, not to mention bars and gelaterias (most places close out of season). If you're **camping**, the *Torre Grande* (☎0783.22.228; May–Sept) lies about 150m from the sea and has cabins for hire. If you want a **hotel**, the only choice is the expensive *Del Sole*, a modern block at one end of the Lungomare (☎0783.22.000, fax 0783.22.217; ⑨).

Marina di Torre Grande is on Oristano's Linea Azzurra city **bus** line, and there are also frequent services run by ARST.

San Salvatore

Six kilometres west of Marina di Torre Grande (signposted off the Tharros road), the sanctuary of **San Salvatore** (July–Aug Tues–Thurs 10am–1pm & 4–6pm, and the first week of Sept) is one of Sardinia's *chiese novenari* – churches open for just nine days a year, when devotees live in nearby *cumbessias*, or pilgrims' lodgings. The *novena* of San Salvatore takes place between August and September, culminating in one of Sardinia's most interesting festas, the **Corsa degli Scalzi** – a barefoot race run on the first weekend of September in a re-enactment of a frantic rescue mission undertaken four centuries ago to save the statue of San Salvatore from Moorish attackers. Departing from Cabras, 8km away, the first part of the race is run on the Saturday at dawn by a throng of the town's boys, barefoot and clad only in white shirts and shorts. The following day, the boys return, bearing aloft the holy statue from his sanctuary to safe custody in Cabras. It's a spirited caper, infused with the rowdy enthusiasm of the many participants and spectators.

The rest of the time the place is deserted, the outwardly unexceptional sixteenth-century church slumbering in an eerie calm in the middle of a wide area lined by one- or two-room pilgrims' shacks. If it all looks vaguely familiar, it may be because the place was used as a set for various spaghetti westerns in the sixties and seventies; indeed, San Salvatore recalls nothing so much as an adobe-built Mexican ghost-town. Belying its unassuming appearance, the church reveals a fascinating past, since it was built on top of an ancient **pagan sanctuary** dedicated to Mars and Venus, and connected in nuraghic times with a water cult. When the building is open, a guide will accompany you down into the fourth-century subterranean chambers, where you can just make out some faded frescoes of Venus, Cupid and Hercules.

In addition to these, there are black-inked drawings and graffiti from a number of sources, most intriguingly a repeated "RF". This may be a Carthaginian prayer for healing (*Rufu* in their semitic language), but the use of the Latin alphabet suggests that a degree of Punic culture survived later into the Roman era than was previously thought. Greek and Arabic writing also indicates a thoroughly cosmopolitan melange, which can be explained by the fact that the holy site lay close to Tharros, which was still an important port. The pictures of boats – including a Sard *fassonis* and a Spanish galleon – were possibly ex-voto drawings, while an image of a person in a cage could well be a prisoner's doodle from when the chambers were used as a gaol during the Spanish period.

There's a **bar** at the entrance to the huddle of *cumbessias*: *Abraxas* (closed Mon in winter), appropriately decked out to look like a western saloon, offering snacks and beers.

The Sinis coast

Outside the holiday season, an air of profound calm lies over the peninsula's western coast, and even in summer there is a stillness and sense of space here, at least away from the beaches. Straight roads branch westwards over the Sinis peninsula to a string of undeveloped **beaches** (there is no coast road), and even if the crowds get oppressive, it is always possible to wander a short distance north or south to find an unoccupied stretch of sand.

Is Arutas has a large unshaded car park (pay in summer, 8am–9pm L1500 per hour, L5000 for four hours, L10,000 for 12hrs, camper vans cost 50 percent more), a bar, and pedalos for rent in summer. The long white strand is lent a little more interest by rocky outcrops to north and south, beyond which more sand extends in both directions. Apart from passing ships, the only feature punctuating the horizon is a small island 10km out, the oddly-named **Mal di Ventre** ("stomach ache"). The origin of the name is uncertain, but sailing conditions here are sometimes fierce, and it may either refer to seasickness, or be a corruption of *Malu Entu*, dialect for bad wind. The island is uninhabited and has recently been made a marine reserve, though boats call here daily in summer from Putzu Idu (see below). The remains of a double-towered nuraghe testify to the island's occupation in prehistoric times.

Three kilometres further north (drivers have to backtrack inland, then head north and west again), the beach at **Mari Ermi** presents a similar picture to Is Arutas, with bar and beach facilities, but here the sands back onto a small lagoon, and there is a high headland a brief distance north, **Capo Sa Sturaggia**. North again, there is a much larger lagoon, the **Stagno de Is Benas**, and more signs of life – and ugly holiday homes – around the peninsula's only developed resort at **Putzu Idu**. There is a sheltered beach here, but you'll find better swimming on the north side of the peninsula, from **Cala Su Pallosu** and the endless **Is Arenas**. You can reach the first of these with your own transport; for the second you have to walk, from either Putzu Idu or Santa Caterina di Pittinuri (see p.187).

San Giovanni di Sinis

The fifth-century church of **San Giovanni di Sinis** vies with Cágliari's San Saturnino for the title of oldest church in Sardinia. It stands on the roadside at the base of the limb of land on which Tharros sits, 4km south of San Salvatore. With its red dome, irregular stonework and roof slung low over an asymmetrical facade, the paleochristian church presents quite an oriental – or at least Byzantine – appearance. That it should still be standing at all after its long years of exposure to pirate raids is largely thanks to the French Vittorini monks who took it over in the eleventh century. The interior has been stripped clean, and restorations are continuing; if you want to see inside, ask at the nearby *Casas* restaurant at Via Garibaldi 26.

Near the seashore behind the church, look out for the thatched huts, or *domus di cruccuri*, long used by local fishermen, now converted into happily unobtrusive holiday homes. Opposite the church, a line of bars, pizzerias and restaurants caters to the coach parties visiting Tharros, immediately beyond a perfect arc of beach about a kilometre up the road. The combined effect of the bustle around the beach and the comings and goings of buses and cars makes for a fair amount of confusion here in high summer.

Tharros

In shape, the spit of land on which **Tharros** was built resembles a clenched fist, with a sturdy Spanish watchtower dominating its highest point. Protruding into the Golfo di Oristano, the peninsula, which ends at Capo San Marco, afforded a perfect vantage point for any military installation based there, and also provided safe anchorage on either side, according to the direction of the wind. Inevitably,

The elongated Stagno di Sale Porcus, stretching out behind Putzu Idu, often dries out completely in summer. In winter it hosts a swarm of flamingoes. The area is managed by LIPU (Italian bird protection society).

The Sinis peninsula

given its strategic advantages, Phoenicians settled the site during their period of expansion, as early as 800 BC. Tharros flourished under Carthaginian occupation and then, after 238 BC, maintained its importance under the Romans, who furnished it with the baths and streets that you see today. The town had already declined by the Imperial era, however, and with the demise of the *Pax Romana*, it withered, falling prey to Moorish raids, and was finally abandoned in 1070 in favour of the more secure Oristano.

You can tour the site (daily 9am–8pm, 9am–5pm in winter; L8000) on your own, but it makes more sense to accept the company of a guide for at least part of the way to get a full picture of what there is here. There is usually one available who speaks English, though you may have to wait for a sizable group to form (and note that guides are usually not available between 1 and 4pm).

For the most part, the site consists of Punic and Roman houses arranged on a grid of streets, of which the broad-slabbed **Decumanus Maximus** and **Cardo Maximus** are the most impressive, the latter with a deep open sewer visible down the centre, now partly covered over. This was probably the main shopping street – a large number of coins have been found along it, along with other clues such as a slab of stone with a groove for a sliding door and holes at either end to support it. At the top of the Cardo Maximus, a basalt Roman wall stands near the remains of a **tophet** (burial ground) from the earlier Punic settlement, and the hill is crowned by the former Carthaginian acropolis, with a wide ditch alongside that was used for defence by the Carthaginians and as a burial site by the Romans, as evident from the tubular-shaped tombs dug up here.

But the site's most prominent remains are the two strikingly white **Corinthian columns**, remnants of a first-century BC Roman temple (the portico would originally have had four). Alongside lies the site's best-preserved Carthaginian structure, a **cistern** walled with large rectangular blocks. Towards the sea, east of here, stand the remains of a bath house from the end of the second century AD, though these are not as large or impressive as the **thermal complex** on the southern edge of the site, which dates from a century later. The sheltered site to the north of the earlier baths, overlooking the sea, was probably used for a theatre by the Romans; seating has been provided for the performances that take place in summer. The Romans also built a minuscule amphitheatre; its remains are still visible on the hill near the Punic tophet.

Although Tharros has much in common with Nora, there are also significant differences. Tharros was a much bigger, more important centre for far longer than Nora, which soon decayed into a summer resort for Romans from Karalis before being abandoned completely, several centuries before Tharros was evacuated in favour of Oristano. However, like Nora, Tharros has much more waiting to be revealed, submerged underwater as a result of subsi-

Tickets for the performances of Greek theatre, classical and light music and poetry which take place at Tharros more or less weekly between mid-July and mid-August are available directly from the site's ticket office. Events begin around 9.30 or 10pm; prices are L13,000– 15,000. For details, contact the site at ☎0783.370. 019.

dence, and marine archeologists periodically return to fish out more valuable traces.

The ticket to the site will also admit you to the **Torre Spagnola** (daily 9am–1pm & 3–5pm, 3–8pm in summer; L3000, or free with Tharros ticket), a restored Spanish watchtower overlooking the ancient city, which offers sweeping views over the peninsula and the Sinis area.

South of Oristano: Santa Giusta and Arborea

The flat lands south of Oristano really make up the northern reaches of the Campidano plain – a scenically uninspiring landscape, but by no means devoid of interest. The first stop out of Oristano should be the Romanesque church of **Santa Giusta**, a Pisan construction that remains central and relevant to the local community which shares its name. From here the 131 superstrada swerves southeast towards Cágliari, by-passing the extensive reclaimed *bonifica* that is one of the most enduring legacies of the Fascist era in Sardinia. To see this and its main town **Arborea**, founded only in 1928, take the south-bound SS126, the main artery across this prosperous landscape, from which roads shoot off to the mainly sandy coast to the west. Most of this littoral remains undeveloped, though there is a handful of hotels for those who want to spend time on the beach; one of them, set amid the thick belt of pine woods that backs onto the beach, is one of the island's premier bases for **horseriding**. The road ends at the **Stagno di Marceddi**, a natural frontier between Oristano's cultivated plains and the rugged hills of Cágliari province, where the small village of **Marceddi** offers a choice of fish restaurants by the waterside.

Santa Giusta

Three kilometres south of Oristano, eucalyptus woods round the **Stagno di Santa Giusta** provide shade for picnics and birdwatchers intent on the itinerant population of aquatic wildfowl that continues to feed here, despite the passing traffic and the industry along the lagoon's western shore. Both the lagoon and the nearby village of **SANTA GIUSTA** – once the Punic town of Othoca, now little more than a suburb of Oristano – are named after the austere Romanesque **Basilica di Santa Giusta**, one of the earliest of that string of Tuscan-style constructions which went up in the eleventh to fourteenth centuries across northern Sardinia. This one, whose severe lines suggest Lombard influence, dates from around 1135 and was elevated to cathedral-status in the sixteenth century. Prominently sited at the top of a flight of steps behind a public garden in the centre of town, the church's facade displays a black basalt cross and a triple-mullioned

*The Basilica di
Santa Giusta is
still the
centrepiece for
four days of
celebration
around its
saint's day of
14 May.*

window, topped by a typically Pisan recessed rhomboid motif in the
tympanum. Below the cross, the tall portal is flanked by two truncated columns and a pair of stone lions. Three rusting cannons lie within a railed area to the right, while the main entrance is on the left side
of the building.

Inside, a wooden-beamed ceiling covers the nave, which is illuminated by slit windows cut into the walls and apses, and lined with a
motley array of marble and granite columns. Fluted and plain, some
of these were taken from the ruined city of Tharros, while the first
two columns on the left and the second on the right show evidence
of Arab workmanship. Round arches give access to brick-vaulted
aisles and a series of lateral chapels, the first of which on the right
has a painted altar and ceiling and a wooden crucifix. Otherwise
there is little concession to ornament in the basilica's interior.
Round the back of the church, the square, rather graceless belltower is less than a hundred years old, a poor replacement for the original *campanile*.

A short distance to the south on Via Giovanni XXIII, the church of
Santa Severa stands amid the necropolis of Punic Othaca. The
unmatched sandstone masonry of the church betrays its different
periods of construction, going back to the fourteenth century. The
spiral staircase next to it leads down to the subterranean tombs, part
of a funerary area discovered in 1861 and excavated in 1910 and
again from 1984 to 1989. The tombs are of different types, and
include one monumental example immediately south of the church,
apparently intended for a high-ranking official, judging by similar
ones found in Morocco, Tunisia, Cyprus and southern Spain.
Probably originating with the Phoenicians around the seventh century BC, the necropolis remained in use until the Roman period in the
first century BC, and has yielded Phoenician, Carthaginian, Greek
and Etruscan ceramics, as well as gold and silver jewels, seals,
amulets and weapons of bronze and iron, most of these now preserved in the Cágliari's archeological museum. The much simpler
Roman tombs have also brought to light ceramics, glass and coins.
The site is normally locked – visitors should apply for access at the
Pro Loco on Via Ampsicora (☎0783.358.160).

*On the first
Sunday of
August a
regatta is held
on the Stagno
di Santa
Giusta, using
the fassonis,
the traditional
reed-made
boats of the
area (see
p.169).*

Around the corner from the church on Via Garibaldi, *Da
Leonardo* pizzeria/ristorante offers simple, reasonably-priced
meals, just across from the pale-green *Killtime* disco (see p.168).

Arborea and around

Another smaller lagoon, the **Stagno di S'Ena Arrubia**, 5km south of
the Stagno di Santa Giusta, has a greater variety of birdlife, including
sandpipers, herons and the rare whiteheaded ducks. Although this
area has been left a protected site, the land south of here, the
Bonifica di Arborea, was reclaimed and rehabilitated as cultivable
fields after 1919.

The quiet rural centre of **ARBOREA** is a twentieth-century settlement whose name is a conscious throwback to the old *giudicato*.
Founded in 1928 during the campaign to maximize Sardinia's
domestic production, the town was originally called "Mussolinia",
and was intended to house the rural colonies introduced into the area
from the Veneto, Friuli and Emilia-Romagna regions of Italy, to
which the town owes its incongruous northern Italian appearance.
This is most noticeable in the main square, Piazza Maria Ausiliatrice,
where a formal garden with neat flowerbeds and palm trees is overlooked by a red-brick parish church and town hall, all surrounded by
right-angled, tree-lined streets.

The whole place exudes the cardinal Fascist values of planning
and orderliness, and the neo-Gothic church, **Cristo Redentore**, even
sports a tidy grotto carved into the left side, with a Madonna presiding. At the opposite end of the square, the grand Liberty-style town
hall houses a small but immaculately-kept collection of archeological
finds from the locality, the **Collezione Archeologica** (open when the
town hall is open, usually Mon & Tues 10am–1pm & 3.30–5.30pm;
Wed–Fri 10am–1pm; Sat 9am–noon; free). Six display cases show
items mainly from the Punic and Roman settlements in the area:
bracelets, rings, urns, oil-burners and amphorae, as well as bits of
ceramics and glass, and bronze coins from different periods. Many of
the exhibits were unearthed during the land-reclamation work of
1932, when a Punic necropolis and numerous Roman sepulchres
came to light. Most striking of these is the unusual second- or third-
century-BC vase in the shape of a child's head.

Beyond the main square, the neat appearance of the houses ends
abruptly, and there's precious little to warrant any further exploration. The town could make a useful alternative to staying in
Oristano, however, especially as it possesses a comfortable and cheap
hotel right on the main square, the endearingly old-fashioned *Gallo
Blanco* (☎0783.800.241; ①). The attached **restaurant** (closed
Thurs except for hotel guests) offers a three-course meal plus coffee
for around L32,000. If you want food to take away, Via Sardegna, off
the south side of the square, has a baker and an indoor **market** (open
9am–1pm and 4–7.30pm except Wed afternoon and Sun).

Marina di Arborea

Outside Arborea, the fruits of the large-scale land-reclamation
scheme that made the town possible are readily apparent: the whole
district, formerly a malarial swamp, has been transformed by
drainage, canalization and irrigation into a richly productive zone.
Fruit and vegetables, vineyards, tobacco and beetroot all thrive here,
and the area also supports herds of dairy cows, which account for
most of the island's milk production.

Much of the coast is fringed by a dense pine forest, interspersed
with the occasional wartime pillbox and some superb sandy beaches,

East of
Oristano:
into the
mountains

all within sight of Tharros across the Golfo di Oristano and accessible along any of the straight roads leading westward. At the end of one of these, you come upon **MARINA DI ARBOREA** – little more than a handful of houses behind the shore. One of them is a small **restaurant** and **hotel**, *Il Canneto* (☎0783.800.561; ②), right on the sandy beach – its eight rooms fill quickly in summer.

A much grander affair, the *Ala Birdi* hotel complex (☎0783.801.083, fax 0783.801.086; ⑤), lies just up the coast (reachable from the turn-off opposite the unattractive *La Pineta* hotel, on the main road north of Arborea), where there are good facilities for families, with a pool and the beach just a few steps away beyond the curtain of pinewoods. The main attraction here, though, is the hotel's **riding facilities**, among the best in all Sardinia. All ages and levels are catered for, and excursions organized along the coast, through the woods, and inland. The hotel also has one- and two-room apartments for rent. Ask about family rates, discounts for longer stays and half-board, which may be compulsory in summer.

Marceddi

South of Arborea, Terralba and its surrounding country is interesting only for its wine production; the reclaimed land west of here is also flat and fertile, but is lent more character by the placid lagoon, the **Stagno di Marceddi**, that separates this area from the hilly region on the other side, part of Cágliari province. The banks of the lagoon, which lies 11km south of Arborea off the SP69, have tables and benches under the pines for picnics. Near the mouth of this stretch of water, the sleepy village of **Marceddi** has a low-key port, or *porticciolo*, where fishing boats and pleasure craft are anchored, and a small selection of restaurants, among which *Da Lucio* (closed Thurs except June–Sept) has good seafood dishes and quantities of the renowned Terralba wine; *panini* and *pizzette* are available from bars nearby. A narrow causeway runs south across the mouth of the lagoon to Sant'Antonio di Santadi and the Costa Verde (see p.135).

East of Oristano:
into the mountains

There are two or three places **east of Oristano** that are worth seeking out, all in the former territory of medieval Arborea. The SS388 veers inland through nondescript villages and landscape that is initially flat and uninteresting, but soon becomes hillier and more varied. **Fordongianus** is the prime attraction in these parts, the site of some well-preserved Roman baths on the banks of the Tirso river and an interesting 400-year-old Aragonese home. The village's volcanic trachyte stone – brownish-red, pink or grey – is the predominant building material in this area, quarried around the old Roman resort.

Further east, the roads become more tortuous and the villages more isolated. Near the textile town of **Samugheo**, there is a good expedition to be made on foot or by car to the splendidly isolated **Castello Medusa**, right on the confines of Nuoro province.

ARST **buses** to and from Oristano stop at Fordongianus and Samugheo; **hotels** are few and far between but, where they exist, generally cheap.

Fordongianus and around

Twenty-eight kilometres up the Tirso river from Oristano, **FORDONGIANUS** was a Roman spa town founded at the end of the first century AD under the emperor Trajan; the present name is a corruption of Forum Traiani. The town conserves its old Roman bridge over the river, and the baths are still in fairly good condition and visitable on the river bank at the bottom of the town.

Near the western entrance to Fordongianus, a signposted left turn soon brings you to the **Casa Aragonese** (9am–1pm & 3–5.30pm; L5000, including Terme Romane), marked out by the pillared portico fronting it. The distinctive red trachyte dwelling is thought to date from the end of the sixteenth or beginning of the seventeenth century, and to have been built for a noble Catalan family. Until 1998 the building housed the local library, and there are moves afoot to install a museum or gallery here, but for the present the rooms are utterly bare, showing few signs of the people who once inhabited them. Even without anything more engaging to view, and despite some unfortunate cement restorations from the 1980s, the house is worth a quick whirl round. Guides show you round the interior, pointing out the Gothic decorated windows and doors, and the window seats where the ladies of the household would sit and sew.

You may already have noticed some trachytic stone **sculptures** displayed in front of the house, and there are several more in the garden at the back. These are some of the entries in an international competition held annually here; others are exhibited in the streets of Fordongianus and nearby villages. If you're here in July and August, you can see the sculptors chiselling away in the streets of the village.

There is more to see at the **Terme Romane** (9am–1pm and 2.30–5pm; L5000, including Casa Aragonese) on the banks of the Tirso river, though half the pleasure here is the evocative site. You can see the water steaming as it gushes into the river at a temperature of 54° centigrade, and local women still use it to scrub their laundry as they have done for a couple of millennia. The baths retain much of their original structure, the oldest sections including the main pool, while the frigidarium, tepidarium and calidarium date from a third-century enlargement. Behind the main building, part of a forum still stands, from which a stairway leads to what is thought to be either an ancient hotel or butcher's shop, partly frescoed. A pedestrian viaduct leads across the river to a modern thermal complex, due to open in 1999 or 2000.

A kilometre or so west of Fordongianus, the thirteenth-century **chiesa di San Lussório** stands within its walled enclosure by the side of the SS388. The wonky red trachyte facade looks rough and unadorned at first glance, though closer inspection reveals a very eroded relief around the base of the doorway, and another on one of the columns around the apse, where excavations of a paleochristian necropolis are currently under way.

If you're looking for somewhere to eat in Fordongianus, there are a couple of **restaurants** in town – try *La Befana*, a pizzeria on Via Santíssimi Mártiri (closed Tues), or the smarter *Su Montigu* restaurant, nearby at Via Carlo Alberto Dalla Chiesa, which has local dishes (☎0783.60.018; closed Sun in Feb and Thurs all year except Aug; no CCs).

Samugheo and Castello di Medusa

East of Fordongianus, the SS388 twists into the mountains of the Barbagia, passing close to the dam at the southern end of Lago Omodeo (see p.183), and taking in the village of **Busachi** before reaching the mountain town of Sórgono (see p.334). A right turn off this road leads south to Allai (a much shorter route than the zigzagging SP33 going directly there from Fordongianus) and

*Throughout
August, a craft
fair, the
Mostra
dell'Artigiana-
to del
Mandrolisai,
takes place in
Samugheo,
featuring
mountains of
rugs, blankets,
tapestries and
furniture for
sale in the
shops and
stalls.*

SAMUGHEO, a large village famous for its textiles (*tessile*). It's not a particularly exciting place, but it does have a couple of banks, a hotel/restaurant, and – opposite the Municipio in Piazza Sedda – a good-looking church constructed of pink trachyte blocks and worth a brief wander round. Built in the seventeenth century, **San Sebastiano** has an unusual Gothic interior with a low-vaulted altar. The lovely old wooden pulpit, carved with faces, rests on a single stone column.

At Via Vittorio Emanuele 37, the town's only **hotel**, the newish *Bittu* (☎0783.64.190; ①; no CCs), offers standard rooms with bath and a decent restaurant.

Three or four kilometres south of Samugheo on the SP38 Asuni road, a dirt track – indicated by a yellow signpost on the left – leads off towards the **Castello di Medusa**, a ruined redoubt which makes a rewarding jaunt either on foot or with your own transport. On the way you'll pass several *pineddas*, the unusual igloo-type constructions used by the local shepherds; they resemble miniature nuraghi, but are made of much lighter, smaller stones. Look out for glimpses of the distant peaks of the Gennargentu mountains to the east as you follow the high ridge with steep drops below. The castle itself is about 5km along the track: for orientation, aim for the orange church visible on the horizon. The ruins appear suddenly below the track on the left, utterly isolated above a gorge, though the messy evidence of sporadic restoration work detracts from the site's remote flavour.

Little is known of the origins of the castello, but it is thought that this was an outpost of Fordongianus during the Roman occupation, and the fortified site was later used by Arborea's *giudicati*. The straggling ruins give little idea of how the castle appeared when intact, but it's a grand spot nonetheless, for solitary contemplation or for heading off on foot into the surrounding hills. By crossing the river to the track on the other side, it would be feasible to reach Asuni, about 3km south, through high pastoral country, dotted with herds of goats and sheep, dry-stone walls and sudden rocky outcrops.

East of Oristano: into the mountains

North of Oristano

The northern half of Oristano province contains a couple of essential sites – the nuraghic complexes of **Santa Cristina** and **Losa** – and a handful of non-essential but still rewarding spots which you could take in on easy detours from your main route. Unless you're stopping for wine or oranges in the productive region immediately north of the provincial capital, the nuraghi should be your first halts – they're easily the most important such sites in the province. At Abbasanta, near Losa, the SS131Dir branches off the Carlo Felice Highway towards Nuoro. Anyone with an interest in **Antonio Gramsci** should head a couple of kilometres up this road to see the small exhibition of documents and letters relating to the Communist theorist in his former home in the village of **Ghilarza**, just west of the dammed **Lago Omodeo**. Still further up this route, **Sédilo** has the much venerated church of Sant'Antine, also scene of the hectic **S'Ardia** horse race famous throughout the island.

Horses also feature prominently in the village of **Santu Lussurgiu**, west of Abbasanta, where riding skills are put to the test in the local Carnival celebrations. Rounding the northern reaches of the ex-volcano **Monte Ferru** will bring you to **Cúglieri** and within sight of the sea. There are **beaches** below around **Santa Caterina di Pittinuri**, and an atmospheric paleochristian site at **Cornus**.

Any of these places could be visited on day trips from Oristano, and all but the two nuraghi are reachable on ARST **buses**. If they don't mind a walk, train travellers can at least reach Nuraghi Losa and Ghilarza from the train station at Abbasanta, and Paulilátino is also on the main line. **Accommodation** is thin on the ground, however; apart from the Cúglieri area, the only place you'll find any choice is at San Leonardo de Siete Fuentes, near Santu Lussurgiu.

Though Barátili San Pietro is 5km from the Stagno di Cabras, the villagers have perfected the art of making and navigating the reed-built fassonis used in the race held there in August (see pp.169–170.

Santa Cristina and Paulilátino

Travelling up the main SS131 you'll soon be passing through the "Vernaccia triangle", an area bounded by the villages of Zeddiani, Barátili San Pietro and Solarussa, which forms the core of the Vernaccia wine-producing region. Further on, you might stop to buy a kilo or two of what are reputed to be Sardinia's best oranges, grown around **Milis**; the season extends over ten months of the year. Otherwise, keep going up the Carlo Felice highway about 25km north of Oristano, for the signposted exit to the nuraghic complex of **Santa Cristina** (daily 8.30am–sunset; L4000), a wide-ranging site scattered among a shady grove of olive trees, comprising a nuraghe, a sacred well and other nuraghic buildings, some of them dating back to 1800 BC. The main tower, about 15m high, has an egg-shaped "tholos"-type interior, in which niches and alcoves have been hewn away. From the top, the views over the green wooded surroundings take in other fragments of this extensive site, including a **capanna lunga** – a long, stone-built, open-topped structure of unknown function, which has yielded Roman finds from the third century BC. But the most impressive part of the complex is the underground shrine and **sacred well** a short walk away. An extraordinary feat of engineering, the shrine is reached down a flight of perfectly smooth steps between equally well-finished walls; they are so well-preserved you could mistake them for a modern reconstruction. At the bottom, the narrow chamber and well can't have changed significantly since they were first built. Nearby, there is a round meeting room, similar in form to those in other nuraghic sites, and various other less well-preserved fragments of buildings.

It's an impressive grouping, though one of the most attractive aspects of the Santa Cristina complex is its mossy green ambience. Look out for a sprawling, hoary olive tree here, said to be 1000 years old. The entry ticket includes a guided tour of the site, and also allows entry into the **Museo Archeologico-Etnográfico** in the centre of **PAULILÁTINO**, 5km further up the road (Tues–Sun 9am–1pm & 3–5.30pm, 5–8pm in summer). Housed in a handsomely-restored building from the seventeenth century, this disparate and diverting collection includes archeological finds from Santa Cristina on the ground floor, and local photographs, traditional furnishings, tools and other items of folkloric interest on the upper storeys, with temporary exhibitions on the roof and in the courtyard.

Ghilarza

Although born near Oristano, the great political theorist **Antonio Gramsci** spent most of his youth in the village of **GHILARZA**, between Abbasanta and Lago Omodeo. The modest house where he and his family lived at Corso Umberto 57, near the main church on the town's narrow main street, has been converted into the **Casa di Antonio Gramsci** (Mon–Fri 8.30am–12.30pm & 4–7pm; free), a study centre dedicated to Gramsci's life and writings. Much of the small building is taken up by a library, meeting hall, taped reminiscences by people who knew him and innumerable documents. It's a curious mix of the personal – letters to his mother, boyhood photographs, toys – and his academic and political development. The

Antonio Gramsci (1891–1937)

Antonio Gramsci was born in the village of Ales, southeast of Oristano, but grew up in Ghilarza where his father worked with the land registry. Never physically strong, he suffered from rickets as a child, a condition aggravated by poverty after his father was jailed for "administrative irregularities". Despite such obstacles, the young Gramsci doggedly pursued his education, leaving Ghilarza before he was eighteen to attend the lyceum in Cágliari, where his brother Gennaro was already involved in socialist politics.

By the time he was twenty, Antonio had enrolled to study letters at the university of Turin. In that industrial city, he was drawn into working-class politics, and in 1921 became one of the founders of the Italian Communist Party. The following year, he took part in an Italian delegation to Moscow, where he met his future wife, Giulia Schucht. Returning to Italy, he was elected to the Chamber of Deputies, where he became one of the most effective and articulate opponents of Fascism. Inexorably, the regime closed in. "We must prevent this brain from functioning for 20 years," Mussolini is reported to have ordered. Gramsci was arrested in November 1926; he was 35, and would spend the rest of his life in jail, dying of tuberculosis in 1937.

Yet Mussolini's threat proved ineffective, and the publication of Gramsci's *Prison Notebooks* immediately after the end of World War II created a sensation. Paradoxically, Gramsci's imprisonment had allowed him to develop his ideas untainted by Stalinism, and they were to play a crucial role in the reformation of the Italian Communist Party and the development of the "Eurocommunism" that underlay the electoral successes of his fellow Sard Enrico Berlinguer in the 1970s.

prison cell outside Bari where he spent five years for anti-Fascist activities has been reproduced according to the exact measurements. You could spend an absorbing hour or so here (though a knowledge of Italian would help) – but note that the museum, run by volunteers, does not adhere very closely to its official opening hours, and you'd do well to telephone first (☎0785.54.164).

If you need a **snack** in Ghilarza, try the *Paninoteca da Sabina* at Corso Umberto 85 (closed Sun), which serves sandwiches, hot dogs and chips. For a fuller meal, the unnamed restaurant through the arch opposite Corso Umberto 132 (closed Mon) should fit the bill.

Lago Omodeo and Sédilo

East of Ghilarza, **Lago Omodeo** is Italy's largest artificial lake, covering an area of 22 square kilometres. Named after the engineer who planned it in 1923, it supplies electricity to the area as well as drinking water and irrigation. It's extremely scenic, but difficult to get close to the water; if you felt like a paddle, there are places where access is possible, especially on the eastern shores around the village of Bidoni.

Nearby, the town of **SÉDILO** hosts the annual **S'Ardia** horse race, held in honour of the Roman Emperor Constantine in his saintly guise of San Costantino. The race takes place at dawn on July 6 and 7 at breakneck speed and over a danger-strewn course, around the *novena* church (open for nine days a year) of **Sant'Antine di Sédilo**. It's an attractive, woody spot outside the village and within sight of Lago Omodeo, though tranquillity is notably absent during the S'Ardia itself. The risks to participants and spectators alike are increased by people whose sole job is to harass the horses and their riders, to the extent of shooting dud bullets at them. It's a thrilling spectacle, full of hot tempers, commotion and displays of virility. The church of Sant'Antine is also interesting for the copious ex-voto graffiti scribbled on its walls.

Nuraghe Losa

Standing alone in bare flat country just west of the SS131, the **Nuraghe Losa** (daily 9am–1hr before sunset; free) makes an easy and essential stop for anyone following Sardinia's main north–south highway in either direction (look out for the exit signs). It's also possible to reach the site by public tranport, if you don't mind the three-kilometre walk from the train station at Abbasanta. If you're coming this way, turn left out of the station, cross the lines at the level crossing, and follow the road straight, turning right at the signpost.

Dating from the Middle Bronze Age (the second millennium BC), the flat, grassy site is encompassed within a prodigious perimeter wall, giving a better idea of the extent of a nuraghic settlement than other similar structures in Sardinia. Either before or after visiting the nuraghe itself, take a bit of time to follow this wall round for new perspectives on the central structure, and to explore the three shattered **external towers** which provided secondary entrances to the complex. The perimeter wall encloses the scanty remains of a prehistoric village and, just inside the site's main entrance, exposed cinerary urns from the settlement's post-nuraghic phase, the remains of a first- to second-century-AD cemetery.

It is the massive sheer-walled trilobate (three-cornered) nuraghe which commands most of your attention, however, the compact, fortified structure growing in impact as you approach. Composed of regular basalt stones half-covered with a striking orange lichen, the tapering walls of the truncated central tower are smoother than those of most other nuraghi, today reaching a height of nearly thirteen metres. The design and arrangement of the various parts of the complex are, as ever, baffling. Directly in front of the nuraghe's main entrance, a circular meeting chamber leaves little room for coming and going, and there are equally cramped spaces on the nuraghe's western side, where an inner rampart forms an additional protective belt, enclosing a small courtyard accessible through a lintelled door. Two minor defensive towers – now topless – are incorporated into the rampart, furnished with narrow slits for viewing the surrounding area

and for archers to fire through. Cradled within the rampart at the
northern end are more remains of stone buildings, and an entrance –
again tiny – for access to the northern tower of the trilobate.

On the other side of the bastion, the **main tower** is entered
through a narrow corridor with a large recess hacked out of the
right-hand wall (possibly for a sentry). To the left, a flight of stone
steps curls up to a second-floor chamber, continuing on to the open
terrace from which, on a clear day, you can see the peaks of the
Gennargentu mountains to the east. Back on ground level, the main
corridor also has lateral passages leading to the bare windowless
chambers within the bastion's two southern towers. The main central
tower, the oldest part of the structure, has a tall conical interior,
dimly lit by electric lighting, with alcoves and niches punched out of
the walls. With little evidence of the use to which this monument was
put or of the society that created it, one has to resort to imagination
to fill in the gaps, but there is no single explanation: the overall complex shows continuous occupation from the middle Bronze Age
(around 1500 BC) to the seventh century AD, while most of the village to the northeast and southwest of the bastion has yet to be
uncovered.

The site also holds a small **museum** of very fragmentary finds from
the vicinity. Needles and vases from the nuraghic period fill one display case, pottery with zigzag designs from the fifth and sixth centuries AD are in another, and there are photos and notes from other
nuraghi in the area from which some of these finds originate. There
is nothing particularly arresting, however, since the best stuff is on
view or in store in Cágliari (see pp.77–78).

*For more on
Sardinia's
nuraghic
culture, see
pp.148–149.*

Santu Lussurgiu and around

The village of **SANTU LUSSURGIU** sits in the crater of an extinct
volcano some 35km north of Oristano and 15km west of the Carlo
Felice highway on SP15, amid bare craggy hills and woods of olives
and chestnut. This was once a highly volatile seismic zone, though
nowadays there's little suggestion of anything erupting in this
intensely peaceful corner of the island.

Though many of the local dwellings are modern in appearance, the
nucleus of the village is a web of steep cobbled lanes, among which
the heavily buttressed church of **Santa Maria degli Ángeli** stands out
on an elevation. Opposite the public gardens on the left of the main
street, the grey stone and unusual shape of this late fifteenth-century
building is enough to lure you inside, where there's a good wooden
altar – but the church has been closed for years while serious restoration work is carried out, and it shows no imminent sign of reopening.

Immediately past the gardens further down the street, the **Museo
della Tecnologia Contadina** (also known as the Centro di Cultura
Popolare) on Via Deodato Meloni is an admirably comprehensive and
scrupulously-catalogued collection of everyday items from different

eras and different parts of Sardinia. The museum has no fixed opening hours, however – either just turn up and hope to find someone there, or telephone the curator to make an appointment (☎0783.550.617 or 0783.550.706).

The main passion in Santu Lussurgiu, however, is **horses**. Rearing and riding them is in the blood here, and at no time is this more apparent than in the village's annual party, a horse race spread over three days during **Carnival** (usually Sunday, Monday and Shrove Tuesday). As in Oristano's Carnival binge, riders gallop hard through the narrow streets of the old town, though there are few or no costumed theatrics here – this is serious bareback riding, and highly exciting to watch. The village's saint's day, around **21 August**, is also an excuse to saddle up for horseback competitions during four days of festivities. Santu Lussurgiu takes a break from the horses at **Easter**, however, which is celebrated with choral singing, but the local craftwork for sale in the shops includes anything to do with horses, from saddles to pen-knives.

San Leonardo de Siete Fuentes

North of Santu Lussurgiu, weekend picnickers head up the minor road towards Macomer (see p.219) for the wooded area around the hamlet of **SAN LEONARDO DE SIETE FUENTES**. The village's Spanish name is a reference to its highly-prized mineral waters which attract droves of connoisseurs. The crumbly old Romanesque church is the burial place of Guelfo, son of Count Ugolino della Gherardesca, who died in 1292 (see p.130). San Leonardo is also the scene of a **horse fair**; held every June 2, it's one of Sardinia's most important markets of this kind. The two small **pensioni** in the village make excellent places to stay at any time of year: *Malica*, at Via Macomer 5 (☎ & fax 0783.550.756; ②; no CCs), and *Lugas* (☎0783.550.790; ①; no CCs), the latter with shared bathrooms. As they only have twelve and six rooms respectively, you'd better book in advance if you're coming during the fair.

Cúglieri

West of Santu Lussurgiu looms the mainly forested **Monte Ferru** – the name a reminder of the iron once mined here – which reaches a height of over 1000m. This former volcanic zone is now endowed with an abundance of rivers and springs which nourish its thick forests of oak, elm and chestnut. Seventeen kilometres northwest on the twisty SP19, the silver dome of the basilica at the top of the village of **CÚGLIERI** makes a prominent landmark for miles around. If you're in the village, make sure you take in the superb panorama over the sea from this high point; the basilica itself, though, is less spectacular close up than when viewed from afar, its broad brown exterior only feebly enlivened by two marble carvings on either side of the portal.

If you were thinking of **staying** off the beaten track, the village
has one very reasonable choice, *Hotel Desogos* on Vico Cugia (☎ &
fax 0785.39.660; ①; no CCs), off the one-way Via Cugia, the main
road descending through the old town from the basilica. Plain
rooms are available with or without private bathroom, and there is
a restaurant.

Santa Caterina and Cornus

If you prefer a spot nearer the sea, head downhill along the SS292 to
the main resort on this stretch of coast, **SANTA CATERINA DI PIT-
TINURI**, a busy holiday centre in summer, pretty dead at any other
time. The town itself, almost overwhelmed by holiday homes, has little of much interest, but the **beaches** around it are first-class, a mixture of sand and rocks. Above the town's main beach, a protected
sandy bay, there's the modern, unlovely *Baia* **hotel** (☎ & fax
0785.38.105; ③), signposted off the main road, which offers standard accommodation and a restaurant (hotel and restaurant are
sometimes closed in winter). Further down Corso Alagon, there's
another pleasanter and cheaper hotel, *La Scogliera* (☎ & fax
0785.38.231; ②), closer to the beach and with a pizzeria, though
offering only seven rooms.

The area around Santa Caterina is famed for its olive groves, one
of the island's major sources of olives and olive oil. A kilometre or
two south, a dirt road leads off to the left, signposted **CORNUS**: veer
right just before the cemented section of the track to reach the site,
which is always open (free). The settlement here was the focus for
the gathering opposition of the allied Carthaginian and Sard forces –
under the local chieftain Ampsicora – to the growing power of Rome.
The rebellion was swiftly crushed by Roman forces in 216 BC,
Ampsicora took his own life, and with the Carthaginian threat banished for ever, the way was clear for Rome's undisputed domination
of the island.

The battleground itself is a little further inland on a hill, though
there's nothing left to see of the epic conflict. The main site, however, reveals the interesting remains of an early Christian centre of
worship. The outlines of a double-apsed basilica are clearly visible,
with tombs jammed into every available space, even the apses.
Further along, you'll come across the baptistery, marked out by a
well-preserved cruciform font. It's a serene, deserted spot, within
sight of the sea, and ideal for a quiet picnic.

Continuing south on the SS292, there are more good swimming
spots at **Su Archittu** on either side of a ruined watchtower on a point,
including one famous natural rock arch which you can swim through
and climb above. There's a **restaurant** and discotheque, *La
Capanna*, hereabouts to satisfy post-swim cravings, and a **campsite**
a short distance south, *Europa* (May–Sept; ☎0785.38.058), which
also has bungalows for rent.

Travel Details

TRAINS

Abbasanta to: Cágliari (11 daily; 1hr 35min–2hr 15min); Macomer (12 daily; 25min); Olbia (2 daily; 2hr 30min); Oristano (12 daily; 30min); Ozieri-Chilivani (6 daily; 1hr 20min); Paulilátino (9 daily; 10min); Sássari (2 daily; 2hr 10min).

Oristano to: Abbasanta (10 daily; 35min); Cágliari (hourly; 1hr–1hr 40min); Macomer (hourly; 1hr); Olbia (2 daily; 3hr); Ozieri-Chilivani (7 daily; 2hr); Paulilátino (8 daily; 30min); Sássari (2 daily; 2hr 15min–2hr 50min).

Paulilátino to Abbasanta (9 daily; 10min); Cágliari (6 daily; 1hr 25min–2hr 15min); Macomer (9 daily; 35min); Olbia (1 daily; 2hr 30min); Oristano (6 daily; 25min); Ozieri-Chilivani (2 daily; 1hr 30min).

BUSES

Cabras to: Oristano (1–2 hourly; 15min).

Oristano to: Abbasanta (Mon–Sat 9 daily, Sun 1; 2hr); Arborea (Mon–Sat 1–2 hourly; 25min); Bosa (Mon–Sat 6 daily; 2hr); Cabras (1–2 hourly; 15min); Cágliari (5 daily; 1hr 25min); Cúglieri (Mon–Sat 6–7 daily; 1hr 10min); Fordongianus (Mon–Sat 3 daily; 40min); Marina di Torre Grande (Mon–Sat 12 daily, Sun 1; 15min); Nuoro (4 daily; 2hr); Santa Caterina di Pittinuri (July–Aug 2 daily; 40min); Santa Giusta (Mon–Sat 1–2 hourly; 10min); Samugheo (Mon–Sat 5 daily; 1hr 10min); San Giovanni di Sinis (July–Aug 4 daily; 40min); Sássari (4 daily; 2hr 15min); Tharros (July–Aug 4 daily; 45min).

Chapter 5

The northwest coast

S
ardinia's **northwest coast** shelters a trio of the most attractive seaside resorts on the island, interspersed with some really spectacular coastline. The principal resort on this strip, **Alghero**, has become a major package destination without jettisoning its distinctive Catalan character – the result of intense colonization in the fourteenth century. Paradoxically, given this faintly exotic tinge, it is simultaneously the most "Italian" of Sardinia's holiday towns, its old centre a tight web of narrow lanes jammed with boutiques, bars and restaurants. It's often compared to mainland towns like Sorrento or San Remo, and if it lacks their glamorous edge, it's also refreshingly free of their cynical hard sell. Even a short stay should be enough to get acquainted with the abundance of enticing beaches in the vicinity and to investigate the area's most important archeological sites, not to mention the famous **Grotta di Nettuno** on the point at Capo Caccia.

South of Alghero, the rocky coast remains unspoiled by development, and is consequently one of the last habitats in Sardinia of the griffon vulture. At the end of this stretch, the riverside port of **Bosa** is still waiting to be discovered by the big package companies. While not exactly tourist-free, the town has a quiet, undemanding atmosphere perfectly in tune with the slow rhythms of the local fishing community and the languid pace of provincial life. You won't find a huge number of hotels or restaurants here, but a compact medieval warren of streets overlooked by a ruined castle, with enough curious waterside haunts within walking distance to keep boredom at bay.

North of Alghero, the ghost town of **Argentiera** and Sardinia's only natural lake, **Lago Baratz**, make intriguing stops, though the real attraction here is the resort of **Stintino**, at the western end of the Golfo di Asinara. Much smaller than Bosa or Alghero, and more subject to the whims of the tourist industry, the village provides a base from which to enjoy the nearby stretch of largely undeveloped coastline, in particular the once-seen, never-forgotten sands around the point at **La Pelosa**. A handful of hotels and restaurants in Stintino cater to the summer visitors. Many of these come on organized tours,

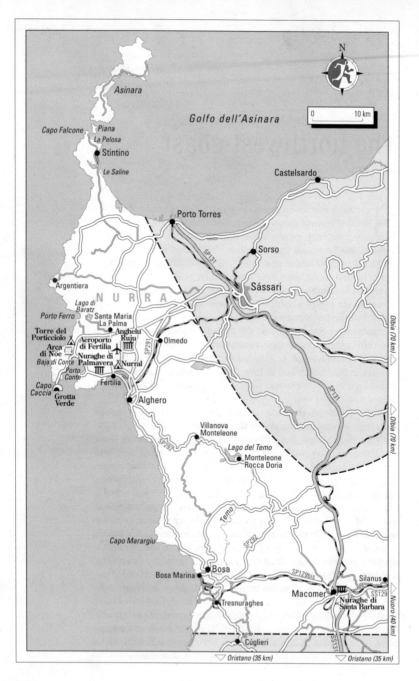

and melt away once August is past, leaving the village to relapse into a somnolent semi-oblivion for much of the year. And while Stintino may lack excitement out of season, it is still a useful stop for beach-bums and fans of exquisite panoramas.

In between these places, the northwest coast presents a wild and rocky aspect, sparsely populated and ideal for roaming. Although **public transport** services are adequate for travelling between the main towns and villages, your own car gives you more freedom, while renting a bike (available from Alghero or Stintino) would be a fun way to cover the shorter distances. **Walkers** will find the terrain rewarding, with few over-strenuous tracts, though they should be aware that the rough and ragged nature of the coast means that much of the alluring Alghero–Bosa stretch, for example, must be tackled on the road – thankfully free of much traffic most of the time.

For more information on bus and train connections, see Travel Details, p.223.

Hotels are not so thick on the ground in Stintino and Bosa. They are much more plentiful in Alghero, though even here availability can be tight in summer, while many places throughout the region close altogether between October and April. **Campsites** are similarly few and far between: the area around Alghero has four of them, but there are none around Bosa or Stintino. The region does contain two of Sardinia's three **hostels**, however, in Fertilia (near Alghero) and Bosa, and these too fill up very quickly.

Alghero and around

ALGHERO is a very rare Italian phenomenon: a tourist town that is also a flourishing fishing port, giving it an economic base entirely independent of the summer swarms. The predominant flavour here is Catalan, owing to a wholesale Hispanicization that followed the overthrow of the Doria family by Pedro IV of Aragon in 1353, a process so thorough that the town became known as "Barcelonetta".

Alghero and around

According to some, Alghero's name is derived from the Arabic, *al-ghar*, meaning cave or cavern, possibly a reference to the celebrated Grotta di Nettuno nearby. Others suggest that its original name was *S'Alighera* (*L'Alguer* in Catalan), meaning "seaweedy" or more specifically "place of algae", though there is little evidence of this today in the clear blue seas hereabouts. In fact it is the purity of the water together with the spectacular coast – not to mention Neptune's Grotto – which have helped to put the town on the map in recent times. Tour operators homed in on Alghero in the post-war holiday boom, which gave birth to the welter of hotels and restaurants that exist today, catering to a constant supply of mostly British and German tourists.

It would have been easy for this over-developed holiday niche to have sold out to quaintness and fakery, but, strangely, none of this has come about, and though it can get pretty busy in high summer, if you come here at any other time you'll find a much lower tourist profile and less foreigner fatigue, and have a far greater possibility of finding hotel vacancies. As you would expect, the choice of accommodation is extensive, but booking is essential at any time. As for the restaurants, the quality of the food is generally high – the presence of the fishermen ensures a regular supply of the freshest seafood, and the local cuisine makes good use of Catalan recipes to augment its already varied repertoire. The town is additionally blessed by its proximity to some of Sardinia's most famous vineyards, producing eminently quaffable wines.

But the real attraction of Alghero is its atmospheric old centre, a puzzle of lanes, at the heart of which the pedestrianized Via Carlo Alberto, Via Principe Umberto and Via Roma have most of the bars and shops. The old town's finest architecture dates from the sixteenth century, built in a congenial Catalan-Gothic style; a walkabout should also take in the series of seven towers which dominate Alghero's centre. The Spanish connection is never far away: the street names are all in the Catalan dialect – *carrer* for "via," *iglesia* for "chiesa," *palau* for "palazzo", and *plaça* for "piazza". Beyond the stout girdle of walls enclosing this historic core, the new town's grid of parallel streets has little of interest beyond its restaurants and hotels.

Most visitors to Alghero make the boat trip to the **Grotta del Nettuno**, justifiably famous and worth the ride, though by no means the only essential stop. If you visit the grotto by boat, you'll pass the glorious deep bay of **Porto Conte**, one of Sardinia's most celebrated beauty spots, favoured by sailors and windsurfers, part of which is set aside as a wildlife reserve. The land journey will take you through the low-key resort of **Fertilia**, an alternative place to stay if Alghero is full, and close to the area's most important nuraghic complex, **nuraghe di Palmavera**, not to mention some fine beaches. Inland, you could drop into another archeological site belonging to an earlier era, the necropolis at **Anghelu Ruju**, nestled within the endless vineyards that produce some of the best of Sardinia's wine.

Further afield, the undeveloped coast **south of Alghero** is a marvellous marriage of rock and sea, ideal for cruising, or else venture inland through empty mountainous terrain towards the village of **Villanova Monteleone**. In the opposite direction, the country **north of Alghero** is much flatter, but there are a couple of places worth exploring: **Lago Baratz**, harbouring protected wildlife, and the abandoned mining centre of **Argentiera**, dominated by the eighteenth-century workings of a once flourishing industry.

Local **buses** from Alghero (service AF) run hourly to Fertilia, less frequently to Porto Conte and Capo Caccia (for Grotta di Nettuno). Other places must be reached by taxi or your own transport, though there is a regular bus service to Villanova Monteleone.

Some history

While archeological finds in the area around Alghero suggest cultural activity going back to 6000 BC, the history of the modern town really begins in the first half of the twelfth century with the fortification of what had been an obscure fishing port by the Doria family of **Genoa**. The town successfully defended itself from assaults by the Pisans and Aragonese until 1353 when, after the conquest of Cágliari and Sássari, a large **Spanish fleet**, supported by the Venetians, routed the Genoans at the nearby bay of Porto Conte and took possession of Alghero. Following an uprising in which the Spanish garrison was massacred, the town was subjected to a thoroughgoing "ethnic cleansing", in which waves of **Catalan settlers** displaced the locals, forcing them to settle at Villanova, a mountain village 25km south. Laws were passed limiting the number of native Sards who could enter, and compelling them to leave town at the sound of a trumpet signal.

Because of its geographic and strategic importance on Sardinia's northwestern coast, Alghero quickly became the foremost port for traffic between Sardinia and Catalonia. Between the fourteenth and sixteenth centuries, its defences were massively strengthened; most of the ramparts and towers still standing today date from this period, when they sheltered a substantial garrison and fleet, providing a powerful bulwark against seaborne incursions against Sássari and the whole western interior.

In 1541, the emperor **Charles V** made a historic visit to the town accompanied by his admiral Andrea Doria – the family were now reconciled to the Spanish – and one of the biggest fleets yet assembled, en route to do battle against the corsair **Hassan Aga** in Algiers. This pirate chief was himself, ironically, a Sard: born of shepherds, he was abducted as a slave, forcibly converted and castrated for harem service, and soon rose to become right-hand man to the feared Khair al-Din, or Barbarossa.

In summer, kids will enjoy Alghero's Trenino Catalano, a miniature train which does a circuit of the old centre every thirty minutes. Tickets (L7000) are available on board.

Alghero and around

The best way to hear the algherese/catalano dialect is to spend time with the fishermen. Alternatively, drop in on one of the church services conducted in the local vernacular at the cathedral and San Francesco. See in church or ask at tourist office for times.

After the expulsion of Alghero's substantial **Jewish community**, or *Aljama*, in 1492, the resulting downturn in the town's economic fortunes forced the Aragonese to reopen it to foreign and Sard traders. The core of the town, however, remained stoutly Catalan in character and culture, and continued to be so after Sardinia was taken over by the **House of Savoy** in 1720. As a marginalized enclave, Alghero declined steadily, a trend which the destruction of the landward-facing walls in the nineteenth century was unable to halt.

New money only began to flow into the town with its discovery and development as a package **tourist resort** in the 1960s, when Sardinia's greatest concentration of hotels and restaurants was built here. Alghero's remoteness from the mainland has enabled it to escape total mass-market annihilation, however, while its well-established port has ensured the continuation of the key role of fishing in the local economy. At the same time, the most obvious index of Alghero's distinctive culture, the *catalano* or *algherese* **dialect**, has largely lost the battle against uniformity. While old people – many of whom still regard themselves primarily as Catalans – are attached to it, few of the post-1960s generations are at all adept, and the existence of evening classes for locals to learn or perfect their knowledge of *catalano* is a significant gauge of its present precarious state.

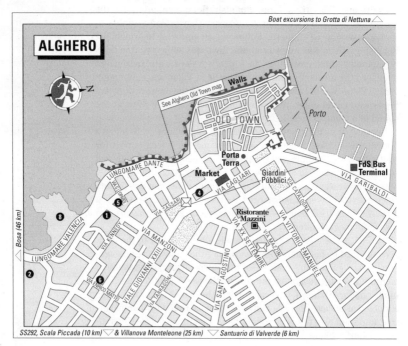

Boat excursions to Grotta di Nettuna

ALGHERO

Walls
See Alghero Old Town map
OLD TOWN
Porto
Porta Terra
Market
Giardini Pùbblici
FdS Bus Terminal
LUNGOMARE DANTE
VIA CAGLIARI
VIA SASSARI
VIA GARIBALDI
CATALOGNA
Ristorante Mazzini
VIA XX SETTEMBRE
VIA MAZZINI
VIA VITTORIO EMANUELE
LUNGOMARE VALENCIA
VIA KENNEDY
VIA MANZONI
VIA SANT'AGOSTINO
VIALE GIOVANNI XXIII
VIA TARRAGONA
VIA ENRICO MATTEI
Bosa (46 km)

SS292, Scala Piccada (10 km) & Villanova Monteleone (25 km) Santuario di Valverde (6 km)

Arrival, information and accommodation

Alghero's **airport** lies 10km inland, outside the town of Fertilia. The building has a **tourist office** whose opening hours vary (roughly Mon–Sat 8.30am–8pm, 9am–3pm & 5–8pm in winter; open daily until 11.30pm in August; ☎079.935.124), but currently no bank or cash machine. If you're aiming to catch a **bus into town**, however, you'll need to move fast if you want to avoid hanging around for another hour, since departures are timed to coincide with plane arrivals. Get tickets from the shop at one end of the terminal (L1,100). Long-distance buses also connect the airport with Sássari, Nuoro and Olbia. Taxis into Alghero cost around L20,000.

FdS **trains** arrive some way out of the centre; the small station is connected to the port by local buses. Buy tickets from the newsagent inside the station – the bus stop is across the road. Buses AP (every 20min) and AF (hourly) run into town (in the opposite direction, the AF runs to Fertilia, for people heading straight to the hostel or campsite there). Local and regional **buses** arrive in Via Catalogna, on the Giardini Púbblici, though FdS buses stop at the port. Alghero's **main tourist office** (May–Sept Mon–Sat 8am–8pm, July & Aug, also Sun, 8am–noon; Oct–April Mon–Sat 8am–2pm; ☎079.979.054), at the top end of the Giardini Púbblici, is easily the most efficient on the

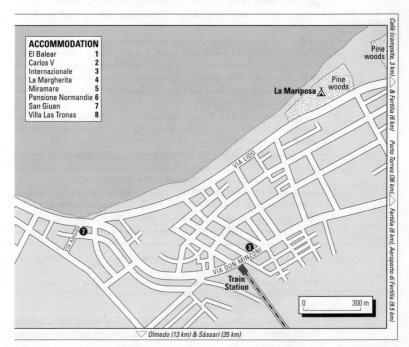

ACCOMMODATION
El Balear — 1
Carlos V — 2
Internazionale — 3
La Margherita — 4
Miramare — 5
Pensione Normandie — 6
San Giuan — 7
Villa Las Tronas — 8

island; its multilingual staff are equipped with reams of maps, accommodation lists and tour details.

For **getting around** town, your feet should be enough for most journeys, though you may use **local buses** for journeys to the train station, the campsites and Fertilia. Fares cost L1,100, tickets from *tabacchi* and bars. A good alternative for short trips around the town and its environs is by **bike**: see "Listings" for details.

Agriturismo lodgings are all dispersed in the country around Alghero: contact the tourist office for possibilities. For apartment rentals, see "Listings" (p.204).

Of the 28 **hotels** listed in Alghero, only seven or eight remain open in winter, of which five are four-stars, greatly reducing choice. However, there's a good chance of finding a room in one of the less expensive options that remain open – better, anyway, than during July and August, when booking is absolutely essential. Prices jump up in these months, though never by more than about 25 percent. The two **campsites** listed here are an easy bus ride from the centre, but both close outside the summer months. The only site that's open all year in the area is located 6km along the coast at Fertilia (see p.208), and there's a fourth, more secluded one at Torre del Porticciolo (p.209). Alghero's youth hostel is also at Fertilia (p.208).

Hotels

El Balear, Lungomare Dante 32 (☎079.975.229). White, boxy building a few minutes south of Piazza Sulis. At least it's bright and modern, overlooking the sea and has attractive rates, only just creeping into its price category. Open April–Oct. ④.

Carlos V (Carlos Quinto), Lungomare Valencia 24 (☎079.979.501; fax 079.980.298). One of the plushest hotels in town, offering quite reasonable rates, especially if you opt for a back-facing room. The air of luxury is fostered by palm trees around the good-sized pool, where a broad terrace sports a chic bar and perfect panorama of the *Villa Las Tronas* hotel (see opposite), and Capo Caccia farther beyond. ⑥.

Internazionale, Via Don Minzoni 126 (☎079.951.208). Standard two-star 150m from the station (and 500m from the beach) with rooms with or without private bath and a restaurant. No CCs. Open mid-April to mid-Oct. ③.

La Margherita, Via Sássari 70 (☎079.979.006). Close to Piazza Sulis and the old town, this old-fashioned three-star is clean and reliable, and one of the cheaper options staying open through winter. All rooms have private bathrooms, some with tubs. Front-facing ones have a small balcony, with the best views from the top (fourth) floor; there's a lift. Breakfast included. ③.

Miramare, Via Giácomo Leopardi 15 (☎079.979.350, fax 079.982.108). Fairly central choice off Lungomare Dante. Smallish rooms have their own toilet and shower. Open May–Sept. ④.

Pensione Normandie, Via Enrico Mattei 6 (☎079.975.302). In the newer part of town, between Via Kennedy and Via Giovanni XXIII, this very cheap but basic place has spacious rooms, though plans to incorporate bathrooms (currently shared) will make them smaller. One single also available, while a third bed adds 45 percent to the bill. No CCs. ②.

San Francesco, Via Machin 2 (☎079.980.330). Alghero's best-value hotel and the only one in the old town, therefore often full. Formerly a convent attached

to San Francesco church (and lying just behind it), it retains a cloistered air;
the 21 rooms are clean and quiet, with telephones and private bathrooms. The
bill includes breakfast. Parking is a problem, but a garage is available nearby
at an extra cost of L10,000 per night. Stays open all year, though may close for
a few weeks in November. ②.

San Giuan, Via Angioy 2 (☎079.951.222, fax 079.951.073). North of the centre – about a 15-minute walk – but near the beaches, this is a modern hotel with
all rooms en suite. In theory, it stays open in winter; in practice it often closes
for weeks at a stretch. Breakfast included. ④.

Villa Las Tronas, Lungomare Valencia 24 (☎079.981.818; fax
079.981.044). At the top end of the market, this castellated former baronial
mansion is full of character, still retaining an aristocratic air with its old-
fashioned furnishings. Superbly sited on a promontory surrounded by small
beaches east of town, it makes a terrific splurge. Capacity is limited, however, with only 31 bedrooms. ⑦.

Campsites

La Mariposa, Via Lido 22 (☎079.950.360). The nearest site to Alghero, 2km
out of town, this has direct access to the beach, part of which is sectioned off
for site users. Eucalyptus and pine provide welcome shade and soft ground.
There are shops and a restaurant, and bungalows and caravans are available
for rent (L38–60,000 for a double). Take bus AP from the station or Alghero's
Giardini Púbblici, or walk 10min from the station (right on Via Minzoni, left on
Via Malta, right on Via Lido). Open April–Oct.

Calik (☎079.930.111). Further out from Alghero than *La Mariposa*, but with
slightly lower prices and fewer campers, this site has similar facilities, direct
access to the beach, and likewise spreads beneath a canopy of trees. Take bus
AF from the station, the Giardini Púbblici, Via Lido or Via Garibaldi. Open
June–Oct.

The town

Alghero's **Giardini Púbblici**, which effectively divide the right-
angled regularity of the new town from the intricate maze of the old,
are the usual starting place for any exploration of the *centro stórico*.
The **Porta Terra**, at the top of the gardens past the tourist office, was
originally one of the two gates into the walled town. Also known as
the Torre del Portal, it has been identified by some scholars with the
Torre dels Ebreus referred to in the Middle Ages and financed by
Alghero's Jewish community, though others believe that this lay elsewhere. Today the tower sports an incongruous Art-Deco-style war
memorial.

Another remnant of the old town's defensive structure lies at the
bottom of the gardens, towards the port, where the huge hollow
shell of the **Bastione La Maddalena** has one of the town's seven
towers, embedded within the crumbling ruins. The bastion forms
the venue for open-air cinema in summer, and also provides the
main access to the centre of the old town, **Piazza Cívica**, an elongated, traffic-free space also reachable from the port. Lined with
expensive bars and boutiques, this elegant arena of scurrying

*The Giardini
Púbblici are a
good place to
cool down if
you have kids;
elsewhere in
town, the pub-
lic garden at
Via Tarragona
has swings and
a climbing
frame.*

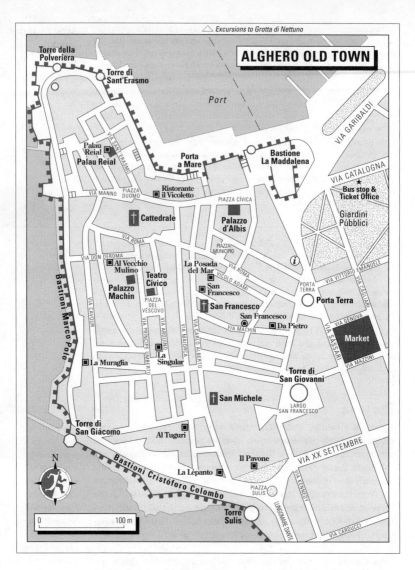

ALGHERO OLD TOWN

Port

Torre della
Polveriera

Torre di
Sant'Erasmo

VIA GARIBALDI

VIA CATALOGNA

★ Bus stop &
Ticket Office

Palau
Reial
Palau Reial

Porta
a Mare

Bastione
La Maddalena

VIA SANT'ERASMO

VIA VITTORIO EMANUELE

Giardini
Púbblici

Ristorante
il Vicoletto

VIA MANNO

PIAZZA
DUOMO

PIAZZA CÍVICA

† **Cattedrale**

**Palazzo
d'Albis**

VIA ROMA

PIAZZA
MUNICIPIO

Al Vecchio
Mulino

La Posada
del Mar

VIA ROMA

PORTA
TERRA

◯ **Porta Terra**

VIA CAGLIARI

VIA DON DEROMA

VICOLO ADAMI

San
Francesco

VIA VITTORIO EMANUELE

**Teatro
Cívico**

† **San Francesco**

San Francesco

Da Pietro

VIA GENOVA

**Palazzo
Machin**

PIAZZA
DEL
VÉSCOVO

VIA MACHIN

Market

VIA SASSARI

VIA ARDUINO

VIA PRINCIPE UMBERTO

VIA MAIORCA

VIA CARLO ALBERTO

VIA MAZZINI

La Muraglia

**La
Singular**

Torre di
San Giovanni

VIA CAVOUR

Bastioni Marco Polo

† **San Michele**

LARGO
SAN FRANCESCO

Torre di
San Giácomo

Al Tuguri

Il Pavone

VIA XX SETTEMBRE

La Lépanto

PIAZZA
SULIS

VIA KENNEDY

N

Bastioni Cristóforo Colombo

LUNGOMARE DANTE

0   100 m

Torre
Sulis

VIA CARDUCCI

locals and dawdling tourists opens on to the **Porta a Mare**, the second of the main gates to the old city, giving access to the port. The
top end of the square holds the Gothic **Palazzo d'Albis** (*Palau
Albis*), the former governor's palace from which the emperor
Charles V addressed the crowds in 1541 before embarking for
Algiers to fight his African campaign against the Turks. He is said
to have uttered the words, long-remembered in local lore as grant-

ing instant nobility to the assembled throng, *Estade todos caballeros* ("You are all knights"), and to have described Alghero as *bonita y bien asentada* ("pretty and well-situated"). Mullioned Gothic and Renaissance windows adorn the facade. Next door, a comfortable-looking sailors' club occupies the ground floor of the former town hall.

The Cattedrale

At the far end of the square, Via Manno leads into Piazza Duomo, where four tall, fluted columns dominate the white Neoclassical facade of Alghero's **Cattedrale** (daily: 6.30am–noon & 5–8pm), a grandiose entry somewhat out of keeping with the sixteenth-century edifice. Founded in 1510, just seven years after Alghero was promoted to city status, the cathedral was not fully completed – and finally consecrated – until 1730, though it had long since been established as the customary place for Spanish viceroys to take a preliminary oath before assuming office in Cágliari.

The **interior** is a bit of a hodgepodge: the alternating pillars and columns on either side of the lofty nave survive from the original construction, while the impressive dome and creamy marble central altar date from the eighteenth century, and the lateral chapels are predominantly Neoclassical or Baroque. Behind the altar, an ambulatory said to derive architecturally from the Islamic mosque of the old Moorish city (and recalling similar designs in cathedrals at Salamanca and Segovia) gives onto five radiating chapels, also part of the original building. The left transept holds the well-executed marble funerary monument of the Savoy Duke of Monferrato, brother of King Carlo Felice, dated 1799. Elsewhere, the flaking walls show the need of a long overdue restoration. A good time to visit would be for one of the services in the local Catalan dialect, currently held at 7.30pm on Saturdays, 6.30pm in winter.

To see an original part of the cathedral's **Gothic exterior**, walk round to the back of the building, where a lovely carved portal at the base of the octagonal campanile makes a pleasant contrast to the overblown entrance. The road stretching south from here, **Via Príncipe Umberto**, is one of the quietest and most attractive of Old Alghero's lanes. Among its older buildings is the decrepit **Palazzo Machin** at no. 9–11; built in the seventeenth century for a local bishop, it still preserves its Catalan-Gothic windows and Renaissance portal. Further up, the currently disused eighteenth-century **Teatro Cívico** occupies one side of Piazza del Véscovo.

North of the cathedral, walk a few steps down Via Sant'Erasmo to take in the elegantly austere **Palau Reial**, whose well-restored exterior is enlivened by elaborate brown and white patterns around the windows. The palace was probably owned by the Jewish Carcassona family before their eviction in 1492; the ground floor is now a restaurant.

Via Carlo Alberto

Of the long lanes running the length of the Old Town, **Via Carlo Alberto** is the busiest, crowded with amblers browsing among the succession of tourist shops and bars between Piazza Cívica and Piazza Sulis. Many of the shops are jewellery stores, specializing in the coral for which Sardinia's northwestern coast in general and Alghero in particular are famous. Halfway along, stop at the fifteenth-century church of **San Francesco** (daily: 6.30am–noon & 5–8.30pm), fronting a small piazza. Architecturally the finest of Alghero's churches, it encompasses several different styles; the Gothic campanile and some of the lateral chapels – survivals from the original construction – blend successfully with the Renaissance ceiling, round arches and swirling carved windows. The centrepiece of the dim interior is a polychrome marble altar, while bound to a column on a pier to the left stands a horribly emaciated (*grattugiato*) figure of Christ which, despite its modernistic appearance, dates from the seventeenth century. Behind the statue, prayers and personal items – even jewellery – are pinned up as ex voto offerings.

Services are held in Catalan in the church of San Francesco at 7pm on Sundays, 6pm in winter. In summer, the cloister is sometimes the venue for al fresco classical concerts.

To the left of the altar, the presbytery, with its happily irregular cross-vaulted Gothic ceiling, gives onto a simple **cloister** with round, rough-hewn arches. Originating at the beginning of the fourteenth century, it was modified at the end of the following century and again in the eighteenth.

Further up Via Carlo Alberto, the majolica-tiled cupola of **San Michele** (open daily from 20min before masses, currently Mon–Sat from about 7pm, Sun from 9am, 10.30am and 7pm, one hour earlier in winter) is a sparkling feature of Alghero's skyline, though from close up the flaky facade does not invite further exploration. In fact, the haughty interior remains true to its seventeenth-century Jesuit origins, with a high, rough-looking ceiling above round arches and swirling columns. One of the elaborately stuccoed and decorated chapels contains a sculpture of St Michael slaying the dragon. Look out too for the gilt wooden choir box over the main entrance.

Via Carlo Alberto ends a few metres further south at Piazza Sulis, site of the stout **Torre Sulis**, also called Torre dello Sperone (*Torre dell'Esperò Real* in Catalan), which dominates the seashore here. The tower is named after its most celebrated prisoner from the time when it served as a place of detention: Vincenzo Sulis, incarcerated here for thirty years for his part in an uprising in Cágliari in the early nineteenth century. Today the area around the tower is a meeting point for many of the town's youth (and their bikes); it's an airy, pleasant space, marking the end of the old town and the start of the traffic.

On the far side of the piazza, next to the Standa supermarket, Alghero's **Aquarium** (April–Sept daily 10am–1pm & 5–9pm in April & May, 5–10pm in June, 5–11pm in July & Sept, 5pm–12.30am in Aug; Oct daily 4–10pm; Nov–March weekends and public holidays

4–9pm; L10,000) makes a diverting place to while away an hour or two. The underground complex is not particularly big, but there's over a hundred species of marine life to be viewed, including piranha and beautiful spotted "leopard" sharks. Via Kennedy runs north from here, past Largo San Francesco, site of another of Alghero's towers, as far as Porta Terra and the Giardini Púbblici.

The waterfront

An alternative route from Piazza Sulis would be along the perimeter of the sea-facing walls, or **bastioni**, girding the old town, reached by turning right out of Via Carlo Alberto. You'll pass three more of the town's defensive towers this way, Torre di San Giácomo, Torre della Polveriera and Torre di Sant'Erasmo, and the views out to Capo Caccia are superb. It makes a good place to escape Alghero's bustle, though evenings and night-time in summer see a fair amount of coming and going between the bars here.

North of the old quarter, most of the tourist activity revolves around the **port** abutting the lofty walls, its wide quay nudged by rows of colourful fishing boats and bordered by more bars. This is the embarcation point for excursions to Neptune's Grotto and along the coast. Further up begin the hotels and beaches, most of them an easy walk from town. Some of the more opulent, older-looking villas were formerly owned by a resident expatriate community, mainly central European refugees who fled here after World War I. The **beaches** themselves aren't particularly alluring: it's worth carrying on a while to where the pinewoods begin, though even here you'll have to share the water with a couple of campsites located within a few steps of the sea, and you can find much better beaches a short drive out of town (see p.209).

Eating and drinking

Alghero's **restaurants** are renowned for their fish and seafood, always fresh, inventively prepared and tastefully presented; spring and winter are the best seasons. You might find *paella* on the menu, following the Catalan tradition, while lobster (*aragosta*) is the local speciality. This is pricey, however; the best way to order it is on one of the set-price menus which feature this dish, usually L60,000–70,000 per person (though one portion is often enough to share). Fixed-price menus are common and offer good value, though as a rule don't expect a wide choice or huge portions. Most places close for a few weeks in winter.

For **snacks**, the fast-food joints by the port aren't bad, though you can do better by doing it yourself: drop in at the daily market (until 1pm) off Via Sássari between Via Génova and Via Mazzini for the freshest fruit and vegetables. Good foodstuffs and *panini* can also be had at the nearby Antica Formaggeria, which does a good line in Sard specialities, on the corner of Via Génova and Via Cágliari.

Restaurants

La Lépanto, Via Carlo Alberto 135 (☎079.979.116). Just off Piazza Sulis, with large windows looking out to sea, this is a top-class restaurant renowned for its fish – take your pick from the enticing choice laid out for inspection. As a rough guide to prices, a good sized *spígola* (sea bass) should cost around L26,000. Meat dishes are excellent too, and there's a delectable range of Sardinian sweets also on view. Closed Mon in winter. Expensive.

Ristorante Mazzini, Via Mazzini 59. A modern-town restaurant with less pretension and lower prices – if less atmosphere – than the places in the *centro stórico*. The food's fine if you stick to basics, and service is friendly. There's a wood-fired oven for pizzas, and minstrels strum their stuff. Moderate.

La Muraglia, Bastioni Marco Polo 7 (☎079.977.254). You can eat outside on the old city walls here, where fixed-price menus are offered at L25,000, L30,000, L40,000 and L60,000, including drinks. Top choice, and expensive, is the *Paella Valenziana*, though this must be ordered beforehand. À la carte items are otherwise reasonably priced. Moderate.

Palau Reial, Via Sant'Erasmo 14 (079.980.688). Occupying the ground floor of a medieval Jewish palazzo, this is a classy joint where you can feast on sea-urchin mousse and other delicacies of *la cucina algherese*. Closed Wed in winter. Expensive.

Il Pavone, Piazza Sulis 3 (☎079.979.584). A few outside tables provide an exclusive enclave to sample some of the best of Alghero's cuisine, including meat dishes. First courses weigh in at around L16,000, main courses at L25,000. Inside, the two small mirrored rooms can get stuffy and over-formal. Closed Wed, also Sun in winter. Expensive.

Da Pietro, Via Machin 20 (☎079.979.645). Fish is, once again, the main item in one of Alghero's oldest establishments. There's a reasonable L35,000 tourist menu (drinks included), or you might opt for the L60,000 lobster menu. Pastas go for about L12,000, fish for L7000 per 100g. The main drawback is the rather crowded dining space. Closed Wed Oct–June. Moderate.

La Posada del Mar, Vícolo Adami 29, off Via Roma. This pizzeria/ristorante in a brick basement is touristy, but not bad value with a L25,000 menu (excluding drinks). If you want to go beyond the limited choice, pastas go for about L10,000, though this goes up to L15,000 if you're not having a main course as well, and fish dishes average at L6500 per 100g. Moderate.

San Francesco, Piazza San Francesco. *Paninoteca*, pizzeria and general fast-food place outside San Francesco church. Pastas also available.

La Singular, Via Arduino 45 (☎079.982.098). If you tire of seafood, come here for a solid selection of land-based dishes such as kid and boar, not to mention the Sard classic, *porcheddu al mirto*, young pig roasted on the spit with myrtle. Fish also features on the menu. Closed Mon except Aug. Moderate.

Al Tuguri, Via Maiorca 57 (☎079.976.772). Minuscule restaurant – two rooms on two floors – specializing in Catalan cuisine. The name is dialect meaning "old abandoned house", helping to explain the faintly rustic ambience. First courses are around L12,000, a plate of fish might be L25,000, but if you can afford it, opt for one of the sampling menus at L50,000, or L65,000 for a five-course feast. Firsts only, unaccompanied by a main course, are not served. Closed Sun. Expensive.

Ristorante il Vicoletto, Piazza Cívica 5. Comparatively modest trattoria at one end of the old town's main square. The one simple vaulted room is sparsely decorated and rarely very crowded. Set menus start at L30,000 including drinks. Closed Thurs and Nov. Moderate.

Al Vecchio Mulino, Via Don Deroma 3 (☎ 079.977.254). An atmospheric low-vaulted cellar in the heart of the old town. You can sample the best on offer with the expensive fixed-price menu (L65,000) but you can eat more cheaply with just a first (L11,000–15,000) or a pizza. Closed Tues in winter. Moderate.

Cafés, bars and birrerias

Surprisingly, Alghero doesn't have a great selection of bars and cafés, and the ones there are can look pretty dismal out of season. Things liven up in summer, of course, when many stay open until the small hours. The following are some of the best places:

L'Arca, Lungomare Dante. Laid-back seafront bar with table football and live music on Friday and Saturday evenings.

Bar Granada, Bastioni Marco Polo. Located on the city walls looking out to sea, with a few outdoor tables where you can sip cappuccinos or cocktails, or snack on toasted sandwiches and *panini*. Open till midnight on summer nights, till 2 or 3am on Fridays and Saturdays.

Café Latino, Piazza Duomo 6. An elegant venue for whiling away an afternoon, with outside tables and wicker chairs beneath white parasols on the walls overlooking the port. *Panini*, pastas and ice creams are also available.

Diva Café, Piazza Municipio 1. Slightly Bohemian in tone, though more restrained than many of Alghero's bars, tucked up a side street off Piazza Cívica. Closed Sun.

Jamaica Inn, Via Príncipe Umberto 57. A pub with snacks and cocktails, open late. Closed Mon.

Mill Pub, Via Maiorca 37. For the homesick, an Italian-style "pub", with regular live music in summer.

Discos

Alghero's small number of discos and clubs in fact represent Sardinia's best choice of nightspots. Most require a car to reach, their out-of-town location pulling in the punters from Sássari and other nearby centres, and most are open in summer only. Count on about L20,000 entry, usually including the first drink; subsequent drinks are around L10,000.

Ex, Via Lido 17 (☎079.953.263). Winter-only disco, and then only Fridays and Saturdays, playing mainstream dance sounds. Open from around 10pm–midnight.

Manpea, Colle San Giuliano (☎079.978.481). One of the most popular discos, and often crammed. Summer only.

Ruscello, about 8km from Alghero on Olmedo road (☎079.953.168). It's on the right, opposite a large supermarket. Open summer only, with open-air dance floors and occasional live bands.

Siesta, Scala Piccada, 10km southeast of town on the SS292 (☎079.980.137). Magnificent views over the deserted coast are the best feature of this outdoor disco, sometimes with live bands, and open Saturday nights only in winter.

Festivals and entertainment

Alghero's Spanish inheritance is particularly manifest during its **Easter** festivities, when the rituals of the *Incontru* (the symbolic meeting of the Virgin with Christ) and *Misteri* (representing the Passion of Christ) are enacted, with statues carried through town amid solemn processions. In contrast, **Carnival** is a pretty feisty affair, involving plenty of masked antics and the burning of the *pupazzo* – a "guy" representing a French soldier, ceremonially put on trial and burnt on the bonfire on Shrove Tuesday. May sees a steady procession of pilgrims to the sanctuary of Valverde, 6km east of town, in thanksgiving for the Madonna's intervention at times of disaster. The other major milestone in the year is **Ferragosto** (August 15), in which the Feast of the Assumption is celebrated with a range of musical and folkloric events, boating competitions and fireworks.

Religion and secular games are mixed on Sant'Agostino's day on August 28, and there are waterborne events and feasting organized as part of the **Sagra dei Pescatori**, or Fisherman's Fair, on a Saturday or Sunday in September, the precise date varying from year to year.

A range of diverse events are staged during the tourist season, and recent years have seen the **World Music Festival**, which started as a one-off extravaganza, become a regular event, usually taking place throughout August. Previous years have seen a range of music from township to Czech grunge; tickets cost around L20,000. Recently, too, concerts have been staged in the Grotta di Nettuno (L22,000 incuding boat ride). Contact the tourist office for details on both events. Theatre and cinema are poorly catered for in Alghero, though there are **open-air film screenings** at the Bastione della Maddalena in July and August, in Italian or, occasionally, Catalan.

Listings

Airport Aeroporto di Fertilia lies 10km north of Alghero. For flight information call ☎079.935.033 or the toll-free Alitalia number ☎147.865.641.

Apartment rentals There is a good choice of private apartments to let, available through Immobiliare agencies, a full list of which can be obtained from the local tourist office. Off-season rates are particularly favourable, though don't expect to find many bargains or any availability at all (unless you've booked far ahead) in August. As an example, 4- to 5-bed apartments range from L800,000–2,000,000 per week during high season, including bills; minimum stay is normally seven days, or three weeks in August. Try contacting the Mario Cau agency at Via Don Minzoni 159 (☎079.952.478).

Banks and exchange Banks in Alghero are generally open Mon–Fri 8.20am–1.15pm and 3–4pm. Most now have cash machines, for example the Banco di Sardegna in Largo San Francesco, and Banca Nazionale di Lavoro at Via Vittorio Emanuele 5, on the Giardini Púbblici. There's also a small exchange office with longer opening hours at Sardinia Tourist Service, Via

Machin 55 (Mon–Sat 9am–1pm & 4.30–7pm), and the main post offices (see below) also change cash and American Express traveller's cheques. Note that there are currrently no exchange facilities at Fertilia Airport.

Bike rental Cicloexpress (tel. 079.986.950 or 0336.327.048), off Via Garibaldi at the port, and Silvio Noleggio, Via Lo Frasso 38 and Via Garibaldi 113 (☎079.974.386 and 0347.596.7924) charge about L60,000 per day for a Vespa, L35,000 for a moped, L20,000 for a mountain bike, and L15,000 for a regular bicycle. Tandems and Honda Shadow VT 600s are also available, and all vehicles can be hired on an hourly basis if preferred. Near the station, Bike Center, Via Don Minzoni 130 (☎079.951.206) charges similar rates.

Boat tours See Tours, on p.206.

Bookshops English books and guides from Il Labirinto, Via Carlo Alberto 3.

Buses ARST ticket office at Via Catalogna, on the Giardino Púbblico, next to the bus stop (☎079.950.179). FdS long-distance buses stop here or at the port; they also run the local bus service (☎079.950.458). Turmo Travel (☎0789.26.101) have one departure daily to Olbia and its airport, leaving in the evening, and Deplanu (☎0784.30.325) connect Fertilia Airport with Nuoro twice daily. There is no PANI service.

Car rental Most of the rental agencies have offices out at Fertilia airport, such as Avis (☎079.935.064), Pinna (☎079.935.130) and Maggiore-Budget (☎079.935.045). In town, you'll find Nolauto Alghero, Via Vittorio Véneto 119 (☎079.953.047), and Avis and Maggiore-Budget also have offices, respectively at Piazza Sulis (☎079.979.577) and Via Sássari 87 (☎079.979.373). Reckon on roughly L130,000 per day for a Panda, L150,000 for a Punto, with unlimited mileage (some agencies offer lower daily rates but charge a supplement per kilometre).

Laundry Central laundries include Marzia, Via Catalogna 4 and Tintoria Flórida, Via Mazzini 20. You have to leave your clothes to be washed and pressed, ready within one or two working days.

Left luggage At the train station (open while station is open, until around 9.15pm); L1500 per piece per day.

Markets Daily food market in the block between Via Cágliari and Via Sássari, and Via Genova and Via Mazzini. Wednesday mornings see a lively fish market on Via de Gásperi, on the southern outskirts.

Pharmacy Farmacia Cabras, at Piazza Sulis 11, is the most central pharmacy (Mon–Sat 9am–1pm & 4–7.20pm). The night-time rota is posted on this and other pharmacy doors.

Post office Main office at Via XX Settembre 112 (Mon–Sat 8.15am–7.10pm, last day of month 8.10am–noon). There's another big office at Via Carducci, off Via Sássari (Mon–Fri 8.10am–1.15pm, Sat 8.10am–12.45pm, last day of month 8.10am–noon). Both have foreign desks which change cash and American Express travellers' cheques.

Supermarket Standa on Piazza Sulis (Mon–Sat 9am–1pm & 3.45–7.45pm); no food hall.

Taxis Rank on Via Vittorio Emanuele, at Giardini Púbblici (☎079.975.396).

Telephones Cabins at Piazza Sulis, the Giardini Púbblici and by the port.

Tennis Public courts in gardens at Via Tarragona, L10,000 per hour during the day, L17,000 for evening play, using lights. Pay at Bar del Tennis (closed Mon morning). Racquets available for hire.

Tours Cooperativa SILT, Via Petrarca 14 (☎079.980.750), organize one- or two-day guided tours of Alghero and the archeology and wildlife of the surrounding district. The agency also provides a number of other tourist services, for example interpreting and short language courses. For boat tours, the main company, Navisarda, has a booth at the port and an office at Via Diaz 3a (☎079.950.603); they arrange a variety of boat tours in the immediate vicinity of Alghero, sailing up and down the coast and including spaghetti lunches and suppers under the stars. These "mini-cruises" last from 2 hours to the entire day.

Train information For info on FdS trains to Sássari, call ☎079.950.458; for FS services call ☎147.888.088.

Western Union Office at Bar Sanna, Via Vittorio Veneto 118 (☎167.464.464, toll-free).

Women's movement L'Ascolta Donna, a Christian group, gives advice and legal help. There's no telephone, but meetings every Tuesday 4–6.30pm at Via Sássari 82.

Short trips out of Alghero

It's almost de rigueur for visitors to Alghero to make the trip out to the **Grotta di Nettuno**, for which frequent boats leave from the port throughout the year. It's a thrilling ride, and one of Italy's most arresting cave complexes, though it's cheaper and in some ways more rewarding to go by bus. Your own vehicle will make it easier to visit a couple of important sites from the nuraghic and prenuraghic eras, the necropolis of **Anghelu Ruju** and the **Nuraghe di Palmavera**, which make a stimulating contrast to the sun-and-sea attractions of the rest of the region.

Fertilia, 7km west of Alghero, was one of Mussolini's projects linked to the local land reclamation programme, though it appears remarkably mute when compared with Alghero's gaiety. More interesting to serious holiday-makers are the excellent **beaches**, much better than Alghero's, particularly around the deep bay of **Porto Conte**. The area could easily be biked, and there's even a protected bicycle lane running for part of the way as far as Porto Conte.

Grotta di Nettuno

The best of the excursions you can take from the port is west to the **Grotta di Nettuno**, or Neptune's Grotto (daily April–Sept 9am–7pm; Oct 10am–5pm; Nov–March 9am–2pm; L13,000), with boats departing hourly in summer, at 9 and 10am, and 3 and 4pm in April, May and October: return tickets cost L16,000, not counting the entry charge to the grotto. The thirty-minute boat ride along the coast takes you past the lovely long bay of Porto Conte as far as the point of **Capo Caccia**, where the spectacular sheer cliffs are riddled by deep marine caves. They include the **Grotta Verde** and **Grotta dei Ricami** – visited on some tours – but the most impressive is the **Grotta di Nettuno** itself, just to the west of the point.

A long, snaking passage delves far into the rock, filled with fantastical, dramatically-lit stalagmites and stalactites. Forty-five-minute tours are led, single-file, on the hour every hour, by guides giving commentaries in Italian, and sometimes also in German, French or English, relating the discovery of the caves by fishermen, and pointing out imagined resemblances to helmeted warriors, toothy witches and popes. Less fanciful are the likenesses of organ pipes and columned cathedral interiors, after which two of the chambers are named. All in all, it's a magnificent work on the part of nature, only partly spoiled by the ceaseless streams of tourists filing through. Signs point out that touching the rock and photography are both forbidden, though no one takes much notice, especially towards the end of the column. The green colouring visible on some of the rock is mould, mostly caused by the lighting system. Navisarda also operates occasional boat departures from Cala Dragonara, an inlet on the western arm of Porto Conte (see p.209).

A cheaper alternative to the boat trip from Alghero – and the only choice in winter when there's no boat service – is to drive or take a **bus** to Capo Caccia from Via Catalogna, a fifty-minute ride (3 daily in summer; 1 in winter; L3400 one-way, L6300 return). Once you are deposited at the end of the line, there's a spectacular 654-step descent down the Escala del Cabirol; the Catalan name means "goat's steps", presumably a reference to the only animal that could negotiate the perilous path before the construction of the stairway in 1954. The sheer cliff-face and dark-blue water below is almost as impressive as the grotto interior itself. Make sure you time your arrival at the cave so that you don't have to wait up to an hour for the next tour: the descent takes 10–15 minutes. On the way back, leave some time before the bus goes for a well-earned ice cream or thirst-quencher at the bar opposite the top of the steps.

Fertilia

At a pinch you could walk out of Alghero to reach **FERTILIA**, an eight-kilometre stroll along the seafront past pine-fringed beaches. Alternatively, take local bus AF from the train station or Giardini Púbblici. Once out of Alghero, you'll pass a long lagoon on the right, the Stagno di Cálich, which collects the outflow of two rivers. Its mouth is crossed by a medieval bridge sinking picturesquely into the water, known locally as the **Ponte Romano**, or "Roman" bridge; it has been superseded by a modern road bridge, and the old structure is now mainly used as a perch for fishermen.

Fertilia itself is nothing special, a creation of Mussolini's in the 1930s, named to evoke the agricultural abundance that local land drainage would bring about (indeed, the rich agricultural land has produced some excellent wines, notably *Torbato*, a fairly sweet white). The arcaded Via Pola is the main avenue through town, connecting Piazza Venezia Giulia with the broad Piazzale San Marco, where a memorial to the migrants who settled the area from the Friuli-Venezia region of northeast Italy rears up next to the sea.

There's little else in the town, and little movement more frenetic than the slow padding of stray dogs.

If hotel space is scant at Alghero, Fertilia would not make a bad place to sleep. The best **hotels** are *Bellavista*, near the seafront on Lungomare Rovigno (April–Sept; ☎079.930.190, fax 079.930.124; ④), and the more downmarket *Hotel Fertilia*, on the airport road (☎079.930.098; ③), both with restaurants. *Dei Giuliani*, Fertilia's **youth hostel** (open all year; ☎ and fax 079.930.353), lies at the western end of town, on the secluded Via Zara. It's an old-fashioned place, and often booked up months in advance, though a new annex may have been opened by the time you read this; at present, dormitories hold four, six, ten or twenty beds, going for L14,000 each. There are no cooking facilities but evening meals are prepared (also L14,000). Non-IYHF members can buy temporary membership for L5000. Call first to check availability.

One hundred metres along the SS291 running north to Santa Maria La Palma, the *Nurral* **campsite** (☎079.930.485) is open all year. Though it's not that close to the sea, it has good facilities and four-bed bungalows to rent – in July and August half-board only is accepted for these, at L100,000 per head (L120,000 full board).

The town has a few **bars and restaurants** – nothing too inspiring, though the *Acquario* close to Piazzale San Marco at Via Pola 34 has a straight-up menu with reasonable prices (closed Mon in winter).

Nuraghe di Palmavera

On the road to Porto Conte, 10km west of Alghero, you'll pass the **nuraghe di Palmavera** (daily: March–Sept 9am–7pm; Oct–Feb 9.30am–4pm; L5000 with guide, L4000 without, or L9000 and L7000 with or without guide including Anghelu Ruju – see p.210), one of the largest in northwest Sardinia's Nurra region. The site on the side of the road comprises a ruined palace dating from the fourteenth and thirteenth centuries BC, surrounded by fifty or so circular huts.

The corridor in the entrance to the central tower has two niches on either side, probably for sentries, and a trap door in the roof for extra security. The interior is of the rounded "tholos" type, with more shallow niches. An elliptical bastion and a minor tower were added to the main building in the second phase of construction, around the ninth century BC, when some of the round huts scattered outside the ramparts were also erected. One of these, the **Capanna delle Riunioni**, distinguished by a low stone bench running round the circular walls, is believed to have been used for meetings and religious gatherings; others were probably dwellings. A third building phase took place a hundred or so years later, when more buildings were added, this time in limestone, as opposed to the softer sandstone of previous stages. The complex is thought to have been abandoned in the eighth or seventh century BC, possibly on account of fire.

Numerous finds from Nuraghe di Palmavera are on display in Sássari's Museo Sanna (see p.231), including a limestone model of a nuraghic tower and the stool retrieved from the centre of the meeting room – the one you see here is a plaster copy. For more on Sardinia's nuraghic culture, see pp.148-149.

Nearby, on the opposite side of the road, a signpost points to the beach of **Le Bombarde**, nearly a kilometre further on at the end of a straight and narrow track. **Windsurfing** courses are held here, and you can rent equipment (Northwest Windsurfing, ☎079.986.567). Another good beach, **Lazzaretto**, guarded by a Spanish watch tower, lies only about 700m further west, at the end of another signposted turn-off. Neither of these beautiful sandy coves facing Alghero across the bay is exactly a well-kept secret, but Lazzaretto has a string of smaller, less popular beaches beyond, and you can count on having these pretty much to yourself on weekdays out of season.

Porto Conte

The lovely inlet of **Porto Conte** lies a couple of kilometres beyond Lazzaretto, about 10km west of Alghero. Romantically named Portus Nimpharum ("Lake of the Nymphs") by the Romans, the intensely blue bay is a favourite anchorage for luxury yachts, which can be admired from the terraces of the clutch of top-notch hotels hidden among the trees. The road tracing the bay's eastern shore ends at a lighthouse; if you're looking for good bathing spots, follow the main road to Capo Caccia, turning left for the beach of **Baja di Conte** near the hotel of the same name. There are some extremely rudimentary **Roman ruins** here – little more than a scattering of broken walls – and **windsurfing and diving** opportunities on the beach.

To the west of Porto Conte, the peak of Monte Timidone (361m) holds the **Arca di Noe** protected wildlife zone, where the flora includes a rich abundance of Mediterranean *macchia*, and among the fauna are forty miniature horses, fifteen asses from Asinara (see pp.222–223), five mouflons, and even twenty Tibetan goats, as well as assorted wild boar, deer, griffon vultures and peregrine falcons. Entry to "Noah's Ark" is restricted, however: to obtain authorization, ask at Alghero's tourist office or apply directly at the Ispettorato Dipartimentale delle Foreste (Viale Dante 37, Sássari, ☎079.208.8818, fax 079.277.128). There's also a toll-free number to call: ☎167.865.065.

The biggest and swishest of the **hotels** in the area, *Baja di Conte* (May–Oct; ☎079.949.000, fax 079.949.021; ⑦), has the full gamut of sports facilities including boating and windsurfing on the bay; the cheapest choice is *Corte Rosada* (☎079.942.038, fax 079.942.158; ⑨), a little further along the road to Capo Caccia, boasting almost as full a range of facilities. For something a lot less grand, there's a good **campsite** about 5km north on the road to Santa Maria La Palma (signposted). Lying on the western coast, *Torre del Porticciolo* (May–Sept; ☎079.919.007) is the largest campsite in the region with tennis courts, a pool and bungalows, though you can always get away from the fuss by slipping down to the beach in the marvellous round bay below. The German admiral Von Tirpitz owned an extensive estate here before World War I, and it is said that the nearby bays and inlets were much-used by submarines for nocturnal rendezvous.

Not for nothing is this coast known as the Costa del Corallo. The two promontories at the southern end of Porto Conte are walled with the coral colonies, mainly in underwater grottos.

For water-skiing and diving at Porto Conte, go to the Base Nautica, where Adventure and Diving (☎079.942.205 and 0368.338.7048) and Nautica Pelloni (☎079.951.959 and 0337.812.220) provide equipment and tuition at various levels.

Anghelu Ruju

The necropolis of **Anghelu Ruju** (daily: March–Sept 9am–7pm;
Oct–Feb 9.30am–4pm; L5000 with guide, L4000 without, or L9000
and L7000 with or without guide including nuraghe di Palmavera –
see p.208), a pre-nuraghic cave complex of some forty hypogea, lies
10km out of Alghero on the road to Porto Torres. The site was discovered by chance in 1903 shortly after the land was purchased by
the Sella e Mosca winery, now one of Sardinia's most celebrated wine
producers. The necropolis – which now stands in the midst of the
vineyards of *cannonau* grapes beneath the planes roaring to and
from Fertilia airport – is a creation of the late Neolithic Ozieri culture
dating back to about 2900 BC, though it was reused throughout the
Copper Age (2900–1500 BC). The tombs, gouged out of the ground
and accessed by low-lintelled doorways, constitute Sardinia's best
examples of the so-called *domus de janas* ("fairy" or "witches' houses"), of which there are scores on the island, for the most part murky
chambers, or groups of them, some connected by sloping passages.
The dead were embalmed within, occasionally in mass burials, sometimes half-cremated, and in some cases skinned before burial.

You are free to scramble around the tombs, though there is little
specific to see: the rich contents have been removed to Cágliari and
Sássari where they are on display in the archeological museums. In
some cases, however, you can just make out, carved on the lintels or
in the depths of the darkness, symbolic shapes including bulls' horns
in tombs A, XXb, XXVIII and XXX, the last of these – carved on the
left wall of the "atrium" – a simple line which could also be a boat.
Bring a torch, and be prepared for some serious stooping.

Copies of some of the finds from Anghelu Ruju, together with diagrams of the site, are contained in *Sella e Mosca*'s **Museo e Tenuta
Vitivinícola**, less than a kilometre north on the Porto Torres road.
The main focus of the museum, however, is winemaking, whose various stages are explained on guided tours taking place every evening
at 5.30pm between mid-June and September, other times by appointment (☎079.997.700). Vittorio Sella's black-and-white photographs
add life to the history of the vineyard. Buy the end product from the
on-site *enoteca* (wine shop), open Monday–Saturday 8.30am–1pm &
3–7.30pm, also Sunday in August.

South of Alghero

There are two routes running **south of Alghero**, both strongly recommended, but very different from each other. As one route runs
inland and the other along the coast, and each ends at Bosa (see
p.212), you could cover both on a round-trip excursion to that town
from Alghero. The inland route follows the **SP292** from the crossroads at the south end of town, signposted Villanova. The road soon
climbs above the coast, affording magnificent views back towards
Alghero. After 25km of increasingly twisty road, you reach **Villanova**

Monteleone, the place to which the original Algherese were banished in 1354 after their town had been taken over by the Spanish. There's precious little to see or do here, though the village would make a lively destination at the end of August, when the local **festival for St John the Baptist** involves processions and horseback races. The local craft speciality is linen embroidered with angular animals and other geometric designs.

A right-turn out of Villanova takes you along a minor, little-used road which eventually winds up in Bosa, an arduous 40km trawl through an empty but often inspiring wilderness of *macchia* and mountain. Alternatively, continue east another 9km on the SS292 to the dammed **Lago del Temo**, from which the eponymous river flows down to Bosa on the coast. It's a good place to mosey around, with some grassy banks ideal for picnics. Rising on a hill just beyond the lake, **Monteleone Rocca Doria** was a Dorian foundation which endured a three-year siege by the combined forces of Aragon, Sássari, Bosa and Alghero, ending with its complete destruction in 1436. Monteleone's refugees joined the Algherese deportees in Villanova, hence that village's composite name.

The **coast road** south of Alghero travels through an equally rugged landscape, though the vistas encompass a diverse succession of coves and inlets – no beaches to speak of, but several places where you could take a dip from the rocks. Ideally, the tract should be walked or biked through at a leisurely pace. The mercifully undeveloped rocky terrain holds Sardinia's only colony of griffon vultures, though only about sixty were thought to exist in 1998, roughly half of the estimated figure of a year earlier. Many of these predators are being wiped out by the poisons left out by local farmers for foxes and stray dogs.

One of the remotest sections of the coast, **Capo Marargiu**, 8 or 9km north of Bosa, achieved a brief notoriety in the 1980s when it was revealed that a secret right-wing commando group, *Gladio*, used the headland as a training ground. There are good swimming spots around here.

North of Alghero

Travelling north from Alghero, Fertilia or Porto Conte, good roads lead across the territory of Nurra to **Lago Baratz**, Sardinia's only natural lake. A path curves round the reeds and marshes of the perimeter, allowing a close-up of some of the protected plants and, if you are lucky, animals, collected around here. Among these are a species of turtle (*Emys orbicularis*), while wildfowl include the little and great-crested grebes as well as a multitude of mallards and coots. The *macchia* which partially encroaches on the shores is a pungent mêlée of rosemary, myrtle, wild lavender and numerous species of wild orchid.

Just over a kilometre westwards from the lake, easily walkable (there is a road for drivers), the bay of **Porto Ferro** is guarded by three watchtowers and framed by a luscious long beach. North of the lake, an unasphalted track crosses a desolate tract of mountain to the hamlet of Palmádula, which can also be reached on the more reliable main roads (it's a long detour though: back towards Sássari, turning left for Porto Torres, then left again). Palmádula's not a place to linger, so continue another 5km west to reach the old abandoned mining town of **Argentiera**.

As its name implies, this was a silver-mining centre, once the greatest producer of silver on the island. Worked since Roman times, the seams were exhausted and extraction halted in 1963, and now the little town sits by itself at the end of a road on one of the most deserted expanses of the western coast. Its forlorn, haunted air is full of the echoes of its former industry. Shafts lie abandoned, miners' quarters stare blindly out, and there is little movement at all outside the months of July and August. There are some good beaches around here, though, one of which you will have passed on the way into town. The wonder is that the whole place has not been bought up and converted into a holiday village, a tribute to the planning laws in force in Sardinia. Still, Argentiera is unlikely to stay the same for very much longer.

Summer sees a little more action, with bathers attracted to the arcs of beaches in the vicinity, and there's a bar attached to a small, unadvertised **trattoria**, *In Piazza*, serving simple meals at good prices (closed mid-Oct to mid-May; no CCs).

For a good leg-stretch, head out to Capo dell'Argentiera, a headland about 3km southwest of the old mining centre.

Bosa and around

As the only town on the brief western seaboard of Nuoro province, **Bosa** has little in common with that inland shepherd's country. Not only does it exude a much stronger historical atmosphere, but it is far more closely related to the sea, despite its location 5km inland. It has a self-contained air, and from whichever direction you arrive, the town appears curiously suspended, stranded in the middle of one of Sardinia's last remaining stretches of undeveloped coast and coccooned from the main currents of Sardinian life. For all of these reasons, and for the placid river flowing through on its way to the coast, it makes a soothing place to hole up for a few days, refreshingly uncommercial yet within reach of some good beaches. The town's low profile until now has not been of its own choosing, and it can only be a matter of time before it succumbs to the blandishments of mass tourism; in the meantime, catch it while you can.

Bosa's coastal offshoot, **Bosa Marina**, equipped with most of the tourist facilities, is connected to **Macomer** by a private rail line which continues on to the provincial capital, Nuoro. Macomer is also on the main north–south FS line and on the SS131, but other than its usefulness as a transport junction, the only reason to visit this dull inland town would be en route to see a couple of notable nuraghic remains in the area.

Bosa has a small selection of **accommodation**, including a youth
hostel, and Macomer also has a few lodgings; always phone through
a reservation in summer.

Bosa

Though built on the banks of the Temo, Sardinia's only navigable
river of any size, **BOSA** has no easy links to any of the island's major
towns. Encircled by mountains, it huddles around the base of a hill
capped by a ruined castle, its very isolation having largely preserved
it from the incursions of ill-considered construction. The lingering
unkempt look of much of the place shows that Bosa has escaped the
makeover to fully-fledged resort, though this also means that not
everything works at maximum efficiency. The castle, river and a couple of churches are the main sights, all easily reached on foot, making this an ideal place to mooch around at leisure. The lower town,
Sa Piana, is cut through by Corso Vittorio Emanuele, running parallel to the river; north of here, the medieval quarter, *Sa Costa*, is a
succession of tight lanes winding round the Serravalle hill. Bosa
Marina is a bit of a toil to reach on foot; buses leave from Via
Nazionale, on the south side of the river.

Some history
Phoenicians and Romans are known to have settled the banks of the
Temo river; the Roman town was located near the site of the church
of San Pietro, a couple of kilometres upstream from the present
town. After the Romans left, Bosa fared badly, and was repeatedly
battered by barbarian and Moorish raids. In the twelfth century the
settlement was refounded by the Ligurian **Malaspina family** around
their fortress on the Serravalle hill. Many who had been living on the
coast, near present-day Bosa Marina, willingly migrated to this more
defensible spot, establishing the Sa Costa quarter on the slopes of
Serravalle.

Bosa changed hands several times during the ensuing vicissitudes
of war, at one time allying itself with the anti-Aragonese coalition
headed by Eleonora d'Arborea, but eventually forged a happy working relationship with the **Spanish**, under whom it prospered. After an
interlude of decay, the town achieved wealth and security in the eighteenth and nineteenth centuries when it was briefly a provincial capital, excelling in the working of precious metals, coral-gathering and
leather tanning. Much of Sa Piana, the lower town, dates from this era.

Arrival and information
Buses to Bosa pull in on Via Nazionale, a couple of hundred metres
from the old town bridge. **Drivers** on the Macomer road will use this
bridge, though there are convenient parking spaces on this side of
the river which will obviate the necessity of negotiating old-town
streets – alternatively find a slot on Lungotemo Álcide de Gásperi, a

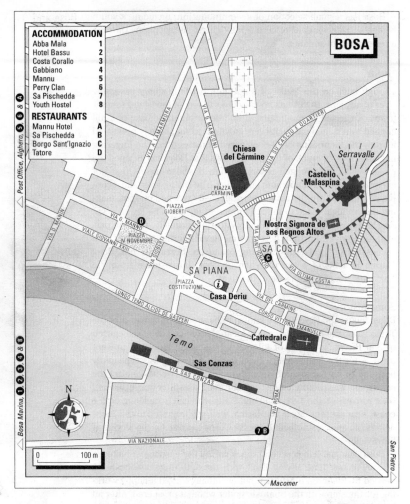

ACCOMMODATION
Abba Mala	1
Hotel Bassu	2
Costa Corallo	3
Gabbiano	4
Mannu	5
Perry Clan	6
Sa Pischedda	7
Youth Hostel	8

RESTAURANTS
Mannu Hotel	A
Sa Pischedda	B
Borgo Sant'Ignazio	C
Tatore	D

BOSA

◁ Post Office, Alghero, **5**, **6** & **4**

◁ Bosa Marina, **1** **2** **3** **4** & **8**

Chiesa del Cármine

Serravalle

Castello Malaspina

PIAZZA CARMINE

PIAZZA GIOBERTI

Nostra Signora de sos Regnos Altos

SA COSTA

SA PIANA

PIAZZA IV NOVEMBRE

PIAZZA COSTITUZIONE

Casa Deriu

Cattedrale

Temo

Sas Conzas

VIA SAS CONZAS

VIA NAZIONALE

N

0   100 m

San Pietro ▷

▽ Macomer

left turn immediately after the bridge. Driving or biking from Alghero, turn left at the first roundabout onto Viale Alghero, which becomes Viale Giovanni XXIII and then Corso Vittorio Emanuele, the pedestrianized main street of the old town; however, one-way systems make this less straightforward in practice. Another newer bridge crosses the river further downstream, nearer Bosa Marina (for which, turn right after crossing). Here, the small FdS station is the terminus for a summer **steam train** service from Macomer, operated mainly for group bookings.

Bosa's **tourist office** is to be found at Corso Vittorio Emanuele 59 (summer daily 10am–1pm & 6–9pm, erratic opening in winter;

☎0785.376.107), though it is currently closed and may reopen in future
at a different address. You might also try the Informagiovani office on
Viale Alghero (Mon–Fri 10am–1pm & 4–7pm; ☎0785.373.410), geared
towards information for youth.

Accommodation

Most of Bosa's **hotels** stay open all year. There are none within the
town's central core, though a couple lie within walking distance. The
lion's share of the accommodation, however, is in Bosa Marina; all of
these hotels are close to the sea, though none has much character.
The modern resort also has one of Sardinia's rare **youth hostels**.
There's no campsite hereabouts, though it would not be impossible
to do some surreptitious "free camping" on the beaches further up or
down the coast.

If you're stuck with nowhere else to go, find out about **rented
apartments** from the tourist office (the management of the *Perry
Clan* hotel also deals with rentals). Most properties are modern and
small, located in Bosa's newer districts or at Bosa Marina.

Hotels

Hotel Bassu, Via Grazia Deledda 15, Bosa Marina (☎ and fax 0785.373.456).
A modest one-star in a bland modern block, 50m from the beach. Rooms with
and without bath are functional and clean, and there's a restaurant. Breakfast
included. ②.

Costa Corallo, Via Colombo, Bosa Marina (☎0785.375.162, fax
0785.375.529). Run by a friendly young family, this smart two-star on the
riverside offers very reasonable rates. Rooms, all with bath, are fairly ordinary
and there's a restaurant. ④.

Gabbiano, Lungomare Mediterraneo, Bosa Marina (☎0785.374.123, fax
0785.374.109). The only three-star in this part of town is an unexceptional
tourist lodge with standard rooms and a basement restaurant. The main advantage is the proximity of the beach, just across the road. Air-conditioning is
available at an extra charge, and half- or full board is required in season. ④.

Mannu, Viale Alghero (☎0785.375.306, fax 0785.375.308). You'll need your
own transport to use this place, as close to Bosa Marina as to the main town
(less than a kilometre in either direction), on the north side of the river. The
main attraction is its plaudit-winning restaurant (see below). The three-star
hotel offers fairly good value for its comfortable facilities, though the location
on a main road is hardly inspiring. Bike and boat rentals and excursions can be
arranged from here. Half- or full board only in summer. ④.

Perry Clan, Viale Alghero 3 (☎0785.373.074). Just off Piazza Dante at the far
end of Corso Vittorio Emanuele, a ten-minute walk from the centre of Bosa,
this is primarily a noisy bar and restaurant with rooms above – rather characterless, but at least it's clean and cheap. Half-board is required in August. ②.

Sa Pischedda, Via Roma (☎0785.373.065). The best choice in Bosa itself, just
across the bridge from the old town, this fine old palazzo is the only hotel with
any atmosphere. A grand staircase leads up to quiet, comfortable rooms; others are currently being renovated on an upper floor. There's a mediocre pizzeria on the ground floor. Booking essential. ②.

Youth hostel and holiday village

Abba Mala, Località Abba Mala, 3km from Bosa (☎0785.375.565). This holiday village offers two-person apartments by the week for L1,200,000 in peak season, though prices drop considerably at other times; three- and four-bed apartments are also available. It's 1.5km inland, though a bus shuttles guests to the beach at Turas twice a day, and there's a pool too. Open May–October.

Malaspina, Via Sardegna 1, Bosa Marina (☎ and fax 0785.374.380). This hostel is scrupulously clean and takes non-IYHF members. Fifty beds in dormitories go for L18,000 each. The lack of a heating system currently forces the hostel to close in winter, usually between Nov and mid-March, though the projected installation of central heating would mean year-round opening. It's closed between 1pm and 3.30pm each day. There's no kitchen; evening meals cost L14,000, and the beach is a five-minute walk.

The town and river

Bosa's colourfully-domed **Cattedrale** lies on the northern side of the bridge, its fifteenth-century origins largely obscured under an overlay of Baroque. The Rococo facade gives access to a lavishly over-the-top interior, a riot of polychrome marble among which there are some individual items to pick out: a marble *Madonna col Bambino* from the sixteenth century, carved lions subduing dragons on the altar steps, and frescos in the apse painted by Emilio Scherer at the end of the nineteenth century. Behind the altar, another fresco from the same period shows a town plan of Bosa; the town's appearance is scarcely different today.

From the cathedral, the main **Corso Vittorio Emanuele** heads west, its tone set by well-preserved palazzi on either side. Halfway along on the right, at no. 159, the nineteenth-century **Casa Deriu** currently houses the Pro Loco, and occasionally hosts art exhibitions. At the Corso's western end, the grand Palazzo Don Carlos, dating from the eighteenth century, overlooks the outdoor bars on **Piazza Costituzione**, beyond which lie the newer outskirts of town. Take any of the lanes to the right of the Corso to penetrate the web of alleys that make up Bosa's Old Quarter, **Sa Costa**. Full of medieval gloom, the corridor-like streets follow up the steep contours of Serravalle, involving a healthy amount of huffing before you reach the brow of the hill and the castle. If this is the direction you are headed, you can't go wrong by taking any way that goes up; it's about a twenty-minute climb. On the way up or down, drop in on the **Chiesa del Cármine**, on Via del Cármine, a richly decorated Baroque edifice with an elegant facade from 1779.

The Castello Malaspina

Only the shell of Bosa's **Castello Malaspina** (daily 10am–noon & 4–7pm, but erratic hours in winter; L5000) survives, but that and the commanding position are enough to give the flavour of this medieval fortress. Erected by the powerful Malaspina family in 1122, the walls incorporate a series of towers, notably the **torre nord**, open-sided in the

fashion of other towers in Oristano and Cágliari, and the **torre maggiore**, taller and more refined than the others, and thought to have been
the work of Cágliari's celebrated military architect Giovanni Capula,
who designed the Torre di San Pancrazio and Torre dell'Elefante in his
home city; the pentagonal **torre ovest** is Aragonese.

Within the walls, the only building standing is the church of
Nostra Signora di Regnos Altos, which contains a rare cycle of
Catalan-style frescos from the fourteenth or fifteenth century. The
church has been undergoing restoration for years, though it may be
open to visitors. The bird's-eye views from the red trachyte ramparts
are worth savouring, allowing a first-hand opportunity to grasp the
area's geography. If the castle's closed, search out the custodian at
Via Última Costa 12, the first road down from the entrance. If you're
on wheels, you can reach the entrance by following signs along the
road skirting the back of town, leading round to the castle gate.

Along the river

From the castle's ramparts, the landscape's clearest feature, the
broad Temo **river**, invites closer investigation. Near the bridge, you
can wander the quayside among **Sas Conzas**, the former leather tan-
neries – relics of an industry that was central to the local economy
from the eighteenth century to World War II. A rank of palms lines
the opposite bank, where most of the fishing boats are moored, their
nets draped over the quay.

The best walk, however, runs 2km east along the south bank,
where a rural road running parallel to the river leads to the former
cathedral of **San Pietro** (also visible from the castle). The original
construction dates from 1073, although the Gothic facade was added
by Cistercian monks at the end of the thirteenth century. Beneath a
trio of small rose windows, the architrave of the west door is embellished with naively-carved vignettes of the Madonna and Child, and
Saints Peter, Paul and Costantinus de Castra, the church's founder.
The square belltower and the apse date from the twelfth century.

The main body of the church, however, is pure Lombard
Romanesque in inspiration, though it was modified at later stages.
The sombre interior has two rows of solid, broad-stoned, rectangular
columns; on one of them, the first on the right, you might just be able
to make out an inscribed dedication by Bishop Constantinus de
Castra. With little other kind of decoration, it's a silent, moody place.
It's rarely open, though: ask at the tourist office for mass times, or if
you stand around and make enough noise the chances are someone
will appear with the key.

Bosa Marina

At various times in its history, Bosa has transferred its site to different points along the banks of the River Temo, one of them being
what is now **BOSA MARINA**, at the mouth of the river. Today it is a

conventional minor resort with a small choice of hotels and trattorias, a terminal for the tourist steam train connecting the town with Macomer in summer, and a broad beach. Guarded by a sullen Spanish watchtower, yachts and fishing boats lie at anchor in the lee of the islet of Isola Rossa, now linked to the mainland by a bridge. In July and August the tower is opened for occasional exhibitions of local arts and crafts. The sheltered beach is a favourite place for windsurfers, with equipment usually available to rent in summer, but can get pretty thronged. Remoter patches of sand lie 2km south in the **Turas** neighbourhood, though if you're looking for true isolation, you're best off visiting the rugged littoral north of Bosa, where you'll find rocks to swim off, but no sandy beaches (see p.211).

Food, drink and entertainment

You'll need to reserve to get a table at Alghero's most rated **restaurant**, attached to the *Mannu* hotel on Viale Alghero (see Accommodation, on p.215), where local specialities such as spaghetti with lobster and fried mussels are expertly prepared. It may be worth booking at the less formal *Sa Pischedda*, too (again, see accommodation listings): the food is rather indifferent, however, and you'll probably fare better at the semi-formal *Borgo Sant'Ignazio*, at Via Sant'Ignazio 33 (an alley above the Corso, signposted), which offers more local specialities (closed Tues). Elsewhere, *Tatore*, at the western end of the Corso on Piazza IV Novembre, has one long room with a painted ceiling, where you can eat good pastas for L12–15,000 (closed Wed in winter; no CCs). For **snacks**, the *Bar-Caffè Taverna* in Piazza Carmine has a terrace where you can have drinks and *panini* (closed Tues Oct–May). Bosa Marina has more restaurants attached to hotels, but the fare is pretty standard. The Bosa area is renowned for its **Malvasia** dessert wine, served at most bars and restaurants.

Bosa's Sagra di Nostra Signora di Regnos Altos festival in September is a great chance to attend an open-air mass at the castle, watch local groups perform traditional songs and dances, and to enjoy local food and drink.

There are two **discotheques** in the locality, open in summer only: *Sas Covas*, at the end of Viale Alghero on the north side of the river, and *Al Paradise* in the Turas neighbourhood, a couple of kilometres south of Bosa Marina; neither deviates too far from mainstream dance beats or Latin salsas. As for **festivals**, the best are centred on the river: the Festa dei Santi Pietro e Paolo on June 29 involves a regatta as far as the church of San Pietro, with local foodstuffs available to be sampled, while in the Sagra di Santa Maria del Mare, on the first Sunday of August, an image of the Madonna is transported by boat from Bosa Marina to the cathedral, returning in the afternoon when an open-air mass is held and fireworks are set off. Carnival is enthusiastically celebrated in Bosa; processions take place at Easter and on the second Sunday of September for the Sagra di Nostra Signora di Regnos Altos, and there's a country festival, the Festa dei Santi Cosma e Damiano, on September 26, accompanied by traditional singing and dancing.

Macomer and around

Thirty kilometres inland of Bosa on the SS129, **MACOMER** is one of Sardinia's main transport junctions, though the town itself has little to recommend anything more than a brief passage. Called Macopissa in Roman times, when it was a major military base, the town was the site of the last serious revolt against the Aragonese by the Sards in 1478. More lately it's become a centre of livestock, dairy farming and wool.

Although Macomer has no intrinsic interest, a few sights in the surrounding area repay the small detour. Chief among these are a couple of nuraghi, the best of an intense concentration of nuraghic sites to be found hereabouts. A kilometre or two north of the centre, signposted between the Bosa road and the Carlo Felice highway, stands the impressive **nuraghe di Santa Barbara**, its mossy central tower reaching 15m, with primitive cupolas, minor towers and bastions tacked on to the main structure. Little is known about the building's origins, though it has been ascertained that it was abandoned in the ninth century BC, but reutilized in the Carthaginian and Roman era as a centre of worship. Nearby, on the other side of the highway, the ruined state of **nuraghe Ruju** (or Ruggiu) reveals a cross-section of how a nuraghic cupola was constructed. *Domus de janas* tombs are scattered about below it, their contents on view at Sássari's Museo Sanna (see p.231).

Twelve kilometres east of town on the Nuoro road (SS129), just outside the village of **Silanus**, the charming little Byzantine chapel of **Santa Sabina** is harmoniously juxtaposed with a small nuraghe close by.

Practicalities

Macomer's **bus and train stations** lie near each other on the western end of town. The rattly old small-gauge trains for Nuoro leave from here approximately every hour. The town has three central **hotels**, of which *Su Talleri* on Via Cavour (☎0785.71.491; ②), three-star with all rooms en suite with telephone and TV, and the two-star *Marghine* (☎ and fax 0785.70.737; ②) on Via Vittorio Emanuele, with rooms with or without bathroom, are the most useful; both have restaurants.

On Sant'Antonio Abate's day, January 17, a mighty bonfire is lit outside Macomer's church of Santa Chiara for the **festa di Su Tuva**.

Stintino and around

Sardinia's northwestern tip, forming the western arm of the **Golfo di Asinara**, is an inhospitable, sparsely populated area of rock and *macchia*. The only town here is **Stintino**, until recently nothing more than a remote jumble of fishermen's cottages jammed between two narrow harbours. Fortunately its discovery by the tourist industry has not drastically altered it, and it remains a small, laid-back, if slightly bland place with a few bars, banks, restaurants and lodgings. The big hotels

have established themselves further up the coast, where most of the sunning and swimming take place around the ravishing beach of **La Pelosa**. At the end of the peninsula, **Capo Falcone** overlooks the isles of **Piana** and **Asinara**, one a tiny blip, the other the only known habitat of a miniature white ass from which the gulf and island both take their name. It's one of Sardinia's more spectacular corners, though increasingly threatened by encroaching tourist developments.

Stintino has a small selection of **hotels**, though if you want to stay nearer the bathing, head further up the coast towards the cape. You'll need a bit of forward planning to find anything available in the summer season, however, with many rooms booked by the week. There is greater scope for finding self-catering apartments, and though most of these are set aside for block bookings by tour companies, you can find some real bargains in low season. There are no campsites in the area, though discreet space for a tent could be found among the remoter tracts.

Stintino is connected by regular **buses** from Porto Torres and Sássari, some of which arrive as far as La Pelosa, though there is a greatly curtailed service outside summer (see "Travel Details" at the end of the chapter for approximate schedules).

Stintino

Some 50km north of Alghero and 30km west of Porto Torres, **STINTINO** was founded little more than a century ago, when the Italian state appropriated the island of Asinara for use as a penal colony. The 45 families of the resident fishing community were transferred to this sheltered spot between two natural inlets. The town today holds a population of about one thousand, to which must be added the thousands more who flock here every year, replacing fishing as the main source of income for many of the locals. While escaping the mass development undergone by other more accessible resorts, Stintino is undeniably a tourist town, even if tourists are extremely scarce for most of the year. The place lives for the summer, and the contrast between the vitality that prevails then and the inertia of the other nine months is striking.

The compact town is simple enough to grasp, a right-angled grid of mainly residential streets spreading out from the main Via Sássari. Two harbours lie on either side of the promontory: to the north, **Porto Nuovo**, also known as Portu Mannu, caters mainly to pleasure craft, while the southern **Porto Vecchio**, or Portu Minori, is crowded with fishing vessels. There is no central piazza, the two ports providing the only reference points.

Next to Porto Nuovo, the **Museo della Tonnara** (June–Sept daily 6pm–midnight; free) outwardly appears like an ordinary quayside warehouse, but is arranged within to reflect the various stages in the process of trapping and killing tuna, once a major activity in these parts, introduced by Ligurians on Asinara. The six rooms from the *Cámera*

Grande to the *Cámera della Morte* ("death chamber") trace the role of tuna in the ecology of the Mediterranean and the intricacies of the centuries-old methods used each year to snare them. Maps, filmed interviews and videos of the final bloody scenes fill out the picture, and will probably tell you all you want to know and more of this practice.

The one-way street running round the seaward side of the promontory, **Lungomare Colombo**, provides a route for an easy stroll around town, which, after a couple of bar stops, and leaving aside Stintino's good restaurants, exhausts the things to do here.

Practicalities

Between two and six **buses** a day go to Stintino from Sássari, and there are also organized trips from Alghero in the summer months. Buses stop on the main Via Sássari. Call in at the small **tourist office** at Via Sássari 77 for general information (Mon–Sat summer 9.30am–1pm & 5–8pm, winter 9.30am–1pm; ☎079.523.788), or see Stintours below.

There are just three **hotels** in town, cheapest of which is the *Lina*, overlooking Porto Vecchio at Via Lepanto 30 (☎079.523.071; ③). Half the plain rooms here (no telephone or TV, but all with private bathroom) have balconies facing the boats, the others have no view but have the same rates, on a first-come basis. Half-board (not obligatory in peak season) costs L30,000 per person on top of the room rate. In Stintino's centre, the smarter *Silvestrino* at Via Sássari 12 (☎079.523.007; ④), has full modern facilities (private bath, TV, telephone), and demands a three-day minimum stay and half- or full board in July and August. The latter requirement shouldn't be too great a sacrifice since its restaurant is one of the region's best (see below). At Via XXI Aprile 4, *Geranio Rosso* (☎079.523.292; ④) is the poshest place, though without any airs, and even has quite a homey feel. Rooms are fully-equipped and tastefully decorated, and there's a pizzeria at street-level (half-board, at L130,000 per person, is the rule from mid-June to mid-August). The Stintours agency on Lungomare Colombo (☎079.523.160, fax 079.523.048) deals with **apartment rentals** in and around Stintino, available even for two or three days for about L30,000–L60,000 per person per night, depending on the season (extras such as laundry and cleaning might be added on).

All of Stintino's **restaurants** specialize in seafood, and the larger ones have fresh lobster on offer. At Porto Vecchio, *Lina* has outdoor seating and reasonable prices for its variable food. Overlooking the northern Porto Nuovo, *Il Portico* is an easy-going outdoor trattoria/pizzeria open in summer only. Undoubtedly the best place to eat is at *Silvestrino*, the hotel on Via Sássari, where a limited menu of fishy firsts and main courses – including lobster soup, seafood risotto and scrumptious prawns – hits all the right buttons (closed Thurs in winter, and Jan). It's also one of the more expensive places in town, with a three-course meal setting you back at least L40,000 per

Try to be in Stintino at the end of August for the Regata della Vela Latina, when the waters are filled with yachts, some of them restored vintage vessels. The other major festival is on September 8, when a procession re-enacts the exodus of Asinara's inhabitants to their new home in Stintino.

head, excluding drinks; it's worth reserving a table if you decide to eat here. Round the corner on Via Marco Polo, *Da Antonio* aspires to the same high standards, but fails on every count: it's over-priced, pretentious and slow.

The Stintours agency (see p.221) is the place for information on almost everything, and you can also **rent cars, mopeds and bikes** from them: for a car, expect to pay around L70,000 per day plus L700 per kilometre, or L180,000 per day with unlimited kilometres; for a moped it's from about L40,000 a day, L250,000 a week, and for a push-bike it's from L25,000 a day, L150,000 a week. Prices drop in low season, and motorboats and dinghies are also available.

Around Stintino

With most of the shore around Stintino rough and rocky, you'll have to go north or south of town to find decent beaches. About a kilometre to the south, near an old watchtower, a narrow road leads to the *macchia*-backed beach of **Le Saline**, once site of a salt works owned by the monks of Santa Maria di Tergu (see p.251). There's a Spanish bastion here, and often a flock of flamingoes attracted to the salt-pan/lagoon here.

North of Stintino, tourist villages clutter the hills backing the coast almost as far as the northern tip of **Capo Falcone**, site of Torre Falcone, a Spanish watchtower. Leading up to the cape, the otherwise idyllic beach of **La Pelosa** is one of Sardinia's premier swimming spots, lapped by a shallow, turquoise sea of crystalline clarity. You probably won't be alone here, and the tiers of holiday homes spreading over the slopes are an annoying blot on the landscape, but the perfect views over the outlying islands of Piana and the much larger Asinara are enchanting, and the swimming is good too.

Piana and Asinara

In summer, regular boat tours depart either from Stintino or La Pelosa to sail round the islands' coasts and make a landing. On **Piana**, what you see is what you get: a tiny flat patch of land with a solitary watchtower standing guard. There is more on **Asinara**, 16km long, though you probably won't be seeing that much of it anyway. Access to the island has been severely restricted since a prison colony was established there in 1885, while the creation of a national park here in 1998 makes it likely that it will continue to be difficult to wander around.

Called Sinuaria by the Romans on account of its indented form, which makes it appear from a distance like a whole archipelago of separate islands, Asinara has been sporadically inhabited in the last two millennia, and was even occupied in 1638 by French pirates as a base for their raiding missions against shipping headed to or from Porto Torres. The Savoyan king sold it to the Duke of Vallombrosa in 1775, but it never yielded a significant income, and was used both as a quarantine hospital for victims of cholera and a place of incarceration. At its northern end, the island's highest point (408m) is poignantly named Punta della Scomúnica ("Excommunication Point").

Asinara's off-limits status has at least meant that it has sheltered a range of wildlife, and it is still used to pasture cattle, who are walked across the shallow straits between Capo Falcone and Piana twice a year, in November and May – worth a photo if you're there. For **tours of Piana and Asinara**, call ☎0337.756.945 or contact Stintours in Stintino (see p.221).

(see p.221)

Practicalities

A range of flashy three- and four-star **hotels** in the vicinity offer surprisingly favourable rates, especially out of season, and are just steps away from the sea. The biggest (and most obtrusive) of these is the *Roccaruja* (May–Sept; ☎079.529.200, fax 079.529.778; ⑥), where there is an Olympic-size pool and an extra L50,000 a week allows you to participate in a number of activities including tennis, windsurfing, canoeing and sailing. With self-contained apartments also available, the hotel makes an ideal place for families, of which you'll see many, as well as groups from northern Italy. Among the other choices, *La Pelosetta* (April–Oct; ☎079.527.188, fax 079.527.020; ⑤) is extensive, right behind the beach of La Pelosa, and boasts a renowned **restaurant** with extraordinary views. The hotel also has a snack bar right on the beach (April–Sept) – both places are open to non-hotel guests. Between mid-June and mid-September, hourly **buses** connect Stintino with La Pelosa (buy tickets on board). At other times, you can reach the beach by taxi or hired bike from Stintino.

Travel Details

TRAINS

Alghero to: Sássari (Mon–Sat 11 daily, Sun 6; 35min).

BUSES

Alghero to: Bosa (Mon–Sat 4 daily, Sun 2; 1hr 15min–1hr 40min); Capo Caccia (1 daily; 50min); Olbia (1 daily; 2hr); Porto Conte (7–8 daily; 30min); Porto Ferro (4 daily; 35min–1hr 5min); Porto Torres (Mon–Sat 5–8 daily, Sun 3; 50min); San Marco (for Anghelu Ruju) (Mon–Sat 4–5 daily, Sun 1; 20min–30min); Sássari (hourly; 1hr); Villanova Monteleone (Mon–Sat 8–11 daily, Sun 6; 40min).

Argentiera to: Sássari (Mon–Sat 5–7 daily; 1hr 5min).

Bosa to: Alghero (Mon–Sat 4 daily, Sun 2; 1hr 15min–1hr 40min); Cúglieri (Mon–Sat 5 daily; 1hr); Olbia (1 daily; 3hr); Oristano (Mon–Sat 5 daily; 2hr); Sássari (Mon–Sat 6 daily, Sun 1; 2hr–2hr 10min); Villanova Monteleone (Mon–Sat 2 daily; 1hr).

Stintino to: Porto Torres (Mon–Sat 5–6 daily, Sun 2–3; 1hr 40min); Sássari (Mon–Sat 5–6 daily, Sun 2–3; 1hr 15min).

Stintino and around

The exceptionally clear waters of La Pelosa and the islands offer limitless opportunities for diving. For equipment rental and courses, contact Asinara Diving Center (☎079.523. 223 or 0338.968.5721) at the Ancora Hotel, 2km north of Stintino.

Chapter 6

Sássari and around

E ncompassing the ancient territories of Logudoro and Anglona, the western half of Sássari province ranges from high tableland riven by unexpected gullies around the provincial capital itself to craggy peaks and valleys further east, and a long sandy arc edging the Golfo dell'Asinara on the northern coast.

Sardinia's second city, **Sássari**, is for many the island's most interesting town, with its crowded medieval centre and Spanish associations. It's a less cosmopolitan place than Cágliari, its inland location accentuating its inward-looking mentality, though there is also a high level of culture here, and enough interest in the city's churches and excellent archeological museum to fill at least a couple of days.

A short ride from Sássari will bring you to some excellent swimming spots on the Golfo dell'Asinara, where the only blot on the otherwise undeveloped coast is the extensive refinery outside **Porto Torres**. Unless you're passing through on one of the ferries to or from the mainland, the principal reason to visit this industrial port is the **Basilica di San Gavino**, considered by many to be the island's finest example of Pisan-Romanesque architecture. It's a superb introduction to the **medieval churches** with which this region of Sardinia is richly endowed, most of them splendidly positioned in improbably remote corners of the countryside, saved from despoliation by their very inaccessibility.

The old territory of **Logudoro**, to the south and east of Sássari, has an impressive collection of these secluded monuments: **Santa Trinità di Saccargia** lies just off the Sássari–Olbia road, though others require a little more perseverance to reach. The medieval refinement of these buildings forms a sharp contrast to the ramshackle grandeur of the nuraghi that are an equally striking feature of the region. The densest concentration of them is at **Torralba**, where there is an outstanding museum of nuraghic culture and, a short distance outside the village (and very near to the SS131), the grand **Nuraghe Santu Ántine**, one of the island's most important nuraghic complexes.

Nuraghs and prenuraghic structures are also scattered across the mountainous **Anglona** region, northeast of Sássari. Its principal

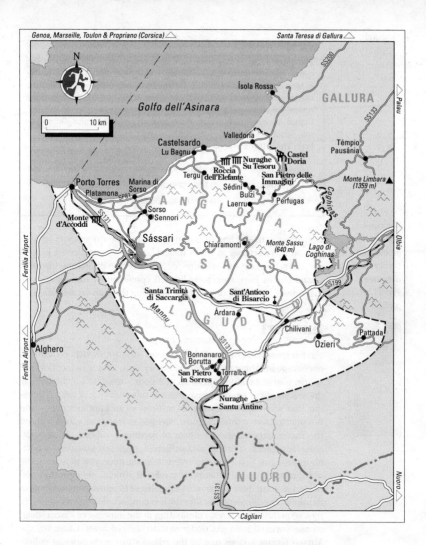

town, **Castelsardo**, occupies a fortified site on the coast; this scenic
location, and the local dexterity with handicrafts, have made it a
magnet for tourists, but don't be put off exploring the old citadel to
enjoy the far-reaching views. There are some good scenic drives
inland from here, while the best beaches lie to the east of town,
around the mouth of the **Coghinas river**, which marks Anglona's
eastern boundary.

Sássari is the area's major transport hub. Apart from the fifteen-
minute **train** connection between Sássari and Porto Torres, and the

Accommodation Price Codes

The hotels listed in this guide have been coded according to price. The codes represent the cheapest available double room in high season (Easter & June–Aug). In cheaper hotels the rooms usually come without en-suite bathroom or shower; some of these places will also have a few en-suite rooms, for which you'll pay more – usually the next category up in price. Higher category hotels nearly always have only en-suite rooms. Out of season, you'll often be able to negotiate a lower price than those suggested here. The categories are:

① under L60,000	④ L120,000–150,000	⑦ L250,000–300,000
② L60,000–90,000	⑤ L150,000–200,000	⑧ over L300,000
③ L90,000–120,000	⑥ L200,000–250,000	

For more information on bus and train connections, see Travel Details, p.258.

occasionally useful line to Ozieri-Chilivani, non-drivers will have to rely on **bus services** to reach most places. The north coast is well-served by frequent buses bound for Santa Teresa di Gallura, but most inland places have extremely limited connections, sometimes with just one or two ARST or FdS buses passing through on weekdays.

Sássari

First impressions of Sardinia's second city, **SÁSSARI**, do little to encourage anything more than a cursory visit; its inland location and sparse tourist facilities might seem a poor substitute for the holiday diversions of the nearby coast. But it is this very lack of tourist glamour that gives Sássari its special interest as an unpretentious – and not unattractive – working town, steeped in tradition, albeit without the rustic and folkloric elements of Sardinia's villages. To the outsider, it presents a proud, self-sufficient, even self-absorbed aspect, an impression that becomes overwhelming once you penetrate the **old quarter**'s dense network of medieval streets, old churches and palazzi, among them some rare examples of Renaissance buildings in Sardinia. This atmospheric labyrinth is connected to the modern city by a sequence of squares, culminating in the impressive Piazza Italia, whose imperial tone sits oddly next to the old town. Close by, the **Museo Sanna** houses one of the island's top archeological collections, second only to Cágliari's.

Sássari has a good range of bars and restaurants, though there is not so much choice when it comes to accommodation. Nonetheless, with its network of transport connections, the town makes a handy base for the many coastal or inland attractions in the vicinity, or else a stimulating diversion from a more permanent base by the sea.

Note that if you're coming to Sássari by **train** from the south or west, you'll probably have to change at the nondescript town of Chilivani (its station is usually referred to as Ozieri-Chilivani).

Sássari's Festivals

One of Sardinia's showiest festivals – **La Cavalcata** – takes place in Sássari on **Ascension Day** (the 40th day after Easter), the highlight of a month of cultural activities. Northern Sardinia's equivalent to Cágliari's Sant'Efisio festival (see p.82), it attracts hundreds of richly costumed participants from villages throughout the province and beyond. Originally staged for the benefit of visiting Spanish kings and other dignitaries, it lapsed in the eighteenth century until it was revived, first in 1899, and then more recently by the local branch of the Rotary Club.

The festival is divided into three stages, the morning featuring a **horseback parade** and a slow **procession** in which the embroidered and decorated costumes unique to each village are displayed. In the afternoon, the scene shifts to the Ippodromo (race track) on the southern outskirts of town, where hectic **horse races** and ever more daring equestrian feats are performed before a large crowd. Saturday night and Sunday evening are devoted to traditional songs and dances in Piazza Italia, showcasing groups from all over the island. The close-harmony singing is especially impressive. A large fair takes over the centre of town during the week leading up to the Cavalcata, so expect lengthy traffic hold-ups.

On the afternoon of **August 14** there is a much more local affair – **Li Candareri** (or *I Candelieri*), linked to the Pisan devotion to the Madonna of the Assumption. It became a regular event when an outbreak of plague in Sássari mysteriously abated – though there is dispute as to which particular plague it was, those of 1528, 1580 and 1652 being the main contenders – since when the ritual has been repeated annually on the eve of the feast of the Assumption as a token of thanks. For all its religious intent, Li Candareri is a crowded, rumbustious occasion, involving bands of *gremi*, or medieval guilds of merchants, artisans and labourers, decked out in Spanish-style costumes, lurching through the old town under the weight of nine gigantic wooden "candlesticks", 8m tall, weighing between 200 and 300kg, and laden with colourful ribbons and other symbols of the guilds they represent. The descent through the town (*La Faradda*) usually begins at Piazza Castello, ending at the church of Santa Maria di Bethlem, with a stop en route at the Teatro Cívico, where the representative of the farmers hails Sássari's mayor with a hearty *A zent'anni* ("May you live a hundred years"), a traditional salute to all the *sassaresi*. The *Faradda* starts at 6pm; if you're in town on the previous afternoon, you should drop in on the *palio*, or bareback horse race, that takes place in the Ippodromo.

Some history

Built on an ancient site known as Tatari, or Tathari, the modern city of Sássari has roots going back to settlers from the Roman colony, Turris Libyssonis, the modern Porto Torres. As the port declined, so the inland town expanded; by the fourteenth century it possessed its own statute of laws and a ring of walls. Sássari was inevitably sucked into the conflict between Pisa and Genoa, making strategic alliances with both sides as the situation demanded. Then, in 1323, James II of Aragon established a power base here and, after a brief interlude under the control of the *giudicato* of Arborea, the city spent the next four centuries as an integral part of the Catalan-Aragonese hegemony, though that did not prevent it from being plundered several times by Moorish pirates. Ten years under Austrian rule preceded the coming of the House of Savoy in 1720, whose cautious programme of reforms and investment was briefly interrupted when an anti-feudal revolt led by a coalition of urban democrats and rural peasants provoked a fierce campaign of repression between 1793 and 1802. In the course of the nineteenth century, the Aragonese castle and walls were demolished, allowing the city to expand gradually.

The Spanish stamp is still evident in Sássari, not least in its churches. The city also has a strong tradition of intellectual independence; in the sixteenth century the Jesuits founded Sardinia's first **university** here, which continues to excel in the spheres of law, medicine and politics. In recent years, Sássari has produced two national presidents, Antonio Segni and Francesco Cossiga, as well as the long-time

head of the Italian Communist Party, Enrico Berlinguer (1922–84) – a cousin, incidentally, of the Christian Democrat Cossiga.

Today, with its 120,000 inhabitants (about half Cágliari's population), Sássari is grappling with rapidly changing economic conditions. Belying the well-to-do urbanity of Via Roma's café society, the city's youth especially is caught between the seemingly intractable problems of unemployment and heroin addiction, which have generated a degree of petty crime. There is little threat to outsiders, however, and most *sassaresi* are rarely less than courteous and hospitable, albeit imbued with a deep cynical streak.

Arrival, information and accommodation

The **train station** is at the bottom of the old town, from which it's a ten-minute walk uphill to Piazza Italia and the modern city. All local and long-distance ARST **buses** arrive at and depart from the semicircular Emiciclo Garibaldi, south of the tourist office, but most make stops at the train station. PANI buses run to and from Piazza Italia, just round the corner from the ticket office at Via Bellieni 5, off Via Roma. ARST buses run the 30-kilometre, 40-minute journey between the bus station and Alghero's **Fertilia airport** (see p.195) six times daily. Note that when ticket offices are closed, you can buy most tickets at some bars, indicated by posters (see Listings, p.239).

Everything of interest in Sássari is easily reached on foot and you're unlikely to need to use **local buses**, though if you want to get to or from the train station quickly, #8 is the most useful service, plying a circular route every 12 minutes between the station, Corso Vittorio Emanuele, Piazza Italia and Via Roma. Buy tickets before boarding at *tabacchi* (L1100, or block of 12 for L10,800). If you're **driving**, make sure you stay on the right side of the parking attendants; seek them out and buy a ticket (L1000 per hour) to avoid a fine during the times when restrictions are in force (Mon–Fri 8.30am–1pm and 4–8pm, Sat 8.30am–1pm). Free spaces can be hard to find: try around the station area, Emiciclo Garibaldi or Viale Umberto. If desperate, use a garage (see Listings, p.239).

Sássari's most useful **tourist office** is right next to the Museo Sanna at Via Roma 62 (Mon–Thurs 9am–1.30pm & 4–6pm, Fri 9am–1.30pm; ☎079.231.777); alternatively the people at the AAST office at Viale Umberto 72 (Mon–Wed 8am–2pm & 4–7pm, Thurs & Fri 8am–2pm; ☎079.231.331), though primarily concerned with administration, are generally helpful and also have maps, accommodation lists and booklets to give away.

Staying in Sássari can be a real problem, as there are few reasonably-priced **hotels** – you'd do well to phone ahead. There are **youth hostels** at Porto Torres (p.242) and Alghero (p.208), respectively 20 and 45 minutes away, and **campsites** in Alghero or on the north coast east of Porto Torres, on a bus route from Sássari.

Hotels

Frank Hotel, Via Armando Diaz 20 (☎ & fax 079.276.456). This and the *Leonardo da Vinci* (see below) form a pair of three-stars in the modern city geared towards groups and conferences, but useful for staying in this part of town. Rooms are spacious, there's a moderate pizzeria/restaurant in the basement (closed Sun), and garage parking. ④.

Garden Hotel, Via Pígliaru 10 (☎079.241.325, fax 079.254.123). An excellent choice if you don't mind the remote location, perched below the viaduct in the Monte Rosello district nearly 2km from the centre of town. True to its name, the hotel occupies a quiet, leafy spot off the main roads, with a view of cultivated fields below. No CCs. ②.

Giusy, Piazza Sant'Antonio (☎079.233.327, fax 079.239.490). Conveniently near the station on Piazza Sant'Antonio, and the only choice in the old town. It's seen better days, and suffers from traffic noise, but all rooms have TV and telephone. No restaurant. Triple rooms are available. ③.

Leonardo da Vinci, Via Roma 79 (☎ & fax 079.280.744). Like the *Frank* but glitzier, with similar accoutrements (garage parking, rooms with TVs, telephones, minibars, etc.). Just up from the museum, it's marginally closer to the centre and has higher prices. There's a bar and breakfast room but no restaurant. ⑤.

Sássari Hotel, Viale Umberto 65 (☎079.239.543). Sássari's only budget choice is an endearingly tumbledown place, with large, sometimes grimy, rooms and old-fashioned plumbing. It's the closest hotel to Piazza Italia. Rooms for three and four available. No CCs. ①.

The modern city

It would be hard to say where the true centre of Sássari lies; the city is split into different, largely self-contained quarters. However, the largest piazza, and the venue of most of the city's festas, is **Piazza Italia**, a magnificent area which can claim to be the grandest piazza in Sardinia, and one of the most monumental public spaces anywhere in Italy. Virtually traffic-free, its generous expanse is a sure cure for any claustrophobic feelings induced by the old town. One whole side of the square is occupied by the imposing **Palazzo della Provincia**, built in 1880, looking more like a presidential palace than a mere provincial office; perhaps surprisingly, the neo-Gothic **Palazzo Giordano** facing it (now the offices of the Banco di Napoli) dates from the same period. Between them, surrounded by palm trees in the middle of the square, a pompous statue of King Victor Emanuel II lends almost a colonial flavour, somewhat deflated by the pigeons perched on his head. The statue's inauguration in 1899 was the occasion for the revival of Sássari's main festival, *La Cavalcata*.

The stately mood of Piazza Italia is continued for a short distance up **Via Roma**, where the succession of smart shops and cafés is abruptly terminated by a stern relic of the Fascist era, the hulking **Palazzo della Giustizia**. Its ponderous dimensions are slyly undermined by the semi-restored Rococo villa opposite at no. 46, sporting a cream-coloured facade adorned with whimsical putti.

A little further up, in its own garden, stands the **Museo Sanna** (Tues–Sat 9am–7pm, Sun 9am–1pm, also July–Sept Thurs–Sat 8.30–11.30pm; L4000), Sardinia's second archeological museum. A modern, well-planned block houses the collection, organized chronologically from prehistoric through nuraghic to Phoenician, Carthaginian and Roman items. Most of the **prehistoric** items date from around 2700 BC, including pottery fragments and necklaces belonging to Sardinia's Ozieri culture, and numerous slivers of the smooth obsidian, used to make arrow heads and cutting tools, which was the island's major export in neolithic times. One room holds a laser image of the unique Copper Age *ziqqurat* temple at Monte d'Accoddi (see p.241), while objects from the Bonnanaro culture include sacred skulls, trepanned for reasons that remain obscure.

It is the finds from the **nuraghic** culture, however, that constitute the museum's prime attraction. Collected on the upper floor, the fragments of pottery, jewellery and household implements are interspersed with plans and cross-sections of nuraghs, and explanations (in English and Italian) of their structure. Most engrossing is the display of bronze statuettes, smaller than the collection in Cágliari but a good taster if you can't make it to see that one; it includes warriors with boldly stylized ox-head helmets, a motif repeated on the boat-prows modelled here, and one figurine of a shepherd holds either a dog or goat on the end of a lead. The material was unearthed at various sites throughout the province, especially the concentration in the Valle dei Nuraghi (see p.257). Some of the finds – a bronze statuette of a bearded man from the Levant, Phoenician ceramics, a necklace of Baltic amber – demonstrate the nuraghic people's strikingly far-flung trading contacts. One of the oldest of these items, a Mycenaean vase from around 1600BC, was recently excavated at Nuraghe Arrubiu.

For more information on Sardinia's nuraghic culture, see pp.148-149.

Back downstairs, the Carthaginian, Roman and classical sections hold a miscellany of coins, ceramics, busts and mosaic floors. From the **Phoenician and Carthaginian** period (sixth–fourth centuries BC), there are beautifully preserved articles of jewellery, terracotta masks, Greek-inspired amphorae painted with battles and sex scenes, and inscribed *stelae*. **Roman** remains include material from Nora and Tharros: statuettes, gold rings, pendants, knives, and a decree carved in stone from AD 69 commanding a group of mountain-dwellers to leave the low-lying region of the Campidano. Elsewhere on the ground floor, space has been set aside for temporary art exhibitions.

If the staff are on hand, free guided tours of the Museo Sanna take place 9am–1pm and 4–7pm (mostly in Italian).

South of Piazza Italia, Via Carlo Alberto leads down to the Emiciclo Garibaldi and the **Giardini Púbblici**, a shady oasis of calm amid the traffic rushing past on all sides. The gardens are home to a permanent exhibition of island art, the **Padiglione dell'Artigianato** (Mon–Fri 9am–1pm & 4–8pm), Sardinia's best showcase for current arts and crafts, with all items for sale. Carpets, ceramics, jewellery and leatherwork jostle for space here; prices are on the high side and, unlike in some other shops, non-negotiable, though quality is guaranteed. Even if you don't intend to buy, it's a good opportunity to see what's available and to check out items which you might find cheaper elsewhere.

At the bottom of Piazza Italia, off its northwestern side, the short arcaded Portici Bargone e Crispo shelters cafés filled with gossiping regulars watching the coming and going between the square and the long sloping Piazza Castello. The site of an Aragonese castle until the nineteenth century, this piazza is still lined on one side by a barracks. This now houses the **Museo della Brigata Sássari** (Mon–Fri 9am–12.30pm & 2.30–4.30pm, Sat 9am–12.30pm; free), dedicated to the renowned Sardinian regiment whose bravery and heavy losses during World War I are taught in every Italian school. Fighting mainly against Austrians in the Alps, the troops were enmeshed in trench warfare with all the horrors that that involved, and lost nearly 4000 missing or dead, with over 9000 wounded. You don't need to be a military buff to enjoy the old photos, posters and documents collected in the half-dozen rooms here, though anyone interested in the period will also appreciate the uniforms, maps and mementos.

The old quarter

The compact **old quarter** is a quirky corrective to the straight lines of Sássari's modern streets. Bounded by Corso Margherita di Savoia and Viale Umberto to south and north, Via Brigata Sássari and Piazza Castello to the east, and Piazza Sant'Antonio and the station area to the west, the area is surrounded by noisy main roads, though little traffic can penetrate the interior network of alleys and piazzas. This makes it a great place to stroll around, easy to get lost in, but equally simple to leave. Although much of it is derelict, it's still got enough in and around it to justify a couple of forays at least.

The main axis, effectively bisecting the old town, is **Corso Vittorio Emanuele**: a long, partly cobbled slope up from Piazza Sant'Antonio, with a few easily-missed medieval doorways, flaking palazzi and fragments of Gothic windows jammed in among the shops and alleys. Look out in particular for the fifteenth-century **Casa Farris** at no. 23, the Catalan-Gothic **Casa di Re Enzo** from a century earlier at no. 42, and, across the road, the **Teatro Cívico**, built by a Piedmontese architect in 1830 as the seat of the municipality. Transformed into a theatre after 1880, and now the only one in Sardinia of any historical note, it's still the place where the city's mayor traditionally meets representatives of the local guilds during the *Candareri* festival (see box, p.227). The facade is elegant enough but badly in need of renovation; the interior, which you might get to see while at a play or concert here, holds little of architectural interest.

For details of drama and classical music at the Teatro Cívico, call ☎079.232.182. Tickets start at about L10,000.

The Duomo and around

At the core of the old town, the **Duomo di San Nicola** is an unexpected eruption of flamboyance amid the cramped jumble of streets. Rearing above the semicircular Piazza del Duomo, its florid seventeenth-century facade is Sardinia's most dazzling example of Baroque architecture, in which statues of the *turritani* saints, Gavino, Proto and Gianuario (see box on p.244) are set, surmounted by San Nicola. Behind this extravagant frontage, however, the basic structure is simpler Aragonese-Gothic work of the fifteenth and sixteenth centuries. The **campanile** alongside is even earlier, a survival from the original thirteenth-century construction, with gargoyles and other Gothic details. The **interior** of the Duomo is mainly Baroque, though you can still make out the Gothic lines. The eighteenth-century choir stalls are worth seeking out, and there's a small museum of ecclesiastical treasures reached from the Cappella Aragonese on the right.

Behind the cathedral, fighting for space on Via Santa Caterina, the **Palazzo Ducale** was designed by a Piedmontese architect at the end of the eighteenth century for the Duke of Asinara, and today houses the *comune* and hosts occasional exhibitions and concerts.

At the back of the Duomo and palazzo, the long **Via Turritana** was a centre of gold- and silver-working, a tradition maintained today by the presence of a few watchmakers and jewellers. Take a right turn off here up Via Università to see the nucleus of Sássari's university in **Piazza Università**. As well as the main library and administration offices, the building still holds the faculty of law, which, with medicine, has been the university's principal field of academic excellence since its foundation by the Jesuits in 1562. Its original late-Renaissance appearance is best appreciated round the back, on the side facing the Giardini Púbblici.

Piazza Tola and around

Sássari's old commercial centre was located on the other side of the Corso Vittorio Emanuele, at the now sequestered **Piazza Tola**, where a daily market recalls its former role. The piazza, known until the last century as *Carra Manna* (Sard for public weighing machine), takes its present name from the judge and historian whose statue stands at its centre, Pasquale Tola (1800–74). Various building styles face the square, most notably the **Palazzo d'Usini**, a Renaissance building dating from 1577.

A much more exquisite relic of the Renaissance stands a short distance away at the end of nearby Via Rosello, another jewellers' lane that leads to the northeastern edge of the old city. The pretty **Fonte Rosello** lies hidden away at the bottom of a flight of dilapidated steps accessible from Corso Trinità. The small, square monument, sculpted by Genoese stonemasons in 1606, is delicately carved with four statues representing the seasons, one on each corner, with dolphins curled around their feet (the statue of San Gavino surmounting it is a copy). The fountain is fed by a spring that was once one of Sássari's principal sources of drinking water, and, until quite recently, still the

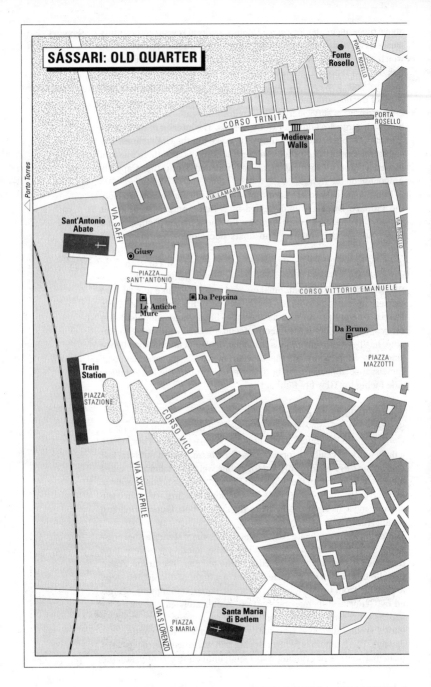

SÁSSARI: OLD QUARTER

Fonte Rosello

PONTE ROSELLO

CORSO TRINITÀ

PORTA ROSELLO

Medieval Walls

Porto Torres

VIA LAMARMORA

VIA SAFFI

VIA ROSELLO

Sant'Antonio Abate

Giusy

PIAZZA SANT'ANTONIO

CORSO VITTORIO EMANUELE

Da Peppina

Le Antiche Mure

Da Bruno

PIAZZA MAZZOTTI

Train Station

PIAZZA STAZIONE

CORSO VICO

VIA XXV APRILE

VIA S LORENZO

VIA S MARIA

PIAZZA S MARIA

Santa Maria di Betlem

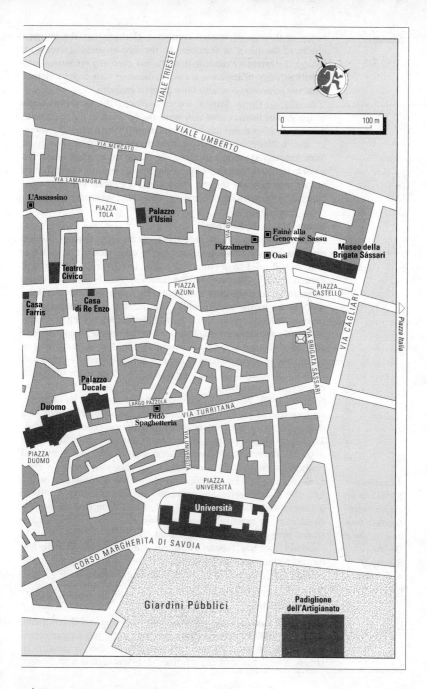

Sássari

scene of throngs of women scrubbing clothes. Now the intimate charm of the place is shattered by the flyover arching overhead, though the extensive renovation of the site currently under way may improve things; in any case, it's worth the short walk to get a view of what the *sassaresi* consider their greatest treasure.

Nearby, in Corso Trinità, are remnants of the **medieval walls** which girdled Sássari until they were pulled down in the nineteenth century. Further down this busy road, turn left onto Via Saffi where, at the bottom of Corso Vittorio Emanuele, the church of **Sant'Antonio Abate** stands above the piazza of the same name. It's a noble Baroque structure of clean lines and elegantly-proportioned arches within, where the star attraction is a gigantic gilded wooden altarpiece, the work of a Genoese master of the seventeenth century.

Santa Maria di Betlem

Piazza Sant'Antonio once held the busy northern gate of the old town; Sássari's northwestern gate, on the other side of the train station, is still used by a stream of traffic to and from Alghero and Fertilia airport. The most striking landmark here is the silver dome of **Santa Maria di Betlem**, one of the city's oldest churches and the one dearest to the local people. The building has accumulated a range of different styles during its long lifetime, with much of its simple Gothic structure overlaid with a heavy Baroque touch. Its best and oldest feature is the Romanesque facade, with its sprinkling of Gothic and even Arab styles in the zigzag cornice, rose window and French Gothic columns. The lowest part dates back to the thirteenth century, to which the upper part containing the rose window was added in 1465. The inside, however, while conserving its fifteenth-century Gothic vaults, is overwhelmingly Baroque, the result of a going-over in the last century, when the elliptical cupola was added. The lateral chapels are still there, though, each one dedicated to one of the local *gremi* (guilds) which became attached to the church and convent in the thirteenth century, when this was the city's chief Franciscan centre. Least retouched of the chapels is the first on the left, the Catalan-style stonemasons' (*muratori*) chapel; others belong to wallmakers, carpenters, tailors and so on. You can see the *candelieri*, or massive wooden candles associated with the guilds, stored here in between their annual outings at the festival of Li Candareri (see box, Sássari's Festivals, p.227), each one heavily festooned with ribbons and decoration. If they're not displayed in the church, they're usually kept in the adjoining cloisters.

An antiques fair is held in Piazza Santa Caterina from 8am to 1pm on the last Sunday of each month.

Restaurants

Sássari has a good range of **restaurants** scattered in different parts, sometimes difficult to track down. In the old town, you'll come across several places serving *fainè*, a popular local dish originating in Genoa, a legacy of that city's former close association with Sássari.

This winter speciality (most *fainè* places are closed in summer) is made of *ceci* (chickpea) flour fried into a sort of thick pancake, served either plain (*normale*), or cooked up with onions (*cipolle*), sausage (*salsicce*), anchovy (*acciughe*), or some combination of these. They're generally dispatched more quickly than pizza, with second and third helpings as the occasion demands; beer is the usual accompaniment. You might find them heavy-going, but they make a good fast-food snack, and are cheap at around L6000 per helping.

Keen carnivores will rejoice to find horsemeat (*cavallo*) especially prized in these parts, and you'll often find donkey (*asinello*) and snails (*lumache* or *monzette*) on the menu too. Fish is not a particular *sassarese* favourite, though you'll usually find it available. Fresh vegetables are good: in season (autumn), sample the local mushrooms (*porcini* or *antunna*).

Fans of edible snails should seek them out in Sássari's restaurants, where monzette are simply roasted in their shells with salt, while the rarer gioghe are boiled and then fried slowly with garlic, parsley and paprika.

L'Angoletto, Via Mazzini 2. Self-service *távola calda* charging L16,000 for first and second courses, *contorno* and a drink. Lunchtime only. No CCs. Closed Sun. Inexpensive.

L'Antica Hostaria, Via Mazzini 27 (☎079.200.066). Small, upmarket place whose creative versions of traditional Sard dishes have earned it a gourmet reputation. Closed Sun & Aug. Expensive.

Le Antiche Mure, Piazza Sant'Antonio. At the bottom of the Corso and close to the train station, this is one of Sássari's nicest restaurants, especially if you choose to eat on the "veranda" (effectively out in the piazza). The interior is smart, and the food is carefully prepared, justifying the highish prices. The *gnocchetti alla furba* is the name here for the ubiquitous *mallorreddus alle sarde*, with tomato, fresh sausage and mild *peperoncino*. Pizzas are available, but there is no carafe wine. Closed Sun. Moderate.

L'Assassino, Vicolo Ospizio Cappuccini 1, off Via Rosello (☎079.235.041). Small, low-vaulted trattoria in the heart of the old town with photos and paintings of Sássari. Specialities are meat-based, but there are seafood dishes too. Nice atmosphere, friendly service. Closed Sun. Moderate.

Da Bruno, Piazza Mazzotti 11. A basic pizzeria, with some seats outside – if you can bear sitting in what must be the ugliest piazza in Sardinia. Try the Sassarese pizza, with *antunna* (local mushrooms) and *melanzane*. At lunch, a L10,000-menu is available, for pizza, drink and ice cream. Closed Wed.

Didò Spaghetteria, Largo Pazzola 8. Much more than a *spaghetteria*, though they do a good range of pastas at very reasonable prices. Their Spaghetti Didò, with sausage, olives and cheese, will leave you reeking of garlic. Closed Sun. Moderate.

Da Peppina, Vícolo Pigozzi, an alley off Corso Vittorio Emanuele. A good place to sample the local specialities of horsemeat, donkey, pork or snails. No CCs. Closed Sun. Inexpensive.

Fainè alla Genovese Sassu, Via Usai 17. An unpretentious central place for *fainè* fans. There's nothing else to eat here, and you can't get wine – only beer, soft drinks or water. Service is brisk and businesslike. No CCs. Closed Sun and June–Sept. Inexpensive.

Florian, Via Bellieni 27 (☎079.236.251). A well-established, top-class restaurant, with excellently-prepared Sard and Italian dishes. Dress up, and don't expect to pay less than L45,000 a head. Closed Sun. Expensive.

Da Gesuino, Via Torres 17 (☎079.273.392). Smartish trattoria, popular with locals and parties, so consider booking. There's an opulent antipasti table, and the *fagottini con salsa di noci* (pasta with nut sauce) is recommended. Pizzas are available in the evenings. Closed Sun. Moderate.

Oasi, Via Usai 7. The first of three restaurant options on this short street linking Piazza Castello and Piazza Tola. This one is a regular trattoria offering the usual regional and national items, with pasta dishes at L8–15,000, including *alle cozze* (with mussels) at L10,000. You can try *fainè* here, or local crepes. Closed Sun. Moderate.

Pizzalmetro, Via Usai 10. Pizzas are ordered here by the metre: just point out how much you want. Prices range from L18,000 to L45,000 per metre; the Antunna, for example, made with local mushrooms, is L36,000. Evenings only. Closed Sun.

Il Posto, Via E. Costa 16. A casually smart trattoria in the new town, its pale pink, vaulted interior hung with tasteful artworks. Pizzas are available alongside a good range of pastas, including *paglia e fieno* ("straw and hay"). Closed Sun.

Drinking and nightlife

There is no lack of good **bars** in Sássari, most of them milling with crowds and open late during summer. The ones in Piazza Castello and along Via Roma are liveliest, sometimes with live music. If you want to dance, there are a few **discos** in town. The most central is *Sergeant Pepper* on Via Asproni, while you'll need a car to reach the *Meccano* (Wed, Fri & Sat) and *Atrium* (winter only, Fri–Sun), located on Sássari's eastern periphery at Via Carlo Felice 33 and Via Milano 40 respectively. Music tends to be technoid pop, entrance charges are L10–25,000, and they close around 6am. The *Atrium* also has live music on a separate floor. Check in the daily *La Nuova Sardegna* for more details on these or other events, and consult the *Sássari'nside* booklet, a monthly preview of what's going on (available from the tourist office and some hotels). It mentions the main **theatre** performances (see Listings opposite for theatre details) and **cinema** programmes, including information on **open-air films** in summer. Otherwise, there's little to appeal to nightbirds from out of town, since, as in Cágliari, social life tends to be concentrated in members-only *círcoli*, or clubs.

For more information on Sássari's festivals, see p.227.

Sássari's biggest **events** are of course the annual festivals, especially the Holy Week processions, the costumed and equestrian shenanigans of the Cavalcata and the mid-August Candareri rumpus – all good times to be here, if you don't mind crowds.

Bars and cafés

Barberry's, Via Roma 18. A late-night crowd-puller, selling the usual beers and ices.

Bar Daniele, Piazza Tola. A comparatively quiet nook for a late drink or snack.

Café al Duomo, Piazza del Duomo. Convenient place for a sit-down in the heart of the old town, with good coffees and pastries.

Caffè Italiano, Via Roma 42. A smart bar with tables outside and stylish decor within. Live music almost every evening, either on the pavement or in an internal room. Closed Sun.

Mokador, Piazza Castello. A favourite hang-out by day or night, serving snacks and ice creams.

Caffè San Carlo, Portici Bargone e Crispo. A traditional people-watching bar selling good ice creams.

Listings

Airport bus For Fertilia airport: at least eight daily departures on ARST buses from Via Margherita di Savoia and Via XXV Aprile, near the train station; for Olbia airport: three departures daily with Nuragica Tour (☎079.510.494), leaving from Emiciclo Garibaldi – call for departure times, or ask at a travel agency.

Airport enquiries For flights from Fertilia airport: Alitalia (☎079.935.033); Meridiana (☎0789.69.300); Italair and Azzurra Air (☎079.935.282). For flights from Olbia, call ☎0789.52.634.

Ambulance Croce Rossa (☎079.234.522) or Sássari Soccorso (☎079.272.222).

Banks It's not hard to find banks in Sássari, nearly all with exchange facilities. Among the central ones with cash machines are: Banca Commerciale Italiana and Banco di Nápoli, Piazza Italia; Banco di Sardegna, train station, Via Pais (corner of Corso Vittorio Emanuele) and Piazza Castello, and Crédito Italiano, Via C. Battisti 2 (corner of Corso Vittorio Emanuele). Most open 8.20am–1.20pm & 3–4.30pm, though note that the BCI in Piazza Italia opens all day Wed 8.20am–5.50pm. You can also change cash and travellers' cheques at the main post office (see p.240).

Bookshops Best for books on Sardinia and English-language novels is Gulliver at Portici Bargone e Crispo (corner of Piazza Italia), open 9am–9pm (closed Sun 1–5pm).

Bus companies ARST (Emiciclo Garibaldi 15, ☎079.260.048) for Alghero; Bosa; Castelsardo; Fertilia; Fertilia airport; Nuoro; Olbia; Porto Torres; Santa Teresa di Gallura; Santa Trinità di Saccargia; Stintino. Ferrovie della Sardegna, or FdS (Emiciclo Garibaldi 15, ☎079.241.301) for Alghero; Bosa; Castelsardo; Fertilia; Palau; Porto Torres; Tempio Pausánia. PANI (Via Bellieni 25, ☎079.236.983) for Cágliari; Macomer; Nuoro; Oristano; Porto Torres. When ticket offices are closed, buy bus tickets at bars nearby, for example *Bar Garibaldi*, on Emiciclo Garibaldi, two doors down from the ARST office.

Car hire Avis, Via Mazzini 2 (☎079.235.547); Eurorent, Via Roma 56 (☎079.232.335); Hertz, Corso Vico (☎079.232.184); Maggiore, Viale Italia 3a (☎079.235.507); Saccargia, Corso Margherita di Savoia 115 (☎079.231.363).

Garage Autorimessa Bonfigli, Corso Margherita di Savoia 8.

Hospital Ospedale Civile Santa Annunziata, Via de Nicola (☎079.220.500).

Left-luggage Train station 6am–8.45pm, L5000 for 12 hours.

Laundry Onda Blu at Via Cavour 67 (off Via Carlo Alberto): self-service coin-operated machines open 8am–10pm.

Markets Every morning (not Sun) in Piazza Tola, mainly household items and clothes, but also some fruit and veg. The main food market is behind, on Via

Mercato, also mornings only, while Monday morning sees a much bigger open-air market of clothes, toys and tools on Piazza Segni, near the stadium (up Via Adua from Piazza Conte di Mariano at the end of Viale Umberto).

Pharmacy Simon night pharmacy open 8.30pm–9.10am at Via Brigata Sássari 2.

Post office Central Ufficio Postale is on Via Brigata Sássari, open Mon–Sat 8.30am–6pm (but closes at 1pm Sat in Aug). Change facility available for cash and some travellers' cheques. Stamps are available from a separate room on the right, and Poste Restante (*Fermo Posta*) from yet another room entered from round the corner.

Supermarkets There's an Upim on Piazza Azuni, in an indoor shopping complex that includes other stores. There's another Upim right next to a Standa on Viale Italia (corner of Piazza Marconi). The Upim closes on Sunday and Monday morning, but Standa is open daily (including Sunday) 9am–1pm & 4–8pm. Super Discount supermarket, 2 or 3km out of town on the Porto Torres road, is also open Sunday.

Taxis Ranks on Emiciclo Garibaldi (☎079.234.630), Piazza Castello (☎079.234.639) and the train station (☎079.260.150). Radiotaxi day or night (☎079.260.060).

Theatres The old Teatro Cívico on Corso Vittorio Emanuele (☎079.232.182) is the ideal place to catch some drama or classical music in Sássari, with tickets starting at about L10,000; otherwise check out the programme at the Teatro Il Ferroviário, next to the train station, where more modern productions are staged (☎079.262.258), and the Teatro Verdi, on Via Politeama (off Piazza Castello), which also has plays, dances and concerts.

Train information FS for Cágliari; Olbia; Oristano; Ozieri; Porto Torres: ☎147.888.088. FdS for Alghero; Nulvi; Sorso: ☎079.241.301.

Travel agencies Agitour (Piazza Italia 13, ☎079.231.757) and Nuove Mete (Via Università 7, ☎079.238.447) for internal and international tickets; CTS (Via E. Costa 48, ☎079.234.585) for international connections only.

Porto Torres and the Sássari Riviera

North of Sássari, the Carlo Felice highway ends its long run from Cágliari at **Porto Torres**, once the main Roman base on this coast. Although surprisingly little of historical interest has survived, what remains easily justifies a sortie: a gem of Pisan church-building, some Roman excavations and an antiquarium. A smoky industrial zone dominates the western side of town, but to the east the coast offers a choice of fine sand **beaches** along the so-called Sássari Riviera. Around Sássari's main resort of **Platamona**, these tend to be very crowded, but further east they soon empty out, sheltered from the SP81 coast road by a curtain of pines, eucalyptus and juniper trees. Inland of Porto Torres, you could make an easy stop at the pre-nuraghic sanctuary of **Monte d'Accoddi**, off the SS131. There are a few **hotels and campsites** on the coast; the alternative is to lodge in Sássari or Porto Torres.

Apart from the fifteen-minute **train** connection between Sássari and Porto Torres, non-drivers will have to rely on **bus services** for all places mentioned in this section. For the Sássari Riviera, there is a good service (marked "Buddi Buddi") leaving Emiciclo Garibaldi every 40 minutes or hourly, stopping at Platamona and the less visited spots along this stretch, and there are onward links as far as Marina di Sorso. Porto Torres is equally well served by frequent buses from the provincial capital, while, for Monte d'Accoddi, you can get off any bus bound for Porto Torres at the turn-off to the site.

Monte d'Accoddi

The stretch of the Carlo Felice highway (SS131) that links Sássari with its parent city, Porto Torres, is mainly dual-carriageway, running northwest through cultivated rolling country. Near the junction for Platamona, 12km out of Sássari, a right turn brings you round to **Monte d'Accoddi** where, surrounded by cereal fields, a sanctuary dating back to the Copper Age (2450–1850 BC) has been unearthed. In fact, there's little visible construction remaining, but the long earthen ramp and the platform at its top are clearly defined. This alone sets the site apart from anything else found in Sardinia, or in the entire Mediterranean for that matter. The flat-topped pyramid would appear to have more in common with Mesopotamian or Aztec temples, hence its popular name, *ziggurat* or *ziqqurat*.

The base, measuring 30 by 38m, tapers inward amid the outlines of various stonewalled dwellings and other buildings, and even a menhir. There are signs that there may have been some kind of sanctuary here from as early as 5000 BC. The first structure appears to have been destroyed by fire and rebuilt. The later altar, at the top of the ramp, was probably used for sacrifices and other ceremonial functions, though you need to make an imaginative leap to picture it as it might have appeared – it helps to have seen the laser images in Sássari's Museo Sanna (see p.231). It's an impressive site, nonetheless, with views back to Sássari and seaward to the Golfo dell'Asinara, over the industrial chimneys of Porto Torres. The site is always open during daylight hours, and **guided visits** theoretically take place between 9am and 6pm (8am–5pm in winter).

Porto Torres

The unprepossessing town of **PORTO TORRES**, 6km further on, is one of the main gateways into Sardinia. There have always been settlements on this site, drawn to its natural harbour and position at the mouth of the Riu Mannu, one of the island's longest rivers. Any trace of its pre-Roman past, however, has long been effaced, though there is considerable evidence of the Roman colony, Turris Libyssonis, which developed as an important shipping stop between the Italian mainland and the Iberian peninsula.

The town subsequently assumed a religious significance as the centre of a cult devoted to the *mártiri turritani* (see box, p.244), and by the tenth century, it had become the capital of one of Sardinia's four *giudicati*. Now called Torres, the town continued to wield commercial influence under the Pisans, though Saracen raids and Genoan assaults eventually led to its decline and a transfer of power inland to Sássari. The building of the Carlo Felice highway linking Porto Torres to the rest of the island contributed to its revival in the nineteenth century, and today the town is thriving once more, its economic role buoyed by the petrochemical works to the west of town as well as constant shipping traffic.

It is not necessary to venture into town, however, to visit its prime attractions: the magnificent Romanesque **Basilica di San Gavino** and various **Roman remains** lie on the outskirts. Perhaps this is just as well – Porto Torres is a gritty working port that does not invite much idle rambling, although it does have a couple of good restaurants and a sensational *gelateria* off its main artery, Corso Vittorio Emanuele.

There are some good-looking **beaches** to the west of town, but their emptiness is explained by the proximity of the oil refinery, and you'll have to go almost as far as Stintino (see p.219) to find safe swimming spots in this direction. To the east, however, there are some enticing sheltered places immediately outside town where you can bathe off the rocks, and a full-scale beach resort at Platamona, 7km out from the centre (see p.245).

Arrival, information and accommodation

Information on sights, events and transport connections can be obtained at the **Pro Loco** (Sept–June Mon–Fri 9am–1pm, July–Aug Mon–Sat 9am–1pm & 3.30–7.30pm, Sun 9am–noon; ☎079.515.000) at the bottom of Corso Vittorio Emanuele. This main street also holds a couple of banks with cash machines and several travel agents.

If you've been deposited by ferry in Porto Torres you may be looking for somewhere to spend the night, though **accommodation** isn't so thick on the ground. Best choice is the *Royal* (☎079.502.278; ②; no CCs) at Via Sebastiano Satta 8 – a side-street reached by taking Via Príncipe di Belmonte up from the Lungomare. The eight rooms are large, if uninspiring, all with TV. If there's no vacancy here, try the *Elisa* right on the port at Via Mare 2 (☎079.513.260; ③), a reasonable three-star with standard rooms, or, further up in the town (on Via Sássari, a left turn off the Corso), the much fancier *Torres* (☎079.501.604, fax 079.501.605; ④), with access to a pool. Porto Torres holds one of Sardinia's three **youth hostels**, on the seafront at Lungomare 91 (June–Sept; ☎079.512.222), though as it's presently undergoing an overhaul, phone first to check it's open (it's possible that the telephone number may change, in which case get

Leaving Sardinia from Porto Torres

If you're leaving Sardinia from Porto Torres, make sure you book as early as possible, especially in peak season, and particularly if you're shipping a vehicle. Tirrenia (for Genoa), Grimaldi (*Grandi Navi*, also for Genoa, mid-June to mid-Sept only) and the French line SNCM (for Marseille and Toulon, March–Sept) are the principal ferry companies operating out of Porto Torres. Departures on each line are once or twice weekly. Tickets on the Genoa run cost between L76,000 and L97,000 for passengers in high season, according to whether or not you book a berth (usually four in a cabin); low-season rates are L57,000–73,000. To Toulon or Marseille, expect to pay around L100,000, with a supplement of L20–40,000 for a berth in a cabin. A medium-size car will cost another L100,000 or so to Genoa, L100,000–200,000 to Toulon or Marseille. CMN, a subsidiary of SNCM, operates a year-round service between Porto Torres and Marseille, with a stop at Propriano, Corsica. This cargo-ferry, with tickets at the same prices as the regular service, also transports vehicles; tickets to Marseille must include cabin accommodation.

If you're leaving on a Tirrenia ship, buy tickets from their office on the Lungomare opposite the port (open Mon–Fri 8.30am–1pm & 2–7.30pm, Sun 3.15–7.30pm, late-June to mid-Aug also Sat & Sun 8.30–10am, mid-Aug to mid-Sept also daily 10pm–midnight). In summer, you'll need to arrive early at the office as there can be a long queue (and note that bookings for sailings not on the same day can only be made until 6pm). Grimaldi Lines passengers must make their way over to the dock in the *zona industriale*, about 2km west of town (signposted *Grandi Navi Veloci*), where there is also a ticket office, or buy tickets in town at Agenzia Paglietti, Corso Vittorio Emanuele 19 (☎079.514.477), also the outlet for tickets for SNCM, CMN and other lines. See Travel Details (p.258) for ferry frequencies and destinations.

the latest info from the Pro Loco). Other hotels and campsites lie along the beaches and resorts east of town (see p.246).

The Basilica di San Gavino

You can find the **Basilica di San Gavino** (daily 7am–noon & 4–7.30pm) signposted to the left on your way into Porto Torres (from the port, continue straight up Corso Vittorio Emanuele). Originally in the open country, its present back-street location diminishes the monument's grandeur, especially in the context of the messy excavations under way on either side of the building. Nonetheless, as Sardinia's largest and (according to some) finest Romanesque structure, it still makes an impressive impact. The slits of windows and blind arcading around the fine yellowy stonework contribute to its austere, fortified appearance, a reminder that it survived innumerable Saracen attacks during the Middle Ages.

The basilica was started by Pisans in around 1050 and finished by 1111, over eight hundred years after the martyrdom of the *mártiri turritani*, and on the site of a Roman necropolis. Unusually, the

A free festival of polyphonic music takes place in the Basilica di San Gavino in the first week of September. Contact the tourist office at Porto Torres for details.

The Mártiri Turritani

The Basilica di San Gavino commemorates the three martyrs, known as
the *mártiri turritani*, upon whom the town's religious fame is based. San
Gavino was a Roman commander based in the city of Turris Libyssonis, as
it was then known, at the time of the emperor Diocletian's last-ditch
attempt to stamp out Christianity. He was converted by two condemned
Christians, Proto and Gianuario, and all three were beheaded in 304 –
Gavino on a small headland to the east of town, where the little church of
San Gavino a Mare now overlooks the sea.

After Diocletian's abdication the following year, the presecutions came to
an end, and within two decades his successor Constantine – commemorated
by an inscription in the crypt – had recognized the new religion. The town
soon became a place of pilgrimage, and by the sixth century a paleochristian church existed on the site. The cult was enhanced during the eleventh
century by the construction of the largest and most impressive basilica on
the island. When the bones of the three martyrs were exhumed in 1614, various miracles and "frequent perfumes" were reported. The saints are commemorated every May 3, when the wooden figures displayed in the nave are
carried in procession from the Basilica to San Gavino a Mare.

church was given a second apse when it was enlarged in the twelfth
century, giving it a slightly confused, directionless look. Of the three
lateral doors, the one on the north side is oldest, decorated with
human and animal figures; the other two are later additions, one of
them, the main entrance, Catalan-Gothic from 1492.

Gloomily lit by the narrow windows and barely decorated, the
three naves of **the interior** are separated by 28 marble columns, dug
up from the old Roman town. The main nave has a harmonious wood-
en roof and, at the back, a prominent catafalque carries wooden
images of the three saints to whom the church is dedicated, near a
dashing seventeenth-century statue of San Gavino on a horse. Across
the nave, stairs lead down to the first of the basilica's two **crypts**
(daily 9am–noon & 4–6pm), a long room lined with statues of saints
and several Roman sarcophagi, one of them elaborately carved with
figures of a seated man and woman – whose tomb this was – surrounded by Apollo and the Nine Muses.

At the far end, a door gives access to the foundations of the original paleochristian church that stood here in the sixth century. From
the ante-crypt, more steps lead down to a lower crypt, where the
bones of the martyrs – placed here in the nineteenth century – are
displayed in arched niches along with more sarcophagi. Free **guided
tours** of the church and crypt are offered in summer,
Monday–Saturday 9am–1pm & 4–6.30pm.

The Roman remains

You'll have to keep your eyes open to locate the poorly-marked
remains of part of the Roman city behind the train station on the
western edge of town (take Via Ponte Romano from the Corso). The

The headland of Capo Testa in the far north of the island

Bear rock, Capo d'Orso

Nuraghic village at Serra Orrios, Nuoro province

The island of Tavolara

JERRY DENNIS

Porto Cervo, Costa Smeralda

ROBERT ANDREWS

Sculpture of Il Redentore, Monte Ortobene

ROBERT ANDREWS

Cork oaks, Gallura

The nuraghic settlement at Su Nuraxi

Prickly pear, Gennargentu National Park

The Cedrino river, near Orosei

Cheisa di Santa Croce, Oleina

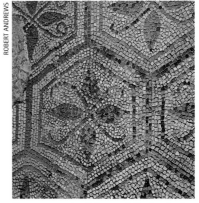

Roman mosaic, Pallazzo della Provincia, Sássari

The main square at La Maddelena

Nuraghe Nuradeo, near Bosa

Ploughing in a vineyard, Oleina

so-called Palace of King Barbarus, or **Palazzo di Re Bárbaro** (Mon–Sat 8am–7pm, Sun 8am–1pm; free) gets its popular name from the Roman governor who presided over the martyrdom of the town's saints. The site principally consists of the main baths complexes of the Roman town, dating from the third or fourth century BC. As well as the shattered *terme*, the best-preserved items are some good mosaic floors and a network of flagstoned roads bordered by stumps of columns. The ruins are used in summer for occasional late-evening exhibitions and concerts.

Next to the site, the **Antiquarium Turritano** (Tues–Sat 9am–1.30pm & 2.30–7.30pm, Sun 9am–1.30pm, also July–Sept 8.30–11.30pm on certain days; free) contains finds from here and other digs in the area of Turris Libyssonis. The ground floor is devoted to objects from the city, including ceramics, votive ornaments, mosaics and frescos from the central baths. The first floor concentrates on the archeological site alongside, among the exhibits a small ceramic gladiatorial shield, though there is also material here from the necropolis on Monte Agellu, where the church of San Gavino now stands.

Another 200m further out of town, taking the left fork, you can glimpse the seven arches of the **Roman bridge** crossing the Riu Mannu near the turn-off for the Stintino–Alghero road. This well-preserved monument was used by traffic until the 1980s, but now looks sadly redundant on the outskirts of town, almost hidden between newer bridges and thick growths of bamboo.

Eating

Porto Torres has a plethora of **eating** places, most of them geared towards fast food. The *Elisa* hotel, for example, has a handy and inexpensive self-service canteen on the ground floor. Better fare is available at *Tana* on Via Cavour, a side street off Corso Vittorio Emanuele; it's a pizzeria/ristorante with swift service, friendly staff, and a wood-burning oven for the tasty pizzas (closed Tues Oct–June; no CCs). On the other side of the Corso, *Gli Ulivi* offers a tourist menu for L18,000 with plenty of choice and pavement seating. For a do-it-yourself lunch or food for the ferry, drop in at the *Enoteca* opposite the port on the Lungomare; they sell *panini* and a range of local cheeses, salamis, wines, yoghurt and bread. Finally, before or after a visit to San Gavino, take time to sample one of the fifty flavours of **ice cream** from *Gelateria Capriccio* at Corso Vittorio Emanuele 114: utterly irresistible, they come in cones, cups and frappés, up to five flavours at a time (closed Mon in winter).

Platamona

A small but hard-working beach resort for exhausted city-dwellers, **PLATAMONA** is just a 20-minute drive from Sássari, linked by hourly buses (every 40min in summer). A right turn off the Porto Torres road brings you through a eucalyptus wood to a brief parade

Porto Torres and the Sássari Riviera

Scopri Sardegna at Via Parini 2, Porto Torres (☎079.512. 209), arranges eco-tours of the surrounding country, venturing as far afield as the island of Asinara (see pp.222–223) and Sopramonte, in the Nuoro region (p.323). Prices for full-day excursions are about L90,000 per head, varying according to number in the party and type of excursion.

of bars, restaurants and lidos. The few sections of pavement are strewn with the wares of Senegalese and Korean traders, while children's play areas, bars, pizzerias, even a pool, stand a stone's throw from the sea. If you want the facilities and don't mind the crowds, you might as well stop here for a swim. At the lidos you'll pay around L13,000 per day for an umbrella and deck chair, L5000 just for the deck-chair, with the use of showers and car park thrown in (elsewhere car parks charge around L1000 per hour).

There are all kinds of fast-food places around, none of them particularly exciting; better fare is available about 500m east from the centre, where the *Grigleria* **restaurant** has tables on a terrace. You can stay here, too, at the adjoining *Toluca* **hotel** (☎ & fax 079.310.234; ⑤), with 25-percent reductions outside peak season; some rooms have balconies with sea views, all have bathrooms and TVs, and there's a pool. You can **camp** 200m inland at the *Cristina* (June–Sept; ☎079.310.230), which also has a pool and tennis court, and caravans are available for rent (L50–94,000 a day for two). Buses from Sássari stop right outside.

East along the coast

Heading eastwards, as the beaches get wilder there's no reason for you not to do a little free camping in the endless pinewoods backing the sands (being extra careful not to start fires). Small lanes disappear north off the SP81 coast road, leading to relatively isolated spots with just enough space for a few vehicles and a bar in summer, and surrounded by sandy wilderness. The buses from Sássari (marked "Buddi Buddi") conveniently stop all along this road, so you can choose your spot and take your chances. If you want the comforts of a three-star **campsite**, however, head for *Li Nibari*, signposted off the road after a few kilometres (Easter–Oct; ☎079.310.303). Bar, restaurants and supermarket cater to a crowd of campers, and there are also sports facilities, but no pool – the sandy shore is just metres away.

There's another concentration of beachside activity at **Marina di Sorso**, albeit on a much smaller scale than at Platamona. The beaches here are nothing special: again, you've only got to shift a few hundred metres to find perfect isolation. Five kilometres inland, the village of **Sorso** lies above a fertile valley whose fruit and vegetable produce liberally fills the pavements. The local *Cannonau* wine is one of Sardinia's best, and the place is also famed for its baskets woven with dwarf-palm leaves. There's not a lot to look at in the village, but there are a couple of **hotels**, cheapest of them the small *Pensione Romangia*, on Via Porto Torres (☎079.352.868; ②; no CCs), which has its own restaurant.

Above Sorso, and almost joined to it, the sister village of Sénnori has a winding road back to Sássari (10km). A general antipathy has traditionally existed between the vine-tenders of Sorso and the Logudorese-speaking villagers of Sénnori, who are more inclined to business.

Anglona

Northeast of Sássari, the compact region of **Anglona** is a mountainous landscape scattered with the remains of a petrified forest. Bound by Logudoro and Gallura to the south and east, the area's rocky northern littoral is the perfect setting for Anglona's main town, Castelsardo, picturesquely draped over a promontory at one end of the Golfo dell'Asinara. The robust fortified citadel here was the Doria power-base in Sardinia for nearly 250 years, and the historic centre preserves a pungent medieval flavour, though the modern lower town is mostly dedicated to milking the coach tours that regularly call in here. Castelsardo makes the area's best **place to stay**, a short drive from some good beaches and the ruined castle of **Castel Doria**, an inland outpost of the Dorias. A scenic but tortuous drive further south brings you to another connection with the powerful Genoan dynasty, the village of **Chiaramonti**, a fast 35-km ride from Sássari.

Non-drivers travelling in Anglona will have to rely on ARST **bus services** for most places mentioned in this section. Castelsardo is well served by frequent buses from Sássari, though the other inland destinations covered here have only infrequent connections.

Castelsardo

Travelling east along the coastal SS200, the first view of CASTEL-SARDO is an impressive one, the reddish-grey houses huddled below the stout castle, with the cathedral's tall campanile visible to one side and a belt of scrub-covered hills to landward. The powerful Genoan Doria dynasty established a stronghold at Castelsardo at the start of the twelfth century, giving it the name of "Castelgenovese". Embroiled in the power clashes between Genoa, Pisa and Spain throughout its ensuing history, the strategically crucial town was one of the last Genoan centres in the Torres *giudicato* to hold out against the Spaniards. When he finally took possession of the town in 1448, Alfonso V immediately changed its name to Castel Aragonese, though the locals were mollified when, in 1511, Charles V accorded the port the same rights and privileges as the rival Spanish sea-base at Alghero. Supported by 4000 French troops, the Dorias made a last, futile effort to recapture their home-base in 1527, then disappeared from the Sardinian scene altogether. The town's present, safely neutral name was given by the Savoyard kings in 1769.

Today, its small port still active, Castelsardo is one of the few fishing centres on the north Sardinian coast, while its well-preserved citadel and photogenic setting above a small beach have assisted its transformation into a fully-fledged holiday resort. Tourists are also lured by the town's pre-eminence as a centre of Sard handicrafts, which are prominently displayed in stores in the lower town and dotted around the narrow lanes of the old quarter (see box on p.248).

Artigianato in Castelsardo

Many people come to Castelsardo purely to shop, and the lower town has plenty of outlets to meet this demand, often geared towards parties on coach stops. All come in search of the famed Castelsardo *artigianato*, or handicrafts, which has grown in the last 20 years from a small cottage industry to a major all-year money-spinner. Cork, coral and ceramic goods are here in abundance, as well as shelves full of the African-looking Sard wooden masks, but the main craft for which Castelsardo is known is *l'intreccio*, or basketwork. Straw, wicker, reeds, raffia and asphodel leaves are all used to create an incredible variety of containers, trays and furniture, though the material most associated with Castelsardo is dwarf-palm leaves, locally picked. You can see plenty of examples in Castelsardo's countless small shops and stores, but you'll have to wade through a large proportion of junk to find the ideal gift or souvenir, and much of it may have been made elsewhere, using synthetic materials.

A good place to visit before any shopping is the museum of basket-weaving in Castelsardo's castle, to get an idea what the best examples of the genre should look like. As for the emporia, don't spend too much time shopping around – you'll see the same products everywhere, with very similar price tags. You should, however, at least view the merchandise at ISOLA on the main road at Via Nazionale 104, a branch of the network of officially-recognized outlets for Sardinian craftwork (Mon–Sat 9.30am–12.30pm & 5.30–8.30pm). Alongside the raffia vases and wicker products on display are carpets, ceramics, wall hangings, metalwork items, masks, handbags and carved wooden ornaments; prices, however, tend to be on the high side. If you've honed your bargaining technique, there's no reason why you shouldn't deal directly with the producers up in the old town, where you can see the locals working the stuff on their doorsteps. This is the place to find cheaper prices, if sometimes cruder products. You can also find some good work in nearby villages such as Tergu (see p.251), where the quality is at least as good as that in town.

It wouldn't be impossible to visit Castelsardo on a day trip from Sássari, just an hour away on frequent buses (last one back at 8.50pm). But despite its somewhat tacky side, it's a pleasant spot to spend a little more time, especially outside August, and an excellent place to break your journey travelling up the coast. The **Easter festivities** are known for the dramatic torchlit procession, *Lunissanti*, a tradition pre-dating the Spanish conquest of the town, in which a cortege of cowled figures threads through the old town on Easter Monday to the accompaniment of medieval choral chants in Latin and Sard.

Arrival, information and accommodation

All ARST buses stop at the central Piazza Pianedda, at the bottom of the old town, and there's another bus stop by the beach in the lower town. If you're driving, leave your vehicle at the piazza, or in the car park reached from the piazza's top-right corner. You *could* drive up the main Via Nazionale and take your chances parking on the road leading to the citadel, but don't get tangled up in the tight web of alleys that make up the old centre unless you want to get involved in frantic reversing and scraped bodywork.

A small **tourist office** operates out of a temporary kiosk in Piazza Pianedda during the summer (June–Aug daily 9am–1pm & 5–9pm – times may vary), and there's a Banco di Sardinia with cash machine just up from the piazza. The seafront, Lungomare Anglona, is where Castelsardo's meagre choice of **accommodation** can be found; it's about a kilometre's walk from the citadel. The cosiest option is the *Pinna* (☎079.470.168; ②), not as small as it appears, above a popular trattoria. The next best, a hundred metres or so along, is the *Cinzia* (April–Sept; ☎079.470.134; ③; no CCs), a middle-range holiday hotel; all rooms have showers, and breakfast is included in the price. Only a few of the rooms have sea views. The next up is quite a jump, the smart *Castello*, closer to town on the same strip (☎079.470.062, fax 079.471.322; ④), with fully-equipped rooms and a good seafront restaurant. Vacancies in any of these are limited in summer; as a last resort try the pensione in Lu Bagnu (p.251). The nearest campsites lie further east (p.253).

The town

It's a steep but rewarding clamber up the streets and steps of Castelsardo's old quarter. Home-made baskets and other artifacts are displayed in doorways, brightly-coloured plants are draped over walls, and time-weathered arches and crumbling doorways adorn the minute lanes. Glimpses of the rocky shore and sea below bring relief from the closed, insular air that survives as a residue of the town's ancient inaccessibility. The best views, of course, are from the top, where the battlements of the heavily restored **castle** (daily: summer 9am–1pm & 2–8pm, winter 9am–1pm & 2–5pm, late-night opening in Aug; L3000) afford long vistas across the gulf to the isle of Asinara, off Sardinia's northwestern point; to the northeast, it's sometimes possible to sight the coast of Corsica – though for this the conditions need to be particularly good. The sunsets here are especially memorable.

The abode of the powerful Doria dynasty for two centuries, and for ten years home to Eleonora d'Arborea and Brancaleone Doria after their marriage in 1376, the castle now houses the **Museo dell'Intreccio Mediterraneo**, a basketwork and weaving museum artfully incorporated into the small chambers. There is much to admire in this assortment of bowls, plates, bottles and lobster traps, often skilfully patterned, some of the most prized items woven from the leaves of the local dwarf-palm. For the most part, these are the traditional tools of everyday life, utilized by bakers, farmers and fishermen; there is even a grass-woven boat here – the truncated-looking *fassoni* used around Oristano (see p.169). But without any labelling of the displays or much explanation of any kind, the exhibition becomes somewhat monotonous to all but a dedicated enthusiast, and it's diverting to find amid this collection a quotation from *Ulysses*, translated into the Sard dialect, daubed onto a door; a remnant of a former art installation, it speaks of local people's attachment to the land.

From the castle, it's a short walk round to the **church of Santa Maria**, a misshapen building squeezed into the available space. The richly decorated church holds a special role among the townspeople, as the repository of the sacred *Critu Nieddu*, or Black Christ, a fourteenth-century crucifix, as well as being the focus of the Easter Monday processions.

After Santa Maria's cramped site, it's a surprise to find, lower down, the relatively large terrace that accommodates Castelsardo's cathedral, **Sant'Antonio Ábate**, but the gradient is not so steep here, and there is even room for a public garden laid out on the rocky slope below. Overlooking reddish boulders washed by the sea, it's a lovely spot, the octagonal campanile with its majolica-tiled cupola adding a splash of colour. The church itself shows little evidence of the original Gothic structure, but its sixteenth-century rebuilding and Baroque accretions are not unsympathetic. The main treasure inside, at the centre of the fussy marble altarpiece, is the *Madonna with Angels*, the work of an unknown local painter in the fifteenth century known simply as Maestro di Castelsardo. Behind the altar, there are some good carved choir-stalls, and the painted wooden pulpit hanging off one of the piers is also worth a look.

There's little else of specific interest to see in the old centre. And, beyond the shops and trattorias, neither does the newer town at sea-level have much to offer. The disordered agglomeration of modern constructions, many of them boxy holiday homes, scars the shoreline, though the rocky cove immediately below and west of the citadel, sheltering an attractive sand beach, is undeniably pretty. Following the coast west, you'll pass the **Porto di Frigianu** fishing anchorage, watched over by an old defensive tower, and the new marina, where posher boats are moored. There are a couple of bars here if you want to sit and watch the bobbing vessels. Eastward, there's another small beach squeezed up among the rocks on the far side of town.

Eating

Castelsardo has some good places to eat and drink. The best **restaurant** in town is *La Trattoria*, halfway up Via Sássari, the main road up to the citadel from Piazza Pianedda. It's a smart, friendly place with a great menu (moderate) which includes the creamy *pasta mazzafrissa*. Just below Castelsardo's castle, *La Guardiola* cooks up quality dishes and has a terrace with romantic views over the sea, but is quite expensive (☎079.470.755; closed Monday in winter). If you're looking for **snacks** with views, head for *Aragona* on Via Manganella, just along from the cathedral, a bar which also serves pasta dishes and other light meals (closed Monday in winter). Near *La Guardiola* at the base of the castle, *La Loggia* is another sit-down bar, good for beers and postcard-writing. There are more trattorias and bars down on the seafront, some with good-value tourist menus, and it's worth remembering that the *Pensione Pinna* here has a fine trattoria with a terrace facing the sea.

Around Castelsardo

Castelsardo makes an ideal base for exploring the rest of the Anglona region, whose contoured terrain is a thinly-inhabited area of stirring vistas. Most of the interest lies inland, where scattered historical relics make good targets for rural expeditions. Of these, a pair of medieval churches at or near the villages of **Tergu** and **Bulzi** are the most impressive, belonging to the same era as the Doria strongholds of **Castel Doria** and **Chiaramonti** deeper in the mountains. Much older remains can be seen at the remarkable **Roccia dell'Elefante**, a huge trachyte wedge in the shape of an elephant, and in the village of **Sédini**, where there are examples of the prehistoric *domus de janas*; Sardinia's nuraghic culture is represented by the nearby **Nuraghe Su Tesoru**. On the coast, the appeal of **Lu Bagnu** and **Valledoria** lies in their seaside locations and holiday facilities – and they're the best places outside Castelsardo to track down **accommodation**.

Lu Bagnu and Tergu

Five kilometres west of Castelsardo, **Lu Bagnu** has good swimming in limpid waters off the rocks at the bottom of cliffs, but the modern holiday surroundings may put you off spending much time here. You might, however, get a taste of the resort's bar-life on a night out from Castelsardo, and you could find yourself **staying** here if that town is full: the cheapest option is *Ampurias*, off the main road on Via Imperia (☎079.474.008, fax 079.474.444; ②), with a restaurant attached.

From Lu Bagnu, a road winds 7km inland to **Tergu**, a small village whose square-faced Pisan-Romanesque church of **Nostra Signora di Tergu** (also called Santa Maria) dates from the early thirteenth century. The facade is the most interesting feature, with blind arcading and red trachyte stone alternating with paler limestone, and there are the ruins of a once-powerful Benedictine monastery alongside. A visit to the village would be a good opportunity to search out examples of local craftwork, often similar to the items on sale in Castelsardo, but cheaper.

Sédini and the Roccia dell'Elefante

Exiting eastwards from Castelsardo, the road soon leaves the sea behind. A right turn for Sédini takes you directly past the famous **Roccia dell'Elefante**, a wind-eroded rock structure whose elephant-shaped profile is featured on hundreds of postcards. It's difficult to

Anglona

After Lunissanti, Castelsardo's other major festival is August 2, when the Madonna degli Ángeli is celebrated with games and traditional dancing.

miss the trachytic monolith on the roadside, its drooping trunk practically swishing the passing vehicles. Clearly the rock has long held
an emblematic power, for there are some pre-nuraghic *domus de
janas* tombs hewn from beneath it; look carefully on the wall of the
right-hand chamber to make out a carving of the curling bull-horns
which are such a pronounced motif on nuraghic figurines.

At **Sédini** itself, another 11km southeast, there are some more of
these ancient tombs gouged out of a massive calcareous rock known
as **La Rocca**, situated right on the main road in the centre of the village. The chambers were utilized as a prison in the Middle Ages,
incorporated into a dwelling in the nineteenth century, and currently holds a small exhibition of agricultural tools and other ethnographic items. In summer, a local group of volonteers is on hand to
provide guided tours of the tombs, at other times you may have to
book at the Comune 200m way (☎079.588.581). Many of Sédini's
houses are Aragonese-Gothic in style, including the church of
Sant'Andrea, dating from 1517, with a fine square portal and a
handsome pointed campanile alongside.

Bulzi, Chiaramonti and around

Arguably the prettiest of the churches scattered around Sássari's hinterland is **San Pietro delle Immágini** (also called San Pietro di
Simbranos). Marooned in a flowery meadow by the side of a small
country road below the village of **Bulzi**, 7km to the south of Sédini,
it makes a picturesque sight. Founded by monks from Monte Cassino
in 1112, the church was an important Benedictine centre during the
twelfth and thirteenth centuries. It owes its excellent state of preservation today to its safe distance from the ravagings of coastal raiders
in the past.

The facade, added together with the apse and transept in the thirteenth century, shows a singular blend of Romanesque and Gothic
styles, with a striped pattern similar to that of Tergu's church, and
possibly worked on by the same builders. The Gothic elements are
stronger here, however, with pointed blind arches on the second
level surmounted by a pediment, and there is no belltower. Above the
door, a lunette holds a crude relief of an abbot with arms raised and
two monks – the images from which the church takes it name. Worth
looking at in the interior is the stoup formed from trunks of petrified
– or more accurately silicified – trees, of which the surrounding area
holds a considerable quantity. You'll be lucky to find the church
open, though: weekends are the best bet, or be here for the Festa di
San Pietro, forty days after Easter.

If you're taking the slow but scenic route back towards Sássari,
you'll pass through the village of **Laerru**, 4km further south, which
boasts an international reputation for the carving of briar, olivewood
and juniper pipes. Shortly before the good SS127 Sássari–Tempio
road, **Chiaramonti** has an intricate network of narrow streets

grouped around the base of a Doria fortification from the twelfth century. Though not particularly high (440m), the ruins offer a fantastic vantage point over the mountains on all sides, most strikingly Monte Limbara (1359m) to the east and Monte Sassu (640m) – a famed haunt of bandits and kidnappers – to the southeast.

Nuraghe Su Tesoru and Valledoria

Alternatively, head east from the Roccia dell'Elefante on the Valledoria road, making a stop almost immediately to see the well-preserved **Nuraghe Su Tesoru** (more properly known as Nuraghe Paddaggiu), erected during the last phase of nuragh-building. The niched central room and stairs up to the second storey still survive.

By the time you reach **Valledoria**, you're back by the sea and in holiday country, with beaches as far as the eye can see, finally giving way to the cliffy rocks around Isola Rossa (see p.301), some 10km away. Of the three **campsites** in the area, the best is *La Foce* (May–Sept; ☎079.582.109), with excellent facilities including a pool, and a lagoon across which a small craft ferries campers to the good sand beach on the other side. ARST buses to Santa Teresa di Gallura stop several times daily at Valledoria, from where you have to walk or hitch. Among the **hotels** in the area, there are three on Valledoria's Corso Europa, including the small but well-equipped *Park Hotel* (☎079.582.800, fax 079.582.600; ③); others lie out of town closer to the sea.

Castel Doria

Inland of Valledoria, you can follow up the course of the Coghinas river for 7 or 8km on the Perfugas road, to where the poetic ruins of **Castel Doria** stand poised over the lake of the same name, a deserted craggy spot full of atmosphere. The castle (now inaccessible) was placed here in the twelfth century to watch over Anglona's eastern approaches. The river feeds the artificially created lake, which marks the boundary with Gallura, and has allowed the drainage of Anglona's only plain of any size to the north. The lake holds one of Sardinia's four main hydrothermal spring sites, whose therapeutic mud baths draw spa devotees from all over Italy.

South of Sássari: Logudoro

The country south of Sássari is sparsely populated, consisting of swathes of sloping fields interspersed by small villages. The historical name, **Logudoro**, or "Land of Gold", probably refers to the past commercial wealth of this southern zone of the Torres *giudicato*, as attested today by the presence of numerous noble churches throughout the region, many of them established by Pisan merchants at a

South of
Sássari:
Logudoro

time when Logudoro covered the whole of Sardinia's northwestern quarter. The present-day territory is much shrunken since then, but retains the distinction of having the purest form of Sard, softer and more rolling than the island's other dialects.

Although few places justify a lengthy stay around here, several are well worth a stop en route to somewhere else, notably the Pisan churches of **Santa Trinità di Saccargia**, **Sant'Antíoco di Bisarcio** and **San Pietro di Sorres**, each stranded in open countryside, though within easy reach of the main roads. Close to the last of these stands one of Sardinia's most important nuraghic complexes, the **Nuraghe Santu Antine**, whose construction and background is lucidly explained in the nuraghic museum at the nearby village of **Torralba**. The area's only town of any size, **Ozieri**, holds remnants of the neolithic culture to which it has lent its name, and also has some of the only **accommodation** to be found hereabouts.

Ozieri-Chilivani is a major rail junction for **trains** to Sássari, Olbia and Cágliari, and Logudoro's former capital of **Árdara** is also on the Sássari line; other places covered here really need a car to reach, though most villages have a sketchy service of one or two **buses** daily from Sássari. Note that the village of Torralba is a stop on the Sássari–Oristano PANI bus route, though visitors to the nuraghic site will have to walk or hitch the last 4km.

Along the SS597: Santa Trinità di Saccargia and Árdara

The most accessible of all the churches covered in this section lies right on the main Sássari–Olbia SS597, some 15km from Sássari (and glimpsable from the Sássari–Chilivani train). Rising in isolation above the flat country, the zebra-striped facade and belltower of **Santa Trinità di Saccargia** conspicuously mark the church's Pisan origins.

Masses are held in Santa Trinità di Saccargia during the weeks leading up to Easter, and during the summer on Sundays at 7.30pm.

It was built in 1116, supposedly owing its remote location to a divine visitation that took place while the *giudice* of Logudoro and his wife were stopped here on the way to Porto Torres, where they were to pray for a child at San Gavino's shrine. During the night, a celestial messenger informed the *giudice*'s wife that the pilgrimage was unnecessary since she was already pregnant, whereupon the grateful *giudice* built an abbey on this spot. The basalt and limestone facade was added some sixty years later, and, like the rest of the structure, has survived remarkably well, although the abbey's outhouses are either ruined or converted into barns. Look out for the carved dogs, cows and other beasts on the lovely Gothic capitals at the top of the porch as you enter. The stark, rather gloomy interior (open every day during daylight hours) shows elements of Lombard architecture and, apart from the gilded wooden pulpit embedded in one wall, has only some faded thirteenth-century frescos in the apse in the way of decoration.

The nondescript village of ÁRDARA, 15km further east along the SS597, shows few traces of its one-time role as capital of the Logudoro region, though the restored basilica of **Santa Maria del Regno**, visible immediately on entering the village, hints at its former glory. Built by Pisans in around 1100, using black and brown basalt, the Romanesque church provided the model for a series of lesser churches in the region. The columned interior features an altar with an ornate tableau of thirty panels on a gold background, the work of various artists in the sixteenth century. The church was the venue for the marriage in 1239 of Enzo, son of Frederick II of Hohenstaufen, by which he came into possession of the *giudicati* of Torres and Gallura, which enabled him to claim the title of king of Sardinia. Though Enzo abandoned wife and island soon afterwards, he clung on to the title, even during the last 23 years of his life spent in prison in Bologna. The church is the focus of a costumed **carnival** with horses every July 29.

There's another solitary Pisan relic visible about 10km further along this road on the left, the church of **Sant'Antíoco di Bisarcio**. Built in 1090, reconstructed in 1170, it was later given cathedral status and was the venue for the coronations of many of Logudoro's *giudici*. Today, though, it is in such a tumbledown state that little of its original splendour can be divined; a walk round the building is enough to appreciate the French-style portico, apse, blind arcading and smashed *campanile*. If you want to explore the rather uninteresting interior, Signora Giuseppa Cammedda in one of the nearby houses holds the key; otherwise, be content with the views over the hills.

Ozieri and around

A signposted right turn from the main SS597 brings you to **OZIERI**, the main centre for this area. Arrayed along a slope that creates a natural amphitheatre, it's a wealthy-looking place, with stuccoed, sometimes faded, Neoclassical houses, though you'll also come across vividly-coloured contemporary murals depicting scenes of rural life and the horrors of war. The town's prominence stems from the surrounding fertile country, mainly used for cattle-rearing and dairy-producing; the best-known local products, however, are the little almond biscuits known as *suspirus* (also called *sospiri*, or *guelfos*), for sale in any of the town's bakeries and most bars.

The town has given its name to a whole era of Sard prehistory, the **Ozieri culture**, which prevailed mainly in the northwest of Sardinia in the fourth and third millennia BC. This is also known as the San Michele culture after the grotto where most of the finds identified with it were discovered, many of which can be seen in the town's **Museo Archeologico** (Tues–Fri 9am–1pm & 4–7pm, Sat & Sun 9.30am–12.30pm, extended opening in summer; L3000, or L5000 with grotto), housed in the cloisters of the convent annexed to the **church of San Francesco**, close to the main Piazza Garibaldi. The

The last Sunday of September sees Ozieri's biggest festa, La Sagra della Madonna del Rimédio, during which groups from all over the island participate in medieval chanting and costumed processions.

first of the low-vaulted display rooms is packed with the bone jewellery and ceramics painted with a spiral pattern that are characteristic of this people; five more rooms contain other objects retrieved
from the local area, including nuraghic ornaments, Punic and Roman
coins, and domestic items from the Middle Ages.

You can visit the **Grotta di San Michele** (guided tours Tues–Fri
9am–12.30pm; L3000, or L5000 with museum) where many of these
finds were unearthed, a walk or brief drive from here along the
panoramic Viale Vittorio Veneto, on the northern edge of town (next
to the sports ground, signposted). The complex of caves consists of
little more than a deep hole in the limestone, with connecting tunnels
and passages, where the key items relating to the Ozieri culture were
discovered in 1914.

Back in the lower part of town, make a stop at Ozieri's **Cattedrale
dell'Immacolata**, whose Neoclassical facade fronts an Aragonese-
Gothic structure overladen with Neoclassical and Baroque additions.
Among several sculptures and paintings here, there's a noteworthy
polyptych, the *Madonna di Loreto*, its seven panels painted by the
so-called Maestro di Ozieri, the foremost Sard painter of the sixteenth century.

Practicalities

*For riding
around
Chilivani,
contact
Associazione
Íppica Monte
Acuto
(☎079.787.
852).*

Ozieri wouldn't be a bad place to **bed down** if you're travelling in
these parts: there's only one place in town, however, the *Mastino*
(☎079.787.041, fax 079.787.059; ③), though there are cheaper
rooms available a short distance out, in Località Sa Uppara, where *Il
Nuraghe* has rooms with or without bath, but no singles
(☎079.788.733, fax 079.788.544; ②); both places have restaurants. Buses connect Ozieri with the train station 10km west towards
Chilivani, a main junction for passengers between Sássari, Olbia and
Cágliari, and close to the island's most important racecourse and
horse-breeding stables (visible from the train).

Pattada

The hilltop village of **PATTADA**, 15km east of Ozieri, is famed for its
shepherds' knives, known as *pattadesa*, for sale in shops all over the
island. You can see numerous examples in the shops here at surprisingly steep prices: all have tough, hand-worked steel blades and the
best have horn handles from ram or mouflon. At 778m, the village is
the highest in the province of Sássari, and there are plenty of good
views and walks in tall pine forests within a short distance. Some
5km to the east, the **Lago di Pattada**, an artificial lake, also provides
good picnic spots.

Torralba and around

Thirty kilometres south of Sássari, an easy detour from the SS131
takes you to the village of **TORRALBA**, whose only interest is a

remarkable nuraghic museum, a short distance from one of Sardinia's greatest prehistoric monuments, the Nuraghe Santu Ántine. It doesn't matter which you visit first – the same ticket will let you into both. Easy to find in the centre of the village, the **Museo di Torralba** (daily: June–Sept 7am–8pm, Oct–May 9am–5pm or 6pm; L5000, including Nuraghe Santu Ántine) focuses on the nearby nuraghic complex, though the ground floor is devoted to enlightening temporary exhibitions of local ethnography, such as *logudorese* costumes or the history and science of olive production. A room here also holds a model of the Nuraghe Santu Ántine, though most of the material relating to this is displayed upstairs in the **Sala Santu Ántine**, including some of the 17,000 shards of pottery found on the site, which testify to the continuous use of the monument and surrounding area from the twelfth century BC until the Roman era. Other items include ceramic combs, smith's tools and projectiles, while bits and pieces of Phoenician and Greek ware illustrate the extensive trading links which this settlement enjoyed. Elsewhere on this floor, the **Sala Romana** has examples of columns and capitals dug up in the area, with displays of coins and pottery fragments, and there are more Roman finds in the garden, reached from the Sala Santu Antine, including a collection of inscribed milestones found alongside the Cágliari–Olbia road, the first one built by the Romans on the island.

The Nuraghe Santu Ántine

The **Nuraghe Santu Ántine** (daily: June–Sept 7am–8pm, Oct–May 9am–5pm or 6pm; L5000, including Museo di Torralba) lies just over 4km south of the village, in the heart of the so-called Valle dei Nuraghi, an area copiously dotted with the ancient structures. This royal palace is the biggest and most impressive of them – hence its common name Nuraghe Majore – and is considered to be technically the finest nuraghic structure on the island. The oldest sections date back to the fifteenth century BC, though the site was continuously worked on and added to during its long history, not least by the Romans. Built of square basalt blocks, the central complex consists of three external bastions, mostly crumbled, connected by a defensive wall and grouped around the original massive three-storey circular tower, with walls up to 5m thick and 17.5m high. The tower is thought to have once reached 21m, before the uppermost of its three circular rooms was demolished in the nineteenth century. Corridors and staircases link the different parts of the tower, and the grounds include a well in an internal courtyard. It's a fascinating place to scramble around, an intricate network of steps, ramps, chambers and curving passages.

From the railed area on top, other *nuraghi* are visible among the cultivated fields – though the closest and most perfect specimen is a recent reconstruction. A scattering of circular huts lies around the walls of the main complex, the ruins of the nuraghic village on which

A handy bar at the entrance to the Nuraghe Santu Ántine serves rolls and other snacks, and there's a shop with guides to the site in English.

Carthaginian and Roman structures were added. Note that guided tours are available, though not always in English. The site lies about a kilometre north of an exit off the SS131.

San Pietro di Sorres

The hilly area north of Torralba holds one of the best-preserved of Sardinia's Romanesque churches, the twelfth-century **San Pietro di Sorres** (Mon–Sat 8.30–11.45am & 3.30–5.45pm, Sun 8.30am–12.30pm & 3.30–7.15pm). Surmounting a bluff with sweeping views over the villages of Bonnanaro and Borutta, the former cathedral is still attached to a Benedictine convent (accounting for its immaculate condition), whose monks have become specialized in book restoration among other fields. The church displays more Tuscan precision than Sardinia's other Pisan churches, while its grand dimensions and ornate style suggest French influence. The striped facade of white and dark grey stone has three levels of blind arcading, each embellished with coloured geometrical motifs and intricate patterning.

The slightly forbidding interior restates the two-tone scheme and contains a few items of interest, in particular a decorated Gothic pulpit supported by four arches and an open sarcophagus from the twelfth century, belonging to a local bishop. Take time to wander round the back of the building, past the monks' plantations in pinewoods, to enjoy the extensive views over the high cultivated country on every side.

Travel details

TRAINS

Ozieri-Chilivani to: Cágliari (5 daily; 2hr 30min–3hr); Macomer (5–6 daily; 1hr); Olbia (10 daily; 1hr–1hr 20min); Sássari (10 daily; 45min).

Porto Torres to: Cágliari (1–2 daily; 4hr–4hr 30min); Sássari (2–5 daily; 20min).

Sássari to: Alghero (Mon–Sat 11 daily, Sun 6; 35min); Árdara (5–7 daily; 40min); Cágliari (3 daily; 3hr 40min–4hr); Macomer (4 daily; 1hr 35min); Olbia (2–4 daily; 2hr); Oristano (4 daily; 2hr 35min–3hr); Ozieri-Chilivani (7–9 daily; 50min); Porto Torres (2–5 daily; 15min).

BUSES

Castelsardo to: Santa Teresa di Gallura (Mon–Sat 5 daily, Sun 2; 2hr); Sássari (Mon–Sat 7–10 daily, Sun 3; 1hr); Sorso (Mon–Sat 5 daily, Sun 3; 20min); Sédini (Mon–Sat 5–6 daily, Sun 2; 35min); Valledoria (Mon–Sat 5 daily, Sun 3; 25min).

Porto Torres to: Alghero (Mon–Sat 3–5 daily; Sun 3; 50min); Fertilia airport (Mon–Sat 1–3 daily, Sun 1–2; 30min); Monte d'Accoddi (1–2 hourly; 10min); Olbia airport (3 daily; 1hr 50min); Santa Teresa di Gallura; Sássari (1–2 hourly; 30min–1hr); Stintino (Mon–Sat 5–6 daily, Sun 2–3; 45min); Torralba (3 daily; 1hr 15min–1hr 45min).

Sássari to: Alghero (1–2 hourly; 45min–1hr); Argentiera (Mon–Sat 5 daily, Sun July–Aug 1; 1hr 5min); Bosa (Mon–Sat 4 daily, Sun 1; 2hr 15min);

Cágliari (7 daily; 3hr 15min–3hr 45min); Castelsardo (Mon–Sat hourly, Sun 5; 1hr); Chiaramonti (Mon–Sat 7 daily, Sun 2; 50min–2hr); Fertilia airport (5–11 daily; 40min); Marina di Sorso (Mon–Sat 3–9 daily; 1hr 35min); Monte d'Accoddi (1–2 hourly; 20min); Nuoro (7–8 daily; 1hr 50min–2hr 30min); Olbia (2 daily; 1hr 45min); Olbia airport (3 daily; 1hr 25min); Oristano (4 daily; 2hr 20min); Ozieri (Mon–Sat 5 daily, Sun 1; 1hr–1hr 25min); Platamona (1–2 hourly; 30min); Porto Torres (1–2 hourly; 35min); Santa Teresa di Gallura (Mon–Sat 5 daily, Sun 2; 3hr); Sédini (Mon–Sat 5 daily, Sun 2; 1hr 30min); Sénnori (Mon–Sat hourly, Sun 5; 25–30min); Sorso (Mon–Sat hourly, Sun 5; 30min); Stintino (Mon–Sat 5–6 daily, Sun 2–3; 1hr 15min); Torralba (4 daily; 45min).

FERRIES

Porto Torres to: Ajaccio, Corsica (May–Sept 2 weekly, 3hr 30min); Genoa (1–2 daily; 13hr); Marseille, France (1–2 weekly, 13–16hr); Propriano, Corsica (2 weekly, 3hr 30min); Toulon, France (1 weekly; May–Sept 9hr, Oct–Apr 16hr).

Chapter 7

Olbia, Gallura and the Costa Smeralda

S ardinia's northernmost region, **Gallura**, is a land of raw granite mountains and startling wind-sculpted rocks, which combine with its extraordinary coastline to imbue the area with a
unique edge-of-the-wilderness appeal.

The largest town in this wedge, **Olbia**, owes its recent phenomenal
growth to the huge annual influx of tourists bound for one of the
numerous holiday spots on this coast. Although not many of them
linger, the town acts as a base for the whole region, and has a good
selection of hotels and restaurants. If you're stuck here for an afternoon, you might as well visit its main item of interest, the Pisan-
Romanesque church of San Símplicio that is the focus for the town's
biggest festa. Otherwise follow the tide to one of the Mediterranean's
loveliest stretches of coast and premier holiday zones, the **Costa
Smeralda**. The five-star development of the "Emerald Coast" has not
only transformed the economy of the region but kick-started the
tourist industry in the entire island, setting new standards of carefully planned, environment-friendly tourism, where the devotion to luxury does not intrude too heavily on the extraordinary natural beauty
of the indented rocky coast – albeit at a price to the consumer.

Fortunately, the Costa Smeralda is only a tiny part of Sardinia's
northeastern littoral, and elsewhere on the coast it's still possible to
have fun without spending stacks of money. **South of Olbia**, the lurking presences of **Tavolara** and **Molara** form a constant feature of the
seascape. They are the largest of a group of islands that may be visited by boat from **Porto San Paolo**. This modern resort and **San
Teodoro**, further south, exemplify the soulless holiday developments
which have defaced much of this coast, overwhelmed in summer,
deserted the rest of the time, though they lie within reach of some
excellent bathing spots and provide a choice of useful bars, restaurants and accommodation.

North of Olbia, there are miles of shoreline still undeveloped and
a profusion of minor islands, over sixty in all, which you can explore

on boat tours from points along the coast. A daily ferry service runs from **Palau** to the biggest islands of **Maddalena** and **Caprera**, part of an archipelago of sunbaked rocks, mainly uninhabited, partly occupied by NATO forces. West of Palau, the SS125 passes a succession of lovely bays before reaching **Santa Teresa di Gallura**, the embarcation point for boats to Corsica. It is also a lively holiday centre, within easy reach of some of the most splendid **beaches** anywhere in Italy. Cradled in coves and inlets, often small and secluded, they demand a degree of effort to track down, but repay the work. When in doubt, hit any dirt track heading seaward. Sailors and windsurfers have long appreciated the perfect wind conditions in the Straits of Bonifacio, briskly channelled between the mountains on either side, and there are numerous outfits around to cater to watersports enthusiasts.

The ever-present backdrop to this indented shore is the jagged line of granite **mountains** which are the dominant motif in Gallura. Hidden within them is the secret heart of the region, a world that most tourists never discover, thickly forested with the cork oaks which, after tourism, provide most of Gallura's revenue. Though now somewhat stranded from the main currents of life in the region, the grey granite town **Tempio Pausánia** conserves a largely uncompromised appearance within sight of the pine-clad slopes of the region's highest mountain, **Monte Limbara**, and within easy reach of some of the interior's best walking routes.

Accommodation is available throughout the coastal area in summer, but harder to find inland and in winter. Prices on the coast shoot skywards during July and August, and vacancies can be rare during that time. The cheapest option is to camp, and there are plenty of sites dotted along the shore, though all get uncomfortably crowded in peak season.

Public transport is adequate for all the towns mentioned here, and there's a fuller service in summer. Olbia is linked to Golfo Aranci **by**

Accommodation Price Codes

The hotels listed in this guide have been coded according to price. The codes represent the cheapest available double room in high season (Easter & June–Aug). In cheaper hotels the rooms usually come without en-suite bathroom or shower; some of these places will also have a few en-suite rooms, for which you'll pay more – usually the next category up in price. Higher category hotels nearly always have only en-suite rooms. Out of season, you'll often be able to negotiate a lower price than those suggested here. The categories are:

① under L60,000	④ L120,000–150,000	⑦ L250,000–300,000
② L60,000–90,000	⑤ L150,000–200,000	⑧ over L300,000
③ L90,000–120,000	⑥ L200,000–250,000	

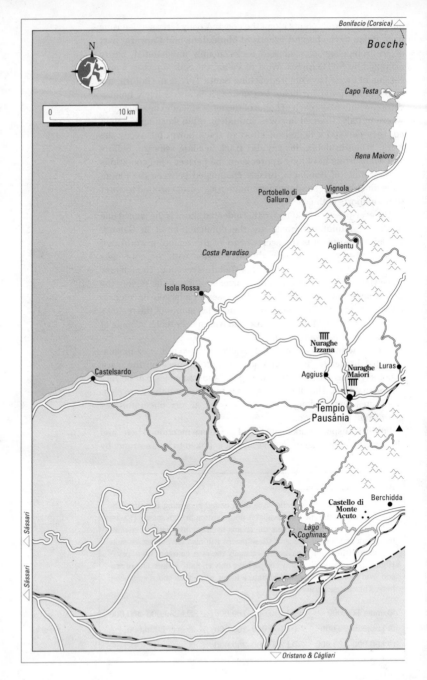

Bonifacio (Corsica) △

Bocche

Capo Testa

Rena Maiore

Portobello di
Gallura

Vignola

Aglientu

Costa Paradiso

Ísola Rossa

Nuraghe
Izzana

Luras

Aggius

Nuraghe
Maiori

Tempio
Pausánia

Castelsardo

Berchidda

Castello di
Monte
Acuto

*Lago
Coghinas*

△ Sássari

△ Sássari

▽ Oristano & Cágliari

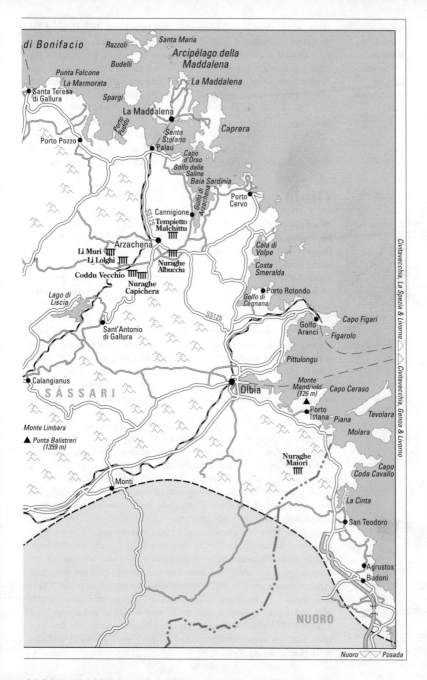

For more information on bus and train connections, see Travel Details, p.308.

train, while a summer-only train service runs twice daily through the mountainous heart of Gallura from Tempio Pausánia to Palau – an appealing if somewhat slow and laborious way to see parts of the region you might otherwise miss. As well as the frequent ARST **bus** connections, some local buses from Olbia are useful for destinations within a short distance of town; #5, for example, plies between Porto Rotondo (across the Golfo di Cugnana from the Costa Smeralda), via Olbia to Porto Istana, a bathing locality east of town. For bus passengers and drivers alike, traffic can be unbearably slow on all Gallura's roads, especially in summer when motor-homes add to the congestion already created by trucks bearing massive loads of quarried granite.

Olbia

When the English barrister John Tyndale visited **OLBIA** in the 1840s, he compared its Greek name, meaning "happy", with the state he found it in: "A more perfect misnomer, in the present condition of the town, could not be found... The whole district suffers severely from *intemperie*. The wretched approach across these marshes is worthy of the town itself. The houses, none of which have an elegant or neat appearance, are built mostly of granite, and are whitewashed, as if to give a greater contrast to the filth and dirt within and around them."

The "intemperie" of which Tyndale complained was malaria, which, together with the marshes and the filth, has long vanished as a result of the land-drainage schemes and DDT-saturation of the 1950s and the tourist invasions of the 1960s. Olbia today is once more a happy place, enjoying its new-found income both as the nearest Sardinian port to the mainland and the main gateway to the Costa Smeralda.

Nonetheless, few of the tourists pouring through the docks and airport stay long in town, for Olbia – the least Sardinian of all the island's centres – holds no more character than most transit towns. The best view of it is from the surrounding hills, a wide panorama embracing the flat hinterland and the wide Golfo di Olbia, where a small group of islands clusters out to sea, most prominently the immense mass of Tavolara. From close up the town is less inviting, awash with traffic and ugly apartment blocks which spoil what might once have been an attractive seafront, and its appeal is scarcely enhanced by tawdry back-streets, crossed by canals, railway lines and flyovers. There is a little more charm in the old centre, where the narrow lanes are lined with bars and restaurants that are generally crammed with tourists, sailors and service personnel from the NATO base further up the coast. Apart from the Pisan-Romanesque church of **San Símplicio**, there is little in the way of sights, but it is at least a manageable place, the airport a short bus ride away, the bus and train stations conveniently located in the centre of town, and the ferry port at no great distance.

Olbia was the first Sardinian town to be taken by the Romans, who captured it in 259 BC, expelling the Carthaginians who had been established here since the fourth century BC. The great Carthaginian general Hanno was killed in the fighting, and was buried with full military honours by the victorious Lucius Cornelius Scipio. Under Rome, the city expanded and flourished as the only natural port on Sardinia's eastern seaboard, though it was also almost permanently afflicted with malaria on account of the marshy lagoons backing onto it.

Having survived numerous Vandal and Saracen raids in the Dark Ages, Olbia – or Civita, as it became – was completely rebuilt by Pisa after 1198. It went on to become one of the principal strongholds of the *giudicato* of Gallura, preserving its independence from Spain until the fifteenth century. Now called Terranova Pausánia (a name which it retained until 1939), the city suffered complete destruction in 1553 at the hands of the Turkish admiral Dragut, in alliance with France against Charles V of Spain, and half its population were carried away as slaves.

Spain's shift of focus towards its Atlantic empire deprived the port of its prominent role, and Olbia languished in neglect. In 1711 the English Admiral Norris briefly occupied the city, and six years after that an Austrian army landed and took possession of the town, intending to march on Alghero. But, according to the story, the priest they commandeered as a guide led them into a trap, and the Austrians were captured and led back to Olbia by a Sardinian force – a triumph of cunning that is still the subject of mirth among the local population.

The last century has seen the arrival of the railway, a good road connecting the port with the SS131, and the eradication of malaria, all of which have helped to restore the fortunes of the city. Sophisticated, wily, but still friendly, the people of Olbia – today numbering over 40,000 – are well-used to having large numbers of foreigners in their midst – not just tourists but sailors from the port and large numbers of US service personnel from the nearby NATO base on Palau and the Maddalena archipelago. The sassy black servicemen with their walkmans and baseball caps are viewed with bemusement by the Senegalese traders crouched on pavements, their wares spread before them.

Arrival, transport and information

Ferries from Civitavecchia, Genoa and Livorno (see box on p.270 for details of services) dock at the island of Isola Bianca, connected to the mainland by a 2km causeway along which you can walk or take an hourly #3 bus; alternatively take a train to Olbia's main station, though these are infrequent. The **Stazione Maríttima** at the port holds the main ferry offices, as well as a bank with cash machine, a bar and a restaurant. There are bus departures from here to

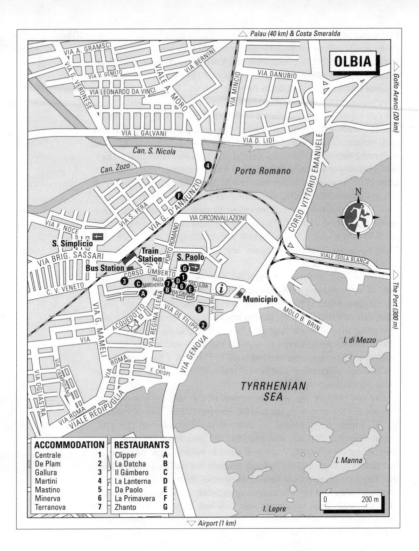

Arzachena, Nuoro, Palau, Santa Teresa di Gallura and Sássari (see Travel Details, p.308). In town, there are shipping agencies at the bottom of the main Corso Umberto.

Of Sardinia's three airports, Olbia's **Aeroporto di Costa Smeralda** is the most convenient, connected with the town by half-hourly bus #2 (hourly on Sun), which takes just ten minutes to reach the central Piazza Regina Margherita (tickets L1300 from the bar in the terminal; last departure 8pm). A summer-only **bus service** (5 daily) departs from the airport for the resorts of Arzachena, Palau and

Santa Teresa di Gallura (see p.295), obviating the need to go to Olbia at all if you're bound for the beach-chequered coast northward. **Taxis** into town charge about L20,000; if you want to reach other destinations directly by taxi from the airport, it'll cost around L75,000 to Arzachena, L90,000 to Palau.

Trains from Sássari and Cágliari arrive several times daily at the station just off Corso Umberto; some trains also stop at the station at the ferry quay. The ARST **bus station** is round the corner from the main train station, also reachable from platform 1. Buy tickets here or from the FS ticket booth at the train station.

Olbia's **tourist office** is on Via Piro, a sidestreet running off Corso Umberto (mid-June to mid-Sept Mon–Sat 8.30am–1pm & 4.30–7.30pm, Sun 8.30am–1pm; mid-Sept to mid-June Mon–Sat 8.30am–1pm; ☎0789.21.453). There is also an office at the airport (open summer only, daily 8am–10pm; no phone).

Accommodation

There is no shortage of **hotels** in Olbia, though most are on the expensive side. The nearest campsites are north of town near the Golfo di Cugnana (see p.278) or south at Porto San Paolo (p.274), both about twenty minutes' drive or bus-ride away.

Hotels

Centrale, Corso Umberto 85 (☎0789.23.017, fax 0789.26.464). Tidy little three-star on the main street, with elegant, smallish rooms. Soundproofing keeps the noise level down. There's a bar serving breakfast, but no restaurant. ⑤.

De Plam, Via de Filippi (☎0789.25.777, fax 0789.22.648). Standard business-class hotel on the seafront, with boxy rooms, some of them enjoying the best views in Olbia. ⑤.

Gallura, Corso Umberto 145 (☎0789.24.648, fax 0789.24.629). Small but smart three-star on the main drag opposite the bus station. The rooms are crowded, though with nice bathrooms, and there's a renowned ground-floor restaurant. Breakfast included. ④–⑤.

Martini, Via D'Annunzio (☎0789.26.066, fax 0789.26.418). Olbia's poshest hotel, with an elegant view over the bay and sumptuous rooms, though not central enough to be useful to anyone wanting to walk around town. There's no restaurant on the premises, though the classy *Bacchus 2* is almost next door. ⑥.

Mastino, Via Vespucci (☎ & fax 0789.21.130). Near the tourist office, this has the cheapest rooms in town, though also the shabbiest; things may improve, as it's in the process of changing hands. No CCs. ②.

Minerva, Via Mazzini 7 (☎ & fax 0789.21.190). Olbia's best budget choice has clean if rather cramped rooms, with or without a private bathroom. It's well situated, off Via Garibaldi and near Piazza Margherita. ②.

Terranova, Via Garibaldi 3 (☎0789.22.395, fax; 0789.27.255). Comfortable rooms in this central choice near Piazza Margherita, which has its own restaurant. Breakfast included. ④.

Bus #2 runs to the airport every 30min from outside the Ragazze Italiane boutique, just past the level crossing, last departure at 7.30pm. Buy tickets from the Small Coffee bar on Piazza Margherita, or from the bar just beyond the bus stop.

Olbia

The town and around

The centre of town is reached from the seafront by the pedestrianized Corso Umberto, at the bottom of which the Art Nouveau **Municipio** (town hall) ranks as one of Olbia's more interesting architectural features. Other than this, the main if not the only sightseeing item in town is the little **Basilica of San Símplicio** (daily 6.30am–12.30pm & 4–7pm), on the street of the same name lying over the level-crossing from Corso Umberto. Set in a piazza apart from Olbia's bustle, the simple granite structure is claimed to be the most important medieval monument in the whole of Gallura.

The Basilica di San Símplicio is the venue for Olbia's biggest festa, three days of processions, costumed dancing, poetry recitations, traditional games and fireworks around May 15, commemorating San Símplicio's martyrdom in the fourth century.

The church formed part of the great Pisan reconstruction programme of the eleventh and twelfth centuries, though also displays distinct Lombard influences. The lower part of the exterior as far as the blind arcading dates from the first period of construction at the end of the eleventh century. The building's best feature, the facade, was added in the twelfth century, capped by a mullioned window.

The narrow windows hardly lighten the murky **interior**, whose three aisles are separated by columns recycled from Roman constructions; even the stoup for the holy water was formerly an urn that held cremated ashes. Along the walls is an array of Roman funerary slabs and milestones from the Olbia–Cágliari road, some with fragments of inscription still visible. Otherwise the building is completely undecorated save for two faded thirteenth-century frescos in the apse, showing San Simplicio on the left and, on the right, a figure possibly representing Vittore Vescovo, a bishop ordained by Pope Gregory the Great in the sixth century. Two carved capitals, also Lombard in inspiration, are also worth peering at, one carved with a human head, the other with a ram's. Outside, the piazza makes a quiet spot for a sit-down, and there's a bar.

The only other church of note in Olbia is **San Paolo** just off Corso Umberto, easily recognisable by its multi-coloured cupola. The church, built in 1747 on the site of a Punic temple, is a good example of Gallura's typical building style of that time. Within the unadorned granite-faced exterior, there is a lovely wooden pulpit of the eighteenth-century Venetian school, with inlaid panels and a canopy from which a wooden hand grasping a crucifix is thrust out. The date 1421, engraved on one of the arches of the nave, suggests San Paolo was raised on a site where there was already a church, or else that its builders utilized material from another church. Other buildings in town display dates from the seventeenth and eighteenth centuries carved into their granite lintels (look on Via Garibaldi), though the prevailing tone of the centre's right-angled lanes is modern and rather faceless.

Out of town, there are a couple of spots you might visit on your way north. One, **Sa Testa**, is a sacred well from the late nuraghic era (eighth–sixth century BC), signposted on the left shortly after the turn-off for Golfo Aranci, about 4km from Olbia. Seventeen steps lead down to a tholos-shaped chamber holding the spring. A spacious circular area surrounding it, bounded by upright stones, was probably a sort of waiting room for devotees who had come to perform their rites; there's even a bench round the walls. The good state of preservation is due to the fact the entire site remained buried until 1938. A little further on, to the right, is Olbia's favourite bathing spot: **Pittulongu**, a wide arc of sand where bars and parasols are set up in season.

Restaurants

The centre of Olbia is generously furnished with fast-food places and more sedate **restaurants**. You'll find good-value tourist menus in most places in summer, when everywhere gets pretty crowded.

Clipper, Piazza Matteotti. This place has definitely got a touch of the Costa Smeralda. Part of a chain with similar restaurants in Porto Rotondo and Porto Cervo, it's slightly twee, but the menu features classic Sard cuisine. The arched and raftered old room can get packed. Closed Sun. Moderate.

La Datcha, Via Cavour 3. Near the central Piazza Margherita, this *osteria* offers good-value dishes of the day. It's a bit touristy and gimmicky; and you can eat at benches outside. Moderate.

Il Gámbero, Via Lamármora 6. Locals and tourists alike go for the rustic trimmings including a broad fireplace, a mantlepiece piled with pots and ceramics, and hangings. The *risotto al carciofo* is small but perfect. Closed Sun. Moderate.

La Lanterna, Via Olbia 13. This subterranean dive off the Corso is good for pizzas, also offering a vegetarian choice, and there's a tourist menu for L25,000. Closed Wed. Moderate.

Da Paolo, Via Garibaldi 18 (entrance also at Via Cavour 17). There are three rooms in this old building (1723 on the lintel), one of them granite-walled with a polished wooden ceiling. Over-anxious service but good food, including excellent *zuppa di verdure*. Closed Sun evening. Moderate.

La Primavera, Via D'Annunzio 16. Outside the main restaurant area, on the other side of the rail tracks, this place is spacious and relaxed and offers a vast choice of dishes including pizzas. Moderate.

Zhanto, Via delle Terme 1b. Just off the Corso, this small and elegant place with a garden offers good value and is always busy with locals; it serves pizzas at lunchtime. Closed Sun. Moderate.

Bars, nightlife and entertainment

On Piazza Margherita, *Caffé Cosimino* is good for coffees and fresh cornetti (closed Sun); sit out or inside, where the walls have faded photos of old Olbia. In the evening, the *Havana* **birreria** at Corso Umberto 32 attracts a young male crowd, including sailors.

Capricorno, on the corner of Via Piro and the Corso, is a semi-exclusive **nightclub** which flings its doors open for free on Saturday after 11pm, for a diet of mainstream dance music. Live music can be heard between Thurs and Sun at *Ajoabi*, Via de Filippi 34 (closed

Sailings from Olbia

To Civitavecchia

Between May and September, Tirrenia (☎0789.24.691) operates fast ferries (*mezzi veloci*) to Civitavecchia (north of Rome). The daily departure at midnight arrives at 6am; from mid-June there is a second departure at 8.30am (arriving at 12.30pm), and according to demand there may also be sailings at 1.30pm and 7pm, taking 4hr–4hr 30min; between October and April, fast ferries leave on Mondays and Tuesdays at 6.30pm, arriving at 10.30pm, and Wed–Sat at midnight, arriving at 6am. For the fastest vessels, tickets cost L50,000–80,000 according to season, medium-size cars are L130,000–160,000; tickets for the slower ones, which travel at 23 knots, cost L40,000–55,000, medium cars pay L125,000–140,000.

To Genoa

Ferries (*traghetti*) of Tirrenia and Grandi Navi Veloci (☎010.589.331) connect Olbia to Genoa. Tirrenia ships leave three times weekly (Tuesday, Thursday and Saturday) between early September and late July, daily in summer, all departures at 8.30pm, arriving at 10am the following day. Fares are L46,000–60,000 for deck class, L57,000–77,000 for a semi-reclinable seat, L73,000–97,000 for a berth. Ferries run by Grandi Navi Veloci operate from the end of June to the end of September, leaving at 9am until mid-August, then at 9pm (journey time 10hr). A reclinable seat costs L72,000–126,000 according to season, a berth in a four-person cabin is L90,000–148,000 (more for a cabin with a porthole), and you'll pay L130,000–190,000 for a medium-sized car. Tirrenia's **fast ferries** leave daily between mid-June and early September, leaving at 4pm, arriving at Genoa at 10pm, and daily except Tuesday and Thursday between early and late September at 12.30pm, arriving at 6pm. Fares are currently L111,000–131,000 per passenger, L136,000–166,000 for a medium-size car.

To Livorno

Moby Lines (☎0789.27.927) boats leave **for Livorno** roughly once or twice daily in winter, three times daily mid-May to mid-Sept, with departures at different times, usually 10am, 8pm and 10pm; crossings take 8hr. Tickets are L36,000–83,000 according to season and whether or not it is a night crossing (which is more expensive); reclinable seats cost an extra L12,000–18,000, and berths an extra L40,000–L100,000. A small-to-medium size car costs L77,000–192,000 according to season, motorbikes L68,000–99,000, and bikes go free. There are additional port taxes to pay of about L3000 per passenger, L3500 per vehicle.

FS and Sardinia Ferries to Livorno and Civitavecchia leave from Golfo Aranci (see box on p.277), 15km up the coast. All **tickets** can be bought from the offices at the Stazione Maríttima or at the agencies at the bottom of Corso Umberto (see "Listings" for opening hours). Ask about discounts, for example for return tickets for car + passengers, and for midweek daytime departures in low season. Book as early as possible for the lowest fares and to guarantee availability, which in August is extemely limited.

Mon). It's a spacious cellar dive, where *panini* and steaks are served alongside the draught beer, staying open until 3am at weekends.

Olbia

Apart from San Símplicio, Olbia's other main **festivals** are on Sant'Agostino's day on June 24 and Santa Lucia's day on the first Sunday of September, both lasting three days. Olbia also hosts a cultural festival, L'Estate Olbiense, with concerts and other events throughout the summer from the end of July.

Listings

Automobile Club d'Italia (ACI) Via Piro 9 (☎116).

Airport Aeroporto di Costa Smeralda lies 3km east of Olbia. Call ☎0789.23.721 or 0789.69.228 for flight information, or call in at a travel agency.

Banks Banco di Sardegna at Corso Umberto 142 (open Mon–Fri 8.20am–1.20pm & 2.35–4.05pm), has a cash machine; Crédito Italiano at Corso Umberto 165 (Mon–Fri 8.20am–1.20pm & 2.50–4.20pm, Sat 8.20–11.50am).

Bike hire Gallura (see Car hire) rents out scooters for about L75,000 a day, or L500,000 per week, for a 150cc. There is no bicycle hire in Olbia.

Boat tours Various tours in July and August from Olbia's Marina di Porto Ottiolu, or Marina di Cugnana: look out for the sign *Escursioni in batello*. Most leave at 9.30am and return at about 6pm, and include circuits of the nearby islands of Tavolara and Molara, and as far as the Maddalena archipelago. Boats to Tavolara leave at 10am, arriving there at noon, with the option of returning at 12.30pm, 4pm or 5pm, tickets L30,000. Others include a spaghetti meal. Ask details from the tourist office or the kiosks by the quayside, or by phoning ☎0789.40.210, 0789.53.065, 0347.378.8432 or 0338.646.7684.

Bookshop Gulliver, Corso Umberto 154, has guidebooks and a few English-language books. Open Tues–Sat 9am–1pm & 4–8pm, Sun 10.30am–1pm & 5–8pm.

Car hire All the major companies have agencies at the airport. Agencies in town include: Ellepi, Via Tavolara 14 (☎0789.23.390); Gallura, Viale Aldo Moro (☎0789.51.518), and Holiday Car, Via Genova 71 (☎0789.46.119). Rates vary according to whether or not you have a kilometre rate; Holiday Car and Ellepi charge about L85,000–125,000 for a Panda for one day, L80,000 for successive days, or L75,000 per day for a week or more, with a supplement of L250–350 per kilometre driven over 150km per day. Gallura, offering unlimited mileage, charges just L100,000 per day for a Panda. Prices may rise about 15 percent in July and Aug.

Ferries At Stazione Maríttima, the Tirrenia office is open Mon–Sat 8am–1pm, also Sun, Mon & Tues 5–10.50pm, Wed & Thurs 5.20–11.50pm; the Moby Lines office is open Mon–Sat 9.30am–12.30pm, also Mon, Wed & Fri 4–7pm, Tues & Thurs 4–10pm, Sun 6–10pm. In town, agencies where you can pick up tickets for Tirrenia, Moby Lines and Sardinia Ferries are at Corso Umberto 1 (☎0789.25.560); Corso Umberto 4 (☎0789.25.200), and Corso Umberto 17 (☎0789.28.533), all open Mon–Sat 8.30am–1pm & 4.30–7.30pm. FS and Sardinia Ferries for Livorno and Civitavecchia leave from Golfo Aranci, 15km up the coast (from Olbia, 4–7 trains daily). Book early for all departures.

First aid ☎0789.54.000.

Hospital Viale Aldo Moro (☎0789.552.200).

Laundrette Self-service laundrette on Via Redipúglia (at the bottom of Via Regina Elena), open summer daily 9am–10pm, winter Mon–Sat 8am–1pm & 3–8pm, Sun 3–8pm. L6000 for washing 6kg, L6000 for drying.

Luggage deposit At train station (daily 8am–9.20pm) and at FS window at Stazione Maríttima (daily 5.10pm–11pm); charge at both is L5000 per piece for 12hr.

Market Covered fruit and veg market in Via Bari, Mon–Sat 8am–1pm & 4.30–8.30pm.

Pharmacy Most pharmacies are open 9am–1pm & 4.15–7.35pm, closed on Sat afternoon & Sun, though Lupacciolu at Corso Umberto 134 stays open weekdays until 10pm. Night rotas are posted on pharmacy doors or in the local newspaper.

Post office Main office at Via Acquedotto, open Mon–Fri 8.15am–6.10pm, Sat 8.15am–1.15pm, last day of month closes at noon. Cash and travellers' cheques changed here.

Supermarket Standa at Corso Umberto 158, open Mon 3.30–7.30pm, Tues–Sat 9am–1pm & 3.30–7.30pm, with food hall. Upim at Corso Umberto 166, same opening hours as Standa but no food hall.

Taxis Ranks at train station (☎0789.22.718, 0789.27.334 or 0338.659.3164) and airport (☎0789.69.150).

Train information ☎147/888088 daily 7am–9pm.

Travel agent CTS, Piazza Matteotti 9 (☎0789.25.965); Unimare, Corso Umberto 1 (☎0789.25.560).

South of Olbia

The coastal stretch **south of Olbia** has rapidly grown from a wilderness of rock and scrub to become a favourite with Olbians and other holiday-makers who throng the area's beaches every summer. The cubic pink and coral-coloured constructions that have sprouted haphazardly in the last couple of decades have sadly blighted much of the landscape, though the seaward view remains thankfully unaltered, dominated by the dramatically looming shapes of the islands of **Tavolara** and **Molara**. You can visit them from points along the coast, most easily from **Porto San Paolo**, a recently developed resort village 14km south of Olbia, catering like other holiday centres along this coast mainly to families. Further south, **San Teodoro** is more of the same, a bland colony of bungalows interspersed with hotels and campsites around a decent, though not terrific, beach.

Porto San Paolo

From Olbia, the southbound SS125 runs past the airport and the first suitable bathing beach at **Lido del Sole** after another four or five kilometres. The road twists just inland of the coast, but always within sight of the monolithic flat-topped islands of Tavolara and Molara. The six-times-daily #5 bus route from Olbia terminates at **Porto Istana**, a sandy bay sheltered by the hulking forms of the islands. A nice excursion around here is to **Capo Ceraso**, the southern tip of the Golfo di Olbia. You can drive most of the way, or walk along a mainly tarmacked road that cuts north about 200m off the SS125 on the Porto Istana road. There are some good beaches among the thick growth of *macchia* and pink rocks, and a stairway once used to reach a World War II gun emplacement leads to the top of **Monte Mandriolo** (126m); the views from here across to Capo Figari north, and the island of Tavolara to the east, are fabulous.

In summer, **boat tours** depart from Porto Istana to visit Tavolara and Molara (see box), though the main embarcation point is a few kilometres further south at **PORTO SAN PAOLO**, a dormitory town and summer resort. Here, beyond the battery of bars and pizzerias, the small quay at Pontile della Marina is used by fishing boats; it's also the embarkation point for tour boats to Tavolara and Molara, which leave hourly costing L15,000 per person (L50,000 if you take

---

Tavolara and Molara

The boat excursion to **Tavolara** and **Molara** is a great way to combine a close exploration of these islands with swimming in the sublime waters around them. The tall eruptions of rock are ever more daunting the nearer you approach, and they harbour some fine beaches lapped by crystal-clear water.

For a return ticket to the islands, expect to pay around L30,000. Between July and August, boats leave at regular intervals from Porto Istana and Porto San Paolo, with less frequent sailings outside the summer months. Most boat companies offer a cruise around Tavolara, with optional swims; once disembarked, find yourself a patch of sand (preferably with shade attached), and concentrate on doing nothing. You can choose to return at different times throughout the afternoon.

Tavolara is the more impressive: a giant wedge 4km long and just 1km wide, its sheer walls towering to a height of 564m. The island's eastern flank is a military zone and therefore off limits, but the western side, which is inhabited and even has a cemetery, is freely accessible; in summer there are bars and a couple of restaurants, *La Corona* and *Da Tonino*. The southern tip of the island holds a couple of good beaches at Spalmatore di Terra.

The island also hosts an open-air **film festival** of non-mainstream Italian movies, screened on the beach during four or five nights in mid-July. Special boat excursions ferry ticket-holders to and from the al fresco arena. Contact the tourist office at Olbia or Porto San Paolo for dates and times, or consult the website: *web.tin.it/cinematavolara*.

Some tours take in the smaller, circular isle of **Molara**; in contrast to calcareous Tavolara, the island is composed of granite, and it's greener too, with a covering of wild olives. On its eastern shore, at Cala di Chiesa, are the remains of a medieval village, **Gurguray**, with the shattered hulk of a church, San Ponziano. You may also make a stop at **Piana**, a tiny rock just big enough to hold a lovely sandy beach.

For more information on excursions, call one of the boat companies (☎0789.40.210, 0789.53.065 or 0347.378.8432), or contact Porto San Paolo's tourist office on ☎0789.40.172.

Peregrine falcons and storm petrels are among the rare birds to look out for on Tavolara, nesting on the vertical cliff walls of the island.

South of Olbia

the 8pm tour that includes supper). Buy tickets from the kiosks here.

Most of the vacationing on this stretch of coast takes place in holiday apartments, accounting for the sparsity of other types of accommodation. The one **hotel** in Porto San Paolo is the swish *San Paolo* (☎0789.40.001, fax 0789.40.622; ⑤), with its tennis court; it's closed mid-October to mid-May, prices fall sharply outside July and August. Three kilometres south of here, the beachside *Tavolara* **campsite** is open between May and September and also has a tennis court and boat rental (☎0789.40.166). Otherwise, contact the **agriturismo** *Lu Striglioni*, signposted at Bivio Diriddò a short way inland (☎0789.40.524 or 0360.616.867). Information on any of these places and on boat tours is on hand at the **Pro Loco** (☎0789.40.172), open summer only.

San Teodoro

Just south of the Sássari-Nuoro provincial boundary, the cape known as **Capo Coda Cavallo**, or "horse's tail", curls round to within 3km of the island of Molara. There's another good **campsite**, *Cala Cavallo* (June–Sept; ☎0789.834.156), on the cape; it's well equipped, with its own pool and tennis court. The views over the islands from this little peninsula are awesome. Eight kilometres further south, past a lagoon used by wading flamingos and cranes, **SAN TEODORO** is another popular beach resort, its modern villas, bars and restaurants thickly planted behind the **Cala d'Ambra** beach. This is the preferable area to stay in if you're looking for accommodation in San Teodoro. Two three-star **hotels**, *L'Eságono* (April–Oct; ☎0784.865.783, fax 0784.866.040; ③) and the *Hotel Bungalow* (mid-May to mid-Oct; ☎0784.865.713, fax 0784.865.178; ④), have relatively cheap rates and provide a range of facilities for children and adults, including tennis courts, pools and riding. Away from the sea, Via del Tirreno has most of the hotels, including the cheap *Al Faro* (mid-May to Sept; ☎0784.865.665, fax 0784.865.565; ③), and one of San Teodoro's two **campsites**, the *San Teodoro* (mid-May to Oct; ☎0784.865.777), which offers bungalows sleeping four for between L100,000 and L150,000 per night. The other site, however, *Cala d'Ambra* (June–Sept; ☎0784.865.650), has lower prices and is situated right by the sea.

One of the finest beaches around San Teodoro is on La Cinta, a long bar of sand separating the Stagno di San Teodoro from the sea.

Nor is San Teodoro short of **places to eat**: *Al Deborah* offers four-course Sard meals for just L30,000 including drinks, while *L'Eságono* hotel has a terrace right on the beach. Other ones to look out for include *La Lámpara* ristorante/pizzeria, with a wood-fired oven for pizzas and meat and fish served on the spit. For afters, treat yourself to good **ice cream** and pastries from the *Anna gelateria/pasticceria* near here. San Teodoro also boasts a good choice of **discos**, including, near the beach, open-air dance floors at *L'Eságono* hotel and *Cala d'Ambra* campsite; nearer the centre, the *Idolhouse* discobar has billiards and serves *panini* too.

Budoni

The minor road south from San Teodoro takes you past more beaches and campsites, eventually rejoining the main SS125. If you're looking for accommodation in the area, **BUDONI**, 10km south of San Teodoro, has a couple of hotels on its main drag, *Isabella* (☎0784.844.048, fax 0784.844.409; ③) and *Solemar* (☎0784.844.081; ③); they're both pretty characterless, though they do stay open all year. The beach neighbourhood of Agrustos has two pricier options, and two of the several campsites in these parts. There's not much to recommend a stay in this area, though, and you might as well press on to the mouth of the Posada river and the Nuorese village of the same name (see p.339).

South of Olbia

In the village of Budoni, Piemme rents out bikes, scooters and cars at Piazza Italia 1 (☎0784.844.444).

Golfo Aranci and the Costa Smeralda

The Golfo di Olbia reaches its northern extent at **Golfo Aranci**, a major port which has taken an increasing portion of Olbia's shipping traffic. Its picturesque name – "Gulf of Oranges" – fails to convey to the more down-to-earth reality, and apart from some decent beaches and a nature reserve in the vicinity, there is no pressing reason to come here unless you need to cross on the daily ferries to the mainland. Much of this long peninsula has been invaded by the uniform holiday villas that become increasingly dominant along this stretch of coast, not least around the modern holiday town of **Porto Rotondo**. However bland the architecture, the vegetation is always exuberant, bougainvillea, tiger lily and hibiscus injecting a tropical brilliance to the granite rock.

This dialogue between nature and artifice is even more pronounced on the **Costa Smeralda**, the "millionaire's playground" which occupies the western shore of the Golfo di Cugnana. At least here, however, the development has been subject to stringent controls which have limited the damage. Accordingly, large areas of *macchia* and mountain have been left undisturbed, though the pockets of development that exist are not always as unobtrusive as they are vaunted to be, and they are growing inexorably, however slowly.

It is not just the natural beauty of the granite littoral which is striking, but the cleanliness and transparency of the sea – another beneficiary of the planning regulations in force here. If you don't mind bathing off rocks, then you can swim virtually anywhere; if it's **beaches** you're after, they're here too, though much less obvious – follow the brown signs, where they exist.

Although Golfo Aranci has a couple of good **accommodation** choices, and there is a campsite just south of the Golfo di Cugnana, don't even think of staying on the Costa Smeralda itself unless you have an invitation. Even three-star hotels have five-star prices, and in any case most of the accommodation here is in the form of rentals by the week. If that's your preferred option, consult the agencies in Porto Cervo, Baja Sardinia or Porto Rotondo, who will probably try to persuade you to spend a little more on a purchase, otherwise stay in Arzachena or camp.

Golfo Aranci

If you have come from Livorno, La Spezia or Civitavecchia, **GOLFO ARANCI** may well be your first landing in Sardinia, not a bad place to touch down if you want to avoid the noise and bustle of Olbia. It's hardly a particularly inspiring town, however, nor a great foretaste of what else Sardinia has in store, but it has good connections to other places in Gallura, with a couple of nice beaches nearby and even a nature reserve, overlooked by most visitors, in the hills behind.

The town developed in the first decades of the twentieth century when the construction of its port facilities and the railway line to Olbia helped it to take over a portion of the shipping coming to that town. The arrival of the FS ferries in 1961 gave a further boost, as did the establishment of a passenger service in the 1970s; the holiday homes followed soon after.

If Golfo Aranci has any centre, it's the port and train station at the far end of town, where there's also a tourist office open daily in summer. Just a few metres up from the station is Golfo Aranci's only item of historical interest, the **Pozzo Sacro Milis**, a rough-hewn sacred well dating from the nuraghic era.

Behind the town rears the immense mass of rock occupying **Capo Figari**, a protected area where the thick *macchia* is interlaced with holm oaks and a juniper wood. A number of Sardinia's long-horned mouflons (wild sheep) have been successfully reintroduced here and on the offshore islet of Figarolo, whose steep slopes are visible from here, similarly clad in *macchia* and twisted old olives. The best **beaches**, however, lie south of town, round the curve of the **Golfo degli Aranci**, where Cala Sássari includes several small sandy coves, one of which, **Sos Aranzos**, lent its name to both the gulf and the major port. The aptly named **Cala Banana** (also called *Pellicano*) is another arc of beach worth seeking out.

Practicalities

Frequent **trains** and (in summer) **buses** connect Golfo Aranci with Olbia. Some trains run right up to the port, though most stop at the central station in town. If you need to stay at Golfo Aranci, there is a handful of **hotels** to choose from, most on or off the long main road connecting the port area with the centre of town. Two are on Via Libertà: *Castello* (☎0789.46.073, fax 0789.46.450; ④) and the much smaller and cheaper *King's* (☎0789.46.075, fax 0789.46.400; ③), both open April–September. A third option lies nearby: *La Lámpara* on Via Magellano (☎0789.615.140; no CCs; ⑤).

Sailings from Golfo Aranci

Tirrenia (☎0789.24.691) operates a **fast-ferry** (*mezzo veloce*) service to La Spezia and Civitavecchia. Departures to **La Spezia** take place between mid-June and early Sept, at 2.30pm mid-June to July and the middle ten days of Aug, at 1am the rest of the time. Crossing time is 5hr 30min and fares are L100,000–112,500 for passengers, L150,000–165,500 for a small car.

Departures to **Civitavecchia** take place during the same period twice daily in June and July, at 1pm and midnight, with an extra 2.15pm departure for the first 10 days of Aug, and only a 1pm departure from late Aug to early Sept. Journeys take 4hr and cost L50,000–80,000 according to season, medium-size cars are L130,000–160,000; tickets for the slower vessels, which travel at 23 knots, cost L40,000–55,000, with medium cars paying L125,000–140,000. Sardinia Ferries (☎0789.46.780) also runs *mezzi veloci* to Civitavecchia between June and Sept, leaving twice daily at 1.10pm and 9.20pm, taking 3hr 30min; passengers pay L65,000–100,000, small cars L160,000–210,000. The same company operates a slower ferry service to Civitavecchia, departing daily at 4.30pm, with an additional 9.30pm departure in Sept, and a reduced service between Oct and April (L40,000–80,000 for passengers, L50,000–150,000 for a cabin, L100,000–150,000 for a car; 7hr), as do FS ferries (☎147/888088) at 10am daily, taking 8hr with similar prices.

Sardinia Ferries also run a service to **Livorno** once or twice daily between April and mid-Oct, at 9.30am and/or 9.30pm (L40,000–90,000 for passengers, L115,000–200,000 for a cabin, L80,000–200,000 for a small vehicle; 9–10hr). Ask about any possible reductions on return crossings, stand-bys, advance bookings, etc. In season, you are advised to book early.

The best **place to eat** is near the port, off the main road at Via de' Caduti, where the plain-looking *Manzoni* (closed Nov; no CCs) offers first-class fish meals for very reasonable prices, and there are pizzas too. The local *sagra di pesce*, or **fish festival**, takes place on August 14, when seafood and wine are doled out to all and sundry.

Porto Rotondo and around

Built in 1963 following the development of Costa Smeralda, **PORTO ROTONDO** does not deviate very far from the main theme. Rows of orange villas snake remorselessly over the *macchia* hills, grouped more thickly around the inevitable round yachting port. Chic boutiques and fashion shops set the tone in the central Piazzetta San Marco, from which a wide stairway leads up to the church of **San Lorenzo**, a modern granite construction holding twenty wooden statuettes on a religious theme. A few metres away, there's an open-air theatre, also granite, built in 1995, where entertainments are staged in summer. There are beaches around the thin headland north of here, **Punta della Volpe**, though these get overwhelmed in summer.

There's nowhere remotely affordable to stay in the area, except for an inland **campsite**; to reach it, back track some 10km from Porto

Rotondo towards the SS125. Turn right before reaching the highway, onto the Porto Cervo road. Having rounded the base of the Golfo di Cugnana, you'll pass almost immediately *La Cugnana*, a campsite (May–Sept; ☎0789.33.184) that's also the nearest to Olbia and the Costa Smeralda, and the cheapest option for staying anywhere near that exclusive zone. Consequently, expect a crowd. Bungalows with bathroom are also available here for L65,000-85,000 per night sleeping three. The site lies 2km from the beach at Marina di Cugnana, and a minibus shuttles campers to some of the Costa Smeralda's best beaches. ARST **buses** between Olbia and Porto Cervo stop right outside. To **rent bikes, scooters and cars**, contact Rubix Motorbikes at Località Castello (☎0789.35.331 or 0338.722.2700).

The Costa Smeralda

The **Costa Smeralda** is a strictly defined 10km strip between the gulfs of Cugnana and Arzachena, beginning some 12km north of Olbia. Legend has it that the Aga Khan Prince Karim IV, Imam and spiritual leader of the Ismaili Muslims, stumbled upon the charms of this idyllic coast when his yacht took shelter from a storm in one of its narrow creeks in 1958. Four years later the fabulously wealthy tycoon headed a consortium of businessmen with the aim of exploiting this wild coastal strip, and was easily able to persuade the local farmers to part with their largely uncultivable land – though stories have circulated ever since of the stratagems used to dupe the locals into selling their property for a fraction of its value.

The consortium's plans were on a massive scale, limited only by the conditions imposed by the regional government. These included proper sewage treatment and disposal, restrictions on building, and the insistence that the appearance of the landscape should not be unduly changed. On this last point the developers were only partial-

Only local building materials may be used along the Costa Smeralda, and only indigenous vegetation planted – barring pines, eucalyptus and poplars, for example, in favour of oleander, mimosa, arbutus and myrtle.

ly successful. Although multi-storey hotels, advertising hoardings, fast-food restaurants and even garish filling stations have been banned, the coast here can hardly be described as pristine, nor will you find a genuine fishing community surviving in these parts, nor anything like the kind of local markets you'll see in other parts of the island. Even the supermarkets are self-consciously discreet, and the red-tiled holiday villages, for all their trappings of luxury, have a bland, almost suburban feel about them.

Shorn of the eruptions of vulgarity, what's lacking is that vital human element or local touch which invigorates most other Italian resorts. Ultimately of course it's a question of taste, and you will make your own choice. If you can afford to be staying here, you will no doubt appreciate the virtues of this form of insulated holiday oasis, though you may soon tire of the ritzy glitzy world of hedonists and hangers-on, and the stifling air of opulence.

The keynote in the best hotels is understated class, and the places which flaunt their extravagance are deemed to have transgressed the unwritten code that decrees a kind of peasant chic, the sophisticated Bohemian tone you'll find in the most sumptuous hotels clustered around **Cala di Volpe**. If you really want to mingle with the in-crowd, however, sip aperitifs in the Piazzetta in **Porto Cervo**, the only real town on this coast, though, again, it's more a simulacrum than the real thing. Needless to say, when the summer's gone, so are the jet set, and the whole area sinks into a kind of dispirited inertia, though this might be the best time to appreciate the truly spectacular coast, undistracted by the shenanigans of the wannabe high-flying élite. June, July and September are the best months to enjoy the glorious **beaches** dotted along the indented coast south of Porto Cervo, which usually require a little enterprise and a good sense of direction to reach.

Cala di Volpe and around

The quiet creeks and inlets north of the Golfo di Cugnana provide numerous anchorages for yachts and often reveal hidden patches of sand from which to bathe. Of the area's broader **beaches**, the most popular include **Rena Bianca**, **Petra Ruia** and **Liscia Ruia**, the latter giving onto the bay of **Cala di Volpe**, a locality holding a concentration of some of Europe's most select hotels. The most exclusive of these, formerly managed by the Aga Khan's Consorzio Costa Smeralda, are now part of the ITT-Sheraton group, though it is unlikely that the rarefied flavour of these bastions of privilege will have been toned down.

Perhaps the most stylish of all is the *Cala di Volpe* (Feb to mid-Nov; ☎0789.976.111, fax 0789.976.617; ⑨) designed by celebrated architect Jacques Couelle and looking something like a mix between an adobe Moorish fortress and a peasant's farmstead, painted in umbers and ochres, all in immaculate taste. Exceptional cuisine, a private harbour, two salt-water pools (one on the hotel's roof) plus a fine sand beach combine to make this a sybaritic delight, if you're loaded: palatial rooms ring in at about L1,800,000 a night in high season (half-board); the low season rate plunges to just L490,000 for a standard room (B&B only).

Head west of Cala di Volpe for the pick of the area's **beaches**: just follow any dirt track – the rougher it is, the more promising – down to the sea. The beaches at **Capriccioli** and **Romazzino** are among the best, facing the offshore islands of Soffi and Mortorio.

Porto Cervo

In the "capital" of Costa Smeralda, **PORTO CERVO**, the tidy rustic-red architecture characteristic of the region becomes almost surreal, embodying the dream of an idealized holiday resort without any of the irritations of real life. Fascinating to wander round, crime- and litter-free, Porto Cervo resembles a film set, or a virtual version of a "Mediterranean village", rather than any authentic resort. The huge

The 18-hole 72-par Pevero golf course on a rolling expanse of green above the Cala di Volpe hotel is one of Europe's most prestigious. It's also a masterwork of design, the creation of architect Robert Trent Jones. It's linked to the Cervo, Romazzino, Cala di Volpe and Pitrizza hotels by a free shuttle service.

yachting marina is a curiosity in itself, awash with the ostentatious baubles of the ultra-rich. The gleaming ranks are overlooked to the west of the centre by the **Stella Maris** church, a rough-textured, whitewashed building which surprisingly houses a couple of good works of art, including a *Mater Dolorosa* by El Greco, the bequest of a Dutch aristocrat. The church was designed in 1968 by the Roman architect Michele Busiri Vici, who was also responsible for the grotto-like shopping arcade in Porto Cervo's centre. At the heart of this warren of paths and passages, the **Piazzetta** is the place to lounge in style, ideally with cocktail in hand and an expensive pair of shades. Drinks at the bars here will knock you back upwards of L10,000, though the price includes a front-seat view of the kind of people who frequent this VIP resort. Steps lead down from here to the **Sottopiazza**, an area of posh boutiques and also site of an ISOLA outlet, selling government-sponsored craftwork.

Designed with the yachter in mind, Porto Cervo has the best marine facilities in Sardinia. There are berths for 650 vessels, each with electricity and fresh water supplies, and rings and bollards in bronze. During the first days of September in uneven years, antique sailing boats gather at the port, usually followed by a race in the Straits of Bonifacio.

There are also banks, phones, pharmacies, travel agents, estate agents, even a supermarket here, not to mention the top-quality tennis facilities, used for tournaments in the summer and at other times open daily to the public. Unless you opt for this, however, there's not much else to do in town once you've had your eyeful of the Fendis and Vespaces, and gawped at the incredibly grand yachts at the marina. If you're hungry, head for the supermarket behind the Piazzetta or else buy an expensive *panino* from a bar. For anything more substantial, there are some slightly cheaper **restaurants** than the swanky affairs tucked away in Porto Cervo's alleys, including *Il Pomodoro*, behind the Piazzetta.

The dominant presence in the centre of the resort is the five-star *Cervo Hotel* (☎0789.931.111, fax 0789.931.613; ⑧), its entrance on the central piazza but still projecting an air of privileged quiet. If you were tempted to stay here, rooms rise from about L230,000 to L850,000 in high season, for which you get use of squash and tennis courts, a pool and, for a secluded swim, a boat-service that whisks guests off to a select beach twenty minutes away.

Beyond the obligatory aperitif in the Piazzetta, Porto Cervo has no nightlife as such, though there are venues within a short drive. A couple of kilometres outside town, on the road south, the *Sopravento* has one of the biggest **discos** in the area, also featuring occasional live bands. Across the road from it, *Sottovento* is a less intense piano bar. For **taxis** call ☎0789.92.250.

Baia Sardinia and around

You'll need your own transport to get to the sequestered **beaches** around Porto Cervo, none of which are clearly marked. North of the resort, one of the best is at **Liscia di Vacca**, an exquisite bay at the end of a long bumpy dirt road. Thankfully, the villas of the nearby *Pitrizza* hotel (mid-May to mid-Oct; ☎0789.930.111, fax 0789.930.611; ⑧), which numbers moguls and minor royals among its guests, are safely fenced off, and do not intrude too much on the beach.

West of here, just outside the controlled zone of the Costa Smeralda though sharing its élite ethos, **BAIA SARDINIA** is dominated by the extensive *Forte Capellini* holiday village, whose lawns and thatched bungalows lie scattered around the granite boulders of the headland here. There are a number of other high-class hotels in and around this modern resort, and also a good **restaurant** that's not excessively expensive, the *Grazia Deledda*, on the Cannigione road (open summer only). Also on this road, the *Aquadream* amusement park is a hit with kids (June–Sept).

The Golfo di Arzachena and Palau

Outside the luxury belt but enjoying many of the Costa Smeralda's natural advantages, the **Golfo di Arzachena** is a deep narrow bay whose western shore holds most of the tourist facilities. **Arzachena** itself is inland and not particularly inspiring, though it has its share of excitement in high season. Apart from its hotels, banks and shops, the town also has a couple of curiosities worth exploring, including, a short distance outside, two of Sardinia's "giants' tombs" – the biggest and best-preserved of this type of nuraghic monument in the whole island. These and other sites lying in the middle of the countryside would make easy targets for walking or biking expeditions.

Most of the tourists gravitate towards the nearby coasts, with a concentration of facilities around **Cannigione** – a small fishing port and yachting resort on the gulf. There are campsites here, while a partly unasphalted road leads round the coast to the **Golfo delle Saline**, one of the area's best swimming spots, before reaching the port of **Palau**. The embarkation point for the Maddalena archipelago, Palau is a drab town, though well supplied with hotels. West of here, **Porto Puddu** has a magnificent beach that encompasses the coast's – if not Sardinia's – best windsurfing location.

Driving, you can reach Arzachena from Olbia in about thirty minutes on the SS125. Three **buses** daily leave Olbia on a route that takes in Arzachena and Palau, and several buses daily link Cannigione with Arzachena. Palau is also the terminus for the small **train service** that currently operates in summer only, and then with a very limited service.

Arzachena and its prehistoric sites

Although **ARZACHENA** lacks the glamour of the nearby upscale resorts, it makes a useful base for the area, with a selection of relatively reasonable hotels and restaurants. At the centre of town, Piazza Risorgimento holds the main tourist office and is the site of nightly entertainments – cabaret, concerts and the like. The tourist

Arzachena has a good market in and around Piazza Risorgimento on Wednesday mornings, for both food and household goods.

office can supply you with material on the sundry archeological sites scattered in or within a short distance of town, which are always open, and free.

The first of these lies only a short walk from the piazza, the **Roccia Il Fungo**, or "mushroom rock" (also called *Monti Incappidatu*), one of Gallura's weathered natural sculptures, conspicuous on a rise at the end of Via Limbara. Fragments found here have convinced archeologists that the formation provided shelter to Neolithic and nuraghic peoples; there's no doubting its choice location, commanding extensive views up and down the coast.

Nuraghe Albucciu and the Tempietto Malchittu

Of the other prehistoric sights around Arzachena, the easiest to visit lies 2km east of town, signposted near the Cannigione junction. Right by the side of the SS125, surrounded by olives, **Nuraghe Albucciu** is one of Gallura's best-preserved nuraghic monuments, with one chamber, on the right of the main corridor, still roofed and intact. Near the entrance to the nuraghe, you can just make out a groove that was probably made by a device for sealing the door. Linked by sight to other nuraghi in the area, the structure is built on an almost rectangular plan, and still displays the jutting supports for the vanished wooden roof.

Opposite the site, the car park contains a small tourist office, behind which a track leads north to another archeological ruin, the **Tempietto Malchittu** (leave your vehicle by the tourist office, for this is a private road). It's an easy stroll, the track winding through fields for less than 2km, curving round a spur in the lee of which lies the roofless ruin, now overgrown with trees and scrub. Little can be said for certain about this rugged oval structure dating from the first nuraghic phase (between 1500 and 1200 BC), except that it's thought to have been a place of worship; finds suggest that sacrifices were made here. The granite walls enclose two rooms connected by a low doorway; very few examples of this kind of construction are known today. Frankly, there isn't a great deal to see, though it makes a pleasant expedition, and could be a point of departure for longer walks in the *macchia*.

Coddu Vecchiu

Four and a half kilometres south of Arzachena, on the road to Sant'Antonio di Gallura, branch right onto the Luogosanto road and turn left after another 2km to reach the site of **Coddu Vecchiu**, one of the most complete of Sardinia's so-called *tombe dei giganti* (giants' tombs). Like other examples of this type of construction, it consists of carved granite slabs laid end-up in a semicircular, or bull-horn-shaped, formation. Their name was given to them by local people who were clearly mystified as to the purpose of these enigmatic objects. They are now known to be works of the nuraghic culture, for

which they were simultaneously collective burial chambers and
places of worship.

The central stele, over 4m tall, resembles an immense doorway,
probably symbolizing the entry into another world. The low opening
at the base, which would presumably have been sealed after burial,
leads into two long chambers, suggesting two distinct periods of construction during the second millennium BC. Excavations here have
thrown up evidence that members of the older Bonnanaro culture
also used this site, and that it was was later adapted by the nuraghic
people.

Nuraghe Capichera and Li Loghi

A kilometre further up this minor road brings you to a nuraghe that
was possibly associated with the Coddu Vecchiu site, **Nuraghe
Capichera** (also known as *La Prisciona*). Built at any time between
2000 and 1000 BC on a height overlooking the whole Arzachena
plain, this trilobate (three-sided) construction stands 6.5m tall. The
central tower is surrounded by three smaller towers and the very
sparse remains of an external wall. Three niches survive in the main
chamber (which is not central in respect of the tower itself). There's
a well in the space between the rampart and the wall, and huts have
been excavated in the vicinity.

*For more
information on
Sardinia's
nuraghic
culture, see box
on pp.148–149.*

You can visit another giants' tomb by continuing west along the
Luogosanto road for nearly 3km, making a right turn and keeping
right for another couple of kilometres. Just off this track on the left,
Li Lolghi has a lower central stele than Coddu Vecchiu, but its inner
chamber is nearly twice as long, and considered to be the finest
example of its type in Gallura. Again, the small arched doorway leads
into a passage containing the two chambers where bodies were laid.
In most respects the site is very similar to Coddu Vecchiu, and no
less striking.

Li Muri

From Li Lolghi it's a short distance to the last and oldest of
Arzachena's major prehistoric sites, **Li Muri**, reached by backtrack-
ing for a couple of hundred metres to take the left-hand (ie west) fork
off the track leading from the Luogosanto road. The track gets pretty rough, so drivers should leave their vehicles at the first suitable
place and proceed on foot, unless thay have a four-wheel drive.

The stone circles that make up the site constituted a necropolis of
the third millennium BC, once thought to belong to a so-called
"Arzachena culture", though it now looks as though this was a variation of the Ozieri culture (3400–2700 BC). Each of the five central
circles (5–8m in diameter) contained a body interred in a crouching
position together with votive offerings, while smaller circles dating
from a subsequent period are distinguished by a double row of stones
with better worked sides. These were probably used in funerary rites

but not as tombs; it has even been suggested they were used for the skinning of the corpse prior to burial. It's a complex site, the rugged setting giving it an appealingly raw grandeur.

Practicalities

You can pick up maps and details on accommodation and excursions in the area from Arzachena's **tourist office** on Piazza Risorgimento, which serves the whole Costa Smeralda region (Mon–Fri 8am–1.30pm & 3–7pm; Sat 8am–1.30pm; ☎0789.82.624). There's another office across the road from the Nuraghe Albucciu on the SS125 south of town (open daily in summer; ☎0789.88.510). The town has four **hotels**, cheapest of which is the *Citti* (☎0789.82.662, fax 0789.81.920; ③), boasting a small pool but with characterless rooms and no restaurant, on the outskirts of Arzachena on the Palau road (Viale Costa Smeralda 197). At the other end of town, off the road to Olbia at Via Torricelli 3, *Casa Mia* (☎0789.82.790, fax 0789.82.056; ④) has small functional rooms and a restaurant, while the glitzy *Albatros* at Viale Costa Smeralda 28 (☎0789.83.333, fax 0789.840.064; ⑦) has low-season rooms in the ④ category, and the nearby *Delfino*, at Viale Costa Smeralda 51 (☎0789.83.420, fax 0789.83.542; ⑤) has gaudily modern rooms, most with a balcony, and there's a roof bar.

There is a dearth of decent **eating places** in town. Apart from the *Casa Mia* hotel, try the *Pizzeria Il Calipso*, behind the Banco di Sardegna on Viale Costa Smeralda, or *Aryes Spaghetteria* below Piazza Risorgimento on Viale Costa Smeralda. There are a couple of other trattorias on this road and the main Via Ruzzittu.

For **Vespa hire**, ask at the *Raimondo Casula* scooter shop on Via Dettori; their charges are high, at L65,000 for 12 hours. Leaving town on the Palau road, Arzachena's **post office** is on the left at Viale Costa Smeralda 159 (open Mon–Fri 8.10am–6.15pm, Sat 8.10am–1.15pm); it also changes cash and American Express traveller's cheques. Otherwise you can **change money** at the nearby *Banco di Sardegna*, also on Viale Costa Smeralda (Mon–Fri 8.20am–1.20pm & 2.35–4.05pm), which has a cash machine.

Buses pull up on Via San Pietro, off Viale Dettori – the road signposted for Luogosanto. At the *Bar Castello*, Viale Dettori 43 (closed Fri), you can buy tickets for Olbia, Palau, Cannigione and Laconia. When this is closed, buy tickets round the corner at the *Bar Smeraldo*, on Via San Pietro (closed Sun). Arzachena's **train station** is about a kilometre west out of town, with trains stopping twice daily in summer on the Tempio Pausánia–Palau line. **Taxis** can be found on the central Piazza Risorgimento.

Cannigione and around

On the western shore of the Golfo di Arzachena lies the resort village of **CANNIGIONE**, a small fishing port and yacht-stop with some decent beaches to the north. Cannigione has a serene, even dull, atmosphere; it's the place to find supermarkets, restaurants, an exchange office (open morning and afternoon) and a small information office at the end of the main street (open daily summer only), but once you've dispatched a *gelato* on a stroll by the portside, you've exhausted its attractions.

The beaches are further up the coast, though most of the **hotels** are in Cannigione itself, and none of them is especially cheap. Virtually all are over the ⑤ mark, and most are open only from Easter to October: the cheapest is the *Baja* at Via Nazionale 35 (April–Oct; ☎0789.88.010, fax 0789.88.053; ④), a modern block on the left of the main street heading into town, with a large swimming pool. Only slightly more expensive and with a more attractive seafront location on Lungomare Andrea Doria, the *Hotel del Porto* hasn't got a pool, but stays open all year (☎0789.88.011, fax 0789.88.064; ④). Both places have restaurants (other dining spots in Cannigione are pricey).

Cannigione also has a couple of **campsites** which are teeming in high summer. The *Golfo di Arzachena* (June–Oct; ☎0789.88.583) is inland just south of Cannigione, with a big pool and caravans and mini-apartments for rent (⑤–⑥), while the preferable *Villaggio Isuledda* (April to mid-Oct; ☎0789.86.003) lies right on the shore north of the resort, in the Laconia district. It has excellent bathing spots, and bungalows and cabins (④–⑤).

Beyond Laconia, the tiny coast road winds round to the **Golfo di Saline**, a bay sheltering a superlative **beach** and the *Club Hotel Li Capanni* (☎0789.86.041, fax 0789.86.200; ⑦), which happily does not impinge too heavily on the undeveloped sandy shores. At the tip of the bay sit the even more lavish four-star *Capo d'Orso* hotel (☎0789.702.000, fax 0789.702.009; ⑧), and the far humbler but still fairly grand eponymous **campsite** (☎0789.702.007), both open from April or May to September. The campsite gets extremely congested in high summer. This and the hotel are named after the nearby headland, **Capo d'Orso**, which in turn takes its name from a huge outcrop nearby, a strange bear-shaped rock (*orso* = bear), known since ancient times and even claimed to be the dwelling-place of the Laestrigonians, the mythical cannibal tribe which destroyed the fleet of Ulysses when it was docked here. To reach it, you have to pass a gate and climb the slopes of the headland. At 122m high, it makes a grand platform to view the sensational panorama, embracing the Maddalena islands, Santa Teresa di Gallura and Corsica.

Palau

Unless you are one of the US personnel billeted here as part of the NATO presence, the main reason for being in **PALAU** is for the ferry out of it. Overdevelopment has taken the soul out of this

small port and resort, though the town is not in itself an unpleas-
ant place to spend an evening, and can even be fun if you're not
looking for anything more demanding than lively bar life. There
are hotels, too, making good bases to explore the superlative
beaches hereabouts.

Practicalities

The **train station** for summer journeys to Arzachena and the interi-
or (see p.281) lies near the port, where the **stazione maríttima**
holds ferry ticket desks. Palau's **information office** lies on the main
road, Via Nazionale 94 (summer daily 8am–1pm & 4–8pm, winter
Mon–Fri 8am–1pm; ☎0789.709.570). Trecentosessantagradi, at
Via Brigate Sássari 12 (☎0789.708.565), and Naus Rental, Via
Nazionale 97 (☎0789.709.083) **rent out cars, motorbikes, scooters and mountain bikes**; a Fiat 500 will cost around L120,000 a day
during July and August. For **boat tours** around the Maddalena
islands, ask at the stazione maríttima or contact the operators of the
Vagabondo (☎0789.735.419 or 0360.825.332) or the *Ausonia*
(☎0789.735.088 or 0368.555.972), both at the port.

As for **accommodation**, most places in Palau close in winter, but
the *Piccada*, a ten-minute walk from the port at Via degli Asfodeli,
off Via Capo d'Orso (☎ & fax 0789.709.344; ④), stays open all
year; it has a good selection of spacious rooms, those with views
and a separate entrance costing a little more. They also rent out
apartments by the week. Other hotels include the slightly swanky
Del Molo, on Via dei Ciclopi, very near the port (☎0789.708.042,
fax 0789.709.859; ⑤); *La Roccia*, Via dei Mille 15 (☎ & fax
0789.709.528; ③), and – cheapest of all – the *Serra* at Via
Nazionale 17 (☎0789.709.519; ②), which has rooms with and
without bath. If you prefer to be near the sea, try renting a cabin

---

Sailings from Palau

As well as connecting Palau with **La Maddalena** (see box on p.289), TRIS
(☎0789.708.631) also runs ferries to **Porto Vecchio** in Corsica on
Saturday at 4pm during April and May, and on Tuesday and Thursday at
8am between June and September. The trip takes two-and-a-half hours,
and tickets cost L21,500 per passenger, L50,000 for a car, L30,000 for a
motorbike and L20,000 for a bicycle. Except for day-trippers, passengers
disembarking at Porto Vecchio have to a pay a landing fee of L9000.

During the same period, Linee Lauro operates a ferry service between
Palau and **Naples**, leaving from Palau on Thursdays and Saturdays at 6pm,
just Saturdays on the last two weeks of September. Crossings take fourteen hours and cost L45,000–90,000 for a space on the deck,
L50,000–100,000 for a reclinable seat, L70,000–180,000 for a berth,
L140,000–L270,000 for a car, L80,000–190,000 for a motorbike. Get
more information and tickets from Agenzia Bulciolu, Via Fonte Vecchio
(☎0789.709.505).

(L25,000–42,000 per person) at the nearest **campsite**, *Baia Saraceno* (May–Oct; ☎0789.709.403), on the other side of a pinewood close to Punta Nera, less than a kilometre east of town – it has access to a fantastic beach.

For nightlife, there's *Il Big* **disco** at Via Capo d'Orso 30 – a favourite with the American service personnel stationed here. If you want to take a boat tour of the islands, tours lasting two and a half hours leave daily in summer, stopping at Budelli and Spargi, a full day's excursion. Pay between L15,000 and L30,000 for a ticket, depending on what tour you take.

West of Palau

Between Palau and the port of Santa Teresa di Gallura, the dramatic rocky coastline is indented by a succession of lovely bays and fjords. The few small resorts here get very busy in summer, but are generally deserted the rest of the time. A handful of hotels and campsites provide accommodation, though most of them close in winter.

Two or three kilometres out of Palau, a right turn brings you 3km along a minor road to **Porto Puddu** (also called Porto Pollo), a scattered locality which has become established as one of Sardinia's busiest watersports centres. A slender isthmus of beach ending in a thick knob of rock divides the two bays of Porto Puddu and Porto Liscia, creating a breakwater and thus ideal conditions for **windsurfing**: downwind of the sand bank, the sea is flat and fast; upwind it's choppy and more suited to experts. There's a whole network of schools and rental operations on hand to cater to the masses of enthusiasts, but even if you're not a surfer, the dune-backed beaches on the two bays are worth going out of your way for. You can also rent dinghies.

At the end of the sandy limb, the *Isola dei Gabbiani* **campsite** takes its name from the bulbous promontory which it completely occupies (April–Oct; ☎0789.704.019). Caravans and bungalows are also available for rent here at L45,000–90,000 for two, and there are more splendid beaches along the shores of this "island". The only **hotel** around is *Le Dune* (April–Oct; ☎0789.704.013, fax 0789.704.113; ④); a three-star less than 100m from the sea, it wouldn't make a bad place to stay (they also rent out mountain bikes). There are plenty of bars and pizzerias around, such as *Il Maestrale*, a bar/pizzeria/*gelateria* complex, and the nearby and groovier *Bar Onda*, a surfies' meeting place which also does breakfasts. *Le Dune* (see above) is also the focus of a social scene, with a bar, *birreria* and restaurant. And there's always the *Sahara* **disco**, which rocks until late in summer.

Among the dozens of windsurf operations, New Windsurf Club (☎0789.704.075) or Paolo Silvestri Surf and Sail Center (☎0789.704.053) should see you right.

The Maddalena Islands

From Palau, the ferry crossing takes just twenty minutes to reach the **Maddalena archipelago**, a cluster of seven larger islands and a sprinkling of smaller ones. The archipelago is a favourite sailing area for yachters, and sees a number of regattas thoughout the year. Boats dock at the largest of the group, **La Maddalena**, where almost all the hotels and restaurants are located; there's also a small museum of naval archeology here. From the main island, you can drive, bike or walk across to neighbouring **Caprera**, where Garibaldi spent the last third of his life. The hero of the struggle for Italian unifica-

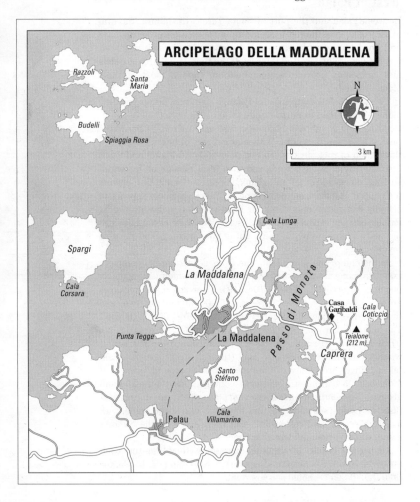

ARCIPELAGO DELLA MADDALENA

Razzoli

Santa
Maria

Budelli

Spiaggia Rosa

N

0   3 km

Cala Lunga

Spargi

La Maddalena

Cala
Corsara

Punta Tegge

La Maddalena

Passo di Moneta

Casa
Garibaldi

Cala
Coticcio

Teialone
(212 m)

Caprera

Santo
Stéfano

Cala
Villamarina

Palau

> ### Getting to La Maddalena
>
> From Palau, TRIS (☎0789.708.631) and Saremar (☎0789.709.270) fer-
> ries leave every 15–30 minutes for the main island of the Maddalena arch-
> ipelago, La Maddalena (L3000 per person, L10,000 for a medium-sized
> car). Be warned that it can be a hectic bustle for tickets in high season, and
> long queues are common, so it's worth arriving half an hour early to bag a
> place. Don't pick fights with queue-jumpers: the chances are they are
> island residents who get priority rights (as well as fare discounts). It's
> much faster for pedestrians, of course; if you don't want to ferry your vehi-
> cle, leave it in the car park behind the ticket office at Palau – cars parked
> in front get fined – and campers cannot be parked at all. When the regular
> service ends at around 11.20pm, a **night service** takes over, run by
> Tremar, with departures every hour (tickets on board).
>
> There are also boat tours to the archipelago from Olbia and Santa
> Teresa di Gallura, for which see pp.271 and 299.

tion is remembered in a museum – his former home, which gives a
fascinating insight into his long career on the world stage and his
reclusive existence on the island.

La Maddalena is also the departure point for a range of boat tours to
the other isles, though there is only limited access to **Santo Stéfano**,
which is almost wholly occupied by a US naval base. The boats also call
at the remote, smaller islands of **Spargi**, **Budelli**, Razzoli and Santa
Maria. Set amid a myriad jutting rocks, they have some perfect scraps
of beach to swim from, but little else besides rock and scrub.

In 1997, the islands were granted **national park** status (extending
as far south as the islands of Martorio and Soffi in the Golfo di
Cugnana, and as far north as Lavezzi and Cavallo in Corsican
waters). The most conspicuous wildlife in evidence on the islands are
gulls, cormorants and herons, which perch on the innumerable granite rocks poking out of the sea. Even before the area was placed
under protection, the archipelago harboured a rich range of wildlife,
which was left relatively undisturbed as a result of the restrictions
imposed by the military base. In effect, the existence of the national
park limits sailing activities, fishing (on the surface and underwater)
and building. Prohibitions are tightest on the northern tip of La
Maddalena, around Caprera's eastern shore, and cover some of the
smaller islands entirely.

La Maddalena

Bearing the same name as the island, the port and sole town of **LA
MADDALENA** is a cheerful place, its regular population of about
12,000 swollen by a large number of Italian and US sailors who lend
the town a garrison feel. Their headquarters are on the eastern side
of town, a drab area of monotonous barracks guarded by armed sentries, which the recruits appear eager to leave every evening in
favour of the distractions of the town.

The Maddalena Islands

Most of the action takes place in the narrow lanes between the main square, Piazza Umberto I, and **Cala Gavetta**, a natural harbour five minutes' walk, heading left, from the ferry port. Now a marina for small boats, this was the original nucleus of the town. The main *passeggiata* takes place here, along Via Garibaldi, but there are few points of specific interest. On Via Améndola, which runs along the seafront between the port and Cala Gavetta, are a few palazzi from the period of the town's main growth in the eighteenth century. Not far from here, the modern-looking church of **Santa Maria Maddalena** contains a couple of silver candlesticks and a crucifix donated by Nelson during his sojourn in the archipelago.

On the Via Panorámica, west of the port in Localitá Mongiardino, the **Museo Archeologico Navale** (Mon–Sat; free) shows finds recovered from ancient wrecks in the area, notably a Roman cargo ship dragged up from the sea near Spargi in the 1950s. The vessel foundered around 120 BC, and the museum's prize exhibit is a reconstructed cross-section of the hull, showing how 202 of the hundreds more amphorae recovered – mostly containing wine from Campania – would have been stored for the sea passage. A second room has lead anchors and various other finds from the sea, as well as photos showing the excavation operations.

Practicalities

La Maddalena's **tourist office** is at Cala Gavetta on Piazza Baron des Geneys (Mon–Fri 8am–2pm & 4–7pm; Sat 8am–2pm, all day in summer; ☎0789.736.321). The town is not particularly well off for **hotels**, considering the volume of tourists; cheapest are the *Arcipélago* at Via Indipendenza Traversa 2 (☎0789.727.328, fax 0789.728.100; ③) – hard to find (but signposted), a fifteen-minute walk from the ferry port, with small but clean and comfortable rooms – and, in the opposite direction, the state-run *Gabbiano* beyond Cala Gavetta at Via Giulio Césare 20 (☎0789.722.507, fax 0789.722.536; ④), excellently sited on a point overlooking Santo Stéfano and Palau. Back in the centre, right on the seafront at Via Améndola 7, the *Excelsior* (☎0789.737.020, fax 0789.739.171; ⑤) enjoys views over the port but has a rather down-at-heel air. All rates drop significantly out of season.

Rooms to rent (*cámere in affito*) are marked in some windows, otherwise pick up a list of addresses from the tourist office, or ask around in bars. There are also three campsites, all outside town (see opposite).

There is an abundance of **eating places** in town, among them *La Terrazza*, just off Piazza Umberto at Via Villa Glori 6 (closed Tues in winter), where you can eat good food at reasonable prices, either inside or on a terrace. Slightly more expensive, *Sottovento* at Via Indipendenza 1 (☎0789.727.792; closed Mon) has a proud array of *antipasti* and a good choice of fresh pasta. Booking is advised in summer.

Buses run to various parts of the island every thirty minutes or one hour in summer (every two hours in winter) from near the Banco di Sardegna at the end of Via XX Settembre – incidentally, the place to **change money**, with a cash machine. The best way of getting around the island is on a **bike or moped**, which can be rented from any of the outlets on the seafront walking towards Cala Gavetta, for L15,000–25,000 a day for a mountain bike, or L35,000–60,000 a day for a scooter òr *motorino*. Fratelli Cuccu at Via Améndola 30 (☎0789.738.528) is one, Noleggio Vacanze at Via Mazzini 1 another (☎0789.735.200). You may be asked for ID or a deposit of L100,000–150,000.

Around the island

The island of La Maddalena invites aimless wandering and offers a variety of sandy and rocky beaches in mostly undeveloped coves. The **beaches** on the northern and western coasts are most attractive, particularly those around the tiny port of **Madonnetta**, 5km west of La Maddalena, and at **Cala Lunga**, 5km north of town. At **Spalmatore**, there's a small sand beach with a jetty, bar and disco. One of the nearest swimming places to town is just 2km southwest at **Punta Tegge**, where the low, flat rocks make access to the sea easy.

The only **places to stay** outside the port are in **campsites**, the two nearest of which lie beyond the barracks east of town: *Il Sole* (mid-June to Oct; ☎0789.727.727), and the better-situated *Maddalena*, in the Moneta district facing Caprera island (June–Sept; ☎0789.728.051). The best location, however, is in the north of the island, where *Abbatoggia* (June–Sept; ☎0789.739.173) lies close to some superb beaches; it also has bungalows, though these are often booked up, there's a ristorante/pizzeria on-site, and you can rent bikes, canoes and windsurf equipment.

Nelson in the Maddalena Islands

Between 1803 and 1805, the fleet of Admiral Nelson was a constant presence in what he called "Agincourt Sound", or the Straits of Bonifacio. It lurked in the waters around the Maddalena archipelago for fifteen months while Nelson stalked the French fleet in the run-up to the Battle of Trafalgar. Throughout this long wait, during which Nelson never once set foot on shore, he sent a stream of letters to the Admiralty in London urging that steps be taken to secure Sardinia – then the only neutral shore in this part of the Mediterranean – for England: "And I venture to predict, that if we do not – from delicacy, or commiseration of the lot of the unfortunate King of Sardinia – the French will." The French, docked at Toulon (nicknamed "Too-Long" by Nelson's impatient sailors), eventually fled to the West Indies before returning to meet Nelson at Trafalgar.

Caprera

A simple bridge built in 1891 stretches for 600m across the **Passo di Moneta** that separates La Maddalena from **Caprera**. Between October and May, half of Caprera is closed off for military purposes, but there is always plenty of space left to roam this protected woody parkland, which is undeveloped apart from Garibaldi's house in the centre and a couple of self-contained tourist complexes, one of them a *Club Med*.

Giuseppe Garibaldi (see box) came to live on Caprera in 1855, after a glorious and highly eventful career in arms, much of it spent in exile from Italy. It was from here that he embarked on his spectacular conquest of Sicily and Naples in 1861, accompanied by his thousand Redshirts, and it was here that he returned after his campaigns to resume a simple farming life. Having first seen the island

---

Giuseppe Garibaldi (1807–82)

The most famous Italian patriot of all, **Giuseppe Garibaldi** was born in Nice of a family of fishermen and coastal traders, and for more than ten years was himself a sailor. By the age of 26 he had served in the navy of the Kingdom of Piedmont-Sardinia, and had aborbed the influence of both Giuseppe Mazzini, the great prophet of Italian nationalism, and the French Socialist thinker, the Comte de Saint-Simon. In 1834, having taken part in a failed mutiny, he was condemned to death by a court in Genoa, but managed to escape, first to France then to South America, where he lived until 1848.

These years in exile formed his education as a guerrilla warrior and wily strategist. Enlisted as a naval captain by a small republic attempting to break free from the Brazilian Empire, Garibaldi later tried his hand as a cowboy, commercial traveller and teacher, but was sucked back into the swashbuckling life when he was put in charge of the Uruguayan navy in another liberation war in 1842. The following year, he took command of a newly formed Italian Legion at Montevideo, the first of the famous "Redshirts" with whom his name was to be permanently linked, and in April 1848 led 60 of them back to Italy to fight for the Risorgimento – Italy's war of independence against the Austrians, French and Spanish. After his services were rejected by both Pope Pius IX and the Piedmontese king Carlo Alberto, Garibaldi went to Milan, where Mazzini had already established himself, and quickly won two engagements against the Austrians before withdrawing across the Swiss frontier. Garibaldi next led a group of volunteers to Rome, from which the pope had recently been expelled, and was elected deputy in the Roman Assembly in February 1849. Taking charge of the defence of the city, he managed to repulse an attack by a French army attempting to restore papal government, and defeat a Neapolitan army soon after. His spirited defence of Rome against an ensuing and ultimately unsuccessful French siege was to became one of the most glorious episodes of the Risorgimento.

Although now renowned internationally as the hero *dei due mondi* ("of the two worlds"), Garibaldi was both envied and feared by the leaders of the Risorgimento in Italy, who saw him as something of a loose cannon,

---

on his flight from Rome in 1849, he subsequently bought the northern part of it for £360, no doubt attracted by its proximity to the Piedmontese naval base. While he lived on Caprera, he devoted his time to writing his memoirs and a handful of bad novels, as well as farming. His neighbour was an Englishman named Collins, with whom he had some celebrated disagreements concerning their wandering goatherds, as a result of which Garibaldi built a wall dividing their properties, which can still be seen. After Collins's death in 1864 a group of English admirers provided the money for Garibaldi to buy the rest of Caprera from his ex-neighbour's family.

At the end of a tamarisk-lined road, the **museum** (daily 9am–1.30pm; L4000) is in Garibaldi's old house, the elegant South American-style **Casa Bianca**, which has been preserved pretty much as he left it. Visitors are escorted past a collection of memorabilia

---

and he once more found himself in exile. After time spent in Tangier, New York and Peru, where he returned to his original trade as a ship's captain, he was allowed to return to Italy in 1854, and the following year he bought part of the Sardinian island of Caprera, which remained his home for the rest of his life.

His career was by no means over, however, and he took up arms again in 1859, when he helped to bring about Piedmont's liberation of Lombardy, and in May 1860, when he set out on the greatest venture of his life, which was to result in the conquest of Sicily and Naples. For this brilliant escapade, he lacked all government support, and when the new kingdom of Italy finally came into being in 1861, Garibaldi was in virtually permanent opposition – he had already been infuriated when, the previous year, his home town of Nice was returned to France (it had become Piedmontese in 1814). At least he had his now legendary fame to fall back on, which led to his being offered a command in the American Civil War by Lincoln, and to his rapturous reception when he came to England in 1864.

Though Garibaldi's military career continued apace, including campaigns in Italy in 1862, 1866, 1867 and 1870–71, he eventually became something of a recluse on Caprera. He still kept abreast of affairs, however, receiving numerous deputations and making regular pronouncements on issues of the day. Towards the end he called himself a Socialist (though Karl Marx disowned him) and even a pacifist, and also proved to be a champion of labour rights and women's emancipation. He showed himself ahead of his time in espousing such unpopular beliefs as racial equality and the abolition of capital punishment, though he also believed in dictatorship, distrusting parliaments which he saw as nests of corruption.

Opinion in Italy is still sharply divided between those who dismiss Garibaldi as an amateur and meddling charlatan, and others who adore him. Indisputably, he deserves his place in history if only as a pioneer of unorthodox guerrilla tactics and for his ability to inspire reckless loyalty. He certainly succeeded better than any of his contemporaries in rousing the Italian people, by whom he is remembered as a professional rebel and indomitable individualist who refused to retire gracefully, continuing to wear his gaucho costume until he died.

which include the famous *camicia rossa* (red shirt) with which he was iconized, the bed where he slept, a smaller one where he died, various scrolls, manifestos and pronouncements, a pair of ivory-and-gold binoculars given to him by the future King Edward VII, and a letter from London, dated 1867, conferring on him honorary presidency of the National Reform League. A stopped clock and a wall calendar indicate the precise time and date of his death.

The tour ends with Garibaldi's grave in the garden, its rough granite contrasting with the more pompous tombs of his last wife and five of his children. Garibaldi had requested to be cremated, but following the wishes of his son Menotti, his corpse was stuffed. In 1932, fifty years after his death, his tomb was opened to reveal the body perfectly intact.

Elsewhere on the island, you can strike out in any direction to reach tranquil spots that are a welcome relief after the bustle of coach parties around Garibaldi's museum. Caprera's flora and fauna are among the most interesting of the islands, especially during spring when the heather, hawthorn and juniper present a multi-coloured mosaic amid the pines, holm oaks and myrtles, and the birdlife includes royal seagulls, shearwaters, sparrow hawks and buzzards. There are several small beaches around the shore, the most popular being **Cala Coticcio**, on the island's east coast (about a forty-minute walk from the bridge, less from the museum). There are also a handful of fortifications dotted around, some built by the Savoy régime in the eighteenth century, and some from around the time of World War I. You can also climb a long stairway leading to the lookout tower on **Teialone**, at 212m the highest point of the islands.

Santo Stéfano, Spargi and Budelli

Halfway between La Maddalena and the coast, the island of **Santo Stéfano** was briefly captured by French forces in 1793 in an abortive attempt to take possession of Sardinia. From here, the young Napoleon Bonaparte, then a Lieutenant-Colonel in the Corsican National Guard, commanded a bombardment of La Maddalena. The island today is mainly occupied by US and Italian military installations, including a nuclear submarine base. The archipelago has always had a strong naval tradition, harbouring a fleet of the Royal House of Savoy long before NATO arrived, and from a boat tour you can spot traces of the fortifications erected here at the end of the eighteenth century. Trippers can disembark on the eastern side of the island, around the **Spiaggia del Pesce** beach, where there are a couple of holiday enclaves. Traces of Neolithic life have been found at **Cala Villamarina**.

The best beach on **Spargi** is on the southern littoral at **Cala Corsara**, with transparent water – though as it's a regular stop for boat tours, it's not exactly untrammelled. Nearby was found the wreck of a Roman vessel from the second century BC, now preserved in La Maddalena's marine museum (see p.290).

On **Budelli** the famous *spiaggia rosa* ("pink beach"), immortalized by the director Michelangelo Antonioni in his film *Il Deserto Rosso* (*Red Desert*, 1965), is also a boat-stop, while the limpid waters around the island draw scuba-divers.

Santa Teresa di Gallura and around

On Sardinia's northern tip, the small town of **Santa Teresa di Gallura** is the main port for ships to Corsica, whose cliffs are clearly visible just 11km away. Not all the people who come here are passing through, however. If beaches are your thing, Santa Teresa must rank as one of the island's most attractive holiday destinations, surrounded by scintillating stretches of sand, with exhilarating views across the Straits of Bonifacio. To cope with the demand, the town has Gallura's widest selection of hotels and restaurants, though few of these stay open outside the summer months, when life grinds to a much slower and duller pace.

Outside Santa Teresa, a local minibus service transports tourists to the beaches on either side of town: to the east, beyond Punta Falcone to **La Marmorata**, and westwards to **Capo Testa**. Buses bound for Castelsardo make stops at the more distant beaches of **Rena Maiore**, **Vignola** and **Ísola Rossa**, on Sardinia's long northwestern littoral. Catch any bus going towards Palau to reach **Porto Pozzo**, presently a small-scale resort, though clearly destined for greater things.

Santa Teresa di Gallura

SANTA TERESA DI GALLURA, Sardinia's most northerly town, is the main embarkation point for Corsica, as well as being one of Sardinia's most full-on holiday resorts in its own right. Though there was a Roman settlement in the region, and fortifications used at different times by the Aragonese and Genoans, the town has a recent history, founded in 1808 by order of the Savoyard King Vittorio Emanuele I, and named after his wife Maria Teresa of Austria. Apart from a Spanish watchtower, however, few buildings of the town date even as far back as the nineteenth century, and it owes its prevailing tone to its development in the late 1950s as a holiday base. In recent years, the growth of Santa Teresa's marina and the swelling pockets of holiday homes on the eastern side of the Longone creek threaten to overwhelm the town and its surrounding area.

Santa Teresa is arranged on a regular grid of modern streets, centring on the main Piazza Vittorio Emanuele, site of the tourist office (see p.296) and a bunch of bars and coral shops. Beyond the square, the Via del Mare ends after a couple of hundred metres at a high bluff dominated by the **Torre Aragonese**, a well-preserved Spanish watch-tower from the sixteenth century, officially known as the Torre di Longosardo (open in summer). There are sweeping views from here over the Straits of Bonifacio, and nearer at hand the minuscule isle of Monica (or Municca). To the east can be seen the burgeoning belt of new developments on the far side of the deep inlet of Longone or Longosardo. A panoramic path leads beyond the tower and down to the waterside, and there are also steps leading west of the tower to the town's main beach, **Spiaggia Rena Bianca**, the focus of most of the fun in the tourist season.

The marina and port area lie out of sight further down the Longone creek, and are best reached from Via del Porto. The kiosks selling tickets for Corsica and the various boat tours are located here, while the capacious marina – also the subject of a continuing programme of expansion – is jammed with yachts and blue and white fishing vessels.

Practicalities

ARST and FdS **buses** arrive and depart from Via Eleonora d'Arborea off Via Nazionale, the main road into town. This is also the terminus for the blue Sardabus **shuttle buses** for beaches in the vicinity (tickets on board). For longer routes, tickets and timetables are available from *Baby Bar* on Via Lu Pultali, just round the corner from the bus stop and from Via Nazionale (closed Tues, when you can buy tickets on board).

Pick up a map of the town and surrounding area, and accommodation listings, from Santa Teresa's **tourist office** on the main Piazza Vittorio Emanuele 24 (June–Sept daily 8.30am–1pm & 3.30–8pm; Oct–May Mon–Fri 9am–1pm & 3.30–6.30pm, Sat 9am–1pm; ☎0789.754.127); there is also a summer-only booth down by the port (usually open June–Sept daily 9.15am–1.15pm & 3.20–8.30pm).

Accommodation

As Sardinia's most northerly port and the main crossing point for ferries to Corsica, Santa Teresa di Gallura has a plentiful collection of central **hotels**, and several more outside town where they are best-placed to take advantage of some of Sardinia's most alluring beaches. Many places close over the winter months, while vacancies can be difficult to come by in summer, particularly in August when groups from the mainland descend on Santa Teresa. The nearest campsite lies 6km west of town beyond Capo Testa (see p.301). See Listings, or ask at the tourist office about **weekly rents** in apartments in and around town.

Hotels

Bellavista, Via Sonnino 8 (☎ & fax 0789.754.162). Considering this hotel's prime position above Rena Bianca beach, you'll find excellent rates for the 16 comfortable doubles, though these are often booked up months in advance. Rooms with balconies and views go first, of course. Open May–Oct. ②.

Canne al Vento, Via Nazionale 23 (☎0789.754.219, fax 0789.754.948). Tastefully decorated family-run hotel on the main road into town. It's quiet enough, provided you ask for a room at the back. The hotel has attracted such stars as Antonioni in the past, and the restaurant is renowned (see Restaurants, below). Open Easter–Sept. ③.

Da Cecco, Via Po 3 (☎0789.754.220, fax 0789.755.634). Superb value in this handsome palazzo above the port, with 36 comfortable rooms. Often closed in winter. ③.

Corallaro, Rena Bianca (☎0789.755.475, fax 0789.755.431). Santa Teresa's classiest hotel, just back from the beach and enjoying superb views over to the Corsican coast from its rooms and terraces. There's a minimum stay of three days, or a week in peak season, and there's a half- or full board requirement in August. Prices drop into category ④ if you come in April–June or September. Open April to mid-Oct. ⑦.

Marinaro, Via Angioy 48 (☎0789.754.112, fax 0789.755.817). In a quiet spot in the centre of town, this solid, old-fashioned building contains a modern, well-designed hotel, smartly painted in cheerful blue and yellow stripes. Rooms on two floors are a good size, fully-equipped. In August guests must take at least half-board, which comes to L125,000 each. ④.

Miramare, Piazza della Libertà (☎0789.754.103, fax 0789.754.675). Occupies Santa Teresa's prime scenic location, for which it commands premium rates, though there are cheaper, simpler rooms in the ground-floor annexe, with shared bathrooms. Open May–Sept. ④.

Moderno, Via Umberto 39 (☎ & fax 0789.754.233). A small, useful lodging halfway between the bus stop and the main Piazza Vittorio Emanuele. Polite management and plain rooms all with bath. Half-board required in July and Aug, when most rooms are booked months ahead. ②.

Sa Domo, Via Genova 18 (☎0789.756.564, fax 0789.754.082). Family-run and family-based hotel in the centre of town, with huge terraces on the second floor. There's a pool, and music, cabaret and children's events are staged nightly in summer, with excursions available by day. ③.

Sandalion, Via Valle d'Aosta (☎0789.754.541, fax 0789.755.406). One of Santa Teresa's cheaper options, plain and clean. Try to bag one of the rooms with a balcony. Open April–Sept. ③.

Scano, Via Lazio 4 (☎0789.754.447). A good, cheap two-star on the west side of town, with relaxed family management and a reasonable restaurant. Basic rooms with and without private bath, often booked up early. ②.

Smeraldo, Via XX Settembre 23 (☎0789.754.175, fax 0789.755.795). Small hotel with only twelve rooms, but centrally located just up from Piazza Vittorio Emanuele, close to the main beach. Street noise can be a problem. There's a restaurant, but no half-board requirement. ④.

Bars and restaurants

Santa Teresa's intense **bar life** is steamy, loud and fun in summer but melts away without trace in the winter months. Recommended stops on or off the main Piazza Vittorio Emanuele include *Bar Conti* at Via Regina Margherita 2 (closed Wed), *Central Bar 80*, which serves *panini* and ice creams, on the corner of the square, and the *Groove Café* on Via XX Settembre, a bar and *paninoteca* with music and an upper floor that stays open late (closed Sun).

The town also has an abundant choice of **restaurants** – again, many of them boarded up after October. For a good, unpretentious meal west of the centre, try *Due Palmi*, a pizzeria/trattoria at Via Capo Testa (closed Thurs in winter). On the corner of Via del Porto, at Via Angioy 59, the *Stella Marina* (closed Tues in winter) is touristy, with a veranda and photos on the walls, but offers some good Sard dishes, and you can sample goat's-milk liqueur from Berchidda. On Via del Porto, *Ristorante Riva* (☎0789.754.392, closed Wed in winter) is a posher restaurant for good fish meals; first courses weight in at around L15,000, seconds for L25,000–30,000. Less snooty but no less elegant, the *Canne al Vento* at Via Nazionale 23 (see Hotels, on p.297), offers seafood cooked in all kinds of ways, and authentic local cuisine such as *suppa cuata* (bread, cheese, and tomato soup, L16,000) and *porcheddu* (roast suckling pig, L18,000). Closer to the sea on Via del Mare, try *La Torre*, a bar-restaurant below the *Miramare* hotel and above the main beach, while the *Tropican* ristorante/pizzeria sits right on the beach in front of the *Corallaro* hotel; for the best **pizzas**, however, head for *Pape Satan*, at Via Lamármora 20. All three places get pretty crowded in high summer, and are closed in winter.

Entertainment

If you feel like a dance, the biggest local **disco** is *Éstasi* (☎0789.755.570), a turn-off on the right two or three kilometres out of town near the church of Buoncammino. It's open-air and removed from other buildings, so your best bet is to follow your ears. More sedate entertainment is provided by the **open-air cinema** on Via Capo Testa, nightly in July and August. Other diversions are never far away in summer, for example a **sagra del pesce**, or fish festival, with samplings, during the second week of July; a **sailing regatta** between Corsica and Sardinia at the end of July, and a religious procession for the Assumption on August 15. Windsurfing championships are also held in the Straits most years.

Sailings from Santa Teresa di Gallura

Moby Lines (☎0789.751.449) and Saremar (☎0789.754.788) operate sailings from Santa Teresa di Gallura to Bonifacio in Corsica (6–22 daily). The crossing takes 50min, single ticket for foot-passengers is L14,000 rising to L18,000 in peak periods, while medium-size cars cost L40,000–60,000. Motorbikes cost L15,000–19,000, push-bikes L6000. Note that passengers disembarking at Bonifacio must pay a landing fee of L4000.

Look out for special discounts for booking specified return dates or for car/passenger packages.

For boat tours, see Listings, opposite.

Listings

ACI Via Genova 4 (☎0789.754.077).

Apartments IST Immobiliare, Via Maria Teresa 15 (☎0789.755.755), and GULP, Via Nazionale 58 (☎0789.755.689), have apartments in town, or at Marmorata and Rena Maiore. The weekly tariff for a two-bed apartment in town ranges from L290,000 in May and June to L1,130,000 in August.

Bank Banco di Sássari in Piazza Vittorio Emanuele, open Mon–Fri 8.20am–1.20pm & 2.30–3.30pm, Sat 8.20–11.20am; has cash dispenser. Banco di Sardegna on Via Nazionale has similar hours. Global Information (see Bike hire) also changes money, open daily in summer 8.30am–1pm & 4–8pm.

Bike rental Global Information on Via Maria Teresa (☎0789.755.080) has mountain bikes (L10,000 per day), mopeds (L25,000) and scooters (up to L50,000) for rent.

Boat hire Contact Lo Squalo Bianco at Spiaggia Rena Bianca (☎0789.750.113) for motorboats, canoes and pedalos.

Boat tours Tours around the coasts and to the islands can be booked at Consorzio delle Bocche, at Piazza Vittorio Emanuele 16 (☎0789.755.850), or ask at booths at the port. The 9.30am departure takes in the western isles of the Maddalena archipelago, including a stop at Santa Maria and Spargi, and a lunch on board, with a return at 5pm, all for L60,000 per person.

Car rental Happy Car, Piazza Villamarina (☎0789.754.741); Sardinia Car, Via Maria Teresa (☎0789.754.2477). The agent for Maggiore-Budget is the Viaggi Sardorama travel agent (see below), and for Hertz the agent is Gulp (see Apartments, above).

Post office Via Eleonora d'Arborea, on the corner of the square where the buses come in, open Mon–Fri 8.10am–1.15pm, Sat 8.05am–12.45pm. Cash and American Express travellers' cheques are changed here.

Taxis Offices on Via Cavour (☎0789.754.286) and by the port (☎0789.755.000). Also try ☎0789.754.422, 0368.554.220, or the 24-hour Mercedes service at 0330.926.741. The run to Olbia airport is priced at around L100,000.

Travel agent Viaggi Sardorama on Via Tíbula (☎0789.754.464 or 0335.611.0501, fax 0789.755.550) can arrange air, sea and rail tickets, as well as excursions in the area and beyond. Also rents cars.

East out of Santa Teresa

Some of Sardinia's most alluring **beaches** lie only a short ride out of Santa Teresa, all with superb views over to Corsica. To reach them from town, turn off at the signposts on the main Via Nazionale, otherwise by-pass the town to get to places to the west, while places east are best reached from the S133bis from Palau.

East of Santa Teresa, **Punta Falcone** is the Sardinian mainland's most northerly point, sheltering a grand beach at **La Marmorata**, an exquisite spot marred by the proximity of vast villa complexes. The swimming, though, is fabulous, with the serrated profile of the Ísola di Marmorata out to sea. The next beach down, **Marazzino**, is reached from the same turn-off from the SS133bis (and both have capacious parking areas). **La Licciola**

*Swimmers,
sailors and
windsurfers
should all
beware of the
strong cur-
rents coursing
through the
Straits of
Bonifacio, par-
ticularly
around the
northernmost
cape of Punta
Falcone.*

also has a scattering of holiday houses, though not enough to overwhelm this small beach.

Porto Pozzo is a small beach and fishing locality about 15km east of Santa Teresa, at the edge of the deepest of the inlets hereabouts, also called Porto Pozzo. Presently this is little more than a bar and a few houses, though things liven up considerably in the season, when you can eat at the beach-side trattoria, and consult the **information office** on the main Via Nazionale (open summer only).

If you want to spend any time in Porto Pozzo, there's a handful of **hotels** on Via Aldo Moro, including the basic *Locanda Porto Pozzo* (☎0789.752.124; ②), opposite the road to the beach, which also leads to the *Arcobaleno* **campsite** (May–Sept; ☎0789.752.040), right next to the sea. **Boat trips** to the islands of Spargi, Budelli and Santa Maria leave from the quay here.

West out of Santa Teresa

Three kilometres west of Santa Teresa, **Capo Testa** is one of Sardinia's finest bathing localities, a rocky promontory at the end of a narrow isthmus, surrounded by turquoise sea. It's extremely popular in summer, though it makes an excellent destination outside the peak months, and has a handful of hotels worth considering as alternatives to staying in town, all open in summer only. The headland has some scraps of sandy beach and even some paltry remains of a Roman settlement called Tibula – truncated granite columns and some fragments of stone by the waterside. Material from the nearby quarries was used both for the columns of the Pantheon in Rome and for Pisa's cathedral. Beyond, standing amid a clutter of surreal, wind-chiselled rock formations, a lighthouse endlessly casts its beam from the point.

Take your pick of the **beaches** on Capo Testa, facing Corsica on one side, the northern Sardinian coast sloping away westward on the other. The most popular ones are the **Spiaggia dei Due Mari** – arrayed on either side of the isthmus, facing north and south – and those actually on Capo Testa, such as **Spiaggia Rosa**. The **Spiaggia Levante** (also called Baia Santa Reparata) on the north side, and **Spiaggia Ponente** (or Cala La Colba) on the south, are the places to rent surfboards and other craft, or enrol in a diving or sailing course.

If you want to go farther afield, there are more beaches and plenty of privacy behind the thick pinewoods flanking the SS200 coastal road south and west. First and best of these is **Rena Maiore** near the tourist village of the same name, and **Vignola**, about 20km west of Capo Testa, signposted off the SS200. The locality is named after the vineyards which produce the region's best wine, Vermentino di Gallura. South of here, the road tracks inland, away from the sea, where a sequence of holiday villa developments lies tucked out of sight at the end of private roads. In fact the coast in these parts is in the process of being privatized, and, following the

example of the Costa Smeralda, has been dubbed **Costa Paradiso**.
There are indeed some heavenly spots here, but be prepared to
backtrack when you reach a barrier across the road with lavish villas on the other side.

Access is easier to the rather mundane tourist village of Ísola
Rossa, reached along a five-kilometre road cutting off right from the
SS200. The site, however, is impressive, on a promontory opposite
the reddish island after which the resort is named. Overlooked by a
stout sixteenth-century watchtower, the indented, cliffy coast here
shelters some small patches of beach among the coves, and there is
a much longer one to the south, with views over to Castelsardo,
30km southwest (see p.247).

Practicalities

The best **hotel** in the Capo Testa area is *Bocche di Bonifacio*
(☎0789.754.202; ③), where you can stay comfortably and cheaply
in clean rooms just a few metres above the sands. Four **apartments**
are also available (to rent by the month only in Aug), and there's also
a wonderful **restaurant** with cheap Sard specialities. Other hotels
here include the much grander *Capo Testa e dei Due Mari* (May to
mid-Oct; ☎0789.754.333, fax 0789.754.482; ⑤), and the appropriately named *Large Hotel Mirage* (June–Sept; ☎0789.754.207, fax
0789.755.518; ④–⑤).

The nearest **campsite** is a couple of kilometres west of Capo
Testa, signposted off the Castelsardo road: *La Liccia* (open mid-May
to Sept; ☎ & fax 0789.755.190), spreading out on a shady elevation
about 400m from the beach. Bungalows are available, costing
L45,000–90,000 for two people.

Buses run to Capo Testa four times daily mid-June to mid-
September, tickets on board cost L1700, or L3200 return. The ride
takes 30 minutes; the last bus back goes at 5.30pm. Other buses
towards Castelsardo can drop you at or near the beaches at Rena
Maiore, Vignola and Ísola Rossa.

Inland Gallura

Although most people are content to admire from afar the dramatic
mountainscape backing onto Gallura's coast, you can't fail to be
intrigued by the spiky pinnacles lying just a short way inland, where
the small towns and villages retain far more of the authentic Galluran
atmosphere than any of the region's coastal resorts. The chief town
in these parts, **Tempio Pausánia**, has a serene dignity lacking on the
coast, and makes a good base for refreshing excursions, with most of
the region's hotels and a great choice of restaurants. The obvious
destination for excursions is nearby **Monte Limbara**, Gallura's highest peak, with glorious views extending in all directions. Southwest
of Limbara, one of Sardinia's many artifical lakes, **Lago Coghinas**,

also makes a great area to hike around, and the nearby village of **Berchidda** provides handy accommodation.

Where the country is not bare and arid, it is covered with a thick mantle of holm oak and cork oak forest, the latter providing the area's main industry. In September and October you are sure to notice lorry-loads of the silver and red bark being transported to processing plants in Olbia and Arbatax, and you can see at all times the lower trunks stripped to their rust-red stems. The main centre for cork-processing is **Calangianus**, a good place to purchase cork products to take home, and close to the village of **Luras**, site of some intriguing prehistoric dolmens. North of here, another lake, **Lago di Liscia**, stands close to a magnificent forest of centuries-old wild olive trees. West of Tempio, **Aggius** is famous for its carpets, and lies close to an extraordinary area of knobbly, rock-strewn slopes.

Come in winter and you'll find the peaks snow-clad, while spring is the best time to appreciate the *macchia*-covered lower slopes, woven with cistus, gorse, juniper, heather, myrtle and a hundred other wild species, pungent with diverse herbal scents. Before leaving, take away with you a jar of the famous bitter honey produced in these parts and for sale in the local shops: you'll probably already have tasted it poured over *sebadas*.

This is one of the few areas in Sardinia where you will see isolated farmsteads, or *stazzi*, originally founded by settlers from Corsica fleeing the strife on that island in the eighteenth century – and the inhabitants of Gallura still have a reputation for the touchy sense of honour and vengeance for which Corsicans are famous.

The area is best reached either from the SS199 running between Olbia and Sássari, or the roads climbing inland from Arzachena, Palau and Vignola. Those without their own transport could make use of the narrow-gauge **railway** that stoically burrows through the region, stopping at Tempio Pausánia, Calangianus and Arzachena on its long, tortuous route from Palau. Beware, though – some of the stations are located in quite remote areas.

Tempio Pausánia and around

"Capital" of Gallura since the Romans established camps here to control the inland tracts of the region, Tempio Pausánia has all the slow-moving solidity of a typical mountain town, conserving an appearance of calm well-being. The town had a greater profile in the eighteenth and nineteenth centuries, when it was the administrative centre of the Gallura region, benefitting also from the presence of therapeutic mineral waters. Though the springs remain, most of the commercial and bureaucratic activity has shifted to the coast in general, and to Olbia in particular. This at least has saved Tempio from the unplanned construction that has blighted much of Olbia since the 1960s, and the present-day town has a homogeneous appearance, its uniform granite-grey centre a pleasant place for a wander, if oddly lacking much of specific architectural interest.

Lowlanders from Olbia and around frequent the resort in the summer, relishing the superb climate which has always kept the area malaria-free. As you might expect at a height of 566m, the air here is crisp and fresh, and long views stretch out on every side, most dramatically towards the region's highest mountain, Monte Limbara (see p.304).

At the centre of town, Tempio's **Municipio** dominates Piazza Gallura, behind which Via Roma leads to the **Cattedrale** in Piazza San Pietro (daily 7am–noon & 3.30–6.30pm). This was originally a fifteenth-century Romanesque construction, though its present appearance owes so much to a drastic nineteenth-century restoration that only the carved wooden portal and belltower are completely original. The interior is now mostly Baroque in appearance, devoid of much interest, though the third and fourth chapels on the left have good wooden altars from the eighteenth century. Opposite the cathedral, the **Oratorio del Rosario** from the same period has an austere but elegant front, mixing Baroque and late-Romanesque motifs. Inside there is another wooden altarpiece, this time decorated with pure gold.

If you are having a meal in Tempio, make sure you sample a glass of the local Vermentino, a strong, dry white wine drunk as an aperitif or with desserts.

Out of town, there are some worthwhile excursions, best made with your own transport. You could walk, though, to the nearest, the **Fonti Rinaggiu**, a wooded spot a couple of kilometres away (follow signs, *Alle Terme*, up Via San Lorenzo from Largo de Gásperi). The waters are prized for their diuretic qualities, and the spring is usually crowded with folk filling up flagons of the stuff. A more compelling sight could also be visited on foot from the centre, 2km north on the Palau road (SS133), where **Nuraghe Maiori** lies signposted off to the right along a dirt road. Surrounded by cork woods, the nuragh has one round room on the right as you enter, another on the left, with a corridor giving access to the main chamber. From here, steps wind up to a parapet, from which there's a wonderful view of Gallura's jagged peaks, also embracing Tempio and Aggius as well as miles of fields and vineyards.

Practicalities

Tempio's **train station** for the summer service to Arzachena and Palau is just west of the centre. ARST **buses** stop here and at two other stops in town. The **tourist office**, on Piazza Gallura (Mon–Fri 9.30am–1pm & 4–7pm or 4.30–7.30pm in summer, Sat 9.30am–1pm; ☎079.631.273), sells bus tickets, and can also point you towards the town's three **hotels**: most central is the *Petit*, at Piazza De Gásperi 9 (☎079.631.134, fax 079.631.760; ⑤), a slick, modern business folks' lodge, whose restaurant has fine views; a kilometre's walk uphill from here, right by the Fonti Rinaggiu, the *Delle Sorgenti* at Via delle Fonti 6 (☎079.630.033, fax 079.671.516; ③)

Tempio's Carnival

Tempio's week-long **Carnevale** celebrations have grown hugely in recent years to become one of Sardinia's principal festivities. The pagan element is strong, featuring parades of outlandish allegorical floats, and the high points include the symbolic marriage of two puppets, Re Giorgo (King George, a sort of Carnival King) and the peasant girl Mennena, on Carnival Sunday, followed by a distribution of corn fritters (*fritelle*); on Shrove Tuesday King George is burned in a ceremonial bonfire.

has a certain run-down character and another rivetting vista, this time from the edge of town; cheapest and remotest is the *Carmà*, east of town off the Olbia road at Via Fosse Ardeatine 14 (☎079.670.685, fax 079.670.800; ②). All three places have restaurants.

In Piazza Gallura, the Banco di Napoli (8.20am–1.20pm & 2.35–3.35pm) can **change money** and has a cash machine. You can **rent cars** from New Car at Viale Don Sturzo 4 (☎079.634.111).

Piazza Gallura has a supermarket where you can stock up with provisions, or you can eat at a good range of **restaurants**. At Via Garibaldi 9, behind the church in Piazza Purgatorio, *Ristorante Il Purgatorio* (closed Mon) is old-fashioned but quite smart and has set-price menus for L12,000 and L16,000, ideal for lunch; in the evenings you can have roast rabbit (*sella di coniglio*) for L14,000, and duck (*ánatra arrosto*) for L18,000. *Il Giardino* (closed Wed) is a pizzeria/ristorante from 1926 at Via Cavour 1, with an open-air veranda; wild boar is one of the specialities. Off Corso Matteotti at Via Piave 4, *Trattoria Gallurese* serves typical local items such as soup (*zuppa gallurese*), pasta with beans (*pasta e fagioli*), and lamb (*scottaditos di agnello*). *Il Fagotto* on Piazza Italia has good take-away **pizzas**.

In the evenings, you can repair to a cosy Irish **pub**, the *Sporting*, on Piazza Don Minzoni 12, which serves *panini* and *piadine* (unleavened bread with mozzarella and tomato) and has occasional live music at weekends. *Millennium*, about 3km outside town on Via Panorámica, has live music on Friday and Saturday in winter; entry is usually free. It's an unusual, octagonal building with a *birreria* below and dance floor upstairs, plus outstanding 180-degree views over the encircling mountains.

Monte Limbara and around

Though not huge by Italian standards, the **Monte Limbara** massif stands shoulders above the rest of Gallura. You can drive to this thickly wooded peak by car by taking a left turn off the main road south to Óschiri after about 8km (signposted). You could park your vehicle here and walk, or else drive up along a narrow road that twists up the pine-clad flanks of the mountain. The road climbs for a long way, affording fantastic views all around, then follows a ridge before reaching the forest of RAI-TV antennas. Near here is a Punto Panorámico where there is a statue of the Madonna and Child, festooned with charms and bracelets, an odd miscellany of personal mementoes, lighters, hair-grips, even strips of gum, donated by the faithful. Nearby, the plain **Chiesa di Santa Madonna della Neve** stands at the site of a spring.

The road passes within a few hundred metres of the highest summit, **Punta Balestrieri** (1359m). There are bracing views, of course, even as far as Tavolara island, and several of the curious contorted rocks that are such a feature of the area. There's an endless choice of paths and tracks to explore around here; the tourist office in Tempio Pausánia can supply you with a very rough map of routes. If you want to take part in a **guided excursion**, contact *Cammina Limbara* in Tempio (☎079.670.704), which charges around L20,000 for its frequent excursions. The peaks of this massif have become the haunt of hiking enthusiasts in recent years, and have also become popular with free climbers.

Lago di Coghinas

The Óschiri road continues south, descending from **Passo della Limbara** (640m); it's a lovely ride through cork forests and *macchia*, the road usually empty but for flocks of sheep. At the bottom of the valley, **Lago di Coghinas** swings into view. Dammed in 1926 to provide a reservoir and hydro-electric power, the artificial lake has a beautiful shore, alternately rocky and sandy, that makes a good picnic spot. Just before the road crosses a bridge over the lake, a lane on the left leads a few hundred metres to *Villa del Lago Coghinas* (☎079.734.231), where you can rent mountain bikes, go riding, and stay in the **agriturismo** here: clean rooms go for about L60,000 per person for bed, evening meal and breakfast.

The FdS **bus** between Tempio and Ozieri makes a stop at the lake, and FS **trains** between Olbia and Ozieri-Chilivani also make a stop at the village of Óschiri, just three of four kilometres east of the lake. Between the lake and Óschiri, the scanty ruins of a medieval castle and church, as well as a Roman fort and nuraghe, all lie close to each other.

Berchidda

East of the lake, just off the main SS199, **BERCHIDDA** is an important producer of Vermentino wine – one of Sardinia's most renowned whites – as well as of pecorino cheese and an intriguing goat's-milk liqueur. It's not a particularly attractive village, though it's the starting point for expeditions to Limbara and around. An easy ramble from the village follows a track leading 4km west to the **Castello di Monte Acuto**, a desolate ruin once the home of Ubaldo Visconti and later an outpost of the Doria and Malaspina families. The walls are mostly rubble now, but it makes an exhilarating ascent, and you can continue for another four or five kilometres along the path to the shores of Lago Coghinas.

There are two reasonably-priced **hotels** in Berchidda if you're looking for a place to stay in the area: *Sos Chelvos*, Via Umberto 52 (☎079.704.935; fax 079.704.921; ②), and the slightly more expensive *Nuovo Limbara*, Via Coghinas (☎079.704.165; fax 079.705.030; ②), both with en-suite bathrooms and restaurants.

Aggius

Ten kilometres west of Tempio, **AGGIUS** is another popular highland retreat, enlivened by its colour-washed granite houses with wrought-iron balconies. The village, which occupies a superb panoramic position, boasts a strong choral tradition, its choir having taken part in the Welsh Eisteddfod. The village is also known for its woven carpets, produced using traditional methods, which you can view between July and September, usually in the Pro Loco on Via Andrea Vasa (☎079.620.803). Cork and granite constitute the foundations of the local economy, helping to account for the well-to-do appearance of the solid-looking houses.

On the first Sunday of October, the **Festa di li 'Agghiani** ("Bachelors' Feast") takes over the village. Traditionally an opportunity for the young folk to meet and make merry, it's now mainly an excuse for the locals to consume a lot of *suppa cuata*, the favourite Gallurese soup dish.

Leaving Aggius northward, a left turn toward Ísola Rossa soon brings you to a wilderness of rocky debris, dubbed **La Valle della Luna**. In this "lunar valley", boulders are strewn across an arena-like hillside, looking – in the words of the travel writer Virginia Waite – "as though a giant has pettishly emptied his playbox of rocks and thrown them carelessly about". Many have been carted away by illegal quarriers, though plenty remain, including some said to resemble human figures – one on the left of the road is said to recall Plato's head. Where the road curves to the left, take a rough track on the right for a few metres to reach the **Nuraghe Izzana**.

A Sardinian Vendetta

In the annals of Aggius's past, the area was the hiding place of a sinister character known as *Il Muto di Gallura* – the mute of Gallura, the last scion of a family locked in a long and deadly nineteenth-century vendetta that claimed 72 lives and left only six survivors. The mute carried on the feud from this lonely eyrie, from which he descended only to polish off his enemies. He ended his terror with the murder of the twelve-year-old son of his principal antagonist, the head of the opposing family. The boy was of an unsurpassing beauty, so the story goes, and was cut down while walking through the cork forests lost in song.

There is no listed **accommodation** in Aggius except for a few agri-turismo outlets in the neighbourhood: try Giovanni Franco Serra at Via Andrea Tortu, in Località Fraiga (☎079.620.559).

Calangianus and around

Seven kilometres east of Tempio, the road skirts Limbara to **CALANGIANUS**, a small town surrounded by a jagged ring of mountains and, closer to hand, cork factories. This is the centre of Sardinia's biggest cork-producing area, and it's no surprise to see the local shops overflowing with the stuff, fashioned into an endless variety of unusual forms. In September, the village stages an exhibition of cork and its various uses.

There's a station on the Tempio-Palau rail line in Calangianus, but nowhere to stay, and, once you've sifted through the shelves of cork, precious little to do. Three kilometres out of town to the north, however, the village of **Luras** – notable for its *logudorese* dialect, as opposed to the *gallurese* spoken elsewhere – has some impressive prenuraghic dolmens, or funerary stones, which date back to the

---

Cork

No one travelling through Gallura can fail to notice the groves of short, spiky **cork oak** (*Quercus suber*), usually stripped at the waist to reveal the reddish inner bark. This evergreen grows abundantly in the Mediterranean region, particularly in Portugal, Spain, parts of France and Italy, and North Africa, usually to a height of about 18m, with a broad, round-topped head and glossy green, holly-like leaves. It is the new outer sheath of bark which is useful, harvested in Gallura since earliest times to fit a variety of uses. Ladles and other kitchen utensils, trays, containers and insulation material are all produced from this versatile substance, and its lightness, flexibility and impermeability make it ideal for a number of other industrial and practical uses – 90 percent of Italy's bottle corks come from Gallura's trees. In recent times it has also been fashioned into a variety of unlikely objects of the souvenir ilk, such as paper and postcards, masks, ornaments and purses.

The cork oak lives about 150 years, and the first cork is not peeled off the trunk until the tree is 25–30 years old. The product of this initial de-barking, or *demaschiatura*, is too porous and plastic to be useful, however; the second stripping, about ten years later, yields a better quality, and thereafter the outer sheath is removed every decade or so. In a healthy tree, 2.5–5cm of new cork forms in 3–10 years, and it may continue to be productive for the rest of its life. The stripping itself is still done by hand, by cutting slits in the outer bark, which is then pried loose and peeled away with the help of levers and wedges, taking care not to injure the regenerative layers of the inner bark. Before it can be used, the peel of cork is boiled or steamed to remove soluble tannic acids and increase its flexibility, and its rough woody surface is scraped clean by hand. Among the many by-products, the fibrous tissues that come away with the bark are used to dye sheep's wool and goat hair.

---

second or third millennium BC. To reach the most impressive of these, **dolmen Ladas**, follow the road north through the village, turn right into the last asphalted street, and follow a dirt track for about 350m, then take the right fork – a couple of kilometres in all. Standing on a low hill, the tall rectangular dolmen measures all of 6m in length and over 2m in width.

The tiny village of **Sant'Antonio di Gallura** lies 18km northeast of Calangianus on the SP427 (and the same distance south of Arzachena along the same road), close to the **lago di Liscia**, the artificial lake which supplies irrigation to much of the coastal region and drinking water to Olbia, Arzachena and the Costa Smeralda. The neighbourhood also holds an ancient forest of wild olive trees, some reaching 14m high and 11m broad, among which is thought to be the oldest wild olive tree in Sardinia, estimated to be 2000 years old. You'll need local advice to find it, however: it's out of sight in a secluded little valley near the banks of the lake. The area is also renowned for its Nebbiolo wines.

Travel Details

TRAINS

Arzachena to: Calangianus (July–Aug 2 daily; late June and early Sept 2 weekly; 1hr); Palau (July–Aug 2 daily; late June and early Sept 2 weekly; 25min); Tempio Pausánia (July–Aug 2 daily; late June and early Sept 2 weekly; 1hr 25min).

Golfo Aranci to: Olbia (Mon–Sat 7 daily, Sun 4–5; 25min).

Olbia to: Cágliari (1–2 daily; 4hr–4hr 30min); Golfo Aranci (Mon–Sat 7 daily, Sun 4–5; 20min); Oristano (1–2 daily; 3hr); Ozieri-Chilivani (5–7 daily; 1hr–1hr 20min).

Olbia (Ísola Bianca) to: Cágliari (1 daily; 4hr 10min–4hr 25min).

Palau to: Arzachena (July–Aug 2 daily; late June and early Sept 2 weekly; 25min); Calangianus (July–Aug 2 daily; late June and early Sept 2 weekly; 1hr 30min); Tempio Pausánia (July–Aug 2 daily; late June and early Sept 2 weekly; 1hr 45min).

Tempio Pausánia to: Arzachena (July–Aug 2 daily; late June and early Sept 2 weekly; 1hr 10min); Calangianus (July–Aug 2 daily; late June and early Sept 2 weekly; 20min); Palau (July–Aug 2 daily; late June and early Sept 2 weekly; 1hr 35min).

BUSES

Arzachena to: Laconia (2 daily); Olbia (12–14 daily; 40min); Palau (hourly; 20min); Santa Teresa di Gallura (6–8 daily; 1hr).

Golfo Aranci to: Arzachena (July & Aug 1 daily; 50min); Olbia (July & Aug 3 daily; 25min); Palau (July & Aug 1 daily; 1hr 5min); Santa Teresa di Gallura (July & Aug 1 daily; 1hr 40min).

Olbia to: Arzachena (12–14 daily; 40min); Golfo Aranci (July & Aug 3 daily; 25min); Nuoro (4 daily; 2hr 30min); Palau (hourly; 1hr); Porto Cervo (4 daily;

2hr 30min); Porto San Paolo (4 daily; 20min); Posada (4 daily; 1hr 10min);
San Teodoro (4 daily; 40min); Santa Teresa di Gallura (7–8 daily; 1hr
45min–2hr 15min); Sássari (1 daily; 1hr 35min); Tempio Pausánia (Mon–Sat
5–8 daily, Sun 3; 1hr 25min).

Olbia (Ísola Bianca) to: Arzachena (3 daily; 45min); Nuoro (3 daily; 2hr
35min); Palau (3 daily; 1hr 10min); Santa Teresa di Gallura (2 daily; 2hr);
Sássari (1 daily; 1hr 40min).

Palau to: Arzachena (hourly; 20min); Olbia (hourly; 1hr); Santa Teresa di
Gallura (Mon–Sat 7–9 daily, Sun 6; 40min).

Santa Teresa di Gallura to: Arzachena (5–6 daily; 40min); Castelsardo
(Mon–Sat 5 daily, Sun 3; 2hr); Sássari (Mon–Sat 5 daily, Sun 3; 3hr).

Tempio Pausánia to: Aggius (8–10 daily; 15min); Arzachena (2 daily; 1hr
15min); Cágliari (1 daily; 3hr 50min); Calangianus (Mon–Sat 8–10 daily, Sun
4; 15min); Ísola Rossa (3–4 daily; 1hr); Palau (2 daily; 1hr 40min); (1hr
30min) Sássari (4 daily; 1hr 15min); to Ploaghe 4 or 5 daily (45min)

FERRIES

Golfo Aranci to: Civitavecchia (1–2 daily; 7–8hr 30min), or by fast ferry (mid-
June to early Sept 2–5 daily; 3hr 30min–4hr); La Spezia (mid-June to early
Sept 1 daily; 5hr 30min); Livorno (April to mid-Oct 1–2 daily; 9–10hr).

Olbia to: Civitavecchia by fast ferry (May–Sept 1–4 daily, Oct–April 6 weekly;
4–6hr); Genoa (3–8 weekly; 10–13hr 30min), or by fast ferry (mid-June to
early Sept 5–7 weekly; 5hr 30min–6hr); Livorno (1–3 daily; 8hr).

Palau to: La Maddalena (2–4 hourly, 1 hourly at night; 20min); Naples
(April–Sept 1–2 weekly; 14hr); Porto Vecchio, Corsica (April–Sept 1–2 weekly; 2hr 30min).

Santa Teresa di Gallura to: Bonifacio, Corsica (6–22 daily; 50min).

Chapter 8

Nuoro province

T he huge central **province of Nuoro** has little in common with Sardinia's modern sun-and-sand image, but for many it's the most interesting part of the island, dotted with isolated villages which have never known the heel of foreign conquerors. Their inhabitants have retained a fierce sense of independence and loyalty to centuries-old practices, which continued unabated in the inaccessible interior long after most of the coastal towns had shed their traditional trappings. The province is consequently the last repository of some of Sardinia's oldest customs, where you won't be surprised to find a few elderly folk still unselfconsciously wearing their local costumes.

All the same, the best place to view the region's huge range of costumes – not to mention masks, musical instruments, jewellery and types of bread – is the ethnographic museum in the provincial capital, **Nuoro**. It's easily the best reason to visit this high inland town, though you'll discover other, more recondite attractions, often connected to the remarkable roster of artists and writers who lived and worked around here before achieving national fame.

For many, Nuoro is the starting point for trips into Sardinia's **Barbagia** region, called *Barbaria* by the Romans who, like Sardinia's other conquerors, never managed to subdue it completely, foiled by the guerrilla warfare for which the rugged recesses proved ideal. Among the hills and high pasture, the Barbagia's population is concentrated in small, self-contained villages, interconnected by twisting mountain roads. These settlements have changed little since the novelist Salvatore Satta described them as "minuscule settlements as remote from one another as are the stars". Although material conditions have improved in recent years, the region seems a world apart from the whitewashed luxury of the Costa Smeralda just a couple of hours' drive away, and it is still common to see black-shawled old ladies trudging up and down the steep streets of the villages, or shepherds in brown corduroy suits, wrapped up against the cold grey air which envelopes these parts for much of the year.

The region is divided into different districts, of which the **Barbagia Ollolai** is the nearest to Nuoro. En route to this area,

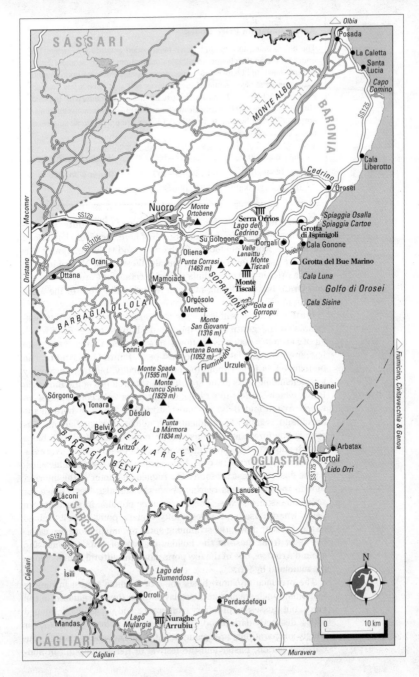

Accommodation Price Codes

The hotels listed in this guide have been coded according to price. The codes represent the cheapest available double room in high season (Easter & June–Aug). In cheaper hotels the rooms usually come without en-suite bathroom or shower; some of these places will also have a few en-suite rooms, for which you'll pay more – usually the next category up in price. Higher category hotels nearly always have only en-suite rooms. Out of season, you'll often be able to negotiate a lower price than those suggested here. The categories are:

① under L60,000   ④ L120,000–150,000   ⑦ L250,000–300,000

② L60,000–90,000   ⑤ L150,000–200,000   ⑧ over L300,000

③ L90,000–120,000   ⑥ L200,000–250,000

Oliena is the best base for expeditions on to **Sopramonte**, the dramatic massif visible from Nuoro. South of here, **Orgósolo** had one of the island's worst reputations for banditry and violence, though it is now best known for its striking murals. Westwards, **Mamoiada** and **Ottana** present two of Sardinia's most spectacular Carnival displays, and **Orani** has a diverting museum featuring the work of the artist Costantino Nivola.

Further south, **Fonni** is one the main gateways to the once impenetrable **Gennargentu** massif, the island's highest range, from which all of Sardinia's major rivers flow – most of them dammed to create fetching mountain lakes. The loftiest peak, **Punta La Mármora,** can be reached on foot without too much difficulty, but there are many less demanding treks in the area. The forested slopes of the **Barbagia Belvì**, which borders this range, shelter more tight communities, of which **Aritzo** and **Belvì** are most attractive. South of here in the **Sarcidano** region, the gradients are milder, though **Láconi**, surrounded by forest, still retains a fresh, mountainous feel. **Ísili** has a superb single-towered nuraghe worth a photo-stop, while **Nuraghe Arrubiu**, below Orroli, is one of the island's grandest nuraghic sites.

The **eastern coast** preserves the rugged character of the interior, though the sheer walls rearing above the sea also leave space for some fantastic beaches. These are more popular in the northern parts, where **Posada** provides a lofty vantage point from its ruined castle. Further down, the swimming spots are much more inaccessible apart from those at the holiday enclave of **Cala Gonone** and around **Arbatax**, one of the few ports along this littoral, connected to the mainland by ferry.

The province of Nuoro hosts some of Sardinia's most intriguing **festivals**, much smaller and less lavish than those organized in the cities, but possessed of a fiery exuberance and occasionally imbued with a distinctly dark mood. Each village has at least one *festa*, for which preparations are made months in advance, though the Carnival period, Easter and the festival of the Assumption in mid-

August are usually the most spectacular, and all provide a good opportunity to see traditional costumes (the tourist office at Nuoro can supply you with an illustrated booklet with full details).

Because of the winter sports and trekking possibilities which draw growing numbers of enthusiasts, there are plenty of **accommodation** choices along the way, though it's always wise to phone first. The province is best explored using your own vehicle, though it would not be impossible to circulate on **public transport**: ARST buses from Nuoro or Cágliari pass through the remotest villages in the area at lest once a day, while PANI buses link Nuoro to Cágliari, Sássari and Oristano. Private FdS trains connect Nuoro with Macomer, and Sórgono, Ísili and Arbatax with Cágliari, though the Cágliari line is a slow one, best treated as a travelling experience rather than as a means of crossing the island.

For more information on bus and train connections, see Travel Details, p.345.

Nuoro

"There is nothing to see in Nuoro: which to tell the truth, is always a relief. Sights are an irritating bore," wrote D.H. Lawrence, though he omitted to mention the town's superb position beneath the soaring peak of Monte Ortobene and opposite the sheer and stark heights of Sopramonte. In many respects **NUORO** is little different from the other villages of the region, insular and parochial, in parts drab and ugly, though the city still occupies a unique place in the island's cultural life, both for its extraordinary literary fame and the artists who lived and worked here.

When Lawrence touched down here during his Sardinian excursion of 1921, it appeared to him "as if at the end of the world, mountains rising sombre behind". Despite the overlay of unsightly apartment blocks, administrative buildings and banks which have overrun the town in the last half-century, little seems to have changed since then. An old-fashioned air hangs over the place, stifling the progressive currents infusing towns such as Olbia and Oristano, and preserving a dignified calm that recalls a grittier reality unleavened by the glossy trappings of the tourist industry.

Nuoro's walls still display faded Fascist graffiti from the 1930s, and the town's biggest attractions are both rooted firmly in the past – the wonderful **ethnographic museum** with its instructive overview of rural culture, and the **Sagra del Redentore**, when you can see many of the costumes on view in the museum brought to vivid life. This festival also reaffirms the strong bond with the nearby **Monte Ortobene**, whose summit, 8km outside Nuoro, marks the end-point of the costumed parade. You can visit the mountain at any time of course, to appreciate the dramatic prospect. There's little else in Nuoro to justify an extended stay, though it makes an obvious base to explore the region, and you may yet be lulled by the town's unpretentious, uncommercialized milieu and its friendly population.

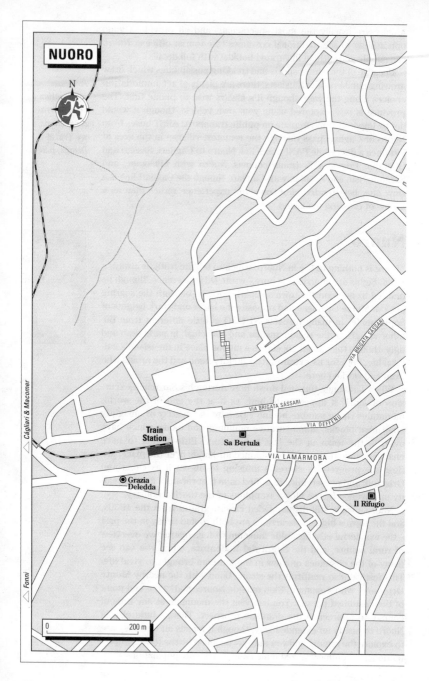

NUORO

N

Cagliari & Macomer

Fonni

Train
Station

Sa Bertula

VIA BRIGATA SÁSSARI

VIA BRIGATA SÁSSARI

VIA DEFFENU

VIA LAMÁRMORA

Grazia
Deledda

Il Rifugio

0   200 m

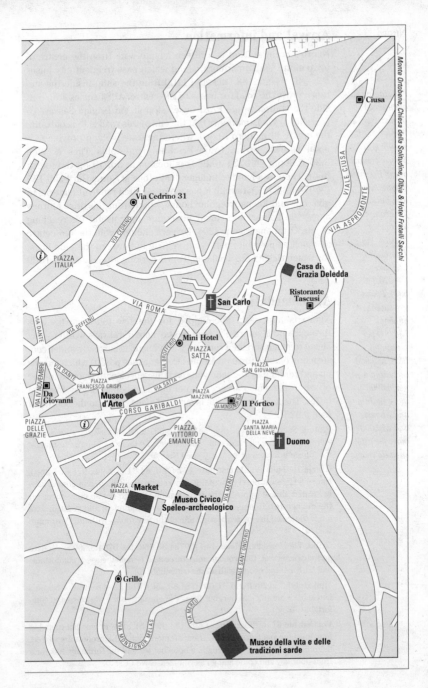

Monte Ortobene, Chiesa della Solitudine, Olbia & Hotel Fratelli Sacchi

- Ciusa
- Via Cedrino 31
- PIAZZA ITALIA
- VIA CEDRINO
- Casa di Grazia Deledda
- VIA ASPROMONTE
- VIALE CIUSA
- VIA ROMA
- San Carlo
- Ristorante Tascusi
- VIA DEFFENU
- VIA DANTE
- Mini Hotel
- PIAZZA SATTA
- VIA BROFFERIO
- PIAZZA SAN GIOVANNI
- VIA IV NOVEMBRE
- VIA DANTE
- PIAZZA FRANCESCO CRISPI
- VIA SATTA
- PIAZZA MAZZINI
- Museo d'Arte
- Da Giovanni
- CORSO GARIBALDI
- Il Pórtico
- VIA MONSIGN
- PIAZZA DELLE GRAZIE
- PIAZZA VITTORIO EMANUELE
- PIAZZA SANTA MARIA DELLA NEVE
- Duomo
- PIAZZA MAMELI
- Market
- Museo Cívico Speleo-archeologico
- VIA MEREU
- VIALE SANT'ONORIO
- Grillo
- VIA MEREU
- VIA MONSIGNOR MELAS
- Museo della vita e delle tradizioni sarde

Arrival and information

Nuoro's **train station** is a fifteen-minute walk from the centre of town along Via Lamármora, along which pass frequent city buses #2, #3, #4 and #8 (tickets L1100 from the shop inside the station); cross the road for buses to the centre. ARST **buses** stop outside the station, while PANI buses stop at Via Brigata Sássari 15 (parallel to Via Lamármora). At the end of this road is **Piazza Italia**, the centre of modern Nuoro, where the town's – and province's – main **tourist office** (Mon–Fri 9am–1pm, plus Tues & Wed 3.30–6.30pm; ☎0784.30.083) is located at no. 19 on the fourth floor. There is a handier independent office at Corso Garibaldi 155 (☎0784.38.777), though it has a more limited range of material to give out and keeps irregular hours. Apart from the brief journey along Via Lamármora, **local buses** are only useful for reaching Monte Ortobene (see p.320). **Drivers** should avoid the old centre as much as possible; park your vehicle in between the blue lines, for which tickets are available from a parking attendant for L1000 per hour.

Accommodation

For staying in agriturismo properties throughout the province of Nuoro, contact one of the main island-wide associations, for example Vacanze e Natura, Viale Trieste 124, Cágliari (☎070.280. 537). Prices are standard, at about L30,000 per person for B&B, L55,000 including dinner, L5000 more in July and August, and L10,000 more for an en-suite room.

Nuoro is hopelessly ill-equipped for the few tourists who pass through, and if you're planning **to stay** here it's always worth calling ahead to make sure of a room. A youth hostel is currently under construction outside town on Monte Ortobene (see p.320) which may be up and running by the time you read this: check with Nuoro's tourist office. There's also a decent hotel up here, connected by frequent buses. The nearest campsite is outside Oliena, 12km to the southeast (see p.325).

Fratelli Sacchi, Monte Ortobene (☎0784.31.200). Not all the rooms have views, but they're all clean and comfortable, and there's a popular restaurant too. Space is limited in August. Closed Nov. ③.

Grazia Deledda, Via Lamármora 177 (☎0784.31.257, fax 0784.31.258). Nuoro's classiest hotel is actually very reasonably priced, and conveniently located almost opposite the train station (though not so convenient for the old centre). Rooms are spacious and well-equipped, and you can save a few thousand lire by requesting one of the few rooms without TV or mini-bar. ③.

Grillo, Via Monsignor Melas 14 (☎0784.38.668, fax 0784.32.005). Modern and characterless, this conspicuous three-star is nonetheless a comfortable and fairly central choice with all the trimmings. ③.

Mini Hotel, Via Brofferio 31 (☎0784.33.159). The most central of Nuoro's hotels has a scruffy exterior, but the seven en-suite rooms are clean and comfortable. ②.

Via Cedrino 31, off Piazza Italia (☎0784.30.675). Signora Iacobini rents out four spacious and clean rooms for one or more nights. Bathrooms are shared, but otherwise it's just like being in a hotel but without the formality. Ask for a front-door key and come and go as you please. No CCs. ②.

The old centre

Nuoro's **old quarter** is the most compelling part of town, spread around the pedestrianized hub of **Corso Garibaldi**, at its best during the buzzing *passeggiata*. Nuoro's newest attraction lies just off here, on the corner of Via Satta and Via Manara. The **Museo d'Arte** (Tues–Sun 10am–1pm & 4–8pm; L5000) occupies four floors of a renovated nineteenth-century *palazzo*, and is filled with the works of some of Sardinia's best-known artists. The ground and top floors are devoted to temporary exhibitions, while the middle two floors have a permanent display of artists from the nineteenth and twentieth centuries, including moody abstracts by Mauro Manca (1913–69), and sculptures by two outstanding locals, Costantino Nivola (1911–88, see p.328) and the Nuorese Francesco Ciusa (1883–1949). The gallery also hosts poetry readings on Thursday evenings and classical and jazz concerts once a month.

More works by two of these artists can be seen a few steps away at the top of Via Satta. In the usually deserted **Piazza Satta**, the poet Sebastiano Satta, who was born nearby (see box on p.318), has been honoured with a cluster of menhir-like granite blocks in which small bronze figures evoking nuraghic *bronzetti* have been placed – the work of Nivola in the 1960s. Just beyond, on the corner of Via Sássari and Via San Carlo Borromeo, a ramshackle house now awaiting renovation was the birthplace of Francesco Ciusa. His tomb lies opposite in the pink rustic-looking church of **San Carlo** (daily 8am–1pm & 4–7pm), which also contains a copy of Ciusa's most powerful work, *Madre dell'Ucciso*, "Mother of the killed man", a bronze statue of a crouching barefooted crone swathed in shawl and headscarf, whose bony face is a poignant display of bitter grief. The original was presented at the Biennale at Venice in 1907, and is now exhibited in Rome's Galleria dell'Arte Moderna.

Corso Garibaldi ends at Piazza San Giovanni, from where a left turn up Via Deledda will bring you to the **Casa di Grazia Deledda**, once the home of the Nobel Prize-winning author (see box on p.318), now containing manuscripts, first editions, photos, clippings and mementoes. The building with period furnishings is a good example of a typical Nuorese family house – though it may have been altered and expanded when the current renovation work is complete.

Turning right from Piazza San Giovanni leads instead to the spacious Piazza Santa Maria della Neve, dominated by Nuoro's nineteenth-century **Duomo**. Framed by two bell-towers, its orangey Neoclassical exterior often crops up on local postcards but lacks much presence from close up. The cool, spacious interior holds various items of religious art, including panels showing the stations of the cross by local twentieth-century artists Carmelo Floris and Giovanni Ciusa Romagna. Try to persuade someone to let you into the **belvedere** to one side of the cathedral, from which there is a superb view of the town and the precipitous valley below.

Nuoro's government-sponsored ISOLA shop has two floors of folk arts and crafts at Via Monsignor Bua, near the Duomo. The quality is generally good, though prices are often steep.

Literary Nuoro

Who knows what makes one town more conducive to great art than any other? In Sardinia, Nuoro seems to have the monopoly where literature is concerned. The best-known Sard poet, **Sebastiano Satta** (1867–1914) was Nuorese – though hardly known outside the island, where he is fêted on innumerable street- and piazza-names. In his home town, he has not only the street on which he lived named after him but also the square at one end of it (Piazza Satta), where bronze statuettes depict him at different stages of his life.

In 1926, the author **Grazia Deledda** (1871–1936) became one of four Italians to win the Nobel Prize for Literature. It was a tribute to a steady writing career devoted to establishing a corpus of work based on the day-to-day trials and passions of simple folk in Nuoro and the villages around. Praised by D.H. Lawrence, she has been compared with Thomas Hardy in her style and subject matter. The house where Deledda grew up, described in her autobiographical work *Cosima*, can be seen at Via Deledda 28 and is now a museum; her tomb is at the bottom of Monte Ortobene, in the church of Santa Maria della Solitúdine, which also recurs in her works.

"Nuoro was nothing but a perch for the crows," for the town's greatest modern writer, **Salvatore Satta** (1902–1975), as he wrote in his semi-auto-biographical masterpiece, *The Day of Judgment*. No relation to his poetic namesake Sebastiano, Salvatore Satta earned his living as a jurist, which placed him at the heart of the tangled intrigues of this provincial town, and though his book – his only literary work, published posthumously – chronicles life in Nuoro at the turn of the twentieth century, much of it still rings true today. The meandering descriptions of the townsfolk and the antagonisms between the local shepherds, peasants and aristocrats tread a fine line between soap opera and existential angst, dry yet easily readable, in some ways recalling Lampedusa's Sicilian epic, *The Leopard*. Salvatore Satta's achievement has not earned him any memorial in his home town apart from the plaque at Via Angioi 1, just up from Piazza Mazzini, which indicates the house where he wrote parts of his only novel.

For details of this publication, and of Grazia Deledda's works in English, see p.363.

Elsewhere in Nuoro's old town, off Piazza Vittorio Emanuele, the **Museo Cívico Speleo-archeologico** displays a range of rocks, ropes and other equipment relating to the caving that this province is particularly suitable for. It's been closed a long time, however, with no information on its reopening.

Museo della Vita e delle Tradizioni Sarde

Nuoro's most stimulating sight lies up on Via Antonio Mereu, a ten-minute walk past the Duomo from the Corso: the **Museo della Vita e delle Tradizioni Sarde** (daily: mid-June to Sept 9am–7pm; Oct to mid-June 9am–1pm & 3–7pm; L4000) – more simply known as the Museo delle Costumi or Museo Etnográfico. Past the rude carts and wine presses that greet you on your way in, the museum has

Sardinia's most comprehensive range of local costumes, jewellery, masks, carpets and other handicrafts, arranged in a modern pur- pose-built complex whose sequence of rooms, steps and courtyards is intended to evoke a Sardinian village.

The most striking exhibits are the **costumes**, showing an incredi- ble diversity of pattern, design and colour, according to both their place of origin and the circumstances in which they were worn: scarves, skirts and bodices for unmarried women or widows; blous- es and shawls for mourning or feasting, and shirts, tunics and pan- taloons for the menfolk. One of the first rooms, however, deviates immediately from the main theme in its presentation, behind glass, of a well-preserved seventeenth-century fresco from a local church. Of unknown authorship, the work shows six of the apostles (pre- sumably there was another fresco portraying the other six) all hold- ing their traditional symbols – Simon the Zealot holds a saw.

The next room, **sala 4**, is devoted to costumes from the Barbagia villages of Bitti, Fonni, Gavoi, Ollolai and Désulo – black hats and boots for the men, lace shawls for the women – while **sala 5** has rugs, carpets and a horizontal-type oak loom from Bono from the second half of the nineteenth century. Funerary carpets on which the deceased were placed during wakes are draped on the walls.

Sala 6 focuses on Sardinia's musical instruments, including vari- ous drums (*tamburi*), flutes made from canes from Barbagia and La Marmilla, and rudimentary clarinets (*benas*) made from oat stems. Some of these were tied together to make *launeddas*, or shepherd's pipes, said to be the island's oldest and most original instrument, made of three tubes of cane of differing lengths and diameters, and differently holed. Other noise-making gadgets include a simple string bass used at Bosa, Sássari and Gavoi during Carnival time, similar to that used in jug bands but resonating in an inflated pig's bladder instead of a box; whistles, triangles and rattles used at Easter, and cork-popping guns fired by children at Christmas. Another display shows sheep- and goat-bells, the various sizes used to identify differ- ent flocks – one of the characteristic accoutrements in Barbagia's masked processions.

The next room has some of the various *dolci* and breads you may have encountered in restaurants and pastry shops throughout Sardinia, but particularly common in the Nuoro region. *Paneddas*, cakes and sweets with bird designs, elaborately designed hearts and bows made of pastry, filled with figs and nuts, are displayed below photos showing how they are prepared. The island's famous *pane carasau* – discs of bread – are also here. Traditionally made once a month, they were at first the preserve of the better-off classes, but are now in general use.

Guns and swords share space in the next room with lacework and basketwork, while **sala 10** – downstairs and across a yard – has solemn photos from the end of the nineteenth century, costumes from Atzara and Samugheo, and more carpets on the walls. **Rooms 11–13** display costumes from Oristano and Cabras, lace from Cágliari, and an impressive collection of jewellery used by men and women, crafted out of silver plate, polychrome glass, precious stones, and silver filigree work. Among the buttons, pins and earrings studded with pearls and coral, wedding and engagement rings of silver and gold, and necklaces made of coral, gold plate and silver, there are pendants and amulets encrusted with turquoise, marble and obsidian, some of them incorporating fragments of shell, shark's teeth, boar's tusks and crystals to ward off evil.

Rooms 14 and 15 have sober dark brown and black garments from Macomer and Íttiri, more flamboyant women's dresses from Ósilo decorated with roses and other flowers, and brocaded wedding and feast gowns from Sénnori, Ploaghe and Bono. The costumes in the last rooms are much more dramatic affairs, including the very sinister-looking black gowns tied with ropes and bells belonging to *Sos Thurpos* of Orotelli – a chain of twenty or thirty hooded and stick-wielding men swathed in thick black cloth to leave only their soot-blackened faces exposed, who leap upon their victims during the village's Carnival procession and truss them up, as seen in the photos displayed here. You can also see the hairy goatskin costumes of Mamoiada's Carnival, the masks at once menacing and tragic (see box on p.327), and those of *Sos Merdules* of Ottana.

Monte Ortobene

On Nuoro's eastern flank, the summit of **Monte Ortobene** affords striking views over the gorge separating Nuoro from Monte Corrasi (1463m) and the Sopramonte massif. The heavily wooded slopes are a favourite destination for the townsfolk at weekends, though there are plenty of areas which feel remote enough to get lost in. The **Farcana** locality, signposted off the only road going up the mountain, has a new sports complex which includes a good-sized open-air pool, tennis courts and stables for riding. There is also a pizzeria close by, and a new youth hostel under construction. Other possibilities for horse-riding include the *Locanda Sedda Ortai*, signposted.

Monte Ortobene forms a central part in Nuoro's annual Festa del Redentore (see box opposite) when a procession weaves up from the town to the bronze **statue** of the Redeemer at the top (955m). Poised in an attitude of swirling motion over the immense void, the statue attracts pilgrims at all times, as shown by the trinkets and other devotional gifts left here, and by Christ's polished right toe – the only part of the statue within reach of the worshippers. The statue makes an awe-inspiring vantage point, with dizzying views down to the valley floor.

The woods hereabouts are perfect for walks and picnics, and there are a few bars and snacks places to provide refreshment. More substantial dishes can be enjoyed a little way past the statue at *Fratelli*

The Sagra del Redentore

Many of the costumes displayed in Nuoro's ethnographic museum are aired in the town's biggest annual festival, the **Sagra del Redentore**. Held at the end of August, it involves participants from all over the island, but especially the villages of the Barbagia. The festival combines solemn religious rites with a flamboyant celebration of Sardinia's cultural heritage: the penultimate Sunday of August is dedicated to dancing and dialect singing, enthusiastically performed in the old town's squares, while on August 29, a long, costumed procession trails through Nuoro as far as the statue of the Redeemer on Monte Ortobene and the nearby church of Nostra Signora di Montenero. Together, these events constitute one of the most vibrant events on the island's calendar, and accommodation at this time is at a premium.

Sacchi (closed Nov), specializing in delicious local recipes, and with superb views to aid digestion; there are also rooms here (see p.316). *Su Redentore*, a little further along, is another recommended restaurant. Frequent local buses (#8 or #81) connect Monte Ortobene from outside Nuoro's train station, Corso Garibaldi and Piazza Vittorio Emanuele; the last bus down is at around 8.20pm.

At the base of Monte Ortobene, where the road up the mountain meets the main road to Siniscola and Olbia, you might stop a few minutes at the **Chiesa della Solitúdine**, an austere granite structure at the top of a flight of shallow steps. The church was designed in the 1950s by local artist Giovanni Ciusa Romagna on the site of an earlier church that was often mentioned in the books of Grazia Deledda, and contains the author's simple granite tomb.

Restaurants

Nuoro is not particularly well off for **restaurants**, though prices are generally very reasonable. For fruit, veg and other takeaway items, the covered **market** is open mornings and evenings at Via Santa Barbara.

Sa Bertula, Via Deffenu 119. Near the train station, this quiet, rather characterless place specializes in Nuorese cuisine and seafood. Closed Sun. Moderate.

Ciusa, at Viale Ciusa 53, on the western end of town. Most popular with the Nuorese is the excellent pizzeria-restaurant, at weekends a merry riot, and rarely quiet at other times (closed Mon Oct–May). Moderate.

Da Giovanni, Via IV Novembre 9. Unmarked first-floor restaurant rated for its local dishes, but a bit tatty and usually empty. Prices, at least, are reasonable. *Filindeu* is a warming winter soup, and they also have polenta and wild boar. Closed Sun. Moderate.

Il Pórtico, Via Monsignor Bua 13. One of Nuoro's smarter choices, though not intimidatingly so, and the food's delicious. Closed Sun. Moderate.

Il Rifugio, Vícolo del Pozzo 4. Plain and popular pizzeria with some pasta and meat dishes. It fills up quickly, but service is brisk and there's a fast turnover. Closed Wed. Inexpensive.

Aranciadda nuorese is a typical local sweet, made with honey and fresh oranges, though it may be too sticky for some. This and other local specialities are available from places on the Corso, for example Zia Marianna at no. 174.

Ristorante Tascusi, Via Aspromonte 11. A good daily-changing fixed-price menu of L17,000 might include *Fusilli al nero di seppia* (pasta with squid ink), roast pork and fish. Side dishes, drinks and fruit are included in the price, and pizzas are also available. Closed Sun. No CCs. Inexpensive.

Bars

Bar Camboso, Via Monsignor Bua 4. On the corner of Piazza Vittorio Emanuele, this is a lively but old-fashioned place with comfy chairs and lots of chat. A good breakfast stop.

Killtime Pub, Via Mereu 45 (corner of Viale Sant'Onofrio). The conspicuous modern green and orange building below the museum combines a bar, cafeteria and nightspot. Serves snacks and Guinness too. Closed Mon.

Bar Majore, Corso Garibaldi 69. The old fittings, beautifully painted ceilings and mirrors give this small bar plenty of atmosphere.

Il Mio Bar, Via Mereu. A handy sit-down place for a lunchtime snack, between the museum and the duomo. Closed Sun.

Bar il Muretto, Via Solferino 18. *Panini caldi*, burgers and chips, plus lots of beers, bottled or draught. Closed Sun afternoon.

Bar Nuovo, Piazza Mazzini. Good old bar offering *pizzette*, *panini*, ice creams and tables outside. Closed Wed.

Sas Grassias, Piazza delle Grazie. Homemade ice creams and, in winter, *cioccolata calda con panna montata* – hot chocolate topped with whipped cream. Closed Thurs.

Entertainment

When the theatre currently under construction in Via Brofferio is completed, it will be the main venue for the city's cultural life. In the meantime, check out the local edition of *La Nuova Sardegna* any day except Monday (when sport predominates) for listings of current events. For music, the *Killtime Pub* on Via Mereu has regular jazz and blues concerts from about 9.30pm. Outside town, *Farcana* and *Nuovo Parco*, both on Monte Ortobene, also have live music in summer.

Listings

Bank Banco di Sardegna, Corso Garibaldi 90 (8.20am–1.20pm & 3.05–4.35pm); Banca Commerciale Italiana, Piazza Italia (same times). Both have cash dispensers, and the post office (see opposite) also changes money.

Bus information ARST ☎0784.32.201; Deplanu (for Olbia) ☎0784.201.518; PANI ☎0784.36.856.

Emergencies ☎113.

First aid ☎0784.240.249.

Hospital ☎0784.240.237.

Market Open mornings and evenings at Via Santa Barbara, mainly fruit and veg, but there are also other stalls selling clothes and various goods.

Pharmacy Gali on Corso Garibaldi (☎0782.30.143). Late-night pharmacies operate on a rota – check on any pharmacy door to see the address of the current one.

Post office Piazza Francesco Crispi, open Mon–Sat 8.15am–7.30pm. Changes cash or American Express travellers' cheques mornings only.

Supermarket Upim on Via Lamármora, opposite the train station (Mon–Sat 9am–1pm & 4–8pm).

Taxi At train station ☎0368.909.471, or ☎0335.399.174.

Train information For FS and FdS services, call ☎147.888.088 between 7am and 9pm daily.

Travel agent La Nuova Barbagia, Via Dante 28 (☎0784.37.777).

The Barbagia Ollolai

South and east of Nuoro, the **Barbagia Ollolai** ranges from the great wall of mountain that is Sopramonte to the much milder plains to the west. Although strictly outside this area, the village of **Oliena** is the first obvious stop from the provincial capital, crouched at the base of Monte Corrasi, with good hiking possibilities and accommodation choices. To the east, **Su Gologone** is another starting point for some excellent excursions into the mountains, including to the nuraghic village of Tíscali. Southwest, **Orgósolo** is famous for its ancient banditry and its vivid murals, but for scenery you need to head south to the **Montes** region. The otherwise unremarkable village of **Mamoiada**, 11km west of Orgósolo and 16km south of Nuoro, is the venue of a highly pagan Carnival romp; **Ottana** is also renowned for its festivities during the Carnival period, and possesses a good Pisan church. Halfway between Mamoiada and Ottana, **Orani** has a wonderful museum dedicated to Costantino Nivola, one of Sardinia's most respected twentieth-century artists.

If you're looking for an overnight stop, choose places either in or around Oliena or Orgósolo. There is practically nothing elsewhere. All villages are accessible by frequent ARST buses from Nuoro.

The most interesting of Oliena's feast days are the Easter S'Incontru, or meeting, between the processions following the figures of the Virgin Mary and Jesus, and the four days of revelry around San Lussorio's day on August 21. The festivals are an opportunity to see the local traditional dress for men and women, an elegant black and white costume.

Oliena and around

The nearest village of any size to Nuoro, **OLIENA** is easily visible from the provincial capital, sprawled along the side of Monte Corrasi to the south. Rising to 1349m, this rugged limestone elevation forms part of the Sopramonte massif, famed as the haunt of bandits until relatively recent times. Oliena itself prefers its reputation as the producer of one of the island's finest wines – a dry, almost black concoction that turns lighter and stronger over the years – and as the best base for hiking excursions in the mountainous terrain surrounding it. You can gain access to Monte Corrasi from Località Maccione, a wooded area 3km south of town off the very squiggly old road to Orgósolo.

Off the Dorgali road, 7km from Oliena, **Su Gologone** makes a good starting point for expeditions onto the mountain; the area is named for a fast-flowing therapeutic spring which emerges from

A walk to Valle Lanaittu and Monte Tíscali

One of the most rewarding expeditions you can make on to Sopramonte is to the **Valle Lanaittu**, for which a signposted track heads off near Su Gologone on the left. You can also drive up this way, though you must leave your vehicle at Grotta sa Oche, about a kilometre up. From here, red and white paint-marks point the way to the right, where a path leads to a fork – follow the paint to the broad path on the left. Keep left at the next crossroads (signed "Grotta Helie's Arias"); when the track levels off after a curve to the left, turn right (south), still following the dots, to a mild ascent. Above a heap of stone on the left, there's a narrow cleft through the rock: follow this, then veer right to a trough where there's a wood surrounded by steep rock walls. Here lie the remains of a nuraghic village, **Tíscali**, clearly a last refuge from foreign incursions at some point during the first millennium BC. The site was inhabited well into Roman and medieval times, but was only rediscovered about a century ago, and is still under excavation. It's a fascinating place, the yellow limestone walls and stalagmites giving it a weird, ghostly atmosphere. Calculate about ninety minutes to hike up to this point from Grotta sa Oche.

From here, either retrace your steps or continue along the path which rises out of the chasm then drops to take you through the Flumineddu valley to the east. Follow the path north, along the course of a riverbed (usually dry), until reaching a wooden gate, which brings you back to the path from Grotta sa Oche. The whole route to and from Grotta sa Oche should not take longer than three hours. There are plenty of side-trips which can be made along the way, for example in the Flumineddu valley, for which you should hook up with a guided party.

underground close to the church of **San Giovanni** and attracts a constant trail of drivers with jerry cans. It makes a good place to picnic under the eucalyptus trees, and you can follow the course of the stream or a choice of tracks leading into the mountains. There's a hotel with a renowned restaurant here too (see opposite). ARST buses stop at the turn-off for Su Gologone.

Practicalities

Oliena is connected by regular **buses** from Nuoro, the last one returning at around 8pm (earlier on Sun). The village's **Pro Loco** (Mon–Fri 2.30–7pm, Sat 9am–1pm; ☎0784.287.612) currently resides in the town library, though they plan to move to new premises soon. The office has limited resources, but can offer some material on hiking in the region and also supply contacts for guided walks as well as agriturismo addresses. There is only one **hotel** in town, the bright and cheerful *Cikappa* at Via Martin Luther King 2 (☎0784.288.721, fax 0784.288.733; ②), which also has a pizzeria and restaurant and can arrange excursions in the vicinity. There is a useful **agriturismo**, however, for once right in the centre of the village at Via Bixio 9 (☎0784.287.066; no CCs; ②), offering clean and comfortable rooms and home cooking. Another agriturismo,

Camisadu (☎0368.347.9502; ②), lies 3km south of town on the Orgosólo road (signposted to the left), an isolated, partially modernized farmstead, with some great walking in the vicinity. Nearer to town, *Cooperativa Enis* (☎0784.288.363) offers clean rooms (②) as well as pitches for **camping** (L10,000 per person) in Località Maccione, a wooded area 3km south of town off the old road to Orgósolo.

One of Sardinia's best-known hotels, *Su Gologone* (☎0784.287.512, fax 0784.287.668; ⑦), lies 7km east of Oliena on the Dorgali road in a rustic setting next to the spring of the same name. It's an expensive choice, equipped with a swimming pool and two tennis courts; though remote, it's a popular destination for both excursionists and food pilgrims drawn to its good **restaurant**. The hotel organizes horse-riding and jeep expeditions onto Sopramonte and a "lunch with the shepherds" – an open-air affair where punters are pampered with a succulent succession of local dishes cooked over an open fire (not recommended for vegetarians).

You can arrange tailor-made **guided expeditions** around Sopramonte's caves and crags from Oliena itself. The main operators in the village are: Barbagia Insólita, Via Carducci 25 (☎0784.288.167 or 0336.608.211); Levamus, Corso Vittorio Emanuele 27 (☎0784.285.190 or 0336.775.731); Tíscali Trekking, Via Casu 8 (☎0368.381.9464) Cooperativa Enis (see above) also organizes excursions.

Orgósolo and Mamoiada

Deeper into the mountains, at the end of a straggly 18km road from Oliena, **ORGÓSOLO** is stuck with its label of bandit capital of the island. The clans of Orgósolo, whose menfolk used to spend the greater part of the year away from home with their flocks, have always nursed an animosity towards the settled crop-farmers on the Barbágia's fringes, a tension that occasionally broke out into open warfare. On top of this there was conflict between rival clans, which found expression in large-scale sheep-rustling and bloody vendettas, such as the *disamistade* (enmity) that engulfed Orgósolo at the beginning of the twentieth century. The feud arose from a dispute over the inheritance of the village's richest chieftain, Diego Moro, who died in 1903, and lasted for fourteen years, virtually exterminating the two families involved. Between 1901 and 1954, Orgósolo – population 4000 – clocked up an average of one murder every two months.

The village's most infamous son is **Graziano Mesina**, the so-called "Scarlet Rose", who won local hearts in the 1960s by robbing only from the rich to give to the poor and only killing for revenge against those who had betrayed him. Roaming at will through the mountains, even granting interviews to reporters and television journalists, he was eventually captured and incarcerated in Sássari prison. Escaping in

The Barbagia Ollolai

In 1953 the first of the post-war kid-nappings, which would soon become endemic to this region of Sardinia, took place near Orgósolo. Vittorio de Seta's film, Banditi di Orgósolo, *came out in 1961.*

1968, he was recaptured near Nuoro and flown by helicopter the same day to appear on television in Cágliari. Mesina last surfaced in July 1992, when he was dispatched to Sardinia from a mainland prison to help negotiate the release of Farouk Kassam, an eight-year-old boy held hostage for seven months in the Barbagia (see box on p.330).

Saddled with this semi-legendary background, it is inevitable that Orgósolo should play host to a constant trickle of visitors hoping to find traces of its violent past amid the shabby collection of grey breeze-block houses, and the locals have obliged by peppering the village's name-plate with bullet holes, and by painting a sinister scarlet and white face onto a rock by the side of the main road into town. But this is just a harbinger of things to come, for Orgósolo's narrow alleys have been daubed with a vivid array of **murals**, more strident and better executed than those found in other Sard villages such as San Sperate (see pp.140–141). Covering whole houses and shop fronts, most have a political element, graphically illustrating themes of exploitation – of the landless and women, for example – or demanding Sardinian independence. Some date back to the 1960s, protesting against the US bombing of Vietnam, while others are more recent, such as recalling the 1993 famine in Somalia; yet others are comic or simply depict village culture. All share a common theme of traditional culture in collision with the modern world. One of the most heavily painted buildings is the Municipio, whose garish collection of cartoon figures and slogans are poignantly shot through with more bullet holes – the work of local hotheads.

You could happily spend an hour or two wandering through this open-air gallery, but there's precious little else to do in Orgósolo, unless, that is, you're here at Ferragosto (August 14–15) when one of the region's most colourful **festivals** takes place around the little church of the **Assunta**, a nondescript, cream-fronted building enclosed behind a wall (but visible below Piazza Caduti). Within easy reach of the village, the high country above Orgósolo is well worth exploring. Following the road through the village, a left turn takes you south out of town and steeply uphill, leading after about 5km to the high plateau of **Montes**, an empty, desolate expanse, green but rugged, suitable for hiking or riding, and site of a good hotel and restaurant (see p.328). A small road continues as far as **Funtana Bona**, at a height of 1052m, only a kilometre or two's walk from the peak of **Monte San Giovanni** (1316m), near the source of the Cedrino river.

Taking the right fork above the village leads instead to **MAMOIA-DA**, a village every bit as straitened as Orgósolo, judging by its drab appearance, but whose distinctive Carnival rituals have made it one of the best-known of Barbágia's villages (see box opposite). In contrast to this intensely theatrical tradition, it's a disappointingly prosaic village, mainly flat and unprepossessing. Unless you're here for the twice-yearly masked festivities, there is little to see or do, though you

Mamoiada's Mamuthones

The **Mamuthones of Mamoiada** are among the best-known of Sardinia's traditional costumed figures, associated with the festivities around Carnival time, but with obscure and tangled roots going back several centuries. Despite their spookily disturbing appearance – decked out in shaggy black or brown sheepskins on which rows of jangling goat bells are strung, and with heavy, oversized masks – the Mamuthones are symbols of abundance and good times, as manifested by the food and drink liberally dispensed during the proceedings.

The main events take place on Shrove Tuesday and the preceding Sunday, usually kicking off at 3pm and 3.30pm respectively. The masked Mamuthones emerge onto the main street, Corso Vittorio Emanuele, in two parallel columns, accompanied by red-jacketed Issohadores – or Issokadores – wielding lassos (*sa soca*). As the Mamuthones solemnly advance along the street they perform curious synchronized leaps, causing the hundreds of goat bells tied across their backs to clang simultaneously, while the Issohadores twirl their lassos and ensnare victims, often from metres away, sometimes targeting spectators watching from balconies along the route. At the end of Shrove Tuesday's procession, marking the end of Carnival, a masked puppet known as *Juvanne Martis* is hauled on a cart through the village by supposedly weeping participants, representing the end of Carnival, though the evening sees a general carousal in Piazza Santa Croce anyway, with plates of pork and beans, traditional sweets and glasses of the local wine offered around, and dancing. In fact there is always plenty of similarly rustic fare to eat and drink during the ceremonies, from stalls and shops around the village.

An alternative opportunity to view these shenanigans comes much earlier, at the traditional beginning of the Carnival period, the festa di Sant'Antonio Abate around January 16 and 17, when bonfires are lit around the village and kept burning through the night, attracting groups of half-drunk revellers passing between them. Locals contend this is the best time to view the Mamuthones, when there are fewer distractions from the other costumed Carnival celebrations on the island, and fewer tourists.

might wander up to the **Fonte Romana** (signposted from Piazza Europa, at the bottom of the Corso), a couple of simple spouts over granite basins; only the lower part is authentically Roman, but the water is drinkable and fresh. The **Biblioteca** (library) in Piazza Europa usually holds an **exhibition of local costumes** during the period of the festivities.

Practicalities

About ten buses a day (two on Sun) ply the route to Orgósolo from Nuoro, so it's not necessary to stay over. Should you want to, however, there are a couple of reasonable **hotels** in town, one, *Sa'e Jana* (☎ & fax 0784.402.437; ②), on Via Lussu, has a restaurant, discotheque and stupendous views; it's slightly above the village on the Mamoiada road, signposted past the well-graffitied school. The other, the *Petit* (☎ & fax 0784.402.009; no CCs; ①), is right in the heart of things on Via Mannu, with less in the way of vistas but rock-bottom prices. Apart from these places, Orgósolo itself has little in the way of restaurants, though drivers can go a few kilometres in the Montes direction to **Località Settiles**, where there is a wonderful restaurant, the *Monti del Gennargentu*, serving up healthy mountain fare (☎ & fax 0784.402.374). You can also stay here, if you wanted to do any walking or riding around here (stables are nearby): *mezza pensione* comes to about L65,000 per person. It's about 3km from the SS389 Nuoro–Arbatax road, from the junction at Pratobello.

Mamoiada is equally well connected to Nuoro, though the village has no hotels or pensions. You can contact the Pro Loco (round the back of the library, ☎0784.56.277; Mon–Wed & Fri–Sat 4.30–8pm), however, about the possibility of staying with local families during the festivities. The Pro Loco will also provide local information, as does the *comune* on the Corso (☎0784.56.023; irregular hours). Mamoiada also has more scope for **eating**, including a basic trattoria, *La Campagnola*, at Corso Vittorio Emanuele 59 (closed Mon), and a simple pizzeria, *Da Mommo*, at Corso Vittorio Emanuele 82. About a hundred metres further up, at Corso Vittorio Emanuele 92, the *Bar Sarvuleddu* has snacks and tables outside. These places may be closed out of the summer season, however. If you're here during Carnival, pick up a steaming pork sandwich freshly grilled in places along the Corso, which also sell chilled wine.

Note that if you're driving here direct from Nuoro, you might prefer to take the fast, straight but poorly signposted route via the Circonvallazione Sud rather than the twisty, but gratifyingly empty, alternative.

Orani and Ottana

The unassuming village of **ORANI** is worth a stop for the museum dedicated to its most famous son, the sculptor **Costantino Nivola** (1911–88). In fact, Nivola only spent a short part of his life in the village, working with his stonemason father until the age of fifteen before studying in Sássari and then fleeing Fascist persecution in 1938. After spending some time in Paris, he emigrated to the United States, where he forged a long association with Le Corbusier and taught at Berkeley and Harvard. Most of the pieces in the **Museo Nivola** (Mon 4–8pm, Tues–Sun 9am–1pm & 4–8pm; L3000), a low yellow villa located above the Q8 petrol station at Via Gonare 2, are from the last period of Nivola's life, and reflect the artist's attitudes towards his homeland upon revisiting it after his long American exile. Small-scale, the very opposite of monumental, the items are arranged in one white, well-lit room on marble plinths, and in a small courtyard outside. Many of the bronze sculptures clearly recall nuraghic *bronzetti*, other works use cement and marble, and the technique of sandcasting (which Nivola pioneered). There are also sketches and models. If you like what you see or want to find out more about Nivola, there's a good bookshop where you can pick up material.

OTTANA, on the northern and western fringes of the Barbagia Ollolai, is reckoned to be the dead centre of Sardinia. The twin chimneys of the chemical plant outside town create an unattractive landmark in the predominantly flat countryside – a rare instance of industry in this province. Although its masked and horned Carnival horrors, *Sos Merdules*, vie with those of Mamoiada, Ottana is a dull place. It does, however, possess a good Romanesque church, **San Nicola**, for once centrally positioned on an elevation above the main square of this small town. Completed in 1160, the structure's dark, lugubrious stone is not exactly endearing, though its bare interior, minimally illuminated by slit windows, has an impressive altarpiece from the mid-fourteenth century. The main Carnival procession starts off from here at around 2.30pm on Shrove Tuesday, and features costumed representatives from the villages of Mamoiada, Fonni, Gavoi and Tonara as well as Ottana. The previous afternoon sees folk dances in the piazza below.

The Gennargentu massif and Barbagia Belvì

The **Gennargentu** chain of mountains – the name means "silver gate", referring to the snow that covers them every winter – holds the island's highest peaks, **Punta La Mármora** (1834m) and **Monte Bruncu Spina** (1829m), and the only skiing facilities. Unlike the granite crags of, say, Gallura, these mountains are round and, above a certain altitude, completely bare. The villages scattered about were traditionally shepherds' communities, but nowadays the shepherds send their children to university, or they go to seek work in mainland Italy and don't come back, leaving behind   32them slowly atrophying communities whose salvation is deemed to lie in a greater awareness of their tourism potential.

Many villages have in fact succeeded in adapting to the new economic reality, serving the expanding leisure industry, even if the season is short and has only a partial impact on the local economy. Though the villages themselves are often unprepossessing and uniform in appearance – **Fonni**, for example, one of the main centres on the northern outskirts of the Gennargentu range, or **Sórgono**, loathed by D.H. Lawrence during his visit to Sardinia – some, such as **Aritzo** and **Belvì**, Sardinia's cherry capital, are beautifully sited and even have good museums. But the real pleasures here are the bits between the villages: the thickly-wooded slopes where you may come across wild pigs, vultures and deer, the lush valleys and distant mountain views.

The villages certainly make good bases for **walking**, best undertaken in spring and summer, and there are good, reasonably-priced

Among the birds to be seen in the Gennargentu mountains are sparrow-hawks, peregrine falcons, goshawks, griffon vultures and eagles.

Banditismo and kidnapping in the Barbagia

Until a short time ago, the villages of the Barbagia were primarily communities of shepherds, whose isolated circumstances and economic difficulties in the postwar years led to widescale emigration and, among those who stayed behind, a crime wave. Sheep-rustling and internecine feuding came to be replaced by the infinitely more lucrative practice of the **kidnapping** and ransoming of wealthy industrialists or their families. This phenomenon reached epidemic proportions during 1966–68, when scores of *carabinieri* were drafted into the area to comb the mountains for the hideouts, rarely with any success. Following a lull in the kidnaps, recent years have seen a resurgence, exemplified by the case of Farouk Kassam, an eight-year-old abducted from the Costa Smeralda in 1992 and held for seven months on Monte Albo, near Sinìscola, suffering the severance of part of his ear by his kidnappers to accelerate the ransom payment.

hotels in the best areas, **Désulo**, for example, and **Tonara**. For fuller details on walks, you can obtain a handy booklet from Nuoro's tourist office (see p.316). As for **getting around**, roads are twisty and slow, and public transport is usually infrequent, but every village is connected by at least one route to large centres. The FdS train service is not as bad as in Lawrence's day, but it's still a cumbersome way to travel, only to be used if you have lots of time and patience.

Fonni and around

Sixteen kilometres due south of Mamoiada, in a hilly area thick with vineyards, corks and oak forests, **FONNI** is, at 1000m, Sardinia's highest village. As a popular destination for skiers and walkers in the Gennargentu mountains – whose loftiest peaks, Bruncu Spina and La Mármora, are visible from the village – Fonni is also one of the Barbagia's biggest centres, a role it has occupied since the seventeenth century when a community of Franciscans helped to make this the focus of the whole region.

The church of **Madonna dei Mártiri** annexed to their convent is still the most significant of the Barbagia's churches, both for its wealth and for its image of the Madonna, said to have been made from the crushed bones of martyrs. You can see the domed church at the highest point of the village, in the centre of a large open space off Piazza Europa, surrounded by *cumbessias* or pilgrims houses. Outside, the trees have been skilfully carved to illustrate religious themes. Originally dating from the seventeenth century but remodelled a hundred years later, the church is a substantial, salmon-coloured building with a tall grey granite spire. The interior is richly painted; an elaborate shrine on the right as you enter holds the artless but much venerated Madonna. The image is escorted through the streets during Fonni's two principal **festivals**, both in June – on the Monday following the first Sunday in June and again for San Giovanni's day on June 24. Both occasions are costumed extravaganzas, with columns of immaculately turned-out women and men on horseback, also in traditional dress, filing through the village.

The village has two three-star **hotels**: the recently modernized and fully-equipped *Cualbu* on Viale del Lavoro, (☎0784.57.054, fax 0784.58.403; ③), signposted on the left as you enter town, and the much smaller *Cinghialetto* on Via Grazia Deledda (☎ & fax 0784.57.660; ③). Both have **restaurants**, or you could seek out the modest *Barbagia* ristorante/pizzeria on Via Umberto, at the southern end of town.

You can eat and sleep on the slopes of **Monte Spada** at the *Sporting Club* (☎0784.57.285, fax 0784.57.220; ④), a large complex 8km south of Fonni, on a signposted left turn off the Désulo road; catering mainly to groups of skiers, it has a full range of facilities. Paths from here wind up to the peak of the mountain (1595m). Alternatively, take the right fork before reaching the hotel to reach **Bruncu Spina**, to which you can approach quite close by a tarmacked road. It's a magnificent landscape, with bracken and other hardy shrubs taking over above the tree-line, covered in snow for a good part of the year. The views from the top extend as far as Gallura and even Corsica to the north. **Skiers** can experience Sardinia's only piste from the ski-station here, while properly-equipped hikers can reach the top of the island's highest peak, **Punta La Mármora**, a little way to the south, in less than three hours. You don't need to be an experienced climber to tackle either of these summits, though a guide is essential; excursions can be organized from the various villages on the flanks of the mountains between May and September.

The Gennargentu massif and Barbagia Belvì

Climbers, cavers and hikers in difficulty and with access to a phone can call for help from SASS (Soccorso Alpino e Speleológico della Sardegna) at ☎070.286.200 or (toll-free) ☎167.272.048. Otherwise call the Carabinieri at ☎113.

Désulo

DÉSULO lies huddled along the steep slope of a deep forested valley 27km south of Fonni, to which it is connected by bus (less frequent services run from Cágliari and Nuoro). As one of the closest villages to the Gennargentu mountains, it makes a useful hiking base, and as such has a choice of **hotels**, including a good-value three-star, the *Gennargentu* (June–Sept; ☎0784.619.270; ②), up Via Kennedy on the left as you enter the village from the north; the *Lamármora* (Dec–March & June–Sept; ☎0784.619.411, fax 0784.619.126; ③), on the main Via Lamármora on the right, and *La Nuova* (☎0784.619.251; no CCs; ①), further up the same road, which has seven basic rooms with a shared bathroom above a restaurant. At the end of Via Lamármora, another hotel, *Maria Carolina* on Via Cágliari (☎ & fax 0784.619.310; ②) has splendid views from its bar, restaurant and pizzeria.

Belvì and Aritzo

West of Désulo, the road descends along a valley to meet the SS295 after about 6km. Turn left (south) to reach **BELVÌ** after another 4 or

5km. This compact cluster of dwellings is, like Désulo, crowded along the side of a valley, and is famed for its cherries. Its former importance is attested by the fact that the village gave its name to the whole of this sector of the Barbagia, but it's a very low-key place now, with little reason to linger apart from its **Museo Scienze Naturali** (daily: summer 8am–noon & 2–7pm, winter 9am–noon & 3–5pm; free), a collection of minerals, fossils and stuffed mammals, lizards and nearly 400 birds, all crammed into a private house on Via Sebastiano (corner of Via Roma). It's a diverting assortment, but the numerous stuffed animals look a little tatty in places; if you're very keen, call first to make sure it's open (☎0784.629.467 or 0784.629.397). Close by on Via Roma, the village has a decent **hotel and restaurant**, *L'Edera* (☎0784.629.898; ②).

Almost immediately after Belvì, **ARITZO** is another grey huddle, though it's larger, and has a livelier aspect than many of the other villages round here. The main road, Corso Umberto, holds everything of interest, including the parish church of **San Michele Archángelo**, a handsome edifice with some traces of its late Gothic construction and a good eighteenth-century *Pietà* on the second chapel on the right, and a seventeenth-century *San Cristóforo* in the last. Outside the church, the curiously square and solitary profile of Monte Téxile (975m) is visible on the horizon.

Aritzo also has an excellent **Museo Etnográfico** (Tues–Sun 10am–1pm & 4–7pm, 3–6pm in winter; L3000), signposted on the right as you enter the village from the north. Currently housed in six or seven rooms in the basement of a school, it's a fascinating jumble, mainly connected with rural culture in the Gennargentu, including agricultural implements, articles for cheese- and wax-making, artisans' tools, a few local costumes and some old photos, all in excellent condition. Aritzo once earned a healthy living selling snow, and you can see here the straw-lined chests with which it was transported. The collection is soon to be moved, probably to the Villa Comunale at the other end of the village.

Beyond the church, the imposing crenellated building on the left as you ascend the main road is the neo-Gothic **Castello Arangino**, its tower and loggia giving it a Tuscan character, though it was only built at the beginning of the twentieth century. The Corso also holds the eighteenth-century **prigione d'Aritzo**, used as a gaol until the 1940s.

There are several **hotels** in Aritzo, making this a feasible place to stay. Cheapest is the *Park Hotel*, on Via Maxia (April–Oct; ☎0784.629.201, fax 0784.629.318; no CCs; ②), and the same street holds *La Capannina* (☎ & fax 0784.629.121; no CCs; ②), a bigger place; both have rooms with or without bath. At the top, southern end of the village, the *Hotel Castello* is a modern two-star with plain and clean rooms, some with views (☎0784.629.266; no CCs; ②). Further up, through an arch, the *Moderno* has more character, with its own little garden and a pleasant restaurant (☎0784.629.299, fax 0784.629.675; ②). There are also a few craft shops and a **bank** on Corso Umberto.

Tonara and Sórgono

Fifteen kilometres north of Aritzo, **TONARA** shares the same forested environment; chestnuts are one of the foundations of the local economy. The village is also famed for the manufacture of cattle bells and for its *torrone* nougat – a rich sticky feast of honey, nuts and eggs, usually for sale wherever there's a village *festa*. Tonara also has a couple of small hotels: on the left, the *Belvedere* on the street of the same name (☎ & fax 0784.63.756; ②), and *Su Toni* on Via Italia (☎0784.63.420; ①). Both places have **restaurants**, or you can eat informally at *Aquarium*, a cosy pizzeria/*paninoteca* on the main drag.

D. H. Lawrence in Sardinia

D.H. Lawrence arrived in Sardinia in January 1921 in response to a restless desire to take a break from Sicily, where he was then living with his wife Frieda: "Comes over one an absolute necessity to move," begins his travelogue, *Sea and Sardinia*. The result was the briefest tour of the island, just six days, for most of which he was in trains and buses, having decided to travel the hardest route – straight up through the interior from Cágliari on the painfully slow narrow-gauge railway ("Oh, wooden wearisome railway carriage, we are so sick of you!") as far as Sórgono, from which the Lawrences changed onto a bus to Nuoro, and thence to Olbia, where they took the ferry. In Sórgono – which at first appeared like "some little town in the English West Country" with "glades of stripling oaks and big slopes with oak trees and on the right a sawmill buzzing, and on the left the town, white and close, nestling round a baroque church-tower" – there was just one hotel, the *Risveglio*, where the only bedroom available contained "a large bed, thin and flat with a grey-white counterpane, like a large, poor, marble-slabbed tomb in the room's sordid emptiness; one dilapidated chair on which stood the miserablest weed of a candle I have ever seen: a broken wash-saucer in a wire ring: and for the rest, an expanse of wooden floor as dirty-grey-black as it could be, and an expanse of wall charted with the bloody deaths of mosquitoes." A stroll through the village did not improve his mood: "A dreary hole! a cold, hopeless, lifeless, Saturday-afternoon-weary village, rather sordid, with nothing to say for itself." Things got worse.

Nonetheless, it's a good read: a close-up description of travelling on the cheap, crammed with the details of conversations and the minutiae of buying bread or making tea on the "kitchenette", interspersed with observations on the state of the world in the wake of World War I. Lawrence's tone wasn't always negative: "For us to go to Italy and to *penetrate* into Italy is like a most fascinating act of self-discovery – back, back down the old ways of time. Strange and wonderful chords awake in us, and vibrate again after many hundreds of years of complete forgetfulness." For details of publication, see p.362.

The
Gennargentu
massif and
Barbagia
Belvì

West of Tonara, the road careers through forests of chestnut and oak for 10km before reaching the small town of **SÓRGONO**, the northernmost point of the FdS narrow-gauge railway from Cágliari. D.H. Lawrence and his wife Frieda disembarked here in 1921, en route to Nuoro, and hated it. As the centre of the Mandrolisai wine region, the town enjoys a certain fame, but it's a long, dull sprawl, devoid of any great interest and useful only as a transport junction and hotel stop. The FdS station is at the eastern end of the village, off the main street, where the Banco di Sardegna has a cash machine. There is little to distinguish between the two **hotels**: one, *Da Nino*, is on Via IV Novembre (☎ & fax 0784.60.127; ③), the other is *Villa Fiorita* on Viale Europa (☎0784.60.129; ③); both have **restaurants**.

The Sarcidano: Láconi, Ísili and the Nuraghe Arrubiu

On the southern edges of the Barbagia, the **Sarcidano** district is a quickly changing landscape of verdant hills and desolate basalt plains. There is ample evidence here of Sardinia's murky prehistory, starting with a fascinating collection of menhirs in the museum at **Láconi**, a village cradled in a fold of the hills at the top of this area. Further south, **Ísili** – considered the economic, cultural and administrative centre of Sarcidano – has the imposing **Is Parras** nuraghe on its outskirts, while outside the town of Orroli, between the Flumendosa and Mulargia lakes, the **Nuraghe Arrubiu** is one of the island's grandest monuments from this era.

Either Láconi or Ísili would be good places to break your journey, the latter having the area's best choice of **hotels**, though the former is the more attractive village. Both places are stops on the FdS line, and these villages and Orroli are linked by ARST buses, though you will need your own transport to view Nuraghe Arrubiu.

Láconi

On the fringes of the mountains, the village of **LÁCONI** retains a fresh, wooded feel; it's a pleasurable place to explore, with a surprising number of varied attractions. Not the least of these is its elegant Neoclassical **Municipio** on the main Corso Garibaldi, designed in 1846 by Sardinia's greatest architect, Gaetano Cima (1805–78). Below and behind it is housed Láconi's excellently presented **Museo delle Statue Menhir** (daily: summer 9.30am–1pm & 4–7.30pm; winter 9am–1pm & 4–6pm; closed 1st Mon of month; L4000), signposted simply Museo Archeologico, but mainly dedicated to Sardinia's extraordinary prehistoric menhirs, of which the area has a concentration. Although most of the bigger ones, reaching up to seven metres in height (as seen in photographs here), have been left in their original sites, the museum has a fine selection of smaller

The
Sarcidano:
Láconi, Ísili
and the
Nuraghe
Arrubiu

Sant'Ignazio da Láconi

Born Vincenzo Peis, though apparently called Il Santerello even in his youth because of his extreme piety, Sant'Ignazio da Láconi became a lay Capuchin monk in 1721, and spent the next 60 years practising penitence, humility and charity; as an inscription in his birthplace relates, *Conobbe le cose occulte, penetrò il segreto dei cuori, ed ebbe il dono dei miracoli* ("he knew occult things, he penetrated the secrets of the heart, and he had the gift of miracles..."). For 40 of those years he lived in Cágliari, where he performed various miracles, dying there in 1781 and spawning an enthusiastic cult. Beatified in 1940, he was canonized in 1951.

pieces, imaginatively displayed and grouped according to the genre they represent.

The majority of the menhirs, which are mainly of trachyte stone, date back to the Neolithic cultures of Ozieri and Arzachena of the second half of the fourth millennium BC, and are a principal source of information for this obscure era, particularly regarding its divinities. The earliest have few if any characteristic marks, though later ones bear primitive facial characteristics, mainly nose and eyes. Of these, the most interesting are the "anthropomorphic" ones, especially common around Láconi, which represent either male or female forms. The "males" are distinguished by the horn-shaped tridents embossed on one side, perhaps indicating membership of a warrior class, while "feminine" menhirs have a more inchoate form, though one, in Sala 2, shows a grooved circle below the "neck", perhaps representing a hair arrangement. Others are "asexual", though still retaining the facial features. The museum also displays Neolithic ceramics and obsidian arrowheads.

Opposite the Municipio, the cobbled Via Sant'Ignazio leads to the **Casa Natale di Sant'Ignazio**, family home of one of Sardinia's most revered saints. Even non-believers can find something interesting in the house, though you need to go round to the back to appreciate how it must have originally appeared – the rough stonework here is quite unlike the spruced-up exterior of the front. The house is usually left open: a bare room with a typical wood-beamed and bamboo-covered ceiling holds a shrine, and there are benches for prayer and meditation.

Further down Via Sant'Ignazio, turn left at Piazza XXIX Agosto and walk up Via Don Minzoni to reach the church dedicated to **Sant'Ignazio**, conspicuous by its metal dome and square, pointy campanile. The bronze sculpted doors, carved in the 1980s, depict miracles and scenes from the saint's life, and you can see the chapel where he received his baptism.

Below the church, the bosky terraced **Parco Aymerich di Láconi** (8am–sunset) makes an ideal place to take a breather or have a picnic. Once over a bridge that crosses a pretty stream, you'll find a

The Sarcidano: Láconi, Ísili and the Nuraghe Arrubiu

marvellous shady retreat full of surprises – not just springs, waterfalls, a lake with goldfish and much bigger, darker fish lurking, grottoes, great overhanging rocks, and beautifully crafted rustic benches – but, buried within the thick groves, the **Castello Aymerich**, a ruined redoubt parts of which go back to 1051. The building has pleasing details, such as the small carving of a castle on the gate and the windows oddly resembling an ace of spades. In front of the roofless hall there's a grassy terrace with fine views over the valleys and countless paths curving round the hill. Everything is verdant, damp and mossy. All around are trees from Europe, Asia and the Americas (they are labelled, and a list at the entrance gives their scientific nomenclature, their names in Italian, and in the Láconi dialect).

Practicalities

Láconi has a good, friendly and cheap hotel, the *Sardegna*, (☎0782.869.033, fax 0782.867.005; ①), above a restaurant at the top of the main street. ARST buses stop right outside here as well as in front of the Municipio (tickets from the kiosk to its left), and the village is a stop on the FdS line, the station a ten-minute walk to the west of town. The Banco di Sardegna on Via Santa Maria – signposted left off the main street heading north – has a *cambio* but no cash dispenser (open Mon–Fri 8.20–1.20pm).

Ísili

A right turn off the SS128 southward takes you along the SS197 to the Giara di Gésturi, La Marmilla and Barúmini (see pp.144–152). Staying on the SS128 leads another 8km across a calcareous landscape studded with outcrops to ÍSILI. Like so many of Sardinia's inland villages, it makes little visual impact, though it has a couple of attractions and some good country worth exploring in the vicinity. In recent years it has been a popular base for free climbers, attracted to the sheer rock faces of the surroundings, though the village has a longer-established fame as a centre of *artigianato*, particularly copperware, which is readily available in the shops in and around the central Corso Vittorio Emanuele III. There are also several **domus de janas** in the vicinity – the so-called fairy-houses which were actually prenuraghic tombs. A couple of them are easily visitable on foot from the western end of the Corso: a sign points the way along a cul-de-sac on the edge of the village, from where a path leads to square-cut openings giving onto low-roofed chambers.

Far more compelling is the **Is Parras** nuraghe (daily 9am–noon & 2–5pm; free) on Ísili's northern outskirts, unmissable from the SS128 from Láconi or from the FdS train. Splendidly sited on a bare hillock, this is one of Sardinia's most impressive single-towered nuraghic monuments, whose smooth-walled tholos interior is also, at 12m, the highest in the island. There's a small chamber in front of the main entrance, and a niche for a sentry on its right-hand side. It's an exposed place, with wild olive growing out of its walls. Outside the normal opening times, it's easy enough to jump the walls to have a poke around.

Free climbers and passing visitors alike can enjoy some of the desolate sites lying within a short distance of Ísili. The **Lago di San Sebastiano**, visible from the village's western side, is a dammed lake with the ruins of a church poised above. Also west of town, the canyon of **Is Borroccus**, carved out by the Mannu river, is one of the rare nesting sites in Sardinia of Bonelli's eagle.

Practicalities

Ísili's main FdS station is on the southern end of town, though there is another station to the north. Owing to its fame as a centre of crafts and climbing, Ísili boasts four **hotels**, making it a useful overnight stop. Of these, the small *Giardino* lies nearest to the main FdS station, just across from the Agip petrol station on Corso Vittorio Emanuele (☎0782.802.014; no CCs; ②), though it's also the dingiest; two mini-apartments have private bathrooms, the other six rooms share facilities. Of the other choices, the smartest and most modern is the two-star *Del Sole* (☎0782.802.024, fax 0782.802.371; ②), at the western end of Corso Vittorio Emanuele, though the *Pioppo* (☎0782.802.117, fax 0782.803.091; ②), on the corner of Via Dante Alighieri and the Corso – some of whose comfortably-sized rooms have TVs – and the *Cardellino*, a modern, three-storey yellow block next to a public garden on Via Dante (☎0782.802.004, fax 0782.802.438; ②), are fine too. All hotels have their own restaurants and charge very similar rates, and all, apart from the *Giardino*, have rooms with en-suite facilities.

Nuraghe Arrubiu and Perdasdefogu

From the SS128, the SS198 branches eastward about 8km south of Ísili, from which the towns of Nurri and **ORROLI** are reachable along the SP10. Neither village has any immediate appeal, though the latter has a useful and well-appointed **hotel and pizzeria**, the *Igalan* on the main Corso Cavour (☎0782.845.135, fax 0782.845.002; ③).

From Orroli, continue south for another kilometre along the SP10 for the turn-off leading to one of Sardinia's most important nuraghic sites, **Nuraghe Arrubiu** (daily: summer 9.30am–1pm & 3–8.30pm, winter 9am–5pm; L5000), occupying an exposed, wind-blown plain another 3 or 4km down this road. Dating from around the seventh century BC, this formidable ruin is the only five-towered nuraghic complex in existence, and is thought to have originally had a much older 30-metre central tower, of which nothing now remains. The complex takes its name ("red") from the basalt trachyte stone and the lichen that lend it its distinctive hue. The site has only been open since 1996 after a long period of excavation. Curiously, no nuraghic finds have so far been unearthed, only Punic and Roman artefacts,

The Sarcidano: Láconi, Ísili and the Nuraghe Arrubiu

For excursions around the Orroli area, including canoeing in the nearby lakes of Flumendosa and Mulargia, contact Orroli's Is Janas agency, at Via Eleonora d'Arborea 30 (☎0330.435. 551, website www.web.tin.it /orroli).

For more information on Sardinia's nuraghic culture, see box on pp.148-149.

The
Sarcidano:
Láconi, Ísili
and the
Nuraghe
Arrubiu

though continuing excavations are expected to throw up more valuable material. The Roman finds, which include mills, basins and stone tools used for pressing olives and grapes, are displayed in a separate walled area to the left as you enter the site.

Because of the continuing work being carried out, visitors must be guided round the complex; tours last about an hour. If you're in the area on a summer night, you can sign up for one of the illuminated **nocturnal tours** offered by the local *cooperativa*, an atmospheric way to view the remains. Just a couple of hundred metres across from the site, an agriturismo complex offering accommodation, horse-riding facilities and treks should have been completed by the time you read this. If not, you can pick up refreshments from a snack bar at the site.

The country south and east of here is rugged and empty, though growing greener and gentler once past the Flumendosa river. Continue south to reach the mountainous Gerrei district (see p.95), or head west at Escalaplano for the highly scenic and gloriously deserted minor road that runs through **PERDASDEFOGU** before climbing north again towards the Ogliastra region (see p.344). Perdasdefogu is an undistinguished village whose name ("Fire stones") is thought to derive from either the bituminous coal and anthracite which was mined here in the nineteenth century, or the local silica, used by primitive tribes to light fires.

These days, with its military base, the town has little to recommend a stay, though there are some wonderful walks to be enjoyed in the area, for example in the **Santa Barbara** wood, less than a kilometre from town, and to a lovely set of 70-metre waterfalls, the **Cascate di Luesu**, to the south (on the right of the new road to Tertenia). The main Corso Vittorio Emanuele has a Banco di Sardegna and post office, and a useful **hotel and restaurant** at no. 55, the *Mura* (☎0782.94.603; ②).

The eastern coast

Nuoro province's long **eastern seaboard** is highly developed around the resorts of **Posada** and **Orosei**, but further south it preserves its desolate beauty, virtually untouched apart from a couple of isolated spots around **Cala Golone** and, further down, the small port of **Arbatax**. The SS125 follows the coast down from Siniscola. Frequent daily buses connect Cágliari and Nuoro with Tortolì, which is close to Arbatax. Tortolì and Arbatax are also on the FdS narrow-gauge railway which follows an inland route from Mandas, which has connections with Cágliari; the full journey from the coast to Cágliari takes seven dawdling hours.

The **beaches** along this coast are some of Sardinia's wildest. Near Orosei, **Cala Liberotto** has some extremely swim-worthy stretches of sand, as does Orosei's Marina, from where another small road leads a

338   THE GUIDE: CHAPTER 8

little further south to some more secluded bathing spots. **Hotels** are easy to come by, and the coast also has a good choice of **campsites**.

Posada

Northeast of Nuoro, the SS131dir. highway follows the course of two river valleys, passing close to the inland town of Siniscola, the main centre of the rich agricultural land around here. The main road reaches the coast at **POSADA**, sited on a rise a little way inland, near the mouth of the river of the same name. Once a power-base for the surrounding districts, the town was prey to repeated attacks by sea-borne raiders during the Middle Ages, and now only the ruins of its once impregnable castle – still commanding impressive views for miles around – attest to its former importance,

To get to the castle, climb up into the old centre; drivers should leave their vehicles in Piazza Eleonora d'Arborea or lower. The **Castello della Fava** (always open; free) is a five-minute climb up steps above the square, now little more than a single oblong upright tower ringed by broken-down walls. Visitors must climb up five levels of wooden steps and iron rungs to reach the trapdoor at the top, but are rewarded by a sweeping panorama over the citrus groves around the coast and banks of the Posada river, south past lagoons to the resort of La Caletta, and inland to the peaks of Barbagia. The castle owes its strange name – "Bean Castle" – to a medieval legend according to which, when besieged here by Moors, the *giudice* of Gallura took a homing pigeon, forced a broad bean down its gullet, and attached a message addressed to a fictitious army of rescuers. As planned, the Moors intercepted the bird. When they read the message and found the broad bean in its stomach, they concluded that not only was there an army on the way, but that the besieged Sards had plenty of provisions (enough to waste on pigeons, anyway), and promptly withdrew.

Most of Posada's **hotels** are located on the road to the sea, though there is the small three-star *Sa Rocca* in the village (☎0784.854.139, fax 0784.854.166; ②), an attractive hotel below the castle in Piazza Eleonora d'Arborea, with half- or full board required in summer. On Via Gramsci, between Posada and La Caletta, the *Donatella* has much more capacity (☎0784.854.521, fax 0784.854.433; ③). The **restaurants** in either place can supply good pastas and pizzas. If you want to spend any time in the area, *Dea Centro Escursioni* can arrange trekking, mountain biking, caving and canoeing at all levels (☎ & fax 0784.854.580).

Posada hosts a jazz festival over three or four days around August 20, when bands from Sardinia and the mainland play for free in Piazza Belvedere.

The coast to Orosei

South of Posada, **La Caletta** is a small resort close to a watchtower and some good beaches, with a choice of hotels and snack bars. The fine white sands lie to the south of the small port. For refreshments,

Skipper is just around the corner from the beach, a *birreria* with *panini* and music on Via Lungomare (closed Mon), while the nearby *Caffè Concerto* has snacks including crepes and ice creams. *Fantasy*, on Piazza Berlinguer, rents out bikes, tandems and cars. **Santa Lucia**, 5km further south, is another holiday resort with a Spanish watchtower. Close to the beach, under pinewoods, are two adjacent **campsites**, *Selema* (mid-May to mid-Oct; ☎0784.819.068) and *La Mandragola* (mid-May to Sept; ☎0784.819.119), both fully-equipped (the bigger *Selema* has better sports facilities). A little further south in the La Mandras neighbourhood, there's a remoter site, *Cala Pineta* (mid-June to mid-Sept; ☎0784.819.184), which also has a tennis court. Of the three, only *La Mandragola* has cabins (①), which are rudimentary.

Six or seven kilometres south, a turn-off left leads another couple of kilometres on to **Capo Comino**, Sardinia's easternmost point, a wild and desolate spot of jagged rocks and abundant *macchia*. An enticing arc of sand just to the north of the point is backed by more holiday homes and a couple of bars. A further 12km to the south, **Cala Liberotto** is yet another small-scale holiday centre, lacking much in the way of shops, but the pinewoods are scattered with villas and a clutch of **campsites**, including *Cala Ginepro*, right on the sea (☎0784.91.017); it's got bungalows at up to L180,000 for four, much less in low season (and it's open all year). The *Mariposa* here supplies good **pizzas**.

From Cala Liberotto, the SS125 tracks away from the sea for 12km before crossing the Cedrino river, thick with reeds, to the town of **OROSEI**, the main centre of the Baronia region. Though it now stands 3km from the sea in a flat and fertile zone planted with vines and citrus groves, medieval accounts of Turkish raids suggest that Orosei must have been a harbour before the silting up of the nearby river pushed the shore back. Orosei shows signs of a prosperous past, in the many fine Spanish palazzi scattered around its interesting old quarter, and in its splendid ecclesiastical architecture, not least the church and towers of **Sant'Antonio**, fifteenth-century but much restored and remodelled. The church precincts, entered through an ogival arch from Piazza Sant'Antonio, consist of a cobbled space surrounded by *muristenes*, temporary pilgrims' dwellings (known as *cumbessias* in Sardinia's other provinces), in the centre of which stands a Pisan tower, converted into a private residence.

Orosei's central Piazza del Pópolo has another group of medieval buildings worth seeking out, foremost among which is **San Giácomo**, a cluster of tiled cupolas and a campanile fronted by a plain white Neoclassical facade at the top of a flight of steps. More steps on the other side of the road lead to Piazza Sas Ánimas, holding the dreadfully neglected remains of a fourteenth-century castle that was later used as a gaol, for which it's called **Castello Prigione Vecchia**. Next to it stands the pretty eighteenth-century **Chiesa delle**

Ánime, made of rough brick and stonework with a tiled cupola and good portal. A brief walk away (and well signposted) lie two more churches: San Gavino and the ruin of San Sebastiano, which you could take in on a brief stroll through the old town's streets.

Practicalities

Orosei's **Pro Loco** sits below the church of San Giácomo, and can put you in touch with people willing to guide you round the backstreets pointing out things of interest. There are only three or four **hotels** in town, none particularly cheap. Best is *Su Barchile* on Via Mannu (☎0784.98.879, fax 0784.998.113; ④), a modern and friendly three-star with a great restaurant attached, though the *S'Ortale* on Via S'Ortale has more space and is cheaper (☎0784.998.055, fax 0784.998. 056; ③), and also has a restaurant. When it comes to **restaurants**, however, the first choice must be *Su Barchile*, with delicious local dishes such as *makkarrones de busa* and *porcetto* cooked in myrtle. There's a Banco di Sardegna (Mon–Fri 8.20am–1.20pm & 2.35–4.05pm) on Via Nazionale, with a cash dispenser.

Dorgali and around

Centre of the renowned **Cannonau** wine-growing region, **DORGALI** attracts a lot of tourists in summer, both for its craftwork and on account of the recent growth of Cala Gonone, a small port 10km away. Along with a couple of significant attractions in the neighbourhood, this is the main reason people come here, though you could visit the town's small **Museo Archeologico** on Via Vittorio Emanuele.

Dorgali's restaurants and hotels are generally cheaper than those by the coast, making it a useful base if you're planning to spend some time in the area. The *San Pietro* (☎0784.96.142; ①) has bargain lodgings in the centre of town on Via La Mármora; on the same street, but at the northern entrance to town, is the next cheapest hotel, the modern three-star *Querceto* (☎0784.96.509, fax 0784.95.254; ③), closed between November and March. Both places have **restaurants**; alternatively you'll find Sardinian specialities at *Cólibri* on Via Gramsci, near the northern entry into town from the SS125. Ask at the **Pro Loco** (Mon–Sat 9am–1pm; ☎0784.96.243) about excursions to the nearby archeological sites and trekking expeditions, or call Escursarda Neulé (☎0784.94.897 or 0330.663.850).

The Ispinigoli Grotto

Between Orosei and Dorgali, the **Grotta di Ispinigoli** (L9000) is signposted a little way off the main road. This deep cave contains one of nature's most magnificent works of art, a mind-bending collection of stalagmites and stalactites dominated by one 38-metre column that appears to hold the whole lot up. Inside have been found traces of some distant human presence – jewels, amphorae and bones, probably dating from Phoenician times. The local name for the cave, Abisso delle Vérgini, probably owes more to popular imagination than to fact, but it is likely that such an impressive natural phenomenon would have attracted some kind of religious ritual.

Tours inside the grotto leave on the hour 9am–6pm in summer; between October and April visitors must contact the Pro Loco in Dorgali (☎0784.96.243) for access. The half-hour tour costs L9000 per person. There's a good **restaurant** close to the entrance.

Serra Orrios

Eleven kilometres northwest of Dorgali, near the SS129 running between Nuoro and Orosei, **Serra Orrios** (daily: 9am–noon & 4–6pm, 2–4pm in winter; L5000) makes a fascinating stop. Though it doesn't have a nuraghe as such, it's still one of the most interesting nuraghic sites in the region, showing how a typical community was arranged. Located in a small plain surrounded by olive trees and overlooked by the peaks of Monte Albo to the north, the remains of the village lie within a long walled enclosure at the end of a 500-metre path through an olive grove.

Entered through a lintelled doorway, the extensive site consists chiefly of the closely packed circular walls of the seventy-odd village buildings, about two metres high and separated by paths. Among them are two rectangular temples labelled "Tempietto A" and "Tempietto B", the first of which lies within a round walled area, and is thought to have been used by visiting pilgrims. Tempietto B was probably the villagers' centre of worship – a long building surrounded by a wall, with a doorway at one end topped by a curved slab and a low bench running along the inside. All in all, it's an attractive site to wander round; guides provide a commentary in Italian but are mainly there to keep you off the walls. Before setting off, spend some time examining the diagram near the entrance showing how the village must once have appeared. There's a bar and *paninoteca* here, too.

Cala Gonone

A couple of kilometres south out of Dorgali, a left turn into a tunnel brings you through the mountain wall and corkscrewing down through groves of cork to an azure bay. Beautifully sited at the base of the 900-metre-high mountains, **CALA GONONE** was once a tiny settlement huddled around a harbour, until recently accessible only by boat. Now hotels and villas dominate the scene, though these have not entirely spoilt the sense of isolation, and it is worth a visit if only to take advantage of the numerous boat tours to the secluded coves up and down the coast.

At the small port crowded with pleasure craft, you can hire dinghies and book boat excursions. There's a curve of sand next to the port, which improves as you continue further south, though the best beaches by far are those accessible only by boat (see box opposite). A car

Boat tours from Cala Gonone

Running between March and September, the best boat tours from Cala
Gonone take you to **Cala Luna** and **Cala Sisine**, secluded beaches at the
base of soaring cliffs, respectively 6 and 11km south of the port. These and
some of the other sandy inlets beaches round here are truly spectacular
swimming spots, and most cruises take in brief explorations of the deep
grottoes that pit the shore.

The most famous of these is the **Grotta del Bue Marino** – touted as the
last refuge of the Mediterranean monk seal, or "sea ox", in Italian waters.
Whether or not you catch a glimpse of one, it's a good expedition, since
this is among Sardinia's most spectacular caves, a luminescent gallery
filled with remarkable natural sculptures resembling organ pipes, wedding
cakes and even human heads – one of them is known as "Dante", after a
fondly imagined resemblance to the poet.

Pick any of the agencies at the Porto Turístico to book tickets for any of
the various excursions. Prices vary seasonally: to go to the Grotta di Bue
Marino it's about L18,000 per person, but a typical minicruise – heading
south for around two hours as far as Arco di Goloritzè or Spiaggia Aguglia
for diving, swimming and a *grigliata* lunch (included in the price), then
returning with stops at Cala Mariolu, Cala Biriola, Cala Sisine, Cala Luna,
and Grotta del Bue Marino – would cost about L60,000. Boats depart at
about 9.30am, returning at around 7pm. General information can be
obtained from the Nuovo Consorzio Trasporti Maríttimi in Via Millelire
(☎0784.93.305). Book the day before, if possible, and take a sun hat.

or bike would do for a pair of idyllic swimming places at **Spiaggia
Cartoe** and **Spiaggia Osalla**, accessible from the narrow road dug out
of the mountains north of the town that connects up with the SS125.

Practicalities

ARST **buses** pull up right by the port on Via Marco Polo, or in the
pine woods above town if you have a hotel here. Most of the **hotels**
in Cala Gonone are closed out of season. At the bottom of the long
Viale Colombo, about 50m up from the port, the *Píccolo*
(☎0784.93.232; ③) is one of the cheapest, with views through pine
trees to the sea. It's theoretically always open; if you find it closed
out of season, call ☎0784.93.035. Below, right on the portside, the
Pop is a good-value hotel with a range of facilities (☎0784.93.185,
fax 0784.93.158; ③). At the south end of Via Lungomare, the
bougainvillea-covered *Cala Luna* (April to mid-Oct;
☎0784.93.133, fax 0784.93.162; ③) is a lively place with rooms
with balconies and direct access to the beach. On the same road, try
La Conchiglia (March to mid-Oct; ☎0784.93.448; ③), smaller and
smarter, also with seafront views. There's a choice of **eating places**
too, ranging from fast food to gourmet parlours. In the latter category, the *Miramare* hotel, on Piazza Giardini, is rated highly. Just
beyond it, *Al Faro* on Via Dándolo does pizzas and seafood dishes,
and *La Terrazza* pizzeria/ristorante next door to the *Cala Luna* on

> ### Hikes from Cala Gonone and Dorgali
>
> South of Cala Gonone lies one of Sardinia's last truly untouched tracts: swerving inland along the ridge of the Flumineddu River, walled on the other side by the Sopramonte massif, the new road brings you into a majestic mountain landscape, largely devoid of human life. Stefano Ardito, in his *Backpacking and Walking in Italy*, outlines two **long-distance hikes** in these wild parts, which he describes as among the best in the whole Mediterranean basin.
>
> One of these walks – a two- to three-day hike – follows the coast from **Cala Gonone to Cala Sisine**, at which point the route wanders inland, up the Sisine canyon, as far as the solitary church of **San Pietro**, from which a track leads down to **Baunei**. The second, shorter hike follows the course of the **Flumineddu River** from **Dorgali** and takes you after a couple of hours into the **Gorropu Gorge**, though further exploration requires mountaineering skills and even dinghies to negotiate the small lakes in the heart of the gorge. This hike also terminates at Baunei.
>
> A good first port of call for those interested in guided walks and excursions is *Sa Domu De S'Orku*, a bunker-like building near the turn-off for Urzulei. It houses a bar, shop and informal hiking centre, the Società Gorropu (☎0782.649.282), where you can look at routes and maps and talk to the staff about options.

Via Lungomare has alfresco eating in summer. By the port, *Il Pescatore* on Via Marco Polo does a busy trade in fish dishes, and the next-door *Pop* hotel also has a popular restaurant with set-price menus ranging from L15,000 to L25,000.

Tortolì and Arbatax

From Baunei the road descends steeply to **TORTOLÌ**, 5km inland from the port of **ARBATAX**, itself little more than a paper factory, a few bars and restaurants, and a port from which ferries ply to Genoa and Civitavecchia two or three times weekly. The small beach here is famous for its red rocks, but there are better bathing spots outside town – especially to the south, where there is a series of sand and rock beaches at Porto Frailis, San Gemiliano and, further down, Lido Orri. **Porto Frailis** is the nearest and the liveliest spot, site of most of the local hotels and restaurant, and connected by #2 buses from Viale Arbatax. The best **beaches** in the area are at **Lido Orri**, though you'll need to drive to reach it, 4km down the coast accessible from the SS125 south of Tortolì.

Practicalities

There is a **tourist office** at Arbatax station (June–Sept daily 7.30–10am, noon–1.30pm & 5–9pm, open until 10 or 10.30pm in July and Aug; ☎0782.667.690) with information on sea **excursions**, including the Grotta del Bue Marino for L35,000 (see box on p.343) – in winter Tortolì's Pro Loco on Via Mazzini is open 9am–noon (☎0782.622.824).

Ferries from Arbatax

Tirrenia runs a regular **ferry service** to the mainland from Arbatax, sometimes via Cágliari or Olbia. Departures are once or twice weekly to Civitavecchia (near Rome) and Genoa. The crossing to Genoa is a slow one, taking up to 21 hours, since it usually makes a stop for a couple of hours at Olbia. A typical fare between Arbatax and Civitavecchia in high season would be around L82,000 in a second-class cabin, L65,000 in a semi-reclinable seat, L135,000 for a small or medium-size car, or respectively L61,000, L46,000 and L100,000 in low season. In summer, an additional fast ferry service (*mezzo veloce*) connects Arbatax with Fiumicino, near Rome, in less than six hours, with fares at L65,000–90,000 per person, L120,000–140,000 for a small-to-medium-sized car. See Travel Details below for full schedules.

Tickets should be booked as early as possible, especially in summer. The Tirrenia office is on the right near the port, at Via Venezia 10 (Mon–Fri 8.30am–1pm & 4–7.30pm, Sat 8.30am–2pm, plus Sun & Wed 10pm–midnight; ☎0782.667.067).

There are several small **hotels** in the Arbatax area, most of them difficult to reach on foot. The only reasonably priced one in Arbatax itself, the *Gabbiano* (☎0782.623.512; ③), is actually a couple of kilometres south of the port in the Porto Frailis district, near a good beach; it only has four rooms, however, and may be closed in winter. Otherwise, head towards Tortolì, where there is a small selection, including the pleasant *Splendor* on Viale Arbatax (☎0782.623.037; ②) – opposite the Esso station on the other side of the rail tracks – and, further up on the left (on the corner with Via Sarcidano), *Dolce Casa* (June–Sept; ☎0782.624.235; no CCs; ②), a clean and comfortable place run by an expatriate Englishwoman and her husband. There's a **campsite** in Porto Frailis, *Telis* (☎0782.667.323), open all year with bungalows and caravans to rent by the week; another one at San Gemiliano, *Sos Flores* (June–Sept; ☎0782.623.671), and a third further south at Lido Orrì, *Orrì* (May–Sept; ☎0782.624.927). Frequent buses connect Tortolì, Arbatax and Porto Frailis.

As for **restaurants**, there are a few seafront joints in Arbatax itself; in the Porto Frailis district, look out for *Il Faro*, overlooking the beach, and with a good choice of fish. There's also *La Baia* pizzeria/ristorante near the *Telis* campsite. A good place for pizzas and full meals as well as late drinks, the *Caffè del Mare* on the Spiaggia di San Gemiliano also has live music.

Travel Details

TRAINS

Arbatax to: Mandas (April Sun only, May–Sept 1–2 daily; 4hr 30min).

Ísili to: Cágliari (Mon–Sat 5 daily; 1hr 45min); Láconi (May–Aug Sat & Sun only 1 daily; 30min); Mandas (Mon–Sat 6 daily; 20min); Sórgono (May–Aug Sat & Sun only 1 daily; 2hr 20min).

Láconi to: Mandas (May–Aug Sat & Sun only 1 daily; 50min); Sórgono (May–Aug Sat & Sun only 1 daily; 2hr 20min).

Nuoro to: Macomer (6–9 daily; 1hr 30min).

Sórgono to: Ísili (May–Aug Sat & Sun only 1 daily; 2hr 20min); Láconi (May–Aug Sat & Sun only 1 daily; 1hr 30min); Mandas (May–Aug Sat & Sun only 1 daily; 2hr 45min).

BUSES

Arbatax to: Dorgali (Mon–Sat 1 daily; 2hr); Nuoro (Mon–Sat 1 daily; 3hr); Tortolì (Mon–Sat 3–4 daily; 10min).

Aritzo to: Barúmini (1 daily; 1hr 25min); Belvì (2 daily; 5min); Cágliari (2 daily; 2hr 10min–2hr 45min); Désulo (1 daily; 30min); Fonni (1 daily; 1hr 20min); Ísili (1 daily; 20min); Láconi (2 daily; 45min); Sanluri (1 daily; 2hr); Tonara (1 daily; 30min).

Belvì to: Aritzo (2 daily; 5min); Barúmini (1 daily; 1hr 30min); Cágliari (2 daily; 3hr); Désulo (Mon–Sat 2 daily, Sun 1; 25min); Fonni (1 daily; 1hr 15min); Ísili (1 daily; 25min); Láconi (2 daily; 50min); Mamoiada (Mon–Sat 2 daily, Sun 1; 1hr 25min); Nuoro (Mon–Sat 2 daily, Sun 1; 2hr); Sanluri (1 daily; 2hr); Tonara (1 daily; 25min).

Bitti to: Nuoro (Mon–Sat 7 daily, Sun 3; 1hr 5min).

Désulo to: Aritzo (1 daily; 50min); Barúmini (1 daily; 2hr 15min); Belvì (Mon–Sat 2 daily, Sun 1; 25–45min); Cágliari (1 daily; 3hr 35min); Fonni (Mon–Sat 4 daily, Sun 1; 40min); Láconi (1 daily; 1hr 40min); Mamoiada (Mon–Sat 1 daily; 1hr); Nuoro (Mon–Sat 1 daily; 1hr 30min); Sanluri (1 daily; 2hr 45min).

Dorgali to: Arbatax (Mon–Sat 1 daily; 2hr); Cala Gonone (Mon–Sat 7–10 daily, Sun 4–7; 20min); Nuoro (Mon–Sat 7–9 daily, Sun 3–5; 45min); Oliena (Mon–Sat 3–5 daily, Sun 2–4; 25min); Orosei (Mon–Sat 2–3 daily; 25min).

Fonni to: Abbasanta (Mon–Sat 1 daily; 2hr 50min); Aritzo (1 daily; 1hr 20min); Belvì (1 daily; 1hr 15min); Cágliari (1 daily; 4hr 15min); Désulo (Mon–Sat 1 daily; 40min); Ísili (1 daily; 2hr 40min); Macomer (1 daily; 1hr 50min); Mamoiada (Mon–Sat 4 daily; 25min); Nuoro (Mon–Sat 13–14 daily, Sun 6; 50min–2hr); Orani (4–5 daily; 50min–1hr); Oristano (Mon–Sat 2 daily, Sun 1; 3hr); Ottana (6–9 daily; 1hr 20min–1hr 35min); Porto Torres (1 daily; 3hr 35min); Sássari (1 daily; 3hr); Sórgono (Mon–Sat 3 daily, Sun 1; 1hr 20min); Tonara (Mon–Sat 3 daily, Sun 2; 50min–1hr).

Ísili to: Aritzo (1 daily; 45min); Belvì (1 daily; 50min); Cágliari (1 daily; 1hr 35min); Fonni (1 daily; 2hr 35min); Láconi (2 daily; 25min); Mamoiada (1 daily; 3hr); Mandas (1 daily; 25min); Nuoro (1 daily; 3hr 25min); Tonara (1 daily; 1hr 45min).

Láconi to: Aritzo (2 daily; 45min); Barúmini (Mon–Sat 2 daily, Sun 1; 35min); Belvì (2 daily; 50min); Cágliari (Mon–Sat 3 daily, Sun 2; 2hr–2hr 35min); Désulo (1 daily; 1hr 15min); Fonni (1 daily; 2hr 5min); Ísili (1 daily; 25min); Mamoiada (1 daily; 2hr 25min); Mandas (1 daily; 50min); Nuoro (1 daily; 3hr); Oristano (Mon–Sat 5 daily, Sun 1; 1hr 50min–2hr 20min); Sanluri (Mon–Sat 2 daily, Sun 1; 1hr 5min–1hr 20min); Tonara (1 daily; 1hr 15min).

Mamoiada to: Aritzo (1 daily; 1hr 40min); Belvì (1 daily; 1hr 35min); Cágliari (1 daily; 4hr 35min); Fonni (Mon–Sat 3 daily, Sun 2; 20min); Ísili (1 daily; 3hr); Láconi (1 daily; 2hr 25min); Mandas (1 daily; 3hr 25min); Nuoro (Mon–Sat 10–12 daily, Sun 4; 30min); Tonara (1 daily; 1hr 10min).

Nuoro to: Alghero and Fertilia airport (2 daily; 2hr 25min); Arbatax (Mon–Sat 1 daily; 3hr); Aritzo (1 daily; 2hr 10min); Belvì (Mon–Sat 2 daily, Sun 1; 2hr); Bitti (Mon–Sat 7–8 daily, Sun 3; 1hr 5min); Cágliari (6 daily; 2hr 30min–5hr); Cala Gonone (2–3 daily; 1hr 10min); Désulo (Mon–Sat 1 daily; 1hr 30min); Dorgali (Mon–Sat 7–9 daily, Sun 3–5; 45min); Fonni (Mon–Sat 13–14 daily, Sun 6; 50min–2hr); Ísili (1 daily; 3hr 30min); Láconi (1 daily; 3hr); Mamoiada (Mon–Sat 9–13 daily, Sun 4; 30min); Mandas (1 daily; 4hr); Olbia and Olbia airport (3–5 daily; 1hr 45min); Oliena (Mon–Sat 9–11 daily, Sun 4; 20min); Orgósolo (Mon–Sat 9–11 daily, Sun 4; 35min); Oristano (4 daily; 2hr); Orosei (Mon–Sat 4–5 daily, Sun 3; 1hr 5min); Ottana (Mon–Sat 5–8 daily; 30min); Porto Torres (3 daily; 3hr); Posada (2 daily; 2hr 10min); Sássari (6 daily; 2hr 30min); Sórgono (Mon–Sat 1 daily; 1hr 35min); Tonara (1 daily; 1hr 40min).

Oliena to: Dorgali (Mon–Sat 3–5 daily, Sun 2–4; 25min); Nuoro (Mon–Sat 9–11 daily, Sun 4; 20min).

Orani to: Fonni (3–4 daily; 1hr); Ottana (3–4 daily; 15min).

Orgósolo to: Nuoro (Mon–Sat 9–11 daily, Sun 4; 35min).

Orosei to: Dorgali (Mon–Sat 3–4 daily, Sun 1; 25min); Nuoro (Mon–Sat 4–6 daily; 1hr); Olbia (1 daily; 1hr 40min); Posada (2 daily; 1hr 20min).

Ottana to: Fonni (6–9 daily; 1hr 20min–1hr 35min); Nuoro (Mon–Sat 7–10 daily; 30min); Orani (3–4 daily; 20min); Oristano (Mon–Fri 2 daily; 1hr–1hr 15min); Sórgono (3–5 daily; 1hr 5min).

Posada to: Nuoro (1 daily; 2hr 25min); Olbia (Mon–Sat 8 daily, Sun 5; 1hr 5min); Orosei (1 daily; 1hr 20min).

Sórgono to: Abbasanta (Mon–Sat 1 daily; 1hr 20min); Désulo (Mon–Sat 2 daily, Sun 1; 45min); Fonni (Mon–Sat 2 daily, Sun 1; 1hr 30min); Nuoro (Mon–Sat 1 daily; 1hr 35min); Oristano (Mon–Sat 7 daily, Sun 2; 1 hr 45min–2hr 50min); Ottana (3–4 daily; 1hr 5min); Tonara (Mon–Sat 7 daily, Sun 2; 20min).

Tonara to: Aritzo (1 daily; 30min); Belvì (1 daily; 25min); Cágliari (1 daily; 3hr 25min); Désulo (Mon–Sat 3 daily, Sun 1; 25min); Fonni (1 daily; 50min); Ísili (1 daily; 1hr 50min); Láconi (1 daily; 1hr 15min); Mamoiada (1 daily; 1hr 10min); Mandas (1 daily; 2hr 15min); Nuoro (1 daily; 1hr 40min); Sórgono (Mon–Sat 4 daily, Sun 1; 20min).

FERRIES

Arbatax to: Cágliari (2 weekly; 5hr); Civitavecchia (2 weekly; 9hr); Fiumicino (mid-July to mid-Sept 2 weekly; 5hr 30min); Genoa, via Olbia (2 weekly; 16hr 30min–20hr 30min); Olbia (1–2 weekly; 4hr 30min).

Contexts

The historical framework

Sardinia's position at the centre of the Mediterranean has ensured that the island has rarely been left to its own devices, and for most of its history it has been subject not only to the great power struggles which convulsed this inland sea, but also to the depredations of casual opportunists for whom the island's exposed shores were an irresistible target. Only in remote prehistory did the island enjoy relative freedom from external interference, and this period is inevitably the one we know least about.

Prehistoric times

No one can say where the first Sards came from, though various theories have suggested that they were the followers of Sardus, son of Heracles, or else the descendants of the Libyan Shardana people; the island's name could have derived from either of these sources, or neither – we don't know. But the earliest phase of the island's development is also the most intriguing, and our curiosity is rekindled every time we gaze on one of the mysterious remnants of that distant era which dot the landscape of modern Sardinia.

Though recent discoveries indicate the presence of communities in the Paleolithic era, the first traces of human settlement go back to before 6000 BC, when a hunting and pastoral society lived in grottoes, creating tools and

weapons of flint and obsidian, and crudely decorated ceramic bowls. In the fourth millennium BC, a more advanced culture, called **Bonu Ighinu** after the grotto near Mara where their most significant remains have been found, appeared on the scene. They seem to have inhabited villages of huts and practised more advanced systems of agriculture. Finds show that they had trading links with Corsica, southern Italy and the south of France, while statuettes suggest a cult based on a mother-goddess; their dead were interred in caves.

Around the end of the fourth millennium and the first centuries of the third, another culture, called the San Michele or **Ozieri culture**, after the grotto of San Michele at Ozieri, achieved dominance in the island. This was a significantly advanced society of hunters, shepherds and farmers, who worked copper as well as flint, obsidian and ceramics, all in a greater variety of forms than seen until then. The cult of the dead was also much developed; the bodies were interred in rock-cut caves, often decorated, which came to be called *domus de janas* (fairy-houses) by later generations ignorant of their function. The sanctuary of Monte d'Accoddi, near Porto Torres, is one of the most important religious relics from this era.

Sardinia's **Bonnanaro culture** held sway during the first centuries of the second millennium, though this was to be overshadowed by the new emerging **nuraghic culture**, which has yielded the most ubiquitous and imposing remains of any of Sardinia's historical phases, and which survived until the third century BC or later. The first nuraghic phase, between about 1800 and 1500 BC, overlapped in many aspects with the preceding Ozieri culture, including the use of *domus de janas* and menhirs. The second, lasting until around 1200 BC, saw the development of the nuraghic towers and the *tombe dei giganti* – "giants' tombs", or collective burial chambers. During the third phase (1200–900 BC), the nuraghic towers became elaborate complexes sheltering sizeable villages, such as those at Su Nuraxi and Santu Antine; sacred wells suggest the presence a water cult.

The nuraghic culture reached its apogee between the tenth and eighth centuries BC, trading abroad and cultivating at home. Its fate was sealed, however, when Sardinia became embroiled in the commercial and military rivalries of other Mediterranean powers. The last nuraghic phase is characterized by the increasing engagement of the indigenous people with these more powerful forces, even as they were producing items of growing sophistication such as the *bronzetti*. These bronze statuettes have provided invaluable insights into nuraghic society, suggesting a tribal and highly stratified social organization comprising an aristocracy, priests, warriors, artisans, shepherds and farmers.

The Phoenicians, Carthaginians and Romans

The *bronzetti* and other artifacts reveal the extent of the mercantile network of which Sardinia formed a part, encompassing Italy, North Africa and Spain. From the eastern Mediterranean, **Phoenicians** first began trading in Sardinia around 900 BC, and soon established peaceful commercial bases at Bythia and Nora, both southwest of Cágliari; Monte Sirai and Sant'Antíoco (*Sulki*, or *Sulcis*), further west; Tharros, near Oristano, and Cágliari itself (*Karalis*). The Phoenicians were also attracted by the island's mineral resources – as were every subsequent group of settlers and invaders.

From the sixth century BC onwards, the main protagonists on the scene were the much more warlike **Carthaginians**, whose capital was less than 200km away across the Mediterranean near present-day Tunis, and for whom the island was of crucial strategic importance in their rivalry with the Greek cities of Italy. Intent on drawing Sardinia into their sphere of influence, the Carthaginians took over and expanded the main Phoenician settlements, to the extent that almost all traces of the Phoenician presence were eradicated, and proceeded either to wipe out or assimilate as much as they could of the nuraghic culture.

They were stopped only by the need to concentrate on the thrusting new power of **Rome**, which eventually, in 259 BC, was turned against Sardinia itself. The Sards – now in league with Carthage – fervently struggled against the new aggressors, at first with some success, but their inevitable defeat occurred in 232 BC, followed five years later by the institution of the *provincia* of Sardinia and Corsica.

Resistance continued, however, and after the Second Punic War a concerted attempt to shake off the Roman yoke was organized under **Ampsicora**, a Sard of Carthaginian culture who rallied the opposition but suffered a crushing defeat at Cornus, north of Oristano, in 216 BC. Other revolts followed, including one in 177 BC when 12,000 of the islanders were slaughtered and many more sent away as slaves to the mainland. The survivors of these rebellions, and others who refused to bow to the Romans, fled into the impenetrable central and eastern mountains of the island where they retained their independence, in an area called Barbaria by the Romans, and known today as Barbagia.

Under the **Roman occupation**, Sardinia was bled of its resources – minerals and agricultural produce mainly, especially grain – and its taxes, without any great benefit accruing to its people. Although the island was rewarded for supporting Caesar's side in Rome's civil wars, little was done over seven centuries to instil Roman values or develop the island, which was often entrusted to corrupt officials.

The attitude of the Romans towards the island was summed up in the use they found for it as a place of exile for "undesirable elements," including 4000 Jews sent by the emperor Tiberius, and early Christian subversives, who helped to spread the Gospel in Sardinia. Apart from some impressive remains at Nora and Tharros, traces of Roman building on the island are few when compared to, say, Sicily. The most notable are at Porto Torres, seat of an important colony (Turris Libyssonis); the baths at Fordongianus (Forum Traiani), east of Oristano; the Tempio di Antas in the Iglesiente, which showed the integration of Roman and Sardinian cults, and the amphitheatre at Cágliari. Rome's most lasting contribution was perhaps the strong Latin element that can still be heard in the Sard dialect today.

The Giudicati, Pisa and Genoa

With the eclipse of the Roman empire in the 5th century AD, Sardinia shared the fate of other former territories in becoming vulnerable to barbarian raids and plundering that reached far inland. For a short period the island was held by the

Vandals, then, after 534 AD, the **Byzantines**. It was too remote an outpost of Byzantium to benefit greatly from this new rule, though the island was given some protection in fighting off incursions of Goths and Lombards from the European mainland. One survival of Byzantine rule was the division of the island into **giudicati** for administrative purposes, a system which was to endure all through the Middle Ages. There were four main *giudicati*: Cágliari, Arborea (around Oristano), Torres (or Logudoro) in the northwest and Gallura, each a small kingdom with an elected king – originally a judge, or *giudice*.

In practice, however, these were the preserve of local oligarchies, and the island was left to its own devices, increasingly prey to raids from the new Muslim empires of North Africa and Spain, which were to continue sporadically after 700 for over 1000 years. In southern Sardinia in particular, travellers today can hardly fail to notice the dozens of watchtowers along the coasts, built to warn against these attacks. Though most date from a later era, fear of sudden death or slavery at the hands of the corsairs was a fact of life in Sardinia throughout this period, and had the long-term effect of depopulating the island's coasts. Another reason for the move inland was the increasing prevalence of malaria on the coasts and lowlands, the result of neglected irrigation works, deforestation and the silting-up of rivers. This combination of marauders and malaria led to the downgrading of agriculture on the island, and the rise of sheep and livestock farming in the safe highland pastures of the interior.

The threat posed by the Arabs was not confined to localized attacks: larger forces occupied Cágliari in 720 and a substantial part of the island in 752. In 1015, a substantial force from the Arab emirate in Spain landed and threatened to occupy the entire island; the Italian mercantile republic cities of Pisa and Genoa, which were then extending their commercial operations, were encouraged by the pope to come to the defence of the beleaguered island. With the help of the Sards, they succeeded in ousting the invading force. In the end, however, they proved harder to dislodge themselves, and from this time onwards Sardinia was increasingly open to trading and political links with the Italian mainland. Monastic orders from Provence were also influential; granted special privileges on the island, they played an important part in restoring the decayed irrigation works and industries such as salt extraction.

By means of lending their support in the various conflicts between the *giudicati*, the competing cities of **Pisa** and **Genoa** were able to take an increasingly active role in their internal affairs. The driving forces were individual families, not specifically linked to either of these cities – for example the Visconti family in Logudoro, della Gherardesca in Iglesias, and the Malaspina in Bosa – though the Doria clan were closely connected with the city of Genoa. At the end of the eleventh century, the principal Pisan merchants had been granted privileges in the northern *giudicato* of Torres, where their influence was evident in the string of remote churches such as San Gavino in Porto Torres, and Santa Trinità di Saccárgia and San Pietro di Sorres, both southeast of Sássari – all apparently transplanted ready-built from Tuscany. In Arborea, there was Santa Giusta, outside Oristano, while further south, Pisa's influence was centred on Cágliari, where the defences built around that city's citadel still stand. By the end of the thirteenth century, the balance had swung entirely in the favour of Genoa, whose power-bases were in Torres, specifically Castelsardo, on the northern coast, and Alghero.

However, there was now a new player on the scene: Aragon, whose king, Pedro III, had recently taken possession of Sicily. Keen to resolve the dynastic crisis there, Pope Boniface VIII managed to persuade Pedro's successor James II of Aragon to give up the Aragonese claim to Sicily in return for being granted rights over the newly created kingdom of Sardinia and Corsica in 1297. The title was a mere paper formality, however, since Aragon was very far from asserting any control over the island, and the ensuing struggle lasted more than a century. The campaign proved easier in the south of the island, with Cágliari taken from the Pisans in 1326; in the north, the biggest obstacle was the Doria family – of whom the king of Aragon was nominally feudal overlord – and there was continual fighting between Aragonese forces and the alliance between Sards, Genoans and the mixed-blood aristocracy.

The islanders' cause was led by the *giudicato* of Arborea, and championed in particular by **Eleanora d'Arborea**, a warrior queen who granted Sardinia its first written Code of Laws, the *Carta di Logu*, which – after the Spanish had extended its use throughout the island – remained in force for the next four centuries. Despite numerous betrayals, Eleanor succeeded in stemming the Aragonese advance, but after her death in 1404, Sardinian resistance crumbled. Following a decisive victory at Sanluri in 1409, the Aragonese finally triumphed.

The Spanish in power

With the unification of the kingdoms of Aragon and Castile in 1479, Sardinia became a colony of a united Spain. Although, when compared with the turmoil that had prevailed in previous centuries, this was an unusually peaceful period in the island's history, the three centuries during which Spain ruled Sardinia left many vestiges but little of great significance, and there were few attempts to develop or even maintain the infrastructure. Like Sicily, the island was ruled by viceroys who were uninterested in the island's welfare and in any case unable to effect any improvements in their short three-year terms. The island's trading links with the Italian mainland were cut while the shift of focus towards Spain's Atlantic empire left Sardinia marginalized and neglected.

The Spanish introduced a **feudal system**, according to which the land was parcelled up and distributed among Catalan-Aragonese nobles who enjoyed absolute powers within their domains. The great landlords rarely lived on the island, however, leaving their affairs in the hands of bureaucrats, though the smaller potentates such as the Castelvi, Zatrillas and Alagon families resided on their estates and had a more direct input into the well-being of their territories.

Spanish influence was strongest in the cities, which were given a brusque introduction to Catalan Gothic architecture and later a heavy sprinkling of Baroque in the churches and palazzi – notably in Sássari, Iglesias and Alghero. On the coasts, the most visible contribution was the series of defensive towers that still line Sardinia's shores, which provided only a partial defence against the attacks from North African corsairs, who remained a constant threat. The Spanish king (and Holy Roman emperor) **Charles V** attempted to end these destructive assaults by assembling huge fleets in 1535 and 1541, with which he hoped to extirpate the raiders from their lairs in Tunis and Algiers. But these armadas had only short-term success, and Charles and his successor Philip II were too preoccupied with their far-flung empire and the threat posed by the Protestant Reformation to devote much time to the island's welfare.

Throughout this period Sardinia was particularly hard hit by the malaria that was rife in all but the highest points of the island. A devastating toll was also extracted by two other calamities which swept across the island during the **seventeenth century**: plague, which is thought to have dispatched 25 percent of the population during the 1650s, and famine, which might have accounted for around 80,000 deaths in 1680–81. On the positive side, universities were founded in Cágliari in 1626 and Sássari in 1634, encouraging the growth of a professional class which no longer had to leave the island in order to pursue a career.

Overall, however, Spain had only a superficial impact on Sardinia, and the period is a barren one in the island's history. Relegated to an exploited and deprived backwater, Sardinia shared in the lethargy and decay which infected Spain itself, whose power was ebbing and institutions were moribund. Nonetheless, its hold on the island was never seriously questioned, and the mere hint of a rebellion in Cágliari in 1688 resulted in a harsh repression.

The Kingdom of Sardinia

As Spain declined, events in Europe began to impinge on Sardinia's destiny. During the War of the Spanish Succession in 1701–13, Cágliari was bombarded by an English fleet in 1708 and briefly occupied. In the ensuing negotiations the island was ceded first to Austria, then, according to the Treaty of London of 1718, to the Piedmontese House of Savoy, a duchy on the French-Italian border. The united possessions of Vittorio Amedeo II of Savoy became the new **Kingdom of Sardinia**.

Although Sardinia's Savoy period is associated with the beginnings of reconstruction, reforms did not take place quickly enough to stem the simmering discontent engendered by high expectations. The frustration manifested itself in a variety of forms during the **eighteenth century**. *Banditismo* – the phenomenon of factional fighting, clan warfare, robbery and kidnapping that had always existed in the interior – assumed chronic proportions, while the enforced adoption of Italian as the language of government alienated an aristocracy for whom Spanish was the mother tongue.

For the majority of Sardinia's population, the chief problems included the failings of the education system, in which schools were dominated by the church and illiteracy was almost universal; the island's continued vulnerability to seaborne attacks, and Sardinia's very sparse population. The government attempted to solve the last of these by a poorly-organized and ultimately unsuccessful attempt to introduce foreign colonies to the island. The most deep-rooted cause of Sard hostility to the new ruling elite, however, concerned the continuing existence of the feudal system.

Matters came to a head after the French Revolution and the war which followed it had exposed not only the intransigence of the regime vis-à-vis Sardinia's plight, but also the drawbacks inherent in the island's links to the House of Savoy, as the latter's quarrels became Sardinia's. In 1793 French troops attempting to invade the island succeeded in occupying the island of San Pietro, but another force which included the young **Napoleon** was repulsed at La Maddalena, as was a fleet which bombarded Cágliari. Though the Savoyard king rewarded his Piedmontese officials for their part in the rout, the role of the islanders was unacknowledged. What rankled even more was the refusal of the royal court to respond to a delegation from Sardinia bearing the *Cinque Domande*, or "Five Demands", which called for a full constitutional reform, including the restoration of ancient privileges and the regular convocation of an island parliament.

Between 1794 and 1796, an **insurrection** in Cágliari forced the viceroy and his entourage to take flight, and full-scale revolts subsequently broke out all over Sardinia, which ended with Sássari being taken by the rebels. At their head was **Giovanni Maria Angioy**, an aristocrat whose anti-feudal stance made him popular among the peasants, but whose increasingly radical demands for a Sardinian republic alienated the more moderate elements and eventually led to his downfall. In 1796, Angioy was driven out of Sardinia and died in exile in Paris – leaving behind a name which has been given to streets and squares throughout the island – and his followers were savagely persecuted by the Piedmontese.

The French were not the only ones to cast a hungry eye over Sardinia. Even **Admiral Horatio Nelson** expressed an interest in the island as a potential base, during the fifteen months he spent hovering around its coasts in his pursuit of the French fleet that ended at Trafalgar in 1805. "God knows," he wrote in his dispatches home, "if we could possess one island, Sardinia, we should want neither Malta, nor any other: this which is the finest island in the Mediterranean, possesses harbours fit for arsenals, and of a capacity to hold our navy, within 24 hours' sail of Toulon..."

The most noteworthy Savoyard kings in the **nineteenth century** were Carlo Felice (1821–31), who did much to modernize the island's infrastructure, not least by building the Carlo Felice highway – today the SS131 – that runs the length of the island from Cágliari to Porto Torres, and Carlo Alberto (1831–49), responsible for the final **abolition of the feudal system** in 1836–43. Although this led to a bitter conflict over the introduction of enclosures to demarcate private land in the mountains, which limited the ancient liberty of shepherds to wander freely in search of fresh pasturage, it was an essential prelude to rural reform.

Unified Italy

The Kingdom of Sardinia came to an end with the **unification of Italy** in 1861, when Vittorio Emanuele II, son of Carlo Alberto, became the new nation's first king (1861–78). Sardinia played a crucial role in the Risorgimento (the struggle for nationhood), providing both a genuine king to stand as the figurehead of a united Italy, and the base from which Giuseppe Garibaldi, who led the military campaign, embarked on both his major expeditions.

Sardinia's problems entered a new phase with unification. Adjusting to its role as a part of a modern nation-state has been the main theme of recent times, and attempts to force the island to integrate into the new centralized, bureaucratic Italy gave rise to a host of resentments whenever old, traditional ways came up against the new. Colonial attitudes towards the island persisted, its natural resources were ruthlessly plundered, accounting for much of the deforestation still evident today, and wages remained low. Agriculture also suffered, leading to soaring unemployment, which in turn fuelled the banditry that was still widespread and was brutally suppressed. There was little money available to improve the root causes of the problem and less interest in doing so. Although there was a degree of political reform, voting rights were still only available to less than five percent of the island's population by the end of the nineteenth century, leaving the vast majority without a voice or representation.

Nonetheless, Sardinia contributed notably to both world wars, with the Sássari Brigade in particular achieving lasting distinction during **World War I**, albeit at a heavy cost. The experience of war radicalized many Sards, and elections now based on universal suffrage in 1920 and 1921 saw the creation of the **Partito Sardo d'Azione**, or Sardinian Action Party, whose manifesto demanded autonomy; four of its members were elected as deputies, thus making it the island's second biggest party.

Mussolini and World War II

Ironically, Sardinia had to wait for a ruthless centralizing dictatorship before real changes began to make themselves felt. **Mussolini** saw the backward island as fertile ground for his social and economic experiments and his push for Italian self-sufficiency in the wake of sanctions imposed following his invasion of Ethiopia. In the 1920s and 1930s, the Fascist government initiated a series of schemes which led to genuine improvements: the island's many rivers were harnessed and dammed to provide irrigation as well as power, land was drained and made fertile, agricultural colonies were implanted to exploit the new resources, and the new towns of Carbonia and Fertilia were founded – though the industrial projects were mostly failures.

The island also suffered as a result of its participation in **World War II**, as Cágliari endured some of the heaviest bombing of all Italian cities in 1943, with 75 percent of its houses destroyed. Traumatized, the island awoke to a post-war era in which nothing seemed to have changed. Once more it felt itself to be a second-class member of the Italian state, subject to a remote bureaucracy and irrelevant legislation.

A genuine attempt to offset this was made in 1948, when the *regione* of Sardinia was granted **autonomy** on the same lines as that also given to Sicily and two other areas on the Austrian and Yugoslav borders, allowing the regional government direct control over such areas as transport,

tourism, police, industry and agriculture. Two years later the central government's fund to speed up the development of the South of Italy, the Cassa per il Mezzogiorno, was extended to Sardinia, and the island began to receive hefty injections of capital investment. Perhaps more significantly, through the intervention of the US Rockefeller Foundation, Sardinia was saturated with enough DDT in the years immediately following World War II to rid it once and for all of malaria, the centuries-old scourge that had sabotaged all local initiative.

Sardinia today

The success of this combined effort to haul Sardinia up from a peripheral, third-world status is everywhere apparent, and some areas of Sardinian life are as streamlined and sophisticated as anywhere on the mainland. Visitors to the island today will recognize a piece of Italy – the same shops, cars and language – to the extent that it is growing ever harder to distinguish "the real Sardinia" underneath the Italian gloss.

Much of the island's present-day landscape is a direct result of two crucial decisions made in the same year, 1962. This was when the Italian parliament finally authorized a programme of industrialization, which led to the introduction of heavy-duty petrochemical plants completely at odds with the island's traditional activities. At the same time, the Aga Khan's development of the Costa Smeralda and the subsequent opening-up of the tourist industry has given Sardinia a new role which has by and large been embraced by the islanders, and has brought genuine wealth to a substantial section of the population.

These developments have gone hand-in-hand with a new appreciation of the traditional culture of the island, a re-evaluation of its dialect and folklore, and a corresponding pride in the Sard identity that had always previously been repressed. The other side of the coin is the often unrestrained and irreversible development of some of the island's most beautiful spots, unregulated construction and the degradation of its natural environment in pursuit of short-term profit – for all its attempts to harmonize with the surroundings, the modern tourist complex has little in common with the primitive rugged solidity of the nuraghi.

Still, with its relatively prosperous population of 1.6 million, Sardinia today seems comfortable enough with its modern role. Despite certain stains on the surface which most people would prefer to overlook – the pockets of pollution, the high rates of unemployment, a worrying level of drug addiction in the cities, and the occasional kidnapping in the Barbagia which continues to baffle the police – there is a general satisfaction with the island's place within Italy and the European Union. Italian bureaucracy still infuri- ates, and there is still a good deal of rancour directed at the Italian state which has imposed on the island, among other things, the largest NATO concentration in the Mediterranean. Campaigning against this presence, and in the longer term for complete independence, the Partito Sardo d'Azione is too marginal to exert much influence, and the general tenor of the island is quiet contentment.

Sardinian wildlife

Sardinia shares with all islands that spark of uniqueness that arises from isolation, in which plants and animals evolve differently from those on the mainland. Many species are found only here, or are shared with neighbouring Corsica (with which Sardinia has much in common), while the proximity of Africa gives the local fauna and flora a distinct, almost tropical character; the only other place in Europe in which the Barbary partridge, for example, can be found is Gibraltar. In addition, Sardinia's location on a key bird migration route between Africa and Europe accounts for the seasonal visitations of a number of bird species.

Sardinia's island ecology also means that a number of species present on the mainland are absent here – notably poisonous snakes, but also wolves, otters and moles. Those species which are present display a brilliant diversity, linked to the range of different terrains – mountain, forest, plain and coast – that exist within a relatively limited area. The climate is typically Mediterranean, with rainfall between 24 inches (600mm) on the plains to 39 inches (990mm) in the mountains.

The principal habitats

Sardinia boasts a significant proportion of Italy's internationally important **lagoons** and **wetlands**, as well as extensive areas of **maquis**, remnant forests, hot **plains** and high **mountains**. The overwhelming presence of mountains accounts for the island's numerous rivers, of which the Tirso and Flumendosa are the most important.

Lagoons

In ornithological terms the **lagoons** (*stagni*) and wetlands are perhaps the most important feature of the island. While wetlands around the world have been extensively drained for agriculture and have become one of the most endangered habitats, Sardinia still has 13,000 hectares of protected lagoons. Constituting 25 per cent of the Italian resource, they are internationally designated both for their importance during migration time and for the presence of rare breeding birds.

The richest *stagni* are to be found in the vicinity of Oristano and Cágliari, where it is common to spot flocks of pink **flamingoes**; they have long used both of these areas as a stopoff on their migrations between Africa and the Carmargue region of France, though recently they have also started nesting and breeding on the island. Along with the flamingoes, the lagoons of Sardinia shelter a remarkable range of wetlands species, most notably **spoonbill**, **crane**, **avocet**, **black-winged stilt** (in Italian the "cavalier of Italy" for its extraordinary appearance), **cattle egret**, **tern**, **cormorant**, **glossy ibis**, **white-headed duck**, **osprey**, **pratincole**, **purple gallinule**, **ferruginous duck**, **marsh harrier** and **Andouin's gull**.

In winter, there are large numbers of duck and cormorant, their "V" shaped skeins a prominent feature in the skies, not to mention plenty of waders and great wheeling flocks of **lapwing**. The spring and autumn migrations see significant numbers of passage birds, and this is a good time to see the **curlew sandpiper**, **Caspian tern**, **short-toed eagle** and **red-footed falcon**.

The area around Oristano has the island's best-protected lagoons, not least those on the Sinis peninsula, where the flatlands around the lakeside town of Cabras has the Pauli e Sali reserve, sheltering reeds and a wide range of waterfowl. The nearby Stagno di Sale Porcus is the place to see the extremely rare European crane. Another general feature of these wetlands are the reed beds, home to **great reed**, **fan-tailed** and **Cetti's warblers** and hunted over by the fast, acrobatic **hobby**.

The coastal zones

In coastal areas, **Aleppo** and **maritime palms** lend a tropical feel, while the long **sand dunes** on the west coast of the provinces of Cágliari and Oristano create a more arid environment, notably around Piscinas and Is Arenas. **Turtles** use these and other remote beaches to lay eggs.

On the other side of the island, Sardinia's eastern coast is mainly cliffy and undeveloped. The Gennargentu mountains end in a sheer rocky wall of limestone where, at Capo di Monte Santu (at the southern end of the Gulf of Orosei), there is a significant colony of the highly unusual **Eleonora's falcon**, a "semi-colonial" nesting falcon. One of a small number of colonies on Sardinia, these are only found in the Mediterranean, named after Queen Eleanora, the medieval warrior queen who decreed that only she was permitted to hunt with it. This large bird is one of Europe's rarest and most enigmatic raptors, with long, thin, rapier-fast wings. As a migratory falcon, it is most likely to be seen during the autumn, since the species breeds late to feed its young on autumn-passage birds, catching its prey on the wing.

The Gulf of Orosei is also important as the last home of the monk or **Mediterranean seal** (in Italian "sea-ox"), sadly facing extinction with at best only a handful of individuals remaining scattered in the coves and grottoes of this rocky coast.

Off the Stintino peninsula in the northwest, the island of Asinara, which is due to be made a National Park, is most famous for its unique and diminutive **albino asses**. Some of these tiny creatures are also to be found south of the peninsula on the massive cliffs of Capo Caccia, where the Arca di Noe reserve also contains **mouflons** (long-horned wild sheep), **wild boars** and immense **griffon vultures**. The latter have been successfully reintroduced a few kilometres further south, on the desolate Alghero–Bosa coast, and this now constitutes the largest Italian colony. Also near Alghero, Lago di Baratz, Sardinia's only natural lake, has a species of **freshwater tortoise** and a system of pine-covered dunes and maritime *macchia*.

Plains and plateaux

Sardinia's **plains** constitute another highly important habitat, largely bare and cultivated, with scattered vines and wheatfields. Flatlands such as these are being agriculturally "improved" across much of Europe, but here in Sardinia they still shelter a range of flora and fauna. The Marmilla region between Cágliari and Oristano is characterized by odd-looking bare hummocks and a series of high tablelands which are virtually empty of homes or developments. Here, red, white, blue and yellow flowers make a carpet of colour with **poppies**, **lavender**, **buttercups**, **daisies**, **asphodel** and **euphorbia** all in abundance.

The largest of these high plateaux is the Giara di Gésturi, where the boundaries of the provinces of Cágliari, Oristano and Nuoro meet. This high basalt plateau is an excellent place to find a concentration of the island's most interesting plants, including a number of rare species of **orchid**; it is also Sardinia's principal habitat of the famous *cavallini* – miniature **wild horses** whose origins are shrouded in mystery and which are notoriously difficult to track down – and shelters a range of other wildlife including hares, boars and foxes.

The most important bird of these plains is the little **bustard**, a turkey-like creature that was once much hunted by aristocratic falcons, providing spectacular sport. The whole bustard family is imperilled in much of Europe, but Sardinia is one of the few places where this particular member of the bustard family is expanding and flourishing in the mosaics of pasture particularly favoured by this species. The plains are also a rich habitat for **partridge**, **buntings**, **woodchat** and **shrike**, while the vividly colourful exotics – **roller**, **hoopoe** and **bee-eater** – are all found here. It is best to visit these areas in springtime when the *macchia* and grasslands are a riot of colour.

The macchia

Sardinia's rocky slopes are everywhere covered with a thick layer of Mediterranean **maquis**, known on the island as *macchia*. This invasive scrub flourishes after fire or the felling of ancient forests and also colonizes abandoned cultivated land. Tangled, heavily scented and richly colourful, *macchia* includes **juniper**, **lentisk**, **myrtle** and **arbutus** (strawberry trees); **heather** and the yellow-flowering **broom** and **gorse** are also common, as are the pink and white petals of the **cistus** family. Leaves here are often thick and gummy to help prevent water loss, and the shrubs are intermingled with herbs and flowers and orchids in more open patches.

Near the coast, the *macchia* has a maritime flavour, while in the drier areas it is interspersed with **prickly pear** cactus (introduced from Mexico by the Spanish), the fruit of which ("Indian fig") is considered a delicacy by Italians. The typical **warblers** here are all interesting: **Sardinian**, **Marmora's**, **subalpine**, **spectacled** and **Dartford**. At night one can hear the calls of **Scops owl** and the echoing warm, low churring of the **nightjar** intermingling with the cicadas.

Mountain and woodland areas

The shrub layer can secede into taller **woodland** where trees such as cork and holm oak start to appear. Here, the richly lyrical **blackcap** and the **Orphean warbler** become more predominant as the thickening canopy shades out the *macchia*. Traditional, low-intensity olive groves and fruit orchards are very important for a number of species, the most important of which is the rare **wryneck**. Alder and the pink blossom of oleander may mark the line of water courses, often totally dried out in summer, while on the more established streams the semi-aquatic **dipper** can sometimes be seen. This is also the sort of place where one might catch a glimpse of the **Sardinian salamander**.

Sardinia has the highest level of forest cover of all the Italian regions, and the interior is criss-crossed by ancient trackway ideal for the adventurous explorer or naturalist. **Cork oak** forest stretches from Gallura to the northern Barbagia (the central zone of mountains), providing one of Europe's main sources of cork – the plantations are particularly thick in the area around Tempio Pausánia. The **holm oak** is another ubiquitous tree in Sardinia: the Gennargentu mountains and the Abbasanta plateau near Oristano hold the remnants of a holm oak forest that once covered much of the island. At Sas Badas and Su Lidone on the Sopramonte massif are remains of ancient forest which has never been felled, its gnarled specimens numbering among the last remaining examples in Europe. Sardinia even has a petrified forest near Soddi on the shore of Lake Omodeo, the trees submerged by a primeval volcanic eruption.

Higher up in these mountains, where the gentle chiming of sheep and goat bells are a constant accompaniment, the species in the tree line change and one finds **bay oaks** and **maples** whose red leaves give a blaze of colour in autumn. Scattered smaller clumps of **holly** and **yew** are residual vegetation from a cooler era. It is here that other rare wildlife is to be found: **golden eagle** and the rare **Bonelli's eagle** soar in these skies above deep and rugged valleys that cut into the mountains, while **goshawk** and **peregrine falcon** prey on the flocks of **wood pigeon** which multiply in years when there are rich falls of acorn. The **jay** is also common. Towards the summits of the mountains the forests largely disappear, and are replaced by grassland, scattered **junipers** and **dwarf palm trees** bent by the Mistral wind.

Many species of rare and unique mountain plants are to be found in the Gennargentu, but pride of place goes to the **peony**, or "mountain rose" as it is known locally, whose blooming announces the arrival of spring. A notable mammal to be found in this terrain is the **Sardinian stag**, a few hundred of which have survived here and in the forests around Cágliari, for example Monte Arcosu, in the mountains of Sulcis – also the place to see **martens**, **wildcats** and **boar**.

Mouflon, or wild sheep, which have been hunted to the edge of extinction across much of Italy, are now found only in the mountains of Sardinia, and on Corsica and Cyprus. Numbers here have recovered quite well, and if one keeps a good eye open, herds of this extraordinary animal, with its enormous, regal curved horns, can be glimpsed perched high on an inaccessible cliff. Lower down, the groves of hazel, almond, walnut and chestnut carpeting the slopes of the interior are grazed by both wild *cinghiali* (boar) and the more domesticated

Timing

Anyone thinking of a visit to Sardinia with its natural history in mind should always consider carefully the timing. A visit in spring or autumn combines the advantages of bird migration with the flowering of many species of plants and shrubs, many of which bloom first in spring and again in autumn, after the summer drought.

pig which in many cases has interbred with its wild cousin. Although Sardinia's wild boar are hunted assiduously both for the sport and their meat, their numbers have not declined significantly in recent years.

Sardinians are unreconstructed hunters, and will shoot at anything that moves. This can be nearly as disturbing as it is destructive, when you come across heavily armed hunting parties of men trailing through the *macchia*, though European public opinion is having an impact on reducing the damaging effects of this "sport", and the provision of protected areas is increasing.

A checklist of Sardinian wildlife sites

Alghero–Bosa coast – where Italy's largest colony of griffon vultures lives. See p.210.

Arca di Noe – this reserve has some of the rare mouflon (long-horned wild sheep), as well as wild boar and griffon vultures, though these are more common further south, on the Alghero–Bosa coast. See p.210.

Capo Figará – mouflon have been reintroduced on this cape and on the offshore islet of Figarolo. See p.276.

Caprera – dense maquis and woods, where sea and land birds nest. See p.292.

Foresta di Minniminni and Monte dei Sette Fratelli – rugged terrain sheltering deer, boar, wildcat, and various birds of prey. See p.98.

Gennargentu – thickly forested central mountain range has boars and – more visibly – wild pigs. See p.329.

Giara di Gésturi – high basalt plateau famous as the island's main habitat of the miniature wild horses (*cavallini*), but also a good place to see rare species of orchid. See p.150.

Monte Arcosu – for the Sardinian stag and other forest fauna. See p.108.

Pauli e Sali – this marsh and lagoon shelters a huge range of birdlife. See pp358–359.

Piscinas – dune system where esparto grasses and even wild lilies take root in the sands. See p.135.

San Pietro – the island's western cliffs are the habitat for rare sea birds. See p.122.

Sopramonte – eagles and other predators can be seen circling above the mountains here. See p.323.

Stagno di Sale Porcus – lagoon sheltering various aquatic birds. See p.173.

Stagno di S'Ena Arrubia – good variety of aquatic birdlife outside Oristano. See p.176.

Tavolara – the sheer cliffs of this island shelter a range of birdlife. See p.273.

Books and films

There are only a few modern writers who have travelled in and written about Sardinia, though the island has provided the inspiration for a few works of literature. Most of the books listed below are in print and those that aren't shouldn't be too difficult to track down (out-of-print books are indicated by o/p). Wherever a book is in print the UK publisher is listed first, followed by the publisher in the US – unless the title is available in one country only, in which case we've specified the country. Where paperback editions are available, these are listed in preference to hardcover.

Travel and general

Russell King *Sardinia* (David & Charles o/p). One of the *Islands* series, this is an informed and comprehensive read, with chapters on archeology, industry and bandits. If you can't track down a copy for sale, you'll usually find it in public libraries.

D.H. Lawrence *Sea and Sardinia* (Penguin). Lawrence's hurried six-day journey through Sardinia in 1921 did not give the island much of a chance, and his account is imbued with impatience and irritation. Travelling up from Cágliari to Nuoro and Olbia in the company of the Queen Bee (Frieda Lawrence), his highly personal travelogue alternates between disgust and rapture, though his descriptions sparkle with closely-observed cameos and the book repays rereading.

Amelie Posse-Brázdová *Sardinian Sideshow* (Routledge, o/p). You may find this entertaining romp in a secondhand bookshop. Translated

from the Swedish in 1932, it relates the experiences of the Swedish protagonist and her Middle-European companions in exile during World War I in Alghero. Illuminating mainly for its close observation of the people of the resort and elsewhere in the island in the days before package tourism.

Alan Ross *The Bandit on the Billiard Table* (Collins Harvill, o/p). A well-written account of a journey through Sardinia in the 1950s, full of sympathetic descriptions of people and places, informative and readable if a mite old-fashioned.

Virginia Waite *Sardinia* (Batsford, o/p). A rambling but well-researched trek through the island, with lots of historical background and first-hand descriptions of the festivals.

Specific guides

Stefano Ardito *Backpacking and Walking in Italy* (Bradt/Hunter, both o/p). The only thing there is in English on serious hiking in Sardinia, with a very short chapter on the island featuring two walks on the mountainous east coast, along the Flumineddu river and the Gorropu canyon, and between Cala Gonone and Cala Sisine.

Egad Trinity *Sardinia Diving Guide* (Swan Hill Press). Recent, lavishly illustrated guide outlining Sardinia's principal underwater ecosystems and describing thirty dives, with details of the marine life and, where they exist, wrecks to explore. Maps and diagrams show the sites, while colour photos help to identify fish and other sea life.

History and archeology

Robert H. Tyke and Tames K. Andrews *Sardinia in the Mediterranean: A Footprint in the Sea* (Sheffield Academic Press). Comprehensive (and highly expensive) study of Sardinian archeology that may be available in some libraries for anyone interested; covers Paleolithic and Neolithic cultures, including nuraghic, Phoenician, Punic, Greek and Roman settlements on the island.

Gary S. Webster *A Prehistory of Sardinia, 2300–500 BC* (Sheffield Academic Press in UK, Almond Press in US). Another heavyweight academic tome bringing together all the research on Sardinian prehistory, with particular attention given to nuraghic society.

Music

Bernard Lortat-Jacob and Teresa Lavender Fagan *Sardinian Chronicles* (University of Chicago Press). Part of the Chicago Studies in Ethnomusicology series, this work examines the music of the island through twelve vignettes of locals who continue to practise the tradition of choral singing.

Sardinian literature

Grazia Deledda *After the Divorce* (Quartet Encounters), *Cosima* (Quartet Encounters), *Elias Portolu* (Quartet Encounters), *La Madre* (Dedalus Modern Classics). Grazia Deledda's Sardinia is a raw place of passion and instinct, which she evokes in her simple, unsentimental tales set around her hometown of Nuoro. In *After the Divorce*, first published in 1902, she writes of the grim sense of exclusion from the tribal mores prevailing in the village of Orlei, where the main protagonist, Giovanna Era, is driven to betray her husband who has been convicted of murder. *Cosima* is an autobiographical novel published posthumously, vividly evoking the experiences of a Nuorese girlhood. *Elias Portolu* (1900) relates the moral and social dilemmas of a convict returned to his rigid shepherd's society, and *La Madre*, published in 1920, deals with the frustrated love of a village priest and the efforts of his mother to dissuade him from giving up his vocation in order to follow his passion. The writing is full of what D.H. Lawrence called "uncontaminated human instinct" and "the indescribable tang of the people of the island, not yet absorbed into the world." Deledda won the Nobel Prize for Literature in 1927.

Salvatore Satta *The Day of Judgment* (Collins Harvill). The respected jurist Salvatore Satta wrote just this one work of fiction, which was not published until after his death in 1975. Like Deledda's work, it is set in Nuoro, peopled by a procession of theatrical characters who seem to inhabit a bleak dreamscape of a long-dead past. Lacking any storyline, the book is a powerful evocation of a lost world, set in the remotest recesses of Sardinia's impoverished interior.

Sardinian films

Banditi a Orgosolo (directed by Vittorio de Seta, 1961). *Bandits of Orgosolo* capitalized on the publicity given to the kidnapping and violence as practised by the outlaws living in the hills around the village of Orgósolo, outside Nuoro. The first feature film of this Sicilian-born director, made with minimal technical and financial facilities, it was enthusiastically received at the 1961 Venice Film Festival, but has disappeared almost without trace now.

Il Deserto Rosso (*Red Desert*, directed by Michelangelo Antonioni, 1965). Filmed on Budelli – one of the Maddalena islands – and responsible for propelling its *spiaggia rosa* or "pink beach" to instant fame, the movie has almost sunk without trace, not making it on to anyone's list of best Antonioni films.

Padre Padrone (directed by Paolo and Vittorio Taviani in 1977). This is the most famous film to come out of Sardinia, and the island's rugged mountain backdrops are used to full effect. All the same, it was hated by Sard audiences for giving a negative portrayal of the island, even if its main theme is chiefly an exploration of a boy's relationship with his tyrannical and sadistic father. Based on the autobiography of the writer Gavino Ledda, it relates how he was dragged out of school to tend sheep until army service gave him the opportunity to educate himself and finally rebel against his father. The cruelty and bleak poverty of the shepherd society is perhaps overplayed, but it's a strongly atmospheric piece, the first film to win both the Palme d'Or and International Critics' Prize at Cannes, and for years de rigueur viewing at Communist Party gatherings. Roberto Rossellini, head of the Cannes jury, declared that the film: "embodies everything which is most impressive, vigorous and coherent, and most daring, socially and artistically, in the Italian cinema."

Language

The ability to speak European languages other than Italian is increasingly widespread in Sardinia, and you will often find the staff in museums, tourist offices and hotels, as well as guides, able to communicate in English, and students in particular are frequently willing to show off their knowledge. Outside the tourist areas, however, few people actually know more than some simple words and phrases – those more often than not culled from pop songs or computer programs.

Some tips

Anyone interested in Sardinia and the Sards will find their experience immeasurably enriched by some attempt to learn a few basic phrases of **Italian**. Even if only a very superficial knowledge from a phrasebook is gained in the limited time available, just the ability to ask for a glass of water will make you feel less helpless. In any case, it's one of the easiest European languages to learn, especially if you already have a smattering of French or Spanish, both extremely similar grammatically.

The rules of **pronunciation** are easy, since every word is spoken exactly as it's written: articulate each syllable of every word – the louder and clearer the better. The only difficulties you're likely to encounter are the few **consonants** that are different from English:

c before **a**, **o** or **u** is hard, as in cat; before **e** or **i** it is **e** or **i** is pronounced as in church, while **ch** before the same vowels is hard.

sci or **sce** are pronounced as in sheet and shelter respectively. The same goes with **g** – soft before **e** and **i**, as in gentle; hard when followed by **a**, **o** or **u**, or by an **h**, as in garlic.

gn has the ni sound of our 'onion'.

gl in Italian is softened to something like li in English, as in vermilion.

h is not aspirated, as in hour.

When **speaking** to strangers, the third person is the polite form (ie *Lei* instead of *Tu* for "you"); using the second person is a mark of disrespect or stupidity. It's also worth remembering that Italians don't use 'please' and 'thank you' half as much as we do: it's all implied in the tone, though if you're in doubt, err on the polite side.

All Italian words are **stressed** on the penultimate syllable unless an **accent** denotes otherwise, although accents are often left out in practice. Thus it is not Cagliari or Sassari, but Cágliari and Sássari. Note that the ending -**ia** or -**ie** counts as two syllables, hence *trattoria* is stressed on the i. We've put accents in, throughout the text and below, wherever it isn't immediately obvious how a word should be pronounced: for example, in *Maríttima*, the accent is on the first i; conversely *Olbia* should theoretically have an accent on the **o**. Other words where we've omitted accents are common ones (like *Isola*, stressed on the I), some names (*Domenico*, *Vittorio*), and words that are stressed similarly in English, such as *archeologico* and *Repubblica*.

Lastly, it's pleasantly surprising how much can be communicated by the use of body language alone – gestures, gesticulations, facial expressions and miming – an art at which Italians are supremely adept.

The Sard dialect

It is only a little over 130 years that Italy has been a separate state, and what is now known as standard Italian was originally the parole of an educated elite deriving from a literary Tuscan dialect. In fact each of the regions of Italy speaks its own local dialect which has only very recently taken second place to "standard" Italian. But in

AN ITALIAN LANGUAGE GUIDE

BASICS

good morning	*buongiorno*	tomorrow	*domani*
good afternoon/		day after tomorrow	*dopodomani*
evening	*buona sera*	yesterday	*ieri*
good night	*buona notte*	now	*adesso*
hello/goodbye	*ciao* (informal; when	later	*più tardi*
speaking to strangers use the phrases above)		wait a minute!	*aspetta!*
goodbye	*arrivederci* (formal)	in the morning	*di mattina*
yes	*sì*	in the afternoon	*nel pomeriggio*
no	*no*	in the evening	*di sera*
please	*per favore*	here/there	*qui/lì*
thank you	*grázie (molte/mille*	good/bad	*buono/cattivo*
(very much)	*grazie)*	big/small	*grande/píccolo*
you're welcome	*prego*	cheap/expensive	*económico/caro*
alright/that's OK	*va bene*	early/late	*presto/ritardo*
how are you?	*come stai/sta?*	hot/cold	*caldo/freddo*
(informal/formal)		near/far	*vicino/lontano*
I'm fine	*bene*	vacant/occupied	*líbero/occupato*
do you speak English?	*parla inglese?*	quickly/slowly	*velocemente/lentamente*
I don't understand	*non capisco*	slowly/quietly	*piano*
I haven't understood	*non ho capito*	with/without	*con/senza*
I don't know	*non lo so*	more/less	*più/meno*
excuse me/sorry	*scusa* (informal)	enough, no more	*basta*
excuse me/sorry	*mi scusi/prego* (formal)	Mr...	*Signor...*
excuse me	*permesso*	Mrs...	*Signora...*
(in a crowd)		Miss...	*Signorina...*
I'm sorry	*mi dispiace*	(*il signore, la signora, la signorina* when	
I'm here on holiday	*sono qui in vacanza*	speaking about someone else)	
I live in...	*abito a...*	first name	*primo nome*
today	*oggi*	surname	*cognome*

ACCOMMODATION

hotel	*albergo*	it's expensive	*è caro*
is there a hotel nearby?	*c'è un albergo qui vicino?*	is breakfast included?	*è compresa la prima colazione?*
do you have a room...	*ha una cámera...*	do you have anything cheaper?	*ha niente che costa di meno?*
for one/two/three people	*per una persona, due/tre persone*	full/half board	*pensione completa/ mezza pensione*
for one/two/three nights	*per una notte, due/tre notti*	can I see the room?	*posso vedere la cámera?*
for one/two weeks	*per una settimana/ due settimane*	I'll take it	*la prendo*
with a double bed	*con un letto matrimoniale*	I'd like to book a room	*vorrei prenotare una cámera*
with a shower/bath	*con una doccia/ un bagno*	I have a booking	*ho una prenotazione*
with a balcony	*con una terrazza*	can we camp here?	*possiamo fare il campeggio qui?*
hot/cold water	*acqua calda/fredda*		
how much is it?	*quanto costa?*	*continued over page*	

AN ITALIAN LANGUAGE GUIDE (continued)

is there a campsite nearby?	*c'è un camping qui vicino?*	cabin	*cabina*
tent	*tenda*	youth hostel	*ostello per la gioventù*

QUESTIONS AND DIRECTIONS

where? (where is/are…?)	*dove? (dov'è/ dove sono?)*	can you tell me when to get off?	*può dirmi quando devo scendere?*
when?	*quando?*	what time does it open?	*a che ora apre?*
what? (what is it?)	*cosa? (Cos'è?)*	what time does it close?	*a che ora chiude?*
how much/many?	*quanto/quanti?*	how much does it cost	*quanto costa?*
why?	*perché?*	(…do they cost?)	*(quanto costano?)*
it is/there is (is it/is there…?)	*è/c'è (è/c'è…?)*	what is it called in Italian?	*come si chiama in italiano?*
what time is it?	*che ora è/che ore sono?*	left/right	*sinistra/destra*
how do I get to…?	*come arrivo a…?*	go straight ahead	*sempre diritto*
how far is it to…?	*quant'è lontano a…?*	turn to the right/left	*gira a destra/ sinistra*
can you give me a lift to...?	*mi può dare un passaggio a...?*		

TRANSPORT

aeroplane	*aeroplano*	port	*porto*
bus	*autobus/pullman*	a ticket to…	*un biglietto a…*
train	*treno*	one-way/return	*solo andata/andata e ritorno*
car	*mácchina*		
taxi	*taxi*	can I book a seat?	*posso prenotare un posto?*
bicycle	*bicicletta*	what time does it leave?	*a che ora parte?*
ferry	*traghetto*		
ship	*nave*	when is the next bus/train/ferry to…?	*quando parte il próssimo pullman/ treno/traghetto per…?*
hydrofoil	*aliscafo*		
hitch-hiking	*autostop*		
on foot	*a piedi*	where does it leave from?	*da dove parte?*
bus station	*autostazione*		
railway station	*stazione ferroviaria*	which platform does it leave from?	*da quale binario parte?*
ferry terminal	*stazione maríttima*		

informal family or social circles, it is often still the dialect that is instinctively spoken.

Sardinia, isolated in the middle of the Mediterranean, has a dialect so dense that it almost constitutes a separate language. Not only the island, but every area of the island, almost every village, has its own variation, as you might expect in a place that is both mountainous and from ancient times poorly integrated. These local strains will include a concoction of ingredients according to each area's particular historical circumstances. Thus on the isle of San Pietro off the southwest coast of Sardinia,

a strong Piedmontese dialect is spoken, owing to its settlement by a colony of Ligurians, invited by King Carlo Emanuele III in 1737. At around the same time there was a wave of immigration from Corsica into the northern region of Gallura, which still retains a dialect close to that spoken in the southern parts of Sardinia's sister island. And the people of Alghero still speak a variety of Spanish Catalan over 600 years after the Aragonese king made the town his main base in northern Sardinia and flooded it with Catalonians. Visitors there will find Catalan street names in the old quar-

do I have to change?	*devo cambiare?*	it to?	*autobus per...?*
how many kilometres is it?	*quanti chilómetri sono?*	where's the road to...?	*dov'è la strada a...?*
how long does it take?	*quanto ci vuole?*	next stop please	*la próssima fermata, per favore*
what number bus is	*que número di*		

SOME SIGNS

entrance/exit	*entrata/uscita*	to let	*affitasi*
free entrance	*ingresso líbero*	platform	*binario*
gentlemen/ladies	*signori/signore*	cash desk	*cassa*
wc	*gabinetto, bagno*	go/walk	*avanti*
vacant/engaged	*líbero/occupato*	stop/halt	*alt*
open/closed	*aperto/chiuso*	customs	*dogana*
arrivals/departures	*arrivi/partenze*	do not touch	*non toccare*
closed for restoration	*chiuso per restauro*	danger	*perícolo*
closed for holidays	*chiuso per ferie*	beware	*attenzione*
pull/push	*tirare/spíngere*	first aid	*pronto soccorso*
out of order	*guasto*	ring the bell	*suonare il campanello*
drinking water	*acqua potábile*	no smoking	*vietato fumare*

DRIVING

parking	*parcheggio*	road closed/up	*strada chiusa/guasta*
no parking	*divieto di sosta/sosta vietata*	no through road	*vietato il tránsito*
		no overtaking	*vietato il sorpaṣso*
one way street	*senso único*	crossroads	*incrocio*
no entry	*senso vietato*	speed limit	*límite di velocità*
slow down	*rallentare*	traffic light	*semáforo*

PHRASEBOOKS AND DICTIONARIES

The best phrasebook is *Italian: A Rough Guide Phrase Book* (Penguin; $3.50/$5), which has a large but accessible vocabulary, a detailed menu reader and useful dialogues. As for dictionaries, *Collins* publish a comprehensive series: their *Gem* or *Pocket* dictionaries are fine for travelling purposes, while their *Concise* is adequate for most language needs.

---

ter, even if they are unable to distinguish the differences in speech.

The influence of Spanish permeates all the island's various dialects – hardly surprising in a place that was a Spanish colony for three centuries. The evidence is also on maps, where you will see examples like *riu* used for a river, where the Italian would be *fiume*. The Sard dialects also have large infusions of Latin, a residue of the much older Roman occupation. "House," for example, in Italian *casa*, is called *domus* in areas of Sardinia, the same as Latin. The words for "the" in northern Sardinia – *su* and *sa* in the sin-gular, *sos* and *sas* in the plural – are derived from the Latin noun-endings. In the south of the island, "the" is *is*, from the Latin *ipse*. Again, you will find copious examples on the maps. The region which has the greatest preponderance of Latin in its dialect is Logudoro, once covering the whole northwestern quarter of Sardinia. Its inhabitants boast of speaking the purest form of dialect, which in effect means the form least corrupted by later influences. Added to the innate insularity of islanders, Sards have a particular reputation for being *isolani*, meaning that they are not only insular but a closed and introspective people, with little interest in anything beyond immediate concerns. Whether or not this is still true today, the trait has influenced – and been influenced by – the local variations in speech. Within the artificially imposed provincial boundaries of Cágliari, Sássari, Nuoro and Oristano, Sardinia is a conglomerate of diverse regions – Campidano, Arborea, Logudoro, Gallura, the Iglesiente and Barbágia, to name but the principal ones – each with distinct traditions and a fierce awareness of their differences from one another. The use of dialect became not just a colloquial mode of speech but a symbol of local solidarity, enabling Sards to identify each other according to the particular area of the island they inhabit, just by listening.

The result of this linguistic confusion is that Italian has become the only means for people of different areas of the island to communicate effectively, and it has been learned, as a foreign language is learned, to perfection. Indeed it is claimed that Sards speak the most correct form of Italian anywhere. Television, of course, has also played its part, and it is extemely improbable that you could ever unearth today a non-Italian speaking Sard.

Some Sardinian Dialect Words	
abba	water
bruncu	protuberance, promontory
flumineddu	river
genna	gate
mannu	big
riu	river
sa (pl. sas)	the (feminine)
su (pl. sos)	the (masculine)

Glossaries

Artistic and architectural terms

APSE Domed recess at the altar end of a church.

ARCHITRAVE The lowest part of the entablature.

ATRIUM Forecourt, usually of a Roman house.

CAMPANILE Bell tower.

CAPITAL Top of a column.

CATALAN-GOTHIC Hybrid form of architecture, mixing elements from fifteenth-century Spanish and Northern European building styles.

CAVEA The seating section in a theatre.

CELLA Sanctuary of a temple.

CUPOLA A dome.

DECUMANUS The main street in a Roman town.

ENTABLATURE The part of the building above the capital on a classical building.

EX-VOTO Decorated tablet designed as thanksgiving to a saint.

HYPOGEUM Underground vault, often used as an early Christian church.

LOGGIA Roofed gallery or balcony.

NAVE Central space in a church, usually flanked by aisles.

POLYPTYCH Painting or carving on several joined wooden panels.

PORTICO The covered entrance to a building.

PUNIC Carthaginian/Phoenician.

STELAE Inscribed stone slabs.

THERMAE Baths, usually elaborate buildings in Roman villas.

TRIPTYCH Painting or carving on three joined wooden panels.

Italian words

ANFITEATRO Amphitheatre.

AUTOSTAZIONE Bus station.

BELVEDERE A look-out point.

CAPPELLA Chapel.

CASTELLO Castle.

CATTEDRALE Cathedral.

CENTRO Centre.

CHIESA Church (Chiesa Matrice/Madre, main "mother" church).

COMUNE An administrative area; also, the local council or the town hall.

CORSO Avenue/boulevard.

DUOMO Cathedral.

ENTRATA Entrance.

FESTA Festival, carnival.

FIUME River.

GOLFO Gulf.

LAGO Lake.

LARGO Square (like piazza).

LUNGOMARE Seafront promenade or road.

MARE Sea.

MERCATO Market.

MEZZO VELOCE High-speed ferry.

MUNICIPIO Town Hall.

PALAZZO Palace, mansion or block (of flats).

PARCO Park.

PASSEGGIATA The customary early evening walk.

PIANO Plain (also "slowly", "gently").

PIAZZA Square.

PINETA Pinewood.

SANTUARIO Sanctuary.

SPIAGGIA Beach.

STAZIONE Station (Train Station, Stazione Ferroviaria; Bus Station, Autostazione; Ferry Terminal, Stazione Maríttima).

STRADA Road/street.

TEATRO Theatre.

TEMPIO Temple.

TORRE Tower.

TRAGHETTO Ferry.

USCITA Exit.

VIA Road (always used with name; as Via Roma).

ZONA Zone.

Acronyms

AAST Azienda Autónoma di Soggiorno e Turismo (local tourist office).

ACI Italian Automobile Club.

APT Azienda Provinciale di Turismo: provincial tourist office.

CAI Club Alpino Italiano: Italian climbing club.

DC Democrazia Cristiana: the Christian Democrat party, now the Partito Popolare.

EPT Ente Provinciale per il Turismo: provincial tourist office.

ESIT Ente Sardo Indústrie Turístiche: regional tourist office.

FdS Ferrovie della Sardegna.

FMS Ferrovie Meridionali Sarde.

FS Italian state railways.

IVA Imposta Valore Aggiunto: VAT.

MSI-DN Movimento Sociale d'Italia-Destra Nazionale: the Italian Neo-Fascist party.

PDS Partito Democrático della Sinistra: the former Italian Communist Party.

PS d'Az Partito Sardo d'Azione: Sardinian Action Party.

PSI Partito Socialista d'Italia: the Italian Socialist Party.

RAI The Italian state TV and radio network.

SP Strada Provinciale: a minor road, eg SP70.

SS Strada Statale: a main highway, eg SS195.

Index

Stay in touch with us!

ROUGH*NEWS* **is Rough Guides' free newsletter. In four issues a year we give you news, travel issues, music reviews, readers' letters and the latest dispatches from authors on the road.**

ROUGH GUIDES: Travel

Amsterdam
Andalucia
Australia

Austria
Bali & Lombok
Barcelona
Belgium &
  Luxembourg
Belize
Berlin
Brazil
Britain
Brittany &
  Normandy
Bulgaria
California
Canada
Central America
Chile
China
Corfu & the
  Ionian Islands
Corsica
Costa Rica
Crete
Cuba
Cyprus
Czech & Slovak
  Republics

Dodecanese
Dominican
  Republic
Egypt
England
Europe
Florida
France
French Hotels &
  Restaurants 1999
Germany
Goa
Greece
Greek Islands
Guatemala
Hawaii
Holland
Hong Kong
  & Macau
Hungary
India
Indonesia
Ireland
Israel & the
  Palestinian
  Territories
Italy
Jamaica
Japan
Jordan

Kenya
Laos
London
London
  Restaurants
Los Angeles
Malaysia,
  Singapore &
  Brunei
Mallorca &
  Menorca
Maya World
Mexico
Morocco
Moscow
Nepal
New England
New York
New Zealand
Norway
Pacific Northwest
Paris
Peru
Poland
Portugal
Prague
Provence & the
  Côte d'Azur
The Pyrenees
Romania

St Petersburg
San Francisco
Sardinia
Scandinavia
Scotland
Scottish Highlands
  & Islands
Sicily
Singapore

South Africa
Southern India
Southwest USA
Spain
Sweden
Syria
Thailand
Trinidad & Tobago
Tunisia
Turkey
Tuscany & Umbria
USA
Venice
Vienna
Vietnam
Wales
Washington DC
West Africa
Zimbabwe &
  Botswana

AVAILABLE AT ALL GOOD BOOKSHOPS

ROUGH GUIDES: Mini Guides, Travel Specials and Phrasebooks

MINI GUIDES
Antigua
Bangkok
Barbados
Big Island of
  Hawaii
Boston
Brussels
Budapest

Dublin
Edinburgh
Florence
Honolulu
Jerusalem
Lisbon
London
  Restaurants
Madrid
Maui
Melbourne
New Orleans
Seattle
St Lucia

Sydney
Tokyo
Toronto

TRAVEL SPECIALS
First–Time Asia
First–Time
  Europe
Women Travel

PHRASEBOOKS
Czech
Dutch

Egyptian Arabic
European
French
German
Greek
Hindi & Urdu
Hungarian
Indonesian
Italian
Japanese

Mandarin
  Chinese
Mexican
  Spanish
Polish
Portuguese
Russian
Spanish
Swahili
Thai
Turkish
Vietnamese

ROUGH GUIDES:
Reference and Music CDs

REFERENCE
Classical Music
Classical:
  100 Essential CDs
Drum'n'bass
House Music
Jazz
Music USA

Internet
Millennium

Opera
Opera:
  100 Essential CDs
Reggae
Reggae:
  100 Essential CDs
Rock
Rock:
  100 Essential CDs
Techno
World Music
World Music:
  100 Essential CDs
English Football
European Football

ROUGH GUIDE MUSIC CDs
Music of the
  Andes
Australian
  Aboriginal
Brazilian Music
Cajun & Zydeco

Classic Jazz
Music of
  Colombia
Cuban Music
Eastern Europe

Music of Egypt
English Roots
  Music
Flamenco
India & Pakistan
Irish Music
Music of Japan
Kenya & Tanzania
Native American
North African
Music of Portugal

Reggae
Salsa
Scottish Music
South African
  Music
Music of Spain
Tango
Tex-Mex
West African
  Music
World Music
World Music Vol 2
Music of
  Zimbabwe

AVAILABLE AT ALL GOOD BOOKSHOPS

the perfect getaway vehicle

low-price holiday car rental.

rent a car from holiday autos and you'll give yourself real freedom to explore your holiday destination. with great-value, fully-inclusive rates in over 4,000 locations worldwide, wherever you're escaping to, we're there to make sure you get excellent prices and superb service.

what's more, you can book now with complete confidence. our £5 undercut* ensures that you are guaranteed the best value for money in holiday destinations right around the globe.

drive away with a great deal, call holiday autos now on **0990 300 400** and quote ref RG.

holiday autos miles ahead